MKTG¹⁴

Principles of Marketing

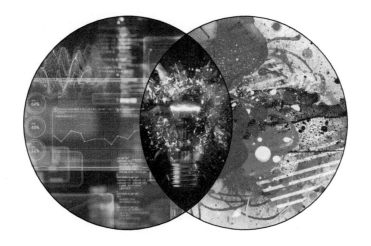

Charles W. Lamb
Texas Christian University

Joe F. Hair
Louisiana State University

Carl McDaniel
University of Texas Arlington

❄ Cengage

Australia • Brazil • Canada • Mexico • Singapore • United Kingdom • United States

MKTG, **14th Edition**
Charles W. Lamb, Joe F. Hair, Carl McDaniel

SVP, Product: Cheryl Costantini

VP, Product: Thais Alencar

Portfolio Product Director: Joe Sabatino

Portfolio Product Manager: Heather Thompson

Senior Subject Matter Expert: Stephanie Hall

Senior Content Manager: Allie Janneck

Learning Designer: Danae Kesel

Digital Project Manager: Jessica Ivanovic

Associate Director, Product Marketing:
Mary Reynolds

Associate Product Marketing Manager:
Melanie Kessler

Content Acquisition Analyst: Rida Syed

Production Service: MPS Limited

Designer: Sara Greenwood

Cover Image Source: 87731443: Gordan/
Shutterstock; 2280735495: Alones/Shutterstock;
1388687270: Yuichiro Chino/Moment/
Getty Images

For product information and technology assistance, contact us at
**Cengage Customer & Sales Support, 1-800-354-9706
or support.cengage.com.**

For permission to use material from this text or product, submit all requests online at **www.copyright.com.**

Library of Congress Control Number: 2023916386

ISBN: 978-0-357-92921-6

Cengage
5191 Natorp Boulevard
Mason, OH 45040
USA

Cengage is a leading provider of customized learning solutions. Our employees reside in nearly 40 different countries and serve digital learners in 165 countries around the world. Find your local representative at **www.cengage.com.**

To learn more about Cengage platforms and services, register or access your online learning solution, or purchase materials for your course, visit **www.cengage.com.**

Printed in the United States of America
Print Number: 02   Print Year: 2024

MKTG 14th Edition is dedicated in memory of Carl McDaniel Jr. (1941–2023), whose invaluable contributions shaped the development of MKTG, the title that launched 4LTR Press. His legacy will continue to inspire and guide marketing students for generations to come.

Brief Contents

Contents

Acknowledgments

We deeply appreciate the assistance of Stephanie Hall, Jeff Penley, Susan Fant, Deb Tech, LEAP, for creating and/or reviewing the MindTap and supplemental content. Many talented professionals at Cengage, MPS Limited, and Lumina have contributed to the development of this book. We are especially grateful to Heather Thompson, Allie Janneck, Stephanie Hall, Danae Kesel, Sara Greenwood, Mary Reynolds, Melanie Kessler, Joe Sabatino, Jess Ivanovic, Erika Longstreth, Manas Pant, Rida Syed, Saveedha Miniane, Parthiban Shanmugam, Dharani Kumar, and Dhivya Sathiyamoorthy. Their inspiration, patience, support, and friendship are invaluable.

We extend our gratitude to our contributing authors, Kara Bentley and Lucy Matthews, for this edition.

Kara Bentley is an Assistant Professor of Marketing at Chapman University in Orange, California. She teaches principles of marketing at the undergraduate level and marketing management at the graduate level. Bentley has coauthored several articles in scholarly journals and has presented her work at many academic conferences. Her research is primarily focused on social influence and digital marketing strategies. She is a member of The Association for Consumer Research, The American Marketing Association, and The Society for Consumer Psychology. Bentley grew up in Fort Worth, Texas, and received her Bachelor's of Business Administration (BBA) degree with a Marketing focus from Texas Christian University in 2009. After graduating from TCU, she worked for a digital marketing agency and owned her own small business before deciding to pursue a PhD. She completed her doctorate degree at the University of South Carolina in 2017.

Dr. Lucy M. Matthews has a B.S. in Marketing and Management from Indiana University and an MBA with a concentration in Marketing from Georgia State University. She worked in sales and management for over 15 years before returning for her doctorate at Kennesaw State University. Her research interests include sales, burnout, engagement, grit, and cross-discipline areas such as innovation and entrepreneurship. Matthews has over 35 peer-reviewed publications and 3,500 citations of her research in journals; they include *Industrial Marketing Management, Journal of Business & Industrial Marketing, Journal of Professional Selling & Sales Management, Journal of Business Ethics, European Business Review,* and *Journal of Business Research.* Dr. Matthews was the recipient of the MTSU Outstanding Teaching Award in 2022, E. W. "Wink" Midgett Distinguished Research Award in 2019, the State Farm Outstanding Professor Award in 2018, and the Outstanding EXL Faculty Award in 2018 and 2023. Outside of MTSU, Dr. Matthews is a 2021 Rutherford ATHENA Award Nominee and the Overall Best Paper in Conference at the 2017 Society for Marketing Advances Conference in Louisville, KY. She is a Past-President and current Board of Governors member of the Atlantic Marketing Association and the Society for Marketing Advances.

MKTG¹⁴

Principles of Marketing

Monkey Business Images/Shutterstock.com

Part 1

Chapter 1

An Overview of Marketing

Learning Outcomes

After studying this chapter, you will be able to . . .

1-1 Define the term marketing

1-2 Describe four marketing management philosophies

1-3 Discuss the differences between sales and market orientations

1-4 Describe several reasons for studying marketing

1-1 What Is Marketing?

1-1 Define the term marketing

What does the term *marketing* mean to you? Many people think *marketing* means personal selling. Others think it means advertising. Still others believe that marketing concerns making products available in stores, arranging displays, and maintaining inventories of products for future sales. Marketing includes all these activities and more.

Marketing has two facets. First, it is a philosophy, an attitude, a perspective, or a management orientation that stresses customer satisfaction. Second, marketing is an organizational function and a set of processes used to implement this philosophy.

The American Marketing Association's (AMA) definition of marketing focuses on the second facet. According to the AMA, **marketing** is the activity, set of institutions, and processes for creating, communicating, delivering, and exchanging offerings that have value for customers, clients, partners, and society at large.[1]

Marketing involves more than just activities a group of people performs in a defined area or department. In the often-quoted words of David Packard, co-founder of Hewlett-Packard (HP), "Marketing is too important to be left only to the marketing department." Marketing entails processes that focus on delivering value and benefits to customers, not just selling goods, services, and/or ideas. It uses communication, distribution, and pricing strategies to provide customers and other stakeholders with the goods, services, ideas, values, and benefits they want when and where they want them. It involves building long term, mutually rewarding relationships when these benefit all parties concerned. Marketing also entails an understanding that organizations have many connected stakeholder "partners," including employees, suppliers, stockholders, distributors, and others.

Research showed that an investment portfolio of companies that promote a culture of health, safety and well-being outperformed the stock market 2 percent per year over a 10-year period.[2] In 2022, Cisco, Hilton, and Wegman's Food Markets secured the top three positions on Fortune's "100 Best Companies to Work For" list. These organizations prioritized diversity, equity, inclusion, and belonging programs, which encouraged employees to express their authentic selves without any fear of rejection. Compared to the average workplace, approximately 90 percent of employees felt comfortable being themselves. Additionally, these companies expanded their resources for mental health assistance, support services for older adults, child care, and well-being. They also provided financial and professional assistance to their employees during layoffs and furloughs, and offered COVID-19 care during the pandemic.[3]

> **"Marketing is too important to be left only to the marketing department."**
>
> —David Packard, co-founder of Hewlett-Packard

One desired outcome of marketing is an **exchange**—people giving up something to receive something else they would rather have. Normally, we think of money as the medium of exchange. We "give up" money to "get" the goods and services we want. Exchange does not require money, however. Two (or more) people may barter or trade such items as baseball cards or oil paintings.

An exchange can take place only if the following five conditions exist:

1. There must be at least two parties.
2. Each party has something that might be of value to the other party.
3. Each party is capable of communication and delivery.
4. Each party is free to accept or reject the exchange offer.
5. Each party believes it is appropriate or desirable to deal with the other party.[4]

Exchange will not necessarily take place even if all these conditions exist, but they must exist for exchange to be possible. For example, suppose you place an advertisement

Ken Worter/Shutterstock.com

Cisco was #1 on *Fortune*'s "100 Best Companies to Work For" in the 2021 national survey of employees. The company takes great care of its employees across many aspects of their lives. It also has initiated diversity, equity, inclusion and belonging programs throughout the company.

marketing the activity, set of institutions, and processes for creating, communicating, delivering, and exchanging offerings that have value for customers, clients, partners, and society at large

exchange people giving up something to receive something else they would rather have

on Craigslist or Facebook Marketplace stating that your used automobile is for sale at a certain price. Several people may contact you to ask about the car, some may test-drive it, and one or more may even make an offer. All five conditions necessary for an exchange to occur exist in this scenario. But unless you reach an agreement with a buyer and sell the car, an exchange will not take place.

Notice that marketing can occur even if an exchange does not occur. In the example just discussed, you would have engaged in marketing by advertising the car, even if no one bought it.

1-2 The Four Marketing Management Philosophies

1-2 Describe four marketing management philosophies

Four competing philosophies strongly influence an organization's marketing processes. These philosophies are commonly called production, sales, market, and societal marketing orientations.

1-2a Production Orientation

A **production orientation** is a philosophy that focuses on the firm's internal capabilities rather than on the desires and needs of the marketplace. A production orientation means that management assesses its resources and asks these questions: "What can we do best?" "What can our engineers design?" "What is easy to produce, given our equipment?" In the case of a service organization, managers ask, "What services are most convenient for the firm to offer?" and "Where do our talents lie?" The furniture industry is infamous for its disregard of customers and for its slow cycle times. For example, most traditional furniture stores (think Ashley or Haverty's) carry the same styles and varieties of furniture they have carried for many years. They always produce and stock sofas, coffee tables, chairs, and end tables for the living room. Bedroom suites always include at least a queen- or king-sized bed, two dressers, and two nightstands.

Regardless of what customers may be looking for, this selection is what they will find at these stores—and they have been so long-lived because what they produce has matched customer expectations. This industry has always been production oriented.

There is nothing wrong with assessing a firm's capabilities; in fact, such assessments are major considerations in strategic marketing planning (refer back to Chapter 2). A production orientation can fall short if it does not consider whether the goods and services that the firm produces most efficiently also meet the needs of the marketplace. On the other hand, sometimes what a firm can best produce is exactly what the market wants. Apple has a history of production orientation, creating computers, operating systems, and other gadgetry because it can and hopes to sell the result. Some items have found a waiting market (early computers, iPod, iPhone). Other products, like the Newton, one of the first versions of a personal digital assistant (PDA), were simply flops.

In some situations, as when competition is weak or demand exceeds supply, a production-oriented firm can survive and even prosper. More often, however, firms that succeed in competitive markets have a clear understanding that they must first determine what customers want and then produce it, rather than focus on what company management thinks should be produced and hope that the product is something customers want.

1-2b Sales Orientation

A **sales orientation** is based on the belief that people will buy more goods and services if aggressive sales techniques are used and that high sales result in high profits. Not only does this approach emphasize sales to the final buyer, but intermediaries are also encouraged to push manufacturers' products more aggressively. To sales-oriented firms, marketing means selling things and collecting money.

The fundamental problem with a sales orientation, as with a production orientation, is a lack of understanding of the needs and wants of the marketplace. Sales-oriented companies often find that, despite the quality of their sales force, they cannot convince people to buy goods or services that are neither wanted nor needed.

1-2c Market Orientation

The **marketing concept** is a simple and intuitively appealing philosophy that focuses on a market orientation. It states that the social and economic justification for an organization's existence is the satisfaction of customer wants and needs while meeting organizational objectives. What a business thinks it produces is not of primary importance to its success. Instead, what customers think

---

production orientation a philosophy that focuses on the firm's internal capabilities rather than on the desires and needs of the marketplace

sales orientation the belief that people will buy more goods and services if aggressive sales techniques are used and that high sales result in high profits

marketing concept the idea that the social and economic justification for an organization's existence is the satisfaction of customer wants and needs while meeting organizational objectives

Examples of a Sales-Oriented Business

A sales orientation is common for businesses selling products or services in highly competitive markets. This orientation is also used when the consumer is not actively pursuing a company's product. Several examples of industries that tend to use a sales orientation follow.

1. The Insurance Industry

In the insurance industry, companies create the products and then sell them through representatives, advertising, and other sales techniques. Insurance policies are not influenced by consumer input or demand. Insurance is a product that most consumers feel is necessary, and it requires a sales orientation to educate and drive purchases from consumers. While consumers do shop rates, a sales orientation drives the business of auto, home, health, and other policies.

2. The Automotive Industry

While the vehicle itself is often built according to market orientation, vehicle parts and mechanical services are sales oriented. Consumers require salespeople to provide information and to understand their needs. Ultimately, the knowledge on the parts and mechanical side primarily drives the sales of parts and services.

3. Business-to-Business Sales

Business-to-business (B2B) sales also provide an example of a sales-oriented business approach. Companies develop products that may benefit a business and then rely heavily upon aggressive marketing tactics to sell them. Examples of products sold in this type of market can include advertising sales or technologies such as point-of-sale software and machinery that will allow the business to run more efficiently and profitably. Chances are the business owner was not initially looking for the product, but bought it because the salesperson showed them some benefit to buying it.

Sources: Zach Lazzari, "Examples of a Sales-Oriented Business," https://yourbusiness .azcentral.com/examples-salesoriented-business-11277.html, May 7, 2018; Jared Lewis, "Examples of a Sales-Oriented Business," https://smallbusiness.chron.com /examples-salesoriented-business-25083.html, accessed January 18, 2023.

---

they are buying—the perceived value—defines a business. The marketing concept includes the following:

- Focusing on customer wants and needs so that the organization can distinguish its product(s) from competitors' offerings
- Integrating all the organization's activities, including production, to satisfy customer wants and needs
- Achieving long-term goals for the organization by satisfying customer wants and needs legally and responsibly

The recipe for success is to develop a thorough understanding of your customers and your competition, your distinctive capabilities that enable your company to execute plans based on this customer understanding, and how to deliver the desired experience using and integrating all the firm's resources. For example, toy manufacturers are making big changes toward sustainability in their product design and packaging to respond to demands from parents and toy retailers. Hasbro and LEGO are among the companies that have committed to eliminating all plastic packaging. Meanwhile, Mattel has pledged to use only recycled, recyclable, or bio-based plastics in its toys. Green Toys, a California-based company, has been using recycled milk jugs in its toys for over a decade and has expanded from a small startup to become a key competitor in the toy industry.[5]

---

market orientation a philosophy that assumes that a sale does not depend on an aggressive sales force but rather on a customer's decision to purchase a product; it is synonymous with the marketing concept

Firms that adopt and implement the marketing concept are said to be **market oriented**, meaning that they assume that a sale does not depend on an aggressive sales force but rather on a customer's decision to purchase a product. Achieving a market orientation involves obtaining information about customers, competitors, and markets; examining the information from a total business perspective; determining how to deliver superior customer value; and implementing actions to provide value to customers.

Some firms are known for delivering superior customer value and satisfaction. For example, in 2022, J.D. Power and Associates ranked Lexus highest in customer satisfaction with dealer service among luxury automotive brands, while Mini ranked highest among mass-market brands.[6] Rankings such as these, as well as word-of-mouth from satisfied customers, drive additional sales for these automotive companies.

Understanding your competitive arena and competitors' strengths and weaknesses is a critical component of a market orientation. This understanding includes assessing what existing or potential competitors intend to do tomorrow and what they are doing today. For example, Tesla was once the undisputed leader in the electric vehicle (EV) market. However, Tesla's share of the EV market fell to about 65 percent in 2022 from about 72 percent in 2021. Car companies have cut into their market share with new electric models that in some areas outperform Tesla. Ford has developed an electric version of its F-150 pickup truck, and Dodge released a prototype of an all-electric version of the Charger, which is designed to drive like a traditional muscle car.[7]

1-2d Societal Marketing Orientation

The **societal marketing orientation** extends the marketing concept by acknowledging that some products customers want may not really be in their best interests or society's best interests. This philosophy states that an organization exists not only to satisfy customer wants and needs and to meet organizational objectives but also to preserve or enhance individuals' and society's long-term best interests. Marketing products and containers that are less toxic than normal, are more durable, contain reusable materials, or are made of recyclable materials are consistent with a societal marketing orientation. The AMA's definition of *marketing* recognizes the importance of a societal marketing orientation by including "society at large" as one of the constituencies for which marketing seeks to provide value. Concerns such as climate change, the depleting of the ozone layer, fuel shortages, pollution, and health issues have caused consumers and legislators to become more aware of the need for companies and consumers to adopt measures that conserve resources and cause less damage to the environment.

Corporate responsibility has transformed from a "nice-to-have silo" to an essential strategic priority.[8] Today, companies of all sorts are spurring change across a broad range of issues, including climate change, education, and poverty. Many have also made a commitment to eliminate waste and reuse valuable materials within their own walls.

Gap, for instance, was established with the objective of providing opportunities to the individuals and communities impacted by their business. Therefore, corporate social responsibility has always been a crucial aspect of their company, even before the term became widely used. Today, as a global brand, Gap is addressing the issue of waste in fast fashion, implementing a sustainable and transparent supply chain, protecting endangered species, reducing energy consumption, using 100 percent renewable energy, minimizing waste, and tackling climate change.[9]

1-2e Who Is in Charge?

The internet and the widespread use of social media have accelerated the shift in power from manufacturers and retailers to consumers and business users. This shift began when customers started using books, electronics, and the internet to access information, goods, and services. Customers use their widespread knowledge to shop smarter; leading executives such as former Procter & Gamble CEO A. G. Laffey to conclude that "the customer is boss."[10] GM CEO Mary Barra believes that the "customer is our compass." The following quotation, attributed to everyone from L.L. Bean founder, Leon Leonwood Bean, to Mahatma Gandhi, has been a guiding business principle for many companies: "Customers are the most important visitor on our premises. [They are] not dependent on us. We are dependent on [them]. [They are] not an interruption in our work, [they are] the purpose of it."[11] And as the use of the internet and mobile devices becomes increasingly pervasive, that control will continue to grow. This evolution means that companies must create strategy from the outside in by offering distinct and compelling customer value.[12] This goal can be accomplished only by carefully studying customers and using deep market insights to inform and guide companies' outside-in view.[13]

1-3 The Differences Between Sales and Market Orientations

1-3 Discuss the differences between sales and market orientations

The differences between sales and market orientations are substantial. The two orientations can be compared in terms of five characteristics: the organization's focus, the firm's business, those to whom the product is directed, the firm's primary goal, and the tools used to achieve the organization's goals.

1-3a The Organization's Focus

Personnel in sales-oriented firms tend to be inward looking, focusing on selling what the organization makes rather than making what the market wants. Many of the historic sources of competitive advantage—technology, innovation, and economies of scale—allowed companies to focus their efforts internally and prosper. Today, many successful firms derive their competitive advantage from an external, market-oriented focus. A market orientation has helped companies such as Zappos.com and Bob's Red Mill Natural Foods to outperform their competitors. These companies put customers at the center of their business in ways most companies do poorly or not at all.

Gap Inc. is committed to protecting natural resources and ensuring healthy communities for generations to come.

Source: Gap, Inc.

societal marketing orientation the idea that an organization exists not only to satisfy customer wants and needs and to meet organizational objectives but also to preserve or enhance individuals' and society's long-term best interests

Customer Value

The relationship between benefits and the sacrifice necessary to obtain those benefits is known as **customer value**. Customer value is not simply a matter of high quality. A high-quality product that is available only at a high price will not be perceived as a good value, nor will bare-bones service or low-quality goods selling for a low price. Price is a component of value (a $4,000 handbag is perceived as being more luxurious and of higher quality than one selling for $100), but low price is not the same as good value. Instead, customers value goods and services that are of the quality they expect and sold at prices they are willing to pay.

Value can be used to sell a Mercedes-Benz as well as a Tyson frozen chicken dinner. In other words, value is something that shoppers of all markets and at all income levels look for. Lower-income consumers are price sensitive, so they may respond positively to special offers and generic brands. Low-income consumers who are both paid and shop by the day may respond to reduced packaging sizes that lower the cost per unit while still offering quality and value for the money. Conversely, higher-income customers may value—and be willing to pay for—high-quality products and superior customer service. Apple offers superior value to its customers, resulting in strong brand loyalty. Apple's products, while expensive, are easy to use and last longer than other brands. Its products have great resale value. Apple's products have style, and they set the bar for sleek, sophisticated design. They also get better with time because the company releases significant software updates every year. Its products all work well together. For example, the iPhone and MacBook are more than just two separate devices; they are extensions of one another. Finally, Apple offers its customers a great service experience.[14]

Customer Satisfaction

The customers' evaluation of a good or service in terms of whether that good or service has met their needs and expectations is called **customer satisfaction**. Failure to meet needs and expectations results in dissatisfaction with the good or service. Some companies, in their passion to drive down costs, have damaged their relationships with customers. Bank of America, Comcast, Dish Network, and AT&T are examples of companies for which executives lost track of the delicate balance between efficiency and service.[15] Firms that have a reputation for delivering high levels of customer satisfaction do things differently

Apple provides value to its customers with superior products and service.

from their competitors. Top management is obsessed with customer satisfaction, and employees throughout the organization understand the link between their job and satisfied customers. The organization's culture is to focus on delighting customers rather than on selling products. Trader Joe's is known for delivering exceptional customer experiences, offering high-quality products, and employing, friendly, knowledgeable staff. As a result, it has developed a loyal customer base that prioritizes the value proposition Trader Joe's provides over the price of its products.[16]

One of the most important ways to make sure customers are satisfied with a company is to track their expectations and experiences. Hyatt's hotel chain popularity is partially due to its willingness to listen to what its customers think and to use that information to enhance customers' experiences. The company collects feedback mainly through website surveys and social media. It has a specific website where customers can share their experiences about a recent stay, and it offers incentives so customers will be more likely to take the survey. Moreover, Hyatt tracks customer feedback through social media sites like Instagram and Twitter, now known as X, to understand where they might have issues to address. By investing resources into collecting customer feedback, the company saw increased return on its investment and surpassed the industry average in customer satisfaction.[17]

Building Relationships

Attracting new customers to a business is only the beginning. The best companies view new-customer attraction as the launching point for developing and enhancing a long-term relationship. Companies can expand market share in three ways: attracting new customers, increasing business with existing customers, and retaining current customers. Building relationships with existing customers directly addresses two of the three possibilities and indirectly addresses the other. Katherine Barchetti, founder K. Barchetti Shops, has famously said, "Make a customer, not a sale."[18]

---

customer value the relationship between benefits and the sacrifice necessary to obtain those benefits

customer satisfaction customers' evaluation of a good or service in terms of whether it has met their needs and expectations

The Elements of Value

When customers evaluate the value of a product or service, they weigh its perceived quality against its price. While this process may sound simple, understanding what customers value can be difficult. Academic research can help. A group of scholars has discovered four elements of value that each address a basic consumer need. Each element contains multiple attributes. These are: as follows

1. Functional. The first, and most basic, value is functional. Consumers look for products that save time, reduce risk, reduce effort, or help them organize. The Container Store and TurboTax are examples of retailers that help consumers organize their things or assets.

2. Emotional. This value includes attributes such as meeting emotional needs, including reducing anxiety, good product design and aesthetics, fun and entertainment, and wellness.

The products made by Dyson, such as the dual-cyclone-technology vacuum cleaners, the Supersonic hairdryers, and the Dyson Zone headphones are examples of good product design that is satisfying to consumers. Streaming television service providers such as Netflix offer fun and entertainment.

3. Life-Changing. This value provides hope, motivation, and a feeling of belonging and self-actualization. Fitbit's exercise-tracking programs address the motivation to get healthier. A $10,000 Leica camera offers not only the high quality of the brand, but also self-actualization that arises from the pride of owning a camera that famous photographers have used for a century.

4. Social Impact. This value meets the need to give back and help others, which translates into self-transcendence. Giving to nonprofit organizations like United Way or cancer research foundations shows examples of social impact.

In practice, many companies offer combinations of these elements and attributes. For example, Amazon started by focusing on functional attributes, such as reducing cost and saving time. Then, with Amazon Prime offering services like streaming media and unlimited photo storage, it expanded its value to include fun and entertainment and reducing risk. Restaurants address the attributes of quality, sensory appeal, variety, and design/appeal.

The relevance of the elements varies according to industry. For example, nostalgia or wellness may not mean much to customers buying gas for their cars. Researchers have found that the right combination of elements and attributes results in stronger customer loyalty, greater consumer willingness to try a brand, and sustained revenue growth.[19]

Relationship marketing is a strategy that focuses on keeping and improving relationships with current customers. It assumes that many consumers and business customers prefer to have an ongoing relationship with one organization rather than switching continually among providers in their search for value. Activision, a leading publisher of the U.S. video game market, engages in relationship marketing by providing continued service to its gamers. For example, Activision monitors social media conversations that are relevant to its products and follows up on those conversations.[20] This long-term focus on customer needs is a hallmark of relationship marketing.

Most successful relationship marketing strategies depend on customer-oriented personnel, effective training programs, employees with the authority to make decisions and solve problems, and teamwork.

Customer-Oriented Personnel For an organization to be focused on building relationships with customers, employees' attitudes and actions must be customer oriented. An employee may be the only contact a particular customer has with the firm. In that customer's eyes, the

employee *is* the firm. Any person, department, or division that is not customer oriented weakens the positive image of the entire organization. For example, a potential customer who is greeted discourteously may well assume that the employee's attitude represents that of the whole firm.

Customer-oriented personnel come from an organizational culture that supports its people. In addition, a company culture that includes job benefits such as competitive wages, a healthy work-life balance, ample family and sick leave, and a commitment to diversity and equal pay, also tends to boost the company's bottom line. Salesforce has a "chief equality officer" and a "chief people officer," and it is at the top of the software industry in its treatment of workers and its commitment to workplace diversity, equity, and inclusion. The company has also been recognized for its focus on mental health issues, which spiked during the COVID-19 pandemic.[21]

Some companies, such as Coca-Cola, Delta Air Lines, Hershey, Kellogg, and Nautilus, have appointed chief

---

relationship marketing a strategy that focuses on keeping and improving relationships with current customers

customer officers (CCOs). These customer advocates provide an executive voice for customers and report directly to the CEO. Their responsibilities include ensuring that the company maintains a customer-centric culture and that all company employees remain focused on delivering customer value.

The Role of Training Leading marketers recognize the role of employee training in customer service and relationship building. Atlantic Health System is a company that has been voted one of America's Best Companies to Work For. Employees are offered free courses—many for college credit. There are classes in clinical and nonclinical care, technology, management, leadership, and customer experience, among others. These classes help spark innovation and engagement within the company.[22]

Empowerment In addition to training, many market-oriented firms are giving employees more authority to solve customer problems on the spot. The term used to describe this delegation of authority is **empowerment**. Employees develop ownership attitudes when they are treated like part owners of the business and are expected to act the part. These employees manage themselves, are more likely to work hard, account for their own performance and that of the company, and take prudent risks to build a stronger business and sustain the company's success. To empower its workers, the Ritz-Carlton chain of luxury hotels developed a set of 12 "Service Values" guidelines. These brief, easy-to-understand guidelines include statements such as "I am empowered to create unique, memorable and personal experiences for our guests" and "I own and immediately resolve guest problems." The 12 Service Values are printed on cards distributed to employees, and each day, a particular value is discussed at length in Ritz-Carlton team meetings. Employees talk about what the value means to them and offer examples of how the value can be put into practice that day.[23]

Teamwork Many organizations that are frequently noted for delivering superior customer value and providing high levels of customer satisfaction, such as Google and Walt Disney World, assign employees to teams and teach them team-building skills. **Teamwork** entails collaborative efforts of people to accomplish common objectives. Job performance, company performance, product value, and customer satisfaction all improve when people in the same department or work group begin supporting and assisting each other and emphasize cooperation instead of competition. Performance is also enhanced when cross-functional

---

empowerment delegation of authority to solve customers' problems quickly—usually by the first person the customer notifies regarding a problem

teamwork collaborative efforts of people to accomplish common objectives

Thanks to Costco's high pay, generous benefits, and trust in its employees, the company's turnover rate is less than 6 percent—significantly lower than that of its competitors.[30]

teams align their jobs with customer needs. For example, if a team of telecommunications service representatives is working to improve interaction with customers, back-office people such as computer technicians or training personnel can become part of the team, with the goal of delivering superior customer value and satisfaction. A study of software engineers showed that those who connected with others and helped them with their projects both earned the trust of their peers and were more productive themselves.[24]

1-3b The Firm's Business

A sales-oriented firm defines its business (or mission) in terms of goods and services. A market-oriented firm defines its business in terms of the benefits its customers seek. People who spend their money, time, and energy expect to receive benefits, not just goods and services. This distinction has enormous implications. For example, Microsoft's original mission was "A computer on every desk and in every home," which is product centered. Its current, benefit-oriented mission is "To empower every person and every organization on the planet to achieve more.[25] It answers the question "What is this firm's business?" in terms of the benefits customers seek instead of goods and services; it offers at least the following three important advantages:

- It ensures that the firm keeps focusing on customers and avoids becoming preoccupied with goods, services, or the organization's internal needs.

- It encourages innovation and creativity by reminding people that there are many ways to satisfy customer wants.

- It stimulates an awareness of changes in customer desires and preferences so that product offerings are more likely to remain relevant.

Market-oriented firms that successfully create a connection with their customers and employees tend to create loyal customers, which can increase overall profitability. These companies shape their mission statements around their core values and in terms of customer benefits. Some examples of good mission statements: are as follows

1. Patagonia: "We're in business to save our home planet," This statement is a more succinct update from its previous mission statement, "Build the best product, cause no unnecessary harm, use business to inspire and implement solutions to the environmental crisis."

2. American Express: "Become essential to our customers by providing differentiated products and services to help them achieve their aspirations." American Express has a list of core values, many of which emphasize teamwork and supporting employees so that the people inside the organization can be in the best position to support their customers.

3. IKEA: "To create a better everyday life for the many people." The statement could have been one of beautiful, affordable furniture (product oriented), but instead, it's to make *everyday life better* for its customers (market oriented).[26]

Having a market orientation and a focus on customer wants does not mean offering customers everything they want. It is not possible, for example, to profitably manufacture and market automobile tires that will last for 100,000 miles for $25. Furthermore, customers' preferences must be mediated by sound professional judgment about how to deliver the benefits they seek. Consumers have a limited set of experiences. They are unlikely to request anything beyond those experiences because they are not aware of the benefits they may gain from other potential offerings. For example, before the internet, many people thought that shopping for some products was boring and time-consuming but could not express their need for electronic shopping.

1-3c Those to Whom the Product Is Directed

A sales-oriented organization targets its products at "everybody" or "the average customer." A market-oriented organization aims at specific groups of people. The fallacy of developing products directed at the average user is that relatively few average users exist. Typically, populations are characterized by diversity. An average is simply a midpoint in some set of characteristics. Because most potential customers are not "average," they are not likely to be attracted to an average product marketed to the average customer. Consider the market for shampoo as one simple example. There are shampoos for oily hair, dry hair, and dandruff. Some shampoos remove gray or color hair. Special shampoos are marketed for infants and older adults. There are even shampoos for people with average or normal hair (whatever that is), but this segment is a small portion of the total shampoo market.

A market-oriented organization recognizes that different customer groups want different features or benefits. It may therefore need to develop different goods, services, and promotional appeals. A market-oriented organization carefully analyzes the market and divides it into groups of people who are similar in terms of selected characteristics. Then the organization develops marketing programs that will bring about mutually satisfying exchanges with one or more of those groups. For example, the more than 120-year-old department store chain Nordstrom has introduced initiatives to attract millennial shoppers, who typically avoid department stores. These initiatives include themed pop-up shops, shop-in-shops featuring new fashion designers, and Nike concept shops.[27]

Customer Relationship Management

Beyond knowing to whom they are directing their products or services, companies must also develop a deeper understanding of their customers. One way of doing this is through *customer relationship management*. **Customer relationship management (CRM)** is a company-wide business strategy designed to optimize profitability, revenue, and customer satisfaction by focusing on highly defined and precise customer groups. This strategy is accomplished by organizing the company around customer segments, establishing and tracking customer interactions with the company, fostering customer-satisfying behaviors, and linking all company processes, from its customers through its suppliers. The difference between CRM and traditional mass marketing can be compared to shooting a rifle versus a shotgun. Instead of scattering messages far and wide across the spectrum of mass media (the shotgun approach), CRM marketers now are homing in on ways to effectively communicate with each customer (the rifle approach).

Vytautas Kielaitis/Shutterstock.com

IKEA offers a wide variety of affordable home furnishings.

---

customer relationship management (CRM) a company-wide business strategy designed to optimize profitability, revenue, and customer satisfaction by focusing on highly defined and precise customer groups

Companies that adopt CRM systems are almost always market oriented, customizing product and service offerings based on data generated through interactions between the customer and the company. This strategy transcends all functional areas of the business, producing an internal system in which all the company's decisions and actions are a direct result of customer information.

As more customers are moving toward online and social media interactions with companies, the use of **big data** is becoming increasingly important. Big data is the discovery, interpretation, and communication of meaningful patterns in data. The amount of time that millions of people spend on Google, Facebook, Instagram, and other social media sites generates a large amount of data every day. All the actions people take create digital footprints that companies can tap to find valuable insights into customer behavior. For example, Sweetgreen Inc. is a California-based salad chain that uses a mobile app to gather data on their guests' allergies and tastes. When guests place mobile orders, they are asked to select from a list of dietary restrictions that includes soy, nuts, and gluten. Selections cause menu items containing those ingredients to be flagged with a red asterisk so the guests know to avoid them. These selections are saved for future orders and give the company detailed data on what their guests like and why. These insights can then be used to shape future menus.[28] We will examine specific applications of CRM and big data in several chapters throughout this book. Also, refer to Chapter 9 and the Appendix for more information on big data.

The emergence of **on-demand marketing** is taking CRM to a new level. As technology evolves and becomes more sophisticated, consumer expectations of their decision- and buying-related experiences have risen. Consumers (1) want to interact anywhere, anytime; (2) want to do new things with varied kinds of information in ways that create value; (3) expect data stored about them to be targeted specifically to their needs or to personalize their experiences; and (4) expect all interactions with a company to be easy. In response to these expectations, companies are developing new ways to integrate and personalize each stage of a customer's decision journey, which in turn should increase relationship-related behaviors. On-demand marketing delivers relevant experiences throughout the consumer's decision and buying process that are integrated across both physical and virtual environments. Trends

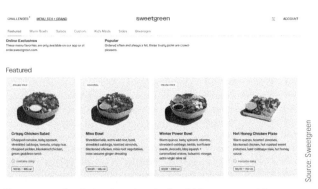

Sweetgreen's mission is to inspire healthier communities by connecting people to real food. The firm offers apps for ordering using iOS or Android.

such as the growth of mobile connectivity, better-designed websites, inexpensive communication through technology, and advances in handling big data have allowed companies to start designing on-demand marketing programs that appeal to consumers. For on-demand marketing to be successful, companies must deliver high-quality experiences across all touch points with the customer, including sales, service, product use, and marketing. Because weather patterns affect the way people purchase online, British online retailer Very has personalized its content based on local weather patterns. For example, in hot weather, Very can deliver product recommendations for light, cool clothing options. If it's going to rain, Very can suggest raincoats and umbrellas.[29]

Many more companies are offering on-demand services. For example, Instacart will deliver groceries to a customer's door, typically within an hour of ordering. Many restaurant chains are now a part of online service GrubHub, which allows customers to type in their zip codes, pick a restaurant, and order items for delivery—all without leaving the GrubHub website. Uber and Lyft provide on-demand

---

big data the discovery, interpretation, and communication of meaningful patterns in data

on-demand marketing delivering relevant experiences, integrated across both physical and virtual environments, throughout the consumer's decision and buying process

The marketing mix provides the tools for marketers to bring about mutually satisfying exchanges with target customers.

transportation by connecting customers to drivers using their own cars—a service that Uber has leveraged into a GrubHub competitor called UberEats.

1-3d The Firm's Primary Goal

A sales-oriented organization seeks to achieve profitability through sales volume and tries to convince potential customers to buy, even if the seller knows that the customer and product are mismatched. Sales-oriented organizations place a higher premium on making a sale than on developing a long-term customer relationship. In contrast, the goal of most market-oriented organizations is to make a profit by creating customer value, providing customer satisfaction, and building long-term relationships with customers. The exception is nonprofit organizations that exist to achieve goals other than profits. Nonprofit organizations can and should adopt a market orientation. Nonprofit organization marketing is explored further in Chapter 12.

1-3e Tools the Organization Uses to Achieve Its Goals

Sales-oriented organizations seek to generate sales volume through intensive promotional activities, mainly personal selling, and advertising. In contrast, market-oriented organizations recognize that promotion decisions are only one of four basic marketing mix decisions that must be made: product decisions, place (or distribution) decisions, promotion decisions, and pricing decisions. A market-oriented organization recognizes that each of these four components is important. Furthermore, market-oriented organizations recognize that marketing is not just the responsibility of the marketing department. Interfunctional coordination means that skills and resources throughout the organization are needed to create, communicate, and deliver superior customer service and value.

1-3f A Word of Caution

This comparison of sales and market orientations is not meant to belittle the role of promotion, especially personal selling, in the marketing mix. Promotion is how organizations communicate with present and prospective customers about the merits and characteristics of their organization and products. Effective promotion is an essential part of effective marketing. Salespeople who work for market-oriented organizations are generally perceived by their customers to be problem solvers and important links to supply sources and new products. Chapter 18 examines the nature of personal selling in more detail.

1-4 Why Study Marketing?

1-4 Describe several reasons for studying marketing

Now that you understand the meaning of the term *marketing*, why it is important to adopt a marketing orientation, and how organizations implement this philosophy, you may be asking, "What's in it for me?" or "Why should I study marketing?" These are important questions whether you are majoring in a business field other than marketing (such as accounting, finance, or management information systems) or a nonbusiness field (such as journalism, education, or agriculture). There are several important reasons to study marketing: Marketing plays an important role in society, marketing is important to businesses, marketing offers outstanding career opportunities, and marketing affects your life every day.

1-4a Marketing Plays an Important Role in Society

The total population of the United States exceeds 334 million people. Think about how many transactions are needed each day to feed, clothe, and shelter a population of this size. The number is huge. And yet it all works quite well, partly because the well-developed U.S. economic system efficiently distributes the output of farms and factories. The average American eats almost 2,000 pounds of food a year.[30] Marketing makes food available when we want it, in desired quantities, at accessible locations, and in sanitary and convenient packages and forms (such as instant and frozen foods).

1-4b Marketing Is Important to Businesses

The fundamental objectives of most businesses are survival, profits, and growth. Marketing contributes directly to achieving these objectives. Marketing includes the following activities, which are vital to business organizations: assessing the wants and satisfactions of present and potential customers, designing and managing product offerings, determining prices and pricing policies, developing distribution strategies, and communicating with present and potential customers.

All businesspeople, regardless of specialization or area of responsibility, need to be familiar with the terminology and fundamentals of accounting, finance, management, and marketing. People in all business areas need to be able to communicate with specialists in other areas. Furthermore, marketing is not just a job done by people in a marketing department. Marketing is a part of the job of everyone in the organization. Therefore, a basic understanding of marketing is important to all businesspeople.

1-4c Marketing Offers Outstanding Career Opportunities

Between one-fourth and one-third of the entire civilian workforce in the United States performs marketing activities. Marketing offers great career opportunities in such areas as professional selling, marketing research, advertising, retail buying, distribution management, product management, product development, and wholesaling. Marketing career opportunities also exist in a variety of nonbusiness organizations, including hospitals, museums, universities, the armed forces, and various government and social service agencies.

1-4d Marketing in Everyday Life

Marketing plays a major role in your everyday life. You participate in the marketing process as a consumer of goods and services. About half of every dollar you spend pays for marketing costs, such as marketing research, product development, packaging, transportation, storage, advertising, and sales expenses. By developing a better understanding of marketing, you will become a better-informed consumer. You will better understand the buying process and be able to negotiate more effectively with sellers. Moreover, you will be better prepared to demand satisfaction when the goods and services you buy do not meet the standards the manufacturer or the marketer promised.

PeopleImages.com - Yuri A/Shutterstock.com

Chapter 2

Strategic Planning for Competitive Advantage

Learning Outcomes

After studying this chapter, you will be able to . . .

2-1 Explain strategic planning

2-2 Define strategic business units (SBUs)

2-3 Identify strategic alternatives

2-4 Explain how marketers use a marketing plan

2-5 Describe the elements of a marketing plan

2-1 The Nature of Strategic Planning

2-1 Explain strategic planning

Strategic planning is the managerial process of creating and maintaining a fit between the organization's objectives and resources and the evolving market opportunities. The goal of strategic planning is long-run profitability and growth. Thus, strategic decisions require long-term commitments of resources.

A strategic error can threaten a firm's survival. On the other hand, a good strategic plan can help protect and grow the firm's resources. For instance, if the March of Dimes had decided to focus only on fighting polio, the organization would no longer exist because polio is widely viewed as a conquered disease. The March of Dimes survived by making the strategic decision to switch to improving the health of mothers and babies.

Strategic marketing management addresses two questions: (1) What is the organization's main activity at a particular time? (2) How will it reach its goals? Here are some examples of strategic decisions:

- Hershey's made a strategic decision to become less reliant on chocolate in recent years and invested in salty snacks. It bought companies such as SkinnyPop, Pirate's Booty, and Dot's Homestyle Pretzels. Hershey also scaled back internationally and sharpened its focus on North America. These moves helped Hershey change and grow.[1]

- Ford decided to transform its entire North American lineup of cars by going all-in on hybrids, adding more sports utility vehicles, and using more cutting-edge technology. The company has also phased out small cars like the Fiesta, Taurus, Fusion, and regular Focus passenger cars. Also, it has invested in electric and autonomous vehicles and smart mobility solutions that address changes in urban living and transportation.[2]

- Amazon is entering the competitive healthcare market by offering a new prescription service called RXPass. This service allows Amazon Prime members to buy medicines for ongoing health problems and have them delivered to their homes for $5 a month. The company also has pharmacists that are available 24/7 to answer questions. Amazon also acquired One Medical, a healthcare organization that combines in-person, digital, and telehealth services to patients.[3]

All these decisions have affected or will affect each organization's long-run course, its allocation of resources, and, ultimately, its financial success. In contrast, an operating decision, such as changing the package design for Post Grape-Nuts cereal or altering the sweetness of a Kraft salad dressing, probably will not have a big impact on the company's long-run profitability.

Effective strategic planning requires continual attention, creativity, and management commitment. Strategic planning should not be an annual exercise in which managers go through the motions and forget about strategic planning until the next year. It should be an ongoing process because the environment is continually changing, and the firm's resources and capabilities are continually evolving. Perhaps the most critical element in successful strategic planning is top management's support and participation.

Sound strategic planning is based on creativity. Managers should challenge assumptions about the firm and the environment and establish new strategies. For example, major oil companies developed the concept of the gasoline service station in an age when cars needed frequent and elaborate servicing. The major companies stayed with the full-service approach, but independents were quick to respond to new realities and moved to lower-cost self-service and convenience store operations. Major companies took several decades to catch up.

> "There are a lot of great ideas that have come and gone in [the digital advertising] industry. Implementation many times is more important than the actual idea."
>
> —David Moore, CEO of 24/7 Media

2-2 Strategic Business Units

2-2 Define strategic business units (SBUs)

Large companies may manage several very different businesses, called **strategic business units (SBUs)**. Each SBU has its own rate of return on investment, growth potential, and associated risks and requires its own strategies and

---

strategic planning the managerial process of creating and maintaining a fit between the organization's objectives and resources and the evolving market opportunities

strategic business unit (SBU) a subgroup of a single business or collection of related businesses within the larger organization

funding. When properly created, an SBU has the following characteristics:

- A distinct mission and a specific target market
- Control over its resources
- Its own competitors
- A single business or a collection of related businesses
- Plans independent of the other SBUs in the total organization.

In theory, an SBU should have its own resources for handling basic business functions: accounting, engineering, manufacturing, and marketing. In practice, however, because of company tradition, management philosophy, and production and distribution economies, SBUs sometimes share manufacturing facilities, distribution channels, and even top managers.

2-3 Strategic Alternatives

2-3 Identify strategic alternatives

Several tools are available that a company, or SBU, can use to manage the strategic direction of its portfolio of businesses. Three of the most used tools are Ansoff's strategic opportunity matrix, the Boston Consulting Group model, and the General Electric model. Selecting which strategic alternative to pursue depends on which of two philosophies a company maintains about when to expect profits—right away or after increasing market share. In the long run, market share and profitability are compatible goals. For example, Amazon lost hundreds of millions of dollars in its first few years by offering deep discounts on books and movies. Today, Amazon has a strong and loyal customer base, particularly among its Prime members. The company's current strategy is to charge the lowest online prices for just a selection of products and to charge the same or more than other retailers for the rest. This practice has increased overall profitability for the company.[4]

2-3a Ansoff's Strategic Opportunity Matrix

One method for developing alternatives is Ansoff's strategic opportunity matrix (refer to Table 2.1), which matches products with markets. Firms can explore these four options:

1. **Market penetration:** A firm using the **market penetration** alternative would try to increase market share among existing customers. The retail division of CVS pharmacy created its ExtraCare and CarePass rewards programs as a market penetration strategy. On the other hand, customers pay $5 a month or $48 a year for CarePass. This program provides members with benefits including free delivery on most medications and purchases, 24/7 access to pharmacy care, and 20 percent off all CVS Health brand products. Customers also receive a monthly $10 CarePass promotional reward that can be used towards nearly all purchases in-store and online at CVS.com.[5]

2. **Market development:** **Market development** means attracting new customers to existing products. Ideally, new uses for old products stimulate additional sales among existing customers while also bringing in new buyers. When CVS opens stores in new neighborhoods, it is using a market development strategy.

---

market penetration a marketing strategy that tries to increase market share among existing customers

market development a marketing strategy that entails attracting new customers to existing products

Table 2.1 Ansoff's Opportunity Matrix: CVS Retail	Present Product	New Product
Present Market	Market Penetration • ExtraCare Rewards • CarePass rewards program	Product Development • COVID-19 testing • Home delivery • Clinical trial access • Minute Clinic
New Market	Market Development • CVS opens stores in new neighborhoods • Project Health	Diversification • In-home health services • Services to long-term care patients • Primary care in underserved neighborhoods

Jonathan Weiss/Shutterstock.com

Also, the company's Project Health initiative offers free health screenings from mobile units, allowing it to reach out to customers in new neighborhoods.

3. **Product development:** A **product development** strategy entails the creation of new products for present markets. CVS introduced Minute Clinic, an in-store healthcare unit staffed with nurse practitioners and physician assistants to serve its existing customers with convenient walk-in medical clinics close to home. It also offers delivery services, COVID-19 testing, and online services to its present customer base.[6]

4. **Diversification:** **Diversification** is a strategy of increasing sales by introducing new products into new markets. For example, CVS acquired Signify Health to reach at-home patients. Signify Health's network of clinicians, physicians, nurse practitioners, and other medical professionals perform home visits to understand a patient's clinical and social needs, and then connect them to suitable follow-up care and resources.[7]

A diversification strategy can be risky when a firm is entering unfamiliar markets. However, it can be very profitable when a firm is entering markets with little or no competition.

2-3b The Innovation Matrix

Critics of Ansoff's matrix mention that the matrix does not reflect the reality of how businesses grow—that the modern businesses plan is a more fluid process based on current capabilities rather than the clear-cut sectors outlined by the opportunity matrix. To reflect this idea, Bansi Nagji and Geoff Tuff, former global innovation managers

---

product development a marketing strategy that entails the creation of new products for present markets

diversification a strategy of increasing sales by introducing new products into new markets

at Monitor Group, developed a system that enables a company to see exactly what types of assets need to be developed and what types of markets are possible to grow into (or create) based on the company's core capabilities, as shown in Figure 2.1.

The layout of the innovation matrix demonstrates that as a company moves away from its core capabilities (the lower left), it traverses a range of change and innovation rather than choosing one of the four sectors in Ansoff's matrix. These ranges are broken down into three levels:

1. **Core Innovation:** Represented by the light blue area in Figure 2.1, these decisions implement changes that use existing assets to provide added convenience to existing customers and potentially entice customers from other brands. Blue Apron, the subscription meal kit company, sells its kits without a subscription on Amazon, in addition to its subscription model. This strategy should help the company reach more customers as its growth slows.[8]

2. **Adjacent Innovation:** Represented by the pale orange arc in Figure 2.1, these decisions are designed to take company strengths into new markets. This space uses existing abilities in new ways. For example, Botox, the popular cosmetic drug, was originally developed to treat intestinal problems and to treat crossed eyes. Leveraging the drug into cosmetic medicine has dramatically increased the market for Botox.

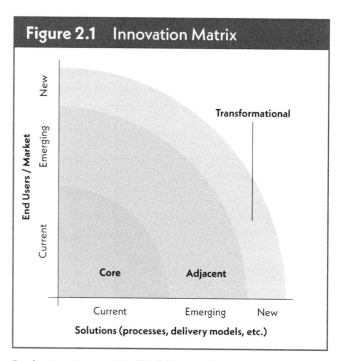

Figure 2.1   Innovation Matrix

Based on Bansi Nagji and Geoff Tuff, "A Simple Tool You Need to Manage Innovation," *Harvard Business Review*, May 2012, https://hbr.org/2012/05/managing-your-innovation-portfolio/ar/1 (accessed June 1, 2012).

3. **Transformational Innovation:** Represented by the light green arc in Figure 2.1, these decisions result in brand-new markets, products, and often new businesses. The company must rely on new, unfamiliar assets to develop the type of breakthrough decisions that fall in this category. Some notable examples are Apple in technology (including the iPhone, iPad, and Apple Watch), Uber in transportation, and Airbnb in hospitality.

2-3c The Boston Consulting Group Model

Management must find a balance among its SBUs that yields the overall organization's desired growth and profits with an acceptable level of risk. Some SBUs generate large amounts of cash, and others need cash to foster growth. The challenge is to balance the organization's portfolio of SBUs for the best long-term performance.

To determine the future cash contributions and cash requirements expected for each SBU, managers can use the Boston Consulting Group's portfolio matrix. The **portfolio matrix** classifies each SBU by its present or forecast growth and market share. The underlying assumption is that market share and profitability are strongly linked. The measure of market share used in the portfolio approach is *relative market share*, the ratio between the company's share and the share of the largest competitor. For example, if a firm has a 50 percent share and the competitor has 5 percent, the ratio is 10 to 1. If a firm has a 10 percent market share and the largest competitor has 20 percent, the ratio is 0.5 to 1.

Figure 2.2 is a hypothetical portfolio matrix for Samsung.[9] The portfolio matrix breaks SBUs into four categories:

1. **Stars:** A **star** is a fast-growing market leader. For example, the flat screen television is one of Samsung's stars. Star SBUs usually have large profits but need lots of cash to finance rapid growth. The best marketing tactic is to protect existing market share by reinvesting earnings in product improvement, better distribution, more promotion, and production efficiency. Management must capture new users as they enter the market.

2. **Cash cows:** A **cash cow** is an SBU that generates more cash than it needs to maintain its market share. It is in a low-growth market, but the product has a dominant market share. For example, home appliances are categorized as cash cows for Samsung in Figure 2.2. The basic strategy for a cash cow is to maintain market dominance by being the price leader and making technological improvements in the product. Managers should resist pressure to extend the basic line unless they can dramatically increase demand. Instead, they should allocate excess cash to the product categories for which growth prospects are the greatest.

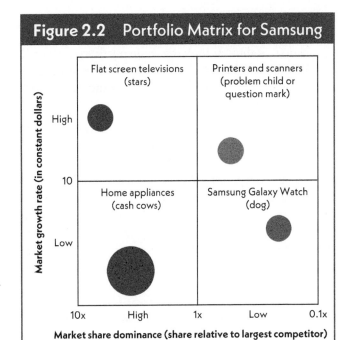

Figure 2.2 Portfolio Matrix for Samsung

3. **Problem children:** A **problem child**, also called a **question mark**, shows rapid growth but poor profit margins. It has a low market share in a high-growth industry. Problem children need a great deal of cash. Without cash support, they eventually become dogs. The strategy options are to invest heavily to gain better market share, acquire competitors to get the necessary market share, or drop the SBU. Sometimes a firm can reposition the products of the SBU to move them into the star category. Compared to the performance of all Samsung's products, its printer can be considered a question mark. High competition in the printer industry and Samsung's small market share of the product contributes to its placement in this category.

4. **Dogs:** A **dog** has low growth potential and a small market share. Most dogs eventually leave the marketplace. The Samsung Galaxy Watch has become a dog due to

---

portfolio matrix a tool for allocating resources among products or strategic business units on the basis of relative market share and market growth rate

star in the portfolio matrix, a business unit that is a fast-growing market leader

cash cow in the portfolio matrix, a business unit that generates more cash than it needs to maintain its market share

problem child (question mark) in the portfolio matrix, a business unit that shows rapid growth but poor profit margins

dog in the portfolio matrix, a business unit that has low growth potential and a small market share

tough competition from competitors like the Apple watch. The iPod could be considered another example of a dog product. It took the company five years to sell 100 million iPods. However, the portable music player market was overtaken by smartphones and the increasing use of music streaming services.[10]

While typical strategies for dogs are to harvest or divest, sometimes companies are successful with this class of product in small, specific markets. For example, while the iPod is in the dog category for Apple, it is still a popular device for young children. It is used in schools because its low price allows each student access to their own device during class activities. Also, many parents say they prefer giving their children an iPod instead of a smartphone because they don't want them to have unlimited access to the internet.[11]

After classifying the company's SBUs in the matrix, the next step is to allocate future resources for each. The following four basic strategies are to:

1. **Build:** If an organization has an SBU that it believes has the potential to be a star (probably a problem child at present), building would be an appropriate goal. The organization may decide to give up short-term profits and use its financial resources to achieve this goal. Samsung invested in creative innovation and strong marketing campaigns to move its Galaxy smartwatch out of the question mark category. It is now second only to Apple in smartwatch market share.[12]

2. **Hold:** If an SBU is a successful cash cow, a key goal would typically be to hold or preserve market share so that the organization can take advantage of the very positive cash flow. Samsung Home Appliances, such as refrigerators, washing machines, and cooking appliances, are the company's cash cows. Over time, Samsung Home Appliances have become a household name and stand for quality and trust. Samsung has been able to attain a good market share across different industry segments and still holds a good potential to grow in the coming future.[13]

3. **Harvest:** This strategy is appropriate for all SBUs except those classified as stars. The basic goal is to increase the short-term cash return without too much concern for the long-run impact. For example, a harvest strategy is appropriate for Samsung's kitchen appliances.

4. **Divest:** Getting rid of SBUs with low shares of low-growth markets is often appropriate. Problem children and dogs are most suitable for this strategy. For Samsung, printers moved from being a question mark to being a dog, so the company sold the printer division to Hewlett-Packard (HP).

2-3d The General Electric Model

The third model for selecting strategic alternatives was originally developed by General Electric (GE). The dimensions used in this model—market attractiveness and company strength—are richer and more complex than those used in the Boston Consulting Group model but are harder to quantify.

Figure 2.3 presents the GE model. The horizontal axis, Business Position, refers to how well positioned the organization is to take advantage of market opportunities. Business position answers questions such as: "Does the firm have the technology it needs to effectively penetrate the market?" "Are its financial resources adequate?" "Can manufacturing costs be held down below those of the competition?" "Can the firm cope with change?" The vertical axis measures the attractiveness of a market, which is expressed both quantitatively and qualitatively. Some attributes of an attractive market are high profitability, rapid growth, a lack of government regulation, consumer insensitivity to a price increase, a lack of competition,

Samsung Galaxy phones are a star product for the company.

Framesira/Shutterstock.com

Figure 2.3 General Electric Model

Market attractiveness		Low	Medium	High
	High	Cautiously Invest	Invest/Grow	Invest/Grow
	Medium	Harvest/Divest	Cautiously Invest	Invest/Grow
	Low	Harvest/Divest	Harvest/Divest	Cautiously Invest
		Low	Medium	High
		Business position		

and availability of technology. The grid is divided into three overall attractiveness zones for each dimension: high, medium, and low.

Those SBUs (or markets) that have low overall attractiveness (indicated by the red cells in Figure 2.3) should be avoided if the organization is not already serving them. If the firm is in these markets, it should either harvest or divest those SBUs. The organization should selectively maintain markets with medium attractiveness (indicated by the yellow cells in Figure 2.3). If attractiveness begins to slip, then the organization should withdraw from the market.

Conditions that are highly attractive—a thriving market plus a strong business position (indicated by the green cells in Figure 2.3) are the best candidates for investment. For example, Google's search engine is has a 70 percent market share and is in the Invest/Grow zone. Google's Chromecast is an innovative product sold at an affordable price. It is in the Cautiously Invest zone. Finally, Google's books are in a highly competitive market and are in the Harvest/Divest zone.[14]

2-4 The Marketing Plan

2-4 Explain how marketers use a marketing plan

Based on the company's or SBU's overall strategy, marketing managers can create a marketing plan for individual products, brands, lines, or customer groups. **Planning** is the process of anticipating future events and determining strategies to achieve organizational objectives in the future. **Marketing planning** involves designing activities relating to marketing objectives and the changing marketing environment. Marketing planning is the basis for all marketing strategies and decisions. Issues such as product lines, distribution channels, marketing communications, and pricing are all delineated in the **marketing plan**. The marketing plan is a written document that acts as a guidebook of marketing activities for the marketing manager. In this chapter, you will learn the importance of writing a marketing plan and the types of information contained in a marketing plan.

2-4a Why Write a Marketing Plan?

By specifying objectives and defining the actions required to attain them, you can provide in a marketing plan the basis by which actual and expected performance can be compared. Marketing can be not only one of the most expensive and complicated business activities, but it is also one of the most important. The written marketing plan provides clearly stated activities that help employees and managers understand and work toward common goals.

Writing a marketing plan allows you to examine the marketing environment in conjunction with the inner workings of the business. Once the marketing plan is written, it serves as a reference point for the success of future activities. Finally, the marketing plan allows the marketing manager to enter the marketplace with an awareness of possibilities and problems. Research shows that marketers who proactively write a marketing plan are 356 percent more likely to report success.[15]

2-4b Marketing Plan Elements

Marketing plans can be presented in many ways. Most businesses need a written marketing plan because a marketing plan is large and can be complex. The details about tasks and activity assignments may be lost if communicated orally. Regardless of the way a marketing plan is presented, some elements are common to all marketing plans. Figure 2.4 shows these elements, which include defining the business mission, performing a situation analysis, defining objectives, delineating a target market, and establishing components of the marketing mix. Other elements that may be included in a plan are budgets, implementation timetables, required marketing research efforts, or elements of advanced strategic planning.

2-4c Writing the Marketing Plan

The creation and implementation of a complete marketing plan will allow the organization to achieve marketing objectives and succeed. However, the marketing plan is only as good as the information it contains and the effort, creativity, and thought that went into its creation. Having a good marketing information system and a wealth of competitive intelligence (covered in Chapter 9) is critical to a thorough and accurate situation analysis. The role of managerial intuition is also important in the creation and selection of marketing strategies. Managers must weigh any information against its accuracy and their own judgment when making a marketing decision.

---

planning the process of anticipating future events and determining strategies to achieve organizational objectives in the future

marketing planning designing activities relating to marketing objectives and the changing marketing environment

marketing plan a written document that acts as a guidebook of marketing activities for the marketing manager

Figure 2.4 Elements of a Marketing Plan

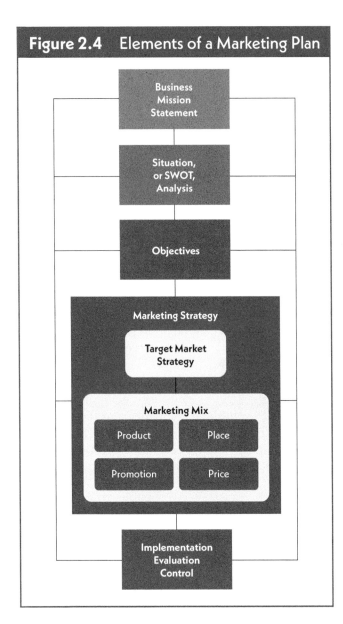

Note that the overall structure of the marketing plan (Figure 2.4) should not be viewed as a series of sequential planning steps. Many of the marketing plan elements are decided simultaneously and in conjunction with one another. Further, every marketing plan has different content, depending on the organization and its mission, objectives, targets, and marketing mix

mission statement a statement of the firm's business based on a careful analysis of benefits sought by present and potential customers and an analysis of existing and anticipated environmental conditions

marketing myopia defining a business in terms of goods and services rather than in terms of the benefits customers seek

components. There is not one single correct format for a marketing plan. Many organizations have their own distinctive format or terminology for creating a marketing plan. Every marketing plan should be unique to the firm for which it was created. Remember, however, that although the format and order of presentation should be flexible, the same types of questions and topic areas should be covered in any marketing plan.

2-5 Elements of a Marketing Plan

2-5 Describe the elements of a marketing plan

As seen in Figure 2.4, there are several elements in a marketing plan. These will be discussed next.

2-5a Defining the Business Mission

The foundation of any marketing plan is the firm's **mission statement**, which answers the question "What business are we in?" The way a firm defines its business mission profoundly affects the firm's long-run resource allocation, profitability, and survival. The mission statement is based on a careful analysis of benefits sought by present and potential customers and an analysis of existing and anticipated environmental conditions. The firm's mission statement establishes boundaries for all subsequent decisions, objectives, and strategies.

A mission statement should focus on the market or markets the organization is attempting to serve rather than on the good or service offered. Otherwise, a new technology may quickly make the good or service obsolete and the mission statement irrelevant to company functions. Business mission statements that are stated too narrowly suffer from **marketing myopia**—defining a business in terms of goods and services rather than in terms of the benefits customers seek. In this context, *myopia* means narrow,

A marketing plan is only as good as the information it contains and the effort, creativity, and thought that went into its creation.

short-term thinking. For example, Frito-Lay defines its mission as being in the snack-food business rather than in the corn chip business. The mission of sports teams is not just to play games but also to serve the interests of the fans.

Alternatively, business missions may be stated too broadly. "To provide products of superior quality and value that improve the lives of the world's consumers" is probably too broad a mission statement for any firm except Procter & Gamble. Care must be taken when stating what business a firm is in. For example, the mission of Ben & Jerry's centers on three important aspects of its ice cream business: (1) Product: "To make, distribute and sell the finest quality all natural ice cream and euphoric concoctions with a continued commitment to incorporating wholesome, natural ingredients and promoting business practices that respect the Earth and the Environment"; (2) Economic: "To operate the Company on a sustainable financial basis of profitable growth, increasing value for our stakeholders and expanding opportunities for development and career growth for our employees"; and (3) Social: "To operate the Company in a way that actively recognizes the central role that business plays in society by initiating innovative ways to improve the quality of life locally, nationally, and internationally."[16] By correctly stating the business mission in terms of the benefits that customers seek, the foundation for the marketing plan is set. Many companies are focusing on designing more appropriate mission statements because these statements are frequently displayed on the companies' websites.

2-5b Conducting a Situation Analysis

Marketers must understand the current and potential environment in which the product or service will be marketed. A situation analysis is sometimes called a **SWOT analysis**—that is, the firm should identify its internal strengths (**S**) and weaknesses (**W**) and examine external opportunities (**O**) and threats (**T**).

When examining internal strengths and weaknesses, the marketing manager should focus on organizational resources such as production costs, marketing skills, financial resources, company or brand image, employee capabilities, and available technology. For example, IBM has a history of reinventing itself and adapting to new opportunities and threats. In 1896, the company started out by manufacturing and selling machinery such as commercial scales and meat and cheese slicers. In 1924, IBM narrowed its focus to business machines, and in the early 1960s, it designed a revolutionary system that made it possible for machines in a product line to work together. IBM introduced its first personal computer in 1981, following market opportunities forged by other computer companies. By the 1990s, however, IBM had lost billions

of dollars because it focused on desktop and personal productivity rather than on pursuing opportunities in business applications. The company rallied and redirected its efforts on building a successful IT and consulting business. Today, IBM has evolved into a cognitive solutions and cloud computing company.[17]

When examining external opportunities and threats, marketing managers must analyze aspects of the marketing environment. This process is called **environmental scanning**—the collection and interpretation of information about forces, events, and relationships in the external environment that may affect the future of the organization or the implementation of the marketing plan. Environmental scanning helps identify market opportunities and threats and provides guidelines for the design of marketing strategy. Increasing competition from overseas firms and the fast growth of digital technology essentially ended Kodak's consumer film business. After emerging from bankruptcy, Kodak has repositioned the firm as a smaller, business-to-business (B2B) company that offers commercial printing and digital imaging services.[18] The six most often studied macroenvironmental forces are social, demographic, economic, technological, political and legal, and competitive. These forces are examined in detail in Chapter 4.

Rapid changes in the environment, such as the emergence, spread, and impact of the COVID-19 pandemic, can make marketing plans developed prior to these environmental changes partially or totally obsolete. In the first quarter of 2020, sales in many product categories plummeted, and businesses were forced to close and/or operate at a set proportion of their capacities (e.g., restaurants only allowed to serve 25 percent of seating capacity and requiring occupants of tables to be seated at least 6 feet from other tables). Consumers were asked or told to self-quarantine except in specific circumstances, such as grocery shopping, seeking healthcare, or other activities identified by state or local governments.

Creative operators ranging from fast food to exclusive restaurants adapted by offering take-out and drive-through services to produce at least some income during closures and to retain some employees. Some restaurants were able to adapt quickly enough to retain a substantial proportion of the sales that they had experienced before the pandemic emerged. Other firms, such as spas, hair salons and other

---

SWOT analysis identifying internal strengths (S) and weaknesses (W) and also examining external opportunities (O) and threats (T)

environmental scanning collection and interpretation of information about forces, events, and relationships in the external environment that may affect the future of the organization or the implementation of the marketing plan

"high touch" organizations had to close longer due to the inability to provide required space between individual service providers and customers.

The emergence and longevity of the COVID-19 pandemic was a surprise to most businesses, investors, and consumers. Careful environmental scanning and adaptation to new environmental conditions may have major long-term effects on the future of specific organizations.

2-5c Competitive Advantage

Performing a SWOT analysis allows firms to identify their **competitive advantage**. A competitive advantage is a set of unique features of a company and its products that are perceived by the target market as significant and superior to those of the competition. It is the factor or factors that cause customers to patronize a firm and not the competition. There are three types of competitive advantage: cost, product/service differentiation, and niche.

Cost Competitive Advantage

Cost leadership can result from obtaining inexpensive raw materials, creating an efficient scale of plant operations, designing products for ease of manufacture, controlling overhead costs, and avoiding marginal customers. IKEA is a global cost leader in home furnishings. IKEA's business model focuses on offering "a wide range of well-designed, functional home furnishing products at prices so low that as many people as possible will be able to afford these products." IKEA does this by constantly discovering and eliminating unnecessary costs, and through efficiencies in production."[19] Having a **cost competitive advantage** means being the low-cost competitor in an industry while maintaining satisfactory profit margins. Costs can be reduced in a variety of ways:

- **Experience curves:** Experience curves tell us that costs decline at a predictable rate as experience with a product increases. The experience curve effect encompasses a broad range of manufacturing, marketing, and administrative costs. Experience curves reflect learning by doing, technological advances, and economies of scale. After 11 years of manufacturing experience,

---

competitive advantage a set of unique features of a company and its products that are perceived by the target market as significant and superior to those of the competition

cost competitive advantage being the low-cost competitor in an industry while maintaining satisfactory profit margins

experience curves curves that show costs declining at a predictable rate as experience with a product increases

Ford Motor Company was able to lower costs of the Model T and increase market share from 10 percent to 55 percent. The company modernized plants and eliminated model changes. In addition, Ford offered the Model T in only black because black paint dried the fastest, thereby increasing production speed.[20] Experience curves allow management to forecast costs and set prices based on anticipated costs as opposed to current costs.

- **Efficient labor:** Labor costs can be an important component of total costs in low-skill, labor-intensive industries such as product assembly and apparel manufacturing. Many U.S. publishers and software developers send data entry, design, and formatting tasks to India, and other countries, where skilled engineers are available at a lower overall cost.

- **No-frills goods and services:** Marketers can lower costs by removing frills and options from a product or service. Aldi is an example of a no-frills retailer. The company, which has been voted number one in price for five years running, has several ways it saves shoppers money. Aldi has a cart deposit system that requires the customer to return the cart for a quarter so employees don't have to chase down carts in the parking lot. Products are displayed in the boxes they arrive in, it's smaller-footprint stores are less expensive to operate, and it limits store hours to the most popular shopping times.[21]

- **Government subsidies:** Governments can provide cash grants and interest-free loans to target industries. These subsidies are given to promote growth or impact business and consumer behavior. Such government assistance has been given for years to the farming and oil industries.[22]

- **Product design:** Cutting-edge design technology can help offset high labor costs. BMW is a world leader in designing cars for ease of manufacture and assembly. Reverse engineering—the process of disassembling a product piece by piece to learn its components and obtain clues as to the manufacturing process—can also mean savings. Reverse engineering a low-cost competitor's product can save research and design costs. Cipla Pharmaceuticals, which is among the largest pharmaceutical companies in India, uses reverse engineering to replicate the chemical composition of drugs developed by other pharmaceutical firms and markets them at a lower cost. For example, its anti-AIDS drugs cost $300 annually, compared to $12,000 charged by other companies.[23]

- **Reengineering:** Reengineering entails fundamental rethinking and redesign of business processes to achieve dramatic improvements in critical measures of performance. It often involves reorganizing functional departments such as sales, engineering, and production into cross-disciplinary teams. Technology is an important part of many reengineering efforts. For example, Kroger's new reengineering program links together shopping, e-commerce, and logistics. Automated fulfillment centers use robots for packing, sorting, and loading groceries, and vans make same-day deliveries to households. Data analytics provide information on consumer trends, and mobile apps distribute customer promotions and coupons. QR codes handle payments online and at self-checkout. These changes have made Kroger one of the most successful grocery retailers in the country.[24]

- **Production innovations:** Production innovations such as new technology and simplified production techniques help lower the average cost of production. Technologies such as computer-aided design (CAD) and computer-aided manufacturing (CAM) and increasingly sophisticated robots help companies such as Boeing, Ford, and General Electric reduce their manufacturing costs.

- **New methods of service delivery:** Medical expenses have been substantially lowered by the use of outpatient surgery and walk-in clinics. Southwest Airlines, the biggest low-cost carrier in the country, offered a new method of service delivery compared to other major airlines. The airline possesses a limited variety of aircraft, conducts operations at smaller and less prominent airports (which offer lower fees), and maintains high aircraft utilization rates by using short-haul flights and rapid turnarounds. The boarding process at Southwest is different as well, with boarding positions distributed to fliers on a first come, first served basis upon check in. Customers are assigned groups and numbers, and board accordingly.[25]

Product/Service Differentiation Competitive Advantage

Because cost competitive advantages are subject to continual erosion, product/service differentiation tends to provide a longer-lasting competitive advantage. The durability of this strategy tends to make it more attractive to many top managers. A **product/service differentiation competitive advantage** exists when a firm provides something that is unique and valuable to buyers beyond simply offering a lower price than that of the competition. Examples include brand names (Lexus), a strong dealer network (Caterpillar for construction work), product reliability (Maytag appliances), image (Neiman Marcus in retailing), or service (Zappos).

PetSmart has partnered with two renowned interior designers, Nate Berkus and Jeremiah Brent, to launch a new collection allowing pets to live more stylishly and comfortably. This collection will also allow pet parents to buy beautiful and functional items that blend with the aesthetics of their homes. For example, the collection includes faux leather and sherpa couches for guinea pigs and hamsters, a mahogany stand to showcase aquatic creatures, and beautiful accessories for lizards and snakes that mimic their natural habitats. This service is not available anywhere else, providing PetSmart with an important competitive advantage.[26]

Niche Competitive Advantage

A **niche competitive advantage** seeks to target and effectively serve a single segment of the market (refer to Chapter 8). For small companies with limited resources that potentially face giant competitors, niche targeting may be the only viable option. A market segment that has good growth potential but is not crucial to the success of major competitors is a good candidate for developing a niche strategy.

Many companies using a niche strategy serve only a limited geographic market. Stew Leonard's is an extremely successful but small grocery store chain found only in Connecticut and New York. Other market niches can be found by looking at consumer characteristics such as demographics (e.g., age or gender), hobbies, income, or life stage. Whole Foods has focused on affluent, health-conscious consumers. The company offered a large selection of organic foods before consumers could find organics everywhere. Lefty's San Francisco is a retailer dedicated to selling products for left-handed people. Although it has only one store, the company has an extensive online presence and has become known as an expert in left-handed products.[27]

Building Sustainable Competitive Advantage

The key to having a competitive advantage is the ability to sustain that advantage. A **sustainable competitive advantage** is one that the competition cannot easily copy. For example, Amazon is the undisputed leader of online retailing. The company has achieved sustainable competitive

---

product/service differentiation competitive advantage the provision of something that is unique and valuable to buyers beyond simply offering a lower price than that of the competition

niche competitive advantage the advantage achieved when a firm seeks to target and effectively serve a small segment of the market

sustainable competitive advantage an advantage that cannot be copied by the competition

advantage through its ability to offer the lowest prices, the widest variety of products, and a well-developed, efficient delivery network. In addition, Amazon has a massive number of users with credit cards on file, making the purchase process quick and easy for customers. Starbucks is the largest coffee company in the world. Along with offering the finest coffee beans, it provides the "Starbucks Experience" that makes customers feel at home through the design and ambience of its stores, creating an emotional connection with customers. Employees foster that connection by providing great service. Starbucks Rewards Card encourages customers to return by offering a host of benefits. Few other coffee companies have this combination of characteristics.[28]

In contrast, consider Blockbuster. The company was the market leader in video stores for a time, but its advantage was not sustainable. Blockbuster ignored the competition and the environment in which it operated,

The emotional connection that Starbucks generates with its customers gives the company its competitive advantage.

---

marketing objective a statement of what is to be accomplished through marketing activities

missing out on innovation in other, more convenient ways to watch movies. Competition from startups like Netflix and other streaming services took Blockbuster down.[29]

The notion of competitive advantage means that a successful firm will stake out a position unique in some manner from its rivals (e.g., Amazon: price and selection; Lexus: quality and luxury; Starbucks: customer experience). Imitation by competitors indicates a lack of competitive advantage and may ensure mediocre performance. Microsoft's Zune MP3 player was a product developed to compete with Apple's iPod. However, the product was too late to market, and its special features, including sharing songs with other Zune owners who were close by, were not enough to beat the iPod.[30] Moreover, competitors rarely stand still, so it is not surprising that imitation causes managers to feel trapped in a seemingly endless game of catchup. They are regularly surprised by the new accomplishments of their rivals.

Rather than copy competitors, companies need to build their own competitive advantages. A sustainable competitive advantage is a function of the speed with which competitors can imitate a leading company's strategy and plans. The sources of tomorrow's competitive advantages are the skills and assets of the organization. Assets include patents, copyrights, locations, equipment, and technology that are superior to those of the competition. Skills are functions such as customer service and promotion that the firm performs better than its competitors. Marketing managers should continually focus the firm's skills and assets on sustaining and creating competitive advantages.

Remember, a sustainable competitive advantage is a function of the speed with which competitors can imitate a leading company's strategy and plans. Imitation requires a competitor to identify the leader's competitive advantage, determine how it is achieved, and then learn how to duplicate it.

2-5d Setting Marketing Plan Objectives

Before the details of a marketing plan can be developed, objectives for the plan must be stated. Without objectives, there is no basis for measuring the success of marketing plan activities.

A **marketing objective** is a statement of what is to be accomplished through marketing activities.

A strong marketing objective for Purina might be "to increase sales on Purina brand cat food between January 1 and December 31, by 15 percent, compared to prior year sales of $300 million."

- **Realistic:** Managers should develop objectives that have a chance of being met. For example, it may be unrealistic for start-up firms or new products to command dominant market share, given other competitors in the marketplace.

- **Measurable:** Managers need to be able to quantitatively measure whether or not an objective has been met. For example, it would be difficult to determine success for an objective that states, "To increase sales of cat food." If the company sells 1 percent more cat food, does that mean the objective was met? Instead, a specific number should be stated, "To increase sales of Purina brand cat food from $300 million to $345 million."

- **Time Specific:** By what time should the objective be met? "To increase sales of Purina brand cat food between January 1 and December 31."

- **Compared to a benchmark:** If the objective is to increase sales by 15 percent, it is important to know the baseline against which the objective will be measured. Will it be current sales? Last year's sales? For example, "To increase sales of Purina brand cat food by 15 percent over 2022 sales of $300 million."

Objectives must be consistent with and indicate the organization's priorities. Specifically, objectives flow from the business mission statement to the rest of the marketing plan.

Carefully specified objectives serve several functions. First, they communicate marketing management philosophies and provide direction for lower-level marketing managers so that marketing efforts are integrated and pointed in a consistent direction. Objectives also serve as motivators by creating something for employees to strive for. When objectives are attainable and challenging, they motivate those charged with achieving the objectives. Additionally, the process of writing specific objectives forces executives to clarify their thinking. Finally, objectives form a basis for control: the effectiveness of a plan can be gauged considering the stated objectives.

2-5e Describing the Target Market

Marketing strategy involves the activities of selecting and describing one or more target markets and developing and maintaining a marketing mix that will produce mutually satisfying exchanges with target markets.

Target Market Strategy

A market segment is a group of individuals or organizations who share one or more characteristics. They therefore may have relatively similar product needs. For example,

parents of newborn babies need formula, diapers, and special foods.

The target market strategy identifies the market segment or segments on which to focus. A **target market** is a group of people or organizations for which an organization designs, implements, and maintains a marketing mix intended to meet the needs of that group, resulting in mutually satisfying exchanges. Thus, parents of newborn babies would be a natural market to target for Proctor and Gamble's Pampers diapers.

This process begins with a **market opportunity analysis (MOA)**—the description and estimation of the size and sales potential of market segments that interest the firm and the assessment of key competitors in these market segments. After the firm describes the market segments, it may target one or more of them. There are three general strategies for selecting target markets.

Target markets can be selected by appealing to the entire market with one marketing mix, concentrating on one segment, or appealing to multiple market segments using multiple marketing mixes. The characteristics, advantages, and disadvantages of each strategic option are examined in Chapter 8. Target markets could be 18- to 25-year-old females who are interested in fashion (*Vogue* magazine), people concerned about sugar and calories in their soft drinks (Diet Pepsi), or parents without the time to potty train their children (special camps where kids are potty trained).

Any market segment that is targeted must be fully described. Demographics, psychographics, and buyer behavior should be assessed. Buyer behavior is covered in Chapters 6 and 7. If segments are differentiated by ethnicity, multicultural aspects of the marketing mix should be examined. If the target market is international, it is especially important to describe differences in culture, economic and technological development, and political structure that may affect the marketing plan. Global marketing is covered in more detail in Chapter 5.

---

marketing strategy the activities of selecting and describing one or more target markets and developing and maintaining a marketing mix that will produce mutually satisfying exchanges with target markets

target market a group of people or organizations for which an organization designs, implements, and maintains a marketing mix intended to meet the needs of that group, resulting in mutually satisfying exchanges

market opportunity analysis (MOA) the description and estimation of the size and sales potential of market segments that are of interest to the firm and the assessment of key competitors in these market segments

2-5f The Marketing Mix

The term **marketing mix (four Ps)** refers to a unique blend of product, place (distribution), promotion, and pricing strategies designed to produce mutually satisfying exchanges with a target market. The marketing manager can control each component of the marketing mix, but the strategies for all four components must be blended to achieve optimal results. Any marketing mix is only as good as its weakest component. For example, the first pump toothpastes were distributed over cosmetics counters and failed. Not until pump toothpastes were distributed the same way as tube toothpastes did the products succeed. The best promotion and the lowest price cannot save a poor product. Similarly, excellent products with poor placing, pricing, or promotion will likely fail.

Successful marketing mixes have been carefully designed to satisfy target markets. At first glance, McDonald's and Wendy's may appear to have roughly identical marketing mixes because they are both in the fast-food hamburger business. However, McDonald's has been most successful at targeting parents with young children for lunchtime meals, whereas Wendy's targets the adult crowd for lunches and dinner. McDonald's has playgrounds, Ronald McDonald the clown, and children's Happy Meals. Wendy's has fresher foods, better customer service, and no playgrounds.

Variations in marketing mixes do not occur by chance. Astute marketing managers devise marketing strategies to gain advantages over competitors and best serve the needs and wants of a particular target market segment. By manipulating elements of the marketing mix, marketing managers can fine-tune the customer offering and achieve competitive success.

Product Strategies

Of the four Ps, the marketing mix typically starts with the product. The heart of the marketing mix, the starting point, is the product offering and product strategy. It is hard to design a place strategy, decide on a promotion campaign, or set a price without knowing the product to be marketed.

The product includes not only the physical unit but also its package, warranty, after-sale service, brand name, company image, value, and many other factors. A Godiva chocolate has many product elements: the chocolate itself, a fancy gold wrapper, a customer satisfaction guarantee,

---

marketing mix (four Ps) a unique blend of product, place (distribution), promotion, and pricing strategies designed to produce mutually satisfying exchanges with a target market

and the prestige of the Godiva brand name. We buy things not only for what they do (benefits) but also for what they mean to us (status, quality, or reputation).

Products can be tangible goods such as computers, ideas like those offered by a consultant, or services such as medical care. Products should also offer customer value. Product decisions are covered in Chapters 10 and 11, whereas services marketing is detailed in Chapter 12.

Place (Distribution) Strategies

Place, or distribution, strategies are concerned with making products available when and where customers want them. Would you rather buy a kiwi fruit at the 24-hour grocery store within walking distance or fly to Australia to pick your own? A part of this P—place—is physical distribution, which involves all the business activities concerned with storing and transporting raw materials or finished products. The goal is to make sure products arrive in usable condition at designated places when needed. Place strategies are covered in Chapters 13 and 14.

Promotion Strategies

Promotion includes advertising, public relations, sales promotion, and personal selling. Promotion's role in the marketing mix is to bring about mutually satisfying exchanges with target markets by informing, educating, persuading, and reminding them of the benefits of an organization or a product. A good promotion strategy, like using a beloved cartoon character such as SpongeBob SquarePants to sell gummy snacks, can dramatically increase sales. Each element of this P—promotion—is coordinated and managed with the others to create a promotional blend or mix. These integrated marketing communications activities are described in Chapters 15 through 17. Technology-driven and social media aspects of promotional marketing are covered in Chapter 18.

Pricing Strategies

Price is what a buyer must give up to obtain a product. It is often the most flexible of the four Ps—the element quickest to change. Marketers can raise or lower prices more frequently and easily than they can change other marketing mix variables. Price is an important competitive weapon and is very important to the organization because price multiplied by the number of units sold equals total revenue for the firm. Pricing decisions are covered in Chapter 19.

2-5g Following Up on the Marketing Plan

One of the keys to success overlooked by many businesses is to actively follow up on the marketing plan.

How Netflix Changed the TV Industry

Kaspars Grinvalds/Shutterstock.com

Netflix revolutionized the television industry. It dominates on-demand media, boasting 223 million global subscribers, and has a strong competitive advantage against other entertainment companies. Netflix has been successful by creating engaging original programming, using big data to analyze users' preferences, and allowing their subscribers to choose when and how to watch content. Netflix was so successful with its on-demand entertainment, it is displacing cable and satellite subscriptions. In fact, approximately 25 million subscribers have discarded their cable subscriptions. To survive, traditional media companies have had to adjust their business models.

Netflix started as a mail-based DVD subscription service. Customers would order a DVD online, receive it in the mail, and return it the same way. Video-rental stores, such as Blockbuster, were its main competition. Ten years after Netflix began, technology improved enough for it to offer streaming services. For a monthly subscription, consumers could access any program at any time on whatever device they wanted. They did not have to be limited to a schedule, interrupted by commercials, or even leave home. This innovation almost killed the video rental business, as well as reduced the number of people going to movie theaters. In response to Netflix, other media companies began offering on-demand content.

In 2013, Netflix branched out and produced its own original content. Soon, it surpassed the established networks, with its series and movies becoming many of the most critically acclaimed and talked about shows on television. Its first original series, *House of Cards,* won four Emmy Awards. One of its original movies, *Roma,* won three Oscars and received 10 nominations. Its popular shows gave rise to the "Netflix Effect," in which actors were propelled to instant fame, and products and ideas related to the shows influenced what people searched for and purchased. For example, *The Queen's Gambit,* was one of Netflix's most-watched limited series. After the show aired, sales of chess sets rose by 87 percent and sales of chess books increased by 603 percent. The show *Bridgerton* caused a 65 percent increase in online searches for embroidery hoops, and a spike in sales of *Bridgerton* influenced fashion and housewares.

Netflix was also the first to upload entire seasons of established TV series at the same time. This approach led to the binge-watching trend because subscribers did not have to wait a week for a new episode in a series. By contrast, broadcast and cable TV still used the once-a-week installment model. Netflix is now testing weekly releases of highly watched shows.

Netflix creates its service around customers. It has an easy-to-use navigation menu, and its system tracks what customers watch so it can recommend shows that are similar. When Netflix expanded globally, it studied each country's target markets to provide a customized experience to its users.

For its newest growth strategy, Netflix has launched an ad-supported option that is 30 percent less expensive than its basic, ad-free tier. With this option, users would be shown four to five minutes of commercials per hour of content, Netflix hopes to attract new users who are price sensitive. Eventually, the company plans to provide personalized ad content similar to the way it provides viewing recommendations.[31]

The time spent researching, developing, and writing a useful and accurate marketing plan goes to waste if the plan is not used by the organization. One of the best ways to get the most out of a marketing plan is to correctly implement it. Once the first steps to implementation are taken, evaluation and control will help guide the organization to success as laid out by the marketing plan.

Four Characteristics of a Marketing Audit

1. **Comprehensive:** The marketing audit covers all the major marketing issues facing an organization—not just trouble spots.

2. **Systematic:** The marketing audit takes place in an orderly sequence and covers the organization's marketing environment, internal marketing system, and specific marketing activities. The diagnosis is followed by an action plan with both short- and long-run proposals for improving overall marketing effectiveness.

3. **Independent:** The marketing audit is normally conducted by an inside or outside party that is independent enough to have top management's confidence and can be objective.

4. **Periodic:** The marketing audit should be carried out on a regular schedule instead of only in a crisis. Whether it seems successful or is in deep trouble, any organization can benefit greatly from such an audit.

2-5h Implementation

Implementation is the process that turns a marketing plan into action assignments and ensures that these assignments are executed in a way that accomplishes the plan's objectives. Implementation activities may involve detailed job assignments, activity descriptions, timelines, budgets, and lots of communication. Implementation requires delegating authority and responsibility, determining a time frame for completing tasks, and allocating resources. Sometimes a strategic plan also requires task force management. A *task force* is a tightly organized unit under the direction of a manager who, usually, has broad authority. A task force is established to accomplish a single goal or mission and thus works against a deadline.

Implementing a plan has another dimension: gaining acceptance. New plans mean change, and change creates resistance. One reason people resist change is that they fear they will lose something. For example, when new-product research is taken away from marketing research and given to a new-product department, the director of marketing research will naturally resist this loss of part of their domain. Misunderstanding and lack of trust also create opposition to change, but effective communication through open discussion and teamwork can be one way of overcoming resistance to change.

Although implementation is essentially "doing what you said you were going to do," many organizations repeatedly experience failures in strategy implementation. Brilliant marketing plans are doomed to fail if they are not properly implemented. These detailed communications may or may not be part of the written marketing plan. If they are not part of the plan, they should be specified elsewhere as soon as the plan has been communicated. Strong, forward-thinking leadership can overcome resistance to change, even in large, highly integrated companies where change seems very unlikely.

2-5i Evaluation and Control

After a marketing plan is implemented, it should be evaluated. **Evaluation** entails gauging the extent to which

---

implementation the process that turns a marketing plan into action assignments and ensures that these assignments are executed in a way that accomplishes the plan's objectives

evaluation gauging the extent to which the marketing objectives have been achieved during the specified time period

control provides the mechanisms for evaluating marketing results in light of the plan's objectives and for correcting actions that do not help the organization reach those objectives within budget guidelines

marketing audit a thorough, systematic, periodic evaluation of the objectives, strategies, structure, and performance of the marketing organization

---

marketing objectives have been achieved during the specified time-period. Four common reasons for failing to achieve a marketing objective are:

1. Unrealistic marketing objectives
2. Inappropriate marketing strategies in the plan
3. Poor implementation
4. Changes in the environment after the objective was specified and the strategy was implemented

Once a plan is chosen and implemented, its effectiveness must be monitored. **Control** provides the mechanisms for evaluating marketing results considering the plan's objectives and for correcting actions that do not help the organization reach those objectives within budget guidelines. Firms need to establish formal and informal control programs to make the entire operation more efficient.

Perhaps the broadest control device available to marketing managers is the **marketing audit**—a thorough, systematic, periodic evaluation of the objectives, strategies, structure, and performance of the marketing organization. A marketing audit helps management allocate marketing resources efficiently.

Although the main purpose of the marketing audit is to develop a full profile of the organization's marketing effort and to provide a basis for developing and revising the marketing plan, it is also an excellent way to improve communication and raise the level of marketing consciousness within the organization. It is a useful vehicle for selling the strategic marketing philosophy and techniques to other organization members.

2-5j Postaudit Tasks

After the audit has been completed, three tasks remain. First, the audit should profile existing weaknesses and inhibiting factors, as well as the firm's strengths and the new opportunities available to it. Recommendations must be judged and prioritized so that those with the potential to contribute most to improved marketing performance can be implemented first. The usefulness of the data also depends on the auditor's skill in interpreting and presenting the data so decision makers can quickly grasp the major points.

The second task is to ensure that the role of the audit has clearly been communicated. It is unlikely that the suggestions will require a radical change in the way the firm operates. The audit's main role is to address the question "Where are we now?" and to suggest ways to improve what the firm already does.

The final post audit task is to make someone accountable for implementing recommendations. All too often, reports are presented, applauded, and filed away to gather dust. The person made accountable should be committed to the project and have the managerial power to make things happen.

iStock.com/Shaun

Chapter 3

Ethics and Social Responsibility

Learning Outcomes

After studying this chapter, you will be able to . . .

3-1 Explain the determinants of a civil society

3-2 Explain the concept of ethical behavior

3-3 Describe ethical behavior in business

3-4 Discuss corporate social responsibility

3-5 Describe the arguments for and against social responsibility

3-6 Explain cause-related marketing

3-1 Determinants of a Civil Society

3-1 Explain the determinants of a civil society

Have you ever stopped to think about the social glue that binds society together? That is, what factors keep people and organizations from running amok and doing harm, and what factors create order in a society like ours? The answer lies in **social control**, defined as any means used to maintain behavioral norms and regulate conflict.[1] **Behavioral norms** are standards of proper or acceptable behavior. Social control is part of your life at every level, from your family to your local community, to the nation, to the global civilization. Several modes of social control are important to marketing:

1. **Ethics: Ethics** are the moral principles or values that generally govern the conduct of an individual or a group. Ethical rules and guidelines, along with customs and traditions, provide principles of right action.

2. **Laws:** Often, ethical rules and guidelines are codified into law. Laws governments create are then enforced by governmental authority. This process is how the dictum "Thou shall not steal" has become part of formal law throughout the land. Law, however, is not a perfect mechanism for ensuring good corporate and employee behavior. Laws often address only the lowest common denominator of socially acceptable behavior. In other words, just because something is legal does not mean that it is ethical. For example, Texas Pete is a hot sauce sold in grocery stores across the country. The packaging for Texas Pete features a lone star, just as the Texas state flag does, and a cowboy holding a lasso. The packaging, along with the name of the product, seems to indicate that the product is made in the state of Texas, or that it is at least made from ingredients sourced in Texas. Texas Pete, however, is produced by TW Garner Foods Company, a company headquartered in North Carolina, more than 800 miles from Texas. A class action lawsuit was filed against the company for false advertising. The lawsuit claimed that consumers were paying a premium price based on their belief that the product originated

in Texas, which has a reputation for spicy food. Texas Pete does not explicitly state that the product is manufactured in Texas and actually lists TW Garner Foods' North Carolina address on the bottle, but the name of the product and the packaging certainly suggest that it is a genuine Texas-based product and could be misleading to consumers.[2] While this presentation is technically legal, is this ethical? What's your opinion? Here's another example: In every state, littering is a problem—and has been for many years. Threats of fines and even jail time are shrugged off as people toss food wrappers, plastic straws and cups, and everything else imaginable out the car window. Many companies are implementing new policies to try and curtail the negative effects of littering. For example, Starbucks in California no longer automatically gives straws and plastic cutlery to customers, but, rather, will only provide these items when customers specifically request them.[3]

3. **Formal and Informal Groups:** Businesses, professional organizations (such as the American Marketing Association and the American Medical Association), and clubs (such as Shriners and Ducks Unlimited) all have codes of conduct. These codes prescribe acceptable and desired behaviors for their members.

4. **Self-Regulation:** Self-regulation involves the voluntary acceptance of standards established by nongovernmental entities, such as the American Association of Advertising Agencies (AAAA) or the National Association of Manufacturers. The AAAA has a self-regulation arm that deals with deceptive advertising. Other associations have regulations relating to child labor, environmental issues, conservation, and a host of other issues.

5. **The Media:** In an open, democratic society, the media play a key role in informing the public about the actions of individuals and organizations—both good and bad. Laundress, a luxury laundry detergent brand that claims to be better for you and better for the environment, came under fire after issuing a safety notice for almost

---

social control any means used to maintain behavioral norms and regulate conflict

behavioral norms standards of proper or acceptable behavior. Several modes of social control are important to marketing.

ethics the moral principles or values that generally govern the conduct of an individual or a group

all of its products. The company released the notice on its social media accounts but provided very little information about the reason for the notice. It was later revealed that the majority of the products the brand manufactured between January 2021 and September 2022 contained heightened levels of bacteria that were causing severe skin rashes and other physical ailments.[4] Many major media outlets, including *The New York Times* and *USA Today*, published articles to inform the public of this safety notice and the product recall that eventually followed.

6. **An Active Civil Society:** An informed and engaged society can help mold individual and corporate ethics, as well as socially responsible behavior. Research reveals that 56 percent of U.S. consumers stop buying from companies they believe are unethical.[5] In the United Kingdom, 53 percent of consumers reported that they would completely stop buying from a brand accused of sourcing from unethical suppliers.[6]

3-2 The Concept of Ethical Behavior

3-2 Explain the concept of ethical behavior

It has been said that ethics is something everyone likes to talk about but nobody can define. Others have suggested that defining ethics is like trying to nail Jell-O to a wall. When you begin to think you understand it, it starts squirting out between your fingers.

Simply put, ethics can be viewed as the standard of behavior by which conduct is judged. Legal standards may not always be ethical, and vice versa. Laws are the values and standards the courts enforce. Ethics, then, consists of personal moral principles. For example, no legal statute makes it a crime for someone to "cut in line." Yet, if someone does not want to wait in line and cuts to the front, it often makes others very angry.

If you have ever resented a line-cutter, then you understand ethics and have applied ethical standards in life. Waiting your turn in line is a social expectation that exists because lines ensure order and allocate the space and time needed to complete transactions. Waiting your turn is an expected but unwritten behavior that plays a critical role in an orderly society.

So it is with ethics. Ethics consist of those unwritten rules we have developed for our interactions with each other. These unwritten rules govern us when we are sharing resources or honoring contracts. "Waiting your turn" is a higher standard than the laws passed to maintain order. Those laws apply when physical force or threats are used to push to the front of the line. Assault, battery, and threats are forms of criminal conduct for which the offender can be prosecuted. But the law does not apply to the stealthy line-cutter who simply sneaks to the front, perhaps using a friend and a conversation as a decoy. No laws are broken, but the notions of fairness and justice are offended by one individual putting themself above others and taking advantage of others' time and position.

Ethical questions range from practical, narrowly defined issues, such as a businessperson's obligation to be honest with customers, to broader social and philosophical questions, such as whether a company is responsible for preserving the environment and protecting employee rights. Many ethical dilemmas develop from conflicts between the differing interests of company owners and their workers, customers, and the surrounding community. Managers must balance the ideal against the practical—that is, they must produce a reasonable profit for the company's shareholders while maintaining honesty in business practices and concern for environmental and social issues.

3-2a Ethical Theories

People usually base their individual choice of ethical theory on their life experiences. The following are some of the ethical theories that apply to marketing.[7]

Deontology

The **deontological theory** states that people should adhere to their obligations and duties when analyzing an ethical dilemma. This theory means that a person will follow their obligations to another individual or society because upholding one's duty is considered ethically correct. For instance, a deontologist will always keep their promises to a friend and follow the law. A person who follows this theory will produce very consistent decisions because those decisions will be based on the individual's set duties.

Deontological theory is not necessarily concerned with the welfare of others. For example, suppose a salesperson has decided that it is their ethical duty (and very practical) to always be on time for meetings with clients. Today they are running late. How are they supposed to drive? Is the deontologist supposed to speed, breaking the law to uphold their duty to society, or is the deontologist supposed to arrive at their meeting late, breaking their duty to be on time? This scenario of conflicting obligations does not lead us to a clear, ethically correct resolution, nor does it protect the welfare of others from the deontologist's decision.

---

deontological theory ethical theory stating that people should adhere to their obligations and duties when analyzing an ethical dilemma

Utilitarianism

The **utilitarian ethical theory** is founded on the ability to predict the consequences of an action. To a utilitarian, the choice that yields the greatest benefit to the most people is the ethically correct choice. One benefit of this ethical theory is that the utilitarian can compare similar predicted solutions and use a point system to determine which choice is more beneficial for more people. This point system provides a logical and rational argument for each decision and allows a person to use it on a case-by-case basis.

There are two types of utilitarianism: act utilitarianism and rule utilitarianism. *Act utilitarianism* adheres exactly to the definition of utilitarianism as just described. In act utilitarianism, a person performs the acts that benefit the most people, regardless of personal feelings or societal constraints like laws. *Rule utilitarianism*, however, considers the law and is concerned with fairness. A rule utilitarian seeks to benefit the most people but through the fairest and most just means available. Therefore, added benefits of rule utilitarianism are that it values justice and doing good at the same time.

As is true of all ethical theories, however, both act and rule utilitarianism contain numerous flaws. Inherent in both are the flaws associated with predicting the future. Although people can use their life experiences to attempt to predict outcomes, no human being can be certain that their predictions will come true. This uncertainty can lead to unexpected results, making the utilitarian look unethical as time passes because their choice did not benefit the most people, as they had predicted.

Another assumption a utilitarian must make is that they can compare the various types of consequences against each other on a similar scale. However, comparing material gains such as money against intangible gains such as happiness is impossible because their qualities differ so greatly.

Casuist

The **casuist ethical theory** compares a current ethical dilemma with examples of similar ethical dilemmas and their outcomes. This theory allows one to determine the severity of the situation and to create the best possible solution according to others' experiences. Usually, one will find examples that represent the extremes of the situation so that a compromise can be reached to include the wisdom gained from the previous situations.

One drawback to this ethical theory is that there may not be a set of similar examples for a given ethical dilemma. Perhaps that which is controversial and ethically questionable is new and unexpected. Along the same line of thinking, this theory assumes that the results of the current ethical dilemma will be similar to the results in the examples. This assumption may not be true and would greatly hinder the effectiveness of applying this ethical theory.

Moral Relativism

Moral relativism is a belief in time-and-place ethics, that is, the truth of a moral judgment is relative to the judging person or group. According to a moral relativist, for example, stealing is not always wrong—if you are a parent and your child is starving, stealing a loaf of bread is ethically correct. The proper resolution to ethical dilemmas is based on weighing the competing factors at the moment and then deciding to take the lesser of the evils as the resolution. Moral relativists do not believe in absolute rules. Their beliefs center on the pressure of the moment and whether the pressure justifies the action taken.

Virtue Ethics

Aristotle and Plato taught that solving ethical dilemmas requires training—that individuals solve ethical dilemmas when they develop and nurture a set of virtues. A **virtue** is a character trait valued as being good. Aristotle taught the importance of cultivating virtue in his students and then having them solve ethical dilemmas using those virtues once they had become an integral part of his students' being through their virtue training.

Some modern philosophers have embraced this notion of virtue and have developed lists of what constitutes a virtuous businessperson. Some common virtues for businesspeople are self-discipline, friendliness, caring, courage, compassion, trust, responsibility, honesty, determination, enthusiasm, and humility. You may see other lists of virtues that are longer or shorter, but here is a good start for core business virtues.

---

utilitarian ethical theory ethical theory that is founded on the ability to predict the consequences of an action

casuist ethical theory ethical theory that compares a current ethical dilemma with examples of similar ethical dilemmas and their outcomes

moral relativism a theory of time-and-place ethics; that is, the belief that ethical truths depend on the individuals and groups holding them

virtue a character trait valued as being good

3-3 Ethical Behavior in Business

3-3 Describe ethical behavior in business

Depending on which, if any, ethical theory a businessperson has accepted and uses in their daily conduct, the action they take may vary. For example, faced with bribing a foreign official to get a critically needed contract or shutting down a factory and laying off a thousand workers, a person following a deontology strategy would not pay the bribe.

Why? A deontologist always follows the law. However, a moral relativist would probably pay the bribe.

While the boundaries of what is legal and what is not are often fairly clear (e.g., do not run a red light, do not steal money from a bank, and do not kill anyone), the boundaries of ethical decision making are predicated on which ethical theory one is following. The law typically relies on juries to determine if an act is legal or illegal. Society determines whether an action is ethical or unethical. In 2022, Oracle, an information technology company, was forced to pay $23 million to settle charges of violating the Foreign Corrupt Practices Act (FCPA). The U.S. Department of Justice and the Securities and Exchange Commission (SEC) allege that subsidiaries of the company in India, Turkey, and the United Arab Emirates used discount schemes and sham marketing reimbursements to finance funds that were then used to bribe foreign officials. Michael Egbert, corporate communications VP for Oracle, stated that "The conduct outlined by the SEC is contrary to our core values and clear policies, and if we identify such behavior, we will take appropriate action."[8]

Morals are the rules people develop as a result of cultural values and norms. Culture is a socializing force that dictates what is right and wrong. Moral standards may also reflect the laws and regulations that affect social and economic behavior. Thus, morals can be considered a foundation of ethical behavior.

Morals are usually characterized as good or bad. "Good" and "bad" have many different connotations. One such connotation is "effective" and "ineffective." A good salesperson makes or exceeds the assigned quota. If the salesperson sells a new computer system or an OLED TV to a disadvantaged consumer—knowing full well that the person cannot keep up the monthly payments—is that still a good salesperson? What if the sale enables the salesperson to exceed their quota?

"Good" and "bad" can also refer to "conforming" and "deviant" behaviors. A doctor who runs large ads offering discounts on open-heart surgery would be considered bad, or unprofessional, because they are not conforming to the norms of the medical profession. "Good" and "bad" also express the distinction between law-abiding and criminal behavior. And, finally, different religions define "good" and "bad" in markedly different ways. A Muslim who eats pork are considered bad by other Muslims, for example. Religion is just one of the many factors that affect a businessperson's ethics. Academic researchers have examined how consumers react to the trade-offs between highly competent but less moral service providers and less competent but highly moral service providers. Their study found that consumers valued competence more than morality.[9] In other words, purchasers of services want someone who can do the job right . . . even if that person might be a bit shady. For example, a house-painting company that does excellent work but has had some legal problems in the past would be preferred over a mediocre painting company that has never had complaints or legal problems.

3-3a Morality and Business Ethics

Today's business ethics consist of a subset of major life values learned since birth. The values businesspeople use to make decisions have been acquired through family, educational, and religious institutions.

Ethical values are situation specific and time oriented. Everyone must have an ethical base that applies to conduct in the business world and personal life. One approach to developing a personal set of ethics is to examine the consequences of a particular act. Who is helped or hurt? How long do the consequences last? What actions produce the greatest good for the greatest number of people? A second approach stresses the importance of rules. Rules come in the form of customs, laws, professional standards, and common sense. "Always treat others as you would like to be treated" is an example of a rule.

3-3b Ethical Decision Making

Ethical questions rarely have cut-and-dried answers. Studies show that the following factors tend to influence ethical decision making and judgments:[10]

- **Extent of ethical problems within the organization:** Marketing professionals who perceive fewer ethical problems in their organizations tend to disapprove more strongly of "unethical" or questionable practices than those who perceive more ethical problems. Thus, the healthier the ethical environment, the more likely it is that marketers will take a strong stand against questionable practices.

- **Top management's actions on ethics:** Top managers can influence the behavior of marketing professionals by encouraging ethical behavior and discouraging unethical behavior. Top management set an example for lower-level employees about what types of behavior are acceptable, so the top managers in an organization must behave ethically to show employees what is expected of them. When top management prioritizes behaving ethically themselves, their behavior leads to a stronger ethical culture throughout the entire organization.[11]

---

morals the rules people develop as a result of cultural values and norms

- **Potential magnitude of the consequences:** The greater the harm done to victims, the more likely that marketing professionals will recognize a problem as unethical.

- **Social consensus:** The greater the degree of agreement among managerial peers that an action is harmful, the more likely that marketers will recognize a problem as unethical. Research has found that a strong ethical culture among coworkers decreases observations of ethical misconduct. In large companies with strong ethics and compliance programs, 33 percent of workers reported observing misconduct. This percentage is significantly less than the 62 percent of workers who reported observing misconduct at large companies with weak ethics and compliance programs.[12]

- **Probability of a harmful outcome:** The greater the likelihood that an action will result in a harmful outcome, the more likely that marketers will recognize a problem as unethical.

- **Length of time between the decision and the onset of consequences:** The shorter the length of time between the action and the onset of negative consequences, the more likely that marketers will perceive a problem as unethical.

- **Number of people to be affected:** The greater the number of persons affected by a negative outcome, the more likely that marketers will recognize a problem as unethical.

As you can tell, many factors determine the nature of an ethical decision. In recent years, more and more fast-food restaurants are making efforts to use cleaner, higher-quality ingredients and to get rid of anything artificial on their menus. Panera was one of the first fast-food restaurants to clean up its menu—the company began using only natural ingredients in all of its food, focusing on fresh, seasonal ingredients so the company did not need to rely so heavily on preserved food, and Panera is completely transparent about what is in its food.[13]

On the other hand, consider fast-food chains such as McDonald's, Taco Bell, and Pizza Hut, all of which recently came under fire after the media obtained and published results from a study showing that chemicals linked to numerous health problems had been detected in food from these chains. More specifically, the study found that more than 80 percent of foods at these chains contained a chemical that has been linked to reproductive health issues.[14]

Panera was one of the first fast-food chains to embrace the clean-eating trend and get rid of all artificial ingredients on its menus, including unnatural flavors, preservatives, sweeteners, and colors.

3-3c Ethical Guidelines and Training

In recent years, many organizations have become more interested in ethical issues. Yet interest and action are not always the same thing. Although some companies are now appointing a Chief Ethics Officer (sometimes called a Chief Compliance Officer), this role is still not present at many companies. It is very common, however, for companies of various sizes to develop a **code of ethics** as a guideline to help marketing managers and other employees make better decisions. Creating ethics guidelines has several advantages as follows:

- A code of ethics helps employees identify what their firm recognizes as acceptable business practices.

- A code of ethics can be an effective internal control of behavior, which is more desirable than external controls, such as government regulation.

- A written code helps employees avoid confusion when determining whether their decisions are ethical.

- The process of formulating the code of ethics facilitates discussion among employees about what is right and wrong and ultimately leads to better decisions.

Ethics training is an effective way to help employees put good ethics into practice. The Ethics & Compliance Initiative's State of Ethics and Compliance in the Workplace Report found that 84 percent of employees who work for a company with a strong ethics and compliance program perceived their organization as having a strong ethical culture. Comparatively, only 13 percent of employees working for an organization classified as having an underdeveloped ethics and compliance program felt that their organization had a strong ethical culture. Strong ethical cultures give employees the

---

code of ethics a guideline to help marketing managers and other employees make better decisions

appropriate guidance to handle situations involving potential wrongdoing and lead to lower rates of misconduct.[15] Still, simply giving employees a long list of *dos* and *don'ts* does not really help employees navigate the gray areas or adapt to a changing world market. In Carson City, Nevada, all governmental lobbyists are required to attend a course on ethics and policy before they can meet with lawmakers. The training outlines exactly how and when lobbyists are allowed to interact with lawmakers and how to report any money they spend. A clear understanding of ethical expectations is essential to an industry like lobbying, where illicit—often illegal—actions are taken to promote individual causes.

Because artificial intelligence (AI) is becoming so pervasive in marketing interactions with consumers, it must also be taught about ethical decision making. Already Microsoft, Adobe, and IBM, along with smaller firms and start-ups, are developing ethical guidelines and best practices for their AI use.

Type "gymnast" into Google's image search and the vast majority of the top results are female, as are the results for "nurse." The term "parents" shows almost exclusively heterosexual couples. The results of these searches are driven by AI, which isn't explicitly taught to discriminate. Rather, these prejudices are the result of the data submitted to the AI algorithm.[16] "There is increasing concern that algorithms used by modern AI systems produce discriminatory outputs, presumably because they are trained on data in which societal biases are embedded," notes Madalina Vlasceanu, an Assistant Professor of Psychology at New York University, whose research explores biases in internet search algorithms and the potential impact of these biased search results on society.[17]

The Most Ethical Companies

Each year, *Ethisphere* magazine (targeted toward top management and focused on ethical leadership) examines more than 5,000 companies in 30 separate industries, seeking the world's most ethical companies. It then lists the top 100. The magazine uses a rigorous format to identify true ethical leadership. A few of the selected winners are shown in Table 3.1.

3-3d Ethics in Other Countries

Ethical beliefs often vary between cultures. Certain practices, such as the use of illegal payments and bribes, are far more acceptable in some places than in others, though enforced laws are increasingly making the practice less accepted. One such law, the **Foreign Corrupt Practices Act (FCPA)**, was enacted because Congress was concerned about U.S. corporations' use of illegal payments and bribes in international

Table 3.1 Selected Winners of the World's Most Ethical Companies

Company	Industry	Country
3M	Industrial manufacturing	USA
Accenture	Consulting Services	Ireland
Aflac	Accident and life insurance	USA
Apple	Technology	USA
Colgate-Palmolive	Consumer products	USA
Dell	Technology	USA
EDP	Energy and utilities	Portugal
General Motors Company	Automotive	USA
Illy	Food, beverages, and agriculture	Italy
Kao	Health and beauty	Japan
L'Oreal	Health and beauty	France
Mastercard	Payment Services	USA
Natura	Health and beauty	Brazil
Parsons	Engineering and design	USA
Salesforce	Application software	USA
U.S. Bank	Banks	USA
Workday	Software & Services	USA

Source: "The 2022 World's Most Ethical Companies Honorees List," https://worldsmostethicalcompanies.com/honorees/ (accessed January 30, 2023).

business dealings. This act prohibits U.S. corporations from making illegal payments to public officials of foreign governments to obtain business rights or to enhance their business dealings in those countries. The act has been criticized for putting U.S. businesses at a competitive disadvantage. Many contend that bribery is an unpleasant but necessary part of international business, especially in countries such as China, where business gift giving is widely accepted and expected. But, as

Foreign Corrupt Practices Act (FCPA) a law that prohibits U.S. corporations from making illegal payments to public officials of foreign governments to obtain business rights or to enhance their business dealings in those countries

prosecutions under the FCPA have increased worldwide, some countries are implementing their own antibribery laws. For example, even though China is among the three countries with the most international corruption cases prosecuted under the FCPA, the country is working to develop its own antibribery laws. President Xi Jinping has vigorously attacked corruption and bribery in the Communist party, investigating almost 5 million members for corruption and formally charging 553. This anti-corruption campaign has been one of the president's key policies and has won him a lot of favor with the public.[18]

---

corporate social responsibility (CSR) a business's concern for society's welfare

stakeholder theory ethical theory stating that social responsibility is paying attention to the interest of every affected stakeholder in every aspect of a firm's operation

3-4 Corporate Social Responsibility

3-4 Discuss corporate social responsibility

Corporate social responsibility (CSR) is a business's concern for society's welfare. This concern is demonstrated by managers who consider both the company's long-range best interests and its relationship to the society within which it operates.

3-4a Stakeholders and Social Responsibility

An important aspect of social responsibility is **stakeholder theory**. Stakeholder theory says that social responsibility is paying attention to the interest of every affected stakeholder in every aspect of a firm's operation. The stakeholders in a typical corporation are shown in Figure 3.1.

Figure 3.1   Stakeholders in a Typical Corporation

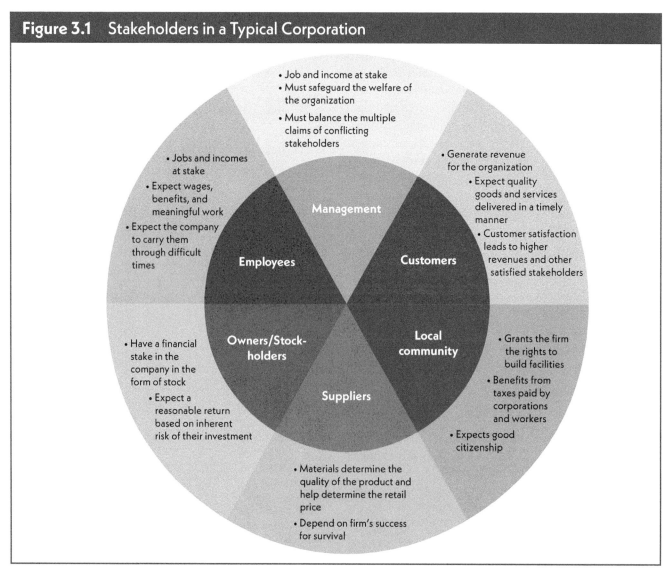

- *Employees* have their jobs and incomes at stake. If the firm moves or closes, employees often face a severe hardship. In return for their labor, employees expect wages, benefits, and meaningful work. In return for their loyalty, workers expect the company to carry them through difficult times.

- *Management* plays a special role because they also have a stake in the corporation. Like employees, managers have their jobs and incomes at stake. On the other hand, management must safeguard the organization's welfare. Sometimes this means balancing the multiple claims of conflicting stakeholders. For example, stockholders want a higher return on investment and perhaps lower costs by moving factories overseas. Their goals may naturally conflict with the interests of employees, the local community, and perhaps suppliers.

- *Customers* generate the revenue for the organization. In exchange, they expect high-quality goods and services delivered in a timely manner. Customer satisfaction leads to higher revenues and the ability to enhance the satisfaction of other stakeholders.

- *The local community*, through its government, grants the firm the right to build facilities. In turn, the community benefits directly from local taxes the corporation pays and indirectly by property and sales taxes the workers pay. The firm is expected to be a good citizen by paying a fair wage, not polluting the environment, and so forth.

- *Suppliers* are vital to the firm's success. For example, if a critical part is not available for an assembly line, then production grinds to a halt. The materials supplied determine the quality of the product produced and create a cost floor, which helps determine the retail price. In turn, the firm is the customer of the supplier and is therefore vital to the supplier's success and survival. A supplier that fails to deliver quality products can create numerous problems for a firm. Takata is global supplier of vehicle airbags. The National Highway Traffic Safety Administration (NHTSA) has warned that tens of millions of cars with Takata airbags face an increased chance of exploding during a collision after prolonged exposure to hot and humid conditions. NHTSA says that across 34 brands, there are 67 million defective Takata airbags in 42 million U.S. vehicles. When the bags explode, they can send metal shards into the passenger cabin. As of the end of 2022, the defective bags have injured more than 400 people and caused 23 deaths. Automakers such as Ford, Nissan, Toyota,

Tasoph/Shutterstock.com

and Mazda have paid out hundreds of millions of dollars to settle consumer loss claims.[19]

- *Owners* have a financial stake in the form of stock in a corporation. They expect a reasonable return based on the amount of inherent risk on their investment. Sometimes managers and employees receive a portion of their compensation in company stock. When Freshworks, a software company based in India, debuted on the U.S. stock exchange, it created 500 employee millionaires, with 70 of these employees being under the age of 30.[20]

3-4b Pyramid of Corporate Social Responsibility

One theorist suggests that total CSR has four components: economic, legal, ethical, and philanthropic. The **pyramid of corporate social responsibility** portrays economic performance as the foundation for the other three responsibilities (refer to Figure 3.2). At the same time that it pursues profits (economic responsibility), however, a business is expected to obey the law (legal responsibility); to do what is right, just, and fair (ethical responsibilities); and to be a good corporate citizen (philanthropic responsibility). These four components are distinct but together, they constitute the whole. Still, if the company does not make a profit, then the other three responsibilities are moot.

pyramid of corporate social responsibility a model that suggests corporate social responsibility is composed of economic, legal, ethical, and philanthropic responsibilities and that a firm's economic performance supports the entire structure

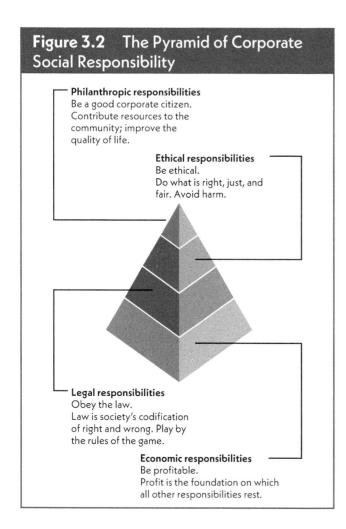

Figure 3.2 The Pyramid of Corporate Social Responsibility

Philanthropic responsibilities
Be a good corporate citizen.
Contribute resources to the
community; improve the
quality of life.

Ethical responsibilities
Be ethical.
Do what is right, just, and
fair. Avoid harm.

Legal responsibilities
Obey the law.
Law is society's codification
of right and wrong. Play by
the rules of the game.

Economic responsibilities
Be profitable.
Profit is the foundation on which
all other responsibilities rest.

3-5 Arguments For and Against Social Responsibility

3-5 Describe the arguments for and against social responsibility

CSR can be a divisive issue. Some analysts believe that a business should focus on making a profit and leave social and environmental problems to nonprofit organizations and government. Economist Milton Friedman believed that the free market, not companies, should decide what is best for the world.[21] Friedman argued that when business executives spend more money than necessary—to purchase delivery vehicles with hybrid engines, pay higher wages in developing countries, or even donate company funds to charity—they are spending shareholders' money to further their own agendas. It would be better to pay dividends and let the shareholders give the money away if they choose.

On the other hand, CSR has an increasing number of supporters based on several compelling factors. One is

that it is simply the right thing to do. Some people claim that societal problems, such as pollution and poverty-level wages, have been brought about by corporations' actions; it is the responsibility of business to right these wrongs. Businesses also have the resources, so businesses should be given the chance to solve social problems. For example, businesses can provide a fair work environment, safe products, and informative advertising.

A socially responsible firm tends to build trust in that organization. Even the smallest transactions in a free-enterprise society are based upon trust. Trust keeps society running. Just ordering a pizza requires faith that the dough will be well-made, that the pizzeria will not abuse the customer's credit card information, and that the delivery person will not eat the pizza. Trust makes the commitment of resources to an activity where its outcome depends upon the cooperative behavior of others[22]—in this case, the pizza maker, cashier, and delivery person.

Research has found that being socially responsible and training frontline employees about social responsibility can have a positive impact on the firm. In a business-to-business environment, researchers found that social responsibility activities can raise customer trust and identification with the firm. These factors, in turn, build customer loyalty, which often leads to higher profits.[23]

Content employees tend to do their jobs better and offer improved customer service. A significant part of that contentment is respecting and admiring their firm, which adds meaning to their lives. Netflix has several policies and programs that target social responsibility, including offering benefits that support their employees. The streaming-service company offers 52 weeks of paid parental leave, which is nearly three times as long as the other tech companies. Netflix is also very active in supporting social causes. The company often uses its social media platforms to support movements such as Black Lives Matter and Pride month.[24]

If a customer has a bad experience with a firm, an active social responsibility program can dampen negative word-of-mouth and social media comments. Even corporations convicted of illegal acts can benefit from being socially responsible. The average fine levied against a firm convicted of bribery under the Foreign Corrupt Practices Act (FCPA) is 40 percent lower if the firm has a comprehensive social responsibility program.[25]

Another, more pragmatic, reason for being socially responsible is that if businesses do not act responsibly, government will create new regulations and perhaps levy fines against them.

Finally, social responsibility can produce a direct profit. Smart companies can prosper and build value by tackling social problems. Recent research found that corporate social responsibility practices can have a direct impact on

a company's return on investment (ROI), increase a company's market value by up to 6 percent, and can reduce systematic risk by up to 4 percent.[26]

Every year, Disney releases a corporate social responsibility report that documents the progress that the company has made regarding its social efforts. In recent years, Disney has focused its corporate social responsibility efforts on promoting diversity, equity, and inclusion throughout the company, increasing its environmental sustainability, and supporting its communities through programs such as Disney VoluntEARS, a program through which Disney cast members can donate their time to volunteering with charities around the world.[27]

PepsiCo's sustainable business philosophy, "Performance with Purpose," is deeply engrained into the company's workplace culture. Performance with Purpose was launched by former PepsiCo CEO Indra Nooyi, the first woman of color to hold this title. The program aims to create healthier products, reduce the environmental impact of the company, and empower employees, and, in turn, has resulted in large profit growth and has allowed PepsiCo to positively impact communities around the world.[28]

3-5a Growth of Social Responsibility

The social responsibility of businesses is growing around the world. Companies are coming under increasing pressure from governments, advocacy groups, investors, prospective employees, current employees, and consumers to make their organizations more socially responsible. In turn, firms are seeing social responsibility as an opportunity. Research has found that consumers, particularly millennial and Gen Z consumers, are four to six times more likely to shop with purpose-driven companies. Further, many consumers will completely stop doing business with companies that they view as irresponsible. For instance, 76 percent of consumers reported that they would not

shop with a company that opposes their views. The good news is that when companies do engage in corporate social responsibility efforts, consumers take note, and this attention can lead to positive outcomes for the company. In a recent study, 80 percent of consumers reported that they would engage in word-of-mouth support about a company's corporate social responsibility programs.[29]

United Nations Global Compact

One way that U.S. firms can do more is by joining the United Nations Global Compact (UNGC). The UNGC, the world's largest global corporate citizenship initiative, has seen its ranks swell over the past few years. In 2001—the first full year after its launch—just 67 companies joined, agreeing to abide by ten principles. More information about "The Ten Principles of the United Nations Global Compact" can be found on the United Nations Global Compact website (https://unglobalcompact.org/what-is-gc/mission/principles). Today, the initiative has more than 21,000 participants across 162 countries.[30]

3-5b Becoming a B Corp

Smaller companies that wish to join the social responsibility and sustainability movement are turning to the B Corp movement. B Corps are for-profit companies certified by the nonprofit B Lab to meet rigorous standards of social and environmental performance, accountability, and transparency. Today, a growing community of over 6,300 Certified B Corps from 89 countries represents 159 different industries.[31] To become a B Corp Certified company, a firm must pass a 200-point assessment. Criteria include things like fair compensation for workers, how much waste the company produces, and the company's work with local businesses. Firms such as Patagonia, Ben & Jerry's, online crafts marketplace Etsy, and Danone have qualified. New Seasons Market, a grocery store chain in Oregon, stamps the B Corp logo on all of its grocery bags and gives employees B Corp badges to wear. The logo helps attract socially minded shoppers and helps in recruiting new workers.

Elissa Foster, former Environmental Analyst for Patagonia, says:

> The Assessment incentivized us to quantitatively measure the performance of our programs. We provide several opportunities for employees to participate in environmental or social activism. But we didn't know how many employees participated and to what degree. The Assessment gathers all the information in one place, it allows us to really recognize our strengths as well as see where we have room for improvement.[32]

Sustainability

A significant part of the B Impact Assessment is measuring a firm's **sustainability**. Sustainability is the idea that socially responsible companies will outperform their peers by focusing on the world's social, economic, and environmental problems. Sustainable companies view these problems as opportunities to build profits and help the world at the same time. Environmental sustainability is concerned with the physical environment. Environmentally sustainable companies believe that threats to the environment should be minimized or eliminated. For example, developing long-term sources of clean water improves health and preserves local ecosystems while creating a competitive advantage. Social sustainability means developing processes and structures that not only meet the needs of a current community but benefit future generations as well. Building schools and providing means for children to attend those schools is an example of creating social sustainability. In a business context, economic sustainability is the efficient use of assets so that a company can continue operating profitably over time. A company cannot be socially or environmentally responsible if it goes out of business.

3-5c Green Marketing

An outgrowth of the social responsibility and sustainability movements is green marketing. **Green marketing**

---

sustainability the idea that socially responsible companies will outperform their peers by focusing on the world's social problems and viewing them as opportunities to build profits and help the world at the same time

green marketing the development and marketing of products designed to minimize negative effects on the physical environment or to improve the environment

greenwashing adding a minimal number of green product attributes to promote a product as green

is the development and marketing of products designed to minimize negative effects on the physical environment or to improve the environment. One approach that firms use to indicate that they are part of the green movement is to use third-party eco-logos. Examples include the chasing-arrows recycling logo (the product is either recyclable or contains recycled materials); the Energy Star logo (the product is energy efficient); and Certified Organic (the U.S. Department of Agriculture created standards relative to soil quality, animal raising practices, pest and weed control, and the use of additives). These logos can enhance a product's sales and profitability.

Movement toward green marketing by manufacturers has not always been self-motivated. Powerful retailers including Walmart, Whole Foods, Target, and others have mandated sustainability requirements for their suppliers. Typically, these mandates have not taken place in a collaborative spirit but are implemented on a formal "Here is what we need you to do basis."[33] Even large manufacturers, such as Procter & Gamble (P&G), Heinz Foods, and Colgate-Palmolive, feel compelled to comply. They can't afford the huge loss of shelf space if they don't.

P&G, whose products include Mr. Clean and Comet, and Reckitt Benckiser Group, the maker of Easy-Off oven cleaner, have been pressured by retailers to disclose—and in some cases remove—ingredients that are harmful to the environment and consumers. The government is getting into the sustainability movement as well. For example, a New York law went into effect on January 1, 2023, that limits the amount of a potentially cancer-causing chemical that can be present in cleaning and personal-care products. Many products from popular brands, such as Tide Original laundry detergent, had to be pulled from the shelves due to this new law.[34]

Many consumers are dedicated to buying sustainable products and services. A study from GreenPrint, an environmental technology company, found that 78 percent of American consumers are more likely to purchase a product that is labeled as environmentally friendly. Further, this research found that 64 percent of American consumers are willing to pay more for sustainable products, while a different research study conducted by a European Commission found that 77 percent of European respondents were willing to pay more for green products.[35]

To benefit from consumers' willingness to pay more, some companies are promoting conventional products as green by adding a few green attributes. This approach is called **greenwashing**. Aquafina sold water in an "ECO-FINA Bottle," a conventional plastic bottle made with 50 percent less plastic. Dasani water was sold in a "Plant Bottle," but it was a plastic bottle made with 30 percent plant ingredients. Herbal Essences shampoo

Patagonia's decision to a responsible economy is so strong that the company advises customers not to buy its products if they don't absolutely need to buy them.

Many consumers are motivated to purchase sustainable products and services and are often even willing to pay more to purchase from companies with sustainable practices.

was promoted as "crafted with bio:renew" by adding an ingredient, histidine, that is derived from corn sugar but did not remove other chemicals found in conventional shampoos. Huggies "pure and natural" diapers claimed to be made from organic cotton but only the outer shells were cotton. The inside of the diaper was still similar to conventional diapers. Researchers have found that consumers have a negative attitude toward greenwashed products. Consumers also began to question the ethics of the firm's actions.[36]

For a product to be labeled "green," it must meet regulatory guidelines issued by the Federal Trade Commission (FTC).[37] Major retailers Kohl's and Walmart have been fined $5.5 million by the FTC for misleading environmental claims.[38] These and other companies are now barred from labeling and advertising rayon textiles as being made of bamboo.

3-5d Leaders in Social Responsibility

Two names at the top of many social-responsibility lists are Patagonia and Unilever. Patagonia is a private outdoor clothing manufacturer founded by Yvon Chouinard, but it is now headed by Ryan Gellert. Gellert first joined Patagonia in 2014 and was later appointed CEO in 2020. Upon his initial arrival at the company, Gellert helped to launch the "Save the Blue Heart of Europe" program, which works with activists in the Balkan region of Europe to protect wild rivers. Since taking over as CEO, one of his top priorities has been to increase the brand's efforts to "repair and resell" merchandise, rather than disposing of used goods, in an effort to increase sustainability.[39]

It's not always easy to think about profits and social responsibility at the same time, and Gellert is often tested. He says that "there is a real tension" when it comes to

both caring about the planet and manufacturing consumer goods that are unnecessary. Sustainability is, however, a core aspect of Patagonia's business and will always be something the company is focused on.

Unilever is a $126 billion corporation, run by Alan Jope, that strongly believes in "doing well by doing good." That idea means making more money by acting virtuously. The firm sells environmentally friendly detergent, has installed thousands of water pumps in African villages, and has removed gender stereotypes for Unilever's advertising. Since taking over as CEO, Jope championed an effort to achieve a full 100 percent reduction of emissions in its operations by year 2030.[40] Unilever staffers have fanned out across India and Africa to install toilets, which will significantly reduce the incidence of infectious diseases. In Vietnam, Unilever employees have visited over 1,000 villages to encourage people to wash their hands. For children, ages 8 to 10, they teach "the handwashing dance." It goes like this: "Rub your left palm with your right hand, then clap, now right, clap, up, down, thumbs, knuckles, clap. Then repeat, scrubbing vigorously." After the dance, the students are encouraged to pick up free Lifebuoy soap and P/S toothpaste at the school clinic. Naturally, it's all made by Unilever.[41]

3-6 Cause-Related Marketing

3-6 Explain cause-related marketing

Another subset of social responsibility is **cause-related marketing**. Often referred to as simply "cause marketing," it is the cooperative efforts of a for-profit

---

cause-related marketing the cooperative marketing efforts between a for-profit firm and a nonprofit organization

firm and a nonprofit organization for mutual benefit. The for-profit firm hopes to generate extra sales, and the nonprofit in turn hopes to receive money, goods, and/or services. Any marketing effort that targets social or other charitable causes can be referred to as cause-related marketing. Cause marketing differs from corporate giving (philanthropy), as the latter generally involves a specific donation that is tax deductible, whereas cause marketing is a marketing relationship not based on a straight donation.

The financial benefits of cause-related marketing was estimated to be over $2.2 billion in 2022, which was an increase of approximately 5 percent from the year prior.[42] It's no wonder why: cause-related marketing creates good public relations and will often stimulate sales for the brand. One study found that 94 percent of consumers are more likely to trust a company that practices cause-related marketing, and 93 percent report that they will be more loyal to such a company.[43] Examples of cause-related marketing used by large companies are abundant. The Body Shop, a beauty and wellness company, created the "Time to Care" campaign in which they donate personal cleaning products to shelters and assisted-living communities. The company advocates for prioritizing self-care and wants to ensure that everyone has an opportunity to practice self-care. Starbucks supports the transgender community through the company's #WhatsYourName campaign, an advertising campaign that features a transgender youth using the Starbucks service system to try out their chosen name. Starbucks also collaborates with the charity Mermaids, which supports transgender and gender-diverse youth, by selling mermaid tail–shaped cookies and donating a portion of these proceeds to the charity. Walmart and Sam's Club have both supported the Children's Miracle Network Hospitals since the late 1980s. For six weeks each year, Walmart employees solicit donations for the cause at checkout. For a dollar or more, customers can put their name on a Miracle Worker balloon or dedicate it to a loved one.

Red Nose Day, which originated in the United Kingdom, is now doing very well in the United States.

Once a year, Walgreens encourages customers to buy and wear red noses. The money raised goes to helping raise children out of poverty.

Walgreens sponsors the six-week campaign each year. The idea is for customers to purchase red noses and wear them for group pictures and other Red Nose Day fund-raising events to spread awareness. The campaign stands out because of its fun and playful nature. Proceeds from the red nose sales go toward helping lift children out of poverty in the United States. In 2022, the campaign raised a record-breaking $37 million through the sale of over red noses at Walgreens.[44]

Clearly, cause-related marketing is becoming a more common practice. Many customers, particularly younger customers such as millennials, not only expect brands to contribute to charities through financial contributions and partnerships, but they are also demanding it. One survey found that 67 percent of respondents between the ages 18 and 34 felt that it is important for a brand that they are purchasing from to have a charitable component, and 71 percent indicated that they would pay more for a product if some of the proceeds would be going to charity. A strong corporate social responsibility program allows companies to contribute to society while also providing increased value for customers—a win-win!

Rawpixel.com/Shutterstock.com

Chapter 4

The Marketing Environment

Learning Outcomes

After studying this chapter, you will be able to...

4-1 Explain how the external environment affects a firm's marketing activities

4-2 Describe the social factors that affect marketing

4-3 Explain how diversity, equity, and inclusion (DEI) influences marketing

4-4 Describe how the economy affects marketing

4-5 Identify the impact of technology on a firm

4-6 Discuss the political and legal environment of marketing

4-7 Explain how competition affects marketing

4-8 Discuss how environmentalism affects marketing

4-1 The External Marketing Environment

4-1 Explain how the external environment affects a firm's marketing activities

Perhaps the most important decisions a marketing manager must make relate to creating the marketing mix. Recall from Chapters 1 and 2 that a marketing mix is the unique combination of product, place (distribution), promotion, and price strategies. The marketing mix is under the firm's control and is designed to appeal to a specific group of potential buyers, or target market. A **target market** is a group of people or organizations for which an organization designs, implements, and maintains a marketing mix intended to meet that group's needs, resulting in mutually satisfying exchanges.

Managers must alter the marketing mix because of changes in the environment in which consumers live, work, and make purchasing decisions. As markets mature, some new consumers become part of the target market; others drop out. Those who remain may have different tastes, needs, incomes, lifestyles, and buying habits than the original target consumers. For example, emerging technologies have resulted in changes in consumers' buying habits. Digital photography has sent 35-millimeter film the way of the horse and buggy, which ultimately led to the bankruptcy of Eastman Kodak, the leading film producer. Smartphones and Amazon have disrupted numerous industries. Artificial intelligence (AI) is on the way to changing our lives and many businesses.

Although managers can control the marketing mix, they cannot control elements in the external environment that continually affect markets. Think, for example, about how social media have changed your world. In contrast, managers can shape and reshape the marketing mix to influence the target market. That is, managers react to changes in the external environment and attempt to create a more effective marketing mix to satisfy customers and remain competitive.

4-1a Environmental Scanning

Unless managers understand the external environment, the firm cannot intelligently create a marketing plan. Thus, many organizations assemble a team of specialists to continually collect and evaluate environmental information, a process called **environmental scanning**. The goal in environmental scanning is to gather the data needed to identify future market opportunities and current threats because a SWOT analysis requires (more about SWOT analyses are discussed in Chapter 2). Companies collect and analyze information about, for example, population shifts, numbers of people in different age or income categories, or what trends are occurring in their industries. Environmental scanning also allows companies to understand their current customers and the desires of potential customers. For example, Ford recognizes the value in regularly conducting SWOT analyses to better understand market trends. The company even has a "Chief Futurist" whose main duty is to monitor consumer trends and understand how these trends may present opportunities or threats for the car company. Every year, Ford puts together a trend report that explores environmental factors that are impacting consumer wants and needs. Recent Ford trend reports revealed that a top concern for many consumers is sustainability. Consumers want to purchase products that are environmentally friendly and help to fight the climate change crisis. Thus, examining the external environments allowed Ford to identify an opportunity in the market to create more electronic vehicles. In response to this finding, Ford has increased its focus on manufacturing electronic vehicles, including the F-150 Lighting, an electronic version of their popular F-150 truck.[1]

It is also important for firms to use environmental scanning to determine who their competitors are and what activities those competitors are engaged in. Early detection of competitors is critical for marketers, particularly those competitors evolving to serve the same customers with an alternative product or technology, as can be seen in the Kodak example above.

Credit card companies like Mastercard, Visa, and American Express, that are locked in a battle to maintain existing customers and attract new ones, frequently use environmental scanning. A credit card is essentially a commodity, so card issuers have continually tried to differentiate their products and services by offering customers rewards such as airline miles, cash back, and concierge service. However, these programs may not appeal to all consumers. For example, younger people often prefer debit cards to credit cards, so benefits such as rewards may not convince them to change this practice. Credit card companies can use environmental scanning to better understand the financial needs of these group members. In fact, credit card companies have started making the customer experience key to the entire service design process. For instance, Citibank used technology to integrate its card and retail units, which had been separate, to create a more seamless experience for customers.

---

target market a group of people or organizations for which an organization designs, implements, and maintains a marketing mix intended to meet the needs of that group, resulting in mutually satisfying exchanges

environmental scanning the continual collection and evaluation of environmental information to identify market opportunities and threats

EtiAmmos/Shutterstock.com

DVKi/Shutterstock.com

Spotify allows users to personalize their playlists.

Some card companies have relied on beating their competitors with more rewards programs instead of focusing on the emerging competitors that threaten them. Companies offering different payment choices, nontraditional players, and changing consumer preferences have resulted in a decline in credit card usage. For example, technology-driven mobile payment solutions such as Apple Pay, PayPal, or Venmo are becoming more popular. New programs also provide fixed-term installment plans such as Affirm, offered at Walmart for example, so customers can finance their purchases directly with a retailer.[2]

Environmental scanning is critical to the success of an organization's marketing plans. The practice allows companies to more effectively and efficiently create their products and services, acquire new customers, retain existing customers, and remain competitive.

4-1b Understanding a Rapidly Changing Environment

Successful firms realize that creating value for the customer is the key to larger profits and market share. A rapidly changing business environment makes understanding customer needs critical to long-term success. Mars Petcare is one of the biggest pet-food manufacturers in the world, marketing brands such as Pedigree, Cesar, and Whiskas. Just as "natural" and "organic" products of all types are popular with customers, these trends are also evident in the pet-food market. Mars makes several versions of natural pet food, such as its smaller U.K. brand James Wellbeloved. Its bigger brands also offer natural pet food, including Sheba, Pedigree, and Perfect Fit Natural Vitality. What's more, the company has created these brands at different price points so consumers with a range of incomes can afford this benefit.[3]

Today, companies must operate in an environment that is becoming more demographically diverse, with customer needs and expectations becoming more individualized. Thus, companies are reshaping their marketing mix to meet these challenges. Target has teamed up with Shipt to offer same-day grocery deliveries, thus providing more convenience. Spotify enables each person to listen to only the music that they want to hear via its personalized playlist. In order to create individualized playlists, Spotify tracks members' listening habits, such as what songs or artists they search for and save and what songs they skip. The more often that a user listens to Spotify, the more individualized their playlist will be because the company will have more data to base the playlist on. Lego is using sugarcane as a sustainable alternative to plastic in its toys, which appeals to consumers who are concerned about the earth's environment.[4]

4-1c Understanding the Needs of the Firm's Most Valuable Customers

Often, 20 percent of a firm's customers produce 80 percent of the firm's revenue. An organization must understand what drives that loyalty and then take steps to ensure that those drivers are maintained and enhanced. Airlines use loyalty programs to satisfy and retain this top 20 percent of customers. For example, Alaska Airlines' Mileage Plan members only need 5,000 miles to fly up to 700 miles one way in coach seating. As the award increases, in distance or seating class, more miles are required, giving customers an incentive to fly more on Alaska Airlines.

4-1d Understanding the Firm's Competition

Successful firms know their competitors and attempt to forecast those competitors' future moves. Competitors threaten a firm's market share, its profitability, and its very existence. Competitors that crop up because of new technologies can create a challenging competitive environment for traditional old-line firms. Uber and Lyft, for example, have made life difficult for traditional taxicab companies. Travel websites such as Expedia, Kayak, and Travelocity have nearly eliminated the need for human travel agents. Amazon took over the market for books, which caused many traditional bookstores to close.

Paper newspapers are currently fighting to survive against online media and blogs. News brands have responded by creating podcasts, digital audio, and email newsletters, which have helped to increase customer loyalty. Media companies are also giving their customers more personalized experiences by incorporating artificial intelligence into their products.[5]

anek.soowannaphoom/Shutterstock.com

People in all cultures count family as an important value.

4-2 Social Factors

4-2 Describe the social factors that affect marketing

Social change is perhaps the most difficult external variable for marketing managers to forecast, influence, or integrate into marketing plans. Social factors include our attitudes, values, and lifestyles. People typically have a set of values that guide their attitudes and lifestyles through interaction with family, friends, and other influencers such as teachers, religious leaders, and politicians. In turn, values influence the products people buy; the prices paid for products; the effectiveness of specific promotions; and how, where, and when people expect to purchase products. Some typical values are family, self-sufficiency, equality, religious beliefs, and achievement.

People typically purchase brands that reflect their values. For example, research shows 78 percent of consumers said they made a purchase decision based on their values. In addition, 53 percent of consumers said they would pay more for a product that was consistent with their social values.

Many companies have profited from aligning with social values held by consumers. For example, Harley-Davidson showed support for current social values when it dropped a major dealer that made racist comments on Facebook. Moreover, while in the 1970s, Harley Davidson sold Confederate Edition bikes, it has not only stopped selling these bikes, but it also does not allow dealers to use the Confederate flag on any of its products.[6]

An individual's culture influences what they value. For example, a recent survey found that family was a value people in all cultures shared. Freedom of speech was found to be valued higher in North America and the Middle East than other countries. Respect was ranked higher in Africa and Central/South America than other countries.[7]

demography the study of people's vital statistics, such as age, race, gender, and location

Therefore, companies need to be aware of a peoples' culture when marketing in different countries. For example, in Germany, technology consumers prefer to see rational information about such features as a product's performance, software upgrades, and how it works with other programs. By contrast, consumers in the United Kingdom prefer a more emotional approach. They would want to see how a technology product integrates into and improves their lives, perhaps by showing how its speed or convenience lets them spend more time with loved ones.[8]

4-2a How Demographic Factors Impact Our Behavior

Another aspect of the social environment is **demography**, the study of people's vital statistics, such as age, race, gender, and location. Demographics are significant because the basis for any market is people. Demographic characteristics are strongly related to consumer buying behavior in the marketplace.

Demographics are always evolving. For example, companies frequently target consumers by age. While a major focus of companies has been members of the age groups Generations X, Y, and Z, these customers have grown older, and their needs and wants have likely changed over time. We now recognize a new generation—Generation Alpha, whose members are children born between 2010 and 2024. Consider how brand-loyalty programs might differ across age groups. Studies have shown that members of Gen X exhibit the highest rate of brand loyalty compared to other generations. They are not as interested in trying new brands as members of other age groups. To create brand loyalty with GenXers, it is important to build solid relationships with them. They also respond strongly to excellent customer service and support. By contrast, members of Gen Y, otherwise known as millennials, tend to have less brand loyalty. They came of age around the 2008 recession, so they are more frugal. In fact, 80 percent of this group are willing to switch brands if they can save money. Therefore, tying discounts to loyalty programs should appeal to millennials.[9]

Companies also target consumers by factors such as location (e.g., urban, or rural), household life cycle, gender, and income. Learn more details about demographics in Chapter 8.

4-2b How Social Media Have Changed Our Behavior

Social media are web-based and mobile technologies that allow the creation and exchange of user-generated content. Social media encompasses a wide variety of formats—sites such as Facebook, YouTube, Twitter, now known as X, TikTok, Instagram, and Pinterest, each of which serves a different function (refer to Chapter 18). These media have changed the way we communicate, keep track of others, browse for products and services, and make purchases. There are now 4.76 billion social media users around the world, equating to 59.4 percent of the total global population. People spend roughly 15 percent of their waking lives using social media.[10]

Beyond accessing the internet via computer, tablet, or smartphone, today many people have embraced the Internet of Things. The number of "things" (thermostats, washing machines, fitness trackers, and light bulbs, for example) connected to the internet has grown exponentially. For example, an internet-connected sensor called Moocall was developed to detect when a pregnant cow will deliver her calf. The device is attached to the cow's tail several days before she is due. Based on her tail movements, an alert is sent when she is ready to calve.[11] Similarly, Medtronic makes a wireless cardiac monitor that doctors can use to monitor people for health risks in real time. The Internet of Things has changed many areas of our lives.

Online reviews play an increasingly important role in consumer behavior as more Americans opt to purchase items online. Consumers can access product reviews, follow influencers who may guide consumers in which brands to purchase, find ads online, and easily compare products and prices.

Social networking has changed the game when it comes to opinion sharing. Now, consumers can reach many people at once with their views—and can respond to brands and events in real time. In turn, marketers can use social media to engage customers in their products and services. Marketers have learned that social media are not like network television, where a message is pushed out to a mass audience. Instead, social media enable firms to create conversations with

Hellman's uses its social media accounts to engage with consumers by posting recipes and meal prep tips.

customers and establish meaningful connections. In other words, social media marketing can humanize brands. Marketers for brands like Solo Stove and Hellman's Mayonnaise post custom videos about their products to Instagram and then invite feedback. For example, Hellman's often posts recipe ideas and meal prep tips to its social media accounts. The mayonnaise company recently posted a video on Instagram that demonstrates how to use its mayo to make light and fluffy biscuits and another post featured a recipe for potato salad.

Videos posted on social media are becoming the new normal for marketing a brand. Marketers know that many consumers would prefer to watch a video about a product than read about it. When online marketers use videos showing their brands, they see increased dwell time, traffic, leads, and sales. They also receive fewer support questions from consumers. Moreover, consumers use videos about brands as an important part of their research and purchasing decisions. "Explainer" videos have found particular success.[12]

4-2c The Influence of Pop Culture on Marketing

Pop culture has been defined as the products and forms of expression and identity that are frequently encountered or widely accepted, commonly liked, or approved, and characteristic of a particular society at a given time.[13] Pop culture is created by the interactions between people as they engage in their day-to-day activities and includes everything from styles of dress and use of slang to greeting rituals and foods. It comes from various sources, including

---

Pop culture the products and forms of expression and identity that are frequently encountered or widely accepted, commonly liked, or approved, and characteristic of a particular society at a given time

music, art, literature, cyberculture, sports, movies, fashion, advertising, and television. For example, hip-hop culture has had a large influence on styles of dress, slang, and greeting rituals. Sometimes brand symbols, such as the Nike Swoosh or McDonald's golden arches, become important symbols in pop culture. Pop culture can change quickly, and it is typically initiated and transmitted by mass media, especially social media. For example, TikTok is a social platform that has both developed and diffused new pop culture trends.[14]

Using pop culture in marketing can help companies to connect with their target customers. It can enhance customers' attention to brands and advertising and help them relate to a company's brand on an emotional level, increasing their loyalty. In effect, a brand can develop a personality and feel more approachable, which can lead to increased sales.[15]

There are numerous examples of how marketers have incorporated pop culture into their strategies.[16] The streaming show *Yellowstone,* about a ranching family in Montana, has become a pop culture sensation and has initiated the current Western wear trend. Western wear companies are profiting as U.S. customers are increasing their purchases of "Cowboy Core" or "Western Core" apparel, such as boots, hats, and flannel shirts. The Western wear market has also exploded in other countries, such as China and India. Cowboy hatmaker Stetson, established in 1865, is seeing increasing demand because of *Yellowstone*'s popularity.[17] Similarly, Boot Barn has experienced a sharp uptick in cowboy boot sales.[18]

Another pop culture phenomenon currently influencing marketing is South Korea's K-pop music and its artists, who have a large influence on young shoppers and create buzz on social media. Capitalizing on this social influence, luxury brands have been targeting younger customers using K-pop artists as brand ambassadors. As an example, two days after Dior named K-pop favorite Jimin as its global ambassador, the company's market price soared.[19] A red tweed cardigan from Zara that star Jisoo showed on her Instagram account sold out right after posting.[20]

For a more detailed look at the influence of social factors on consumer decision making, refer to Chapter 6. In addition, Chapter 18 covers social media in depth.

---

diversity refers to people's race, religion, gender, ethnicity, nationality, socioeconomic status, age, and abilities.

equity fairness in procedures, processes, and distribution of resources

inclusion the action of including people of diverse backgrounds

4-3 Diversity, Equity, and Inclusion in Marketing

4-3 Explain how diversity, equity, and inclusion (DEI) influences marketing

---

Diversity, equity, and inclusion (DEI) is a major external environmental force that has come to the forefront in recent years. **Diversity** refers to people's race, religion, gender, ethnicity, nationality, socioeconomic status, age, and abilities. **Equity** is fairness in procedures, processes, and distribution of resources. **Inclusion** means that people of diverse backgrounds can participate. Overall, the concept involves creating a place where everyone is welcome and has the resources they need.[21] DEI initiatives are typically applied in a management context (e.g., hiring, team building, advancement). However, DEI also has important implications for marketing. It can influence activities such as attracting new customers and retaining current ones, customer service, increasing revenues, supply chain choices and advertising.

Research shows that almost two-thirds of consumers find diversity and inclusion to be essential. This sentiment is highest among parents with small children, Black people, and younger generations. Many people say they are more loyal to brands that stand for diversity and inclusion, and a large proportion of Black people, Hispanic people, and those who identify as LGBTQIA+ stopped using a brand because of lack of representation. Nintendo is an example of a company committed to DEI. In an industry where 61 percent of game developers identify as male, Nintendo put together a gender-balanced, inclusive team to design its *Animal Crossing: New Horizons* game. This game was eventually purchased by an even number of males and females, something also not typically seen in the video game market. The result for the brand was that it became the second-highest launch sales in history for Nintendo Switch.[22]

An inclusive marketing organization helps companies access diverse markets. What's more, consumers are more likely to buy from companies in which they perceive themselves represented. For example, Fenty Beauty, a brand created by pop star Rihanna, created 40 different foundation makeup shades to represent all skin tones—by far the most shades offered by any other beauty company at the time. After its launch, the product was consistently sold out in stores.[23]

Customer service employees are a critical factor in how a consumer interacts with a company, and the more diverse those people are, the more they can relate to a diverse customer base. TIAA, a financial services company, was ranked ninth on a DiversityInc Top 50 Companies for Diversity list for creating a culture that reflects the diversity

Beautyimage/Shutterstock.com

how to use a razor created a meaningful bonding experience between the two. Adobe's Instagram feed highlights artists from different races, genders, sexual orientations, and other diverse groups.[29] Companies are also creating more opportunities for people with disabilities to engage with their brands. For example, some are optimizing websites for voice search for those who are visually impaired. Florida's inclusive "Limitless Florida" campaign provides travelers who have accessibility issues with the resources they need to get the most from their visit to the state.[30]

To summarize, DEI initiatives in marketing can benefit companies in many ways. The examples cited here only represent the tip of the iceberg of what organizations are doing to incorporate DEI into their marketing strategies. You will continue to notice other examples of DEI marketing throughout the remainder of this book.

4-4 Economic Factors

4-4 Describe how the economy affects marketing

In addition to social and demographic factors, marketing managers must understand and react to the economic environment. The three economic areas of greatest concern to most marketers are consumers' incomes, inflation, and recession.

4-4a Consumers' Incomes

The latest figures in the United States show an average annual household income of a little over $87,000.[31] Income also varies between different states, Mississippi has the lowest, and Maryland has the highest.[32] Looking beyond the United States, examples of countries with the highest income include Luxembourg, Norway, Switzerland, Austria, Canada, Germany, and the Netherlands.[33] Countries with the lowest income include Afghanistan, Somalia, Yemen, and Syria.[34]

Education is the primary determinant of a person's earning potential. For example, those with a college degree gain

of the clients it serves. It became one of the first financial services companies to encourage employees to specify pronouns in their email signatures as part of a focus on nonbinary gender inclusion.[24]

Moreover, more diverse organizations tend to outperform those that are less diverse. DEI increases the knowledge base of teams, which benefits the productivity and work culture of the entire company. It also promotes creativity and innovation within the organization, particularly in terms of leadership. In fact, companies that invested in leadership diversity reported a 19 percent higher innovation revenue than companies with below-average leadership diversity.[25]

Increasing diversity in the supply chain can also demonstrate a company's commitment to inclusiveness. Best Buy pledged to spend $12 billion with supply chain businesses owned by members of the Black, Indigenous, and people of color communities, as well as other diverse suppliers. Likewise, the Coca-Cola company has committed to spending $500 million over five years with Black-owned suppliers.[26]

In-store merchandising provides an opportunity to become more inclusive. Companies can make the brands they put on store shelves more reflective of a diverse customer base. Gap, Macy's, and Sephora, for example, have signed the Fifteen Percent Pledge's call for 15 percent of retail shelf space to be dedicated to Black-owned brands. Ulta Beauty places Black-owned brands in prime locations and has been increasing the use of Black-owned brands in email marketing.[27]

Finally, more advertising is appealing to a diverse audience. Sixty-four percent of consumers are more likely to consider, and even purchase, a product after discovering an ad for it that was diverse or inclusive.[28] For example, a Gillette ad shows how a Black father teaching his transgender son

Song_about_summer/Shutterstock.com

a substantial earnings boost. Annual median earnings for bachelor's degree holders are 84 percent higher than those with only a high school diploma. The jobless rate for those with a bachelor's degree is less than 2 percent. Moreover, the level of poverty among bachelor's degree holders is 3.5 times lower than it is for those with high school degrees.[35]

4-4b Purchasing Power

Even when incomes rise, a higher standard of living does not necessarily result. Increased standards of living are a function of purchasing power. **Purchasing power** is measured by comparing income to the relative cost of a standard set of goods and services in different geographic areas, usually referred to as the *cost of living*. Another way to think of purchasing power is income minus the cost of living (i.e., expenses). In general, a cost-of-living index considers housing, food and groceries, transportation, utilities, healthcare, and miscellaneous expenses such as clothing, services, and entertainment. When examining household income by state, and then adjusting it for the cost of living, purchasing power varies substantially from state to state. A high household income does not necessarily translate into high household purchasing power. California has one of the highest household incomes, but the high cost of living erodes buying power, moving it to the midrange of all the states. The states with the greatest household purchasing power are New York, Massachusetts, Washington, and California. The states at the lower end of household purchasing power are Mississippi, West Virginia, Arkansas, and Alabama. Some states, such as Mississippi, have a relatively low cost of living, but a low household income still places them toward the bottom of the list.[36]

When income is high relative to the cost of living, people have more discretionary income. That means they have more money to spend on nonessential items (in other words, on wants rather than needs). This information is important to marketers for obvious reasons. Consumers with high purchasing power can afford to spend more money without jeopardizing their budget for necessities like food, housing, and utilities. They also can purchase higher-priced necessities—for example, a more expensive car, a home in a more expensive neighborhood, or a designer handbag versus a purse from a discount store.

4-4c Inflation

Inflation is a measure of the decrease in the value of money, generally expressed as the percentage reduction in value since the previous year, which is the rate of inflation. Thus, in simple terms, an inflation rate of 5 percent means you will need 5 percent more units of money than you would have needed last year to buy the same basket of products. If inflation is 5 percent, you can expect that, on average, prices have risen by about 5 percent since the previous year. Of course, if pay raises are matching the rate of inflation, then employees will be no worse off in terms of the immediate purchasing power of their salaries.

America's inflation rate over the last three years has risen rapidly. In 2020, the rate was 3 percent. It climbed to 9 percent in the summer of 2022, the highest rate since the late 1970s. Currently, the rate has dropped to around 6 percent.[37] While inflation has decreased over this period, many consumers are still struggling. The percentage of people who feel financially well off dropped to its lowest level in 5 years. This response is more pronounced for Black and Hispanic consumers.[38] People are looking for bargains and cutting back on nonessential purchases to get by.

There are numerous reasons behind the current inflation. Shifts in consumer spending and government stimulus money because of the COVID-19 pandemic combined with supply chain disruptions fed inflation. Russia's invasion of Ukraine caused prices for food, energy, and other commodities to dramatically increase. In the service sector, demands for workers exceeded supply, causing wage gains.[39]

Companies can use marketing strategies to handle inflationary pressure. For example, some companies are intensifying their focus on private brands because these are generally less expensive than manufacturer's brands. Elimination of work can help with labor shortages and increasing labor costs. Snack and beverage company Mondelez International trimmed manufacturing by eliminating 25 percent of products in its portfolio. Hotels everywhere are limiting housekeeping by letting guests opt-in or opt-out of the service.[40] Inflation can also create opportunities for some companies. For example, off-price and discount retailers are well positioned to benefit when consumers cut back on spending. Dollar General and Dollar Tree have both increased the number of new stores opened during the current inflationary period.[41]

4-4d Recession

A **recession** is a period of economic activity characterized by negative growth. More precisely, a *recession* is defined as occurring when the gross domestic product

---

purchasing power a comparison of income versus the relative cost of a standard set of goods and services in different geographic areas

inflation a measure of the decrease in the value of money, expressed as the percentage reduction in value since the previous year

recession a period of economic activity characterized by negative growth, which reduces demand for goods and services

falls for two consecutive quarters. Gross domestic product (GDP) is the total market value of all final goods and services produced during a specific time period. The COVID-19 pandemic-related recession resulted in the unemployment rate increasing 10.3 percent from March to April 2020 to a record high of 14.7 percent. This is the highest rate and the largest over-the-month increase in the history of the Bureau of Labor Statistics. By the end of April 2020, 23.1 million people had become unemployed. Federal, state, and local restrictions on businesses and quarantines resulted in furloughs and terminations in companies of all sizes. This forced millions of Americans to turn to food banks, apply for government aid, or to stop paying rent and other bills. Congress approved nearly $3 trillion in funds to help businesses, unemployment aid, and to receive a relief check. By May 2020, unemployment had fallen to 13.3 percent as 2.5 million jobs were added. This job surge was mostly due to states reopening their economies. The profound jolt of the business lockdowns and the quarantines has impacted many areas of marketing.

4-5 Technology and Innovation

4-5 Identify the impact of technology on a firm

Technological success is based on innovation, and innovation requires imagination and risk taking. Bringing new technology to the marketplace requires a corporate structure and management actions that will lead to success. Great corporate leaders must embed innovation into the lifeblood of the company, and workers should be told not to fear innovation failure. Some of the greatest innovations in recent years, such as 3D printing, hydraulic fracturing, quantum computing, autonomous vehicles, and artificial intelligence, all had setbacks before a successful product was created.

McKinsey & Company, a global consulting firm, recognizes four stages that an existing firm may go through when faced with an innovative, disruptive technology.[42] Stage one occurs when a new technology comes on the market but is yet to be disruptive. This stage is called "Signals Amidst the Noise." Most incumbent firms notice little, if any, impact on their core businesses at this stage, so management is simply not motivated to act. A company that *does* act at this stage must change long-standing beliefs about how to make money in the industries where it competes. To compete with Amazon and other online retailers, Walmart acquired FlipKart, the largest e-commerce company in India. Best Buy is using its crowdsourcing service Instacart to offer the same service.

In stage two, "Change Takes Hold," the core technology and economic factors of the disruptive force are validated. This stage is the one at which companies need to establish footholds in the new technology. At this point, the disruptive technology still does not have a major impact on the bottom line of the incumbent firms. Even as online classified ads for cars and real estate began to take off, most newspapers did not react.

Stage three is called "The Inevitable Transformation." This stage is when the future is pounding at the door. If established companies had the foresight to begin creating new ventures in stage two, they need to aggressively shift resources to these ventures in stage three. And if they did nothing in stage two but maintained the status quo, a major reallocation of resources to the disruptive technology is needed to create a new, and perhaps sole, economic engine for the firm. Faced with the disruptive technology of online retail entering phase three, Best Buy changed its whole philosophy of doing business. One thing the company has that Amazon does not have is more than 1,000 big-box stores. Best Buy saw the benefit of using them as showrooms, which the company calls "showcases." It also decided to open its showcases to high-tech firms. Best Buy was among the first chains to feature Apple boutiques. Next came Samsung showrooms and then Microsoft. Amazon, and Google received space to display their smart-home technologies. Best Buy revamped its website and supply chain and began offering price-matching. The Geek Squad has evolved to become in-home technology advisors.[43]

"Adapting to the New Normal" is the last stage. At this stage, the disruption has reached the point at which companies must accept the fact that the industry has fundamentally changed. Firms that were slow to react must either restructure, consolidate, or go bankrupt. Kodak declared bankruptcy in 2012 after failing to capitalize on the market's migration from film to digital cameras. Yellow Cab of San Francisco declared bankruptcy not long

Best Buy has adapted well to changes in technology over time.

Felipe Sanchez/Shutterstock.com

after Uber and Lyft came to town. Traditional banks may find themselves behind if they don't adapt to accelerating changes in technology. A Chinese firm called Ant has developed an app for borrowing money on the fly while shopping. The app senses your voice and passes it to online algorithms for identity recognition; other algorithms gather information on your bank accounts, credit history, and social media profile; further algorithms weigh all these factors and a suitable credit offer appears on your phone, all within seconds.[44]

4-5a Research

The United States, historically, has excelled at both basic and applied research. **Basic research** (or *pure research*) attempts to expand the frontiers of knowledge but is not aimed at a specific, pragmatic problem. Basic research aims to confirm an existing theory or to learn more about a concept or phenomenon. For example, basic research might focus on high-energy physics. **Applied research**, in contrast, attempts to develop new or improved products. The United States has dramatically improved its track record in applied research. For example, the United States leads the world in applying basic research to aircraft design and propulsion systems. Many companies, particularly small and medium-sized firms, cannot afford the luxury of basic research.

The United States became a global leader in research and development (R&D) spending in the 20th century, funding as much as 69 percent of annual global R&D after World War II. Expenditures continue to rise with funding primarily by business, the federal government, and institutions of higher education.[45] In 2023, R&D expenditures reached $191 billion, a nearly 13 percent increase over the previous year. The National Institutes of Health, the National Science Foundation, the U.S. Department of Energy, and NASA's science programs were all major beneficiaries.[46]

4-5b How Innovation in Technology Affects Marketing

Innovation in technology has been occurring at a rapid pace, and companies must learn how a given technology might be useful. For example, the technology that allows marketers to gather and analyze big data has allowed companies to gain important insights into how consumers think, feel, and behave. This information then aids

---

basic research pure research that aims to confirm an existing theory or to learn more about a concept or phenomenon

applied research research that attempts to develop new or improved products

marketers in deciding who to target and in designing, pricing, distributing, and communicating about their products for that target. Electric vehicles are no longer a novelty on the road.

The COVID-19 pandemic shutdown caused major disruptions to many industries. Research shows companies that increased investments in technology during the pandemic outperformed their competition. The most instrumental technologies used by businesses during the pandemic were mobile cellphone technology, cloud-computing technology, and artificial intelligence—particularly in the context of customer service. For example, many companies automated their customer service during the COVID-19 pandemic by using artificial intelligence (AI) in the form of chatbots. Deliveries made by drones and robots helped to ease pandemic-related delays and labor shortages. In addition, manufacturing firms used technology to enhance the productivity of their factories.[47]

The COVID-19 pandemic inspired many other innovations in business. It forced consumers to shop more online with their computers and phones. Company websites, social media, and apps became more important in the purchase journey. Contactless payment solutions surged. Walgreens has been opening automated pharmacies where robots fill most prescriptions, freeing pharmacists to spend more time interacting with customers.[48] Virtual reality (VR) is being used to provide immersive shopping experiences. For example, Alo Yoga's virtual store can be visited by customers via mobile phones, desktop computers, or a Meta Quest 2 VR headset from where they can shop the store's collections, and design custom outfits.[49] Machine learning and AI have also dramatically changed companies' abilities to identify customer targets and model consumer behavior.[50]

> "Adapt or Perish, now as ever, is nature's inexorable imperative."
>
> —H. G. Wells

4-6 Political and Legal Factors

4-6 Discuss the political and legal environment of marketing

Business needs government regulation to protect innovators of new technology, the interests of society in general, one business from another, and consumers. In turn, government needs business because the marketplace generates taxes that support public efforts to educate our youth, pave our roads, protect our shores, and the like.

Every aspect of the marketing mix is subject to laws and restrictions. It is the duty of marketing managers or their legal assistants to understand these laws and conform to them because failure to comply with regulations can have major consequences for a firm. Sometimes just sensing trends and taking corrective action before a government agency steps in can help avoid regulation.

4-6a Federal Legislation

Federal laws that affect marketing fall into several categories of regulatory activity: competitive environment, pricing, advertising and promotion, and consumer privacy. The key pieces of legislation in these areas are summarized in Table 4.1. The primary federal laws that protect consumers are shown in Table 4.2. The Patient Protection and Affordable Care Act (ACA), commonly called Obamacare, has had a significant impact on marketing since it was signed into law in 2010. A few key provisions of the Act are the following:

- Large employers must offer coverage to full-time workers.

- Workers cannot be denied coverage.

- A person cannot be dropped when they are sick.

- A worker cannot be denied coverage for a preexisting condition.

- Young adults can stay on their parents' plans until age 26.

In 2018, several changes were made to the ACA. For example, one new rule states that people living in areas where there is only one insurer selling ACA plans can qualify for an exemption. Additionally, insurers are no longer required to provide a standardized set of benefits.[51]

In 2010, Congress passed the Dodd–Frank Wall Street Reform and Consumer Protection Act, which brought sweeping changes to bank and financial market regulations. The legislation created the Consumer Financial Protection Bureau (CFPB) to oversee checking accounts, private student loans, mortgages, and other financial products. The agency deals with unfair, abusive, and deceptive practices. Some groups have expressed concerns that the CFPB is assembling massive databases on credit cards, credit monitoring, debt cancellation products, auto loans, and payday loans. CFPB officials claim that they need the information to make effective rules and enforce those policies. One way or another, the CFPB has certainly had a significant impact on several U.S. businesses—the bureau has overhauled mortgage lending rules, stopped abusive debt collectors, prosecuted hundreds of companies, and extracted nearly $12 billion from businesses in the form of canceled debts and consumer refunds. Recently, Regions Bank was fined $191 million for allegedly charging surprise overdraft fees to customers.[52]

Table 4.1 Primary U.S. Laws That Affect Marketing

Legislation	Impact on Marketing
Sherman Antitrust Act of 1890	Makes trusts and conspiracies in restraint of trade illegal; makes monopolies and attempts to monopolize illegal.
Clayton Act of 1914	Outlaws discrimination in prices to different buyers; prohibits tying contracts (which require the buyer of one product to also buy another item in the line); makes illegal the combining of two or more competing corporations by pooling ownership of stock.
Federal Trade Commission Act of 1914	Created the Federal Trade Commission (FTC) to deal with antitrust matters; outlaws unfair methods of competition.
Robinson-Patman Act of 1936	Prohibits charging different prices to different buyers of merchandise of like grade and quantity; requires sellers to make any supplementary services or allowances available to all purchasers on a proportionately equal basis.
Wheeler-Lea Amendments to FTC Act of 1938	Broadens the FTC's power to prohibit practices that might injure the public without affecting competition; outlaws false and deceptive advertising.
Celler-Kefauver Antimerger Act of 1950	Strengthens the Clayton Act to prevent corporate acquisitions that reduce competition.
Hart-Scott-Rodino Act of 1976	Requires large companies to notify the government of their intent to merge.
Foreign Corrupt Practices Act of 1977	Prohibits bribery of foreign officials to obtain business.

Table 4.2 Selection of Primary U.S. Laws Protecting Consumers

Legislation	Impact On Marketing
Consumer Credit Protection Act of 1968	Requires that lenders fully disclose true interest rates and all other charges to credit customers for loans and installment purchases.
Public Health Cigarette Smoking Act of 1971	Prohibits tobacco advertising on radio and television.
Consumer Product Safety Act of 1972	Created the Consumer Product Safety Commission, which has authority to specify safety standards for most products.
Child Protection Act of 1990	Regulates the number of minutes of advertising on children's television.
Children's Online Privacy Protection Act of 1998	Empowers the FTC to set rules regarding how and when marketers must obtain parental permission before asking children marketing research questions.
Do Not Call Law of 2003	Protects consumers against unwanted telemarketing calls.
CAN-SPAM Act of 2003	Protects consumers against unwanted email, or spam.
Restoring American Financial Stability Act of 2010	Created the Consumer Financial Protection Bureau to protect consumers against unfair, abusive, and deceptive financial practices.
Patient Protection and Affordable Care Act of 2010	Overhauled the U.S. healthcare system; mandated and subsidized health insurance for individuals.

4-6b State and Local Laws

Legislation that affects marketing varies state by state. Oregon, for example, limits utility advertising to 0.125 percent of the company's gross revenues. California has forced industry to improve consumer products and has enacted legislation to lower the energy consumption of refrigerators, freezers, and air conditioners.

Many states and cities are attempting to fight consumers' poor health habits by regulating fast-food chains and other restaurants. For example, California and New York have passed a law banning trans fats in restaurants and bakeries, New York City chain restaurants must now display calorie counts on menus, and Boston has banned trans fats in restaurants. New York City enacted a law prohibiting restaurants from selling soft drinks larger than 16 ounces, but the ban was overturned a day before it was to go into effect.

4-6c Regulatory Agencies

Although some state regulatory bodies actively pursue violators of their marketing statutes, federal regulators

---

Consumer Product Safety Commission (CPSC) a federal agency established to protect the health and safety of consumers in and around their homes

generally have the greatest clout. The Consumer Product Safety Commission, the Consumer Financial Protection Bureau (discussed in Section 4-6a), the Federal Trade Commission, and the Food and Drug Administration are the four federal agencies most directly and actively involved in marketing affairs. These agencies, plus others, are discussed throughout the book, but a brief introduction is in order here.

Consumer Product Safety Commission

The sole purpose of the **Consumer Product Safety Commission (CPSC)** is to protect the health and safety of consumers in and around their homes. The CPSC has the power to set mandatory safety standards for almost all products consumers use and can fine offending firms if they don't comply. For example, Peloton was recently fined over $19 million by the CPSC because the company did not report a treadmill defect that was potentially dangerous. In 2008, Congress passed the Consumer Product Safety Improvement Act. The law is aimed primarily at children's products; children are defined as those used by individuals 12 years old or younger. The law addresses items such as cribs, electronics and video games, school supplies, science kits, toys, and pacifiers. The law requires mandatory testing and labeling and increases fines and prison time for violators.

Food and Drug Administration

The **Food and Drug Administration (FDA)**, another powerful agency, is charged with enforcing regulations against selling and distributing adulterated, misbranded, or hazardous food and drug products. In 2009, the Tobacco Control Act was passed. This Act gave the FDA authority to regulate tobacco products, with a special emphasis on preventing their use by children and young people and reducing the impact of tobacco on public health. Four e-cigarette makers were recently cited for not getting the FDA's authorization to sell their products in the United States.[53] Another recent FDA action is the "Bad Ad" program. It is geared toward healthcare providers to help them recognize misleading prescription drug promotions, and it gives them an easy way to report the activity to the FDA.

Federal Trade Commission

The **Federal Trade Commission (FTC)** is empowered to prevent persons or corporations from using unfair methods of competition in commerce. The FTC consists of five members, each holding office for seven years. Over the years, Congress has greatly expanded the powers of the FTC. Its responsibilities have grown so large that the FTC has created several bureaus to better organize its operations. One of the most important is the Bureau of Competition, which promotes and protects competition. The Bureau of Competition:

- reviews mergers and acquisitions, and challenges those that would likely lead to higher prices, fewer choices, or less innovation;

- seeks out and challenges anticompetitive conduct in the marketplace, including monopolization and agreements between competitors;

- promotes competition in industries where consumer impact is high, such as healthcare, real estate, oil and gas, technology, and consumer goods; and

- provides information and holds conferences and workshops for consumers, businesses, and policy makers on competition issues for market analysis.

The FTC has a Bureau of Consumer Protection which "stops unfair, deceptive, and fraudulent business practices by collecting reports from consumers and conducting investigations, suing companies and people that break the law, developing rules to maintain a fair marketplace, and educating consumers and businesses about their rights and responsibilities."[54] A popular laser vision correction company was recently cited by the FTC for using bait-and-switch advertising that claimed patients would only pay $300 for the procedure, while charging them far more.[55] The FTC and the Consumer Financial Protection Bureau coordinate efforts so they could protect consumers

while avoiding duplication of federal law enforcement and regulatory efforts. The objective of the agreement is to avoid overlapping responsibilities and duplications of effort. Another important FTC bureau is the Bureau of Economics. It provides economic analysis and support to antitrust and consumer protection investigations.

4-6d Consumer Privacy

Many consumer protection issues today involve the internet. The popularity of the internet for targeted advertising, for collecting consumer data, and as a repository for sensitive consumer data has alarmed privacy-minded consumers. In 2003, the U.S. Congress passed the CAN-SPAM Act to regulate unsolicited email advertising. The act prohibits commercial emailers from using false addresses and presenting false or misleading information, among other restrictions.

Internet users who once felt anonymous when using the web are now disturbed by the amount of information marketers collect about them and their children as they visit various sites in cyberspace. The FTC, with jurisdiction under the Children's Online Privacy Protection Act, requires website operators to post a privacy policy on their home page and a link to the policy on every page where personal information is collected. Despite federal efforts, online tracking has become widespread and pervasive. A vast amount of personal data is collected through apps.

Tracking has allowed the digital advertising market to grow. The global digital advertising market in 2023 was valued at $681—more than the amount spent on TV advertising. Digital media's share of total advertising is 69 percent.[56] Most companies are collecting data about users, and data collectors piggyback on each other. When a user visits a website that has a code for one type of tracking technology, the data collection triggers other tracking technologies that are not embedded on the site. Piggybacking means that websites really do not know how much data are being gathered about their users.

Acxiom is a company that collects, analyzes and sells customer and business information used for targeted marketing campaigns. The firm has created the world's largest consumer database, containing information on more than 700 million consumers worldwide, with data on more than 1,500 consumer traits such as location,

---

Food and Drug Administration (FDA) a federal agency charged with enforcing regulations against selling and distributing adulterated, misbranded, or hazardous food and drug products

Federal Trade Commission (FTC) a federal agency empowered to prevent persons or corporations from using unfair methods of competition in commerce

age, and household income.[57] Acxiom's database provides more than 3,500 specific behavioral insights, such as one's propensity to make a purchase. The company's customers include firms like Ford, Macy's, and many other major firms seeking consumer insights. Acxiom integrates data from numerous sources, include social media sites, public records, loyalty programs, web browser cookies, credit cards, and mobile apps, to create in-depth consumer behavior portraits.

Many consumers don't want to be part of huge databases—they want their privacy back. They are also concerned about major data breaches, which are occurring more frequently. For example, data recently leaked from 500 million LinkedIn profiles was found to be for sale on a hacker forum. The profiles leaked included mostly professional information, such as full names, email addresses, phone numbers, and workplace information.[58]

In the United States, there is no single, comprehensive federal law regulating the collection and use of personal data. However, in May 2018, the European Union (EU) passed the General Data Protection Regulation (GDPR). It applies to any business that handles personal data of European member residents. The rule covers just about any data point that can be linked to an individual: credit card numbers, addresses, travel records, religion, web search history, biometric data, and more. The world's 500 largest corporations are spending around $7.8 billion to comply with GDPR. Each firm is required to have a "data protection officer." The law applies to all firms using personal data from EU citizens even if the firm has no physical presence in the EU Firms can collect only data needed immediately and not stockpile it. Data collection policies must be clear and available. Fines can go as high as 4 percent of a company's annual global revenues.[59]

4-7 Competitive Factors

4-7 Explain how competition affects marketing

The competitive environment encompasses the number of competitors a firm must face, the relative size of the competitors, and the degree of interdependence within the industry. Management has little control over the competitive environment confronting a firm.

4-7a Competition for Market Share and Profits

As U.S. population growth slows, technology rapidly changes, global competition increases, costs rise, and available resources tighten, firms find that they must work harder to maintain their profits and market share, regardless

of the form of the competitive market. Sometimes technological advances can usher in a whole new set of competitors that can change a firm's business model. Bed Bath & Beyond became a phenomenal success not long after it opened in 1971. The company was a retail pioneer, becoming so large it dominated its industry. Bed Bath & Beyond sells towels, bedding, and other home-related items and has outlasted its major competitor, Linens 'n Things. Yet, strong competition over the last several years has resulted in declining profits and sales. At the same time, more customers started shopping online for home décor. Bed Bath & Beyond was focused on their physical stores. Moreover, customers could find less expensive alternatives on sites such as Amazon and a wider selection of home goods on sites like Wayfair. During the COVID-19 pandemic, the company temporarily closed their stores while competitors stayed open. These factors together resulted in the company struggling to stay in business, and the company eventually filed for bankruptcy. Overstock.com ultimately purchased the Bed Bath & Beyond brand name and relaunched the brand's website, but all of the Bed Bath & Beyond physical retail stores remain closed.[60]

Building strong customer loyalty helps companies to guard against competitors. One study found that 72 percent of customers across the globe felt loyal to their favorite brands, which motivated their purchasing decisions. Over half of Americans stated that they were loyal to a brand for life. Loyalty results from building strong relationships with customers. When a company has enough loyal customers, it does not have to rely as heavily on attracting new customers or on losing customers to competitors. Moreover, monitoring consumer preferences allows a firm to detect and adapt to changes. Adapting could mean offering new products, improving existing products, offering more competitive pricing, or providing a more meaningful experience for customers.[61] Apple, Starbucks, IKEA, and Trader Joe's are all examples of companies that have a substantial base of loyal customers.

4-7b Global Competition

Global competition in many industries is fierce. For example, the United States and China are locked in a competitive battle in the technology sector. The United States maintains an edge with its strong research universities, sizeable private sector companies such as Apple and Amazon, and robust start-up culture. However, China is closing the gap with numerous government-led strategies. Today, the Indo-Pacific region, an area inclusive of the Indian Ocean and the western Pacific Ocean, contributes 52 percent of the world economy, up from 37 percent in 2000. In addition, over the next five years two-thirds of global economic growth is predicted to come from Indo-Pacific countries.[62]

Boeing is an example of a savvy international business competitor. Now Airbus, Boeing's primary competitor, is assembling planes in the United States. Many foreign competitors also consider the United States to be a ripe target market. Thus, a U.S. marketing manager can no longer focus only on domestic competitors. In automobiles, textiles, watches, televisions, steel, digital devices, and many other areas, foreign competition has been strong. In the past, foreign firms penetrated U.S. markets by concentrating on price, but the emphasis has switched to product quality. Nestlé, Volvo, and Rolls-Royce are noted for quality, not cheap prices.

4-8 Environmentalism

4-8 Discuss how environmentalism affects marketing

Environmentalism is a concern about, and action aimed at, protecting the environment. It focuses on the preservation, restoration, and improvement of the natural environment and earth-based elements or processes, such as the climate. It often is associated with a movement to control pollution or to protect plant and animal diversity. Research has

Sheila Fitzgerald/Shutterstock.com

found that sustainable companies and products are important to 78 percent of respondents. Similarly, over half of consumers are willing to pay more for eco-friendly brands, and 84 percent say that poor environmental practices will alienate them from a brand or company. Some study responses varied by country. For example, consumers in Brazil, China, Austria, and Italy are the most likely to have made a significant or total change toward a sustainable lifestyle, while those in the United States trail behind.[63]

Concern for the environment has led companies to develop a diverse array of products and packaging. For example, plant-based diets have become more popular. It has been shown that a person can reduce their carbon footprint by up to 73 percent by not eating meat or dairy. Plant-based "meats" like the Impossible Burger and Chick-fil-A's new Cauliflower Sandwich are examples of foods for this type of diet. Electric vehicles and bikes reduce CO_2 emissions dramatically. Companies are adopting sustainable materials for packaging, such as substituting bamboo rather than using single-use plastics. Compared to wood flooring, bamboo flooring releases more oxygen and absorbs four times as much carbon dioxide. It is also strong, water resistant, and cheaper to produce than wood. Large contributors to recycling will be manufacturers and producers, who will also encourage consumers to do the same. Smart technology in thermostats and large appliances will save energy in consumers' homes. Renewable energy sources, such as a heat pump, provides heat or electricity to homes without having to rely on fossil fuels.[64]

In response to increasing demand from consumers for products that are more environmentally conscious, big companies are taking action to improve their sustainability. Tanger Factory Outlet Centers has made significant progress toward its environmental goals. The company has invested in renewable energy by installing new solar system panels in several of its centers. It has also committed to emissions reductions by adding 165 electric vehicle charging stations at some of its locations and by planning to change all the vehicles in its operational fleet to electric by 2030.[65]

Allbirds is a shoe company that responded to the trend of sustainability by developing eco-friendly shoes. Instead of materials like plastic, it chose to make shoes with natural materials, such as wool. Kindness to the planet is one of the company's strongest selling points. Many competitors have imitated Allbirds shoes, and instead of litigating, the company cofounder encouraged rivals and shared the recipe for the shoes' plant-based soles to anyone who asked.[66]

Environmentalism a concern about, and action aimed at protecting the environment

Our Favorites

FOR EVERYDAY   FOR RUNNING   FOR TRAVEL

Tree Dasher 2   **Tree Flyer**   **Trail Runner SWT**

Comfy, Breezy, Everyday Runs   Light, Bouncy, Long Distance Runs   Durable, Grippy, Off Road Terrain

Source: allbirds

Patagonia, an outdoor apparel firm, is among the best-known environmentally conscious companies in the world. Protecting the planet has been one of Patagonia's core values since the company started in 1973. Its products, packaging, channels of distribution, programs and messaging all revolve around sustainability. Patagonia uses 100 percent organic cotton in making its apparel. An advanced method of technology they use to dye their denim uses 84 percent less water than the standard methods used to color denim. Additionally, recycled materials are used in 87 percent of the items they produce. In fact, it makes polyester from recycled soda bottles! Patagonia recycles the plastic bags used to protect products during shipping, and it encourages its shipping partners to do the same.

The company has created the "Worn Wear" program so that customers can trade-in and buy used Patagonia clothing. This endeavor reduces the number of textiles that end up in landfills. Patagonia's website mentions sustainability on every page. Moreover, they give 1 percent of total sales to support numerous environmental groups. To date, Patagonia has donated $89 million to these causes, giving more than any other apparel industry companies.[67]

Patagonia takes environmentalism seriously. Everything the company does revolves around its core value of not harming the planet.

Sander van der Werf/Shutterstock.com

PopTika/Shutterstock.com

Chapter 5

Developing a Global Vision

Learning Outcomes

After studying this chapter, you will be able to . . .

5-1 Identify the importance of global marketing

5-2 Discuss the impact of multinational firms on the world economy

5-3 Describe the external environment facing global marketers

5-4 Organize the five methods of entering the global marketplace from low to high risk

5-5 List the basic elements involved in developing a global marketing mix

5-6 Describe how the internet is affecting global marketing

5-1 Rewards of Global Marketing and the Shifting Global Business Landscape

5-1 Identify the importance of global marketing

Global marketing—marketing that targets markets on a worldwide scale—has become an imperative for most large and many middle-sized businesses. Even smaller firms are beginning to invest in global marketing, often via digital methods.

Managers must develop a global vision not only to recognize and react to international marketing opportunities but also to remain competitive at home. Often a firm's toughest domestic competition comes from foreign companies. Consider how Spotify, founded in Sweden, impacted Apple Music and Sirius XM, for example. Moreover, a global vision enables a manager to understand that customer and distribution networks operate worldwide. In summary, having a **global vision** means recognizing and reacting to international marketing opportunities, using effective global marketing strategies, and being aware of threats from foreign competitors in all markets.

Adopting a global vision can be very lucrative for a company. It is no accident that global firms like Apple, Microsoft, Walmart, Amazon, and Johnson & Johnson are among the largest and most successful multinational firms in the world.[1] Each has a global vision that managers understand and follow.

The foundation of a successful global vision is a corporate structure that provides a continual flow of fresh ideas. One firm that has such a structure is Dunkin'. Dunkin' is a multinational coffee and donut company that was founded in 1950 in Quincy, Massachusetts and is now part of Inspire Brands.[2] The firm has over 11,300 Dunkin' restaurants worldwide with 3,200 outside of the United States in 36 countries. To satisfy global consumer preferences, Dunkin' has adapted its menu to include grapefruit Coolattas in Korea, pork floss donuts in China, and mango chocolate donuts in Lebanon.[3]

Of course, global marketing is not a one-way street whereby only U.S. companies sell their wares and services throughout the world. Foreign competition in the domestic market was once relatively rare, but now it is found in almost every industry. In fact, in many industries, U.S. businesses have lost significant market share to imported products. In electronics, cameras, automobiles, fine china, tractors, leather goods, and a host of other consumer and industrial products, U.S. companies have struggled at home to maintain their market shares against foreign competitors.

5-1a Why Nations Trade

One might think that the best way to protect workers and the domestic economy would be to stop trade with other nations. Then all production and consumption would stay within a country's borders. But then how would countries get resources they cannot produce, like the United States needing to obtain nonrenewable resources? The United States is 100 percent reliant on other countries to produce 12 commodities and obtain 31 critical minerals, accounting for 50 percent of its consumption.[4] Manganese is essential in steel making; gallium is used in the manufacture of high-speed semiconductors needed to make telephones; and vanadium is used for steel alloys. The United States must import these minerals because it either does not produce them or uses more than it produces.

A country has an **absolute advantage** when it can produce and sell a product or service at a lower cost than any other country or when it is the only country that can provide a product or service. The United States, for example, has an absolute advantage in some genome-editing biopharmaceutical technology and other high-tech items. Suppose that the United States has an absolute advantage in pharmaceuticals and that Italy has an absolute advantage in footwear. The United States does not have the infrastructure and skilled artisans to make footwear, and Italy lacks the technology to develop pharmaceuticals. Both countries would gain by exchanging pharmaceuticals for footwear.

Even if the United States had an absolute advantage in both footwear and pharmaceuticals, it should still specialize and engage in trade. Why? The reason is the **principle of comparative advantage**, which says that each country should specialize in the products and services that it can produce most readily and cheaply and trade those products and services for goods and services that foreign countries can produce most readily and cheaply. This specialization ensures greater product availability and lower prices.

global marketing marketing that targets markets on a worldwide scale

global vision recognizing and reacting to international marketing opportunities, using effective global marketing strategies, and being aware of threats from foreign competitors in all markets

absolute advantage when a country can produce a product or service at a lower cost than any other country or when it is the only country that can provide the product or service

principle of comparative advantage each country should specialize in the products or services that it can produce most readily and cheaply and trade those products or services for goods and services that foreign countries can produce most readily and cheaply

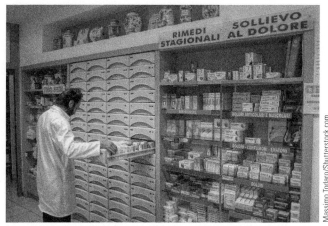

Italy has an absolute advantage in producing quality footwear, and the United States has an absolute advantage in creating and producing pharmaceuticals. Both countries can gain through trade.

For example, China has a comparative advantage in assembling robotics because of lower labor costs, close proximity to component parts manufacturers, and production technology. The United States has an advantage in more efficient agricultural production in grains such as corn and soybeans. Both nations are better off with trade. Trade is not a zero-sum game but creates opportunities for mutual gain.

Thus, comparative advantage acts as a stimulus to trade. When nations allow their citizens to trade whatever goods and services they choose without government regulation, free trade exists. **Free trade** is the policy of permitting individuals and businesses in a country to buy and sell in other countries without restrictions. The opposite of free trade is **protectionism**, in which a nation protects its home industries from foreign competition by establishing artificial barriers such as tariffs and quotas (discussed later in the chapter). Global Trade Alert, a Swiss-based independent trade-monitoring group, records policy change initiatives around the globe that hurt trade with other countries. Since 2008, products of iron and steel represent the sector with the greatest amount of harmful interventions.[5]

5-1b Importance of Global Marketing to the United States

Many countries heavily depend on international commerce. For example, France, the United Kingdom, Canada, and Germany derive 62, 55, 61, and 89 percent of their respective **gross domestic product (GDP)** from world trade—considerably more than the United States' 23 percent.[6] GDP is the total market value of all final goods and services produced in a country for a given period (usually a year or a quarter of a year). *Final* in this sense refers to final products that are sold, not to intermediate products used to assemble a final product. For example, if the value of a semiconductor (an intermediate product) and that of a laptop (the final product) were both counted, the semiconductor would be counted twice. Therefore, GDP counts only final goods and services in its valuation of a country's production.

Traditionally, only very large multinational companies have seriously attempted to compete worldwide. However, more and more small and medium-sized companies have begun pursuing international markets, and some are even beginning to play a critical role in driving export growth. Today, 98 percent of U.S. exports are produced by small businesses. Considering fewer than 5 percent of U.S. businesses export, small businesses make up the bulk of this form of trade.[7] The U.S. government is working with these firms to expand small business trade. The Export–Import Bank of the United States, for example, helps thousands of small businesses each year. Essentially, the bank provides two main types of export services. One is accounts receivable insurance, which lets small exporters extend sales terms to their buyers for up to six months. The other is trade financing to foreign buyers, which is primarily used by larger firms. If a foreign purchaser wants to buy ships from U.S. manufacturer General Dynamics Corporation but doesn't have the funds to do so, given the long turnaround time for

---

free trade policy of permitting individuals and businesses in a country to buy and sell in other countries without restrictions.

protectionism where a nation protects its home industries from foreign competitors by establishing artificial barriers, such as tariffs and quotas

gross domestic product (GDP) the total market value of all final goods and services produced in a country for a given time period

such expensive orders, the Export–Import Bank will provide the financing.[8]

The Small Business Administration (SBA) is a U.S. government agency that provides support for small businesses that export or desire to start exporting. The SBA will provide up to an 85-percent guarantee to lenders for up to $150,000 and 75 percent for amounts greater than $150,000, not to exceed $5 million, that the small business will repay.[9] Other SBA support includes participation in foreign trade missions and market sales trips, aid in designing international marketing strategies, export trade show exhibits, and training.[10]

Job Outsourcing and Inshoring

The notion of **outsourcing** (sending U.S. jobs abroad) has been highly controversial for several decades. Many executives have said that it leads to corporate growth, efficiency, productivity, and revenue growth. Most companies see cost savings as a key driver in outsourcing. But outsourcing also has a negative side. For instance, cities could suffer if many of their manufacturing facilities were to shut down and relocate around the world. U.S. companies employ about 14 million workers in their overseas affiliates. General Electric, the maker of industrial and commercial machinery, employs 66 percent of its workforce overseas. Similarly, The Coca-Cola Company has 88 percent of its employees outside of U.S. borders. Other U.S. firms with large overseas workforces include Microsoft, Apple, Johnson & Johnson, Walmart, Procter & Gamble, and Intel.[11]

Some companies have begun to suspect that outsourcing's negatives outweigh its positives. Improperly designed parts and products have caused production delays, and rising wages in the developing world have rendered U.S. rates more competitive. Increased fuel and transportation costs associated with long-distance shipping, coupled with falling U.S. energy costs, have given impetus to **inshoring**, or reshoring, returning production jobs to the United States. Supply chain and other issues that resulted from the COVID-19 pandemic prompted more than 1,500 U.S. companies to return over 161,000 jobs to the United States the following year.[12] However, with the accelerated adoption of remote work during the pandemic, white-collar positions are the new target for outsourcing. Further, companies are relying heavily on contractors rather than hiring full-time employees. This trend is evidenced by a 56 percent increase in contractor payments in the United States over a three-year period.[13]

outsourcing sending U.S. jobs abroad

inshoring returning production jobs to the United States

Benefits of Globalization

Traditional economic theory says that globalization relies on competition to drive down prices and increase product and service quality. Business goes to the countries that operate most efficiently, have lower labor costs, and/or have the technology to produce what is needed. In summary, globalization expands economic freedom, spurs competition, and raises the productivity and living standards of people in countries that open themselves to the global marketplace. For less developed countries, globalization also offers access to foreign capital, global export markets, access to new cultures, and advanced technology, while breaking the monopoly of inefficient and protected domestic producers. Faster growth, in turn, increases household income, encourages democratization, and promotes higher labor and environmental standards. Though government officials in developing countries may face more difficult choices because of globalization, their citizens enjoy greater individual freedom. In this sense, globalization acts as a check on governmental power by making it more difficult for governments to abuse their citizens' freedom and property.

Globalization deserves credit for helping lift many millions out of poverty and for improving standards of living of low-wage families. Between 1980 and 2010, Mexico saw an increase in GDP by 22 percent after the government loosened trade restrictions and adopted an outward-oriented economic development plan.[14] Likewise in developing countries around the world, globalization has created a vibrant middle class that has elevated the standard of living for hundreds of millions of people.

Costs of Globalization

Countries restrict trade and create barriers for a number of reasons (many of which are discussed later in the chapter). In theory, if a country can boost exports and limit imports, then more jobs are created and there is less competition for domestic businesses. While globalization was a major factor in job losses in the United States in the 1980s and 1990s, technology and automation have caused the vast majority of job losses between 2001 and 2018; that loss was estimated at 3.7 million jobs.[15]

5-2 Multinational Firms

5-2 Discuss the impact of multinational firms on the world economy

The United States has many large companies that are global marketers. Many of them have been very successful. Further, many companies headquartered outside of the United States are also successful globally. A company that is heavily engaged in international trade, beyond exporting and importing, is called a **multinational corporation**. A multinational corporation moves resources, goods, services, and skills across national boundaries without regard to the country in which its headquarters is located. Additionally, it generates a minimum of 25 percent of its revenue from countries outside where it is headquartered.[16]

Multinationals often develop their global business in stages. In the first stage, companies operate in one country and sell into others. Second-stage multinationals set up foreign subsidiaries to handle sales in one country. In the third stage, multinationals operate an entire line of business in another country. The fourth stage has evolved primarily owing to the internet and involves mostly high-tech companies. For these firms, the executive suite is virtual. Their top executives and core corporate functions are in different countries—wherever the firms can gain a competitive edge through the availability of talent or capital, low costs, or proximity to their most important customers.

Many U.S.-based multinationals earn a large percentage of their total revenue abroad. Apple receives 56 percent of its revenue from outside the Americas. Other large U.S. multinationals include Walmart, ExxonMobil, Berkshire Hathaway, and Amazon.[17]

5-2a Are Multinationals Beneficial?

Although multinationals comprise far less than 1 percent of U.S. companies, they account for about 20 percent of all private jobs and 25 percent of all private wages.[18] For decades, U.S. multinationals have driven an outsized share of U.S. productivity growth, the foundation of rising standards of living for everyone.

The role of multinational corporations in developing nations is a subject of controversy. The ability of multinationals to tap financial, physical, and human resources from all over the world and combine them economically and profitably can benefit any country. They also often possess and can transfer the most up-to-date technology. Critics, however, claim that often the wrong kind of technology is transferred to developing nations. Usually, it is **capital intensive** (requiring a greater expenditure for equipment than for labor) and thus does not substantially increase employment. A "modern sector" then emerges in the nation, employing a small proportion of the labor force with relatively high productivity and income levels and with increasingly capital-intensive technologies. A supply chain is a group of entities interlinked in the flow of goods and services from the initial suppliers to the ultimate customers (refer to Chapter 13). Many multinationals have found that the global complexities of worldwide supply chains create more problems than advantages. These problems include partners stealing or copying the firm's technology, complex government regulations and harassment from officials,

and lower global profits. For example, Ford and General Motors make more than 85 percent of their profits in North America. Some successful, old-line multinationals, such as Coca-Cola, Unilever, and Procter & Gamble, have prospered by running a loose federation of national businesses instead of creating complex global supply chains. Others have begun to see the wisdom in this approach, cutting back on global expansion and returning operations closer to home.

A survey of U.S. and European manufacturing companies indicated that more than 60 percent expect to inshore part of their Asia production over the next three years.[19] Reasons for the change include government subsidies, supply chain disruptions, desire for better communication, and continued COVID-19-related shutdowns. Manufacturers are beginning to shift inventory management from just-in-time to "just in case" after shortages in inventory experienced during the pandemic.

Government policies and other funding can also spur job creation by multinational corporations. The U.S. Congress passed the CHIPS and Science Act of 2022 to invest billions of dollars in domestic semiconductor manufacturing. Companies like Micron, Qualcomm, GlobalFoundries, First Solar, Honda, and Toyota have announced plans to build new manufacturing facilities, which are expected to add more than 642,000 jobs.[20] The Advanced Manufacturing Fund, established by Apple, awarded Corning Inc. $45 million to increase capacity at their U.S. manufacturing facilities; Corning Inc. is expected to add 1,000 jobs.[21]

5-2b Global Marketing Standardization

Traditionally, marketing-oriented multinational corporations have operated somewhat differently in each country. They use a strategy of providing different product features, packaging, advertising, and so on. However, Ted Levitt, a former Harvard professor, has described a trend toward what he refers to as "global marketing," with a slightly different meaning.[22] He contends that communication and technology have made the world smaller so that almost all consumers everywhere want all the things they have heard about, seen, or experienced. Thus, he sees the emergence of global markets for standardized consumer products on a huge scale, as opposed to segmented foreign markets with different products. In this book, *global marketing* is defined as individuals and organizations using a global vision

---

multinational corporation a company that is heavily engaged in international trade, beyond exporting and importing

capital intensive using more capital than labor in the production process

to effectively market goods and services across national boundaries. To make the distinction, we can refer to Levitt's notion as **global marketing standardization**.

Global marketing standardization presumes that the markets throughout the world are becoming more alike. Firms practicing global marketing standardization produce "globally standardized products" to be sold the same way all over the world. Most smartphones and tablets, for example, are standardized globally except for the languages displayed. These devices allow the user to switch easily from one language to another. Uniform production should enable companies to lower production and marketing costs and increase profits. Levitt has cited Coca-Cola, Colgate-Palmolive, and McDonald's as successful global marketers. His critics point out, however, that the success of these three companies is really based on variation, not on offering the same product everywhere. McDonald's, for example, modified the Big Mac in Greece by using pita bread instead of a bun. It sells ham and egg pasta in Hong Kong and poutine in Canada.[23] Further, the fact that Coca-Cola and Colgate-Palmolive sell some of their products in more than 200 countries does not signify that they have adopted a high degree of standardization for all their products globally. Only three Coca-Cola brands are standardized, and one of them, Sprite, has a different formulation in Japan.

Companies with separate subsidiaries in other countries can be said to operate using a multidomestic strategy. A **multidomestic strategy** occurs when multinational firms enable individual subsidiaries to compete independently in domestic markets. Simply put, multidomestic strategy is how multinational firms use strategic business units (refer to Chapter 2). Colgate-Palmolive uses both strategies: Axion dishwashing paste detergent, for example, was formulated for developing countries, and Sorriso toothpaste was made for the Brazilian market.

5-3 External Environment Faced By Global Marketers

5-3 Describe the external environment facing global marketers

A global marketer or a firm considering global marketing must consider the external environment. Many of the same environmental factors that operate in the domestic market also exist internationally. These factors include culture, economic development, the global economy,

global marketing standardization production of uniform products that can be sold the same way all over the world

multidomestic strategy when multinational firms enable individual subsidiaries to compete independently in domestic markets

political structure and actions, demographic makeup, and natural resources.

5-3a Culture

Central to any society is the common set of values its citizens share to determine what is socially acceptable. Culture underlies the family, the educational system, religion, and the social class system. The network of social organizations generates overlapping roles and status positions. These values and roles have a tremendous effect on people's preferences and thus on marketers' options. A company that does not understand a country's culture is doomed to failure in that country. Cultural blunders lead to misunderstandings and often perceptions of rudeness or even incompetence. For example, making a circle with the pointer finger and thumb while extending the other three fingers on one's hand is considered the "okay" sign in the United States; however, in Turkey, officially the Republic of Türkiye, and Brazil, this gesture is literally comparing someone to a rear end. In China, if you arrive on time, you are late since it is customary to arrive 15 minutes early; in Latin American countries, the opposite is true. When attending a dinner at a French or German home, giving the host a bouquet of yellow roses indicates their partner is cheating on them.

When Walmart entered Germany in 1997 after buying two established German retail chains, it made various mistakes that resulted in pulling out of the market in 2006 with losses of nearly $1 billion. First, the giant retailer entered the market using penetration pricing, which is a low-pricing strategy to attract more customers; they hoped to win customers with lower prices than local German markets. The other retailers appealed to Germany's high court, and Walmart was ordered to raise prices. From a cultural standpoint, employees were instructed to smile at customers, instructed to chant, "Walmart, Walmart, Walmart" while doing light exercises on breaks, and not permitted to be romantically inclined with coworkers. Further, if an employee knew of a romantic situation, they were required to tell on the rule breakers or face being fired themselves. These practices were not in line with German organizational culture, leading Walmart to have trouble with German unions. Walmart was unable to use its traditional strategies due to the unique culture and business practices in the German market.

Language is another important aspect of culture that can create problems for marketers. Marketers must take care in translating product names, slogans, instructions, and promotional messages to avoid conveying the wrong meaning. When Pepsi introduced its product to China, the slogan, "Pepsi brings you back to life" was translated to "Pepsi brings your ancestors back from the grave."

Walmart's low-pricing strategy and corporate culture was unsuccessful in the German market due to cultural differences.

Clairol, the hair product company, released a curling iron in Germany called the "Mist Stick." However, the term "mist" is German slang for manure, translating the product name into "manure stick." Free translation software, such as BabelFish or Google Translate, allow users to input text in one language and output in another language. But marketers must take care using the software because it can have unintended results—the best being unintelligible, the worst being insulting. Alternative options are to hire professional translators or local experts to avoid these types of mistakes.

Each country has its own customs and traditions that determine business practices and influence negotiations with foreign customers. In many countries, personal relationships are more important than financial considerations. Therefore, being culturally aware is necessary to be successful. For instance, when conducting business in France and not speaking French, one is expected to apologize for the lack of fluency. Punctuality is essential in Australia because being on time or running even five minutes late is considered rude. Gift giving is expected in China, even though the gift is customarily refused three times before being accepted. In Middle Eastern countries, the left hand is considered the bathroom hand and should not be used to shake hands, eat, or pass documents.

Making successful sales presentations abroad requires a thorough understanding of the country's culture. In Mexico, it is expected that negotiations will progress slowly with small talk and sharing of beverages beforehand. Business is more formal in France and the Netherlands. Suits are the norm in France. In the Netherlands, it is appropriate to call someone by their first name only when asked to do so. Lengthy speeches are typical in China, and it is very disrespectful to interrupt. The Japanese culture values silence and sees it as a sign of credibility, so visitors should suppress the need to fill gaps of silence when in Japan.[24]

5-3b Economic Factors

A second major factor in the external environment the global marketer faces is the level of economic development in the countries where it operates. In general, complex and sophisticated industries are found in developed countries, and more basic industries are found in less-developed nations. Average family incomes are higher in more-developed countries than in less-developed countries. Larger incomes mean greater purchasing power and demand, not only for consumer goods and services, but also for the machinery and workers required to produce consumer goods.

According to the World Bank, the average *gross national income (GNI)* per capita for the world is $12,026.[25] GNI is a country's GDP (defined earlier) together with its income received from other countries (mainly interest and dividends), less similar payments made to other countries. The U.S. GNI per capita is $70,930, but it is not the world's highest. Switzerland's GNI is $90,600. Of course, there are many very poor countries: Somalia $430; Burundi $220; India $2,150; and Haiti $1,430. GNI per capita is one measure of a country's citizens' ability to buy various goods and services. A marketer with a global vision can use these data to help measure market potential in countries around the globe.

Not only is per capita income a consideration when doing business abroad, but so is the cost of doing business in a country. Although it is not the same as the cost of doing business, the most expensive places in the world to live are New York in the United States and Singapore in Asia. Locations with the greatest increases in inflation include Caracas, Venezuela, at a rate of 132 percent; Istanbul, Turkey at 86 percent; Buenos Aires, Argentina at 64 percent; and Tehran, Iran at 57 percent.[26]

The Balance of Trade and the Balance of Payments

The more U.S. firms that export their wares, the better the country's **balance of trade**—the difference between the value of a country's exports and the value of its imports over a given period. A country that exports more goods or services than it imports is said to have a favorable balance of trade; a country that imports more than it exports is said to have an unfavorable balance of trade. In other words, when imports exceed exports, more money flows out of the country than flows into it.

The United States has trade surpluses with South and Central America, the Netherlands, Singapore, Australia, Belgium, and Switzerland, but it has substantial trade deficits with China, the European Union, Vietnam, Mexico,

---

balance of trade the difference between the value of a country's exports and the value of its imports over a given period

Canada, India, Japan, South Korea, Taiwan, Malaysia, Saudi Arabia, and Israel.[27] Indeed, although U.S. exports have been doing well, the country imports more than it exports. The U.S. balance of trade deficit was $79.6 billion in 2022. As long as the United States continues to buy more goods than it sells abroad, it will have a deficit and an unfavorable balance of trade.

If Americans consumed less, the deficit would contract along with the broader economy, as happened throughout the COVID-19 pandemic. This leaves workers no better off. To increase production, U.S. companies could export more or take market share from imports. Government actions (discussed next) can make this happen, but they often create more problems in the process. The U.S. dollar appreciated in value relative to other currencies in 2022. It was up more than 22 percent against the Japanese yen and over 13 percent against the Euro over a 9 month period of time.[28] A strong dollar makes U.S. goods more expensive overseas and imports less expensive in the United States, widening the trade deficit. America's largest trade deficit is with China. America exports $36.9 billion less to China than what they import into the United States.[29]

The difference between a country's total payments to other countries and its total receipts from other countries is its **balance of payments**. This figure includes the balance of imports and exports (the balance of trade), long-term investments in overseas plants and equipment, government loans to and from other countries, gifts and foreign aid, military expenditures made in other countries, and money deposits in and withdrawals from foreign banks.

The United States had a favorable balance of payments from about 1900 until 1971. Since then, the country's overall payments have exceeded its receipts—due largely to U.S. foreign aid and a higher level of imports than exports.

5-3c The Global Economy

A global marketer today must be fully aware of the intertwined nature of the global economy. In the past, the size of the U.S. economy was so large that global markets tended to move up or down depending on its health. It was said, "If America sneezes, then the rest of the world catches a cold." This fact is still true today, but less so than in the past. Unfortunately, politics is playing an increasingly important role in the development of the BRICS countries (Brazil, Russia, India, China, and South Africa). Brazil, once considered a fast-rising economy, has been struggling with a multitude of crises, including government scandals, inflation, and deindustrialization.[30] In 2022, Russia

---

balance of payments the difference between a country's total payments to other countries and its total receipts from other countries

invaded Ukraine, resulting in a decrease to GDP of 3 percent rather than an increase of 3 percent.[31] Within eleven months, more than 1,200 companies publicly announced they are choosing to curtail their operations in Russia in response to the war.[32] China, now the world's second largest economy behind the United States, has a GDP ($18 trillion) more than double the combined other four BRICS countries (Brazil: $1.6 trillion; Russia: $1.8 trillion; India: $3.2 trillion; and South Africa: $400 billion).[33] By 2035, China will overtake the United States as the world's largest economy.

Outside of China, perhaps the brightest light among the BRICS is India; its economy grew around 6.3 percent in 2022.[34] India is less dependent on exports than are the other BRICS countries, making it less vulnerable to slowing economics worldwide. Lower energy prices have helped India as well because it is a major energy importer. This move is poised to spur major economic growth resulting from global offshoring, energy transition, and digitization over the next five years. Such a growth is expected to position India as the third-largest economy before 2030.[35]

5-3d Political Structure and Actions

Political structure is a fourth important variable facing global marketers. Government policies run the gamut from no private ownership and minimal individual freedom to little central government and maximum personal freedom. As rights of private property increase, government-owned industries and centralized planning tend to decrease. But a political environment is rarely at one extreme or the other. India, for instance, is a republic with elements of socialism, monopoly capitalism, and competitive capitalism in its political ideology.

Regulation gives businesses the framework they need to grow and prosper. For example, a well-designed land administration system can provide reliable data on the ownership of property and the protection of property rights.

Regulation can also produce fairer outcomes when one business or position is much more powerful than another. In a country with no labor laws, an employer might force employees to work 14 hours a day or longer, for little pay, and under dangerous working conditions.

On the other hand, regulation can overburden businesses and make it virtually impossible for them to operate. The most difficult countries in which to start a new business are Chad, Haiti, and Libya. (The easiest places to start a new business are the United Kingdom, Singapore, and Norway.[36]) It is no surprise, then, that multinationals shy away from the most difficult countries. If resolving a commercial dispute takes too much time (1,402 days in Guatemala), potential clients and suppliers might be hesitant to do business with companies based in that country.

The United Kingdom is one of the easiest places in the world to start a new business.

Legal Considerations

As you can tell, legal considerations are often intertwined with the political environment. In France, nationalistic sentiments led to a law that requires pop music stations to play at least 40 percent of their songs in French (even though French teenagers love American and English music).

Many legal structures are designed to either encourage or limit trade. Recent trends have leaned toward the latter. Nevertheless, the most common legal structures affecting trade are:

- **Tariff:** a tax levied on the goods entering a country. Because a tariff is a tax, it will either reduce the profits of the firms paying the tariff or raise prices to buyers, or both. Normally, a tariff raises prices of the imported goods and makes it easier for domestic firms to compete.

- **Quota:** a limit on the amount of a specific product that can enter a country. Several U.S. companies have sought quotas as a means of protection from foreign competition. The United States, for example, has a quota on chocolate.

- **Boycott:** the exclusion of all products from certain countries or companies. Governments use boycotts to exclude companies from countries with which they have a political dispute. South Koreans have boycotted products made in Japan.

- **Exchange control:** a law compelling a company earning foreign exchange (money) from its exports to sell it to a control agency, usually a central bank. A company wishing to buy goods abroad must first obtain a foreign currency exchange from the control agency. For example, if Whirlpool has a plant in Argentina that makes washing machines and then exports them to other South American countries, the money made on those sales is foreign currency and must be sold to a control agency in Argentina. When Whirlpool needs to buy, say, water pumps for the washing machine from Brazil, it goes to the control agency to get the funds. Some countries with foreign-exchange controls are Argentina, China, South Korea, and the Philippines.[37]

- **Market grouping (also known as a common trade alliance):** occurs when several countries agree to work together to form a common trade area that enhances trade opportunities. The best-known market grouping is the EU (European Union), which will be discussed later in this chapter.

- **Trade agreement:** an agreement to stimulate international trade. Not all government efforts are meant to stifle imports or investment by foreign corporations. The largest Latin American trade agreement is **MERCOSUR**, which has Brazil Paraguay, Uruguay, and Argentina as full members. Venezuela was suspended from membership in 2016. Associate members are Suriname, Guyana, Colombia, Ecuador, Peru, Bolivia, and Chile. Brazil and Argentina account for about 90 percent of MERCOSUR's GDP.[38] Associate members do not have full voting rights or free access to member markets. MERCOSUR made big strides in 2019 by reaching a trade deal with the EU to eliminate tariffs on 90 percent of the exports of MERCOSUR countries. However, concerns regarding protection of the Amazon Rainforest and beef export/imports are ongoing. Although the EU deal has brought about an increase in trade, the MERCOSUR is a flawed union with several restrictions. The members are also conflicted on the level of free trade and protectionism that should be achieved with the trade agreement.[39]

The Trade War

Former President Trump was concerned about the U.S. trade deficit and, therefore, on March 23, 2018, he imposed tariffs on steel and aluminum from many countries, including China. That prompted China to levy $3 billion on U.S. exports to China. Historically, when one country raises tariffs to protect domestic industries, other countries retaliate, which causes the initial country to raise other tariffs—and escalation continues. America quickly announced exemptions to the steel and aluminum tariffs for the European Union (discussed in one of the next sections), Canada, Mexico, South Korea, and other nations. Effectively, those tariffs apply to only three major steel exporters—China, Russia, and Japan. In September 2018, Japan and the United States agreed to launch negotiations on a "Trade Agreement on Goods." America is seeking concessions on the agricultural sector, as well as in automobile tariffs. Later discussions would cover insurance, pharmaceuticals, and digital trade.

MERCOSUR the largest Latin American trade agreement; full members include Argentina, Brazil, Paraguay, Uruguay. Associate members are Suriname, Guyana, Chile, Colombia, Ecuador, Peru, and Bolivia.

In September 2018, President Trump announced additional tariffs of 10 percent on goods coming from China. Predictably, China announced retaliatory tariffs on $60 billion in U.S. goods as trade tensions between the world's two largest economies grew.[40] The United States had imposed around $260 billion in tariffs on imports from China. During the G20 meeting in June 2019, Presidents Xi and Trump agreed to resume trade negotiations.

A complicating factor in the trade negotiations is the Chinese company Huawei. Huawei is the world's largest manufacturer of telecommunications gear. U.S. officials were worried that certain Huawei products could be used for spying on governments and companies. By early 2019, Huawei was effectively banned from the U.S. market. During June 2019, then-President Trump agreed to let Huawei buy and sell high-tech gear in the United States, but only if it did not impact national security. China, in turn, agreed to increase its purchase of U.S. farm products.

Imposing tariffs can create complicated, and sometimes unintended, consequences. Under tariffs that the United States placed on Chinese goods in 2018, Chinese-made finished loudspeakers can enter the United States from China without penalty. However, speaker components (intermediate goods) made in China face a 25-percent tariff. So, a Chinese loudspeaker avoids the tariffs, but one assembled at JL Audio's facility in Florida faces a 25-percent duty on key parts next year. A European loudspeaker also would avoid the tariffs, even if it uses Chinese components.[41]

As mentioned at the beginning of the chapter, the law of comparative advantage dictates that trade is beneficial to nations. Trade does not mean that one country wins and the other loses. The notion that "they are stealing our jobs" doesn't hold in today's economy. The imposition of tariffs on steel and aluminum was purportedly taken "to bring steel and aluminum production jobs back to the United States." Yet, the primary reasons for job losses in these industries were due to technology and lower labor costs elsewhere. The United States imports lower-cost steel and aluminum to make finished goods. This importation results in lower prices to U.S. consumers. It has been estimated that the steel and aluminum tariffs by themselves will result in net job losses of 70,000 in U.S. manufacturing. That is, 10,000 new jobs in the metals-producing section would be offset by 80,000 jobs lost in metal-consuming sections.[42]

An escalating trade war does not benefit either the United States or China. Both countries, in fact, would benefit from free trade. There are, however, serious Chinese trade abuses to address. China unfairly subsidizes targeted industries to give them an unfair export advantage. It has also unfairly restricted access to key markets for foreign markets and forced businesses to divulge proprietary technology and trade secrets to enter Chinese markets. These matters should be referred to the World Trade Organization (WTO, discussed below) if an agreement between the United States and China cannot be reached.

A number of positive signs, in early 2019, gave hope to the possibility of a trade settlement. One Chinese official recently noted that "China's and America's economies are inseparable." China has resumed purchases of American soybeans and announced cuts on auto-import tariffs. China is also examining how state-owned companies can form part of a healthy market economy, provided they enjoy no special advantages. After a flurry of approvals, it can be argued that China is opening its economy to foreign firms. Tesla is on track to be the first foreign carmaker to have a wholly owned manufacturing facility in China. UBS, a Swiss bank, recently became the first foreign firm to be allowed a majority stake in a Chinese brokerage. Exxon-Mobil has started to build a wholly owned petrochemical complex, which until recently, foreign firms could not do. China has also published tougher rules for protecting intellectual property, which foreign companies have long demanded.[43]

Yet, the COVID-19 pandemic created an unprecedented decline in global trade in 2020. This decline has further complicated efforts to reach a trade agreement between the United States and China. President Biden retained $360 billion in tariffs imposed under Trump's administration, sanctioned individual Chinese associated with human rights abuses, and introduced export controls that restrict advanced technology from Beijing.[44] It appears an agreement continues to elude the two countries.

United States–Mexico–Canada Agreement (USMCA)

Former President Trump used the threat of tariffs to push Canada and Mexico into scrapping the North American Free Trade Agreement (NAFTA). The new accord is entitled the **United States–Mexico–Canada Agreement (USMCA).** This new free trade agreement between the United States, Mexico, and Canada took effect on July 1, 2020.[45] Key provisions of the new agreement are:

- **Country of origin rule:** Cars and trucks must have 75 percent of their components manufactured in Mexico, United States, or Canada to qualify for zero tariffs. The goal is to boost auto-parts manufacturing in North America.

- **Labor provisions:** 40 to 45 percent of automobile content must be made by workers who earn at least $16 an hour by 2023. The goal is to drive Mexican wages up and/or shift production to the United States and Canada. The USMCA allows each country to sanction the others for labor violations that impact trade.

- **U.S. farmers gain more access to the Canadian dairy market:** Canada agreed to open its dairy market, which has closely regulated how much of each dairy product can be produced and placed strict tariffs and quotas on imports.

- **Intellectual property protections and digital trade provisions:** The agreement extends a copyright from 50 years beyond the life of an author to 70 years. It also extends protection to new biologic drugs from 8 years to 10. This agreement will extend protection for drug manufacturers against generic competition. Also, there will be no duties on products purchased electronically, such as music or eBooks. In addition, internet companies are not held liable for content their users produce.

- **Creates a special dispute mechanism:** The new agreement sets up an independent mechanism to resolve trade disputes between countries (rather than going to domestic courts).[46]

The agreement also says that if a country makes a free-trade agreement with a "nonmarket economy," then USMCA could be terminated. This stipulation is designed primarily to discourage individual agreements with China.[47] It is an attempt to build a North American alliance when negotiating with China.

The World Trade Organization (WTO)

The **World Trade Organization (WTO)** was established in 1995 to foster global trade and replaces the General Agreement on Tariffs and Trade (GATT). There are 164 members (nations) in the WTO, representing 98 percent of global trade. Over the years, the WTO has been very successful in lowering barriers to trade. This success has been accomplished through member negotiations called "rounds." The **Uruguay Round**, led to the creation

The World Trade Organization helps its members improve the lives of their citizens by raising the living standards, and creating jobs through trade.

Martin Good/Shutterstock.com

of the WTO, reducing tariffs worldwide by one-third.[48] The underlying principle of the WTO is the notion of "most favored nation." This notion means that, as a WTO member, if a nation reduces a tariff imposed on goods from another country, it will do the same for all other member nations. So, for example, when China entered in 2001, it benefited from reduced tariffs between the European Union and the United States.

At the WTO, disputes between countries are handled by "panels," not courts. There is a dispute-settlement panel and a more powerful appellate body consisting of only seven members. More than 350 rules and laws of the WTO have enabled more than 600 disputes to be settled through new "rounds."[49]

The last round of WTO trade talks began in Doha, Qatar, in 2001. For the most part, the periodic meetings of WTO members under the Doha Round were very contentious. One of the most contentious goals of the round was for the major developing countries (BRICS) to lower tariffs on industrial goods in exchange for European and U.S. tariff and subsidy cuts on farm products. Concerned that lowering tariffs would result in an economically damaging influx of foreign cotton, sugar, and rice, China and India demanded a safeguard clause that would allow

---

United States–Mexico–Canada Agreement (USMCA) free trade agreement between the United States, Mexico, and Canada which replaces the North American Free Trade Agreement (NAFTA)

World Trade Organization (WTO) a trade organization with 164 nations that replaced the General Agreement on Tariffs and Trade (GATT)

Uruguay Round a trade agreement to dramatically lower trade barriers worldwide and created the World Trade Organization (WTO)

them to raise tariffs on those crops if imports surged. At a December 2015 meeting of the WTO, trade ministers from more than 160 countries failed to agree that they should keep the negotiations going. After 14 years of talks, members of the WTO effectively ended the Doha Round of negotiations. It became clear in recent years that the talks, which were originally supposed to conclude in 2005, were paralyzed because neither developed economies (like the United States and the European Union) nor developing countries (like China and India) were willing to make fundamental concessions.

The failure of the Doha Round has left the WTO seriously out of date in the complex global economy. Digital trade remains outside the WTO system. Trade in the services sector is inconsistently covered by existing rules. China's subsidized state-owned enterprises have created overcapacity in the global marketplace overwhelming producers elsewhere. Also, China has pressured U.S. companies wanting to do business in China to transfer their technology to Chinese partners. The Chinese government acknowledges that WTO rules forbid making the transfer of technology a condition for access to a nation's economy. But it argues that the practice is "voluntary" because U.S. firms aren't forced to do business in China—their other option is to stay out of the country. U.S. companies and officials say it's a form of extortion because U.S. firms should have access to the Chinese market, as they do to markets in Europe and elsewhere, without losing their intellectual property.

Although the Chinese practice violates WTO rules, it is difficult to bring a successful technology-transfer case because U.S. companies fear retaliation by Beijing if they complain openly or provide detailed evidence that the U.S. government can be used in pursuing such a case.[50]

Back under the Trump administration, it was believed that the rules under which the WTO operates were outdated and incapable of dealing with China's unfair trade practices. Thus, America began blocking the appointment of new judges to the WTO appellate panel. As a result, two of the three appellate-body judge terms expired, leaving the system with a lack of the necessary members to achieve a quorum to hear appeals. This action halted dispute settlement and brought into question the WTO's role in enforcing trade rules.[51]

The Comprehensive and Progressive Agreement for Trans-Pacific Partnership (CPTPP)

The Comprehensive And Progressive Agreement For Trans-Pacific Partnership (CPTPP) was signed in March 2018 in Santiago, Chile. Originally called the "Trans-Pacific Partnership," the name was changed after former President Trump withdrew from joining the organization. The CPTPP consists of Canada and 10 Asia-Pacific counties, which include: Australia, Brunei, Darussalam, Chile, Japan, Malaysia, Mexico, New Zealand, Peru, Singapore, and Vietnam. The objective is to cut tariffs and create common trade laws and regulations. The CPTPP plans to open service sectors, restrict state-owned organization subsidies (like state-owned factories that export at low prices owing to subsidies), protect trade secrets, create higher labor standards, and settle environmental issues through a dispute-settlement panel.[52] The most controversial aspect of CPTPP is its investor-settlement–dispute-settlement mechanism, generally known as ISDS. It means that companies can sue individual governments in the agreement by arguing that they were denied access to that country's market. Countries argue that this term means governments cannot make policy without fear of facing a lengthy and costly legal case.[53]

The Regional Comprehensive Economic Partnership (RCEP)

The Regional Comprehensive Economic Partnership (RCEP) trade agreement was signed in late 2020 and entered into force beginning in 2022 following eight years of discussions.[54] There are 15 member countries, including Australia, Brunei, Cambodia, China, Indonesia, Japan, South Korea, Laos, Malaysia, Myanmar, New Zealand, the Philippines, Singapore, Thailand, and Vietnam, with seven of the countries also included in CPTPP. These member nations, including the largest economies in Asia, represent about 30 percent of the world's population, making this agreement the largest as of the time of its signing. The agreement reduces or eliminates approximately 90 percent of the tariffs over 20 years following the date in force. China is one of the primary beneficiaries of the RCEP agreement. Compared to CPTPP, RCEP does not have as extensive of commitments. For example, CPTPP eliminates 99 percent of tariffs and is effective for more sectors than RCEP. Not being a member, the United States may feel an impact as member nations shift commercial activity to tariff reduced countries rather than continuing with U.S. suppliers.

Comprehensive and Progressive Agreement for Trans-Pacific Partnership (CPTPP) a trade agreement between Canada and 10 Asia-Pacific countries, which include: Australia, Brunei, Darussalam, Chile, Japan, Malaysia, Mexico, New Zealand, Peru, Singapore, and Vietnam

The Regional Comprehensive Economic Partnership (RCEP) a trade agreement that began in 2022 with 15 member countries including Australia, Brunei, Cambodia, China, Indonesia, Japan, South Korea, Laos, Malaysia, Myanmar, New Zealand, the Philippines, Singapore, Thailand, and Vietnam, with seven of the countries also included in CPTPP

The Pacific Alliance

The **Pacific Alliance** was signed in 2012 by Chile, Colombia, Mexico, and Peru to create a single region for the free movement of goods, services, investment, capital, and people. Implementation of the Pacific Alliance began in 2014 with the goal of abolishing tariffs on 92 percent of merchandise trade as soon as possible, with the remainder being eliminated by 2020. Costa Rica was recently accepted as a fifth member of the Pacific Alliance, with full membership effective in 2023.[55]

This agreement has received the attention of many countries around the world since it is the eighth-largest economic power and export force globally. Sixty-three nations act as observers at Alliance meetings.[56] This interest derives from Alliance members' commitment to free markets, free trade, and democracy—which cannot be said of some South American countries (including Brazil and Venezuela).

Dominican Republic–Central America Free Trade Agreement (CAFTA–DR)

The **Dominican Republic–Central America Free Trade Agreement (CAFTA–DR)** was instituted in 2005. Because it joined after the original agreement was signed, the Dominican Republic was amended to the original agreement title (Central America Free Trade Agreement, or CAFTA). In addition to the United States and the Dominican Republic, the agreement includes Costa Rica, El Salvador, Guatemala, Honduras, and Nicaragua.

Most goods imported and/or exported to CAFTA-DR countries do so duty free and without processing fees. The agreement is in effect until January 2025. The agreement covers consumer and industrial goods, intellectual property rights, transparency, electronic commerce, and telecommunications. The CAFTA-DR is America's third-largest export market in Latin America, right after Mexico and Brazil. CAFTA-DR has benefited U.S. exporters of petroleum products plastics, paper, and textiles. It has also aided manufacturers of motor vehicles, machinery, medical equipment, and electronics.[57]

European Union (EU)

Encompassing much of Europe, the **European Union (EU)** is one of the world's most important free trade zones. Actually, much more than a free trade zone, it is also a political and economic community comprised of more than 510 million citizens. As a free trade zone, however, the EU guarantees the freedom of movement of people, goods, services, and capital between member states. It also maintains a common trade policy with outside nations and a regional development policy. The EU represents member nations in the WTO.

The EU currently has 27 member states: Austria, Belgium, Bulgaria, Croatia, the Republic of Cyprus, Czech Republic, Denmark, Estonia, Finland, France, Germany, Greece, Hungary, Ireland, Italy, Latvia, Lithuania, Luxembourg, Malta, the Netherlands, Poland, Portugal, Romania, Slovakia, Slovenia, Spain, and Sweden. The member states remain independent and retain sovereignty but pool together some of their decision-making powers on specific issues for the common interest at the EU level. Therefore, the European Parliament, European Council, European Commission, and Council of the European Union were created with representatives making decisions on behalf of the member states. The United Kingdom left the European Union in 2021. The term for its leaving is "Brexit." The EU-UK Withdrawal Agreement allows residency rights and travel without needing a visa for the citizens of the United Kingdom and EU.

The EU's economy is the second largest in the world, behind the United States; China's is the third largest. The EU and the United States have the largest bilateral trade relationship, and the two unions have a highly integrated economic relationship, even though there is no specific free trade agreement between the two. The U.S. total investment in the EU is four times higher than its investment in the Asia-Pacific region.[58] The EU's total investment in the United States is 10 times higher than its investment in India and China combined. Almost every other country in the global economy calls either the EU or the United States its largest trade and investment partner.

America and the EU

The United States and the EU together account for about 42 percent of the global economic output. In 2021, the U.S. and the EU agreed to a five-year suspension on tariffs imposed on certain goods including aircraft, chocolate, tobacco, luggage, wine, and seafood. Months after the suspension, the EU and United States announced the world's first carbon-based sectoral arrangement related to steel and aluminum trade. The arrangement is open to other countries interested in joining.

Pacific Alliance a single region for the free movement of goods, services, investment, capital, and people between Chile, Colombia, Mexico, and Peru

Dominican Republic-Central America Free Trade Agreement (CAFTA-DR) a trade agreement instituted in 2005 that includes Costa Rica, the Dominican Republic, El Salvador, Guatemala, Honduras, Nicaragua, and the United States

European Union (EU) a free trade zone encompassing 27 European countries

The European Council is made up of the 27 EU member states' heads of government in addition to the European Council President and the President of the European Commission.

EU Governance

The European Commission comprises one member from each EU country. The Commission is responsible for proposing legislation, implementing decisions, and managing the day-to-day business of the EU. The European Commission's Directorate General for Competition handles dominant market abuses, collusion, and other anticompetitive practices.

Recall from Chapter 4 that the EU has passed the 260-page General Data Protection Regulations (GDPR). The law requires any firm doing business with EU citizens to explain how their data will be used, allow them to see what is collected, obtain consent, then permit them to withdraw consent at any moment and demand that their data be deleted. It is estimated that within the Financial Times Stock Exchange (FTSE), 100 companies in the banking sector spend approximately $83.4 million to be compliant with GDPR, which is three times greater than the next closest industry sector.[59] Before the passage of GDPR in 2018, France's privacy regulator extended the "right to be forgotten" to all of a company's websites anywhere in the world. In 2015, France fined Google $115,527 for not complying.[60] In 2018, Google appealed this fine to the EU's Court of Justice. In January 2019, Google was fined $57 million for breaching the European Union online privacy rules.[61] Per GDPR, violators can be fined up to

---

World Bank an international bank that offers low-interest loans, advice, and information to developing nations

International Monetary Fund (IMF) an international organization that acts as a lender of last resort, providing loans to troubled nations, and also works to promote trade through financial cooperation

Group of Twenty (G20) a forum for international economic development that promotes discussion between industrial and emerging-market countries on key issues related to global economic stability

4 percent of global revenue. French regulators are holding the largest global search engine responsible for its lack of clarity and transparency on the way that personal data is handled without consent.

The World Bank, the International Monetary Fund, and the G20

Two international financial organizations are instrumental in fostering global trade. The **World Bank** offers low-interest loans to developing nations. Originally, the purpose of the loans was to help these nations build infrastructure, such as roads, power plants, schools, drainage projects, and hospitals. Now the World Bank offers loans to help developing nations relieve their debt burdens. To receive the loans, countries must pledge to lower trade barriers and aid private enterprises. In addition to making loans, the World Bank is a major source of advice and information for developing nations. The **International Monetary Fund (IMF)** was founded in 1945, one year after the creation of the World Bank, to promote trade through financial cooperation and eliminate trade barriers in the process. The IMF makes short-term loans to member nations that are unable to meet their budgetary expenses. It operates as a lender of last resort for troubled nations, such as the Ukraine. In exchange for these emergency loans, IMF lenders frequently extract significant commitments from the borrowing nations to address the problems that led to the crises. These steps may include curtailing imports or even devaluing the currency. For 2022, the Ukraine economy decreased by more than 30 percent due to the Russian attacks to the country's infrastructure.[62] The IMF provided nearly $2.75 billion to Ukraine to help with the long-term needs of the country in the post COVID-19 pandemic environment. Additionally, the IMF was the first to provide financial support in March 2022 in the amount of $1.4 billion following the onset of the war. Later in 2022, emergency funding of $1.3 billion was provided under the newly established IMF Food Shock Window to help Ukraine after a major shortfall in cereal exports.[63] With challenges remaining in the Ukraine, further IMF involvement and support is likely.

The **Group of Twenty (G20)** finance ministers and central bank governors was established in 1999 to bring together industrialized and developing economies to discuss key issues in the global economy. The G20 is a forum for international economic development that promotes discussion between industrial and emerging-market countries on key issues related to global economic stability. By contributing to the strengthening of the international financial system and providing opportunities for discussion on national policies, international cooperation, and international financial institutions, the G20 helps support growth and development across the globe. The members of the G20 are shown in Table 5.1.

Table 5.1	Members of the G20		
Argentina	European Union	Italy	Saudi Arabia
Australia	France	Japan	South Africa
Brazil	Germany	Mexico	Turkey, officially the Republic of Türkiye
Canada	India	Republic of Korea	The United Kingdom
China	Indonesia	Russia	The United States

The G20 sharpened its focus on countries that serve as tax shelters and those that haven't agreed to new international standards on tax transparency and information sharing. The G20 even declared that it would enforce "punitive sanctions" against uncooperative tax-shelter countries. The G20 members account for more than 80 percent of the global economic output.[64]

5-3e Demographic Makeup

Two primary determinants of any consumer market are wealth and population. It took hundreds of thousands of years for the global urban population to reach 1 billion and in 200 years, it grew seven times that rate to achieve 7 billion in 2011. Just 11 years later, another billion was added, taking the world population to 8 billion people in November of 2022.[65]

China, India, and Indonesia are three of the most densely populated nations in the world. But that fact alone is not particularly useful to marketers. They also need to know whether the population is mostly urban or rural because marketers may not have easy access to rural consumers. Belgium, for example, with about 90 percent of its population living in urban settings, may be a more attractive market.

Over the past quarter-century, world economic growth has lifted 1.25 billion people out of poverty. In 1990, 37 percent of the world's population was in extreme poverty,

defined by the World Bank as living on less than $2.15 a day.[66] Today, the bank estimates that about 685 million people continue to live in extreme poverty. While progress has been made since 1990, the COVID-19 pandemic and the invasion in Ukraine has slowed the progress. The increased consumption that helped pull so many people out of poverty was spurred largely by massive population growth. Between 2015 and 2030, however, 75 percent of global consumption growth will be driven by individuals spending more. Three groups will generate about half the world's consumption growth: the retiring and older adults in developed countries, China's working-age population, and North America's working-age population.

By 2030, individuals over the age of 65 are expected to exceed 1 billion.[67] Many older adults in developed nations have saved sufficiently for retirement. Older adults also spend more per person than those under 65 do because of their increasing healthcare needs. It is expected that by 2030, the spending by older adults will be just under $15 trillion, which is nearly double the spending in 2020.

Within the next 10 years, China's upper-middle income households are expected to increase by nearly 70 percent to almost 400 million people. This total would be just below those of the United States and Europe combined.[68] This group has the very real potential to reshape global consumption, just as America's baby boomers—the richest generation in history—did in their prime years.

In 2018, about 130 million people in America worked full-time. Incomes tend to gradually increase with age among workers in their 20s and 30s. There is, however, a plateau among workers that lasts from their late 30s to their early 60s.[69] The average starting salaries for college graduates in 2023 was about $55,000 a year.[70]

Even though the retiring and adults over 65 are an important part of consumption growth, they present challenges as well. Most notably, the world's population is getting older. While aging has been evident in developed economies for some time—Japan and Russia have seen their populations age for several years running—the demographic deficit is now spreading to China and will soon reach Latin America. China's labor force peaked in 2015.[71] Thailand's fertility rate was 5 births in the 1970s

Sinti Lu/Shutterstock.com

but has declined to 1.5 today.[72] This decline is a result of many factors, including many couples electing to not have children, a growing single population, and modern lifestyles coupled with the cost of raising a child.

5-3f Natural Resources

A final factor in the external environment that has become more evident in recent years is the distribution of natural resources.

Due to rapid improvements in shale oil production technology, the United States produces around 12.49 million barrels of oil per day in 2023 and is projected to produce 12.65 million barrels in 2024.[73] In 2018, the United States became the top crude oil producer in the world. In 2021, five countries produced over 50 percent of the world's crude oil. These five countries are the United States (14.5 percent), Russia (13.1 percent), Saudi Arabia (12.1 percent), Canada (5.8 percent), and Iraq (5.3 percent).[74] The United States is also the world's leading natural gas producer followed by Russia, Iran, China, and Qatar.[75]

Fresh water makes up less than 3 percent of the total volume of the world's water, with 70 percent of the total fresh water in the Amazon region of Brazil. With the population increases, many countries' water resources cannot meet the increasing demand.[76] This lack of water will impact agriculture, the location of production facilities, demand for water-conservation products, and many other goods and services.

Some natural resources are already found in just a few select countries. This enables these countries to restrict supply and, therefore, inflate prices. Two rare earth elements, scandium and terbium, are used in everything from the powerful magnets located in wind turbines to the electronic circuits in smartphones. Although they are not as rare as the name suggests, 97 percent of the world's supply of these materials comes from China. Similarly, plants cannot grow without phosphorus, a key ingredient in fertilizer. Phosphate rock is found in only a handful of countries, including the United States, Morocco, and China.

Natural resources can have a major impact on international marketing. Warm climate and lack of water mean that many of Africa's countries will remain importers of foodstuffs. The United States, on the other hand, must rely on Africa for many precious metals. Vast differences in the locations and quantities available of natural resources create international dependencies, huge shifts of wealth, inflation and recession, export opportunities for countries with abundant resources, and even a stimulus for military intervention.

---

exporting selling domestically produced products to buyers in other countries

RAW-films/Shutterstock.com

5-4 Global Entry Methods

5-4 Organize the five methods of entering the global marketplace from low to high risk

---

A company should consider entering the global marketplace only after its management has a solid grasp of the global environment. Companies decide to "go global" for a number of reasons. Perhaps the most important is to earn additional profits. Managers may believe that international sales will result in higher profit margins or more added-on profits. A second stimulus is that a firm may have a unique product or technological advantage not available to other international competitors. Such advantages should result in major business successes abroad. In other situations, management may have exclusive market information about foreign customers, marketplaces, or market situations not known to others. While exclusivity can provide an initial motivation for international marketing, managers must realize that competitors can be expected to catch up with the firm's information advantage. Finally, saturated domestic markets, excess capacity, and potential for economies of scale can also be motivators to go global. Economies of scale mean that average per-unit production costs fall as output is increased.

Many firms form multinational partnerships—called "strategic alliances"—to assist them in penetrating global markets; strategic alliances are examined in Chapter 7. Five other methods of entering the global marketplace are, in order of risk from least to most, exporting, licensing and franchising, contract manufacturing, joint venture, and foreign direct investment (refer to Figure 5.1).

5-4a Exporting

When a company decides to enter the global market, exporting is usually the least complicated and least risky alternative. **Exporting** is selling domestically produced products to buyers in other countries. A company can sell directly to foreign importers or buyers. China is currently the world's largest exporter, but the United States and Germany are not far behind.

Figure 5.1 Risk Levels for Five Methods of Entering the Global Marketplace

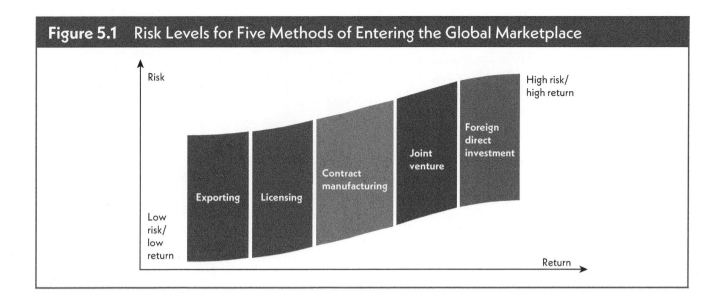

Global trade supports more than 40 million U.S. jobs. Exports support approximately 9 million jobs.[77] Exports from Texas, California, and New York support the most jobs, most of them due to the export of goods. America's largest exports are petroleum, machinery including computers, electronics, vehicles, and pharmaceuticals being the largest product groups. Interestingly, BMW's South Carolina plant exports nearly 60 percent of its vehicles made there, making it the biggest U.S. car exporter.

The U.S. Commercial Services, part of the Department of Commerce, helps U.S. businesses export goods and services to markets worldwide. This organization has offices in more than 70 countries and stations employees in U.S. embassies in nine additional markets. Among its various duties, the Commercial Services holds conferences around the United States to explain the benefits, types, and avenues of exporting. For example, one conference held in Scottsdale, Arizona, focused on helping advanced manufacturers learn about specific global markets. Top managers were invited to meet one on one with U.S. commercial diplomats visiting from abroad. The program also featured panel discussions on the latest industry export trends and how to identify opportunities in new and emerging markets.

The Services also provides marketing research information and conducts trade shows featuring U.S. products and services in countries around the world. Potential exporters can also join trade missions, whereby U.S. companies in specific industries travel together as a delegation, attend market briefings, participate in site visits and networking receptions, and have one-on-one matchmaking appointments with potential buyers.

Instead of selling directly to foreign buyers, a company may decide to sell to intermediaries located in its domestic market. The most common intermediary is the export merchant, also known as a **buyer for export**, which is usually treated like a domestic customer by the domestic manufacturer. The buyer for export assumes all risks and sells internationally from its own account. The domestic firm is involved only to the extent that its products are bought in foreign markets.

A second type of intermediary is the **export broker**, who plays the traditional broker's role by bringing buyer and seller together. The manufacturer still retains title and assumes all the risks. Export brokers operate primarily in agricultural products and raw materials.

The biggest car exporter in America is BMW. It exports 60 percent of the vehicles produced in its South Carolina plant.

buyer for export an intermediary in the global market that assumes all ownership risks and sells globally for its own account

export broker an intermediary who plays the traditional broker's role by bringing buyer and seller together

Export agents, a third type of intermediary, are foreign sales agents/distributors who live in the foreign country and perform the same functions as domestic manufacturers' agents, helping with international financing, shipping, and so on. The U.S. Department of Commerce has an agent/distributor service that helps about 5,000 U.S. companies each year find an agent or distributor in virtually any country in the world. A second category of agents resides in the manufacturer's country but represents foreign buyers. This type of agent acts as a hired purchasing agent for foreign customers operating in the exporter's home market.

5-4b Licensing and Franchising

Another effective way for a firm to move into the global arena with relatively little risk is to sell a license to manufacture its product to someone in a foreign country. **Licensing** is the legal process whereby a licensor allows another firm to use its manufacturing process, trademarks, patents, trade secrets, or other proprietary knowledge. The licensee, in turn, pays the licensor a royalty or fee agreed on by both parties.

A licensor must make sure it can exercise sufficient control over the licensee's activities to ensure proper quality, pricing, distribution, and so on. Licensing may also create a new competitor in the long run if the licensee decides to void the license agreement. International law is often ineffective in stopping such actions. Two common ways of maintaining effective control over licensees are shipping one or more critical components from the United States and locally registering patents and trademarks to the U.S. firm, not to the licensee. Garment companies maintain control by delivering only so many labels per day; they also supply their own fabric, collect the scraps, and do accurate unit counts. An example of a license agreement would be universities licensing the use of their logo to others.

Franchising in the global marketplace has grown rapidly in recent years. Some of the world's largest franchisors are McDonald's, KFC, Burger King, 7-Eleven, Subway, Marriott International, RE/MAX, Dunkin', and InterContinental Hotels and Resorts. InterContinental is based in the UK; the remainder are American.[78] Why are fast-food franchises so popular? They offer consistency. Whether

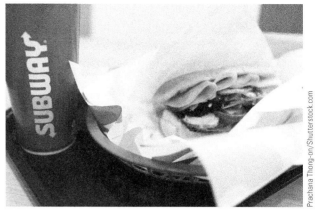

Subway has more than 42,000 shops worldwide

they're in Indiana or California, McDonald's customers can expect the same Big Mac and fries. In international markets, however, chains often have to adapt to local tastes and cultures. In Europe, for example, drinking an espresso is the norm after lunch. To avoid standing in line twice or drinking a cold espresso after a burger and fries, McDonald's customers in much of Europe are given a token with their meal. They simply put the token in a self-serve machine, and out comes a steaming espresso.

Sometimes a franchise has to change its recipes to adapt to local cultures. In India, Taco Bell added crunchy potato tacos, and extra-spicy burritos filled with paneer, a fresh Indian cheese to accommodate local tastes because Hindus do not eat beef and Muslims do not eat pork.[79] Also in India, Subway offers not only the traditional turkey and tuna, but chicken tikka and roast lamb subs. In China, KFC removed coleslaw from the menu and instead offers seasonal vegetables like bamboo shoots or lotus root. Dunkin' adjusted its menu in South Korea to include sweet potato muffins, sesame tofu rings, and a 12-grain latte made from roasted brown rice, barley and other grains.

PIRTEK is a hydraulic and industrial hose maintenance and replacement service company that services construction, equipment rentals, transport and logistics operations, manufacturing, and waste industries. Headquartered in Australia, the company uses franchising for expansion. PIRTEK is an example of a business-to-business franchising company with more than 400 locations in 23 countries.

5-4c Contract Manufacturing

Firms that do not want to become involved in licensing or to become heavily involved in global marketing may engage in **contract manufacturing**, which is private-label manufacturing by a foreign company. The foreign company produces a certain volume of products to specification, with the domestic firm's brand name on the goods. The domestic company usually handles the marketing.

---

export agent an intermediary who acts like a manufacturer's agent for the exporter; the export agent lives in the foreign market

licensing the legal process whereby a licensor allows another firm to use its manufacturing process, trademarks, patents, trade secrets, or other proprietary knowledge

contract manufacturing private-label manufacturing by a foreign company

Thus, the domestic firm can broaden its global marketing base without investing in overseas plants and equipment. After establishing a solid base, the domestic firm may switch to a joint venture or foreign direct investment. One industry that uses a lot of contract manufacturing is electronics.

5-4d Joint Venture

Joint ventures are somewhat similar to licensing agreements. In an international **joint venture**, the domestic firm buys part of a foreign company or joins with a foreign company to create a new entity. For example, Chainalysis, a blockchain data platform, and Notabene, a company that helps other organizations abide by crypto transaction laws, partnered so crypto service providers can obtain the know-your-customer (KYC) information that is required for compliance. Immediately following a transaction, information about the originators and beneficiaries is provided. This information allows crypto transactions to abide by the laws of more than 60 countries.[80]

As the example demonstrates, global joint ventures are often made to gain access to a skill, technology, or market that one partner might not otherwise have. Similarly, IHS, a large owner, operator, and developer of telecommunication infrastructure, and MTN Nigeria, a communication service provider, came together to form a joint venture.[81] They formed a new tower company with the purpose of expanding the network efficiency of the voice and data capacity in Africa, which would benefit both organizations.

Not all international joint ventures involve a foreign corporation, however. Two U.S. companies, Chainalysis, a blockchain data platform provider, and Notabene, a company that helps organizations abide by laws that govern crypto transactions, partnered to provide information about the customer and forward that information to the other side of the transaction to ensure compliance.

While potentially very lucrative, joint ventures can also be very risky. Many fail. Sometimes, joint venture partners simply cannot agree on management strategies and policies. Often, joint ventures are the only way a government will allow a foreign company to enter its country. Joint ventures enable the local firm or government to acquire managerial skills and new technology.

5-4e Foreign Direct Investment

Foreign direct investment (FDI) occurs when a business in one country invests in a business interest in another country. This investment usually takes the form of active ownership of a foreign company or of overseas manufacturing or marketing facilities. Foreign direct investment by U.S.

firms is more than $6 trillion.[82] The countries receiving the largest amount of direct foreign investment in 2021 were the United Kingdom, the Netherlands, Luxembourg, Ireland, and Canada.[83] Direct investors have either a controlling interest or a large minority interest in the firm, so they have the greatest potential reward and the greatest potential risk.

A firm may make a FDI by acquiring an interest in an existing company or by building new facilities. It might do so because it has trouble transferring some resource to a foreign operation or getting that resource locally. One important resource is personnel, especially managers. If the local labor market is tight, the firm may buy an entire foreign firm and retain all its employees instead of paying higher salaries than competitors.

The United States is a popular place for direct investment by international companies. Foreign direct investment in the United States accounts for approximately $5 trillion.[84] The United States continues to receive more foreign investment flows than any country in the world. Japan is the largest investor in the United States, followed by the Netherlands, Canada, the United Kingdom, and Germany.[85] U.S. affiliates of foreign firms employ nearly 8 million people in the United States. German tech company, Siemens, is opening a second U.S. electric vehicle (EV) charger plant in Texas. The facility is part of a critical power infrastructure manufacturing hub in the southeast. The 80,000-square-foot plant will help fulfill the need for millions of chargers with the adoption of EVs.[86]

While the United States is receptive to FDI, some countries are not. Countries may block FDI completely or restrict it to specific industries. In some cases, governments are trying to protect domestic competitors. In others, they are blocking investment for political reasons. India recently opened up foreign investment in several industries, including retail and civil aviation.

In March 2022, the president of the Philippines signed an act that amended the country's Foreign Investment Act. The amendment allows for foreign investors to fully own enterprises in the Philippines. This is the first time for allowing such ownership. Prior to the amendment, foreign businesses would need to enter a joint venture with a local partner or use franchising to enter the Philippine market. The Philippines were classified as Asia's most restrictive country for foreign investment laws.[87]

---

joint venture when a domestic firm buys part of a foreign company or joins with a foreign company to create a new entity

foreign direct investment (FDI) a business investment in a foreign country, either by establishing business operations or by acquiring business assets in that country

5-5 The Global Marketing Mix

5-5 List the basic elements involved in developing a global marketing mix

To succeed, firms seeking to enter into foreign trade must still adhere to the principles of the marketing mix. Information gathered on foreign markets through research is the basis for the four Ps of global marketing strategy: product, place (distribution), promotion, and price. Marketing managers who understand the advantages and disadvantages of different ways of entering the global market and the effect of the external environment on the firm's marketing mix have a better chance of reaching their goals.

The first step in creating a marketing mix is developing a thorough understanding of the global target market. Often, this knowledge can be obtained through the same types of marketing research used in the domestic market (refer to Chapter 9). However, global marketing research is conducted in vastly different environments. Conducting a survey can be difficult in developing countries, where smartphone ownership is growing but is not always common and mail delivery is slow or sporadic. Drawing samples based on known population parameters is often difficult because of the lack of data. In some cities in Africa, Asia, Mexico, and South America, street maps are unavailable, streets are unidentified, and houses are unnumbered. Moreover, the questions a marketer can ask may differ in other cultures. In some cultures, people tend to be more private than in the United States and will not respond to personal questions on surveys. For instance, in France, questions about one's age and income are considered especially rude.

When entering a new market, it is important to understand the gaps in the current market. To do so involves understanding the current market players, offerings, and how they position themselves in the market. When an organization like Walmart enters a new market, they are likely to face not only the local markets but also other large supermarkets, such as Aeon in Japan, Tesco in the United Kingdom, and Ahold Delhaize in the Netherlands. Being familiar with the strategies of each of these competitors can help Walmart in its market positioning.[88]

5-5a Product Decisions

With the proper information, a good marketing mix can be developed. One important decision is whether to alter the product or the promotion for the global marketplace. Other options are to radically change the product or to adjust either the promotional message or the product to suit local conditions.

One Product, One Message

The strategy of global marketing standardization, which was discussed earlier, means developing a single product for all markets and promoting it the same way all over the world. For instance, Procter & Gamble (P&G) uses the same product and promotional themes for Head & Shoulders in China as it does in the United States. Head & Shoulders is now the best-selling shampoo in China, despite costing more than 300 percent more than local brands. P&G markets its rich portfolio of personal-care, beauty, grooming, health, and fabric products in more than 180 countries. The firm has 37 major brands that sell more than $80 billion annually around the world.[89] Some brands, such as Tide, are heavily standardized. P&G has moved away from standardization for other brands, however.

McDonalds is often thought of as leader in global marketing standardization, but even McDonalds takes local markets into account. For example, McDonald's has a very standard menu that includes their popular burgers, fries, and shakes. However, it also adapts to local regulations and customs. In most countries with Muslim majorities, McDonald's serves halal meat that is prepared according to Islamic dietary laws.[90]

Global marketing standardization has paid well for Tesla in China. Tesla's electric car technology aligned perfectly with the Chinese government's priority to reduce pollution. One way that the government controls the number of new cars on the road is by limiting the number of new license plates issued. Drivers have to wait years to get one through a lottery system. One year, 6.2 million people applied for just 36,757 available Beijing plates.[91] Once they get a plate, they are barred from driving one day a week. But plates for electric cars fall under slightly different rules. A greater number of plates are given for drivers of electric vehicles. Before 2023, plug-in hybrid vehicles were given the same concessions as fully electric vehicles, but that is no longer the case. As a result of a

Buying a car in China is not as easy as going to the lot and picking one out. Instead, potential consumers in China must obtain a license plate through the lottery system, which could take years to obtain!

Testing/Shutterstock.com

higher demand for electric vehicles, a Tesla manufacturing facility was built in Shanghai with a capacity to build 550,000 units per year.[92]

When Tesla first entered the Chinese market in 2014, China had too few charging stations. However, the company soon built out a large number of stations, and sales increased. Another factor that helped Tesla gain market share was its direct sales model. New car dealerships in China inflate costs by tens of thousands of dollars through additional fees. Tesla sells direct in China at the same price level that it does in the United States, after currency adjustments.

Global marketing standardization can sometimes backfire. Unchanged products may fail simply because of cultural factors. When Nabisco introduced the Oreo sandwich cookie in China in 1996, the product was the same recipe as the American version. However, the cookie did not appeal to the taste buds in that market as many felt the product was too sweet.

Product Invention

In the context of global marketing, product invention can be taken to mean either creating a new product for a market or drastically changing an existing product. For example, more than 100 unique Pringles potato chip flavors have been invented for international markets. Smoky Paprika and Almond (Ukraine), French Salad (Japan), Parmesan and Olive Oil (Brazil), Sweet Mayo Cheese (Korea), and Chicken Souvlaki (Australia) are some of the many Pringles flavors available outside the United States. After finding that Chinese consumers found Oreo cookies "too sweet," Oreo created a "lightly sweet" version for the Chinese market. Additional research and development was done to compete in the highly desired wafer market. Other products developed by Oreo specific to the Chinese market include the cookie straw, the wafer cookie, green tea-flavored cookies, and the wafer sandwich. These modifications moved Oreo to the top-selling cookie in China.[93]

In the United States, a Kit Kat candy bar is usually just a Kit Kat. But in Japan, where the product comes in 350 flavors, more than 30 of which are on the market at once, the classic candy bar is a trendsetter. The chocolate-covered wafer confection debuted in Japan in 1973, and it enjoys some natural advantages in the country, where

Kit Kat fortuitously translates to "You will surely win."[94] The candy quickly gained status as a good-luck charm for school exams. Fueled by Japan's gift-giving culture, Kit Kat continues to grow in popularity. Two best-selling flavors are Matcha Green Tea and White Creme.[95]

Product Adaptation

Another alternative for global marketers is to alter a basic product to meet local conditions. In India, Starbucks sells a Reshmi Kebab Roll. KFC makes a "Potato Krisper Burger." Burger King sells its classic Whopper hamburger alongside a Veggie and Chicken Tandoori Burger. But Domino's is doing more than simply creating new products in its attempt to woo Indian customers. It has reimagined everything about itself, from changing its flour to maintaining a delicate balance between local tastes and Western influence. This dedication to adaptation has made Domino's enormously successful in India, and its second largest market after the United States.

Other types of modifications globally could include auto manufacturers moving the driver's side to accommodate driving on the other side of the road. Companies may also adjust the product size due to the amount of disposable income available in a given population. Procter & Gamble conducts research in new markets to understand the features that are considered necessary. For diapers in countries with low income, they were able to redesign the product and materials to match the price of purchasing a single egg.[96]

About a year after bringing its Echo speakers to foreign markets, such as the United Kingdom and Germany, Amazon.com Inc. entered the Indian market with voice-controlled hardware. Teams of linguists, speech scientists, developers, and engineers gave the Echo's virtual assistant, Alexa, a decidedly local makeover.

This Alexa uses Hinglish, a blend of Hindi and English, and speaks with an unmistakably Indian accent. Alexa knows Independence Day is August 15, not July 4, and wishes listeners, "Happy Diwali and a prosperous New Year!" Alexa refers to the living room as the "drawing room" and will add *jeera* (cumin), *haldi* (turmeric), and *atta* (flour) to your shopping list. And its cricket jokes are truly, authentically terrible. "We wanted our devices to talk, walk, and feel Indian," says Parag Gupta, head of product management for Amazon Devices in India.[97]

5-5b Promotion Adaptation

Another global marketing strategy is to maintain the same basic product but alter the promotional strategy. For example, bicycles are mainly pleasure vehicles in the United States, but in many parts of the world, they are a family's main mode of transportation. Thus, promotion in these countries should stress durability and efficiency. In contrast, U.S. advertising may emphasize escaping and having fun.

Language barriers, translation problems, and cultural differences have generated numerous headaches for international marketing managers. When Nestlé began selling Gerber baby foods in Africa, it used the U.S. packaging, which featured a baby on the label. However, since most people could not read, the retail companies were having to put a picture on the label of what was inside. Dolce & Gabbana, a luxury brand, released a series of social media posts showing a Chinese woman trying to eat Italian food with chopsticks with a male voice instructing her. The consumers in China threatened to boycott the brand.

Today, 93 percent of marketing professionals are turning to influencer marketing to increase awareness, build trust, and reach their targeted audience. TikTok is utilized by 56 percent of influencers, overtaking Instagram (51 percent), Facebook (42 percent), and YouTube (38 percent). Global spending on influencer marketing has grown from $1.7 billion in 2016 to over $16 billion and growing.[98] From 2019 to 2022, spending more than doubled. Marketers prefer to work with nano- (between 1,000 and 10,000 followers) and micro-influencers (between 10,000 and 50,000 followers) more so than macro-influencers (between 500,000 and 1 million) and celebrities.[99] One of the reasons is that these individuals tend to have a niche or highly engaged audiences. One global study showed that in 2023, 63 percent of those surveyed plan to use artificial intelligence during their campaigns with two-thirds of those respondents using the intelligence for identifying influencers.[100] Brands spend an average of $174 per influencer-generated content.[101]

Zara, headquartered in Spain, is an international fashion giant and does not use conventional advertising such as television commercials, billboards, print ads, or internet advertising. With 2,200 global stores spanning 96 countries, Zara has millions of social media followers. The social media posts consist primarily of pictures and videos showcasing the latest collections. But the company doesn't just post—Zara also engages in user conversations, which has earned a positive response. Regarding fashion, Zara's success in the market is based on being able to quickly adapt to changing trends by assessing the market, designing styles in-house, and getting those styles in stores within weeks.[102]

Using micro-influencers is a means of building relationships with niche audiences. Particularly when entering a global market, these influencers help create awareness and build trust with the brands.

5-5c Place (Distribution)

Solving promotional and product problems does not guarantee global marketing success. The product must still get adequate distribution. For example, Europeans do not play sports as much as Americans do, so they do not visit sporting-goods stores as often. Realizing this difference, Reebok started selling its shoes in about 800 traditional shoe stores in France. In just one year, the company doubled its French sales.

One trend accelerating in the Indian market is the rise of e-commerce and direct-to-consumer (D2C) goods in the beauty and personal-care market. India is the eighth-largest market in the world, with a total value of approximately $15 billion and an expected growth rate of 10 percent. Preferences for natural and clean beauty have resulted in increased sales of products without harmful chemicals like parabens and sulfates toward toxin-free, vegan, and cruelty-free, natural ingredients. However, shopping for beauty products online can pose a challenge because shoppers are no longer satisfied with the general-purpose approach. Rather, these consumers are seeking products tailored to their own skin type. Perfect Corp, a leading augmented-reality and artificial-intelligence tech-solution provider in the beauty and fashion industry, partnered with The Good Glamm Group to launch a virtual AI skin analysis geared toward the D2C market in India. This technology will allow customers a unique shopping experience to try on beauty products virtually with true-to-life results. Further, the AI skin analysis provides a personalized and very detailed skin-care routine in a matter of seconds. For retailers, this D2C channel allows for margins in the 60 to 70 percent range.[103] Global supply chains and distribution systems will be discussed in detail in Chapter 13.

5-5d Pricing

Once marketing managers have determined a global product, distribution, and promotion strategy, they can select the remainder of the marketing mix. Pricing presents some unique problems in the global sphere. Exporters must not only cover their production costs but must also consider transportation costs, insurance, taxes, and tariffs. When deciding on a final price, marketers need to determine how much customers are willing to spend on a particular product. They also need to ensure that their foreign buyers will pay the price. Because developing nations lack mass purchasing power, selling to them often poses special pricing problems. Sometimes, a product can be simplified, or sold in smaller quantities, to lower the price. A firm must not assume that low-income countries are willing to accept lower quality, however.

Gumpanat/Shutterstock.com

Exchange Rates

The **exchange rate** is the price of one country's currency in terms of another country's currency. If a country's currency *appreciates*, less of that country's currency is needed to buy another country's currency. If a country's currency *depreciates*, more of that currency will be needed to buy another country's currency.

How do appreciation and depreciation affect the prices of a country's goods? If, say, the U.S. dollar depreciates relative to the Japanese yen, U.S. residents would need to pay more dollars to buy Japanese goods. For example, if $1.00 was worth ¥134.25. At this exchange rate, a U.S. resident would pay $26,070.67 for a ¥3.5 million Toyota automobile (¥3.5 million divided by ¥134.25 = $26070.67). If the dollar depreciated to being worth ¥98, then the same vehicle would cost the U.S. resident $35,714.28 (¥3.5 million divided by ¥98 = $35,714.28).[104]

Customers can exchange one currency for another at foreign-exchange service providers for a fee. Often the best exchange rates are offered at local banks, automated teller machines (ATM), or credit unions.

As the dollar depreciates, the prices of Japanese goods rise for U.S. residents, so they buy fewer Japanese goods—thus, U.S. imports from Japan may decline. At the same time, as the dollar depreciates relative to the yen, the yen appreciates relative to the dollar. This means prices of U.S. goods fall for the Japanese, so they buy more U.S. goods—and U.S. exports rise.

Although the example above uses depreciation of the U.S. dollar, in reality, the dollar has been appreciating against currencies around the globe in recent years. The U.S. economy is relatively stable and healthier than many other foreign countries. Investors and businesses look for economic strength, stability, and safety in a currency. Thus, money rushes into the United States and its currency.[105]

Traditionally, a strong dollar has been a badge of honor for the United States. However, a strong dollar swells the trade deficit, making imports less expensive and exports more expensive for foreign buyers. The strong dollar, coupled with high inflation rates, has begun to hurt large multinational companies headquartered in the United States as the strength of the dollar decreases profits. For Salesforce, the strong dollar is estimated to cost more than $800 million as it sells its software all over the world.[106]

Currency markets operate under a system of **floating exchange rates**. Prices of different currencies "float" up and down based on the demand for and the supply of each currency. Global currency traders create the supply of and demand for a particular country's currency based on that country's investment, trade potential, and economic strength. Government actions can also impact exchange rates. When sanctions are imposed against a country, such as for invading and creating conflict in a bordering country, they can cause that country's currency to plunge in value. This outcome has happened many times over the course of history and is still happening today.

Theoretically, exchange rates should adjust over time so that one dollar buys the same amount everywhere. However, because so many factors can influence exchange rates, currencies sometimes become overvalued or undervalued. Every year, the *Economist* magazine analyzes the cost of a Big Mac around the world to create a measure of disparity in consumer purchasing power. In other words, the *Economist* converts the cost of a Big Mac from local currencies to U.S. dollars using current exchange rates and

---

exchange rate the price of one country's currency in terms of another country's currency

floating exchange rates a system in which prices of different currencies move up and down based on the demand for and the supply of each currency

sees how they compare. In 2022, the most undervalued currency was Egypt (undervalued by 65.6 percent) followed by Indonesia, Taiwan, the Ukraine, and India. The most overvalued currency was Switzerland by 35.4 percent and then Uruguay at 27.8 percent.

Dumping

Dumping is the sale of an exported product at a price lower than that charged for the same or a like product in the "home" market of the exporter. This practice is regarded as a form of price discrimination that can potentially harm the importing nation's competing industries. Dumping may occur as a result of exporter business strategies that include: (1) trying to increase an overseas market share, (2) temporarily distributing products in overseas markets to offset slack demand in the home market, (3) lowering unit costs by exploiting large-scale production, and (4) attempting to maintain stable prices during periods of exchange-rate fluctuations.

Historically, the dumping of goods has presented serious problems in international trade. As a result, dumping has led to significant disagreements among countries and diverse views about its harmfulness. Some trade economists view dumping as harmful only when it involves the use of "predatory" practices that intentionally try to eliminate competition and gain monopoly power in a market. They believe that predatory dumping rarely occurs and that antidumping rules are a protectionist tool whose cost to consumers and import-using industries exceeds the benefits to the industries receiving protection.

In the United States, the International Trade Commission declares antidumping duties on specific foreign goods. In Canada, the Canada Border Services Agency is the agency responsible for enforcing antidumping duties on unfair foreign competition. The EU has imposed antidumping duties on imports from China for stainless-steel refillable kegs, open mesh fabric of glass fibers originating in China and being consigned from India, Indonesia, Malaysia, Taiwan and Thailand, and aluminum road wheels from Morocco among others.[107]

---

dumping the sale of an exported product at a price lower than that charged for the same or a like product in the "home" market of the exporter

countervailing duty a tax on imported goods to offset a subsidy or other financial assistance given to a foreign exporter by its government that enables the foreign exporter to sell at an artificially low price in the global marketplace

countertrade a form of trade in which all or part of the payment for goods or services is in the form of other goods or services

Based on the *Economist's* Big Mac index, Egypt has the world's most undervalued currency according to the Big Mac currency index.

Dumping problems are a wide concern around the globe.

In addition to antidumping duties, the U.S. International Trade Commission (ITC) levies countervailing duties on foreign suppliers and manufacturers. A **countervailing duty** is when a foreign government provides subsidies or assistance to a local industry, which enables the firms to sell at artificially low prices in the global market. Assistance can be in the form of low-rate loans, tax exemptions, or cash payments. After an investigation by the ITC, a countervailing duty is assessed based on the value of the subsidy.

Countertrade

Global trade does not always involve cash. Countertrade is a fast-growing way to conduct global business. In **countertrade**, all or part of the payment for goods or services is in the form of other goods or services. Countertrade is thus a form of barter (swapping goods for goods), an age-old practice whose origins have been traced back to cave dwellers. The U.S. Department of Commerce says that roughly 30 percent of all global trade is countertrade. In fact, both India and China have made billion-dollar government purchasing lists, with most of the goods to be paid for by countertrade.

One common type of countertrade is straight barter. In the 1980s, before the fall of the Soviet Union, Pepsi was bartering soda for Stolichnaya vodka. However, when the vodka sales dropped due to Americans boycotting Soviet products, the Soviets offered Pepsi navy vessels consisting of 17 submarines, a destroyer, a cruiser, a frigate, and several oil tankers. This offer made Pepsi the sixth largest navy at that time. Many of the vessels in the fleet were in a state of disrepair; therefore, Pepsi recouped the cost of its soda through recycling the scrap, but took pleasure in helping to reduce the number of ships at the Soviet's disposal.

5-6 The Impact of the Internet on Global Marketing

5-6 Describe how the internet is affecting global marketing

In many respects, going global is easier than it has ever been before. Opening an e-commerce site on the internet immediately puts a company in the international marketplace. This gives companies an increased reach to consumers outside of those within a physical proximity. Sophisticated language translation software can make any site accessible to people around the world with internet access. Global shippers such as UPS, FedEx, and DHL help solve international e-commerce distribution complexities, allowing for the delivery of purchased goods. Further, platforms like Shopify offer an integrated commerce system to ease currency conversions by allowing customers to pay in the currency of their choice. Given the vast amount of data available, the internet has made it easier for businesses to personalize their message and customize offers based on an individual's browsing history. They can engage in real-time conversations through social media, digital channels, or chatbots. This data is also helpful in successfully targeting specific customers based on demographics, behaviors, or preferences making data-driven decision making possible to hit strategic goals.

The internet has been especially beneficial to global trade in selling services. It provides a broader reach by breaking down geographic barriers as a means of expanding the customer base by providing services online through video. Physical attendance is no longer a restriction opening the opportunities for engagement in entertainment, training, or social events globally in real time. Some examples of services that can thrive globally include consulting, financial, educational, telehealth or health monitoring, information technology, legal, and marketing. The United States is the largest exporter of services in the world with over $650 billion annually.[108] Not all of these are conducted via the internet, but as you can see, there are many opportunities to do so. One example is Bellroy, an online product design company that specializes in long-lasting products that have a positive impact on the planet. Headquartered in Melbourne, Australia, the company has over 25 countries represented in its employee base to serve a diverse customer base around the globe.[109]

Part 2

Rawpixel.com/Shutterstock.com

Chapter 6

Consumer Decision Making

Learning Outcomes

After studying this chapter, you will be able to . . .

6-1 Explain why marketing managers should understand consumer behavior

6-2 Analyze the components of the consumer decision-making process

6-3 Explain the consumer's postpurchase evaluation process

6-4 Identify the types of consumer buying decisions based on level of consumer involvement

6-5 Describe how some marketers are reconceptualizing the consumer decision-making process

6-6 Describe the cultural factors that affect consumer buying decisions

6-7 Describe the social factors that affect consumer buying decisions

6-8 Describe the individual factors that affect consumer buying decisions

6-9 Describe the psychological factors that affect consumer buying decisions

6-1 The Importance of Understanding Consumer Behavior

6-1 Explain why marketing managers should understand consumer behavior

Consumers' product and service preferences are constantly changing. Marketing managers must understand these desires to create a proper marketing mix for a well-defined market. So, it is critical that marketing managers have a thorough knowledge of consumer behavior. **Consumer behavior** describes how consumers make purchase decisions and how they use and dispose of the purchased goods or services. The study of consumer behavior also includes factors that influence purchase decisions and product use.

Understanding how consumers make purchase decisions can help marketing managers in several ways. For example, if the product development manager for Trek bicycles learns through research that a more comfortable seat is a key attribute for purchasers of mountain bikes, Trek can redesign the seat to meet that criterion. If the firm cannot change the design in the short run, it can use promotion in an effort to change consumers' decision-making criteria. Trek, for example, could promote the ultra-lightweight, durability, and performance of its current mountain bikes.

Buying a mountain bike, or anything else, is all about value. **Value** is a personal assessment of the net worth one obtains from making a purchase. To put it another way, value is what you get minus what you give up. When you buy something, you hope to get benefits like durability, convenience, prestige, affection, happiness, a sense of belonging, relief from hunger . . . the list goes on. To receive these benefits, you must give something up. You may sacrifice money, self-image, time, convenience, effort, opportunity, or a combination thereof. *Value* can also mean an enduring belief shared by a society that a specific mode of conduct is personally or socially preferable to another mode of conduct; this definition will be discussed later in the chapter.

Purchases are made based on **perceived value**, which is what you *expect* to get. The actual value may be more or less than you expected. One of your authors bought a well-known brand of coffee maker with a thermal carafe. This author likes to drink coffee all morning but found that traditional coffee makers' heating elements tended to turn the coffee bitter after a few hours. The thermal carafe has no such heating element, so the coffee stays fresh. That is, if the coffee actually makes it into the carafe. The carafe lid has a valve that lets the coffee drip into the carafe basin. However, the valve tends to stick, and after about a week of use, the valve stuck during a fill-up, and coffee went all over the kitchen counter. No value there! (For the curious, the author has moved on to a new capsule-style coffee maker.)

The value received from a purchase can be broken down into two categories. **Utilitarian value** is derived from a product or service that helps the consumer solve problems and accomplish tasks. Buying a washing machine and dryer gives you a convenient means of cleaning your clothes. Buying a new pair of eyeglasses lets you better view the smartphone screen. Utilitarian value, then, is a means to an end. Value is provided because the purchase allows something good to happen.

The second form of value is **hedonic value**. Hedonic value is an end in itself rather than a means to an end. The purchase tends to give us good feelings, happiness, and satisfaction. The value is provided entirely through the experience and emotions associated with consumption, not because another end is accomplished. Taking a ski vacation or a trip to the beach gives us hedonic value. Spending a day in a spa is a source of hedonic value. A coffee maker provides utilitarian value, but the coffee itself provides hedonic value.

Utilitarian and hedonic values are not mutually exclusive. In some cases, the purchase experience can give you both hedonic and utilitarian value. Morton's The Steakhouse is considered to be one of the top steak restaurant chains in the United States. Going to a Morton's and enjoying the atmosphere and a fine steak will give you hedonic value. At the same time, it satisfies your hunger pangs and thus provides utilitarian value. Some of the best consumer experiences are high in both utilitarian and hedonic value.

Acquiring value comes from making a purchase. How does one go about making the decision to buy? We explore this topic next.

---

consumer behavior processes a consumer uses to make purchase decisions, as well as to use and dispose of purchased goods or services; also includes factors that influence purchase decisions and product use

value a personal assessment of the net worth one obtains from making a purchase, or the enduring belief that a specific mode of conduct is personally or socially preferable to another mode of conduct

perceived value the value a consumer *expects* to obtain from a purchase

utilitarian value a value derived from a product or service that helps the consumer solve problems and accomplish tasks

hedonic value a value that acts as an end in itself rather than as a means to an end

6-2 The Traditional Consumer Decision-Making Process

6-2 Analyze the components of the consumer decision-making process

When buying products, particularly new or expensive items, consumers generally follow the **consumer decision-making process** shown in Figure 6.1: (1) need recognition, (2) information search, (3) evaluation of alternatives, (4) purchase, and (5) postpurchase behavior. These five steps represent the traditional buying process, which can be used as a guide for studying how consumers make decisions. Note, though, that consumers' decisions do not always proceed in order through all of these steps. In fact, the consumer may end the process at any time or may not even make a purchase. Note, too, that technology is changing how people make decisions. A new conceptualization of the buying process is discussed later in the chapter. We begin, however, by examining the traditional purchase process in greater detail.

6-2a Need Recognition

The first stage in the consumer decision-making process is need recognition. **Need recognition** is the result of an imbalance between actual and desired states. The imbalance arouses and activates the consumer decision-making process. A **want** is the recognition of an unfulfilled need and a product that will satisfy it. For example, have you ever gotten blisters from an old running shoe and realized you needed new shoes? Or maybe you saw a friend using a new pair of earbuds and wanted to buy a pair. Wants can be viewed in terms of four goals: economizing, sustaining, treating, and rewarding.[1] The specific goal that a consumer is trying to fulfill influences how they allocate money, time, and effort. Consider a coffee drinker who has just run out of coffee at home. If they wanted to satisfy an economizing goal, they might purchase a particular brand because it is the one that is currently on sale at the grocery store. If, however, they wanted to satisfy a sustaining goal, they would be more likely to purchase their favorite brand because they

consumer decision-making process a five-step process consumers use when buying goods or services

need recognition result of an imbalance between actual and desired states

want recognition of an unfulfilled need and a product that will satisfy it

stimulus any unit of input affecting one or more of the five senses: sight, smell, taste, touch, hearing

Figure 6.1   The Consumer Decision-Making Process

1. Need recognition
2. Information search
3. Evaluation of alternatives
4. Purchase
5. Postpurchase behavior

Cultural, social, individual, and psychological factors affect all steps

prefer the taste over the other two brands they sometimes buy. If they wanted to satisfy a treating goal, they might buy a cup of coffee at Peet's Coffee. Finally, if they wanted to satisfy a rewarding goal, they might opt to order a latte while reading their favorite book at a trendy new cafe.

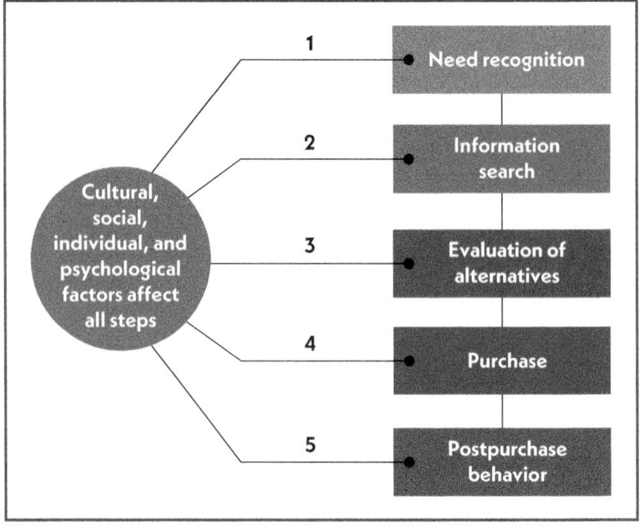

Need recognition is triggered when a consumer is exposed to either an internal or an external **stimulus**, which is any unit of input affecting one or more of the five senses: sight, smell, taste, touch, and hearing. *Internal stimuli* are experiences such as hunger, thirst, or tiredness. For example, you may yawn and then realize you are feeling tired. *External stimuli* are influences from an outside source. In today's digital age, stimuli can come from a multitude of sources. Perhaps it was a TikTok video that created a purchase desire. Perhaps it was a Google search on a smartphone or an interactive advertisement displayed while browsing on a smartphone. Or perhaps it was a friend's video posted on Instagram.

The imbalance between actual and desired states is sometimes called the *want–got gap*. That is, there is a difference between what a customer has and what they would like to have. This gap does not always trigger consumer action. The gap must be large enough to drive the consumer to do something. Just because you yawn once does not mean that you necessarily will stop what you are doing and take a nap.

A marketing manager's objective is to get consumers to recognize this want–got gap. Advertising, sales promotion, and social media often provide this stimulus. Surveying buyer preferences and data mining provides marketers with information about consumer needs and wants that can be used to tailor products and services. Marketing managers can create wants on the part of the consumer. In 2022, Apple unveiled the Apple Watch Ultra, a fitness-focused version of the popular

Apple watch.[2] With the unveiling, Apple launched a campaign that featured athletes using the watch while engaging in different types of fitness activities, including running, mountain climbing, and even scuba diving, to create a desire for the product among consumers who participate in these types of activities. A want can be for a specific product, or it can be for a certain attribute or feature of a product. Thus, avid mountain climbers may purchase the Apple Watch Ultra because they like the highly accurate global positioning system (GPS) or the night mode that eases eye strain in the dark.

6-2b Information Search

After recognizing a need or want, consumers search for information about the various alternatives available to satisfy it. For example, you know you are interested in going out to eat, but you are not sure where to go. So, you visit the Yelp website to find out what is getting great reviews. This search is a type of information search, which can occur internally, externally, or both. In an **internal information search**, the person recalls information stored in the memory. This stored information stems largely from previous experience with a product. For example, when going out to eat with your friends, you may choose to eat at a restaurant where you have dined before because you remember that the restaurant had good food and a friendly wait staff.

In contrast, an **external information search** seeks information in the outside environment. There are two basic types of external information sources: non–marketing-controlled and marketing-controlled. A **non–marketing-controlled information source** is a product information source that is not associated with marketers promoting a product. These information sources include personal experiences (trying or observing a new product), personal sources (family, friends, acquaintances, and coworkers who may recommend a product or service), public sources (such as Yelp, *Consumer Reports*, and other rating organizations that comment on products and services), and social media. Social media, of course, includes both marketing and non-marketing controlled. Once you have read reviews on Yelp to decide which restaurant to go to (public source), you may search your memory for positive restaurant experiences to determine where you will go (personal experience). Or you might rely on a friend's recommendation to try out a new restaurant (personal source). Marketers gather information on how these information sources work and use it to attract customers. For example, car manufacturers know that younger customers are likely to get information from friends and family, so they try to develop enthusiasm for their products via word of mouth and social media.

Living in the digital age has changed the way consumers get non–marketing-controlled information. Consumers can get information from blogs, Amazon, social media, web forums, or consumer opinion sites such as consumerreports.org or tripadvisor.com. Seventy-six percent of U.S. consumers conduct online searches to collect product information, read reviews, and look for better prices before making their final purchase in-store. To give you an idea of the number of searches this total implies, Google averages more than 89 billion searches a month, and this number is only going to expand.[3]

The internet has changed the quality of information available to make purchase decisions. In the past, consumers used quality proxies to help determine what to buy. A proxy could be a brand name ("it is made by Nike so it must be good"), price ("higher price meant higher quality"), or origin ("coffee beans from Ethiopia are the most flavorful"). Today, consumers can appraise a product based on how it is evaluated by others. If you are looking for a hotel in New York City, for example, you can easily view a ranking of all New York hotels based on thousands of reviews on websites like TripAdvisor. This method provides much better information than simply relying on a brand name (such as Hilton) because you have the direct experience of others to guide you. Expedia allows only customers who have purchased a service (such as a flight, car, or hotel room) to write a review. Similarly, Amazon identifies whether a review matches a confirmed transaction. Amazon also bans reviews for which the reviewer received free or discounted items from the company being reviewed.

Social media are playing an ever-increasing role in consumer information search. Eighty-one percent of respondents to a survey reported that social media posts made by family and friends directly impacted their purchase decisions. Seventy-eight percent reported that company posts influenced their buying decisions.[4]

Although a lot of consumption purchases are made online, consumers still make many of their purchases in brick-and-mortar stores. Following the COVID-19 pandemic, consumers were excited and ready to get out of the house and back into physical stores. A recent report found that 45 percent of consumers prefer in-store shopping as opposed to shopping online. Further, the experiential value of shopping in a physical store tends to be of particular importance for younger consumers, who often wish to document and share their shopping experiences on social

---

internal information search the process of recalling information stored in the memory

external information search the process of seeking information in the outside environment

non–marketing-controlled information source a product information source that is not associated with advertising or promotion

Smartphones and social media are playing an ever-increasing role in consumer decision making.

media platforms such as Instagram.[5] However, even when shopping in physical stores, consumers still often consult their smartphones to aid in the information search process to look at price comparisons, product reviews, consult with friends and family, or look at online product demos.[6]

Not every information search is about comparing Product or Service Firm A with Product or Service Firm B. Yet, the online search can still influence purchase patterns. For example, a shopper may browse recipe website or watch cooking demonstration videos before deciding on a dinner party menu. This research helps the shopper decide which ingredients to purchase at the supermarket.

A **marketing-controlled information source** is biased toward a specific product because it originates with marketers promoting that product. Marketing-controlled information sources include mass media advertising (radio, television, magazine, and social media advertising), sales promotion (contests, displays, premiums, and so forth), salespeople, product labels and packaging, and social media. Research shows that developing a social media community with a dedicated fan base, such as an active Facebook page, significantly strengthens customer relationships with a company and brand. Moreover, it has a positive impact on revenue and profits.[7]

The Extent of Information Search

The extent to which an individual conducts an external search depends on their perceived risk, knowledge, prior experience, and level of interest in the good or service. Generally, as the perceived risk of the purchase increases, the consumer enlarges the search and considers more alternative brands. For example, suppose that you want to purchase a new car. The decision is relatively risky because of

the high expense, so you may be motivated to search for information about different models, prices, and features. You may decide to compare many different brands and models because the value of the time expended finding the "right" car will be less than the cost of buying the wrong car.

A consumer's knowledge about the product or service will also affect the extent of an external information search. A consumer who is knowledgeable and well informed about a potential purchase is less likely to search for additional information. In addition, the more knowledgeable consumers are, the more efficiently they will conduct the search process, thereby requiring less time to search. For example, many consumers know that Spirit Airlines and other discount airlines have much lower fares, so they generally use the discounters and do not even check fares at other carriers.

The extent of a consumer's external search is also affected by confidence in one's decision-making ability. A confident consumer not only has sufficient stored information about the product but also feels self-assured about making the right decision. People lacking this confidence will continue an information search even when they know a great deal about the product. Consumers with prior experience in buying a certain product will have less perceived risk than inexperienced consumers. Therefore, they will spend less time searching and limit the number of products they consider.

A third factor influencing the external information search is product experience. Consumers who have had a positive experience with a product are more likely to limit their search to items related to the positive experience. For example, when flying, consumers are likely to choose airlines with which they have had positive experiences, such as consistent on-time arrivals, and avoid airlines with which they have had a negative experience, such as lost luggage.

Finally, the extent of the search is positively related to the amount of interest a consumer has in a product. A consumer who is more interested in a product will spend more time searching for information and alternatives. For example, suppose you are a dedicated runner who reads jogging and fitness magazines and catalogs. In searching for a new pair of running shoes, you may enjoy reading about the new brands available and spend more time and effort than other buyers in deciding on the right shoe. Many brands are capitalizing on consumer interest in a product category through the use of personalized communication campaigns. For example, it is common for brands to track consumers' past purchases, to get a better understanding of product interests and then send them personalized promotions for products that are likely to interest them. Amazon has data on past consumer purchases and

---

marketing-controlled information source a product information source that originates with marketers promoting the product

products that they have rated or indicated that they own. This information is compared with the purchases of other customers and then personalized recommendations are offered, with the assumption that consumers who have similar past purchases will have similar interests for other types of products.

The consumer's information search should yield a group of brands, sometimes called the buyer's **evoked set** (or **consideration set**), which are the consumer's most preferred alternatives. From this set, the buyer will further evaluate the alternatives and make a choice. Consumers do not consider all brands available in a product category, but they do seriously consider a much smaller set. For example, from the many brands of pizza available, consumers are likely to consider only the alternatives that fit their price range, location, take-out/delivery needs, and taste preferences. Having too many choices can, in fact, confuse consumers and cause them to delay the decision to buy, or in some instances, cause them not to buy at all.

6-2c Evaluation of Alternatives and Purchase

After getting information and constructing an evoked set of alternative products, the consumer is ready to make a decision. A consumer will use the information stored in memory and obtained from outside sources to develop a set of criteria. Recent research has shown that exposure to certain cues in your everyday environment can affect decision criteria and purchase. For example, when NASA landed the *Pathfinder* spacecraft on Mars, it captured media attention worldwide. The candy maker Mars also noted a rather unusual increase in sales. Although the Mars bar takes its name from the company's founder and not the planet, consumers apparently responded to news about the planet Mars by purchasing more Mars bars.

The environment, internal information, and external information help consumers evaluate and compare alternatives. One way to begin narrowing the number of choices in the evoked set is to pick a product attribute and then exclude all products in the set that do not have that attribute. For example, assume Nikolas and Theo, both college sophomores, are looking for their first apartment. They need a two-bedroom apartment, reasonably priced and located near campus. They want the apartment to have a swimming pool, washer and dryer, and covered parking. Nikolas and Theo begin their search with all 50 apartments in the area and systematically eliminate complexes that lack the features they need. Hence, they may reduce their list to 10 apartments that possess all of the desired attributes. Now, they can use cutoffs to further narrow their choices. Cutoffs are either minimum or maximum levels of an attribute that an alternative must pass to be

considered. Suppose Nikolas and Theo set a maximum of $1,500 per month for rent. Then all apartments with rent higher than $1,500 will be eliminated, further reducing the list of apartments from 10 to 8. A final way to narrow the choices is to rank the attributes under consideration in order of importance and evaluate the products based on how well each performs on the most important attributes. To reach a final decision on one of the remaining eight apartments, Nikolas and Theo may decide that proximity to campus is the most important attribute. As a result, they will choose to rent the apartment closest to campus.

If new brands are added to an evoked set, the consumer's evaluation of the existing brands in that set changes. As a result, certain brands in the original set may become more desirable. Suppose Nikolas and Theo find two apartments located an equal distance from campus, one priced at $1,300 and the other at $1,150. Faced with this choice, they may decide that the $1,300 apartment is too expensive given that a comparable apartment is cheaper. If they add a $1,400 apartment to the list, however, then they may perceive the $1,300 apartment as more reasonable and decide to rent it.

The purchase decision process described above is a piecemeal process. That is, the evaluation is made by examining alternative advantages and disadvantages along important product attributes. A different way consumers can evaluate a product is according to a categorization process. The evaluation of an alternative depends on the particular category to which it is assigned. Categories can be very general (motorized forms of transportation), or they can be very specific (Harley-Davidson motorcycles). Typically, these categories are associated with some degree of liking or disliking. To the extent that the product can be assigned membership in a particular category, it will receive an evaluation similar to that attached to the category. If you go to the grocery store and notice a new energy drink beverage on the shelf, you may evaluate it on your liking and opinions of energy drinks.

So, when consumers rely on a categorization process, a product's evaluation depends on the particular category to which it is perceived as belonging. Given this factor, companies need to understand whether consumers are using categories that evoke the desired evaluations. Indeed, how a product is categorized can strongly influence consumer demand. For example, what products come to mind when you think about the "morning beverages" category? To the soft drink industry's dismay, far too few consumers include sodas in this category. Several attempts have been made

---

evoked set (consideration set) a group of brands resulting from an information search from which a buyer can choose

to get soft drinks on the breakfast table, but with little success.

Brand extensions, in which a well-known and respected brand name from one product category is extended into other product categories, is one way companies employ categorization to their advantage. Brand extensions are a common business practice. For example, Ferrari, known for its luxurious, high-powered sports cars, recently launched a high-end fashion collection and opened a restaurant in Maranello, Italy.[8]

Another factor that can influence the evaluation process is exposure to the price of the product or service. Imagine that you walk into a department store and notice a display of sweaters that catches your eye. When you walk over to the display, you look at a tag on a sweater to find a price of $49.99. Alternatively, imagine that you walk into the store and notice a rack of clothes labeled with a large $49.99 sign. With this price in mind, you browse through the options and find a sweater that fits your tastes. How might your evaluation of the sweater differ based on whether you notice the product cue versus the price cue first? Researchers have found that when consumers perceive the product cue first (scenario one), evaluation is strongly related to the product's attractiveness or desirability. When the first cue is the price (scenario two), evaluation is related more to the product's value.[9]

While the evaluation process sounds completely rational, behavioral economists point out that this result is not always the case. For example, why do people buy a $5 latte when they're trying to save money? Obviously, they are not making an economically rational decision.

In an experiment, researchers sold Lindt Chocolate Truffles for 26 cents each and Hershey's Kisses for 1 cent each. Equal numbers of people bought each. When researchers dropped the price by 1 cent, 90 percent of the people took the free Hershey's Kiss. Behavioral economists say that "the power of free" often makes consumers irrational.[10]

Behavioral economists talk about using a **nudge**. A nudge is a little push; a little intervention that can stimulate changed behavior but is also easy and cheap to avoid and doesn't forbid other options. Nudges are not mandates. For example, "Keeping America Beautiful" is a nudge, but a sign reading "$1,000 fine for littering" is not.

As another example, it was found in Google's cafeteria that people can be nudged toward healthier eating. Researchers found that employees who poured their drinks at a beverage station 6.5 feet from a snack bar were 50 percent more likely to grab a snack than those who filled their glasses at a beverage station 17.5 feet away from the snack bar. For male Google employees, 11 feet of proximity correlated with gaining one pound of fat each year.[11]

A nudge can be nonprice oriented, such as the Google example, or price oriented. Many companies use short message service (SMS) marketing to reduce online cart abandonment. If, after shopping online and adding products to their online cart, a consumer does not purchase, companies will sometimes send a coupon via text message to incentivize the consumer to ultimately make the purchase. According to Tapcart, a marketing firm focused on push notifications, this type of SMS marketing can reduce cart abandonment rates by as much as 30 percent.[12]

To Buy or Not to Buy

Ultimately, the consumer has to decide whether or not to buy. Specifically, consumers must decide:

1. Whether to buy
2. When to buy
3. What to buy (product type and brand)
4. Where to buy (type of retailer, specific retailer, online or in store)
5. How to pay

If a consumer decides to purchase something online, it has been found that people frequently switch from a mobile device (e.g., smartphone or tablet) to a more fixed device such as a desktop as they move through the purchase process. It seems that mobile devices are used more in the information-seeking process. So, shopping for a new washing machine may entail visiting a Lowe's store and other retailers to compare models, ratings, prices, and so forth, but the actual purchase is made on a desktop or laptop at home. In fact, the average conversion rate is almost twice as high on desktop computers as opposed to mobile devices.[13]

Planned Versus Impulse Purchase

Complex and expensive items are typically purchased only after the consumer has collected a large amount of information. People rarely buy a new home on impulse. Often, consumers will make a *partially planned purchase* when they know the product category they want to buy (shirts, pants, reading lamp, car floor mats) but wait until they get to the store or go online to choose a specific style or brand. Finally, there is the *unplanned purchase*, which people buy on impulse; these purchases are often triggered by a nudge. Impulse purchasing has been on the rise in recent years, driven largely by sponsored posts on social media and the introduction of buy now, pay later.

---

nudge a small intervention that can change a person's behavior

Research has found that 73 percent of adult consumers reported that most of their purchases are impulsive and that consumers spend an average of $314 a month on impulse purchases.[14] Shoppers say that they often make impulse purchases because of a sale or promotion for a product, but also sometimes because of a desire to pamper themselves.[15] A purchase may be in a planned category (e.g., soup), but decisions regarding the brand (Campbell's), package (can), and type (tomato) may all be made on impulse.

Psychological Ownership

Consumers sometimes develop feelings of ownership without even owning the good, service, or brand.[16] For example, think about how you feel when you choose a seat on the first day of class. Then, when you come to class on the second day, where do you usually sit? How do you feel if someone else is sitting in "your" seat? This feeling of "It's mine!" is called psychological, or perceived, ownership. Psychological ownership is important to marketers because when consumers feel a sense of ownership of a product, they are willing to pay more for it and are more likely to tell other consumers about it.[17] Consumers develop this kind of relationship with a product when they are able to control it, when they invest themselves in it, or when they come to know it intimately. Researchers have found that simply touching a product or imagining owning it enhances feelings of psychological ownership. When customers of Threadless T-Shirts were given the opportunity to vote on upcoming shirt designs, their willingness to pay more for the shirts increased because they felt a greater sense of ownership of them. Even liking a social media post can feel like a vote of confidence for a product and can enhance customers' feelings of ownership.[18] Clearly, psychological ownership can have a significant influence on consumer behavior. Marketing managers need to be aware of it when developing their marketing strategies.

Psychological ownership can be triggered by simply touching a product, liking a social media post about a product, or helping to design a product.

6-3 Postpurchase Behavior

6-3 Explain the consumer's postpurchase evaluation process

When buying products, consumers expect certain outcomes from the purchase. How well these expectations are met determines whether the consumer is satisfied or dissatisfied with the purchase. For example, if a person bids on a used Bluetooth speaker from eBay and wins, they may have fairly low expectations regarding performance. If the speaker's performance turns out to be of superior quality, then the person's satisfaction will be high because expectations were exceeded. Conversely, if the person bids on a new Bluetooth speaker expecting superior quality and performance, but the speaker breaks within one month, they will be very dissatisfied because expectations were not met. Price often influences the level of expectations for a product or service.

Have you ever bought a product online or gone to a store to buy a specific item only to find out that it is sold out or not available? This phenomenon is called the **jilting effect**—that is, the anticipation of receiving a highly desirable option only to have it become inaccessible. TikTok, as well as other social media platforms, can dramatically increase product popularity and lead to stock outs. After a TikTok video that featured an influencer wearing a pair of leggings from the clothing company Aerie went viral, the leggings sold out more than six times and accumulated a waiting list of more than 150,000 people.[19] This effect can reduce consumer preferences for the incumbent product or service and increase preferences for alternatives.[20] For a competitor, jilting may represent an opportunity to take market share away from the incumbent brand.

Cognitive Dissonance

For the marketer, an important element of any postpurchase evaluation is reducing any lingering doubts that the decision was sound. When people recognize inconsistency between their values or opinions and their behavior, they tend to feel an inner tension called **cognitive dissonance**. This effect is also sometimes referred to as buyer's remorse. For example, suppose Angelika is looking to purchase an eReader. After evaluating options, she has decided to purchase a Samsung Galaxy Tab, even though it is much more expensive than other dedicated eReaders. Before choosing the Galaxy Tab, Angelika may experience inner tension or anxiety because she is worried that the current

jilting effect anticipation of receiving a highly desirable option only to have it become inaccessible

cognitive dissonance inner tension that a consumer experiences after recognizing an inconsistency between behavior and values or opinions

top-of-the-line technology, which costs much more than the middle-of-the-line technology, will be obsolete in a couple of months. That feeling of dissonance arises as her worries over obsolescence battle her practical nature, which is focused on the lower cost of a Kindle Paperwhite and its adequate—but less fancy—technology.

As another example, imagine that Felix is in need of new tennis shoes. Felix has a budget of $80, but when he gets to the store, he finds a pair of Adidas shoes that he really likes for $120. The salesperson tells Felix that the Adidas shoes have been popular and will likely sell out soon, so Felix decides to exceed his original budget and buy the Adidas shoes. When he gets home, however, he may feel dissonance for spending so much extra money.

Consumers try to reduce dissonance by justifying their decision. They may seek new information that reinforces positive ideas about the purchase, avoid information that contradicts their decision, or revoke the original decision by returning the product. In some instances, people deliberately seek contrary information only to refute it and reduce dissonance. Dissatisfied customers sometimes rely on word of mouth to reduce cognitive dissonance by letting friends and family know they are displeased.

Marketing managers can help reduce dissonance through effective communication with purchasers. For example, a customer service manager may slip a note inside a consumer's package thanking the buyer for their business. Nordstrom employees often send handwritten thank-you notes to new customers, which helps to reduce dissonance and create more loyal relationships. Postpurchase letters sent by manufacturers and dissonance-reducing statements in instruction booklets may help customers feel at ease with their purchase. Advertising that displays the product's superiority over competing brands or guarantees can also help relieve the possible dissonance of someone who has already bought the product. Companies can use social media to ease cognitive dissonance by responding quickly to customer questions and concerns. Research has found that 57 percent of customers expect a response to a question posted on social media within 12 hours, so companies looking to provide top-quality customer service and use social media to reduce potential dissonance need to ensure they keep response times low.[21]

An excellent opportunity for a company to reduce (or, if handled poorly, increase) cognitive dissonance is when a customer has a question or complaint and tries to contact the company. Some firms view their contact centers as cost centers and make it as hard as possible to speak to a customer service representative, which can raise cognitive dissonance and hurt brand loyalty. Marketing-oriented companies

New Africa/Shutterstock.com

perceive the contact center as an opportunity to engage customers and reinforce the brand promise. For example, Bank of America recently launched a highly advanced, AI-driven virtual assistant named Erica. Erica can help with everyday banking, investments, credit cards, and mortgage questions, and customers can interact with Erica over the phone or through text. Bank of America has reported that more than 98 percent of customers get the answers they are looking for through Erica. Bank of America's digital engagement increased 15 percent from 2021 to 2022, in part because of the success that the financial institute found with Erica.[22] Research has shown that consumers whose customer service questions and complaints are resolved during the first point of contact are nearly twice as likely to remain loyal to the product or company and are four times more likely to spread positive word of mouth.[23]

6-4 Types of Consumer Buying Decisions and Consumer Involvement

6-4 Identify the types of consumer buying decisions based on level of consumer involvement

All consumer buying decisions generally fall along a continuum of three broad categories: routine response behavior, limited decision making, and extensive decision making (refer to Table 6.1). Goods and services in these three categories can best be described in terms of the following five factors:

1. Level of consumer involvement
2. Length of time to make a decision
3. Cost of the good or service
4. Degree of information search
5. Number of alternatives considered

The level of consumer involvement is perhaps the most significant determinant in classifying buying decisions. **Involvement** is the amount of time and effort a buyer

---

involvement the amount of time and effort a buyer invests in the search, evaluation, and decision processes of consumer behavior

Table 6.1 Continuum of Consumer Buying Decisions

	Routine Response Behavior	Limited Decision Making	Extensive Decision Making
Involvement	Low	Low to moderate	High
Time	Short	Short to moderate	Long
Cost	Low	Low to moderate	High
Information Search	Internal only	Mostly internal	Internal and external
Number of Alternatives	One	Few	Many

invests in the search, evaluation, and decision processes of consumer behavior.

Frequently purchased, low-cost goods and services are generally associated with **routine response behavior**. These goods and services can also be called *low-involvement products* because consumers spend little time on searching and decision making before making the purchase. Usually, buyers are familiar with several different brands in the product category but stick with one brand. For example, a person may routinely buy Tropicana orange juice. Consumers engaged in routine response behavior normally do not experience need recognition until they are nudged by an advertisement or notice the product displayed on a store shelf. Consumers buy first and evaluate later, whereas the reverse is true for extensive decision making. A consumer who has previously purchased whitening toothpaste and was satisfied with it will probably walk to the toothpaste aisle and select that same brand without spending 20 minutes examining all other alternatives.

Limited decision making typically occurs when a consumer has previous product experience but is unfamiliar with the current brands available. Limited decision making is also associated with lower levels of involvement (although higher than routine decisions) because consumers expend only moderate effort in searching for information or considering various alternatives. For example, what happens if the consumer's usual brand of whitening toothpaste is sold out? Assuming that toothpaste is needed, the consumer will be forced to choose another brand. Before making a final decision, the consumer will likely evaluate several other brands based on their active ingredients, their promotional claims, and the consumer's prior experiences. They may also look online for various brand rankings.

Consumers practice **extensive decision making** when buying an unfamiliar, expensive product, or an infrequently bought item. This process is the most complex type of a consumer buying decision and is associated with high consumer involvement. This process resembles the model outlined in Figure 6.1. These consumers want to make the right decision, so they want to know as much as they can about the product category and available brands. People usually experience the most cognitive dissonance when buying high-involvement products. Buyers use several criteria for evaluating their options and spend much time seeking information. Buying a home or a car, for example, requires extensive decision making.

The type of decision making that consumers use to purchase a product does not necessarily remain constant. For instance, if a routinely purchased product no longer satisfies, consumers may practice limited or extensive decision making to switch to another brand. And people who first use extensive decision making may then use limited or

For many consumers, purchasing a new vehicle is a high involvement decision requiring extensive decision making.

Standret/Shutterstock.com

routine response behavior the type of decision making exhibited by consumers buying frequently purchased, low-cost goods and services; requires little search and decision time

limited decision making the type of decision making that requires a moderate amount of time for gathering information and deliberating about an unfamiliar brand in a familiar product category

extensive decision making the most complex type of consumer decision making, used when buying an unfamiliar, expensive product or an infrequently bought item; requires use of several criteria for evaluating options and much time for seeking information

routine decision making for future purchases. For example, when a family gets a new puppy, they will spend a lot of time and energy trying out different toys to determine which one the dog prefers. Once the new owners learn that the dog prefers a bone to a ball, however, the purchase no longer requires extensive evaluation and will become routine.

6-4a Factors Determining the Level of Consumer Involvement

The level of involvement in the purchase depends on the following factors:

- **Previous experience:** When consumers have had previous experience with a good or service, the level of involvement typically decreases. After repeated product trials, consumers learn to make quick choices. Because consumers are familiar with the product and know whether it will satisfy their needs, they become less involved in the purchase. For example, a consumer purchasing cereal has many brands to choose from—just think of any grocery store cereal aisle. If the consumer always buys the same brand because it satisfies their hunger, then they have a low level of involvement. When a consumer purchases a new category of cereal, such as low in sugar, it likely will be a more involved purchase.

- **Interest:** Involvement is directly related to consumer interests, as in cars, music, movies, bicycling, or online games. Naturally, these areas of interest vary from one individual to another. A person highly involved in bike racing will be more interested in the type of bike they own and will spend quite a bit of time evaluating different bikes. If a person wants a bike only for recreation, however, they may be less uninvolved in the purchase. They may just choose a bike from the most convenient location and in a reasonable price range.

- **Perceived risk of negative consequences:** As the perceived risk in purchasing a product increases, so does a consumer's level of involvement. The types of risks that concern consumers include financial risk, social risk, and psychological risk.

  - Financial risk is exposure to loss of wealth or purchasing power. Because high risk is associated with high-priced purchases, consumers tend to become extremely involved. Therefore, price and involvement are usually directly related: As price increases, so does the level of involvement. For example, someone who is purchasing a new car for the first time (higher perceived risk) will spend a lot of time and effort making this purchase.

  - Social risks occur when consumers buy products that can affect people's social opinions of them (e.g., driving an old, beat-up car or wearing unstylish clothes).

  - Psychological risks occur if consumers believe that making the wrong decision might cause some concern or anxiety. For example, some consumers feel guilty about eating foods that are not healthy, such as regular ice cream rather than fat-free frozen yogurt.

- **Social visibility:** Involvement also increases as the social visibility of a product increases. Products often on social display include clothing (especially designer labels), jewelry, cars, and furniture. All these items make a statement about the purchaser and, therefore, carry a social risk.

High involvement means that the consumer cares about a product category or a specific good or service. The product or service is relevant and important and means something to the buyer. High involvement can take a number of different forms. The most important types are discussed below:

- *Product involvement* means that a product category has high personal relevance. Product enthusiasts are consumers with high involvement in a product category. The fashion industry has a large segment of product enthusiasts. These people are seeking the latest fashion trends and want to wear the latest clothes.

- *Situational involvement* means that the circumstances of a purchase may temporarily transform a low-involvement decision into a high-involvement one. High involvement comes into play when the consumer perceives risk in a specific situation. For example, an individual might routinely buy low-priced brands of liquor and wine. When the boss visits, however, the consumer might make a high-involvement decision and buy more prestigious brands.

- *Shopping involvement* represents the personal relevance of the process of shopping. Some people enjoy the process of shopping even if they do not plan to buy anything. For others, shopping is an enjoyable social activity. Many consumers also engage in **showrooming**—examining merchandise in a physical retail location without purchasing it and then shopping online for a better deal on the same item.

- *Enduring involvement* represents an ongoing interest in some products, such as kitchen gadgets, or activity, such as fishing. The consumer is always searching for opportunities to consume the product or participate

---

showrooming the practice of examining merchandise in a physical retail location without purchasing it and then shopping online for a better deal on the same item

Lay's uses bright, eye-catching packaging to draw customers to what is usually a low-involvement product.

in the activity. Enduring involvement typically gives personal gratification to consumers as they continue to learn about, shop for, and consume these goods and services. Therefore, there is often a link between enduring involvement, shopping, and product involvement.

- *Emotional involvement* represents how emotional a consumer gets during some specific consumption activity. Emotional involvement is closely related to enduring involvement because the things that consumers care most about will eventually create high emotional involvement. Sports fans typify consumers with high emotional involvement.

6-4b Marketing Implications of Involvement

Marketing strategy varies according to the level of involvement associated with the product. For high-involvement product purchases, marketing managers have several objectives. First, promotion to the target market should be extensive and informative. A good ad gives consumers the information they need for making the purchase decision and specifies the benefits and unique advantages of owning the product. For example, Ford recently introduced a new adventure vehicle, the Ford Transit Trail, with many custom options that is being positioned as an alternative to a motor home. This vehicle is being marketed to adventure seeking consumers who like camping and other outdoor activities. One campaign showcased features such as the vehicle's all terrain tires, a heavy-duty towing package for hauling a boat or other adventure toys, and the preinstalled roof vent fan that allows adventurers to get fresh air while hanging out inside of the vehicle. These are all important benefits to consumers looking to invest in an adventure vehicle.[24]

For low-involvement product purchases, consumers may not recognize their wants until they are in the store. Therefore, in-store promotion and targeted mobile ads are important tools when promoting low-involvement products. Marketing managers focus on package design so the product will be eye-catching and easily recognized on the shelf. Examples of products that take this approach are Lay's chips, Tide detergent, Gatorade, and Heinz ketchup. In-store displays and digital coupons also stimulate sales of low-involvement products. A good display can explain the product's purpose and prompt recognition of a want. Displays of snack foods in supermarkets have been known to increase sales many times above normal. Cents-off deals and two-for-one offers also effectively promote low-involvement items.

Researchers have found that another way to increase involvement is to offer products on a "limited availability" basis. Starbucks, for example, only offers its popular pumpkin spice lattes during the fall months. Marketers can use several ways to trigger limited availability, including daily specials (e.g., special soup *du jour*), day of the week (e.g., Sunday brunch), promotional periods (e.g., item availability for a limited time only), harvest time (e.g., corn in the summer), and small production runs (e.g., limited edition items). Limited availability creates a "get it now or never" mentality.

6-5 Reconceptualizing the Consumer Decision-Making Process

6-5 Describe how some marketers are reconceptualizing the consumer decision-making process

Rapid changes in digital technology have given consumers unprecedented power to express likes and dislikes, compare prices, find the best deals, sift through huge numbers of recommendations on sites like TripAdvisor and Yelp, and finally, have items delivered quickly—sometimes on the same day the order was placed. In short, the balance of power has shifted largely from the marketer to the consumer. Because of these remarkable changes, many marketers today are totally reconceptualizing the consumer decision-making process.

6-5a The Consumer Decision Journey

One of the hottest phrases in marketing today is "the consumer decision journey." Figure 6.2 depicts this journey and explains how marketers are trying to regain control from consumers by streamlining the decision-making process.

The consumer decision journey begins when an advertisement or other stimulus causes a consumer to research a number of products or services to meet their needs. Even at

Figure 6.2 The Consumer Decision Journey

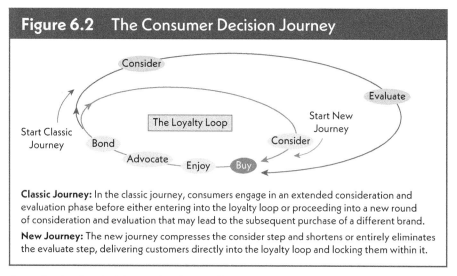

Classic Journey: In the classic journey, consumers engage in an extended consideration and evaluation phase before either entering into the loyalty loop or proceeding into a new round of consideration and evaluation that may lead to the subsequent purchase of a different brand.

New Journey: The new journey compresses the consider step and shortens or entirely eliminates the evaluate step, delivering customers directly into the loyalty loop and locking them within it.

Source: Based on David Edelman and Mark Singer, "Competing on Customer Journeys," *Harvard Business Review*, November 2015.

this early stage, the consumer may drop a number of items from the potential purchase set. The second phase of the journey begins when the consumer evaluates the alternatives, using input from peers, reviewers, retailers, the brand itself, and competitors. At this stage, new brands may be added and options from the initial set may be dropped as the selection criteria shift. The consumer then buys (or doesn't buy) the product and, if they enjoy the purchase, may advocate and bond with the brand. This feedback loop of ratings, rankings, and referrals pressures brands to deliver a superior experience on an ongoing basis. Lush cosmetics, an ethical cosmetics brand that was founded in 1995, has become a billion dollar brand through the use of a strong word-of-mouth marketing strategy.[25] Additionally, 100 percent of the proceeds from one of Lush's body cream products, a product called Charity Pot, are donated to charitable organizations.[26] This approach leads consumers to feel as though they are being prosocial by shopping with the brand, which can help to reduce cognitive dissonance.

Progressive firms armed with new technologies are actively working to exert greater influence over the decision-making journey. To minimize (or, in some cases, eliminate) the "consider and evaluate" phases of the consumer journey, a company must have four distinct but interconnected capabilities:

1. *Automation* streamlines journey steps. One example is letting people take a picture of a check and deposit it through an app rather than depositing it in person. While process automation is highly technical, it should always be done with simple, useful, and increasingly engaging consumer-side experiences in mind.

2. *Proactive personalization* uses information—either based on past interactions or collected through external sources—to instantaneously customize the customer experience. This capability ranges from a website remembering a customer's log-in preferences to an airline automatically adding a frequent traveler to its upgrade list.

3. *Contextual interaction* uses knowledge about where a customer is in the journey to deliver them to the next set of interactions. Consider, for example, a retail website displaying the status of a recent order on its home page. More and more hotels are pushing the boundaries of contextual interaction by configuring their apps to operate like keys when guests approach their rooms.

4. *Journey innovation* extends customer interactions to new sources of value, such as related products or partnered businesses. Many companies mine their data to figure out what adjacent goods or services a shopper might be interested in, then they put those products in front of the shopper in the middle of their journey. The best companies conduct open-ended testing and constantly prototype new services and features to best meet customer needs in the ever-changing, digitally connected market. For example, Alaska Airlines recently formed a partnership with ride-sharing service Lyft so that travelers can earn Alaska Airlines reward miles for all of their Lyft rides, including rides to and from the airport.[27]

To understand how a company can influence the consumer decision journey, let's examine California-based solar panel provider Sungevity. This company's "product" is a seamless, personalized customer journey built on innovative data management about the solar potential of each home. Consider the following Sungevity experience:

> One of the creators of "The Consumer Decision Journey" model (David) experienced the Sungevity journey firsthand. The process began when he received a mailing with the message "Open this to find out how much the Edelman family can save on energy costs with solar panels." The letter within contained a unique URL that led to a Google Earth image of David's house with solar panels superimposed on the roof. The next click led to a page with custom calculations of energy savings, developed from Sungevity's estimates of the family's energy use, the roof angle, the presence of nearby trees, and the energy-generation potential of the 23 panels the company expected the roof to hold.
>
> Another click connected David through his desktop to a live sales rep looking at the same pages David was. The rep expertly answered his questions and instantly

sent him links to videos that explained the installation process and the economics of leasing versus buying. Two days later, Sungevity emailed David with the names and numbers of nearby homeowners who used its system and had agreed to serve as references. After checking these references, David returned to Sungevity's site, where a single click connected him to a rep who knew precisely where he was on the journey and had a tailored lease ready for him. The rep emailed it and walked David through it, and then David e-signed. When he next visited the website, the landing page had changed to track the progress of the permitting and installation, with fresh alerts arriving as the process proceeded. Now, as a Sungevity customer, David receives regular reports on his panels' energy generation and the resulting savings, along with tips on ways to conserve energy, based on his household's characteristics.

Starting with its initial outreach and continuing to the installation and ongoing management of David's panels, Sungevity customized and automated each step of the journey, making it so simple—and so compelling—for him to move from one step to the next that he never actively considered alternative providers. In essence, the company reconfigured the classic model of the consumer decision journey, immediately paring the consideration set to one brand, streamlining the evaluation phase, and delivering David directly into the "loyalty loop."[28]

Another way firms are keeping customers in the loyalty loop is by using automated reordering. Express Scripts, one of the largest pharmacy benefit management organizations in the United States, can automatically reorder customer prescriptions when it is time to refill. Customers also receive reminders that they can save money if they transfer their prescriptions to Express Scripts when they fill prescriptions at local pharmacies. Similarly, when a customer orders an eBook on Amazon, the company uses finely tuned algorithms to suggest other books that they might want to read. Amazon offers automatic order scheduling on thousands of items from diapers to soft drinks. Customers can customize which items are sent, what day of the month they are sent, and how frequently they are sent. Some coffee makers, printers, and washing machines can even use Wi-Fi and special sensors to automatically place orders when supplies run low.

While automation can play a key role in keeping a consumer in the loyalty loop, if used incorrectly, it can cause customer loss. For example, when a problem arises and you call customer service, you go through a long series of automated prompts. Receiving an automated answer that doesn't fully answer the question can cause customer loyalty to decline quickly. A survey based in the United States found that 58 percent of customers feel that good customer service is more important than price and that customers are often willing to pay higher prices to receive good customer service.[29]

13_Phunkod/Shutterstock.com

Researchers have found two loyalty levels among customers: the satisfied and the committed.[30] The satisfied are those who buy regularly, often out of habit, because they are satisfied with the brand's performance over a long period. With consistently good experiences, they perceive the brand to be familiar, easy to buy, and dependable. The brand has become a comfortable habit, and there is no reason to change. For some low-involvement products, the satisfied are the core loyalty group.

The committed have a more intense and involved relationship with the brand. They are more likely to have an emotional attachment, to receive self-expressive benefits, and to have a use experience that goes beyond the functional. They are also more likely to be brand supporters, even telling others about the brand and its use experience.

The satisfied group can be represented by the phrase "one of my favorite brands," which reflects satisfaction and a lack of motivation to change to another brand. The "committed" group can be represented by the phrase "I can't imagine living without," which suggests that there is a functional or emotional attachment that is so intense that the absence of the brand would be upsetting.

Research has identified specific brands that are frequently ranked the highest in terms of both customer satisfaction and customer commitment. Some of the top brands among the high customer satisfaction group include Chewy, Etsy, Gap, and Costco.[31] Top among the high customer commitment group include Amazon, Apple, Instagram, and Nike.[32]

The objective of companies is to maintain lifetime customers, whether they are satisfied or committed loyal customers. Yet, in some industries, heavy competition and perhaps customer dissatisfaction results in people switching companies and/or brands. When a significant number of customers is switching firms or products, it is called **churning**.

---

churning when a significant number of customers are switching brands

In the wireless industry, T-Mobile offers a reimbursement of up to $650 per line to cover early termination fees to customers who are willing to make a switch from another service provider, while Verizon offers a reimbursement of up to $500. This approach creates churn, which destroys customer loyalty and increases competitiveness within an industry.[33]

Yet, firms have begun to realize that lost customers may not be "dead opportunities." Sometimes, exceptional promotional offers can win them back. SiriusXM, for example, offers "free listening" for a period to lost customers in an attempt to regain their business. Once a person has returned, companies should create a proactive strategy of reaching out to these customers to ensure their satisfaction with the product or service. For example, an email stating "we are glad you're back!" followed by a short questionnaire covering reasons for the initial departure and current return and what could be done to improve their satisfaction will provide retention strategies.

6-5b Factors Affecting Consumer Decision Making

Whether framed as the traditional consumer decision-making process or the consumer decision journey, it is important to understand that consumer decision making does not occur in a vacuum. On the contrary, underlying cultural, social, individual, and psychological factors strongly influence the decision process. These factors have an effect from the time a consumer perceives a stimulus and considers the

---

culture the set of values, norms, attitudes, and other meaningful symbols that shape human behavior and the artifacts, or products, of that behavior as they are transmitted from one generation to the next

---

product or service through postpurchase evaluation. Cultural factors, which include culture and values, subculture, and social class, exert a broad influence over consumer decision making. Social factors sum up the social interactions between a consumer and influential groups of people, such as reference groups, opinion leaders, and family members. Individual factors, which include gender, age, household life-cycle stage, personality, self-concept, and lifestyle, are unique to each individual and play a major role in the type of products and services consumers want. Psychological factors determine how consumers perceive and interact with their environments and influence the ultimate decisions they make. These factors include perception, motivation, and learning. Figure 6.3 summarizes these influences, and the following sections cover each in more detail.

6-6 Cultural Influences on Consumer Buying Decisions

6-6 Describe the cultural factors that affect consumer buying decisions

---

Of all the factors that affect consumer decision making, cultural factors exert the broadest and deepest influence. Marketers must understand the way people's culture and its accompanying values, as well as their subculture and social class, influence their buying behavior.

6-6a Culture and Values

Culture is the set of values, norms, attitudes, and other meaningful symbols that shape human behavior and the artifacts, or products, of that behavior as they are

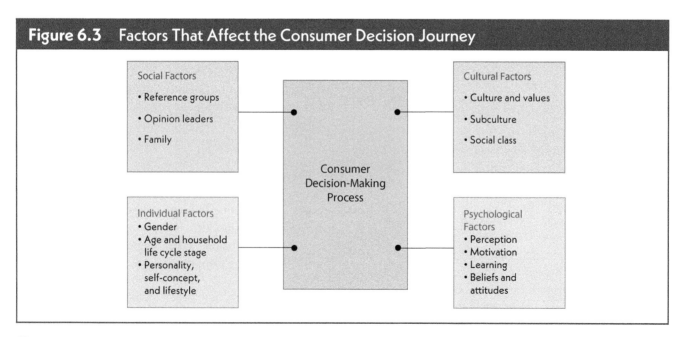

Figure 6.3   Factors That Affect the Consumer Decision Journey

Social Factors
- Reference groups
- Opinion leaders
- Family

Cultural Factors
- Culture and values
- Subculture
- Social class

Consumer Decision-Making Process

Individual Factors
- Gender
- Age and household life cycle stage
- Personality, self-concept, and lifestyle

Psychological Factors
- Perception
- Motivation
- Learning
- Beliefs and attitudes

transmitted from one generation to the next. It is the essential character of a society that distinguishes it from other cultural groups. The underlying elements of every culture are the values, language, myths, customs, rituals, and laws that guide the behavior of the people.

Culture is pervasive. Cultural values and influences are the ocean in which individuals swim, and yet most are completely unaware that it is there. What people eat, how they dress, what they think and feel, and what language they speak are all dimensions of culture. Culture encompasses all the things consumers do without conscious choice because their culture's values, customs, and rituals are ingrained in their daily habits.

Culture is functional. Human interaction creates values and prescribes acceptable behavior for each culture. By establishing common expectations, culture gives order to society. Sometimes, these expectations are enacted into laws. For example, drivers in American culture must stop at a red light. Other times, these expectations are taken for granted: many convenience stores and hospitals are open 24 hours, whereas banks are open only during "bankers' hours," typically nine in the morning until five in the afternoon.

Culture is learned. Consumers are not born knowing the values and norms of their society. Instead, they must learn from family and friends what is acceptable. Children learn the values that will govern their behavior from parents, teachers, and peers. Members of American society learn to shake hands when they greet someone, to drive on the right-hand side of the road, and that burping in public is rude. In China, however, burping after a meal is seen as a compliment to the chef. In Brazil, football (referred to in American culture as soccer) is an important part of the culture and people, even strangers, often greet each other with a hug. People in Indian culture, on the other hand, often greet one another with a Namaste, which is a slight bow with one's hands placed together, and tend to enjoy a game of cricket.

Culture is dynamic. It adapts to changing needs and an evolving environment. The rapid growth of technology in today's world has accelerated the rate of cultural change. American culture is beginning to tell us when it is okay to send a text message and when it is considered impolite. Assume that you are on a first date with someone in a nice, romantic restaurant, and your date is talking to you about their favorite things to do. Pulling out your smartphone to check a text will probably lead to a very short date. Cultural norms will continue to evolve because of our need for social patterns that solve problems.

The most defining element of a culture is its values. Recall that *value* can refer to an enduring belief shared by a society that a specific mode of conduct is personally or socially preferable to another. People's value systems have a great effect on their consumer behavior. Consumers with similar value systems tend to react alike to prices and other marketing-related inducements. Values also correspond to consumption

patterns. For example, Americans tend to live a fast-paced lifestyle and place a high value on convenience. This value has created lucrative markets for products such as breakfast bars, energy bars, and nutrition bars that allow consumers to eat on the go. The French lifestyle, in contrast, is much more leisurely and members of this culture value slowing down to truly enjoy experiences. A traditional family meal in France can last more than two hours! In China, harmony is highly valued, so buildings are designed in a manner that achieves harmony and balance in the space, referred to as feng shui. Values can also influence consumers' television viewing habits or the magazines they read. For instance, people who strongly object to violence avoid crime shows and vegetarians avoid cooking magazines that feature numerous meat-based recipes.

6-6b Subculture

A culture can be divided into subcultures on the basis of demographic characteristics, geographic regions, national and ethnic background, political beliefs, and religious beliefs. A **subculture** is a homogeneous group of people who share elements of the overall culture, as well as cultural elements unique to their own group. Within subcultures, people's attitudes, values, and purchase decisions are even more similar than they are within the broader culture. Subcultural differences may result in considerable variation within a culture in what, how, when, and where people buy goods and services.

Once marketers identify subcultures, they can design special marketing to serve their needs. The growing Hispanic population in the United States has made South and Central American subcultures a prime focus for many companies. For example, recognizing the large Hispanic population presence in Houston, Texas, McDonald's recently launched an advertising campaign that featured El Chapulín Colorado, a popular television character in U.S.-Hispanic households. McDonald's was able to create a campaign that was highly relevant and meaningful specifically to Hispanic Americans, which led to a very positive consumer response.[34]

In the United States alone, countless subcultures can be identified. Many are concentrated geographically. Cajuns are located in the bayou regions of southern Louisiana. Many Hispanic people live in states bordering Mexico, whereas the majority of Chinese, Japanese, and Korean Americans are found on the West Coast. Other subcultures are geographically dispersed. Computer hackers, hippies, Harley-Davidson bikers, military families, and university professors may be found throughout the country. Yet they have identifiable attitudes, values, and needs that distinguish them from the larger culture.

---

subculture a homogeneous group of people who share elements of the overall culture as well as unique elements of their own group

6-6c Social Class

The United States, like other societies, has a social class system. A **social class** is a group of people who are considered nearly equal in status or community esteem, who regularly socialize among themselves both formally and informally, and who share behavioral norms.

Several techniques have been used to measure social class, and several criteria have been used to define it. One view of contemporary U.S. status structure is shown in Table 6.2.

As you can see from Table 6.2, the upper and upper middle classes comprise the small segment of affluent and wealthy Americans. In terms of consumer buying patterns, the affluent are more likely to own their own homes and purchase new cars and trucks and are less likely to smoke. The very rich flex their financial muscles by spending more on vacation homes, jewelry, vacations and cruises, and housekeeping and gardening services. The most affluent consumers are more likely to attend art auctions and galleries, dance performances, operas, the theater, museums, concerts, and sporting events. What types of things do the wealthiest of the wealthy buy? In 2022, Rolls-Royce introduced a one-of-a-kind car called the "Boat Tail." You can't buy one because this car was created for one specific buyer. It is a two-door four-seater with a "hosting suite" in the back of the car that features a dining set, drink cooler and good heater—an entertainer's dream car. The price? Only

The type of products and brands that consumers buy are influenced by their culture and values.

$21 million! The owner is a car collector who displays his car collection in a private museum.[35]

The majority of Americans today define themselves as middle class, regardless of their actual income or educational attainment. This phenomenon most likely occurs because working-class Americans tend to aspire to the middle-class lifestyle, while some of those who do achieve some affluence call themselves middle class as a matter of principle.

The working class is a distinct subset of the middle class. Interest in organized labor is one of the most common attributes among the working class. This group often rates job security as the most important reason for taking a job. The working-class person depends heavily on relatives and the community for economic and emotional support.

Lifestyle distinctions between the social classes are greater than the distinctions within a given class. The most significant difference between the classes occurs between the middle and low income, where there is a major shift in

---

social class a group of people in a society who are considered nearly equal in status or community esteem, who regularly socialize among themselves both formally and informally, and who share behavioral norms

---

Table 6.2 U.S. Income Groups

Upper Income Bracket		
Upper-income bracket	1%	People whose investment decisions shape the national economy; income mostly from assets, earned or inherited; university connections
Upper-middle-income bracket	14%	Upper-level managers, professionals, owners of medium-sized businesses; well-to-do, stay-at-home homemakers who decline occupational work by choice; college educated; family income well above national average
Middle Income Bracket		
Middle-income bracket	33%	Middle-level white-collar, top-level blue-collar; education past high school typical; income somewhat above national average; loss of manufacturing jobs has reduced the population of this class
Working-income bracket	32%	Middle-level blue-collar, lower-level white-collar; income below national average; largely working in skilled or semi-skilled service jobs
Lower Income Bracket		
Low-income bracket	11–12%	Low-paid service workers and operatives; some high school education; below mainstream in living standard; crime and hunger are daily threats
Under-income bracket	8–9%	People who are not regularly employed and receive government assistance; little schooling; living standard below poverty line

Adrian Dennis/AFP/Getty Images

lifestyles. Members of the low-income bracket have annual incomes at or below the poverty level—$13,590 for individuals and $27,750 for families of four (as defined by the federal government).[36]

Social class is typically measured as a combination of occupation, income, education, wealth, and other variables. For instance, affluent upper-class consumers are more likely to be salaried executives or self-employed professionals with at least an undergraduate degree. Working-class or middle-class consumers are more likely to be hourly service workers or blue-collar employees with only a high school education. Educational attainment, however, seems to be the most reliable indicator of a person's social and economic status. Those with college degrees or graduate degrees are more likely to fall into the upper classes, while those with some college experience fall closest to traditional concepts of the middle class.

Marketers are interested in social class for two main reasons. First, social class often indicates which medium to use for promotion. Suppose an insurance company seeks to sell its policies to middle-class families. It might advertise during the local evening news because middle-class families tend to watch more television than other classes do. If the company wanted to sell more policies to upscale individuals, it might place an ad in a business publication like *The Wall Street Journal*. The internet, long the domain of more educated and affluent families, has become an increasingly important advertising outlet for advertisers hoping to reach blue-collar workers.

Second, knowing which products appeal to which social classes can help marketers determine where to best distribute their products. Affluent Americans, one-fifth of the U.S. population, spend more of their discretionary income on one-of-a-kind items. Many lower-income consumers patronize retailers such as Walmart that sell smaller packages of items because customers do not have enough cash to buy more standard-size products. Walmart, of course, sells large economy sizes at low, competitive prices.

6-7 Social Influences on Consumer Buying Decisions

6-7 Describe the social factors that affect consumer buying decisions

Many consumers seek out the opinions of others to reduce their search and evaluation effort or uncertainty, especially as the perceived risk of the decision increases. Consumers may also seek out others' opinions for guidance on new products or services, products with image-related attributes, or products for which attribute information is lacking or uninformative. Specifically, consumers interact socially with reference groups, opinion leaders, and family members to obtain product information and decision approval.

6-7a Reference Groups

People interact with many reference groups. A **reference group** consists of all the formal and informal groups that influence the buying behavior of an individual. Consumers may use products or brands to identify with or become a member of a group. They learn from observing how members of their reference groups consume, and they use the same criteria to make their own consumer decisions.

Reference groups can be categorized very broadly as either direct or indirect (refer to Figure 6.4). Direct reference groups are membership groups that touch people's lives directly. They can be either primary or secondary. A **primary membership group** includes all groups with which people interact regularly in an informal manner, such as family, friends, members of social media, such as Instagram, and coworkers. Today, they may also communicate by email, text messages, Facebook, Zoom, or other social media as well as face to face. In contrast, people associate with a **secondary membership group** less consistently and more formally. These groups might include social clubs, professional groups, and religious groups.

Consumers also are influenced by many indirect, non-membership reference groups to which they do not belong.

---

reference group all of the formal and informal groups in society that influence an individual's purchasing behavior

primary membership group a reference group with which people interact regularly in an informal, face-to-face manner, such as family, friends, and coworkers

secondary membership group a reference group with which people associate less consistently and more formally than a primary membership group, such as a club, professional group, or religious group

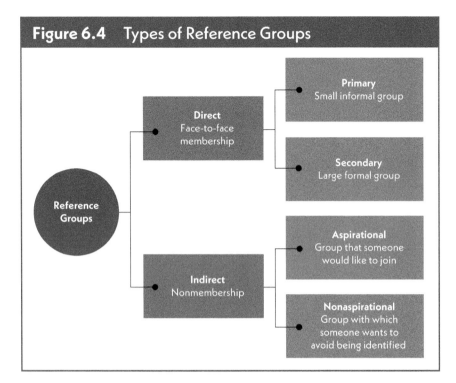

Figure 6.4 Types of Reference Groups

Reference Groups

Direct
Face-to-face
membership

Primary
Small informal group

Secondary
Large formal group

Indirect
Nonmembership

Aspirational
Group that someone
would like to join

Nonaspirational
Group with which
someone wants to
avoid being identified

An **aspirational reference group** is a group a person would like to join. To join an aspirational group, a person must at least conform to the norms of that group. (A **norm** consists of the values and attitudes deemed acceptable by the group.) Thus, a person who wants to be elected to public office may begin to wear suits more often, as other politicians do. They may go to many of the restaurants and social engagements that city and business leaders attend and try to play a role that is acceptable to voters and other influential people.

Nonaspirational reference groups, or *dissociative groups,* influence our behavior when we try to maintain distance from them. A consumer may avoid buying some types of clothing or cars, going to certain restaurants or stores, or even buying a home in a certain neighborhood to avoid being associated with a particular group. The Centers for Disease Control and Prevention (CDC) has helped more than 1 million U.S. adults stop smoking through the use of nonaspirational groups in its "Tips From Former Smokers" advertising campaign. These ads feature powerful stories about the detrimental effects that smoking has had on real smokers' health, such as developing heart disease and cancer. The campaign aims to motivate viewers to dissociate from the "smokers"

---

aspirational reference group a group that someone would like to join

norm a value or attitude deemed acceptable by a group

nonaspirational reference group a group with which an individual does not want to associate

opinion leader an individual who influences the opinions of others

group, by stopping smoking, so that they do not end up with the same health ailments as those featured in the ads.[37]

Reference groups are particularly powerful in influencing the clothes people wear, the cars they drive, the electronics they use, the activities they participate in, the foods they eat, and the luxury goods they purchase. In short, the activities, values, and goals of reference groups directly influence consumer behavior. For marketers, reference groups have three important implications: (1) they serve as information sources and influence perceptions; (2) they affect an individual's aspiration levels; and (3) their norms either constrain or stimulate consumer behavior.

6-7b Opinion Leaders

Reference groups and social media groups (e.g., your friends or social media influencers on Instagram) frequently include individuals known as group leaders, or **opinion leaders**—persons who influence others. Obviously, it is important for marketing managers to persuade such people to purchase their goods or services. They are often the most influential, informed, plugged-in, and vocal members of society.

Opinion leaders can be someone who is an expert in a particular field, such as an advertisement for Colgate toothpaste stating that four out of five dentists recommend their brand, but marketers also often use movie stars, sports figures, and social media influencers to promote products, hoping they are appropriate opinion leaders. The effectiveness of celebrity endorsements varies, though, depending largely on how credible and attractive the spokesperson is and how familiar people are with them. Endorsements are most likely to succeed if a reasonable association between the spokesperson and the product can be established.

Football star Patrick Mahomes, quarterback of the Kansas City Chiefs, signed a ten-year contract for $450 million in 2022. In addition, he has endorsement deals with Adidas, State Farm, Bose, Essentia water, Oakley, and Head and Shoulders shampoo.[38]

Increasingly, marketers are looking to social media to find opinion leaders, but the sheer volume of posts and platforms makes determining true opinion leaders challenging. So, marketers are focusing their attention on platforms such as Instagram and TikTok, because those sites better identify the social trends that are shaping consumer behavior. With their unprecedented ability to network and communicate with each other, people often rely on each other's opinions more than marketing messages when making purchase decisions.

NFL star Patrick Mahomes popularity has led to many lucrative endorsement deals.

MAHOMES 1 IMPACT FLX
Train like a champion.

Decision-making roles among family members tend to vary significantly, depending on the type of item purchased. Family members assume a variety of roles in the purchase process. *Initiators* suggest, initiate, or plant the seed for the purchase process. The initiator can be any member of the family. For example, a younger child in the family might initiate the product search by asking for a new bicycle as a birthday present. *Influencers* are members of the family whose opinions are valued. In our example, a parent or guardian might function as a price-range watchdog, an influencer whose main role is to veto or approve price ranges. Another sibling in the family may give their opinion on certain makes of bicycles. The *decision maker* is the family member who actually makes the decision to buy or not to buy. For example, a parent or guardian is likely to choose the final brand and model of bicycle to buy after seeking further information from the child about cosmetic features such as color and then imposing additional criteria of their own, such as durability and safety. The *purchaser* (probably a parent or guardian) is the one who actually exchanges money for the product. Finally, the *consumer* is the actual user—in this case, the child.

Marketers should consider family purchase situations along with the distribution of consumer and decision-maker roles among family members. Ordinarily, marketing views the individual as both decision maker and consumer. Family marketing adds several other possibilities: sometimes more than one family member or all family members are involved in the decision, sometimes only children are involved in the decision, sometimes more than one consumer is involved, and sometimes the decision maker and the consumer are different people, such is the case in our previous bike purchase example.

Moreover, social media are a popular way for people to communicate their opinions. TikTok is the most popular social media platform for influencer marketing, utilized by 56 percent of brands that use influencer marketing campaigns, followed by Instagram (used by 51 percent) and then Facebook (42 percent).[39] Fast Food chain KFC recently teamed up with popular TikTok influencers to bring awareness to the launch of a new chicken sandwich. One of the most popular posts from the campaign featured Lili Hayes, a 73-year-old mom with nearly 4 million TikTok followers, enjoying the new sandwich while dressed up as Colonel Sanders. Overall, videos from the campaign received over 220 million views and significantly increased sales of KFC's new sandwich, even causing it to sell out at multiple locations.[40]

6-7c Family

The family is the most important social institution for many consumers, strongly influencing values, attitudes, self-concept, and buying behavior. For example, a family that strongly values good health will have a grocery list distinctly different from that of a family that views every dinner as a gourmet event. Moreover, the family is responsible for the **socialization process**, the passing down of cultural values and norms to children. Children learn by observing their parent or guardians' consumption patterns, so they tend to shop in similar patterns.

6-7d Individual Differences in Susceptibility to Social Influences

Social influence plays an important role in consumer behavior, but not all persons are equally influenced in their purchase decisions. Some have a strong need to build the images others have of them by buying products used by other members of their reference groups. Seeking approval of others through the "correct" product ownership is very important to these consumers. Seeking approval is particularly true for conspicuous items (those that others can easily see) such as clothes, jewelry,

Family decisions can range from one family member making a decision, some members, or all persons in the family involved in the purchase decision.

socialization process how cultural values and norms are passed down to children

cars, and even mobile devices. These individuals have a strong desire to avoid negative impressions in public settings.

Consumers differ in their feelings of connectedness to other consumers. A consumer with a **separated self-schema** perceives themself as distinct and separate from others. A person with a **connected self-schema** perceives themself as an integral part of a group. Research has found that individuals who feel connected respond more favorably to advertisements that promote group belonging and cohesion.

The influence of other people on how a consumer behaves is strongest when that consumer knows or feels that they are being watched. Researchers have found this factor to be especially true when individuals are consuming or buying personal products. Some people will not buy memberships to athletic clubs because they don't want to work out with (or even around) a group of people. They fear how they may appear to others.

Source: NFL Enterprises LLC

in gender neutral advertising. For example, the NFL challenged the assumption that football is only for males with its "Run With It" ad that played during the 2023 Super Bowl. This ad showcased the league's support for more women across the world participating in football leagues and was rated as one of the top five ads of that Super Bowl by *USA Today*'s Ad Meter rankings.[41] Cosmetics brand like CoverGirl and Maybelline now feature both males and females in their campaigns, while Nike featured the first transgender Olympian, cyclist Chris Mosier, in an advertising campaign and luxury brand Louis Vuitton created an entire advertising campaign around gender fluidity.

6-8 Individual Influences on Consumer Buying Decisions

6-8 Describe the individual factors that affect consumer buying decisions

While individuality impacts a person's susceptibility to social influences, factors such as gender, age, life-cycle stage, personality, self-concept, and lifestyle also play important roles in consumer decision making. Individual characteristics are generally stable over the course of one's life. For instance, the act of changing personality or lifestyle requires a complete reorientation of one's life. In the case of age and life-cycle stage, these changes occur gradually over time.

6-8a Gender

Physiological differences across genders can result in different needs, although societal shifts in gender identities are redefining the meaning of the term gender and the impact that any differences may play in purchase decisions is lessening. More marketers are challenging gender stereotypes in their communication campaigns and/or engaging

---

separated self-schema a perspective whereby a consumer perceives themself as distinct and separate from others

connected self-schema a perspective whereby a consumer perceives themself as an integral part of a group

6-8b Age and Household Life-Cycle Stage

A consumer's age and household life-cycle stage can have a significant impact on their behavior. How old a consumer is generally indicates what products they may be interested in purchasing. Consumer tastes in food, clothing, cars, furniture, and recreation are often age related.

Related to a person's age is their place in the household life cycle. As Chapter 8 explains in more detail, the *household life cycle* is an orderly series of stages through which consumers' attitudes and behavioral tendencies evolve through maturity, experience, and changing income and status. Marketers often define their target markets in terms of household life cycle, such as "young singles," "young married couples with children," and "middle-aged couples without children." For instance, young singles spend more than average on alcoholic beverages, education, and entertainment. New parents typically increase their spending on healthcare, clothing, housing, and food and decrease their spending on alcohol, education, and transportation. Households with older children spend more on food, entertainment, personal care products, and education, as well as cars and gasoline. After their children leave home, spending by older couples on vehicles and healthcare typically increases. For instance, the presence of children in the home is the most significant determinant of the type of vehicle that's driven off the new car lot. Parents are the ultimate need-driven car consumers, requiring larger cars and trucks to haul their children and all their belongings. It comes as no surprise, then, that for all households with children, SUVs rank either first or second among new-vehicle purchases, followed by minivans.

Marketers should also be aware of the many different types of life-cycle paths that are common today and provide insights into the needs and wants of such consumers as divorced parents, lifelong singles, and couples that choose to not have children. In the 1980s, married couples with children under the age of 18 accounted for about 60 percent of American households. Today, such families make up only 40 percent of all households. Thus, life cycles are evolving due to broader societal changes, so marketers need to ensure this change is reflected in their marketing strategies and communications.

Single Parents

Careers often create a *poverty of time* for single parents. To cope with the dual demands of a career and raising children, single parents are always on the lookout for time-saving products like quick-preparation foods and no-iron clothing. Rightly so, more and more marketers are catering to the single-parent market.

Life Events

Another way to look at the life cycle is to look at major events in one's life over time. Life-changing events can occur at any time. A few examples are death of a spouse, moving, birth or adoption of a child, retirement, job loss, divorce, and marriage. Typically, such events are quite stressful, and consumers will often take steps to minimize that stress. Many times, life-changing events will mean new consumption patterns. For example, the birth or adoption of a new child means purchasing new types of product like diapers, bottles, and cribs. Someone moving to a different city will need a new dentist, grocery store, auto service center, and doctor, among other things. Marketers realize that life events often mean a chance to gain a new customer. The Welcome Wagon helps people who have recently relocated settle into their new area by sending them coupons and advertisements for local businesses in the mail or via email. And when you put your home on the market, you will quickly start receiving flyers from moving companies promising a great price on moving your household goods.

6-8c Personality, Self-Concept, and Lifestyle

Each consumer has a unique personality. **Personality** is a broad concept that can be thought of as a way of organizing and grouping how an individual typically reacts to situations. Thus, personality combines psychological makeup and environmental forces. It includes people's underlying dispositions, especially their most dominant characteristics. Although personality is one of the least useful concepts in the study of consumer behavior, some marketers believe personality influences the types and brands of products purchased. For instance, the type of car, clothes, or jewelry a consumer buys may reflect one or more personality traits.

Self-concept, or self-perception, is how consumers perceive themselves. Self-concept includes attitudes, perceptions, beliefs, and self-evaluations. Although self-concept may change, the change is often gradual. Through self-concept, people define their identity, which in turn provides for consistent and coherent behavior.

Self-concept combines the **ideal self-image** (the way an individual would like to be perceived) and the **real self-image** (the way an individual actually perceives themself). Generally, we try to raise our real self-image toward our ideal (or at least narrow the gap). Consumers seldom buy products that jeopardize their self-image. For example, someone who perceives themself as a trendsetter would not buy clothing that does not project a contemporary image.

Human behavior depends largely on self-concept. Because consumers want to protect their identity as individuals, the products they buy, the stores they patronize, the social media they use, and the credit cards they carry support their self-image. No other product quite reflects a person's self-image as much as the car they drive. For example, many young consumers do not like family sedans like the Honda Accord or Toyota Camry and say they would buy one for their parents but not for themselves. Likewise, younger parents may avoid purchasing minivans because they do not want to sacrifice the youthful image they have of themselves just because they have new responsibilities. To help overcome this obstacle, marketers of the Toyota Sienna minivan decided to reposition it as something other than a "parent car." Several ads in "The Sienna Life" advertising campaign feature groups of friends using the Sienna minivan to take them on an adventure, while another one of the ads features a hip couple driving their minivan through an urban downtown area.

By influencing the degree to which consumers perceive a good or service to be self-relevant, marketers can affect consumers' motivation to learn about, shop for, and buy a certain brand. Marketers also consider self-concept important

---

personality a way of organizing and grouping the consistencies of an individual's reactions to situations

self-concept how consumers perceive themselves in terms of attitudes, perceptions, beliefs, and self-evaluations

ideal self-image the way an individual would like to be perceived

real self-image the way an individual actually perceives themself

Self-concept combines the ideal self-image (the way an individual would like to be perceived) and the real self-image (the way an individual actually perceives themself)

because it helps explain the relationship between individuals' perceptions of themselves and their consumer behavior.

6-9 Psychological Influences on Consumer Buying Decisions

6-9 Describe the psychological factors that affect consumer buying decisions

An individual's buying decisions are further influenced by psychological factors: perception, motivation, and learning. These factors are what consumers use to interact with their world. They are the tools consumers use to recognize their feelings, gather and analyze information, formulate thoughts and opinions, and take action. Unlike the other three influences on consumer behavior, psychological influences can be affected by a person's environment because they are applied on specific occasions. For example, you will perceive different stimuli and process these stimuli in different ways depending on whether you are sitting in class concentrating on the instructor, sitting outside class talking to friends, or sitting in your dorm room streaming a video.

6-9a Perception

The world is full of stimuli. A stimulus is any unit of input affecting one or more of the five senses: sight, smell, taste,

perception the process by which people select, organize, and interpret stimuli into a meaningful and coherent picture

selective exposure a process whereby a consumer notices certain stimuli and ignores others

selective distortion a process whereby a consumer changes or distorts information that conflicts with their feelings or beliefs

touch, and hearing. The process by which we select, organize, and interpret these stimuli into a meaningful and coherent picture is called **perception**. In essence, perception is how we perceive the world around us. We act based on perceptions that may or may not reflect reality. Suppose you are driving to the grocery store, and you see a house with smoke pouring from the roof. Your perception is that the house is on fire, so you quickly stop to warn any occupants and to call 911. As you approach the house, you hear laughter coming from the back yard. As you peek around the corner, you see a family burning a big pile of leaves and the wind carrying the smoke over the roof. There is no house fire. When you get to the grocery store, you see a big, beautiful ripe pineapple and immediately put it in your cart. When you get home, you cut into the pineapple—only to find that it has a rotten core and is inedible. In both cases, you acted based on perceptions that did not reflect reality.

People cannot perceive every stimulus in their environment. Therefore, they use **selective exposure** to decide which stimuli to notice and which to ignore. It is estimated that most Americans are exposed to more than 5,000 ads per day.[42]

The familiarity of an object, contrast, movement, intensity (such as increased volume), and smell are cues that influence perception. Consumers use these cues to identify and define products and brands. Double Tree hotels always have fresh chocolate chip cookies at the reception desk, and the entire area smells like just-baked cookies. For most travelers, this setting cues feelings of warmth and comfort. Cutting-edge consumer research has found that a cluttered, chaotic environment results in consumers spending more. Why does this effect occur? The perception of a cluttered environment impairs self-control. Disorganized surroundings threaten one's sense of personal control, which in turn taxes one's self-regulatory abilities. Researchers have found that cluttered and busy websites with too many communication options (such as forums, Q&A sections, chat rooms, and email) actually reduce the average total amount purchased from the retailer. It seems people will spend more time gathering information and less time shopping.[43]

The shape of a product's packaging, such as Coca-Cola's signature contour bottle, can lead consumers to be more likely to perceive a product. Color is another cue, and it plays a key role in consumers' perceptions. Packaged foods manufacturers use color to trigger unconscious associations for grocery shoppers who typically make their shopping decisions in the blink of an eye. Think of the red-and-white Campbell's soup can and the green-and-white Green Giant frozen vegetable box, for example.

Two other concepts closely related to selective exposure are selective distortion and selective retention. **Selective distortion** occurs when consumers change or distort information that conflicts with their feelings or beliefs. For example, suppose a college student buys a Microsoft Surface Go tablet. After the purchase, if the student gets new information about an alternative brand, such as a Samsung Galaxy Tab, they may distort the information to make it more consistent with the prior view that the Microsoft Surface Go is just as good as the Samsung Galaxy Tab, if not better. Business travelers who are Executive Platinum frequent flyers on American Airlines may distort or discount information about the quality of United Airlines' business class service. The frequent flyer may think to themselves, "Yes, the service is okay, but the seats are uncomfortable, and the planes are always late."

Selective retention is remembering only information that supports personal feelings or beliefs. The consumer forgets all information that may be inconsistent. After reading a pamphlet that contradicts one's political beliefs, for instance, a person may forget many of the points outlined in it. Similarly, consumers may see a news report on suspected illegal practices by their favorite retail store but soon forget the reason the store was featured on the news.

Which stimuli will be perceived often depends on the individual. People can be exposed to the same stimuli under identical conditions but perceive them very differently. For example, two people viewing a television commercial may have different interpretations of the advertising message. One person may be thoroughly engrossed by the message and become highly motivated to buy the product. Thirty seconds after the ad ends, the second person may not be able to recall the content of the message or even the product advertised.

Marketing Implications of Perception

Marketers must recognize the importance of cues, or signals, in consumers' perception of products. Marketing managers first identify the important attributes, such as price or quality, that the targeted consumers want in a product and then design signals to communicate these attributes. For example, consumers will pay more for candy in expensive-looking foil packages. But shiny labels on wine bottles signify less expensive wines; dull labels indicate more expensive wines. Marketers also often use price as a signal to consumers that the product is of higher quality than competing products. Of course, brand names send signals to consumers. The brand names of Supersmile toothpaste, Naturtint hair color, and Caress moisturizing soap, for example, identify important product qualities. Names chosen for search engines and sites on the internet, such as Yahoo! and Amazon, are intended to convey excitement and intensity and vastness.

Consumers also associate quality and reliability with certain brand names. Companies watch their brand identity closely, in large part because a strong link has been established between perceived brand value and customer

Google is consistently recognized as one of the most valuable brands in the world.

loyalty. Brand names that consistently enjoy high perceived value from consumers include Disney, Apple, Mercedes-Benz, and Google. Naming a product after a place can also add perceived value by association. Brand names using the words Santa Fe, Dakota, or Texas convey a sense of openness, freedom, and youth, but products named after other locations might conjure up images of pollution and crime. Marketing managers are also interested in the *threshold level of perception*, the minimum difference in a stimulus that the consumer will notice. This concept is sometimes called the "just-noticeable difference." For example, how much would Apple have to drop the price of its 16-inch MacBook Pro before consumers perceived it as a bargain—$100? $300? $500? Alternatively, how much could Hershey shrink its milk chocolate bar before consumers noticed that it was smaller but selling for the same price?

Besides changing such stimuli as price, package size, and volume, marketers can change the product or attempt to reposition its image. But marketers must be careful when adding features. How many new services will discounter Target need to add before consumers perceive it as a full-service department store? How many sporty features will General Motors have to add to a basic two-door sedan before consumers start perceiving it as a sports car?

Marketing managers who intend to do business in global markets should be aware of how foreign consumers perceive their products. For instance, in Japan, product labels are often written in English or French, even though they may not translate into anything meaningful. Many Japanese associate foreign words on product labels with the exotic, the expensive, and high quality.

---

selective retention a process whereby a consumer remembers only that information that supports their personal beliefs

6-9b Motivation

By studying motivation, marketers can analyze the major forces influencing consumers to buy or not buy products. When you buy a product, you usually do so to fulfill some kind of need. These needs become motives when they are aroused sufficiently. For instance, suppose this morning you were hungry before class and noticed that you needed to eat something. In response to that need, you stopped at Panera Bread for a breakfast sandwich and coffee. In other words, you were motivated by hunger to stop at Panera Bread. A **motive** is the driving force that causes a person to take action to satisfy specific needs.

Why are people driven by particular needs at particular times? One theory is **Maslow's hierarchy of needs**, illustrated in Figure 6.5, which arranges needs in ascending order of importance: physiological, safety, social, esteem, and self-actualization. As a person fulfills one need, a higher-level need becomes more important.

The most basic human needs—that is, the needs for food, water, and shelter—are *physiological*. Because they are essential to survival, these needs must be satisfied first. Ads showing a juicy hamburger or a runner gulping down Gatorade after a marathon are examples of appeals to satisfy the physiological needs of hunger and thirst.

Safety needs include security and freedom from pain and discomfort. Marketers sometimes appeal to consumers' fears and anxieties about safety and security to sell their products. For example, one of Allstate's most popular advertising campaigns features a character referred to as 'Mayhem,' who causes unexpected damage to people's property. The tagline of the commercials is "With Allstate, you're protected from mayhem—like me," indicating that the insurance company can help consumers to feel secure and not have to worry about unexpected property damage.[44] Some companies or industries advertise to allay consumer fears. For example, in the wake of the September 11, 2001, terrorist attacks, the airline industry found itself having to conduct an image campaign to reassure consumers about the safety of air travel.

After physiological and safety needs have been fulfilled, *social needs*—especially love and a sense of belonging—become the focus. Love includes acceptance by one's peers, as well as sex and romantic love. Marketing managers

---

motive a driving force that causes a person to take action to satisfy specific needs

Maslow's hierarchy of needs a method of classifying human needs and motivations into five categories in ascending order of importance: physiological, safety, social, esteem, and self-actualization

learning a process that creates changes in behavior, immediate or expected, through experience and practice

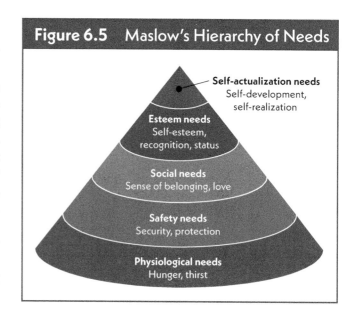

Figure 6.5 Maslow's Hierarchy of Needs

- **Self-actualization needs** — Self-development, self-realization
- **Esteem needs** — Self-esteem, recognition, status
- **Social needs** — Sense of belonging, love
- **Safety needs** — Security, protection
- **Physiological needs** — Hunger, thirst

probably appeal more to this need than to any other. Ads for clothes, cosmetics, and vacation packages suggest that buying the product can bring love.

The next level of needs focus on *esteem needs*. Esteem is acceptance based on one's contribution to the group. *Self-esteem needs* include self-respect and a sense of accomplishment. Esteem needs also include prestige, fame, and recognition of one's accomplishments. Montblanc pens, Porsche automobiles, and Neiman Marcus stores all appeal to esteem needs.

The highest human need is *self-actualization*. It refers to finding self-fulfillment and self-expression, reaching the point in life at which "people are what they feel they should be." Maslow believed that very few people ever attain this level. Even so, advertisements may focus on this type of need. For example, American Express ads convey the message that acquiring an AmEx card is one of the highest attainments in life. The Centurion card, often called simply "the black card," requires a $10,000 initiation fee and carries an annual fee of $5,000.

6-9c Learning

Almost all consumer behavior results from **learning**, which is the process that creates changes in behavior through experience and practice. It is not possible to observe learning directly, but we can infer when it has occurred by a person's actions. For example, suppose you see an advertisement for a new and improved cold medicine. If you go to the store that day and buy that remedy, we infer that you have learned something about the cold medicine.

There are two types of learning: experiential and conceptual. *Experiential learning* occurs when an experience changes your behavior. For example, if the new cold medicine does not relieve your symptoms, you may not buy that brand again. *Conceptual learning*, which is not acquired through direct experience but based on reasoning, is the

The Impact of the COVID-19 Pandemic on Consumer Behavior

For millions of Americans, the COVID-19 pandemic triggered intertwined crises of personal health and personal finance. People were laid off or furloughed because governments were closing workplaces to prevent the virus from spreading. The Coronavirus Aid, Relief, and Economic Security (CARES) Act put cash in the hands of many consumers but did not eliminate the uncertainty about the future. People dramatically reduced most discretionary spending with grave consequences for restaurants and out-of-home entertainment industries such as sporting events. Cancelling vacations meant huge losses for airlines, hotels, and attractions such as Disneyworld. Once COVID-19 restrictions loosened, however, consumers wanted to make up for lost time and the travel industry saw a huge increase in bookings—this behavior has been referred to as "revenge travel." This dramatic increase in consumer travel led to major price increases for airfare and hotels.[45]

The pandemic brought a rapid rise in online purchasing, which has led to a permanent change in how many consumers' shop.

Ninety-two percent of consumers who only began online shopping due to the pandemic converted to primarily shopping online even when in-person stores reopened.[46] Groceries was one of the biggest product categories to see a dramatic increase in online purchasing due to the pandemic. In addition to a higher rate of online shopping, related shopping included a growth in BOLPIS (buy online, pick up in store), curbside pickup, and subscription services.

Having a lot of time at home during quarantines gave many people time to reflect and change their behaviors. Many people decided to try out a new hobby or learn a new skill, such as gardening, to stay busy. Other people started exercising. Sporting goods, musical instruments, gardening equipment, and books all saw drastic increases in sales as people were forced to lockdown at home. Much of these sales were at large retailers such as Amazon and Target, but smaller, personal sellers, such as those that sell through Etsy, also saw a big boost in sales.[47]

---

second type of learning. Assume, for example, that you are standing at a soft drink machine and notice a new diet flavor with an artificial sweetener. Because someone has told you that diet beverages leave an aftertaste, you choose a different drink. You have learned that you would not like this new diet drink without ever trying it.

Reinforcement and repetition boost learning. Reinforcement can be positive or negative. If you see a vendor selling frozen yogurt (stimulus), buy it (response), and find the yogurt to be quite refreshing (reward), your behavior has been positively reinforced. On the other hand, if you buy a new flavor of yogurt and it does not taste good (negative reinforcement), you will not buy that flavor of yogurt again (response). Without positive or negative reinforcement, a person will not be motivated to repeat the behavior pattern or to avoid it. Thus, if a new brand evokes neutral feelings, some marketing activity, such as a price change or an increase in promotion, may be required to induce further consumption. Learning theory is helpful in reminding marketers that concrete and timely strategies are what reinforce desired consumer behavior.

Repetition is a key strategy in promotional campaigns because it can lead to increased learning. Most marketers use repetitious advertising so that consumers will learn what their unique advantage is over the competition. Generally, to heighten learning, advertising messages should be spread out over time rather than clustered together.

A related learning concept useful to marketing managers is **stimulus generalization**. In theory, stimulus generalization occurs when one response is extended to a second stimulus similar to the first. Marketers often use a successful, well-known brand name for a family of products because it gives consumers familiarity with and knowledge about each product in the family. Such brand-name families spur

the introduction of new products and facilitate the sale of existing items. OXO relies on consumers' familiarity with its popular kitchen and household products to sell office and medical supplies; Sony's film division relies on name recognition from its home technology, such as the PlayStation. Clorox bathroom cleaner relies on familiarity with Clorox bleach, and Dove shampoo relies on familiarity with Dove soap. Branding is examined in more detail in Chapter 10.

Another form of stimulus generalization occurs when retailers or wholesalers design their packages to resemble well-known manufacturers' brands. Such imitation conveys the notion that the store brand is as good as the national manufacturer's brand.

The opposite of stimulus generalization is **stimulus discrimination**, which means learning to differentiate among similar products. Consumers may perceive one product as more rewarding or stimulating, even if it is virtually indistinguishable from competitors. For example, some consumers prefer Miller Lite, and others prefer Bud Light.

With some types of products—such as aspirin, gasoline, bleach, and paper towels—marketers rely on promotion to point out brand differences that consumers would otherwise not recognize. This process, called *product differentiation*, is discussed in more detail in Chapter 8. Usually, product differentiation is based on superficial differences. For example, Bayer tells consumers that it is the aspirin "doctors recommend most."

---

stimulus generalization a form of learning that occurs when one response is extended to a second stimulus similar to the first

stimulus discrimination a learned ability to differentiate among similar products

G-Stock Studio/Shutterstock.com

Chapter 7

Business Marketing

Learning Outcomes

After studying this chapter, you will be able to . . .

7-1 Describe business marketing

7-2 Describe trends in B-to-B internet marketing

7-3 Discuss the role of relationship marketing and strategic alliances in business marketing

7-4 Identify the four major categories of business market customers

7-5 Explain the North American Industry Classification System

7-6 Explain the major differences between business and consumer markets

7-7 Describe the seven types of business goods and services

7-8 Discuss the unique aspects of business buying behavior

7-1 What Is Business Marketing?

7-1 Describe business marketing

Business marketing (also called industrial, business-to-business, B-to-B, or B2B marketing) is marketing goods and services to individuals and organizations for purposes other than personal consumption. The sale of a laptop computer to your college or university is an example of business marketing. A **business product**, or **industrial product**, is used to manufacture other goods or services, to facilitate an organization's operations, or to resell to other customers. A **consumer product** is bought to satisfy an individual's personal wants or needs. The key characteristic distinguishing business products from consumer products is intended use, not physical form.

How do you distinguish between a consumer product and a business product? A product that is purchased for personal or family consumption or as a gift is a consumer good. If that same product, such as a laptop computer or a cell phone, is bought for use in a business, it is a business product. Some common items that are sold as both consumer goods and business products are office supplies (e.g., pens, paper, and staple removers). Some items, such as forklifts, are more commonly sold as business products than as consumer goods.

The size of the business market in the United States and most other countries substantially exceeds that of the consumer market. In the business market, a single customer can account for a huge volume of purchases. For example, Apple's purchasing department spends more than $60 billion annually on business products. Procter & Gamble (P&G), Merck, Dell, and Kimberly-Clark each spend more than half of their annual revenue on business products.[1]

Some large firms that produce goods such as steel, computer memory chips, or production equipment market exclusively to business customers. Other firms market to both businesses and consumers. Legend Solar, a solar panel company, initially sold exclusively to homeowners but seized an opportunity for growth when it began marketing its products to businesses. Picky Bars sells energy bars, oatmeal, and granola directly to both consumers and retailers, such as grocery stores, through its website. Many consumers are frequent shoppers at wholesale stores like Costco and Sam's Club, but businesses also purchase products in bulk from these types of stores. Companies that market to both businesses and consumers need to consider what organizational and marketing changes may need to be made to successfully target these different markets.

7-2 Trends in B-to-B Internet Marketing

7-2 Describe trends in B-to-B internet marketing

Over the past decade, marketers have become more and more sophisticated in using the internet. Companies have had to transition from "We have a website because our customer does" to having a site that attracts, interests, satisfies, informs, and retains customers. B-to-B companies are increasingly leveraging the internet as an effective sales and promotion platform (much like B-to-C companies have done for decades). B-to-B companies use the internet in three major ways. First, they use their websites to facilitate communication and orders. Second, they use digital marketing to increase brand awareness. Third, they use digital marketing—primarily in the form of content marketing—to position their businesses as thought leaders and therefore generate sales leads. Companies selling to business buyers face the same challenges as all marketers, including determining the target market and deciding how best to reach it.

Every year, new applications that provide additional information about customers are developed. These applications often also lower costs, increase supply chain efficiency, or enhance customer retention, loyalty, and trust. Increasingly, business customers expect suppliers to know them personally, monitor people's movement within their company, and offer personal interaction through social media, email, and personal mailers. As such, we have understood B-to-B marketers use technology like smartphones and tablets to facilitate orders and enhance customer experiences.

A few years ago, many people thought the internet would eliminate the need for distributors. Why would customers pay a distributor's markup when they could buy directly from the manufacturer with a few mouse clicks? This approach has occurred less frequently than many expected because distributors often perform important functions such as providing credit, aggregating supplies from multiple sources, making deliveries, and processing returns. Many business customers, especially small firms, depend on knowledgeable distributors for information and advice that is not available to them online.

---

business marketing (industrial, business-to-business, B-to-B, or B2B marketing) marketing goods and services to individuals and organizations for purposes other than personal consumption

business product (industrial product) a product used to manufacture other goods or services, to facilitate an organization's operations, or to resell to other customers

consumer product a product bought to satisfy an individual's personal wants or needs

Social media usage has been the most pervasive B-to-B and B-to-C marketing trend in recent years. Most companies use email marketing, search engine optimization, paid search, and display advertising to pull customers to their websites. This field of marketing requires vigilant adjustment to keep track of new applications and platforms, as well as constant evaluation to determine whether these new avenues are beneficial to (or used by) customers. Generally, B-to-C marketers are faster to adopt social media as part of the promotional mix. B-to-B marketers did not initially find the value in these tools. However, that has changed as social media has become more popular.

Content marketing is a strategic marketing approach focused on creating and distributing valuable, relevant, and consistent content. The goal of this content is to attract and retain a clearly defined audience, and ultimately, drive profitable customer action. This strategy has played an important role for B-to-B marketers. Content marketing includes media such as videos, podcasts, webinars, blog posts, white papers, eBooks, slide decks, and more. Sharing valuable insights and interesting content can position a company as a thought leader in an area. A 2022 study by the Content Marketing Institute showed that 73 percent of B-to-B respondents said that they have a content marketing strategy; only 29 percent felt as though their organizations were successful with the content marketing strategy. It was reported that virtual events, webinars, and online courses were the content types that produced the most successful results.[2] Most companies use content marketing to increase brand awareness and generate leads. Increasing engagement comes in a close third. Interestingly, while most B-to-C companies favor Facebook and Instagram as their primary social media platforms, most B-to-B companies perceive LinkedIn as the most beneficial platform through which to distribute content. Regardless of the platform used, the key to social media-based content marketing for B-to-B marketers is to create compelling and useful content for customers. For example, HubSpot and Marketo Engage develop white papers and eBooks on topics such as generating leads through social media for customers and potential customers.

Shopify is an e-commerce platform that provides users tools to help them grow their online businesses. In addition to basic business management tools, such as product sourcing, payment processing, and customer account management, Shopify also offers a number of other resources, such as a business name generator and a logo and slogan maker. Additionally, Shopify offers free courses and guides,

blog posts, and podcasts that can help business owners to succeed with their online business.[3]

As they build reputations in their business areas, many marketers use social media to increase awareness and build relationships and community. Social media platforms like YouTube, LinkedIn, Facebook, and Instagram provide great conversational platforms for doing just that. While building community is important, B-to-B marketers are also using social media to gather leads (as you may have gathered from the HubSpot and Marketo Engage white paper example). Other goals include product promotion, traffic building, search engine optimization (SEO), competitive intelligence and listening, customer feedback and support, and product development.

As platforms such as mobile and streaming video grow, marketers must develop new ways to measure campaign effectiveness. To help marketers with this task, global information and statistical measurement company Nielsen launched Nielsen Digital Ad Ratings, which is designed to provide a more holistic view of how consumers engage with digital media.[4]

According to data collected through this new platform, 40 percent of online advertisement impressions do not reach their intended audience, which is a big waste of money for many companies. Some particularly useful metrics for increasing the success of a social media campaign are awareness, engagement, and conversion. *Awareness* is the attention that social media attracts, such as the number of followers or fans. Awareness is generally used as the first step in the marketing funnel, and social media is often paired with paid digital media like display advertising and text-based ads to increase its effectiveness. *Engagement* refers to the interactions between the brand and the audience, such as comments, reposts, shares, and searches. The engagement is intended to get customers to respond to brand-led posts and to start conversations themselves. *Conversions* occur when action is taken and include everything from downloading a piece of content (like a white paper) to actually making a purchase. Each of these metrics affects the return on investment.

---

content marketing a strategic marketing approach that focuses on creating and distributing content that is valuable, relevant, and consistent

The Top Social Media Tools for B-to-B Marketers

The Content Marketing Institute, CMI, surveyed hundreds of B-to-B marketers regarding their social media usage, and while LinkedIn, Facebook, and Twitter, now known as X, were used by the majority of respondents, LinkedIn was the most used social media tool overall (chosen by 93 percent of respondents). Runners-up were Facebook (80 percent), X (71 percent), YouTube (60 percent), and Instagram (56 percent). LinkedIn is so popular because it drives more traffic and leads than other platforms for B-to-B marketers. The company has only increased its favor among B-to-B marketers by adding new B-to-B-friendly features like sponsored company updates, groups connected to topics, products and services pages, and a thought-leader blogging program.[5]

B-to-B marketers have begun making use of social advertising platforms such as advertisement exchanges on LinkedIn and promoted tweets on X, and many B-to-B marketers are even creating their own blogs. For example, audit and consulting firm Deloitte created an online content hub called Deloitte Insights on which the company uses several different content formats, including blog posts, webcasts, and podcasts, to provide company and industry information to both current and potential customers.[6]

7-3 Relationship Marketing and Strategic Alliances

7-3 Discuss the role of relationship marketing and strategic alliances in business marketing

As explained in Chapter 1, relationship marketing is a strategy that entails seeking and establishing ongoing partnerships with customers. Relationship marketing has become an important business marketing strategy as customers have become more demanding and competition has become more intense. Loyal customers are also more profitable than those who are price sensitive and perceive little or no difference among brands or suppliers.

Relationship marketing is increasingly important, as business suppliers use platforms like Facebook, Instagram, and other social networking sites to advertise themselves to businesses. Social networking sites encourage businesses to shop around and research options for all their needs. This development means that, for many suppliers, retaining their current customers has become a primary focus, whereas acquiring new customers was the focus in the past. Maintaining a steady dialogue between the supplier and the customer is a proven way to gain repeat business.[7]

7-3a Strategic Alliances

A **strategic alliance**, sometimes called a **strategic partnership**, is a cooperative agreement between business firms. Strategic alliances can take the form of licensing or distribution agreements, joint ventures, research and development consortia, and partnerships. They may be between manufacturers, manufacturers and customers, manufacturers and suppliers, and manufacturers and channel intermediaries.

Business marketers form strategic alliances to strengthen operations and better compete. To differentiate its watch from competitors, Apple formed strategic alliances with fashion brands, such as Hermès and Nike, after introducing the Apple Watch to the market. These fashion brands design trendy watchbands that pair with the Apple Watch and allow the product to be sold at high price points. These partnerships have allowed Apple to expand its market to include more fashion-savvy and athletic shoppers who might not purchase the product simply for the high-tech benefits. Because of partnerships like these, Apple has been able to capture 34 percent of the wearable technology market share, making the company the biggest shipper of this type of product.[8]

Sometimes alliance partners are fierce competitors. Take, for example, the partnership between Nestlé, parent company of espresso brand Nespresso, and Starbucks. In 2018, Nestlé and Starbucks formed a global coffee alliance to expand the packaged coffee market and try to make coffee the world's first sustainable agricultural product. This partnership has allowed Starbucks to expand its global market reach and bring its ready-to-drink coffee beverages to new regions, such as Southeast Asia and Latin America. Through the partnership, Nestlé also has the rights to market and distribute Starbucks brand coffee. Additionally, although Starbucks markets its own at-home espresso machines, the partnership allows Starbucks coffee to be manufactured for Nestlé's espresso machines.[9]

Other alliances are formed between companies that operate in completely different industries. For example, John Deere, one of the world's leading agricultural equipment manufacturers, and drone technology company Volocopter recently collaborated to create the VoloDrone, a large agricultural drone that can spray crops with fertilizer or frost-control agents.[10] This technology allows farmers to be more efficient in growing and harvesting crops, which can make farmers more profitable and also allow them to grow more food.

For an alliance to succeed in the long term, it must be built on commitment and trust. **Relationship commitment** means that a firm believes an ongoing relationship with some other firm is so important that it warrants maximum

---

strategic alliance (strategic partnership) a cooperative agreement between business firms

relationship commitment a firm's belief that an ongoing relationship with another firm is so important that the relationship warrants maximum efforts at maintaining it indefinitely

Sometimes alliance partners are from completely different industries.

After Heinz hired the former CEO of Burger King, McDonald's decided to end the 40-year partnership between the two companies.

efforts at maintaining it indefinitely.[11] A perceived breakdown in commitment by one of the parties often leads to a breakdown in the relationship.

Trust exists when one party has confidence in an exchange partner's reliability and integrity.[12] Some alliances fail when participants lack trust in their trading partners. Consider, for example, the fallout between McDonald's and Heinz. The two companies had a partnership for more than 40 years—Heinz supplied ketchup to many of McDonald's restaurants. But when Heinz hired a new CEO, who was also a former CEO of Burger King, one of McDonald's biggest rivals, McDonald's decided to end the partnership. When asked about the reason behind the end of the partnership, McDonald's stated that the main reason was "recent management changes at Heinz."[13] McDonald's felt that it could no longer trust its longtime partner because of Heinz's new ties to one of its main competitors.

The combined effects of the COVID-19 pandemic and tax and tariff conflicts had substantial negative impacts on relationships between the United States and its major trading partners, especially China. These conflicts are still ongoing, and there are no signs of them abating in the near future. Relationship commitments and trust have fallen, leading to shortages and delays in shipping personal protection equipment (PPEs). PPEs such as ventilators, surgical masks, gowns, and shields for healthcare professionals were particularly acute in the first half of 2020. Shortages and shipping delays caused by the pandemic have, however, continued for years in many different industries and are still impacting U.S. companies and consumers. These shortages and delays have added stress to many business alliances, and the efficacy of these trading relationships is being questioned.

---

trust the condition that exists when one party has confidence in an exchange partner's reliability and integrity

keiretsu a network of interlocking corporate affiliates

7-3b Relationships in Other Cultures

Although the terms *relationship marketing* and *strategic alliances* are fairly new and popularized mostly by American business executives and educators, the concepts have long been familiar in other cultures. Businesses in China, Japan, Korea, Mexico, and much of Europe rely heavily on personal relationships.

In Japan, for example, exchange between firms is based on personal relationships that are developed through what is called *amae*, or indulgent dependency. *Amae* is the feeling of nurturing concern for, and dependence on, another. Reciprocity and personal relationships contribute to *amae*. Relationships between companies can develop into a **keiretsu**—a network of interlocking corporate affiliates. Within a *keiretsu*, executives may sit on the boards of their customers or their suppliers. Members of a *keiretsu* trade with each other whenever possible and often engage in joint product development, finance, and marketing activity. For example, all of the major car companies in Japan, as well as all of the major electronic companies, belong to a keiretsu. One of the biggest keiretsu groups is Mitsubishi. The Bank of Tokyo-Mitsubishi is at the top of the keiretsu, with Mitsubishi motors and Mitsubishi Life and Insurance company comprising part of the core group, and companies in other industries, such as insurance, trading, and steel, also serve as integral parts of the keiretsu.[14]

Many firms have found that the best way to compete in Asian countries is to form relationships with Asian firms. Microsoft recently partnered with several Asian companies to expand the availability of its products in China.[15] One such alliance was formed with 21Vianet, a Chinese internet service provider. This alliance allows 21Vianet to operate local Microsoft Office 365 datacenters so that Chinese consumers can access and use Office 365 products and services, all while keeping their data within China.

7-4 Major Categories of Business Customers

7-4 Identify the four major categories of business market customers

The business market consists of four major categories of customers: producers, resellers, governments, and institutions.

7-4a Producers

The producer segment of the business market includes profit-oriented individuals and organizations that use purchased goods and services to produce other products, to incorporate into other products, or to facilitate the organization's daily operations. Examples of producers include construction, manufacturing, transportation, finance, real estate, and foodservice firms. In the United States, more than 13 million firms are in the producer segment of the business market. Some of these firms are small, and others are among the world's largest businesses.

Producers are often called **original equipment manufacturers**, or **OEMs**. This term includes all individuals and organizations that buy business goods and incorporate them into the products they produce for eventual sale to other producers or to consumers. Companies such as General Motors that buy steel, paint, tires, and batteries are said to be OEMs.

7-4b Resellers

The reseller market includes retail and wholesale businesses that buy finished goods and resell them for a profit. A retailer sells mainly to final consumers; wholesalers sell mostly to retailers and other organizational customers. More than 1 million retailers and nearly 700,000 wholesalers are operating in the United States. Consumer product firms like P&G, Kraft Foods, and Coca-Cola sell directly to large retailers and retail chains and through wholesalers to smaller retail units. Retailing is explored in detail in Chapter 14.

Business product distributors are wholesalers that buy business products and resell them to business customers. They often carry thousands of items in stock and employ sales forces to call on business customers. Businesses that wish to buy a gross of pencils or a hundred pounds of fertilizer typically purchase these items from local distributors rather than directly from manufacturers such as Musgrave Pencil Company or Dow Chemical.

7-4c Governments

A third major segment of the business market is government. Government organizations include thousands of federal, state, and local buying units. Collectively, these government

Companies like Kroger are resellers of products offered by P&G and Coca-Cola.

units account for the greatest volume of purchases of any customer category in the United States. The federal government alone spent more than $6 trillion in the 2022 fiscal year.[16]

Marketing to government agencies can be an overwhelming undertaking, but companies that learn how the system works can position themselves to win lucrative contracts and build lasting, rewarding relationships.[17]

Marketing to government agencies traditionally has not been an activity for companies seeking quick returns. The aphorism "hurry up and wait" is often cited as a characteristic of marketing to government agencies. Contracts for government purchases are often put out for bid. Interested vendors submit bids (usually sealed) to provide specified products during a particular time. Sometimes the lowest bidder is awarded the contract. When the lowest bidder is not awarded the contract, strong evidence must be presented to justify the decision. Grounds for rejecting the lowest bid include lack of experience, inadequate financing, or poor past performance. Bidding allows all potential suppliers a fair chance at winning government contracts and helps ensure that public funds are spent wisely.

Federal Government

Name just about any good or service, and chances are that someone in the federal government uses it. The U.S. federal government buys goods and services valued at more than $650 billion per year, making it the world's largest customer.[18]

Although much of the federal government's buying is centralized, no single federal agency contracts for all the government's requirements, and no single buyer

original equipment manufacturers (OEMs) individuals and organizations that buy business goods and incorporate them into the products they produce for eventual sale to other producers or to consumers

in any agency purchases all that the agency needs. We can view the federal government as a combination of several large companies with overlapping responsibilities and thousands of small independent units. One popular source of information about government procurement is the website *SAM.gov*. Until recently, businesses hoping to sell to the federal government found the document (previously called *Commerce Business Daily*) unorganized, and it often arrived too late to be useful. Several online databases now provide timely information about available government contracts and allow contractors to find leads using keyword searches. There are also many different resources available for companies looking to do business with the government. For example, the U.S. Small Business Administration hosts online workshops and webinars such as "Government Contracting 101 Virtual Workshop" and "SBA Federal Contracting Programs."

State, County, and City Government

Selling to states, counties, and cities can be less frustrating for both small and large vendors than selling to the federal government. Paperwork is typically simpler and more manageable than it is at the federal level. But vendors must decide which of the more than 90,000 local government units are likely to buy their wares. State and local buying agencies include school districts, highway departments, government-operated hospitals, housing agencies, and many other departments and divisions.

7-4d Institutions

The fourth major segment of the business market consists of institutions that seek to achieve goals other than the standard business goals of profit, market share, and return on investment. This segment includes schools, hospitals, colleges and universities, churches, labor unions, fraternal organizations, civic clubs, foundations, and other so-called nonbusiness organizations. Some institutional purchasers operate similarly to governments in that the purchasing process is influenced, determined, or administered by government units. Other institutional purchasers are organized more like corporations.[19]

North American Industry Classification System (NAICS) a detailed numbering system developed by the United States, Canada, and Mexico to classify North American business establishments by their main production processes

7-5 The North American Industry Classification System

7-5 Explain the North American Industry Classification System

---

The **North American Industry Classification System (NAICS)** is an industry classification system introduced in 1997 to replace the standard industrial classification system (SIC). NAICS (pronounced *nakes*) is a system for classifying North American business establishments. The system, developed jointly by the United States, Canada, and Mexico, provides a common industry classification system for the United States–Mexico–Canada Agreement (USMCA) partners, previously called the North American Free Trade Agreement (NAFTA). Goods- or service-producing firms that use identical or similar production processes are grouped together.

NAICS is an extremely valuable tool for business marketers engaged in analyzing, segmenting, and targeting markets. Each classification group is relatively homogeneous in terms of raw materials required, components used, manufacturing processes employed, and problems faced. Therefore, if a supplier understands the needs and requirements of a few firms within a classification, requirements can be projected for all firms in that category. The number, size, and geographic dispersion of firms can also be identified. This information can be converted to market potential estimates, market share estimates, and sales forecasts. It can also be used for identifying potential new customers. NAICS codes can help identify prospective users of a supplier's goods and services. The more digits in a code, the more homogeneous the group. A sample of how NAICS codes function is shown in Figure 7.1. For a complete listing of all NAICS codes, refer to the NAICS website.

Figure 7.1   How NAICS Works

The more digits in the NAICS code, the more homogeneous the groups at that level.

NAICS Level	NAICS Code	Description
Sector	51	Information
Subsector	513	Publishing industries
Industry group	5132	Software publishers
Industry	51711	Wired and wireless telecommunications, except satellite
Industry subdivision	513130	Book publishers

7-6 Business Versus Consumer Markets

7-6 Explain the major differences between business and consumer markets

The basic philosophy and practice of marketing are the same whether the customer is a business organization or a consumer. Business markets do, however, have characteristics different from those of consumer markets.

7-6a Demand

Demand for consumer products is quite different from demand in the business market. Unlike consumer demand, business demand is derived, inelastic, joint, and fluctuating.

Derived Demand

The demand for business products is called **derived demand** because organizations buy products to be used in producing their customers' products. For instance, the demand for lumber is derived from, or based on, the demand for new-construction houses. Following the COVID-19 pandemic, the U.S. housing markets saw a huge boom. Houses on the market were receiving multiple offers, housing prices were soaring, and demand for new-construction houses was at an all-time high. The increase in demand for new-construction houses led to an increase in the price of lumber. It was estimated that the increased cost of lumber added an average of over $18,000 to the price of a new-construction house.[20] Because demand is derived, business marketers must carefully monitor demand patterns and changing preferences in final consumer markets, even though their customers are not in those markets. Moreover, business marketers must carefully monitor their customers' forecasts because derived demand is based on expectations of future demand for those customers' products.

Some business marketers not only monitor final consumer demand and customer forecasts but also try to influence final consumer demand. Aluminum producers use digital ads, websites, and videos targeted at final consumers to point out how aluminum can help in the fight against climate change. The Aluminum Association recently launched a "Choose Aluminum" campaign that highlights the sustainable properties of aluminum (100 percent recyclable, durable metal) in an effort to encourage consumers to choose aluminum-based products.[21]

Inelastic Demand

The demand for many business products is inelastic with regard to price. *Inelastic demand* means that an increase or decrease in the price of the product will not significantly affect demand for the product. This idea will be discussed further in Chapter 19.

The Unknown Future of Boeing

The success or failure of one bid can make the difference between prosperity and bankruptcy. The Boeing 787 Dreamliner was once called "the most sophisticated aircraft ever made," but Boeing has encountered a number of different problems with this aircraft. Most recently, problems with production have brought to light certain defects, such as tiny gaps between sections of the aircraft's body that could weaken the structural integrity of the plane. These defects are typically only detected during service and maintenance checks. Because of these production issues, Boeing has more than $25 billion of undeliverable planes, and many customers are canceling orders. The Federal Aviation Administration (FAA) is now requiring that Boeing precisely match new Dreamliners to its FAA-approved designs. Boeing has pledged to fix the problems, but incidents such as this one can cause irreparable damage to a company's sales and long-term image.[22]

The price of a product used in the production of, or as part of, a final product is often a minor portion of the final product's total price. Therefore, demand for the final consumer product is not affected. If the price of automobile paint or spark plugs rises significantly, say, 200 percent in one year, do you think the number of new automobiles sold that year will be affected? Probably not.

Joint Demand

Joint demand occurs when two or more items are used together in a final product. For example, a decline in the availability of memory chips will slow production of microcomputers, which will in turn reduce the demand for disk drives. Likewise, the demand for Hewlett-Packard (HP) ink cartridges exists as long as there is a demand for HP printers. Sales of the two products are directly linked.

Fluctuating Demand

The demand for business products—particularly new plants and equipment—tends to be less stable than the demand for consumer products. A small increase or decrease in consumer demand can produce a much larger change in demand for the facilities and equipment needed to make the consumer product. Economists refer to this phenomenon as the **multiplier effect** (or **accelerator principle**).

---

derived demand the demand for business products

joint demand the demand for two or more items used together in a final product

multiplier effect (accelerator principle) phenomenon in which a small increase or decrease in consumer demand can produce a much larger change in demand for the facilities and equipment needed to make the consumer product

Cummins Inc., a producer of heavy-duty diesel engines, uses sophisticated surface grinders to make parts. Suppose Cummins is using 20 surface grinders. Each machine lasts about 10 years. Purchases have been timed so that two machines will wear out and be replaced annually. If the demand for engine parts does not change, two grinders will be bought this year. If the demand for parts declines slightly, only 18 grinders may be needed, and Cummins will not replace the worn-out ones. However, suppose that next year, demand returns to previous levels plus a little more. To meet the new level of demand, Cummins will need to replace the two machines that wore out in the previous year, the two that wore out in the current year, plus one or more additional machines. The multiplier effect works this way in many industries, producing highly fluctuating demand for business products.

7-6b Purchase Volume

Business customers tend to buy in large quantities. Just imagine the size of Kellogg's typical order for the wheat bran and raisins used to manufacture Raisin Bran. Or consider that the Washington Metro approved a $2.2 billion contract to build the system's new 8000-series railcars, which will feature the latest transit technology, such as digital screens and dynamic maps, to replace its aging fleet.[23]

7-6c Number of Customers

Business marketers usually have far fewer customers than consumer marketers. The advantage is that it is a lot easier to identify prospective buyers, monitor current customers' needs and levels of satisfaction, and personally attend to existing customers. The main disadvantage is that each customer becomes crucial—especially for those manufacturers that have only one customer. In many cases, this customer is the U.S. government.

7-6d Concentration of Customers

Manufacturing operations in the United States tend to be more geographically concentrated than consumer markets. More than half of all U.S. manufacturers concentrate the majority of their operations in the following eight states: California, New York, Ohio, Illinois, Michigan, Texas, Pennsylvania, and Indiana.[24] Most large metropolitan areas host large numbers of business customers.

7-6e Distribution Structure

Many consumer products pass through a distribution system that includes the producer, one or more wholesalers, and a retailer. In business marketing, however, because of

The Washington Metro recently approved a $2.2 billion contract to build new rail cars to replace its aging fleet.

many of the characteristics already mentioned, the channels of distribution are typically shorter. Direct channels, where manufacturers market directly to users, are much more common. The use of direct channels has increased dramatically in the past decade with the introduction of various internet buying and selling schemes. One such technique is called a **business-to-business online exchange**, which is an electronic trading floor that provides companies with integrated links to their customers and suppliers. The goal of B-to-B exchanges is to simplify business purchasing and to make it more efficient. Alibaba.com is a B-to-B e-commerce portal based in China that allows companies from all over the world to purchase goods and services from Chinese suppliers. The website has begun expanding to include suppliers from countries outside China, including the United States. Alibaba.com serves buyers in more than 190 countries worldwide and has suppliers representing more than 40 major product categories. The mission of Alibaba.com is to allow suppliers to reach a global audience and to help buyers quickly find the products and services they need.[25]

7-6f Nature of Buying

Unlike consumers, business buyers usually approach purchasing rather formally. Businesses use professionally trained purchasing agents, or buyers, who spend their entire career purchasing a limited number of items. They get to know the items and the sellers well. Some professional purchasers earn the designation of Certified Purchasing Manager (CPM) after participating in a rigorous certification program.

7-6g Nature of Buying Influence

Typically, more people are involved in a single business purchase decision than in a consumer purchase. Experts from fields as varied as quality control, marketing, and finance, as well as professional buyers and users, may be grouped in a buying center (discussed later in this chapter).

---

business-to-business online exchange an electronic trading floor that provides companies with integrated links to their customers and suppliers

In business marketing, buyers and sellers negotiate product specifications, delivery dates, payment terms, and other pricing matters.

7-6h Type of Negotiations

Consumers are used to negotiating prices on automobiles and real estate. In most cases, however, American consumers expect sellers to set the price and other conditions of sale, such as time of delivery and credit terms. In contrast, negotiating is common in business marketing. Buyers and sellers negotiate product specifications, delivery dates, payment terms, and other pricing matters. Sometimes, these negotiations occur during many meetings over several months. Final contracts are often very long and detailed.

7-6i Use of Reciprocity

Business purchasers often choose to buy from their own customers, a practice known as **reciprocity**. For example, General Motors buys engines for use in its automobiles and trucks from BorgWarner, which in turn buys many of the automobiles and trucks it needs from General Motors. This practice is neither unethical nor illegal unless one party coerces the other and the result is unfair competition. Reciprocity is generally considered a reasonable business practice. If all possible suppliers sell a similar product for about the same price, does it not make sense to buy from the firms that buy from you?

7-6j Use of Leasing

Consumers normally buy products rather than lease them. But businesses commonly lease expensive equipment such as computers, construction equipment and vehicles, and automobiles. Leasing allows firms to reduce capital outflow, acquire a seller's latest products, receive better services, and gain tax advantages.

The leaser, the firm providing the product, may be either the manufacturer or an independent firm. The benefits to the leaser include greater total revenue from leasing as compared to selling and an opportunity to do business with customers who cannot afford to buy.

7-6k Primary Promotional Method

Business marketers tend to emphasize personal selling in their promotion efforts, especially for expensive items, custom-designed products, large-volume purchases, and situations requiring negotiations. The sale of many business products requires a great deal of personal contact. Personal selling is discussed in more detail in Chapter 17.

7-7 Types of Business Products

7-7 Describe the seven types of business goods and services

Business products generally fall into one of the following seven categories, depending on their use: major equipment, accessory equipment, raw materials, component parts, processed materials, supplies, and business services.

7-7a Major Equipment

Major equipment includes capital goods such as large or expensive machines, mainframe computers, blast furnaces, generators, airplanes, and buildings. (These items are also commonly called **installations**.) Major equipment is depreciated over time rather than charged as an expense in the year it is purchased. In addition, major equipment is often custom designed for each customer. Personal selling is an important part of the marketing strategy for major equipment because distribution channels are almost always direct from the producer to the business user.

7-7b Accessory Equipment

Accessory equipment is generally less expensive and shorter-lived than major equipment. Examples include portable drills, power tools, microcomputers, and computer software. Accessory equipment is often charged as an expense in the year it is bought rather than depreciated over its useful life. In contrast to major equipment, accessories are more often standardized and are usually bought by more customers. These customers tend to be widely dispersed. For example, all types of businesses buy laptops and smartphones.

---

reciprocity a practice whereby business purchasers choose to buy from their own customers

major equipment (installations) capital goods such as large or expensive machines, mainframe computers, blast furnaces, generators, airplanes, and buildings

accessory equipment goods, such as portable tools and office equipment, which are less expensive and shorter-lived than major equipment

Local industrial distributors (wholesalers) play an important role in the marketing of accessory equipment because business buyers often purchase accessories from them. Regardless of where accessories are bought, advertising is a more vital promotional tool for accessory equipment than for major equipment.

7-7c Raw Materials

Raw materials are unprocessed extractive or agricultural products—for example, mineral ore, timber, wheat, corn, fruits, vegetables, and fish. Raw materials become part of finished products. Extensive users, such as steel or lumber mills and food canners, generally buy huge quantities of raw materials. Because there is often a large number of relatively small sellers of raw materials, none can greatly influence price or supply. Thus, the market tends to set the price of raw materials, and individual producers have little pricing flexibility. Promotion is almost always via personal selling, and distribution channels are usually direct from producer to business user.

7-7d Component Parts

Component parts are either finished items ready for assembly or products that need very little processing before becoming part of some other product. Caterpillar diesel engines are component parts used in heavy-duty trucks. Other examples include spark plugs, tires, and electric motors for automobiles. A special feature of component parts is that they can retain their identity after becoming part of the final product. For example, automobile tires are clearly recognizable as part of a car. Moreover, because component parts often wear out, they may need to be replaced several times during the life of the final product. Thus, there are two important markets for many component parts: the OEM market and the replacement market.

The availability of component parts is often a key factor in the ability of OEMs to meet their production deadlines. During the COVID-19 pandemic, almost every carmaker around the world was impacted by a shortage of semiconductors, small but critical chips used in the production of cars. A General Motors plant in Kansas City was forced to close down and Porsche buyers were told that they would have to wait an extra 12 weeks to get their cars due to these shortages. The shortage in chips caused major delays in production and shipment of new cars, impacting both carmakers and consumers.[26]

The replacement market is composed of organizations and individuals buying component parts to replace worn-out parts. Because components often retain their identity in final products, users may choose to replace a component part with the same brand the manufacturer uses—for example, the same brand of automobile tires or battery. The replacement market operates differently from the OEM market, however. Whether replacement buyers are organizations or individuals, they tend to demonstrate the characteristics of consumer markets that were discussed in the previous section. Consider, for example, a replacement part for a piece of construction equipment such as a bulldozer or a crane. When a piece of equipment breaks down, it is usually important to acquire a replacement part and have it installed as soon as possible. Purchasers typically buy from local or regional dealers. Negotiations do not occur, and neither reciprocity nor leasing is usually an issue.

7-7e Processed Materials

Processed materials are products used directly in manufacturing other products. Unlike raw materials, they have had some processing. Examples include sheet metal, chemicals, specialty steel, treated lumber, corn syrup, and plastics. Unlike component parts, processed materials do not retain their identity in final products.

Timber, harvested from forests, is a raw material. Fluff pulp, a soft, white absorbent material, is produced from loblolly pine timber by mills such as International Paper Company. The fluff pulp becomes part of a number of different products, including product packaging, paper, disposable diapers, and bandages, among other things.

Most processed materials are marketed to OEMs or to distributors servicing the OEM market. Processed materials are generally bought according to customer specifications or to some industry standard, as is the case with steel and plywood. Price and service are important factors in choosing a vendor.

7-7f Supplies

Supplies are consumable items that do not become part of the final product—for example, lubricants, detergents, paper towels, pencils, and paper. Supplies are normally standardized items that purchasing agents routinely buy. Supplies typically have relatively short lives and are inexpensive compared to other business goods. Because supplies

---

raw materials unprocessed extractive or agricultural products, such as mineral ore, lumber, wheat, corn, fruits, vegetables, and fish

component parts either finished items ready for assembly or products that need very little processing before becoming part of some other product

processed materials products used directly in manufacturing other products

supplies consumable items that do not become part of the final product generally fall into one of three categories—maintenance, repair, or operating—this category is often referred to as MRO items. Competition in the MRO market is intense. Bic and Paper Mate, for example, battle for business purchases of inexpensive ballpoint pens.

7-7g Business Services

Business services are expense items that do not become part of a final product. Businesses often retain outside providers to perform janitorial, advertising, legal, management consulting, marketing research, maintenance, and other services. Contracting an outside provider makes sense when it costs less than hiring or assigning an employee to perform the task, when an outside provider is needed for particular expertise, or when the need is infrequent.

7-8 Business Buying Behavior

7-8 Discuss the unique aspects of business buying behavior

As you probably have already concluded, business buyers behave differently from consumers. Understanding how purchase decisions are made in organizations is a first step in developing a business selling strategy. Business buying behavior has five important aspects: buying centers, evaluative criteria, buying situations, business ethics, and customer service.

7-8a Buying Centers

In many cases, more than one person is involved in a purchase decision. A salesperson must determine the buying situation and the information required from the buying organization's perspective to anticipate the size and composition of the buying center.[27]

A **buying center** includes all the people in an organization who become involved in the purchase decision. Membership and influence vary from company to company. For instance, in engineering-dominated firms like Bell Textron, the buying center may consist almost entirely of engineers. In marketing-oriented firms like Toyota and IBM, marketing and engineering have almost equal authority. In consumer goods firms like The Clorox Company, product managers and other marketing decision makers may dominate the buying center. In a small manufacturing company, almost everyone may be a member.

The number of people involved in a buying center varies with the complexity and importance of a purchase decision.

---

business services expense items that do not become part of a final product

buying center all the people in an organization who become involved in the purchase decision

The average buying center includes more than one person and up to four per purchase.[28] The composition of the buying group will usually change from one purchase to another and sometimes even during various stages of one buying process. To make matters more complicated, buying centers do not appear on formal organization charts.

For example, even though a formal committee may have been set up to choose a new plant site, that committee is only part of the buying center. Other people, like the company president, often play informal yet powerful roles. In a lengthy decision-making process, such as finding a new plant location, some members may drop out of the buying center when they can no longer play a useful role. Others whose talents are needed then become part of the center. No formal announcement of "who is in" and "who is out" is ever made.

Roles in the Buying Center

As in family purchasing decisions, several people may each play a role in the business purchase process:

- The *initiator* is the person who first suggests making a purchase.
- *Influencers/evaluators* are people who influence the buying decision. They often help define specifications and provide information for evaluating options. Technical personnel are especially important as influencers.
- *Gatekeepers* are group members who regulate the flow of information. Frequently, the purchasing agent views the gatekeeping role as a source of their power. An assistant may also act as a gatekeeper by determining which vendors get an appointment with a buyer.
- The *decider* is the person who has the formal or informal power to choose or approve the selection of the supplier or brand. In complex situations, it is often difficult to determine who makes the final decision.
- The *purchaser* is the person who actually negotiates the purchase. It could be anyone from the company president to the purchasing agent, depending on the importance of the decision.
- *Users* are members of the organization who will actually use the product. Users often initiate the buying process and help define product specifications.

Implications of Buying Centers for the Marketing Manager

Successful vendors realize the importance of identifying who is in the decision-making unit, each member's relative influence in the buying decision, and each member's evaluative criteria. Key influencers are frequently located outside the purchasing department. Successful selling strategies often focus on determining the most important buying influences and tailoring sales presentations to the evaluative criteria most important to these buying center members. An example illustrating the basic buying center roles is shown in Table 7.1.

Marketers are often frustrated by their inability to reach C-level (chief) executives who, in today's economy, play an important role in many buying decisions. Marketers who want to build executive-level contacts must become involved in the buying process early on and remain visible and relevant at each stage of the buying process.[29] Additionally, it is important to realize that even most C-level executives are making purchase decisions as a team, not as individuals. Marketers need to target everyone that will be involved in the decision. Executives look for the following four characteristics in sales representatives:

1. The ability to marshal resources

2. An understanding of the buyer's business goals

3. Responsiveness to requests

4. Willingness to be held accountable

Some firms have developed their own strategies to reach executives throughout the buying process and during non-buying phases of the relationship, while other companies may seek external guidance to help them better reach such executives. Many consulting firms specialize specifically in helping firms sell to C-level executives. For example, Grow Digitally, a consulting firm based in Australia, helps B2B companies create strategies for growth, much of which is focused on helping these companies better target the elusive C-level audience.[30]

7-8b Evaluative Criteria

Business buyers evaluate products and suppliers using three important criteria: quality, service, and price.

Quality

In this case, *quality* refers to technical suitability. A superior tool can do a better job in the production process, and superior packaging can increase dealer and consumer acceptance of a brand. Evaluation of quality also applies to the salesperson and the salesperson's firm. Business buyers want to deal with reputable salespeople and companies that are financially responsible. Quality improvement should be part of every organization's marketing strategy.

Service

Almost as much as they want satisfactory products, business buyers want satisfactory service. A purchase offers several opportunities for service. Suppose a vendor is selling heavy equipment. Prepurchase service could include a survey of the buyer's needs. After thorough analysis of the survey findings, the vendor could prepare a report and recommendations in the form of a purchasing proposal. If a purchase results, post-purchase service might consist of installing the equipment and training those who will be using it. Post-sale services may also include maintenance and repairs.

Another service that business buyers seek is dependability of supply. They must be able to count on delivery of what was ordered when it is scheduled to be delivered. Buyers also welcome services that help them sell their finished products. Services of this sort are especially appropriate when the seller's product is an identifiable part of the buyer's end product.

Table 7.1	Buying Center Roles for Computer Purchases
Role	Illustration
Initiator	Division general manager proposes replacing the company's computer network.
Influencers/ evaluators	Corporate controller's office and vice president of information services have an important say in which system and vendor the company will deal with.
Gatekeepers	Corporate departments for purchasing and information services analyze the company's needs and recommend likely matches with potential vendors.
Decider	Vice president of administration, with advice from others, selects the vendor the company will deal with and the system it will buy.
Purchaser	Purchasing agent negotiates the terms of sale.
Users	All division employees use the computers.

In today's economy, C-level executives play an important role in many buying decisions.

Blue Planet Studio/Shutterstock.com

Price

Business buyers want to buy at low prices—at the lowest prices, under most circumstances. However, a buyer who pressures a supplier to cut prices to a point at which the supplier loses money on the sale almost forces shortcuts on quality. The buyer also may, in effect, force the supplier to quit selling to them. Then a new source of supply will have to be found.

7-8c Buying Situations

Often, business firms, especially manufacturers, must decide whether to make something or buy it from an outside supplier. The decision is essentially one of economics. Can an item of similar quality be bought at a lower price elsewhere? If not, is manufacturing it in-house the best use of limited company resources? For example, Briggs & Stratton Corporation, a major manufacturer of four-cycle engines, might be able to save $150,000 annually on outside purchases by spending $500,000 on the equipment needed to produce gas throttles internally. Yet Briggs & Stratton could also use that $500,000 to upgrade its carburetor assembly line, which would save $225,000 annually. If a firm does decide to buy a product instead of making it, the purchase will be a new buy, a modified rebuy, or a straight rebuy.

New Buy

A **new buy** is a situation requiring the purchase of a product for the first time. For example, suppose a manufacturing company needs a better way to page its managers while they are working on the shop floor. Currently, each of the several managers has a distinct ring—for example, two short and one long—that sounds over the plant intercom whenever they are being paged by anyone in the factory. The company decides to replace its buzzer system of paging with handheld wireless radio technology that will allow managers to communicate immediately with the department initiating the page. This situation represents the greatest opportunity for new vendors. No long-term relationship has been established for this product, specifications may be somewhat fluid, and buyers are generally more open to new vendors.

If the new item is a raw material or a critical component part, the buyer cannot afford to run out of it. The seller must be able to convince the buyer that the seller's firm can consistently deliver a high-quality product on time.

Modified Rebuy

A **modified rebuy** is normally less critical and less time consuming than a new buy. In a modified rebuy situation, the purchaser wants some change in the original good or service. It may be a new color, greater tensile strength in a component part, more respondents in a marketing research study, or additional services in a janitorial contract.

Because the two parties are familiar with each other and credibility has been established, the buyer and seller can concentrate on the specifics of the modification. But in some cases, modified rebuys are open to outside bidders. The purchaser uses this strategy to ensure that the new terms are competitive. An example would be the manufacturing company buying radios with a vibrating feature for managers who have trouble hearing the ring over the factory noise. The firm may open the bidding to examine the price, quality, and service offerings of several suppliers.

Straight Rebuy

A **straight rebuy** is a situation vendors prefer. The purchaser is not looking for new information or other suppliers. An order is placed, and the product is provided as in previous orders. Usually, a straight rebuy is routine because the terms of the purchase have been agreed to in earlier negotiations. An example would be the previously cited manufacturing company regularly purchasing additional radios for new managers from the same supplier.

One common instrument used in straight rebuy situations is the purchasing contract. Purchasing contracts are used with products that are bought often and in high volume. In essence, the purchasing contract makes the buyer's decision-making routine and promises the salesperson a sure sale. The advantage to the buyer is a quick, confident decision; the advantage to the salesperson is reduced or eliminated competition. Nevertheless, suppliers must remember not to take straight rebuy relationships for granted. Retaining existing customers is much easier than attracting new ones.

7-8d Business Ethics

As we noted in Chapter 3, *ethics* refers to the moral principles or values that generally govern the conduct of an individual or a group. Ethics can also be viewed as the standard of behavior by which conduct is judged.

Although we have heard a lot about corporate misbehavior in recent years, most people, and most companies, follow ethical practices. To help achieve this standard,

---

new buy a situation requiring the purchase of a product for the first time

modified rebuy a situation in which the purchaser wants some change in the original good or service

straight rebuy a situation in which the purchaser reorders the same goods or services without looking for new information or investigating other suppliers

approximately 80 percent of all major corporations offer ethics training to employees. Many companies also have codes of ethics that help guide buyers and sellers. For example, Home Depot has a clearly written code of ethics available on its corporate website that acts as an ethical guide for all its employees.

7-8e Customer Service

Business marketers are increasingly recognizing the benefits of developing a formal system to monitor customer opinions and perceptions of the quality of customer service. Companies such as FedEx, IBM, and Oracle build their strategies not only around products but also around highly developed service skills.[31] These companies understand that keeping current customers satisfied is just as important as attracting new ones, if not more so. Leading-edge firms are obsessed not only with delivering high-quality customer service but also with measuring satisfaction, loyalty, relationship quality, and other indicators of nonfinancial performance. Delivering consistent, high-quality customer service is an important basis for establishing competitive advantage and differentiating one's company from competitors. Cisco Systems uses a web-based survey to determine the presale and post-sale satisfaction of customers.[32]

Most firms find it necessary to develop measures unique to their own strategies, value propositions, and target markets. For example, Renewal by Andersen assesses the loyalty of its trade customers by their willingness to continue carrying its windows and doors, recommend its products to colleagues and customers, increase their volume with the company, and put its products in their own homes. Basically, each firm's measures should not only ask "What are your expectations?" and "How are we doing?" but should also reflect what the firm wants its customers to do.

Some customers are more valuable than others. They may have greater value because they spend more, buy

Keeping current customers satisfied is just as important as attracting new ones—if not more so. Delivering consistent, high-quality customer service is an important basis for differentiating one's company from competitors.

higher-margin products, have a well-known name, or have the potential of becoming a bigger customer in the future. Some companies selectively provide different levels of service to customers based on their value to the business. By giving the most valuable customers superior service, a firm is more likely to keep them happy, hopefully increasing retention of these high-value customers and maximizing the total business value they generate over time.

To achieve this goal, the firm must be able to divide customers into two or more groups based on their value. It must also create and apply policies that govern how service will be allocated among groups. Policies might establish which customers' phone calls get "fast tracked" and which customers are directed to use the web and/or voice self-service, how specific email questions are routed, and who is given access to online chat and who is not.

Providing different customers with different levels of service is a very sensitive matter. It must be handled very carefully and very discreetly to avoid offending lesser-value, but still important, customers.

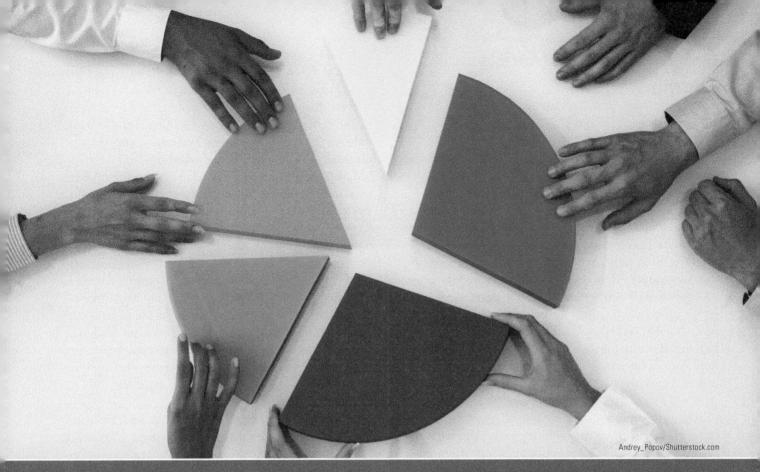

Chapter 8

Segmenting and Targeting Markets

Learning Outcomes

After studying this chapter, you will be able to . . .

8-1 Explain the importance of market segmentation

8-2 Discuss the criteria for successful market segmentation

8-3 Describe the bases commonly used to segment consumer markets

8-4 Describe the bases for segmenting business markets

8-5 List the steps involved in segmenting markets

8-6 Discuss alternative strategies for selecting target markets

8-7 Explain how customer relationship management (CRM) can be used as a targeting tool

8-8 Explain positioning strategies

8-1 Markets and Market Segmentation

8-1 Explain the importance of market segmentation

The term "market" means different things to different people. We are all familiar with the supermarket, stock market, labor market, fish market, and flea market. All these types of markets share several characteristics. First, they are composed of people (consumer markets) or organizations (business markets). Second, these people or organizations have wants and needs that can be satisfied by specific product categories. Third, they can buy the products they seek. Fourth, they are willing to exchange their resources, usually money or credit, for desired products. In sum, a **market** is (1) people or organizations with (2) needs or wants and with (3) the ability, and (4) the willingness to buy. A group of people or an organization that lacks any one of these characteristics is not a market.

Within a market, a **market segment** is a subgroup of people or organizations sharing one or more characteristics that cause them to have similar product needs. At one extreme, we can define every person and every organization in the world as a market segment because each is unique. At the other extreme, we can define the entire consumer market as one large market segment and the business market as another large segment. All people have some similar characteristics and needs, as do all organizations.

From a marketing perspective, market segments can be described as somewhere between the two extremes. The process of dividing a market into meaningful, relatively similar, and identifiable segments, or groups, is called **market segmentation**. The purpose of market segmentation is to enable the marketer to tailor marketing mixes to meet the needs of one or more specific segments.

8-1a The Importance of Market Segmentation

Until the 1960s, few firms practiced market segmentation. When they did, it was more likely a haphazard effort than a formal marketing strategy. Before 1960, for example, the Coca-Cola Company produced only one beverage and aimed it at the entire soft drink market. Today, Coca-Cola offers dozens of different products to market segments based on diverse consumer preferences for flavors, calories, and caffeine content. Coca-Cola offers traditional soft drinks, energy drinks (including Powerade), flavored teas, fruit drinks (Minute Maid), and water (Dasani).

Market segmentation plays a key role in the marketing strategy of almost all successful organizations and is a powerful marketing tool. Most markets include smaller groups of people or organizations with different product needs and preferences. Market segmentation helps marketers define customer needs and wants more precisely. It leads to a deeper understanding of customer lifestyles, values, jobs to be done, need states, and buying occasions. As mentioned in a previous chapter, the increased use of big data has provided new ways companies can reach that understanding. Research has shown that firms that are the best at putting customer needs at the center of everything they do are more able to identify and execute marketing strategies that drive growth.[1]

Because market segments differ in size and potential, segmentation helps decision makers to define marketing objectives more accurately and better allocate resources. In turn, performance can be better evaluated when objectives are more precise. For example, Adidas segments their athletic shoes by sport, including hiking, running, soccer, cycling, and golf shoes. Adidas segments its markets, and develops products to meet the specific needs of customers in those segments.[2]

8-2 Criteria for Successful Segmentation

8-2 Discuss the criteria for successful market segmentation

Marketers segment markets for three important reasons. First, segmentation enables marketers to identify groups of customers with similar needs and to analyze the characteristics and buying behavior of these groups. Second, segmentation provides marketers with information to help them design marketing mixes that specifically match the characteristics and desires of one or more segments. Third, segmentation is consistent with the marketing concept of satisfying customer wants and needs while meeting the organization's objectives.

To be useful, a segmentation scheme must produce segments that meet the following four basic criteria:

1. **Substantiality:** A segment must be large enough to warrant developing and maintaining a special marketing mix. This criterion does not necessarily mean

---

market people or organizations with needs or wants and the ability and willingness to buy

market segment a subgroup of people or organizations sharing one or more characteristics that cause them to have similar product needs

market segmentation the process of dividing a market into meaningful, relatively similar, and identifiable segments or groups

that a segment must have many potential customers. For example, marketers of products such as custom-designed homes and business buildings, commercial airplanes, and large computer systems typically develop marketing programs targeted to a small number of customers. In most cases, however, a market segment needs many potential customers to make commercial sense. In the 1980s, home banking failed because not enough people owned personal computers. Today, a larger number of people own computers, and home banking is a thriving industry.

2. **Identifiability and measurability:** Segments must be identifiable and their size measurable. Data about the population within geographic boundaries, the number of people in various age categories, and other social and demographic characteristics are often easy to get, and they provide concrete measures of segment size. Suppose that a social service agency wants to identify segments by their readiness to participate in a drug and alcohol program or in prenatal care. Unless the agency can measure how many people are willing, indifferent, or unwilling to participate, it will have trouble gauging whether there are enough people to justify setting up the service.

3. **Accessibility:** The firm must be able to reach members of targeted segments with customized marketing mixes. Some market segments are hard to reach—for example, older adults (especially those with reading or hearing difficulties), individuals experiencing homelessness, and those who are uneducated.

4. **Responsiveness:** Markets can be segmented using any criteria that seem logical. Unless one market segment responds to a marketing mix differently than other segments, however, that segment need not be treated separately. For instance, if all customers are equally price conscious about a product, there is no need to offer high-, medium-, and low-priced versions of a product to different market segments.

8-3 Bases for Segmenting Consumer Markets

8-3 Describe the bases commonly used to segment consumer markets

Marketers use **segmentation bases,** or **variables,** which are characteristics of individuals, groups, or organizations, to divide a total market into segments. The choice of segmentation bases is crucial because an inappropriate segmentation strategy may lead to lost sales and missed profit opportunities. The key is to identify bases that will produce substantial, measurable, and accessible segments that exhibit different response patterns to marketing mixes.

Markets can be segmented using a single variable, such as age group, or several variables, such as age group, gender, and education. Although it is less precise, single-variable segmentation has the advantage of being simpler and easier to use than multiple-variable segmentation. The disadvantages of multiple-variable segmentation are that it is often harder to use than single-variable segmentation, usable secondary data are less likely to be available, and as the number of segmentation bases increases, the size of individual segments decreases. Nevertheless, the current trend is toward using more rather than fewer variables to segment most markets, because multiple-variable segmentation is clearly more precise than single-variable segmentation.

Consumer goods marketers commonly use one or more of the following characteristics to segment markets: geography, demographics, psychographics, benefits sought, behavioral patterns and usage rate.

8-3a Geographic Segmentation

Geographic segmentation refers to segmenting markets by region of a country or the world, market size, market density, or climate. Market density means the number of people within a unit of land, such as a census tract. Climate is commonly used for geographic segmentation because of its dramatic impact on residents' needs and purchasing behavior. Snowblowers, water and snow skis, clothing, and air-conditioning and heating systems are products with varying appeal, depending on climate.

Consumer goods companies take a geographic approach to marketing for several reasons. First, firms continually need to find ways to grow. Dollar General's growth strategy includes opening smaller-format stores, called pOpshelf. Targeting people with higher incomes than the typical Dollar General customers, pOpshelf offers products such as home goods, food, paper products and cleaning supplies, most selling for $5 or less. Dollar General is capitalizing on high inflation rates, which makes consumers look for lower prices.[3]

Second, geographic segmentation assists companies in avoiding unnecessary marketing costs because they focus on locations where their products will sell. Nike used geographic segmentation with its "Nothing Beats a Londoner" advertisement. This video targets football fans in London

segmentation bases (or variables) characteristics of individuals, groups, or organizations

geographic segmentation segmenting markets by region of a country or the world, market size, market density, or climate

by showing key landmarks, local football stars, and everyday life in London.[4]

8-3b Demographic Segmentation

Marketers often segment markets based on demographic information because it is widely available and often related to consumers' buying and consuming behavior. Some common bases of **demographic segmentation** are age, gender, income, ethnic background, and household life cycle.

Age Segmentation

Marketers use a variety of terms to refer to different age groups. Examples include newborns, infants, young children, tweens, millennials, Generation X, baby boomers, and the Silent Generation. Age segmentation can be an important tool, as a brief exploration of the market potential of several age segments illustrates.

Generation Alpha (born between 2010–2024) will soon become the largest generation in history. Their lives have been shaped by technology and the COVID-19 pandemic. They are also influenced by their millennial parents, who prefer simple, natural products.[5] Many companies are responding to this influential generation. For example, Amazon has created a service for kids, with the goal of nurturing young readers, called "Amazon Prime Book Box." The company chooses children's books for a monthly subscription that delivers a box of books based on the child's age.[6] Home improvement retailer Lowe's was successful with in-store building workshops for kids. The company is now testing its "Build a Birthday" parties. These parties will give kids options to build things like race cars, wooden castles, and wall shelves. And, if Lowe's can satisfy kids with this program, it may keep them as customers throughout their lives.[7]

Generation Z, whose members were born from 1997 to 2010, has access to $44 billion in buying power. Members of Gen Z shop across both online and physical channels, prefer higher-quality products, and desire to protect the environment.[8] Social platform TikTok is used by 60 percent of members in this generation. Walmart added TikTok to its advertising network to reach Gen Z with its online grocery service.[9]

The millennial cohort, those born between 1981 and 1996, is comprised of approximately 72 million people—more than any other generation.[10] This group is idealistic and pragmatic and is the most technology-proficient generation ever, so social media is an important part of any brand's marketing strategy. The top brand attributes important to millennials include trustworthiness,

Millennial consumers tend to prioritize and spend money on personal experiences, like concerts.

creativity, intelligence, authenticity, and confidence.[11] This group loves experiences. Upscale retailer Barneys New York partnered with blog Highsnobbery to host a weekend-long event aimed at millennials that featured exclusive, limited-edition merchandise and appearances by designers of streetwear. Shoppers could get custom sneakers, tattoos, and piercings. In its first day, the event led to a 25 percent sales increase, with 20 percent of the customers new to Barney's.[12] Millennials love private brands. A typical shopping cart contains 25 percent private label products, while millennials' baskets contain 32 percent private brands. They shop at stores like Aldi and deep discounters, and they shop online more than other age group.[13]

Generation X, those born between 1965 and 1980, is a smaller group than both the millennial and the baby boomer groups; it makes up only 16 percent of the total population. Members of Generation X are at a life stage where they are often supporting their aging parents and young children (earning Gen X the nickname "the sandwich generation"). They grew up spending time alone at home while their parents worked long into the night. They are the best-educated generation—29 percent have earned a bachelor's degree or better. They tend to be disloyal to brands and skeptical of big business. Many of them are parents, and they make purchasing decisions with thought for and input from their families.[14] Gen Xers respond well to nostalgic products and advertising messages. In fact, they have been behind the comeback of many 1990s trends and have revived the concept of "retro." One brand that has capitalized on this trend is Big Chill Appliances. The company designs and sells retro-styled refrigerators, stoves, and dishwashers, many with brightly colored exteriors. Similarly, Urban Outfitters has successfully collaborated with iconic 90s brands like Calvin Klein and Tommy Hilfiger.[15]

People born between 1946 and 1964 are often called baby boomers. This group makes up almost one-third of

---

demographic segmentation segmenting markets by age, gender, income, ethnic background, and household life cycle

the U.S. adult population. They own 51 percent of all the wealth in the country, having $2.6 trillion in buying power. Moreover, baby boomers have high average spending and like to indulge in luxury purchases.[16] They are living longer, healthier, and more active and connected lives, and they will spend time and money doing whatever is necessary to maintain vitality as they age. Those in the baby boomer generation are very loyal to their preferred brands. They stay loyal to companies that have quality, fair pricing, good product selection, and great service. Baby boomers respond positively to companies that share their core values. For years, Ben & Jerry's has appealed to this group, creating marketing campaigns centering around social justice causes.[17] T-Mobile targeted baby boomers by focusing on an affordable way to stay connected with family and friends, something that is important for members of this group. The company introduced a less expensive data plan without extra features, so that older customers could better afford the latest smartphones.[18]

Consumers who were born before 1946 are often called the silent generation because of their ability to quietly persevere through great hardships. The smallest generation of the past 100 years, members of this group were taught to play by the rules. They tend to be cautious, and they are hardworking, disciplined, and place significant value on economic resources.[19] As consumers age, they do require some modifications in the way they live and the products they purchase. For example, aging individuals may need to install well-placed handrails or grab bars, ramps, easy-access bathrooms, easy-access kitchens, stair lifts, widened doors or hallways, and modified sink faucets or cabinets" in their homes. Members of this age group were especially hard hit by the COVID-19 pandemic, and its lockdowns. A U.K. brand that excelled during the first COVID-19 pandemic lockdown was meal-delivery service Oakhouse Foods. To target older customers, the company completely redesigned its online experience for those with poor eyesight or mobility.[20] Companies like Delta, Microsoft, Google and Procter & Gamble are also engaged in addressing the needs of customers with accessibility issues. For example, Delta offers wheelchair service to customers with disabilities throughout their travel journeys. Delta wheelchair assistants can meet customers the moment they arrive at the airport and will stay with them until they are boarded on their flight. Delta also has onboard wheelchairs on most of its aircrafts so customers with mobility issues can safely move through the airplane if needed.

Gender Segmentation

Traditionally many companies have segmented their markets by targeting men or women because there are often differences in what these genders buy. For example, women have typically been the purchasers of products such as

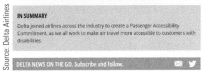

Source: Delta Airlines

Delta Airlines is committed to creating a positive flying experience for consumers with accessibility issues.

cosmetics, apparel, and groceries, not only for themselves, but also for their families, while men have tended to purchase electronics, cars, and sports-related goods. In addition, there are some differences in how and where men and women shop. Women tend to be bargain hunters, while men spend more per item than women. Men often stay focused on purchasing something specific, while women are more likely to consider purchases other than what they were originally shopping for, which can lead women to spend more time shopping.[21]

Women contribute to 37 percent of global gross domestic product (GDP), and in the United States, they drive 80 percent of purchases of consumer goods each year.[22] They are an experienced purchasing group with the responsibility of purchasing many household items. Research including 43 different countries found that 98 percent of baby, laundry and household cleaner ads are targeted at women, along with 71 percent of food advertising and 60 percent of retail ads.[23] On the other hand, many beer and car ads are targeted at men. However, an increasing number of companies are beginning to target some products that have traditionally been aimed at women to men. Grocery shopping is usually the purview of women, but Southern food chain, Lowe's Foods, recognized an opportunity for growth by targeting men. The chain set up gourmet sausage stations and opened an in-store brewery where customers can sit and order a craft beer or order one to enjoy while shopping. These strategies proved successful, as management saw a significant increase in the number of male shoppers after implementing these changes.[24]

Products targeted toward men include men's grooming products, outdoor activities like camping, and sporting events. For example, English soccer star David Beckham launched a grooming brand for men that includes face creams, beard oil, and hair pomades.[25] On the other hand, companies that traditionally have marketed to men are now also targeting women. Johnnie Walker has traditionally marketed mostly to men, but when they began to realize that women also love whiskey, the company started to feature more women in their marketing campaigns. Harry's—the men's innovative direct-to-consumer shaving company—created Flamingo, which is the same service for women.[26]

Today, to embrace diversity, it is important for companies to understand and acknowledge gender identity. An individual's **gender identity** is their internal perception of their gender and how they label themselves, LGBTQIA+ is an acronym to describe one's sexual orientation or gender identity: Lesbian, Gay, Bisexual, Transgender, Queer or Questioning, Intersex, Asexual, and +. The "+" includes all other non-hetero/cis normative identities not included within the LGBTQ acronym. Many companies include the LGBTQIA+ community in their advertising. In some cases, the ad directly targets this community, such as Verizon's television ad campaign "Love Calls Back". It featured calls on the company's phones between four LGBTQIA+ individuals and their family members, who had difficulty with their coming out. The message of the campaign was that it's never too late for love to call back.[27] Other ads aim to promote inclusion. For example, Vrbo's recent Super Bowl ad featured an LGBTQIA+ couple arriving at a Vrbo rental for a family reunion.[28]

Some companies have begun to create gender-neutral marketing. Calvin Klein was one of the first companies to create a beauty product that was marketed as unisex. The company's original CK One fragrance ads featured gender-fluid models with the tagline "One for All." The company recently launched another gender-neutral fragrance call "CK Everyone." Its global advertising campaign was a tribute to individuality and self-expression, featuring people of different genders telling a story about the fragrance.[29] Milk Makeup was one of the first cosmetic companies that marketed to nonbinary people. Seven models of diverse genders and sexual orientations shared their messages about self-identification, attitudes to the world, and makeup in the campaign.[30]

Income Segmentation

Income is a popular demographic variable for segmenting markets because income level influences consumers' wants and determines their buying power. Many markets are segmented by income, including those for housing, clothing, automobiles, and food. Some companies have found success in marketing to low income learners. For example, a former Trader Joe's executive opened two deep discount supermarkets in Boston called Daily Table. The store purchases and resells fresh produce and food products from other groceries, supermarkets, growers, and food distributors that would otherwise have gone to waste. These stores provide delicious and nutritious food options for lower socioeconomic status consumers.[31] Unilever sells smaller, less expensive packages of laundry detergent to low-income consumers in countries such as Indonesia, Sri Lanka, and Bangladesh. Wholesale clubs Costco and Sam's Club also appeal to many income segments with a mix of products. High-income customers looking for luxury want products that exhibit careful craftsmanship, timeless design, prestige, and exclusivity. Luxury brands such as Chanel and Louis Vuitton do not focus on mass popularity, but instead try to set long-lasting standards of good taste.

Ethnicity Segmentation

Many companies segment their markets using ethnicity. **Ethnicity** refers to shared cultural characteristics such as language, ancestry, practices, and beliefs. U.S. statistics show that almost 76 percent of the country is White, 14 percent Black, 20 percent Hispanic, with the rest being Asian, American Indian, Pacific Islander, and others.[32]

In the past, ethnic groups in the United States were expected to conform to a homogenized, Anglo-centric ideals. This was evident in how mass-produced products were marketed as well as in the selective way that films, television, advertisements, and popular music portrayed America's population. Now, Whites, Hispanics, and Blacks are the largest groups in the United States, and these groups are more equally represented in the media and in marketing campaigns. White people still make up the most substantial single group of consumers in this country and hold the largest percent of buying power compared to other groups. However, the U.S. population is becoming more diverse, with people of non-White ethnicities growing not only in numbers, but also in spending power.[33]

To meet the needs and wants of this more diverse population, some companies, such as McDonald's and Google, have marketing campaigns geared toward specific ethnic groups. For example, McDonald's has begun running Lunar New Year, a holiday celebrated in many Asian countries, promotions.[34] Google's launch of its Pixel smartphone to the Hispanic and Latino/Latina communities showed how a live-translate feature could ease language barriers between people. A short film was created about a young Latina woman and a foreign exchange student falling in love. This film showed how the phone could help people overcome culture and language barriers to forge connections, making the love story possible.[35]

Similarly, several companies have begun devoting more resources to target Black Americans. For example,

---

gender identity an individual's internal perception of their gender and how they label themselves

ethnicity shared cultural characteristics such as language, ancestry, practices, and beliefs

Source: Microsoft Corporation

Microsoft's Xbox has honored Black History Month through a variety of initiatives. The brand has introduced new profile themes, wallpaper, and avatar items to be inclusive of the Black community. It is also showcasing more games designed by Black creators. Additionally, Xbox not only supports the Black community in their marketing efforts, but also ensures that their company culture is welcoming to and inclusive of Black people. A Black woman who works as a manager for the company said that her "leadership chain has emphasized what is possible in this field and that I, and people who look like me, belong here."[36]

The Hindu holiday of Diwali is an important South Asian cultural tradition. Knowing this, Ford created a campaign showcasing this holiday to promote its Escape SUV to Canadians of Indian descent. In this campaign, a young mother visits her aging father for their first Diwali together since the start of the COVID-19 pandemic. The message of this campaign focused on how Ford vehicles help to bring families closer together.[37]

More companies are starting to target the Native American community. For example, Xfinity Internet and Mobile, owned by Comcast, spotlighted members of this community in a campaign celebrating Native American Heritage Month. Customers were given free access to a large set of On Demand movies, documentaries, interviews with community leaders, and family-friendly entertainment. The company also allowed customers to connect to the *All Nations Network*, a dedicated network for Indigenous stories, as well as a selection of programs from networks like Peacock and AMC+.[38]

Household Life-Cycle Segmentation

Frequently, consumption patterns among people of the same age and gender differ because they are in different stages of the household life cycle. The **household life cycle (HLC)** is a series of stages determined by a combination of age, marital status, and the presence or absence of children. For example, some adults get married in their 20s, have and raise children together, and then transition to empty

nesters. Some adults may choose to wait to get married until they are in their 50s and not have children. Other adults may choose to never get married and adopt a child to raise as a single parent. It is important for marketers to recognize that there are multiple different varieties of domestic arrangements. Household life cycle patterns can differ across cultures and subcultures, and shift with time.

The household life-cycle stage consisting of the married-couple households used to be considered the standard family in the United States. Today, however, married couples make up just 47 percent of households, down from 72 percent in the 1960s. Twelve percent of households are headed by women, 5 percent are headed by men, and one-person households represent 29 percent of total households.[39] Many companies are recognizing these shifts in household life-cycles and adjusting their strategies accordingly. For example, Hello Fresh offers meal delivery kits specifically for one-person households. Figure 8.1 illustrates some examples of HLC patterns. It is important to recognize other types of families not represented in the figure. For example, blended families, same-sex couple families, single parent families, and families where people are raising their grandchildren, or "grandfamilies."

Consumers are especially receptive to marketing efforts at certain points in the life cycle. For example, families with babies need diapers, toys, and baby clothes, while those with older children may need sports equipment, or dancing lessons. A unique experiential learning company for kids, Kidzania is a place where children go to play and learn. Companies such as Nutella, Walmart, and Sony have collaborated with KidZania to create engaging experiences for kids. What child wouldn't want to pretend to work for Nutella and not only get to see how the products are made but also to try them?[40] Campbell's *Made for Real, Real Life* ad campaign shows a young boy at home with his two dads. An advertisement for Wells Fargo showed a lesbian couple learning sign language to prepare for the adoption of a deaf daughter. Many companies are also targeting individuals and couples that do not have children. The term PANK, professional aunt, no kids, has become a TikTok trend and companies such as Royal Caribbean are creating entire advertising campaigns targeting these consumers. Empty nesters represent another large group of consumers. There are nearly 23 million empty nesters in America, and they are a growing market for real estate.[41] Empty nesters might buy a vacation or second home, possibly with the idea of eventually living in it year-round. They may relocate to a retirement or "over-50" community

---

household life cycle (HLC) a series of stages determined by a combination of age, marital status, and the presence or absence of children

Figure 8.1 Household Life Cycle

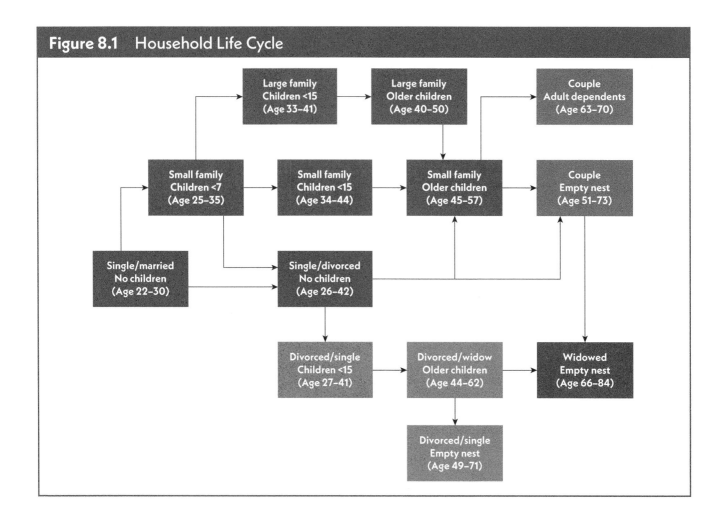

or downsize their homes. When buying a new home, or remodeling where they currently live, empty nesters are likely to want high-end features, such as hardwood floors, granite countertops, and custom cabinets. These are but a few examples of how companies market to different types of families.[42]

8-3c Psychographic Segmentation

Demographic variables are helpful in developing segmentation strategies, but often, they do not paint the entire picture. Demographics provide the skeleton, but psychographics add meat to the bones. **Psychographic segmentation** is market segmentation based on the following psychographic segmentation variables:

- **Personality:** Personality reflects a person's traits, attitudes, and habits. Clothing is the ultimate personality descriptor. People buy clothes that they feel represent their personalities and give others an idea of who they are. For example, research has found that people who

like feminine clothing (e.g., dresses and skirts) tend to be fashion leaders and to show compassion to others. By contrast, those who own more traditional clothing (e.g., shirts and jackets) tend to be sociable and exhibit emotional stability and higher energy.[43]

- **Motives:** Marketers of baby products and life insurance appeal to consumers' emotional motives—namely, to care for their loved ones. Using appeals to economy, reliability, and dependability, carmakers like Subaru and Suzuki target customers with rational motives. On the other hand, carmakers like Mercedes-Benz, Jaguar, and Cadillac appeal to customers with status-related motives.

- **Lifestyles:** Lifestyle segmentation divides people into groups according to the way they spend their time, the importance of the things around them, their beliefs, and socioeconomic characteristics such as income and education. For example, record stores specializing in vinyl are targeting young people who are listening to independent labels and often pride themselves on being independent of big business. Some brands are considered lifestyle brands, such as lululemon. This popular yoga apparel company has developed a

---

psychographic segmentation segmenting markets based on personality, motives, lifestyles, and geodemographics

passionate community of people who like to be active and want premium quality, by promoting a lifestyle of health and wellness.[44]

- **Geodemographics: Geodemographic segmentation** clusters potential customers into neighborhood lifestyle categories. It combines geographic, demographic, and lifestyle segmentations. Geodemographic segmentation helps marketers develop marketing programs tailored to prospective buyers who live in small geographic regions, such as neighborhoods, or who have very specific lifestyle and demographic characteristics. College students, for example, often share similar demographics and lifestyles and tend to cluster around campus. Knowing this, marketing teams for start-ups and tech companies often launch ambassador programs at college campuses. Red Bull has one of the most popular college ambassador programs. Students earn an hourly rate to create, distribute, and monitor social media posts. Ambassadors also go to social and sporting events to promote Red Bull to their fellow students, where they hand out drinks and other branded merchandise.[45]

Psychographic variables can be used individually to segment markets or can be combined with other variables to provide more detailed descriptions of market segments. Based on data from more than 14,000 people in 22 countries, DuPont Nutrition & Health has identified six core consumer segments in the health and wellness area. The segments are based on demographics, geographics, health concerns, brand influences, attitudes, lifestyle choices, and parenting styles. The six groups are Health Helpers, Weight Strugglers, Health Wise, Taste Driven, Good Life, and Just Food. Insights about these segments will help food and beverage manufacturers to understand the motivations, needs, and behaviors of each group and more clearly define market opportunities.[46]

8-3d Behavioral Segmentation

Behavioral segmentation is grouping customers based on the purchasing behaviors they exhibit, including what, where, when, and how they buy. It also includes frequency of use, and how long people continue to use a product. One example of a company that uses behavioral segmentation is Amazon. The company collects data on an individual's past purchase behavior along with the purchase histories of people who buy similar items to make product recommendations. These recommendations represent 35 percent of Amazon's sales.[47]

Email marketing is an excellent tool that marketers can use with behavioral segmentation. To illustrate, they send thank you, confirmation, and shipping emails after consumers purchase a product. If a consumer's online

shopping cart is abandoned, they send reminder emails. For example, the luggage company Away sends cart abandonment emails to shoppers who add products to their cart but do not ultimately purchase. The first line of the email is "Your shopping cart is like your luggage—it should never be left unattended." This is an entertaining way for the company to remind customers about the product in their cart and motivate them to complete the purchase.[48] Many companies also use email marketing to alert consumers about special promotion periods, such as holiday sales.[49]

Hallmark is adept at behavioral segmentation for special occasions. The company stores data when customers purchase a card online, such as time purchased and type of card. Hallmark then uses that information to create reminders to consumers that it is time to buy again. For example, if a consumer buys a birthday card, the company can contact them around the same time the following year, reminding them to buy again.[50]

Usage-rate is one important form of behavioral segmentation. It divides a market by the amount of product bought or consumed. Categories vary with the product, but they are likely to include some combination of the following: former users, potential users, first-time users, light or irregular users, medium users, and heavy users. Segmenting by usage rate enables marketers to focus their efforts on heavy users or to develop multiple marketing mixes aimed at different user segments. Because heavy users often account for a sizable portion of all product sales, some marketers focus on the heavy-user segment.

The **80/20 principle**, or Pareto Principle, holds that 20 percent of all customers generate 80 percent of the demand. Although the percentages usually are not exact, the general idea often holds true. Marketers can focus on understanding the characteristics of their heavy users to develop campaigns aimed at people who have similar characteristics but are not yet customers. For example, those who spend heavily at department stores have been found to be likely to own a smart television and to watch streaming services. They are likely to give gifts more often than other consumers, and they want to be able to buy in one channel (such as online) and return in another (such as in store). A new streaming service could use this information

---

geodemographic segmentation segmenting potential customers into neighborhood lifestyle categories

behavioral segmentation the process of grouping customers based on the behaviors they exhibit, including what they buy, where they buy, when they buy, and how they buy.

80/20 principle a principle holding that 20 percent of all customers generate 80 percent of the demand

to, for instance, create a marketing campaign that targeted department store shoppers.

Companies can also reward heavy users with loyalty initiatives, as airlines do with frequent flyer programs. Loyalty programs can also be effective in attracting new users or encouraging light users to buy more. Research shows that 69 percent of consumers said rewards or loyalty programs influenced their shopping decisions, and 57 percent said saving money was their most important reason for joining a loyalty program.[51]

8-3e Benefit Segmentation

Benefit segmentation is the process of grouping customers into market segments according to the benefits they seek from the product. Benefit segmentation is different because it groups potential customers based on their needs or wants. For example, a snack-food company could divide their market into three benefit segments: nutritional snackers, indulgent snackers, and convenience snackers.

Customer profiles can be developed, for example, by examining demographic information associated with people seeking certain benefits. This information can be used to match marketing strategies with selected markets. A Tesco grocery store in Scotland has what it calls a "relaxed checkout line." It is slower paced than normal lines and is staffed by employees trained by an Alzheimer's group. This checkout line has benefits for anyone who feels they need extra time, such as those with dementia, or perhaps parents with several small children.[52]

8-4 Bases for Segmenting Business Markets

8-4 Describe the bases for segmenting business markets

The business market consists of four broad segments: producers, resellers, government, and institutions. (For a detailed discussion of the characteristics of these segments, see Chapter 7.) Whether marketers focus on only one or on all four of these segments, they are likely to find diversity among potential customers. Thus, further market segmentation offers just as many benefits to business marketers as it does to consumer product marketers.

---

benefit segmentation the process of grouping customers into market segments according to the benefits they seek from the product

8-4a Company Characteristics

Company characteristics, such as geographic location, type of company, company size, and product use, can be important segmentation variables. Some markets tend to be regional because buyers prefer to purchase from local suppliers, and distant suppliers may have difficulty competing in terms of price and service. Therefore, firms that sell to geographically concentrated industries benefit by locating close to their markets.

Segmenting by customer type allows business marketers to tailor their marketing mixes to the unique needs of different types of organizations or industries. For example, a company called BigCommerce has an online platform that helps businesses in different industries, including apparel, health and beauty, and manufacturing, operate online shops. BigCommerce can help entrepreneurs set up their e-commerce store and adapt the storefront to operate in different countries, manage the payment experience, and even allows these companies to set up buy online, pick up in-store options for customers. Ted Baker, Johnnie Walker, and Natori are just a few of BigCommerce's many clients. BigCommerce's website caters to companies' diverse needs with an array of hosting packages and information pages segmented by both business size and business type.[53]

Volume of purchase (heavy, moderate, light) is a commonly used basis for business segmentation. Another is the buying organization's size, which may affect its purchasing procedures, the types, and quantities of products it needs, and its responses to different marketing mixes. Banks frequently offer different services, lines of credit, and overall attention to commercial customers based on their size. Many products, especially raw materials like steel, wood, and petroleum, have diverse applications. How customers use a product may influence the amount they buy, their buying criteria, and their selection of vendors. For example, a producer of springs may have customers who use the product in applications as diverse as making machine tools, bicycles, surgical devices, office equipment, telephones, and missile systems.

8-4b Buying Processes

Many business marketers find it helpful to segment customers and prospective customers based on how they buy. For example, companies can segment some business markets by ranking key purchasing criteria, such as price, quality, technical support, and service. Atlas Door has developed a commanding position in the industrial door market by providing customized products in just 4 weeks, which is much faster than the industry average of 12 to 15 weeks. Atlas's primary market consists of companies with an immediate need for customized doors.

The purchasing strategies of buyers may provide useful segments. Two purchasing profiles that have been identified are satisficers and optimizers. **Satisficers** contact familiar suppliers and place the order with the first one to satisfy product and delivery requirements. **Optimizers** consider numerous suppliers (both familiar and unfamiliar), solicit bids, and study all proposals carefully before selecting one.

The personal characteristics of the buyers themselves (their demographic characteristics, decision style, tolerance for risk, confidence level, job responsibilities, and so on) influence their buying behavior and thus offer a viable basis for segmenting some business markets.

8-5 Steps in Segmenting a Market

8-5 List the steps involved in segmenting markets

The purpose of market segmentation, in both consumer and business markets, is to identify marketing opportunities. The following steps can be used to segment a market:

- **Select a market or product category for study:** Define the overall market or product category to be studied. It may be a market in which the firm already competes, a new but related market or product category, or a totally new market.

- **Choose a basis or bases for segmenting the market:** This step requires managerial insight, creativity, and market knowledge. There are no scientific procedures for selecting segmentation variables. However, a successful segmentation scheme must produce segments that meet the four basic criteria discussed earlier in this chapter.

- **Select segmentation descriptors:** After choosing one or more bases, the marketer must select the segmentation descriptors. Descriptors identify the specific segmentation variables to use. For example, if a company selects demographics as a basis of segmentation, it may use age, occupation, and income as descriptors. A company that selects usage-rate segmentation needs to decide whether to go after heavy users, nonusers, or light users.

satisficers business customers who place an order with the first familiar supplier to satisfy product and delivery requirements

optimizers business customers who consider numerous suppliers (both familiar and unfamiliar), solicit bids, and study all proposals carefully before selecting one

Black Paper Party's Targeting Strategy

Black Paper Party is a Black-owned, woman-owned company that introduced a new type of gift-wrapping paper with images showing Black culture. Madia Willis, J'Aaron "Jae" Merchant, and Jasmine Hudson launched the brand in September 2020, in the middle of the COVID-19 pandemic, because they knew Black families were not well represented in the marketplace, especially on holidays. For example, they discovered that while Black consumers spent 15 percent more than other demographic groups during Christmas, there were no companies creating inclusive seasonal items for Black families on a large scale. There was a noticeable gap in the market for products that Black families could see and celebrate themselves on holidays, which mirrored the women's own experiences as kids.

The company started by manufacturing and marketing Christmas wrapping paper based on Black children, families, and Santas who were smiling and joyful. The women's 25 years of combined experience in textile design, product development and sourcing, merchandise planning and buying, and award-winning illustration, particularly of Black characters, made them uniquely suited to focus on wrapping paper. They sold the paper on their own website at first.

Black Paper Party's distinctive products sold quickly, and by mid-December of 2020, when an overwhelmed postal service could not guarantee delivery by Christmas, the company stopped taking orders. In 2021, revenue grew by six times to nearly $300,000, even though there were supply chain disruptions across the country, The next year, they expected to meet their goal of $1 million in annual revenue.

Black Paper Party has grown its product lines to include culturally relevant ornaments, gift bags, greeting cards, party supplies, accessories, and décor, and the company is working to create a kitchen goods line, as well. Along with the company's website, consumers can now purchase the products at stores such as Target, Macy's, TJ Maxx, Marshalls, and Walmart. The brand also designed an exclusive collection with Walmart of pre-decorated cookies depicting the Black Paper Party kids. Black Paper Party continues to build the brand through licensed partnerships including Zrike for beverageware, housewares, and serve ware, Brand Castle for baking mixes, baking activity kits, prebaked cookies, and décor kits, Mad Engine for apparel, sleepwear, and sleep accessories and Morris National for food gift sets, chocolate, confections, and candy.

The company's founders have committed to the Black community by offering trend relevant, high-quality products that provide authentic representation for all occasions. Their mission is to help promote understanding and appreciation for the diversity within the Black community.[54]

- **Profile and analyze segments:** The profile should include the segments' size, expected growth, purchase frequency, current brand usage, brand loyalty, and long-term sales and profit potential. This information can then be used to rank potential market segments by profit opportunity, risk, consistency with organizational mission and objectives, and other factors important to the firm.

- **Select markets:** Selecting markets is not a part of but a natural outcome of the segmentation process. It is a major decision that influences and often directly determines the firm's marketing mix. This topic is examined in greater detail later in this chapter.

- **Design, implement, and maintain appropriate marketing mixes:** The marketing mix has been described as product, place (distribution), promotion, and pricing strategies intended to bring about a mutually satisfying exchange relationship with a market.

Markets are dynamic, so it is important that companies proactively monitor their segmentation strategies over time. Often, when customers or prospects have been assigned to a segment, marketers think their task is done. Once customers are assigned to an age segment, for example, they stay there until they reach the next age bracket or category, which could be 10 years in the future. Thus, the segmentation classifications are static, but the customers and prospects are changing. Dynamic segmentation approaches adjust to fit the changes that occur in customers' lives.

8-6 Strategies for Selecting Target Markets

8-6 Discuss alternative strategies for selecting target markets

So far, this chapter has focused on the market segmentation process, which is only the first step in deciding whom to approach about buying a product. The next task is to choose one or more target markets. A **target market** is a group of people or organizations for which an organization designs, implements, and maintains a marketing mix

target market a group of people or organizations for which an organization designs, implements, and maintains a marketing mix intended to meet the needs of that group, resulting in mutually satisfying exchanges

undifferentiated targeting strategy a marketing approach that views the market as one big market with no individual segments and thus uses a single marketing mix

intended to meet the needs of that group, resulting in mutually satisfying exchanges.

Because most markets will include customers with different characteristics, lifestyles, backgrounds, and income levels, it is unlikely that a single marketing mix will attract all segments of the market. Thus, if a marketer wishes to appeal to more than one segment of the market, it must develop different marketing mixes. The three general strategies for selecting target markets—undifferentiated, concentrated, and multi-segment targeting—are illustrated in Table 8.1, which also illustrates the advantages and disadvantages of each targeting strategy.

8-6a Undifferentiated Targeting

An **undifferentiated targeting strategy**, sometimes called mass marketing, essentially views the market as a homogeneous market with no individual segments. The firm uses one marketing mix for the entire market. A firm that adopts an undifferentiated targeting strategy assumes that individual customers have similar needs that can be met with a common marketing mix.

The first firm in an industry sometimes uses an undifferentiated targeting strategy. With no competition, the firm may not need to tailor marketing mixes to the preferences of market segments. Henry Ford's approach to marketing the first Model T automobiles was to make them all black, a classic example of an undifferentiated targeting strategy: At

Table 8.1	Advantages and Disadvantages of Target Marketing Strategies	
Targeting Strategy	**Advantages**	**Disadvantages**
Undifferentiated	• Potential savings on production/marketing costs	• Unimaginative product offerings • Company more susceptible to competition
Concentrated	• Concentration of resources • Can better meet the needs of a narrowly defined segment • Allows some small firms to better compete with larger firms • Strong positioning	• Segments too small or changing • Large competitors may more effectively market to niche segment
Multi-segment	• Greater financial success • Economies of scale in production/marketing	• High costs • Cannibalization

one time, Coca-Cola used this strategy with a single product and a single size of its familiar bottle. Marketers of commodity products, such as flour and sugar, are also likely to use an undifferentiated targeting strategy. One brand that has been successful with an undifferentiated strategy is M&Ms, which is owned by Mars. The company targets people of all ages and appeals to anyone looking for sweets. In addition, the product itself has not changed over many years.[55]

One advantage of undifferentiated marketing is the potential for saving on production and marketing. Because only one item is produced, the firm should be able to achieve economies of mass production. Also, marketing costs may be lower when there is only one product to promote and a single channel of distribution. Too often, however, an undifferentiated strategy emerges by default rather than by design, reflecting a failure to consider the advantages of a segmented approach. The result is often sterile, unimaginative product offerings that have little appeal to anyone.

Another problem associated with undifferentiated targeting is that it makes the company more susceptible to competitive inroads. Hershey lost a big share of the candy market to other candy companies, such as Nestle, before it changed to a multi-segment targeting strategy. Coca-Cola forfeited its position as the leading seller of cola drinks in supermarkets to PepsiCo in the late 1950s, when Pepsi began offering several sizes of containers.

You might think a firm producing a standard product such as toilet tissue would adopt an undifferentiated strategy. However, this market has industrial segments and consumer segments. Industrial buyers want an economical, single-ply product sold in boxes of a hundred rolls (or jumbo rolls a foot in diameter to use in public restrooms). The consumer market demands a more versatile product in smaller quantities. Within the consumer market, the product is differentiated with designer print or no print, as cushioned or non-cushioned, and as economy priced or luxury priced. Undifferentiated marketing can succeed in certain situations, though. A small grocery store in a small, isolated town may define all the people who live in the town as its target market. It may offer one marketing mix and generally satisfy everyone in town. This strategy is not likely to be as effective if there are three or four grocery stores in town.

8-6b Concentrated Targeting

With a **concentrated targeting strategy**, a firm selects a market **niche** (one segment of a market) for targeting its marketing efforts. Because the firm is appealing to a single segment, it can concentrate on understanding the needs, motives, and satisfaction of that segment's members and on developing and maintaining a highly specialized marketing mix. Some firms find that concentrating resources

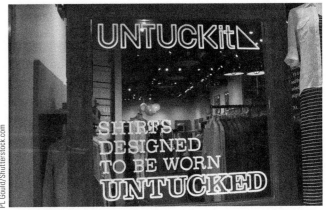

PL Gould/Shutterstock.com

UNTUCKit targets a niche market of men who want to wear their casual shirts untucked

and meeting the needs of a narrowly defined market segment is more profitable than spreading resources over several different segments.

Intelligentsia Coffee & Tea, a Chicago-based coffee roaster/retailer, targets serious coffee drinkers with hand-roasted, ground, and poured super gourmet coffee or tea served by impeccably educated baristas. The company also offers training classes for the at-home or out-of-town coffee aficionado.

Small firms often adopt a concentrated targeting strategy to compete effectively with much larger firms. For example, Enterprise Rent-A-Car, number one in the car rental industry, started as a small company catering to people whose cars were in the shop. Some other firms use a concentrated strategy to establish a strong position in a desirable market segment. To fill an unmet need in the market, UNTUCKit created casual shirts for men who like to wear their shirts untucked. Few of the numerous companies that make men's casual shirts offer those that look stylish when worn untucked. After becoming successful with this niche, UNTUCKit expanded into making additional products. The company now offers other products for men, like polo shirts and jackets, and has also started to target women.[56]

Concentrated targeting violates the adage "Don't put all your eggs in one basket." If the chosen segment is too small or if it shrinks because of environmental changes, the firm may suffer negative consequences. For instance, Totsy was a company that sold luxury fashion brands at discounted prices via limited time flash sales. However, when the economic and social environments shifted, leading flash sales to lose their attractiveness, the company was unable to adapt and eventually went out of business.[57]

---

concentrated targeting strategy a strategy used to select one segment of a market for targeting marketing efforts

niche one segment of a market

A company using a concentrated strategy can also be a casualty of its own success by attracting strong competition. For example, Fab was an online company offering daily design inspiration, featuring and selling third-party items from small designers all over the world Its success resulted in other companies launching exact replicas of Fab's platform, which contributed to its failure.[58] Before Procter & Gamble (P&G) introduced Head & Shoulders shampoo, several small firms were already selling antidandruff shampoos. Head & Shoulders was introduced with a large promotional campaign, and the new brand immediately captured over half the market. Within a year, several of the firms that had been concentrating on this market segment went out of business.

8-6c Multi-segment Targeting

A firm that chooses to serve two or more well-defined market segments and develops a distinct marketing mix for each has a **multi-segment targeting strategy**. Marriott International is an example of a company that uses this kind of targeting by offering several types of properties designed to meet the needs of customers in different market segments. These are some of the Marriott brands and their target markets:

- **Marriott Courtyard:** Targeted at over-the-road travelers.

- **Ritz-Carlton Hotels:** Targeted at luxury travelers.

- **Marriott Conference Centers:** Targeted at businesses hosting small- and midsized meetings.

- **Marriott ExecuStay:** Targeted at executives needing month-long accommodations.

- **Marriott Vacation Clubs:** Targeted at travelers seeking to buy timeshares.[59]

Toyota makes vehicles that appeal to multiple customer segments. Its products include subcompact cars, sport-utility vehicles, pickup trucks, and minivans. For people who want luxury, they make Lexus, for those who wish to have a sporty car, they make Scion, and for environmentally conscious consumers, they make Prius. Its Yaris model is designed for the budget-minded consumer. Toyota also markets vehicles in several hundred countries.[60]

Multi-segment targeting offers many potential benefits to firms, including greater sales volume, higher profits, larger market share, and economies of scale in

---

multi-segment targeting strategy a strategy that chooses two or more well-defined market segments and develops a distinct marketing mix for each

cannibalization a situation that occurs when sales of a new product cut into sales of a firm's existing products

manufacturing and marketing. Yet it may also involve higher costs for product design, production, promotion, inventory, marketing research, and management. Before deciding to use this strategy, firms should compare the benefits and costs of multi-segment targeting to those of undifferentiated and concentrated targeting.

Another potential cost of multi-segment targeting is **cannibalization**, which occurs when sales of a new product cut into sales of a firm's existing products. For example, many cell phone companies now offer refurbished smartphones, which gives consumers the option to purchase a lower-priced, secondhand cell phone rather than a new phone. Apple dominates the secondhand market, followed by Samsung. The appeal of this phenomenon comes from a slowdown in innovation from smartphone manufacturers. Thus, refurbished high-end phones are cannibalizing the low-end market for smartphones, which contributes to slower growth for Apple and Samsung.[61]

8-7 CRM as a Targeting Tool

8-7 Explain how customer relationship management (CRM) can be used as a targeting tool

Recall from Chapter 1 that CRM entails tracking interactions with customers to optimize customer satisfaction and long-term company profits. Companies that successfully implement CRM tend to customize the goods and services offered to their customers based on data generated through interactions between carefully defined groups of customers and the company. CRM can also allow marketers to target customers with extremely relevant offerings. Panera made a promise to its customers that it would (1) create healthy food by removing all artificial flavors, sweeteners, and preservatives from its products, and (2) offer convenience, and then followed through. Moreover, the company nurtures customer relationships with personalization. For example, Panera alerts loyalty members about new food items that match members' taste profiles based on past purchases. Panera also offers business and home delivery, rapid pickup, and catering. These CRM initiatives have resulted in 48 million people becoming Panera loyalty members.[62]

As many firms have discovered, a detailed and segmented understanding of customers can be advantageous. There are at least four trends that will lead to the continued growth of CRM: personalization, time savings, loyalty, and technology.

1. **Personalization:** One-size-fits-all marketing is no longer relevant. Consumers want to be treated as the individuals they are, with their own unique sets of needs and wants. Its personalized nature allows CRM to fulfill this desire. The spice maker McCormick, for

example, personalized a campaign for Black consumers by catering to their interest and creativity around cooking. The brand partnered with award-winning chef Millie Peartree, whose good-tasting food and affordable recipes made her famous in the Black community. McCormick used this campaign to spotlight the history and importance of soul food by making traditional charcuterie boards into "Soul-Cuterie" boards for Black History Month. McCormick built stronger relationships within the Black community because of its attention to celebrating Black culture and food heritage.[63]

2. **Time savings:** Direct and personal marketing efforts will continue to grow to meet the needs of consumers who no longer have the time to spend shopping and making purchase decisions. With the personal and targeted nature of CRM, consumers can spend less time making purchase decisions and more time doing the things that are important to them.

3. **Loyalty:** Consumers will be loyal only to companies and brands that have earned that loyalty and reinforced it at every purchase occasion. CRM techniques focus on finding a firm's best customers, rewarding them for their loyalty, and thanking them for their business. Some companies that offer loyalty programs include Amazon, DSW Shoe Warehouse, Starbucks, and Sephora. For example, Sephora's Beauty Insider loyalty program has over 25 million members. The program is free to join, and members receive free shipping, access to seasonal discounts, and the ability to earn rewards they can redeem for free products.[64]

4. **Technology:** Mass-media approaches will decline in importance as advances in market research and database technology allow marketers to collect detailed information on their customers. New technology offers marketers a more cost-effective way to reach customers and enables businesses to personalize their messages. For example, My.Yahoo.com greets each user by name and offers information in which the user has expressed interest. Similarly, gifts.com helps customers keep track of special occasions and offers personalized gift recommendations. With the help of database technology, CRM can track a business's customers as individuals, even if they number in the millions.

CRM is a huge commitment and often requires a 180-degree turnaround for marketers who have been used to developing and implementing mass-marketing efforts. Although mass marketing will probably continue to be used, especially to create brand awareness or to remind consumers of a product, the advantages of CRM cannot be ignored.

Sephora has a tremendously successful loyalty program. The program is free to join, and members earn points every time they shop, get access to seasonal promotional events, and get free online shipping (with a minimum purchase amount).

8-8 Positioning

8-8 Explain positioning strategies

Marketers segment their markets and then choose which segment, or segments, to target with their marketing mix. Then, based on the target market(s), they can develop the product's **positioning**, a process that influences potential customers' overall perception of a brand, product line, or organization in general. **Position** is the place a product, brand, or group of products occupies in consumers' minds relative to competing offerings. Consumer goods marketers are particularly concerned with positioning. Coca-Cola has multiple cola brands, each positioned to target a different market. For example, Coca-Cola Zero is positioned on its bold taste and zero calories, Caffeine Free Coca-Cola is positioned as a no-caffeine alternative, and Tab is positioned as a cola drink for dieters.[65]

Positioning assumes that consumers compare products based on important features. Marketing efforts that emphasize irrelevant features are therefore likely to misfire. For example, Crystal Pepsi and a clear version of Coca-Cola's Tab failed because consumers perceived the "clear" positioning as more of a marketing gimmick than a benefit.

Effective positioning requires assessing the positions occupied by competing products, determining the

---

positioning developing a specific marketing mix to influence potential customers' overall perception of a brand, product line, or organization in general

position the place a product, brand, or group of products occupies in consumers' minds relative to competing offerings

important dimensions underlying these positions, and choosing a position in the market where the organization's marketing efforts will have the greatest impact. Ben & Jerry's bases its positioning on creative flavors, fun packaging, and a commitment to social and environmental causes. Customers associate the brand with high-quality, delicious ice cream and progressive values.[66]

One positioning strategy that many firms use to distinguish their products from competitors is based on **product differentiation**. The distinctions between products can be either real or perceived. For example, Nike used a product differentiation strategy based on product performance and innovation in the athletic shoe market. The company invented the waffle shoe and targeted its brand to professional athletes. Empowerment is the message of its brand communications, including its tagline "Just Do It" to its namesake, the Greek Goddess of Victory.[67] However, many everyday products, such as bleaches, aspirin, unleaded regular gasoline, and some soaps, are differentiated by such trivial means as brand names, packaging, color, smell, or "secret" additives. The marketer attempts to convince consumers that a particular brand is distinctive and that they should demand it.

Some firms, instead of using product differentiation, position their products as being like competing products or brands. Two examples of this positioning are artificial sweeteners advertised as tasting like sugar and margarine as tasting like butter.

8-8a Perceptual Mapping

Perceptual mapping is a means of displaying or graphing, in two or more dimensions, the location of products, brands, or groups of products in customers' minds. . The perceptual map in Figure 8.2 shows various popular restaurants

---

product differentiation a positioning strategy that some firms use to distinguish their products from those of competitors

perceptual mapping a means of displaying or graphing, in two or more dimensions, the location of products, brands, or groups of products in customers' minds

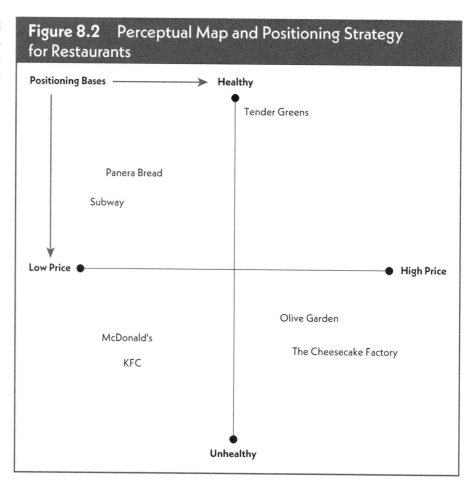

Figure 8.2   Perceptual Map and Positioning Strategy for Restaurants

mapped on the dimensions of healthy/unhealthy and fast food/sit down. A company thinking about opening a new restaurant could use this map to find a space that has less competition, for instance a healthy sit-down restaurant. This tool is also useful for companies wishing to reposition their restaurants. For example, if McDonald's wanted to reposition its offerings as more healthy, it would likely face limited competition based on this map.

8-8b Positioning Bases

Firms use a variety of bases for positioning, including the following:

- **Attribute:** A product is associated with an attribute, product feature, or customer benefit. In engineering its products, Seventh Generation focuses on removing common toxins and chemicals from household products to make them safe for everyone in the household.

- **Price and quality:** This positioning base may stress high price as a signal of quality or emphasize low price as an indication of value. In the watch market, Rolex uses a premium pricing strategy to signal high quality, while Timex markets affordable watches. Consumers who only need a watch to tell time can buy a Timex for $50 - $300. However, other consumers are willing to pay $10,000 or more for the Rolex because they perceive the product to be of very high quality, and a status symbol.[68]

- **Use or application:** Stressing uses or applications can be an effective means of positioning a product with buyers. Vita Coco is a coconut water company that has long marketed to health-conscious consumers as a product that quenches thirst. After starting to develop a reputation as a hangover cure, it decided to position the drink this way. For example, the company collaborated with Postmates and Lyft to market hangover recovery kits that feature its products. The company also partnered with DoorDash for a promotion Monday morning following the 2023 Super Bowl.[69]

- **Product user:** This positioning base focuses on a personality or type of user. Gap Inc. has several different brands: Gap stores offer basic casual pieces, such as jeans and T-shirts, to middle-of-the-road consumers at midlevel prices; Old Navy offers low-priced, trendy casual wear geared to youth and college-age groups; and Banana Republic is a luxury brand offering fashionable, luxurious business and casual wear to 25- to 35-year-olds.[70]

- **Product class:** The objective here is to position the product as being associated with a particular category of products—for example, positioning a margarine brand with butter. Alternatively, products can be disassociated from a category. Amtrak has positioned itself as an alternative to airplanes, citing cost savings, enjoyment, and other advantages.[71]

- **Competitor:** Positioning against competitors is part of any positioning strategy. Brands can position against competitors by having offerings that are unique in an industry. One example is the Airbnb Experiences feature that the vacation rental site designed for its customers. This feature offers a variety of experiences, such as tours, classes, lessons, and excursions that guests book through the company. Some of these experiences offer exclusive opportunities, such as sailing tours at dusk, or photo shoots in unusual locales. Other experiences are offbeat and fun, such as creating a custom perfume. Airbnb Experiences provides the company a great way to position against competitors.[72]

Positioning against competitors can also be done more directly, by using comparative advertising. Popeye's Chicken recently used this technique to position against Chick-fil-A. The latter restaurant is known to be closed on Sundays. When National Sandwich Day fell on a Sunday, Popeye's marketers seized the opportunity to develop a smart comparison ad. In this ad, a man walks up to a highway sign advertising nearby restaurants and prints the words, "Open Sunday" underneath the Popeye's logo. Directly adjacent on the ad are the words "Closed on Sunday" underneath the Chick-fil-A logo.[73]

- **Emotion:** Positioning using emotion focuses on how the product makes customers feel. Emotional positioning has been shown to be effective in helping brands increase brand loyalty, engagement, and purchase intent. For example, in Google's Search stories campaign the company's services are portrayed as being helpful in the everyday lives of individuals. In one ad, Google maps are used to save a family. In another example, a Pepsi ad pictured its product as one that encourages family mealtimes, friends' hangouts, and activities such as dancing and football. Instead of showing rational reasons why consumers should buy a product, these examples focus on consumer emotions.[74]

8-8c Repositioning

Sometimes products or companies are repositioned to sustain growth in slow markets or to correct positioning mistakes. **Repositioning** is changing consumers' perceptions of a brand in relation to competing brands. For example, Gucci has transformed itself from being considered out-of-touch compared to its competitors, to becoming one of the most popular fashion brands in the world. The company started by targeting young consumers. Gucci redesigned its logo, made its products more Instagram-friendly, and started messaging about its progressive stance on sexual fluidity. Because of its strong repositioning, the brand experienced its most profitable period financially in recent history Gucci has also increased its importance among fashion influencers.[75]

---

repositioning changing consumers' perceptions of a brand in relation to competing brands

Chapter 9

Marketing Research

Learning Outcomes

After studying this chapter, you will be able to . . .

9-1 Explain the importance of marketing research to marketing decision making

9-2 Describe the steps involved in conducting a marketing research project

9-3 Discuss the profound impact of the internet on marketing research

9-4 Describe the growing importance of mobile research

9-5 Discuss the growing importance of scanner-based research

9-6 Explain when marketing research should be conducted

9-1 The Role of Marketing Research

9-1 Explain the importance of marketing research to marketing decision making

Marketing research is the process of planning, collecting, and analyzing data relevant to a marketing decision. The results of this analysis are then communicated to management. Thus, marketing research is the function that links the consumer and the public to the marketer through information. Marketing research plays a key role in the marketing system. It provides decision makers with data on the effectiveness of the current marketing mix and insights for necessary changes. Furthermore, marketing research is a main data source for management information systems. In other words, the findings of a marketing research project become data for decision making by management.

Marketing research has three roles: descriptive, diagnostic, and predictive. Its *descriptive* role includes gathering and presenting factual statements. For example, what are the historical sales trends in the industry? What are consumers' attitudes toward a product and its advertising? Its *diagnostic* role includes explaining data, such as determining the impact on sales of a change in the design of the package. Its *predictive* function is to address "what if" questions. For example, how can the researcher use descriptive and diagnostic research to predict the results of a planned marketing decision?

9-1a Management Uses of Marketing Research

Marketing research can help managers in several ways. First, it improves the quality of decision making, allowing marketers to explore the desirability of various alternatives before arriving at a path forward. Second, it helps managers trace problems. Was the initial decision incorrect? Did an unforeseen change in the external environment cause the plan to fail? How can the same mistake be avoided in the future? Questions like these can be answered through marketing research. Third, marketing research can help managers understand very detailed and complicated relationships. Most importantly, sound marketing research can help managers serve both current and future customers accurately and efficiently. This service in turn can mean greater revenue and profits for the firm.

Firms like Dick's Sporting Goods, Cabela's, and Bass Pro Shops continually tweak their inventory to meet the needs of existing customers and to attract new ones. One such display area in these stores is camping gear and supplies.

RossHelen/Shutterstock.com

Marketing research can aid retailers in determining the amount and type of camping equipment they should carry in their stores.

So, the questions become, "Are more people camping?" "Fewer?" and "Who's camping?" The COVID-19 pandemic had a big impact on how many people took camping trips since many consumers felt that camping was safer than traveling to busy locations or staying in a hotel. Marketing research determined that 28 percent of campers went on more camping trips due to the pandemic, and 43 percent of Gen Z campers started camping during the pandemic.[1] More than 9 million households tried camping for the first time in 2021. Researchers have found that social influences can play a big role in camping-related purchasing decisions, with many campers turning to friends and social media to get information about camping gear. Many people view camping as a time to relax, escape stress, and clear their minds. Tent usage remains high, with 64 percent of campers primarily using tents. The Baby Boomer generation is the most likely to use an RV for camping (34 percent) or to camp in a cabin (24 percent). Armed with these and other research data, a sporting goods retailer can update its camping gear inventory to increase sales. Certainly, one factor would be having a variety of styles and types of tents to meet buyers' needs. In-store displays or online pictures should emphasize relaxation and a tilt toward younger campers.

Marketing research can also help managers understand whether and when changes should be made to customer service. Suppose a large retail apparel chain is considering adding more associates to the floor to improve customer satisfaction. Marketing research can be useful in making this type of strategic decision. For example, research has found that customers are turning away from hands-on, personalized service from store associates and instead turning to friends, family, and social media for advice. Eighty-five

---

marketing research the process of planning, collecting, and analyzing data relevant to a marketing decision

percent want to be able to check prices at scanners rather than asking someone. Also, 42 percent of millennial consumers find it important to be able to research apparel online and try it on in a store before making a purchase. Technology in apparel store dressing rooms that assist with shopping was deemed important by only 17 percent. Almost 30 percent of consumers want to be able to pay a sales associate from anywhere in the store (using mobile point-of-sale), and 29 percent of consumers appreciate apps that provide personal recommendations.[2] Thus, this research would suggest that the retailer should focus on in-store technological improvements to improve customer satisfaction, rather than increasing the number of sales associates.

9-1b Understanding the Ever-Changing Marketplace

Marketing research helps managers to understand what is going on in the marketplace and to take advantage of opportunities. Now, with big data analytics (discussed later in the chapter), we can understand the marketing environment like never before. One of the hottest trends in technology today is the Internet of Things (IoT). This term refers to everyday devices—such as refrigerators, toys, light bulbs, and hot water heaters—connecting wirelessly to a network to improve their functionality. An early leader in this market was the Nest Thermostat. Nest learns the temperatures you like throughout the week and then turns itself down when you are away. It can be controlled via an app, so you can increase or decrease the temperature while lying in bed. So, what does this trend mean to manufacturers of appliances, clothing, fitness devices, and countless other items? Survey data found that 38 percent of households own at least one IoT device, and 44 percent of households plan to purchase an IoT device in the coming year.[3] Adoption of wearable IoT technology (such as smart watches and fitness devices) is also expected to increase; 45 percent of households in India, 40 percent of household in the United States, and 32 percent of households in Germany own these types of devices. Further, a separate research study found that 25 percent of women and 18 percent of men wear, specifically, smartwatches.[4] The IoT is expected to have revenues of over $620 trillion by 2030.[5]

9-2 Steps in a Marketing Research Project

9-2 Describe the steps involved in conducting a marketing research project

Virtually all firms that have adopted the marketing concept engage in some marketing research because it offers decision makers many benefits. Some companies spend millions on marketing research; others, particularly smaller firms, conduct informal, limited-scale research studies.

Whether a research project costs $200 or $2 million, the same general process should be followed. The marketing research process is a scientific approach to decision making that maximizes the chance of getting accurate and meaningful results. Figure 9.1 traces the seven steps in the research process, which begins with the recognition of a marketing problem or opportunity. As changes occur in the firm's external environment, marketing managers are faced with the questions "Should we change the existing marketing mix?" and, if so, "How?" Marketing research may be used to evaluate product, promotion, distribution, or pricing alternatives.

A large online retailer felt that there was plenty of room for improvement on its website. The firm decided to examine Amazon, Target, and Walmart to find out whether some web page elements were more important than others. The market research found that shoppers that browsed all three companies' product pages were most likely to buy from

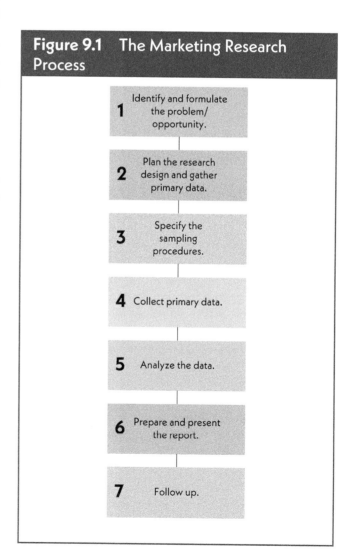

Figure 9.1   The Marketing Research Process

1. Identify and formulate the problem/opportunity.
2. Plan the research design and gather primary data.
3. Specify the sampling procedures.
4. Collect primary data.
5. Analyze the data.
6. Prepare and present the report.
7. Follow up.

Walmart. Walmart's pages had a larger product image, a visible and user-friendly "add to cart" section, and visible and user-friendly size and quantity options. The product image area with Walmart was twice as big as the same area with Amazon and 1.5 times bigger than Target's. Also, Walmart's "add to cart" section was large and had sizable buttons. It was positioned close to the product image and highlighted important details such as price, discount, and shipping fees. Ninety-two percent noticed this section on the Walmart page, 86 percent on the Amazon page, and only 34 percent on the Target page. Amazon's strategy of using complementary products, that is, showing products that were frequently bought together, tended to significantly boost sales. Target and Walmart showed alternative products. So, if a page featured women's running shoes, an alternative product strategy would be to show more shoes. A complementary strategy would, perhaps, show socks or a gym bag. The researchers found that a complementary products section holds 30 percent more of viewers' attention than an alternatives product section.[6] Armed with this information, the online retailer was able to significantly improve its website.

This example illustrates an important point about problem/opportunity definition. The **marketing research problem** involves determining what information is needed and how that information can be obtained efficiently and effectively. The **marketing research objective**, then, is the goal statement. The marketing research objective defines the specific information needed to solve the marketing problem and provides insightful decision-making information. This requires specific pieces of information needed to solve the marketing research problem. Managers must combine this information with their own experience and other information to make proper decisions. The research problem of the online retailer being discussed was to determine what factors led to greater online views, click-throughs to "add to cart" sales, and add-on sales. The marketing research objective was to increase sales through a rebuilt website.

By contrast, the **management decision problem** is action oriented. Management problems tend to be much broader in scope and far more general than marketing research problems, which must be narrowly defined and specific if the research effort is to be successful. Sometimes, several research studies must be conducted to solve a broad management problem. The online retailers' management decision problem was determining whether a rebuilt website would increase the firm's market share and profits.

9-2a Identifying and Formulating the Problem/Opportunity

A valuable tool throughout the research process, particularly in the problem/opportunity identification stage, is **secondary data**—data previously collected for any purpose other than the one at hand. Secondary information originating within the company includes the company's websites, annual reports, reports to stockholders, blogs, product testing results perhaps made available to the news media, YouTube videos, social media posts, and house periodicals composed by the company's personnel for communication to employees, customers, or others. Often, this information is incorporated into a company's internal database.

Innumerable outside sources of secondary information also exist, some in the forms of government departments and agencies (federal, state, and local) that compile and post summaries of business data. Trade and industry associations also publish secondary data. Still more data are available in business periodicals and other news media that regularly publish studies and articles on the economy, specific industries, and even individual companies. The unpublished summarized secondary information from these sources corresponds to internal reports, memos, or special-purpose analyses with limited circulation. Competitive considerations in the organization may preclude publication of these summaries.

Secondary data save time and money if they help solve the researcher's problem. Even if the problem is not solved, secondary data have other advantages. They can aid in formulating the problem statement and suggest research methods and other types of data needed for solving the problem. In addition, secondary data can pinpoint the kinds of people to approach and their locations and serve as a basis of comparison for other data. The disadvantages of secondary data stem mainly from a mismatch between the researcher's unique problem and the purpose for which the secondary data were originally gathered, which are typically different. For example, suppose that a company wanted to determine the market potential for a fireplace log made of coal rather than compressed wood by-products. The researcher found plenty of secondary data about total wood consumed as fuel, quantities consumed in each state, and types of

---

marketing research problem determining what information is needed and how that information can be obtained efficiently and effectively

marketing research objective the specific information needed to solve a marketing research problem; the objective should be to provide insightful decision-making information

management decision problem a broad-based problem that uses marketing research for managers to take proper actions

secondary data data previously collected for any purpose other than the one at hand

wood burned. Secondary data were also available about consumer attitudes and purchase patterns of wood by-product fireplace logs. The wealth of secondary data would provide the researcher with many insights into the artificial log market, but could not provide the research with specific information about whether consumers would buy artificial logs made of coal.

The quality of secondary data may also pose a problem. Often, secondary data sources do not give detailed information that would enable a researcher to assess their quality or relevance. Whenever possible, a researcher needs to address these important questions: Who gathered the data? Why were the data obtained? What methodology was used? How were classifications (such as heavy users vs. light users) developed and defined? When was the information gathered?

The Growing Importance of Social Media Data

Meta owns and controls data collected from 2 billion daily and nearly 3 billion monthly active users.[7] The user databases of social media sites like Twitter, now known as X, Facebook, and Instagram tell these companies' marketers who your friends are, where you are, and what you like and dislike. One study found that the pattern of Facebook likes can accurately predict personal attributes such as relationship status, emotional stability, age, and political views, among other things.[8]

Data brokerages like Acxiom and Oracle combine social data collected from social media sites with data from other sources to get a highly detailed and very accurate understanding of consumers, what their interests are, and how they make purchase decisions. These firms also get data from online cookies, data collected from loyalty-card programs, and even data from credit card companies. All of the collected data is then aggregated, typically on an anonymous basis, and provides an in-depth understanding about which items and brands consumers buy. Pepsi uses this type of data to show different ads based on whether a user regularly buys Pepsi or Diet Pepsi or is a Pepsi switcher (i.e., a person who tends to switch soda brands and is more price sensitive).

Another Facebook tool allows advertisers to calculate their *return on investment* (total profit minus expenses divided by the investment made) on Facebook ads by tallying the actions taken by ad viewers. These actions include click-throughs, registrations, shopping cart checkouts, and other metrics. The tool also enables

If you notice these buttons, Facebook may be tracking your browsing history—whether you click on them or not.

marketers to deliver ads to people who are most likely to make further purchases.

Facebook has shifted much of its focus from tracking cookies (small files stored on users' machines that track online activity) to Facebook log-ins. The goal of this shift is to improve ad targeting by associating views with a person's account instead of a particular device or IP address. (A number of people might use the same computer, but each likely has their own Facebook account.) This move has helped Facebook ensure that the 10 million advertisers who buy views from specific age groups and/or genders actually reach the people they want to.

The Incredible World of Big Data and Market Analytics

Big data is the exponential growth in the volume, variety, and velocity of information and the development of complex new tools to analyze and create meaning from such data. In the past, the flow of data was slow, steady, and predictable. All data were quantitative (countable)—many firms collected sales numbers by store, by product line, and at most, perhaps by a few other measures. Today, data are constantly streaming in from social media as well as other sources. Advanced databases of big data allow the analysis of unstructured data such as emails, audio files, and YouTube videos.

Market analytics is applying quantitative techniques that enable companies to identify hidden customer shopping patterns and produce actionable insights. These insights enable marketing managers to create the right marketing mix to drive customer satisfaction. Marketing analytics also uncover new opportunities in the marketplace as well as drive efficiency in pricing strategies, supply chain management (discussed in Chapter 13), promotional campaigns, and product development. Market analytics is covered in detail in the Appendix at the end of the book.

9-2b Planning the Research Design and Gathering Primary Data

Good secondary data and big data can help researchers conduct a thorough situation analysis. With that

---

big data the exponential growth in the volume, variety, and velocity of information and the development of complex, new tools to analyze and create meaning from such data

information, researchers can list their unanswered questions and rank them. Researchers must then decide the exact information required to answer the questions. The **research design** specifies which research questions must be answered, how and when the data will be gathered, and how the data will be analyzed. Typically, the project budget is finalized after the research design has been approved.

Sometimes research questions can be answered by gathering more secondary data; otherwise, primary data may be needed. **Primary data**, or information collected for the first time, are used for solving a particular problem under investigation. The main advantage of primary data is that it can answer specific research questions that secondary data cannot. Dollar stores, or deep-discount retailers, have fared quite well in a market dominated by Walmart and Amazon. Contributing to the continual patronage of dollar stores is their image. Customers tend to abandon stores quite rapidly if they develop a negative image. So, market research was done to assess their image. Marketing research found that, in the U.S., dollar stores (such as Dollar General, Dollar Tree, and Family Dollar) have favorability ratings around 60 percent. These retailers focus on low-income consumers. Research by California State University Monterey Bay found that well-known brand-names will introduce lower priced products to be sold at these retailers, referred to as downward brand extensions. Having access to popular brands gives lower-income consumers a favorable shopping experience and positively impacts their self-worth. Further, offering such well-known brands helps dollar stores to maintain a positive image.[9]

Each of the dollar stores have localized their community support strategy, and most dollar stores tend to support local, as opposed to national, causes. For example, Dollar General focuses most of its giving on the Dollar General Literacy Foundation, a program aimed at helping employees and customers within 15 miles of its stores. Family Dollar concentrates on small grants to local community groups that provide "basic necessities," such as local food banks. People living in low-income areas and/or rural areas tend to have the most positive image of the dollar stores.[10] Overall, marketing research found that public image of dollar stores was positive and that these retailers did not need to invest in changing their image.

Primary data are current, and researchers know the source. Sometimes researchers gather the data themselves rather than assign projects to outside companies. Researchers also specify the methodology of the research. Secrecy can be maintained because the information is proprietary. In contrast, much secondary data is available to all interested parties for relatively small fees or for free.

Dollar stores such as Family Dollar have a positive image in the local communities that they serve.

Gathering primary data can be expensive; costs can range from a few hundred dollars for a limited survey to several million. Several factors can impact the cost of collecting primary data, including the methodology that a marketer is using, the target audience, and then incentives. For instance, online surveys are less expensive than other survey methods such as phone surveys, since phone surveys require live people to administer the surveys, or focus groups, which typically require more time of participants. Because primary data gathering is so expensive, many firms do not bother to conduct in-person interviews. Instead, they use the internet. Larger companies that conduct many research projects use another cost-saving technique—*piggyback studies*—in which data are gathered on two different projects using one questionnaire. Nevertheless, the disadvantages of primary data gathering are usually offset by the advantages. It is often the only way of solving a research problem. And with a variety of techniques available for research—including surveys, observations, and experiments—primary data can address almost any marketing question.

Survey Research

The most popular technique for gathering primary data is **survey research**, in which a researcher either interacts

---

research design specifies which research questions must be answered, how and when the data will be gathered, and how the data will be analyzed

primary data information that is collected for the first time; used for solving the particular problem under investigation

survey research the most popular technique for gathering primary data, in which a researcher interacts with people to obtain facts, opinions, and attitudes

with people or posts a questionnaire online to obtain facts, opinions, and attitudes. Table 9.1 summarizes the characteristics of traditional forms of survey research.

In-Home Personal Interviews In-home personal interviews often provide high-quality information. They can be very expensive if interviewers have to travel to respondents' homes, but personal interviews via video conferencing, through platforms such as Zoom, are becoming more common, which can be more cost-effective. These types of interviews are often set up in advance to ensure participation by the interviewee.

Telephone Interviews Telephone interviews cost less than personal interviews, but the cost is rapidly increasing owing to respondent refusals to participate. Most telephone interviewing is conducted from a specially designed phone room called a **central-location telephone (CLT) facility**.

A CLT facility has many phone lines, individual interviewing stations, headsets, and sometimes monitoring equipment. The research firm typically will interview people nationwide from a single location. The federal "Do Not Call" law does not apply to survey research.

---

central-location telephone (CLT) facility a specially designed phone room used to conduct telephone interviewing

Most CLT facilities use computer-assisted interviewing. The interviewer reads the questions from the screen and enters the respondent's data directly into the database, saving time. One of the main benefits of using computer assistance for these interviews is that it can save time. For example, computer-assisted interviewing technology can automatically update the flow of questions based on participant responses. If Chobani was looking for feedback about a new flavor of yogurt that it had recently released, one question might be whether or not the participant had tried the new flavor. If yes, the computer-assisted interviewing technology could automatically display questions to assess the participants' attitudes toward the new flavor. If not, the technology could automatically display questions to assess participant interest in trying the new flavor. This method would be much quicker than the interviewer having to search through a script to find the correct questions. Additionally, the researcher can stop the survey at any point and immediately print out the survey results, allowing the research design to be refined as necessary.

Mail Surveys

Mail surveys are those that are directly mailed to potential respondents. Mail surveys have several benefits: relatively low cost, elimination of interviewers and field supervisors,

Table 9.1	Characteristics of Traditional Forms of Survey Research					
Characteristic	In-Home Personal Interviews	Central-Location Telephone Interviews	Mail Surveys	Mail Panel-Surveys	Executive Interviews	Focus Groups
Cost	Moderate to high	Moderate	Low	Moderate	High	Low
Time span	Moderate	Fast	Slow	Relatively slow	Moderate	Fast
Use of interviewer probes	Yes	Yes	No	Yes	Yes	Yes
Ability to show concepts to respondent	Yes (also taste tests)	No	Yes	Yes	Yes	Yes
Management control over interviewer	Low	High	N/A	N/A	Moderate	High
General data quality	High	High to moderate	Moderate to low	Moderate	High	Moderate
Ability to collect large amounts of data	High	Moderate to low	Low to-moderate	Moderate	Moderate	Moderate
Ability to handle complex questionnaires	High	High, if computer aided	Low	Low	High	N/A

centralized control, and actual or promised anonymity for respondents (which may draw more candid responses). A disadvantage is that mail questionnaires usually produce low response rates. The resulting sample may therefore not represent the surveyed population. Another serious problem with mail surveys is that no one probes respondents to clarify or elaborate on their answers. If a respondent uses the word "convenience," there is no way to clarify exactly what is meant. Convenience could refer to location, store hours, or a host of other factors.

Mail panels offer an alternative to the one-shot survey. A panel consists of a sample of respondents recruited to participate in mail surveys for a given period. Panel members often receive gifts or payment in return for their participation. Essentially, the panel is a sample used several times. In contrast to one-time surveys, the response rates from panels are higher. Rates of 70 percent (of those who agree to participate) are not uncommon.

Executive Interviews An **executive interview** usually involves interviewing businesspeople at their offices concerning industrial products or services, a process that is very expensive. First, individuals involved in the purchase decision for the product in question must be identified and located, which can itself be expensive and time consuming. Once a qualified person is located, the next step is to get that person to agree to be interviewed and to set a time for the interview. Finally, an interviewer must go to the particular place at the appointed time. Long waits are frequently encountered; cancellations are not uncommon. This type of survey requires the very best interviewers because they are frequently interviewing on topics that they know very little about. Many of these interviews have moved online.

Focus Groups A **focus group** is a type of personal interviewing. In focus groups, researchers recruit 7 to 10 people with certain desired characteristics. These qualified consumers are usually offered an incentive (typically $30 to $150) to participate in a group discussion. Focus groups can take place in person, in which the meeting is typically recorded and the viewing room may have a one-way mirror so that clients (manufacturers or retailers) can watch the session, or focus groups can also take place online. During the session, a moderator, hired by the research company, leads the group discussion. Focus groups can be used to gauge consumer response to a product or promotion and are occasionally used to brainstorm new-product ideas or to screen concepts for new products. Focus groups also represent an efficient way of learning how products are actually used in the home. Lewis Stone, former manager of Colgate-Palmolive's research and development division, says the following about focus groups:

"If it weren't for focus groups, Colgate-Palmolive Co. might never know that some women squeeze their bottles of dishwashing soap, others squeeeeeze them, and still others squeeze out the desired amount. Then there are the ones who use the soap "neat;" that is, they put the product directly on a sponge or washcloth and wash the dishes under running water until the suds run out. Then they apply more detergent."

Stone was explaining how body language, exhibited during focus groups, provides insights into a product that are not apparent from reading questionnaires on habits and practices. Panelists' descriptions of how they perform tasks highlight need gaps, which can improve an existing product or demonstrate how a new product might be received.

Questionnaire Design All forms of survey research require a questionnaire. Questionnaires ensure that all respondents will be asked the same series of questions. Questionnaires include three basic types of questions: open-ended, closed-ended, and scaled-response (refer to Table 9.2). An **open-ended question** encourages an answer phrased in the respondent's own words. Researchers get a rich array of information based on the respondent's frame of reference (What do you think about the new flavor?). In contrast, a **closed-ended question** asks the respondent to make a selection from a limited list of responses. Closed-ended questions can either be what marketing researchers call dichotomous (Do you like the new flavor? Yes or No.) or multiple choice. A **scaled-response question** is a closed-ended question designed to measure the intensity of a respondent's answer (To what extent did you like the new flavor? 1—Did not like the flavor at all, 2—Somewhat disliked the flavor, 3—Neither disliked nor liked the flavor, 4—Somewhat liked the flavor, 5—Liked the flavor very much).

Closed-ended and scaled-response questions are easier to tabulate than open-ended questions because response choices are fixed. On the other hand, unless the researcher

---

executive interview a type of survey that usually involves interviewing businesspeople at their offices concerning industrial products or services

focus group 7 to 10 people who participate in a group discussion led by a moderator

open-ended question an interview question that encourages an answer phrased in the respondent's own words

closed-ended question an interview question that asks the respondent to make a selection from a limited list of responses

scaled-response question a closed-ended question designed to measure the intensity of a respondent's answer

Table 9.2 Types of Questions Found on Questionnaires for National Market Research

Open-Ended Questions	Closed-Ended Questions	Scaled-Response Question

1. What advantages, if any, do you think ordering online offers compared to shopping at a local retail outlet? (Probe: What else?)
 	
2. What flavors of breakfast burritos do you typically buy?
 	
3. What is it about the color of the eye shadow that makes you like it the best?
	Dichotomous
	1. Did you heat the breakfast burrito before eating It?
	   Yes 1
	   No 2
	2. The packaging of the chips was appealing.
	   Agree 1
	   Disagree 2
	Multiple Choice
	1. I'd like you to think back to the last footwear of any kind that you bought. I am going to read a list of descriptions and would like for you to tell me which category they fall into. (*Read list and circle proper category.*)
	   Dress and/or formal 1
	   Casual 2
	   Canvas/trainer/gym shoes 3
	   Specialized athletic 4
	   Boots 5
	2. In the past three months, have you used Noxzema skin cream . . . . (*Circle all that apply.*)
	   As a facial wash 1
	   For moisturizing the skin 2
	   For treating blemishes 3
	   For cleansing the skin 4
	   For treating dry skin 5
	   For softening skin 6
	   For sunburn 7
		Now that you have tried our new flavor of chips, would you say that you . . . (*Circle one.*)
		Would definitely buy it 1
		Would probably buy it 2
		Might or might not buy it 3
		Probably would not buy it 4
		Definitely would not buy it 5

designs the closed-ended question very carefully, an important choice may be omitted. For example, suppose a food study asked this question: "Besides meat, which of the following items do you normally add to tacos that you prepare at home?"

Avocado	1	Olives (black/green)	6
Cheese (Monterey Jack/cheddar)	2	Onions (red/white)	7
Guacamole	3	Peppers (red/green)	8
Lettuce	4	Jalapeños	9
Mexican hot sauce	5	Sour cream	0

The list seems complete, doesn't it? However, consider the following responses: "I like to add roasted sweet potatoes to my tacos," "I cut up a mixture of lettuce and spinach," "I'm a vegetarian—I don't use meat at all," and "My taco is filled only with guacamole." How would you code these replies? As you can tell, the question needs an "other" category.

A good question must be clear and concise and avoid ambiguous language. The answer to the question "Do you live within 10 minutes of campus?" depends on the mode of transportation (maybe the person walks), driving speed, perceived time, and other factors. Language should also be clear. Therefore, jargon should be avoided, and wording should be geared to the target audience. A question such as "What is the level of efficacy of your preponderant dishwasher powder?" would probably be greeted by a lot of blank stares. It would be much simpler to say, "Are you (1) very satisfied, (2) somewhat satisfied, or (3) not satisfied with your current brand of dishwasher detergent?"

Stating the survey's purpose at the beginning of the interview may improve clarity, but it may also increase the chances of receiving biased responses. Many times, respondents will try to provide answers that they believe are "correct" or that the interviewer wants to hear. To avoid bias at the question level, researchers should avoid leading questions and adjectives that cause respondents to think of the topic in a certain way.

Finally, to ensure clarity, the interviewer should avoid asking two questions in one—for example, "How did you like the taste and texture of the KIND granola bar?" This should be divided into two questions, one concerning taste and the other texture.

Observation Research

In contrast to survey research, **observation research** entails watching what people do or using machines to watch what people do. Specifically, it can be defined as the systematic process of recording the behavioral patterns of people, objects, and occurrences without questioning them. A market researcher using the observation technique witnesses and records information as events occur or compiles evidence from records of past events. Carried a step further, observation may involve watching people or phenomena and may be conducted by human observers or machines. Examples of these various observational situations are shown in Table 9.3.

Some common forms of people-watching-people research are one-way mirror observations, mystery shoppers, and behavioral targeting. A one-way mirror allows the researchers to observe the participants, but the participants cannot view the researchers.

Mystery Shoppers **Mystery shoppers** are researchers posing as customers to gather observational data about a store (e.g., are the shelves neatly stocked?) and collect data about customer/employee interactions. The interaction is not an interview, and communication occurs only so that the mystery shopper can observe the actions and comments of the employee. Mystery shopping is, therefore, classified as an observational marketing research method, even though communication is often involved. Restaurant chains like Subway use mystery shoppers to evaluate store cleanliness and quality of service.

Behavioral Targeting **Behavioral targeting (BT)**, sometimes simply called "tracking," began as a simple process by placing cookies in users' browsers or mobile apps to track which websites they visited, how long they lingered, what they searched for, and what they bought. All of this information can be tracked anonymously—a "fly on the wall" perspective. While survey research is a great way to find out the "why" and the "how," behavioral targeting lets the researcher find out the "how much," the "how often," and the "where." Also, through **social media monitoring**—using automated tools to monitor online buzz, chatter, and conversations—a researcher can learn what is being said about the brand and the competition. Tracking is the basis for input into online databases. Companies like Tapad track customers across multiple devices—laptops, smartphones, and tablets, for example. If a customer is using multiple devices at the same time, Tapad knows, and knows what is being done on each.

Ethnographic Research Ethnographic research comes to marketing from the field of anthropology. The technique is becoming increasingly popular in marketing research. **Ethnographic research**, or the study of human behavior in its natural context, involves observation of behavior and physical setting. Ethnographers directly observe the population they are studying. As "participant

Table 9.3	Observational Situations
Situation	**Example**
People watching people	Observers stationed in supermarkets watch consumers select frozen Mexican dinners; the purpose is to find out how much comparison shopping people do at the point of purchase.
People watching an activity	An observer stationed at an intersection counts traffic moving in various directions.
Machines watching people	Cameras record behavior as in the people-watching-people example above.
Machines watching an activity	Traffic-counting machines monitor traffic flow.

observation research a research method that relies on four types of observation: people watching people, people watching an activity, machines watching people, and machines watching an activity

mystery shoppers researchers posing as customers to gather observational data about a store

behavioral targeting (BT) a form of observation marketing research that combines a consumer's online activity with psychographic and demographic profiles compiled in databases

social media monitoring the use of automated tools to monitor online buzz, chatter, and conversations

ethnographic research the study of human behavior in its natural context; involves observation of behavior and physical setting

observers," ethnographers can use their intimacy with the people they are studying to gain richer, deeper insights into culture and behavior—in short, what makes people do what they do?

While conducting research on organic products, a marketing consultant asked participants, "Do you normally purchase organic foods?" One woman, a single mother with limited income, replied, "Are you kidding me? It's too expensive for me. I'll never buy organic products. I can't afford them." Six months later, the consultant was doing ethnographic research and went to the same woman's apartment, where she saw a catalog on the desk for organic products. The consultant asked, "Are you buying those?" and she said, "Yes, definitely." The price of the products was more expensive than the organic products you'd typically find in the supermarket.

After discussing it with her, the consultant discovered that the woman didn't care singularly about the price. She bought the products because they were organic, but most of all, because they were sold through parties, similar to shopping parties that are commonly held by consultants for brands like BeautyCounter and Herbalife. The parties, and thus the products, enabled her to meet her new neighbors.

It makes you think—if you're working with an organic brand or a company that sells organic products, you might want to explore new ways of distribution that add relationship and/or socialization benefits. The consultant never would have discovered this fact if they used only surveys to conduct their research. The woman might have responded "organic never" in one survey and "organic often" in the next. The consultant never would have understood why that change occurred without ethnographic research. This example shows the richness of the human being: people might have contradictory behaviors on paper, but they're often driven by emotional motivators that aren't always evident.

Virtual Shopping Advances in computer and virtual reality technology have enabled researchers to simulate an actual retail store environment on a computer screen or in a headset. For example, the Meta Quest 2 is a widely used virtual reality headset that consumers can use for gaming and other virtual social experiences, but these types of technologies are also being used by marketers to collect data through simulated shopping experiences. Depending on the type of simulation, a shopper can "pick up" a package by touching its image on the monitor and rotate it to

examine all sides. Like buying on most online retailers, the shopper touches the shopping cart to add an item to the basket. During the shopping process, the computer unobtrusively records the amount of time the consumer spends shopping in each product category, the time the consumer spends examining each side of a product, the quantity of the product the consumer purchases, and the order in which items are purchased.

Imagine that an apparel retailer is trying to better understand how its customers shop for clothing. With the use of a computer-simulated environment the retailer found that older consumers, their primary target market, tend to shop for an entire outfit, that is, buying a shirt, matching sweater, and pants all at the same time, rather than just buying single pieces of clothing. With this knowledge, the apparel chain could redesign the way that it organizes its merchandise—rather than organizing clothing by product type, it could group matching items together so that consumers can more easily put their outfits together.

Virtual shopping research is growing rapidly. Thousands of new consumer packaged goods are introduced every year. All are vying for very limited retail shelf space. Any process, such as virtual shopping, that can speed up product development time and lower costs is always welcomed by manufacturers. Some companies outside of retail have even begun experimenting with virtual shopping and other simulated-environment tools—many telecom, financial, automotive, aviation, and fast-food companies are using such tools to better serve their customers.

Experiments

An **experiment** is a method that a researcher can use to gather primary data. The researcher alters one or more variables—price, package design, shelf space, advertising theme, advertising expenditures—while observing the

Virtual reality has enabled researchers to simulate a retail store environment. Merchandise shelf positioning, store layouts, point-of-purchase displays, and other variables can easily be tested.

---

experiment a method of gathering primary data in which the researcher alters one or more variables while observing the effects of those alterations on another variable

effects of those alterations on another variable (usually sales). The best experiments are those in which all factors except one are held constant. The researcher can then observe what changes in sales, for example, result from changes in product packaging.

Holding all other factors constant in the external environment is a monumental and costly, if not impossible, task. Such factors as competitors' actions, weather, and economic conditions are beyond the researcher's control. Yet market researchers have ways to account for the ever-changing external environment. Mars, the candy company, was losing sales to other candy companies. Traditional surveys showed that the shrinking candy bar was not perceived as a good value. Mars wondered whether a bigger bar sold at the same price would increase sales enough to offset the higher ingredient costs. The company designed an experiment in which the marketing mix stayed the same in different markets, but the size of the candy bar varied. The substantial increase in sales of the bigger bar quickly proved that the additional costs would be more than covered by the additional revenue. Mars increased the bar size—along with its market share and profits.

9-2c Specifying the Sampling Procedures

Once the researchers decide how they will collect primary data, their next step is to select the sampling procedures they will use. A firm can seldom take a census of all possible users of a new product, nor can they all be interviewed. Therefore, a firm must select a sample of the group to be interviewed. A **sample** is a subset from a larger population.

Several questions must be answered before a sampling plan is chosen. First, the population, or **universe**, of interest must be defined. This is the group from which the sample will be drawn. It should include all the people whose opinions, behavior, preferences, attitudes, and so on, are of interest to the marketer. For example, in a study whose purpose is to determine the market for a new canned dog food, the universe might be defined to include all current buyers of canned dog food.

After the universe has been defined, the next question is whether the sample must be representative of the population. If the answer is yes, a probability sample is needed. Otherwise, a nonprobability sample might be considered.

Probability Samples

A **probability sample** is a sample in which every element in the population has a known statistical likelihood of being selected. Its most desirable feature is that scientific rules can be used to ensure that the sample represents the population.

One type of probability sample is a **random sample**—a sample arranged in such a way that every element of the population has an equal chance of being selected as part of the sample. For example, suppose a university is interested in getting opinions from a cross section of students on a proposed sports complex to be built using student activity fees. If the university can acquire an up-to-date list of all the enrolled students, it can draw a random sample by using random numbers from a table (found in most statistics books) to select students from the list. Common forms of probability and nonprobability samples are shown in Table 9.4.

Nonprobability Samples

Any sample in which little or no attempt is made to get a representative cross section of the population can be considered a **nonprobability sample**. Therefore, the probability of selection of each sampling unit is not known. A common form of a nonprobability sample is the **convenience sample**, which uses respondents who are convenient or readily accessible to the researcher—for instance, employees, friends, or relatives.

Nonprobability samples are acceptable as long as the researcher understands their nonrepresentative nature. Because of their lower cost, nonprobability samples are sometimes used in marketing research.

Types of Errors Whenever a sample is used in marketing research, two major types of errors may occur: measurement error and sampling error. **Measurement error** occurs when there is a difference between the information the researcher desires and the information the measurement

---

sample a subset from a larger population

universe the population from which a sample will be drawn

probability sample a sample in which every element in the population has a known statistical likelihood of being selected

random sample a sample arranged in such a way that every element of the population has an equal chance of being selected as part of the sample

nonprobability sample any sample in which little or no attempt is made to get a representative cross section of the population

convenience sample a form of nonprobability sample using respondents who are convenient or readily accessible to the researcher—for example, employees, friends, or relatives

measurement error an error that occurs when there is a difference between the information the researcher desires and the information the measurement process provides

Table 9.4 Types of Samples

Probability Samples	
Simple Random Sample	Every member of the population has a known and equal chance of selection.
Stratified Sample	The population is divided into mutually exclusive groups (such as gender or age); then random samples are drawn from each group.
Cluster Sample	The population is divided into mutually exclusive groups (such as geographic areas); then a random sample of clusters is selected. The researcher then collects data from all the elements in the selected clusters or from a probability sample of elements within each selected cluster.
Systematic Sample	A list of the population is obtained—e.g., all persons with a checking account at Chase Bank—and a skip interval is obtained by dividing the sample size by the population size. If the sample size is 100 and the bank has 1,000 customers, then the skip interval is 10. The beginning number is randomly chosen within the skip interval. If the beginning number is 8, then the skip pattern would be 8, 18, 28, ...
Nonprobability Samples	
Convenience Sample	The researcher selects the population members from whom it is easiest to obtain information.
Judgment Sample	The researcher's selection criteria are based on personal judgment that the elements (persons) chosen will likely give accurate information.
Quota Sample	The researcher finds a prescribed number of people in several categories—e.g., owners of large dogs versus owners of small dogs. Respondents are not selected on probability sampling criteria.
Snowball Sample	Additional respondents are selected on the basis of referrals from the initial respondents. This method is used when a desired type of respondent is hard to find—e.g., persons who have taken round-the-world cruises in the past three years. This technique employs the old adage "Birds of a feather flock together."

process provides. For example, people may tell an interviewer that they purchase Crest toothpaste when they do not. Measurement error generally tends to be larger than sampling error.

Sampling error occurs when a sample somehow does not represent the target population. Sampling error can be one of several types. Nonresponse error occurs when the sample actually interviewed differs from the sample drawn. This error happens because the original people selected to be interviewed either refused to cooperate or were inaccessible.

Frame error, another type of sampling error, arises if the sample drawn from a population differs from the target population. For instance, suppose a telephone survey is conducted to find out Chicago soda drinkers' attitudes

toward Pepsi. If a Chicago telephone directory is used as the *frame* (the device or list from which the respondents are selected), the survey will contain a frame error. Not all Chicago soda drinkers have landline phones, many phone numbers are unlisted, and people may own cell phones with a different area code. An ideal sample (in other words, a sample with no frame error) matches all important characteristics of the target population to be surveyed. Could you find a perfect frame for Chicago soda drinkers?

Random error occurs when the selected sample is an imperfect representation of the overall population. Random error represents how accurately the chosen sample's true average (mean) value reflects the population's true average (mean) value. For example, we might take a random sample of soda drinkers in Chicago and find that 16 percent regularly drink Pepsi. The next day, we might repeat the same sampling procedure and discover that 14 percent regularly drink Pepsi. The difference is due to random error. Error is common to all surveys, yet it is often not reported or is underreported. Typically, the only error mentioned in a written report is sampling error.

9-2d Collecting the Primary Data

Marketing research field service firms are used to collect some primary data. A **field service firm** specializes in interviewing respondents on a subcontracted basis. A

---

sampling error an error that occurs when a sample somehow does not represent the target population

frame error an error that occurs when a sample drawn from a population differs from the target population

random error an error that occurs when the selected sample is an imperfect representation of the overall population

field service firm a firm that specializes in interviewing respondents on a subcontracted basis

Figure 9.2 Social Media Platforms Cross-Tabulation

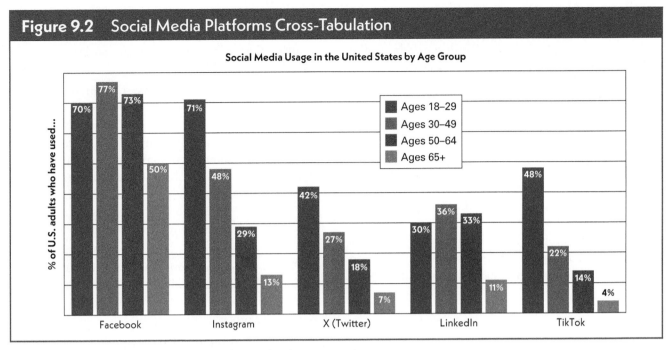

Source: https://www.pewresearch.org/internet/2021/04/07/social-media-use-in-2021/

typical marketing research study involves data collection in several cities, which may require the marketer to work with a comparable number of field service firms. Besides conducting interviews, field service firms provide focus group facilities, test product storage, and kitchen facilities to prepare test food products.

9-2e Analyzing the Data

After collecting the data, the marketing researcher proceeds to the next step in the research process: data analysis. The purpose of this analysis is to interpret and draw conclusions from the mass of collected data. The marketing researcher tries to organize and analyze those data by using one or more techniques common to marketing research: one-way frequency counts, cross-tabulations, and more sophisticated statistical analysis. Of these three techniques, one-way frequency counts are the simplest. One-way frequency tables simply record the responses to a question. For example, the answers to the question "What social media platform have you used?" would provide a one-way frequency distribution. One-way frequency tables are always done in data analysis, at least as a first step, because they provide the researcher with a general picture of the study's results. A **cross-tabulation** lets the analyst look at the responses to one question in relation to the responses to one or more other questions. For example, in Figure 9.2, what is the association between age and social media platform usage?

Researchers can use many other more powerful and sophisticated statistical techniques, such as hypothesis testing, measures of association, and regression analysis. A description of these techniques goes beyond the scope of

this book but can be found in any good marketing research textbook. The use of sophisticated statistical techniques depends on the researchers' objectives and the nature of the data gathered.

9-2f Preparing and Presenting the Report

After data analysis has been completed, the researcher must prepare the report and communicate the conclusions and recommendations to management. This is a key step in the process. If the marketing researcher wants managers to carry out the recommendations, they must convince them that the results are credible and justified by the data collected.

Researchers are usually required to present both written and oral reports on the project. Sometimes the written report is no more than a copy of the PowerPoint slides used in the oral presentation, while other times it is a much more detailed and formal document. Whatever kind of report is used, it should be tailored to the audience. The report should begin with a clear, concise statement of the research objectives, followed by a complete but brief and simple explanation of the research design or methodology employed. A summary of major findings should come next. Typically, the main report does not provide in depth information about specific numbers and statistical analyses (these may be included in an appendix in case management

---

cross-tabulation a method of analyzing data that lets the analyst look at the responses to one question in relation to the responses to one or more other questions

wants to explore the numbers in more detail), but more so focuses on the major trends in the data and the implications of these trends. Graphs and other visuals should be used to present the results; visuals make it much easier for managers to interpret the results. The conclusion of the report should also present recommendations to management.

Most people who enter marketing will become research users rather than research suppliers. Thus, they must know what to notice in a report. As with many other items we purchase, quality is not always readily apparent. Nor does a high price guarantee superior quality. The basis for measuring the quality of a marketing research report is the research proposal. Did the report meet the objectives established in the proposal? Was the methodology outlined in the proposal followed? Are the conclusions based on logical deductions from the data analysis? Do the recommendations seem prudent, given the conclusions?

9-2g Following Up

The final step in the marketing research process is to follow up. The researcher should determine why management did or did not carry out the recommendations in the report. Was sufficient decision-making information included? What could have been done to make the report more useful to management? A good rapport between the product manager, or whoever authorized the project, and the market researcher is essential. Often, they must work together on many studies throughout the year.

9-3 The Profound Impact of the Internet and Smart Devices on Marketing Research

9-3 Discuss the profound impact of the internet on marketing research

Nearly 90 percent of marketing researchers regularly use online surveys. Online survey research has replaced computer-assisted telephone interviewing as the most popular mode of data collection.

9-3a Advantages of Online Surveys

The huge growth in the popularity of online surveys is the result of the many advantages the internet offers. The specific advantages of internet surveys, which are often sent to mobile devices, are many:

- **Rapid development, real-time reporting:** Digital surveys can be broadcast to thousands of potential respondents simultaneously. Respondents complete

surveys simultaneously; then results are tabulated and posted for corporate clients to view as the returns arrive. The effect: survey results can be sent to the client very quickly.

- **Dramatically reduced costs:** The internet can cut costs by 25 to 40 percent and provide results in half the time it takes to do traditional surveys. Traditional survey methods are labor-intensive efforts, incurring training, telecommunications, and management costs. Online methods eliminate these completely. While costs for traditional survey techniques rise proportionally with the number of interviews desired, digital solicitations can grow in volume with little increase in project costs.

- **Personalized questions and data:** Online surveys can be highly personalized for greater relevance to each respondent's own situation, thus speeding the response process.

- **Improved respondent participation:** Smartphone surveys take half as much time to complete as phone interviews, can be accomplished at the respondent's convenience (e.g., after work hours), and are much more stimulating and engaging. As a result, online surveys enjoy much higher response rates.

- **Contact with hard-to-reach groups:** Certain groups—doctors, high-income professionals, top management in Global 2000 firms—are among the most surveyed on the planet and are also the most difficult to reach. Many of these groups are well represented online. Internet surveys provide convenient anytime/anywhere access that makes it easy for busy professionals to participate.

9-3b Uses of the Internet and Smart Devices by Marketing Researchers

Marketing researchers use the internet to administer surveys, conduct focus groups, and perform a variety of other types of marketing research.

Methods of Conducting Online Surveys

There are several basic methods for conducting online surveys: web survey systems, survey design and web-hosting sites, and online panel providers.

Web Survey Systems Web survey systems are software systems specifically designed for web questionnaire construction and delivery. They consist of an integrated questionnaire designer, web server, database, and data delivery program designed for use by nonprogrammers.

The web server distributes the questionnaire and files responses in a database. The user can query the server at

Web survey systems enable the researcher to query the survey at any time to examine survey results to date.

any time via the web for completion statistics, descriptive statistics on responses, and graphical displays of data. Some popular online survey research software packages are SurveyMonkey, Typeform, Google Forms, and SurveyPlanet.

Free versions of all these tools and paid versions offer added capabilities, such as:

- **Survey logic:** Survey logic uses information from previous answers to determine which questions to go to next. For example, do you own an imported car? If the user answers yes, then the next question might be, "What brand?" If the respondent answers no, then the survey would skip to the next section of questions.

- **Export data:** Many tools won't let you export your data unless you use the paid version.

- **Customer logo:** Paid versions let you get rid of the tools logo and replace it with your own logo.

- **A wider range of question types:** Most free survey creators offer plenty of question options, including multiple choice radio buttons, drop downs, rating scales, and others. Usually, paid versions offer more options such as the ability to select multiple options in a drop-down menu, star rankings, grids, and others.

Using any of these tools you could create and publish your own survey. Then you are left with the issue of getting people to take your survey. The survey can be done via an email list, where invitations are sent to people on the list, or you could use an online panel like the ones discussed below.

SurveyMonkey Audience SurveyMonkey has created a platform that allows market researchers to create their surveys, find respondents for the survey, and do basic analyses on the data collected. Researchers can specify the type of respondents they are looking for, based on demographic and geographic variables and profession, among other variables. Next, researchers can create their survey on the SurveyMonkey platform, and then the platform also offers data analysis tools to help researchers interpret and understand the data. The data analytics tools include text analysis, basic statistical analyses such as cross-tab analyses, and the ability to export to more sophisticated statistical software, such as SPSS. For a simple five question survey, the approximate cost to use SurveyMonkey Audience is $1 per response.[11]

Online Panel Providers Often, researchers use online panel providers for a ready-made sample population. Online panel providers such as Survey Sampling International and e-Rewards pre-recruit people who agree to participate in online market research surveys.

Some online panels are created for specific industries and may have a few thousand panel members, while the large commercial online panels have millions of people waiting to be surveyed. When people join online panels, they answer an extensive profiling questionnaire that enables the panel provider to target research efforts to panel members who meet specific criteria.

In addition to effective panel recruitment, online panel providers must have effective ongoing management of their panel to ensure a high level of quality. Panels must continually realize that their participants have positive experiences with every research project. Among other components, good panel management includes frequency controls to realize that panel members are not surveyed too little or too much. Panel members should be given enough survey opportunities to stay effectively engaged in the research process, but not surveyed so much as to be burdened with survey invitations. Other keys to guaranteeing a positive experience for panel members is providing respondent privacy, safeguarding personal information, and protecting members from bogus research that attempts to use online surveys as a sales channel (this is the practice of *sugging*—selling under the guise of research).

Panel providers are continually recruiting new members to keep up with the growth in demand for online samples, as well as replacing any panel members who may drop out. Even with exceptional panel member retention, some panel members will become less active in responding to surveys. In addition, panels will often recruit new members to assist in growing certain hard-to-reach segments and/or balancing the panel to have maximum representation of the overall population. Ensuring a growing supply of engaged, active panel members is a constant goal of every panel provider.

Finally, panel management includes ensuring panel freshness. As panel members change, their profiles must be updated. A single, 22-year-old college student with an annual income of $17,000 from three years ago may now be a married 25-year-old accountant with a new baby and a household income of $55,000. Updating profiles ensures that panel providers are able to consistently target qualified people for surveys.[12] Some panel providers are now using marketing analytics and big data to compose a much more detailed profile of all of their panel members.[13]

Online Focus Groups

Many research firms conduct focus groups entirely online. The process is fairly simple. The research firm builds a database of respondents via a screening questionnaire on its website. When a client comes to a firm with a need for a particular focus group, the firm goes to its database and identifies individuals who appear to qualify. It sends an email to these individuals, asking them to log on to a particular site at a particular time scheduled for the group. Many times, these groups are joined by respondents on mobile devices. The firm pays them an incentive for their participation.

The firm develops a discussion guide similar to the one used for a conventional focus group, and a moderator runs the group by typing in questions online for all to view. The group operates in an environment similar to that of a chat room so that all participants find all questions and all responses. The firm captures the complete text of the focus group and makes it available for review after the group has finished.

Online focus groups also allow respondents to view things such as a concept statement, a mockup of a print ad, or a short product demonstration video. The moderator simply provides a URL for the respondents to open in another browser window.

More advanced virtual focus group software reserves a frame (section) of the screen for stimuli to be shown. Here, the moderator has control over what is shown in the stimulus area. Many online groups are now conducted with audio and video feeds as well. One advantage of this approach is that the respondent does not have to do any work to notice the stimuli. There are many other advantages of online groups as follows:

- **Better participation rates:** Typically, online focus groups can be conducted over the course of days; once participants are recruited, they are less likely to drop out because of time conflicts.

- **Cost-effectiveness:** Face-to-face focus groups incur costs for facility rental, airfare, hotel, and food. None of these costs is incurred with online focus groups.

- **Broad geographic scope:** Time is flexible online; respondents can be gathered from all over the world.

- **Accessibility:** Online focus groups allow access to individuals who otherwise might be difficult to recruit (e.g., business travelers, senior executives, mothers with infants).

Online Research Communities

An online research community is a carefully selected group of consumers who agree to participate in an ongoing dialogue with a particular corporation. All community interaction takes place on a custom-designed website. During the life of the community—which may last anywhere from six months to a year or more—community members respond to questions the corporation regularly poses. In addition to responding to the corporation's questions, community members talk to one another about topics that are of interest to them.

Hyatt used a community of travel enthusiasts from the United States, the United Kingdom, France, Australia, Chile, and Mexico to gain insights about various travel-related topics. Hyatt learned, for example, that sampling local cuisine is one of the best parts of business travelers' trips. After several travelers expressed an interest in selecting their rooms online, Hyatt launched an initiative examining what it might take to add that functionality to its system. When Procter & Gamble (P&G) was developing scents for a new product line, it asked members of its online community to record the scents that they encountered over the course of a day that made them feel good. By week's end, P&G had received images, videos, and simple text tributes to cut grass, fresh paint, Play-Doh, and other aromas that revealed volumes about how scent triggers not just nostalgia, but also

Prostock-studio/Shutterstock.com

Vita Monart/Shutterstock.com

feelings of competence, adventurousness, comfort, and other powerful emotions.

9-4 The Growing Importance of Mobile Research

9-4 Describe the growing importance of mobile research

Most Americans who have a mobile phone have a smartphone. Because so many people are connected through their phones, mobile phones are a natural vehicle for conducting marketing research surveys. Sixty-four percent of U.S. marketing research organizations currently conduct mobile research surveys.[14]

Mobile surveys are designed to fit into the brief cracks of time that open up when a person waits for a plane, is early for an appointment, commutes to work on a train, or stands in a line. Marketers strive to engage respondents "in the moment" because mobile research provides immediate feedback when a consumer makes a decision to purchase, consumes a product, or experiences some form of promotion. With mobile research, participants can not only send and respond to direct and immediate questions but also share the videos, photos, stories, and moments that are important to them. As new and better apps make the survey experience easier and more intuitive, the use of mobile surveys will continue to rise. New responsive-design technology automatically adjusts the content and navigation of a website to fit the dimensions and resolution of any screen on which it is viewed.

One advertiser wanted to conduct a survey on the televised advertisements that ran during the Super Bowl. The client wanted to measure real-time reactions, but most people do not sit in front of their laptop during the big game. They do, however, multitask using their smartphones. Respondents were recruited in advance of game day, and then during the game, surveys were pushed out in real time to collect feedback on commercials as they aired.

Mobile research offers several advantages in addition to real-time reactions:

- **Increased response rates:** Respondents respond at higher rates (and more quickly) on mobile devices.

- **Increased convenience:** Respondents have better experiences when they can provide feedback when and where they want to.

- **Broader reach:** The ability to reach respondents in developing and remote countries creates a huge opportunity to capture insights from those regions.

- **Richer content:** Respondents can easily share media (e.g., photos, videos, voice recordings) via mobile devices.

- **Broader demographic reach:** Respondent cooperation from all demographic groups is higher.

- **Immediate feedback:** Mobile surveys provide immediate feedback on research questions concerning marketing campaigns, ad testing, and more.

- **Cost savings:** Researchers receive faster replies to surveys, shortening project completion time.

- **Additional options:** Can be used as a mobile recruiting tool to direct respondents to online surveys or connect with hard-to-reach groups. It is another way of reaching people on the go.[15]

9-5 Scanner-Based Research

9-5 Discuss the growing importance of scanner-based research

Scanner-based research is a system for gathering information from respondents by continuously monitoring the advertising, promotion, and pricing they are exposed to and the things they buy. Scanner-based research also entails the aggregation of scanner data from retailers, analysis, and identification of sales trends by industry, company, product line, and individual brand. The variables measured are advertising campaigns, coupons, displays, and product prices. The result is a huge database of marketing efforts and consumer behavior.

The two major scanner-based suppliers are Information Resources Inc. (IRI) and the Nielsen Company. Each has a significant share of the market, but IRI is the founder of scanner-based research. IRI's Shopper Data Cloud is a scanner-based sales-tracking service for the consumer packaged-goods industry. Retail sales, detailed consumer purchasing information (including measurement of store loyalty and total grocery basket expenditures), and promotional activity by manufacturers and retailers are monitored and evaluated for all bar-coded products. Data are collected weekly from supermarkets, drugstores, and mass merchandisers. For example, scanner-based data has revealed that snack food consumption in the United States has increased significantly. In 2022, the snack food industry was worth approximately $150.6 billion and is expected to grow to nearly $170 billion by 2027. According to data from IRI, consumers in the Baby Boomer Generation and Generation X tend to only snack in the afternoon, but millennial consumers often snack throughout the day. Additionally,

---

scanner-based research a system for gathering information from a single group of respondents by continuously monitoring the advertising, promotion, and pricing they are exposed to and the things they buy

during the COVID-19 pandemic, consumption of late-night snacks increased. These shifts in eating patterns have contributed to the overall sales increase in the snack food industry. It is important for marketers of food and beverage products to be aware of these findings so that they can adjust their strategic marketing decisions accordingly—either by introducing new snack food products to meet consumer demands or by repositioning current products to be perceived as snack food options.[16]

Some companies have begun using neuromarketing to study microscopic changes in skin moisture, heart rate, brain waves, and other biometrics to understand how consumers react to things such as package designs and ads. **Neuromarketing** is the process of researching brain patterns and measuring certain physiological responses to marketing stimuli. It is a fresh attempt to better understand consumers' responses to promotion and purchase motivations.

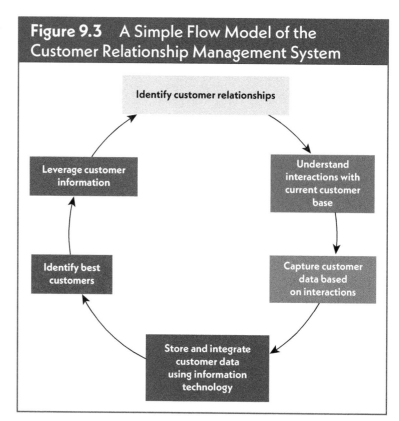

Figure 9.3 A Simple Flow Model of the Customer Relationship Management System

9-6 When Should Marketing Research Be Conducted?

9-6 Explain when marketing research should be conducted

When managers have several possible solutions to a problem, they should not instinctively call for marketing research. In fact, the first decision to make is whether to conduct marketing research at all.

Some companies have been conducting research in certain markets for many years. Such firms understand the characteristics of target customers and their likes and dislikes about existing products. Under these circumstances, further research would be repetitive and waste money. P&G, for example, has extensive knowledge of the coffee market. After it conducted initial taste tests with Folgers Instant Coffee, P&G went into national distribution without further research. Sara Lee followed the same strategy with its frozen croissants, as did Quaker Oats with Chewy Granola Bars. This tactic, however, can backfire. Marketers may think they understand a particular market thoroughly and so bypass market research for a product, only to have the product fail and be withdrawn from the market.

If information were available and free, managers would rarely refuse more, but because marketing information can require a great deal of time and expense to accumulate, they might decide to forgo additional information. Ultimately, the willingness to acquire additional decision-making information depends on managers' perceptions of its quality, price, and timing. Research should be undertaken only when the expected value of the information is greater than the cost of obtaining it.

9-6a Customer Relationship Management

Recall from the beginning of the chapter that databases and big data play a key role in marketing decision making. A key subset of data management systems is a customer relationship management (CRM) system. CRM was introduced in Chapters 1 and 8. The key to managing relationships with customers is the CRM cycle (Figure 9.3).

To initiate the CRM cycle, a company must *identify customer relationships with the organization*. This step may simply entail learning who the customers are or where they are located, or it may require more detailed information about the products and services they are using. Next, the company must *understand the interactions with current customers*. Companies accomplish this step by collecting data on all types of communications a customer has with the company.

---

neuromarketing a field of marketing that studies the body's responses to marketing stimuli

Using this knowledge of its customers and their interactions, the company then *captures relevant customer data on interactions*. Big data analytics are used not only to enhance the collection of customer data but also to *store and integrate customer data* throughout the company, and ultimately to "get to know" customers on a more personal level. Customer data are the firsthand responses that are obtained from customers through investigation or by asking direct questions.

Every customer wants to be a company's main priority. Yet not all customers are equally important in the eyes of a business. Consequently, the company must *identify its profitable and unprofitable customers*. Marketing analytics compile actionable data about the purchase habits of a firm's current and potential customers. Essentially, analytics transform customer data into customer information a company can use to make managerial decisions. Once customer data are analyzed and transformed into usable information, the information must be *leveraged*. The CRM system sends the customer information to all areas of a business because the customer interacts with all aspects of the business. Essentially, the company is trying to enhance customer relationships by getting the right information to the right person in the right place at the right time.

Part 3

Chapter 10

Product Concepts

Learning Outcomes

After studying this chapter, you will be able to...

10-1 Define the four product classification types

10-2 Define the terms product item, product line, and product mix

10-3 Describe marketing uses of branding

10-4 Describe marketing uses of packaging and labeling

10-5 Discuss global issues in branding and packaging

10-6 Describe why product warranties are important marketing tools

10-1 What Is a Product?

10-1 Define the four product classification types

The product offering, the heart of an organization's marketing program, is usually the starting point in creating a marketing mix. A marketing manager cannot determine a price, design a promotion strategy, or create a distribution channel until the firm has a product to sell. Moreover, an excellent distribution channel, a persuasive promotional campaign, and a fair price have no value when the product offering is poor or inadequate.

A **product** may be defined as everything, both favorable and unfavorable, that a person receives in an exchange. A product may be a tangible good like a pair of shoes, a service like a haircut, an idea like "don't litter," or any combination of these three. Packaging, style, color, options, and size are some typical product features. Just as important are intangibles such as service, the seller's image, the manufacturer's reputation, and the way consumers believe others will view the product.

To most people, the term *product* means a tangible good. However, services and ideas are also products. (Chapter 12 focuses specifically on the unique aspects of marketing services.) The marketing process identified in Chapter 1 is the same whether the product marketed is a good, a service, an idea, or some combination of these.

10-1a Types of Consumer Products

Products can be classified as either business (industrial) or consumer, depending on the buyer's intentions. The key distinction between the two types of products is their intended use. If the intended use is a business purpose, the product is classified as a business or industrial product. As explained in Chapter 7, a business product is used to manufacture other goods or services, to facilitate an organization's operations, or to resell to other customers. A consumer product is bought to satisfy an individual's personal wants or needs. Sometimes the same item can be classified as either a business or a consumer product. Examples include light bulbs, pencils and paper, and computers.

We need to know about product classifications because business and consumer products are marketed differently. They are marketed to different target markets and tend to use different distribution, promotion, and pricing strategies.

Chapter 7 examined seven categories of business products: major equipment, accessory equipment, component parts, processed materials, raw materials, supplies, and services. This chapter examines an effective way of categorizing consumer products. Although there are several ways to classify them, the most popular approach includes these four types: convenience products, shopping products, specialty products, and unsought products. This approach classifies products according to how much effort is normally used to shop for them.

Convenience Products

A **convenience product** is a relatively inexpensive item that merits little shopping effort—that is, a consumer is unwilling to shop extensively for such an item. Cereal, bottled water, toothpaste, small hardware items, dry cleaning, and car washes fall into the convenience product category.

Consumers buy convenience products regularly, usually without much planning. Nevertheless, consumers do know the brand names of popular convenience products, such as Cheerio's cereal, Dasani water, and Crest toothpaste. Convenience products normally require wide distribution to sell sufficient quantities to meet profit goals. For example, the gum brand Orbit is available everywhere, including Walmart, Walgreens, gas stations, newsstands, and vending machines.

Shopping Products

A **shopping product** is usually more expensive than a convenience product and is found in fewer stores. Consumers usually buy a shopping product only after comparing several brands or stores on style, practicality, price, and lifestyle compatibility. They are willing to invest some effort into this process to get the desired benefits.

There are two types of shopping products: homogeneous and heterogeneous. Consumers perceive *homogeneous* shopping products as basically similar—for example, washers, dryers, refrigerators, and televisions. With homogeneous shopping products, consumers typically look for the lowest-priced brand that has the desired features. For example, a consumer shopping for a new television may want a smart television that has 4K technology and a 40-inch screen. Once they identify several options having these desired features, they will likely purchase the option that has the lowest price.

In contrast, consumers perceive *heterogeneous* shopping products as essentially different—for example, furniture, clothing, housing, and universities. Consumers often have

---

product everything, both favorable and unfavorable, that a person receives in an exchange

convenience product a relatively inexpensive item that merits little shopping effort

shopping product a product that requires comparison shopping because it is usually more expensive than a convenience product and is found in fewer stores

Custom built homes are specialty items.

trouble comparing heterogeneous shopping products because the prices, quality, and features vary so much. The benefit of comparing heterogeneous shopping products is "finding the best product or brand for me"; this decision is often highly individual. For example, it would be difficult to compare a small, private college with a large, public university, or IKEA with La-Z-Boy.

Specialty Products

When consumers search extensively for a particular item and are very reluctant to accept substitutes, that item is a **specialty product**. Omega watches, Rolls-Royce automobiles, Bose speakers, Ruth's Chris Steak House, and highly specialized forms of medical care are generally considered specialty products. For example, if a consumer who is shopping for an Omega watch finds out that the specific watch that they want is on backorder, they will likely wait until the watch they want is available rather than buying another brand of watch.

Marketers of specialty products often use selective, status-conscious advertising to maintain a product's exclusive image. Distribution is often limited to one or a very few outlets in a geographic area. Brand names and quality of service are often very important.

---

specialty product a particular item for which consumers search extensively and are very reluctant to accept substitutes

unsought product a product unknown to the potential buyer or a known product that the buyer does not actively seek

product item a specific version of a product that can be designated as a distinct offering among an organization's products

product line a group of closely related product items

product mix all products that an organization sells

Unsought Products

A product unknown to the potential buyer or a known product that the buyer does not actively seek is called an **unsought product**. New products fall into this category until advertising and distribution increase consumer awareness of them.

Some goods are always marketed as unsought items, especially needed products we do not like to think about or care to spend money on. Insurance, burial plots, and similar items require aggressive personal selling and highly persuasive advertising. Salespeople actively seek leads to potential buyers. Because consumers usually do not seek out this type of product, the company must go directly to them through a salesperson, direct mail, or direct response advertising.

10-2 Product Items, Lines, and Mixes

10-2 Define the terms product item, product line, and product mix

Rarely does a company sell a single product. More often, it sells a variety of things. A **product item** is a specific version of a product that can be designated as a distinct offering among an organization's products. Coca-Cola's Sprite is an example of a product item (refer to Table 10.1).

A group of closely related product items is called a **product line**. For example, the column in Table 10.1 titled "Soft Drinks" represents one of Coca-Cola's product lines. Different container sizes and shapes also distinguish items in a product line. Coca-Cola, for example, is available in cans and various plastic containers. Each size and each container are separate product items.

An organization's **product mix** includes all the products it sells. All Coca-Cola's products—soft drinks, juices, waters, sports drinks, teas, and more—constitute its product mix. Each product item in the product mix may require a separate marketing strategy.

In some cases, however, product lines and even entire product mixes share some marketing strategy components. For example, Samsung promotes its various products with the tagline "Do what you can't" to demonstrate how their products can help customers do things that were once thought to be impossible. Organizations derive several benefits from organizing related items into product lines. They include:

- **Advertising economies:** Product lines provide economies of scale in advertising. Several products can be advertised under the umbrella of the line. Coca-Cola can use the slogan "Taste the Feeling" to promote the entire line.

- **Package uniformity:** A product line can benefit from package uniformity. All packages in the line may have

Table 10.1 Coca-Cola Company's Product Lines and Product Mix

		Soft Drinks	Juice	Water	Sports Drinks	Tea
Depth of the Product Lines	**Depth**	Coca-Cola Coca-Cola Vanilla	Minute Maid Orange Juice	Aquarius	Powerade	Fuze
		Sprite	Simply Orange	Dasani	Powerade Zero	Gold Peak sweetened
		Barq's Root Beer	innocent	Topo Chico	BODYARMOR	Gold Peak unsweetened
		Fresca	Ades	Smartwater		Peace Tea Peachy
		Fanta		Vitamin Water		Peace Tea Mango Green Tea

Width of the Product Mix

←――――――――――――――――――――――――――→

a common look and still keep their individual identities. Coca-Cola's soda packaging is again a good example. Coca-Cola Classic, Diet Coke, and Coke Zero Sugar all share certain colors and design elements, but each is recognizably unique.

- **Standardized components:** Product lines allow firms to standardize components, thus reducing manufacturing and inventory costs. For example, General Motors uses the same parts on many automobile makes and models.

- **Efficient sales and distribution:** A product line enables sales personnel for companies like Procter & Gamble to provide a full range of choices to customers. Distributors and retailers are often more inclined to stock the company's products if it offers a full line. Transportation and warehousing costs are likely to be lower for a product line than for a collection of individual items.

- **Equivalent quality:** Purchasers usually expect and believe that all products in a line are about equal in quality. Consumers expect that all Campbell's soups and all Gillette razors will be of similar quality.

Product mix width (or breadth) refers to the number of product lines an organization offers. In Table 10.1, for example, the width of Coca-Cola's product mix is five product lines. **Product line depth** is the number of product items in a product line. As shown in Table 10.1, the sports drink product line consists of three product items; the water product line includes five product items.

Firms increase the *width* of their product mix to diversify risk. To generate sales and boost profits, firms spread risk across many product lines rather than depending on only one or two. Firms also widen their product mix to capitalize on established reputations. For example, sportswear company Adidas recently added virtual gear to its

product mix as virtual environments like the metaverse are becoming more popular among consumers.

The new collection will allow people to dress their metaverse avatars in limited edition Adidas gear. The company is working to widen its product mix across both physical and virtual goods.[1]

Firms increase the *depth* of their product lines to attract buyers with different preferences, increase sales and profits by further segmenting the market, capitalize on economies of scale in production and marketing, and even out seasonal sales patterns. For example, yogurt maker Chobani releases its yogurt products in seasonal flavors every fall, such as pumpkin spice Greek yogurt.[2]

10-2a Adjustments to Product Items, Lines, and Mixes

Over time, firms change product items, lines, and mixes to take advantage of new technical or product developments or to respond to changes in the environment. They may adjust by modifying products, repositioning products, or extending or contracting product lines.

Product Modification

Marketing managers must decide if and when to modify existing products. **Product modification** is a change in one or more of a product's characteristics:

---

product mix width the number of product lines an organization offers

product line depth the number of product items in a product line

product modification changing one or more of a product's characteristics

The cleaning product 'The Pink Stuff" is a product item.

- **Quality modification:** a change in a product's dependability or durability. Reducing a product's quality may let the manufacturer lower the price and appeal to target markets unable to afford the original product. Conversely, increasing quality can help the firm to better compete in the market, increase customer satisfaction and loyalty, offer greater opportunities to increase prices, and create new opportunities for market segmentation. For example, the Apple iPhone 14 uses a highly durable and scratch-resistant glass called Ceramic Shield that offers greater screen protection if the phone is dropped than what was used on earlier versions of the iPhone. This increase in durability led consumers to be more satisfied with the product.[3]

- **Functional modification:** a change in a product's versatility, effectiveness, convenience, or safety. Many car companies, including Hyundai, Kia, BMW, and Audi, now offer 360-degree cameras in vehicles that give drivers a complete picture of their surroundings. These cameras eliminate blind spots for drivers, make

backing out of parking spaces easier, and, overall, make cars safer to drive.[4]

- **Style modification:** an aesthetic (how the product looks) product change rather than a quality or functional change. Clothing and auto manufacturers commonly use style modifications to motivate customers to replace products before they are worn out.

Planned obsolescence is a term commonly used to describe the practice of modifying products so that those that have already been sold become obsolete before they actually need replacement. For example, products such as printers and cell phones become obsolete because technology changes so quickly.

Some argue that planned obsolescence is wasteful; some claim it is unethical. Marketers respond that consumers favor style modifications because they like changes in the appearance of goods such as clothing and cars. Marketers also contend that consumers, not manufacturers and marketers, decide when styles are obsolete.

Repositioning

Repositioning, as Chapter 8 explained, involves changing consumers' perceptions of a brand. For several years, Taco Bell was perceived as an outdated, low quality, cheap Mexican food brand. Sales were down and competition in the fast-food industry was strong. Taco Bell repositioned their brand as youthful and fun by opening more modern and upscale Taco Bell "Cantina" locations, which featured open kitchens, new menu items, and alcoholic beverages. The company introduced a vegetarian menu and started using higher quality ingredients in all of its food products. Additionally, they began using the tagline "Live Más" to demonstrate that eating at Taco Bell is an experience that goes beyond the food. These efforts paid off and Taco Bell is now one of the top franchises in the United States.[5]

Changing demographics, declining sales, changes in the social environment, and competition often motivate a firm to reposition an established brand. To better compete in the health and wellness category, Weight Watchers has rebranded itself as WW and overhauled its products and services to focus more on healthy living than on weight loss alone. This repositioning includes a new logo, color palette, corporate images, and the slogan "Wellness that works." A new program was created called "WellnessWins," which rewards members for tracking their meals, physical activity, weight, and workshop attendance. These actions qualify for "wins" that can be exchanged for exclusive products, services, and experiences designed to inspire members on their wellness journey."[6]

Product Line Extensions

A **product line extension** occurs when a company's management decides to add products to an existing product line to compete more broadly in the industry. Lysol, a

---

planned obsolescence the practice of modifying products so those that have already been sold become obsolete before they actually need replacement

product line extension adding additional products to an existing product line to compete more broadly in the industry

popular brand of cleaning products, recently extended their line of cleansing wipes with the introduction of Lysol® Biodegradable Disinfecting Wipes.[7] Consumers are increasingly motivated to purchase eco-friendly products, so this product line extension helps Lysol to meet this consumer need.

A company can add too many products, or over time demand can change for the type of products that were introduced. When this happens, a product line is overextended. Product lines can be overextended when:

- Some products in the line do not contribute to profits because of low sales or they cannibalize sales of other items in the line.

- Manufacturing or marketing resources are disproportionately allocated to slow-moving products.

- Some items in the line are obsolete because of new-product entries in the line or new products offered by competitors.

Product Line Contraction

Sometimes marketers can get carried away with product extensions. (Does the world really need 53 flavors of Cheez-Its?) Contracting product lines is a strategic way to deal with overextension. In 2020, Coca-Cola announced that it would be discontinuing products from its core Coca-Cola and Diet Coke lines, such as Coca-Cola Life and Diet Coke Feisty Cherry. Eliminating these products allowed the company to allocate resources more effectively to their more profitable products.[8]

Indeed, three major benefits are likely when a firm contracts an overextended product line. First, resources become concentrated on the most important products. Second, managers no longer waste resources trying to improve the sales and profits of poorly performing products. Third, new-product items have a greater chance of being successful because more financial and human resources are available to manage them.

10-3 Branding

10-3 Describe marketing uses of branding

The success of any business or consumer product depends in part on the target market's ability to distinguish one product from another. Branding is the main tool marketers use to distinguish their products from those of the competition.

A **brand** is a name, term, symbol, design, or combination thereof that identifies a seller's products and differentiates them from competitors' products. A **brand name** is that part of a brand that can be spoken, including letters (GM, YMCA), words (Chevrolet), and numbers (WD-40,

---

brand a name, term, symbol, design, or combination thereof that identifies a seller's products and differentiates them from competitors' products

brand name that part of a brand that can be spoken, including letters, words, and numbers

---

Interbrand's Best Global Brands

In 2022, Interbrand announced that Apple, Microsoft, and Amazon were the top three most valuable brands in the world. Apple has held the top position for 10 years. Apple's brand value grew by 18 percent, Microsoft's brand value grew by 32 percent, and Amazon's brand value grew by 10 percent. Other brands in the Top 10 were Google, Samsung, Toyota, Coca-Cola, Mercedes-Benz, Disney, and Nike with a growth of 28 percent, 17 percent, 10 percent, 0 percent, 10 percent, 14 percent, and 18 percent, respectively. Many of the 100 Best Global Brands came from five industry sectors: Automotive, Financial Services, Luxury, and Fast-Moving Consumer Goods. The combined total value of the Top 100 brands crossed the $3 trillion mark—a 16 percent increase from 2021.[9]

01 **Apple**	02 **Microsoft**	03 **Amazon**
+18% 482,215 $m	+32% 278,288 $m	+10% 274,819 $m

Source: Interbrand

Patcharaporn Puttipon4289/Shutterstock.com

Table 10.2 The Power of Brand Equity	
Product Category	**Dominant Brand Name**
Children's Entertainment	Disney
Laundry Detergent	Tide
Tablet Computer	Apple
Toothpaste	Crest
Microprocessor	Intel
Soup	Campbell's
Bologna	Oscar Mayer
Ketchup	Heinz
Bleach	Clorox
Greeting Cards	Hallmark
Overnight Mail	FedEx
Copiers	Xerox
Gelatin	Jell-O
Hamburgers	McDonald's
Baby Lotion	Johnson & Johnson
Tissues	Kleenex
Acetaminophen	Tylenol
Coffee	Starbucks
Information Search	Google

7-Eleven). The elements of a brand that cannot be spoken are called the **brand mark**—for example, the well-known Mercedes-Benz and Nike symbols.

10-3a Benefits of Branding

Branding has three main purposes: product identification, repeat sales, and new-product sales. The most important purpose is *product identification*. Branding allows marketers to distinguish their products from all others. Many brand names are familiar to consumers and indicate quality.

The term **brand equity** refers to the value of a company or brand name. A brand that has high awareness, perceived quality, and brand loyalty among customers has high brand equity—a valuable asset indeed. Refer to Table 10.2 for some classic examples of companies that leverage their brand equity to the fullest.

The term **global brand** refers to a brand that obtains at least one-third of its earnings from outside its home country, is recognizable outside its home base of customers, and has publicly available marketing and financial data. Yum! Brands, which owns Pizza Hut, KFC, and Taco Bell, is a good example of a company that has developed strong global brands. Yum! management believes that it must adapt its restaurants to local tastes and different cultural and political climates. In Japan, for instance, KFC sells tempura crispy strips. In northern England, KFC focuses on gravy and potatoes, and in Thailand, it offers rice with soy or sweet chili sauce.

---

brand mark the elements of a brand that cannot be spoken

brand equity the value of a company or brand name

global brand a brand that obtains at least one-third of its earnings from outside its home country, is recognizable outside its home base of customers, and has publicly available marketing and financial data

brand loyalty consistent preference for one brand over all others

The best generator of *repeat sales* is satisfied customers. Branding helps consumers identify products they wish to buy again and avoid those they do not. **Brand loyalty**, a consistent preference for one brand over all others, is quite high in some product categories. More than half the consumers in product categories such as mayonnaise, toothpaste, coffee, headache remedies, bath soap, and ketchup are loyal to one brand. Many students go to college and purchase the same brands they used at home rather than choosing by price. Brand identity is essential to developing brand loyalty.

The third main purpose of branding is to *facilitate new-product sales*. Having a well-known and respected company and brand name is extremely useful when introducing new products.

10-3b Branding Strategies

Firms face complex branding decisions. They may choose to follow a policy of using manufacturers' brands, private (distributor) brands, or both. In either case, they must then decide among a policy of individual branding (different brands for different products), family branding (common names for different products), or a combination of individual branding and family branding.

Manufacturer's brands and private brands often compete for retail shelf space.

Manufacturers' Brands Versus Private Brands

The brand name of a manufacturer—such as McDonald's, Hewlett-Packard (HP), and Levi's—is called a **manufacturer's brand**. Sometimes "national brand" is used as a synonym for "manufacturer's brand," but this term is not always accurate because many manufacturers serve only regional markets. Using "manufacturer's brand" precisely defines the brand's owner.

A **private brand**, also known as a private label or store brand, is a brand name owned by a wholesaler or a retailer. Private labels tend to be more successful in markets where product differentiation is low. Many food and beverage products are privately branded, for example. High inflation rates following the COVID-19 pandemic led to an increase in the number of customers shopping for private brands. One survey found that 87 percent of consumers buy private brands in food and beverage categories. Frozen appetizers, cooking oils, refrigerated pasta, and shelf stable beverages, in particular, saw a significant increase in the growth of private brand sales. This research also found that 45 percent of customers are driven to purchase private brands because they have lower prices[10] Sensing these trends, Amazon has created more than 100 private brands, including apparel, batteries, lighting, computer cables, paper shredders, and pet products to name a few. For example, Amazon sells products in multiple different categories, including batteries, workout equipment, and kids' toys, under the Amazon Basics brand name. Under the brand name Buttoned Down, Amazon sells professional button-down shirts.[11]

Retailers love consumers' greater acceptance of private brands. Because overhead is low and there are no marketing costs, private-label products bring 10 percent higher profit margins, on average, than manufacturers' brands. More than that, a trusted store brand can differentiate a chain from its competitors. Table 10.3 illustrates key issues that wholesalers and retailers should consider in deciding whether to sell manufacturers' brands or private brands. Many firms offer a combination of both.

---

manufacturer's brand the brand name of a manufacturer

private brand a brand name owned by a wholesaler or a retailer

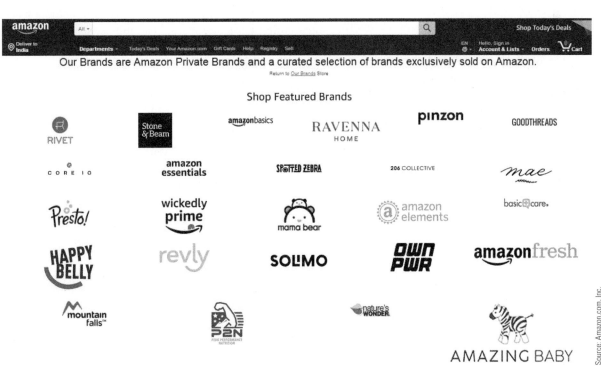

Private brands owned by Amazon.

Table 10.3 Comparison of Manufacturer's and Private Brands from the Reseller's Perspective

Key Advantages of Carrying Manufacturers' Brands	Key Advantages of Carrying Private Brands
• Heavy advertising to the consumer by manufacturers such as Procter & Gamble (P&G) helps develop strong consumer loyalties.	• A wholesaler or retailer can usually earn higher profits on its own brand. In addition, because the private brand is exclusive, there is less pressure to mark down the price to meet competition.
• Well-known manufacturers' brands, such as Nike and Fisher-Price, can attract new customers and enhance the dealer's (wholesaler's or retailer's) prestige.	• A manufacturer can decide to drop a brand or a reseller at any time or even become a direct competitor to its dealers.
• Many manufacturers offer rapid delivery, enabling the dealer to carry less inventory.	• A private brand ties the customer to the wholesaler or retailer. A person who wants to buy Charles Shaw wine must go to Trader Joe's.
• If a dealer happens to sell a manufacturer's brand of poor quality, the customer may simply switch brands and remain loyal to the dealer.	• Wholesalers and retailers have no control over the intensity of distribution of manufacturers' brands. Target store managers don't have to worry about competing with other sellers of Kindfull pet food. They know that this brand is sold only in Target stores.

Instead of marketing private brands as cheaper and inferior to manufacturers' brands, many retailers are creating and promoting their own **captive brands**. These brands carry no evidence of the store's affiliation, are manufactured by a third party, and are sold exclusively at the chains. This strategy allows the retailer to ask a price similar or equal to manufacturers' brands, and the captive brands are typically displayed alongside mainstream products. This strategy is particularly important as millennials come to dominate the grocery shopping arena. One study found that members of this group are more loyal to their stores of choice than their parents were. They are well informed about where specific brands and foods come from, read labels, are equally aware of national brands and store brands, and look for good value. Millennials also desire products that are clean, natural, and organic. Whole Foods Market's store brand 365 consists of food, cleaning, and personal products that ban hundreds of ingredients that may be potentially harmful. This line of products is especially popular among millennial consumers.[12] Similarly, Kroger has found much success with its Simple Truth and Simple Truth Organic lines of private label products. Over half of Kroger shoppers buy products from these lines.[13]

captive brand a brand manufactured by a third party for an exclusive retailer, without evidence of that retailer's affiliation

individual branding using different brand names for different products

family branding marketing several different products under the same brand name

co-branding placing two or more brand names on a product or its package

Individual Brands Versus Family Brands

Many companies use different brand names for different products, a practice known as **individual branding**. Companies use individual brands when their products vary greatly in use or performance. For instance, it would not make sense to use the same brand name for a pair of dress socks and a baseball bat. P&G targets different segments of the laundry detergent market with Bold, Cheer, Dash, Dreft, Era, Gain, and Tide.

By contrast, a company that markets several different products under the same brand name is practicing **family branding**. Jack Daniel's family brand includes whiskey, coffee, barbeque sauce, heat-and-serve meat products like brisket and pulled pork, mustard, playing cards, and clothing lines.

Co-Branding

Co-branding entails placing two or more brand names on a product or its package. Three common types of co-branding are ingredient branding, cooperative branding, and complementary branding. *Ingredient branding* identifies the brand of a part that makes up the product. For example, Ritz and Oreo partnered to create a new snack sandwich that features a Ritz cracker on one side of the sandwich, an Oreo cookie on the other side, and a filling of peanut butter mixed with Oreo cream.[14] *Cooperative branding* occurs when two brands receiving equal treatment (in the context of an advertisement) borrow from each other's brand equity. Uber and Spotify launched a "Soundtrack for Your Ride" campaign that featured Uber passengers enjoying their personal Spotify playlists while on their rides.[15] Finally, with *complementary branding*, products are advertised or marketed together to suggest usage, such as a Betty Crocker brownie mix recommending adding Hershey's chocolate chips to make it extra delicious.

Co-branding is a useful strategy when a combination of brand names enhances the prestige or perceived value of a product or when it benefits brand owners and users. Co-branding may also be used to increase a company's presence in markets where it has little room to differentiate itself or has limited market share. For example, French luxury brand Louis Vuitton teamed up with *League of Legends*, a popular video game, to create both physical and in-game products. The creative director for Louis Vuitton collaborated with artists from the video game to create unique designs and patterns for the products. Physical products from the collection included clothing that featured characters from the game, a high-tech watch, and luxury sneakers. The collaboration will help Louis Vuitton gain acceptance among a new, younger consumer base.[16]

10-3c Trademarks

A **trademark** is the exclusive right to use a brand or part of a brand. Others are prohibited from using the brand without permission. A **service mark** performs the same function for services, such as H&R Block and Weight Watchers. Parts of a brand or other product identification may qualify for trademark protection. Some examples are:

- Sounds, such as the MGM lion's roar.
- Shapes, such as the Jeep front grille and the Coca-Cola bottle.
- Ornamental colors or designs, such as the decoration on Nike tennis shoes, the black-and-copper color combination of a Duracell battery, Levi's small tag on the left side of the rear pocket of its jeans, or the cutoff black cone on the top of Cross pens.
- Catchy phrases, such as BMW's "The Ultimate Driving Experience," McDonald's "I'm Lovin' It," and Nike's "Just Do It!"
- Abbreviations, such as Bud, Coke, or the Met.

It is important to understand that trademark rights come from use rather than registration. An intent-to-use application is filed with the U.S. Patent and Trademark Office, and a company must have a genuine intention to use the mark when it files and must actually use it within three years of the granting of the application. Trademark protection typically lasts for 10 years.[17] To renew the trademark, the company must prove it is using the mark. Rights to a trademark last as long as the mark is used. Normally, if the firm does not use it for two years, the trademark is considered abandoned, and a new user can claim exclusive ownership of the mark.

The Digital Millennium Copyright Act (DMCA) explicitly applies trademark law to the digital world. This law includes financial penalties for those who violate trademarks or register an otherwise trademarked term as a domain name. The DMCA has come under some criticism for its more restrictive provisions. For example, some are concerned that this law has been abused by governments to silence political criticism on the internet.[18]

Companies that fail to protect their trademarks face the possibility that their product names will become generic. A **generic product name** identifies a product by class or type and cannot be trademarked. Former brand names that were not sufficiently protected by their owners and were subsequently declared to be generic product names by U.S. courts include aspirin, cellophane, linoleum, thermos, kerosene, monopoly, cola, and shredded wheat.

Companies such as Rolls-Royce, Xerox, Lucky, Frigidaire, and McDonald's aggressively enforce their trademarks. Rolls-Royce, Coca-Cola, and Xerox have even run newspaper and magazine ads stating that their names are trademarks and should not be used as descriptive or generic terms. Evermore Parks, a Utah-based theme park, recently sued Taylor Swift for trademark infringement, claiming that her album entitled "Evermore" violated its trademark rights. The theme park claimed that Swift's album took over Google searches for the term "Evermore," which negatively impacted their business, although the lawsuit was eventually dropped.[19]

To try to stem the number of trademark infringements, violations carry steep penalties. But despite the risk of incurring a penalty, infringement lawsuits are still common. Serious conflict can occur when brand names resemble one another too closely. Tiffany & Co. was in a lawsuit battle against Costco for more than eight years for trademark infringement after the warehouse club created display signage and other in-store marketing that used terms such as "Tiffany Setting" to describe non–Tiffany-brand diamond rings. The case was eventually thrown out after a judge determined that customers should be wise enough to realize that genuine Tiffany's rings were not being sold at Costco.[20]

Companies must also contend with fake or unauthorized brands. Knockoffs of trademarked clothing lines are easy to find in cheap shops all over the world, and loose imitations are found in some reputable department stores as well. Today, whole stores are faked in China. These stores are selling copied versions of brands such as Louis Vuitton, Prada, Apple, and New Balance. The offerings of these stores are unauthorized, and their brands are

---

trademark the exclusive right to use a brand or part of a brand

service mark a trademark for a service

generic product name identifies a product by class or type and cannot be trademarked

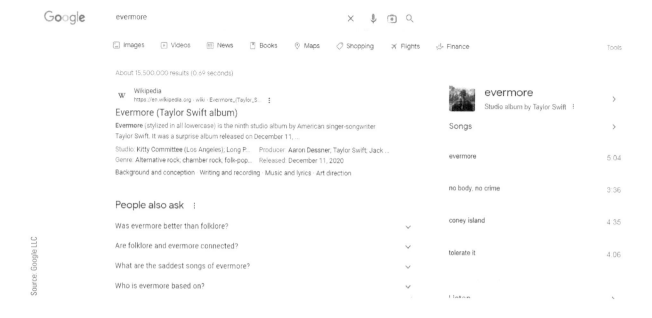

fake. Above the door on one fake Louis Vuitton store, the "Louis" is spelled "Loius." In Beijing, a fake Apple store complete with automated iPhone check-ins and a faux Genius bar was shut down by local authorities.[21] In Europe, you can sue counterfeiters only if your brand, logo, or trademark is formally registered. Formal registration used to be required in each country in which a company sought protection. However, today a company can register its trademark in all European Union member countries with one application.

10-4 Packaging

10-4 Describe marketing uses of packaging and labeling

Packages have always served a practical function—that is, they hold contents together and protect goods as they move through the distribution channel. Today, however, packaging is also a container for promoting the product and making it easier and safer to use.

10-4a Packaging Functions

The three most important functions of packaging are to contain and protect products; promote products; and facilitate the storage, use, and convenience of products. A fourth function of packaging that is becoming increasingly important is to facilitate recycling and reduce environmental damage.

Containing and Protecting Products

The most obvious function of packaging is to contain products that are liquid, granular, or otherwise divisible.

Packaging also enables manufacturers, wholesalers, and retailers to market products in specific quantities, such as ounces.

Physical protection is another obvious function of packaging. Most products are handled several times between the time they are manufactured, harvested, or otherwise produced and the time they are consumed or used. Many products are also shipped, stored, and inspected several times between production and consumption. Some, like milk, need to be refrigerated. Others, like beer, are sensitive to light. Still others, like medicines and bandages, need to be kept sterile. Packages protect products from breakage, evaporation, spillage, spoilage, light, heat, cold, infestation, and many other conditions.

Promoting Products

Packaging does more than identify the brand, list the ingredients, specify features, and give directions. A package differentiates a product from competing products and may associate a new product with a family of other products from the same manufacturer. However, some products' packaging lacks useful information. The Food and Drug Administration (FDA) is looking to remedy inconsistent and incomplete food packaging information by adding more facts to nutrition labels. These changes include listing the number of servings in each container and printing the calorie count for each serving in larger, bolder type. The FDA hopes that these changes will catch consumers' eyes and help them better manage their health.[22] Similarly, the Canadian government is proposing mandatory front-of-package labeling for foods high in ingredients that are a public health concern, such as sugars, sodium, and saturated fat.[23]

Knockoff retail outlets can be found in many parts of the world.

Packages use designs, colors, shapes, and materials to try to influence consumers' perceptions and buying behavior. For example, marketing research shows that health-conscious consumers are likely to think that any food is probably good for them as long as it comes in green packaging. Packaging can influence other consumer perceptions of a brand as well. For example, research has found that white packaging conveys a sense of cleanliness, and thus would be appropriate for personal-care products. Dark blue portrays a sense of professionalism whereas light-blue packaging can lead the product to be perceived as more creative. Green packaging is not only associated with health but also with natural and organic.[24]

Facilitating Storage, Use, and Convenience

Wholesalers and retailers prefer packages that are easy to ship, store, and stock on shelves. They also like packages that protect products, prevent spoilage or breakage, and extend the product's shelf life.

Consumers' requirements for storage, use, and convenience cover many dimensions. Consumers are constantly seeking items that are easy to handle, open, and reclose, although some consumers want packages that are tamper-proof or childproof. Research indicates that hard-to-open packages are among consumers' top complaints—especially when it comes to clamshell electronics packaging. There is even a Wikipedia page devoted to "wrap rage," the anger associated with trying to open clamshells and other poorly designed packages.[25] As oil prices force the cost of plastics used in packaging skyward, companies such as Amazon, Target, and Walmart are pushing suppliers to do away with excessive and infuriating packaging. Such packaging innovations as zipper tear strips, hinged lids, tab slots, screw-on tops, simple cardboard boxes, and pour spouts were introduced to solve these and other problems. Easy openings are especially important for kids and aging Baby Boomers.

Some firms use packaging to segment markets. For example, a C&H sugar carton with an easy-to-pour, reclosable top is targeted to consumers who do not do a lot of baking and are willing to pay at least 20 cents more for the package. Different-sized packages appeal to heavy, moderate, and light users. Campbell's soup is packaged in single-serving cans aimed at the elderly and singles market segments. Packaging convenience can increase a product's utility and therefore its market share and profits.

Facilitating Recycling and Reducing Environmental Damage

One of the most important packaging issues today is eco-consciousness, a trend that has recently been in and out of consumer and media attention. Studies conflict about whether consumers will pay more for eco-friendly packaging, though consumers repeatedly iterate the desire to purchase such products. One study, which surveyed consumers in North America, South America, and Europe, showed that 67 percent of consumers believe that reusable packaging is important when choosing products.

Consumers under the age of 44 appear to be especially motivated to purchase products with eco-friendly packaging.[26] Many companies have responded by looking for alternative packaging materials that are more ecologically friendly. For example, Monday's Child is a kid's clothing brand that designs their packaging to turn in to a dollhouse. When customers place an order with this brand, they get both a new outfit and a new toy for their child, while also acting in a sustainable manner. As another example, Soapack shampoo is packaged in bottles made from soap that can be melted in hot water once the bottle is empty.[27]

10-4b Labeling

An integral part of any package is its label. Labeling generally takes one of two forms: persuasive or informational. **Persuasive labeling** focuses on a promotional theme or logo, and consumer information is secondary. Note that the standard promotional claims—such as "new," "improved," and "super"—are no longer very persuasive. Consumers have been saturated with "newness" and thus discount these claims.

Informational labeling, by contrast, is designed to help consumers make proper product selections and

---

persuasive labeling   a type of package labeling that focuses on a promotional theme or logo; consumer information is secondary

informational labeling   a type of package labeling designed to help consumers make proper product selections and lower their cognitive dissonance after the purchase

lower their cognitive dissonance after the purchase. Most major furniture manufacturers affix labels to their wares that explain the products' construction features, such as type of frame, number of coils, and fabric characteristics. The Nutritional Labeling and Education Act of 1990 mandated that detailed nutritional information appear on most food packages, as well as standards for health claims on food packaging. An important outcome of this legislation has been guidelines from the FDA for using terms such as *low fat*, *light*, *reduced cholesterol*, *low sodium*, *low calorie*, *low carb*, and *fresh*. Getting the right information is very important to consumers, so some corporations are working on new technologies to help consumers shop smart. For example, microsensor technology is being developed to sense the freshness of food. On-package sensors indicate a food's shelf life and alert customers when it is safe to consume, to avoid early disposal or excessive purchasing.[28]

Greenwashing

Numerous products in every product category use *greenwashing* to try to sell products. Greenwashing is when a product or company attempts to give the impression of environmental friendliness, whether or not it is environmentally friendly.

---

universal product codes (UPCs) a series of thick and thin vertical lines (bar codes) readable by computerized optical scanners that represent numbers used to track products

As consumer demand for green products appeared to escalate, green certifications proliferated. Companies could create their own certifications and logos, resulting in more than 300 possible certification labels, ranging in price from free to thousands of dollars. Consumer distrust and confusion caused the Federal Trade Commission (FTC) to issue new rules. In 2011, new regulations started applying to labeling products with green-certification logos. If the same company that produced the product performed the certification, that relationship must be clearly marked. This benefits organizations such as Green Seal, which uses unbiased, third-party scientists and experts to verify claims about emissions or biodegradability and hopes to increase consumer confidence in green products.[29]

10-4c Universal Product Codes

The **universal product codes (UPCs)** that appear on most items in supermarkets and other high-volume outlets were first introduced in 1974. Because the numerical codes appear as a series of thick and thin vertical lines, they are often called *bar codes*. The lines are read by computerized optical scanners that match codes with brand names, package sizes, and prices. They also print information on cash register tapes and help retailers rapidly and accurately prepare records of customer purchases, control inventories, and track sales. The UPC system and scanners are also used in scanner-based research (refer to Chapter 9).

Creative Packaging Design Trends

Product package design can have a large influence on what consumers choose. As human needs are changing, package design must evolve to remain relevant and address those needs. Some of the top packaging design trends include:

1. Simplicity. Minimalist package design has been around for a long time, and feedback from buyers shows it to be a continuing trend. Simple designs involve presenting signs and symbols that everybody can relate to, so this can be a challenging thing for designers.

2. Pastels. Pastel colors have fragile characteristics that bring out a calming effect that bright colors cannot. Many people recognize pastels as a message that welcomes them to the products.

3. Outstanding shapes and materials. Unusual shapes and packaging materials can attract children and those who love art. A resin package that is designed to look like a sheltering tree trunk or a juice can is designed to look like a bamboo segment can stand out from other packages and speak to the emotional side of customers.

4. Doodles. This design element speaks to consumers' kid side. When a package design incorporates doodles into its design, it brings out the fun side of a product, and can attract a wide range of target markets.

5. Vintage design. With vintage designs, consumers are reminded of the past. In many cases this design type represents important aspects of our history and culture.[30]

Nutrition Facts	
6 servings per container	
Serving size	**1 cup (230g)**

Amount per serving	
Calories	**250**

	% Daily Value*
Total Fat 12g	**14%**
Saturated Fat 2g	**10%**
Trans Fat 0g	
Cholesterol 8mg	**3%**
Sodium 210mg	**9%**
Total Carbohydrate 34g	**12%**
Dietary Fiber 7g	**25%**
Total Sugars 5g	
Includes 4g Added Sugars	**8%**
Protein 11g	
Vitamin D 4mcg	20%
Calcium 210mg	16%
Iron 4mg	22%
Potassium 380mg	8%

*The % Daily Value (DV) tells you how much a nutrient in a serving of food contributes to a daily diet. 2,000 calories a day is used for general nutrition advice.

The Nutrition Facts label has been a mandatory part of most foods' packaging since 1990. The informational label has been revised several times since its introduction, the most recent major revision being in 2016.

10-5 Global Issues in Branding and Packaging

10-5 Discuss global issues in branding and packaging

When planning to enter a foreign market with an existing product, a firm has the following three options for handling the brand name.

1. **One brand name everywhere:** This strategy is useful when the company markets mainly one product and the brand name does not have negative connotations in any local market. Nike, McDonald's, and Dunkin' all use a one-brand-name strategy. The advantages of a one-brand-name strategy are greater identification of the product from market to market and ease of coordinating promotion from market to market. For example, McDonald's famous golden arches are displayed outside of nearly all of the company's 38,000 McDonald's locations. Additionally, when Dunkin' Donuts updated their branding to just "Dunkin'," the company initiated this change in U.S. stores but eventually also carried the updated branding over to its international markets.[31]

2. **Adaptations and modifications:** A one-brand-name strategy is not possible when the name cannot be pronounced in the local language, when the brand name is owned by someone else, or when the brand name has a negative or vulgar connotation in the local language. The Iranian detergent Barf, for example, might encounter some problems in the U.S. market.

3. **Different brand names in different markets:** Local brand names are often used when translation or pronunciation problems occur, when the marketer wants the brand to appear to be a local brand, or when regulations require localization. Unilever's Axe line of male grooming products is called Lynx in England, Ireland, Australia, and New Zealand. PepsiCo changed the name of its eponymous cola to Pecsi in Argentina to reflect the way the word is pronounced with an Argentinian accent.

In addition to global branding decisions, companies must consider global packaging needs. Three aspects of packaging that are especially important in international marketing are labeling, aesthetics, and climate considerations. The major *labeling* concern is properly translating ingredient, promotional, and instructional information on labels. Care must also be employed in meeting all local labeling requirements. Several years ago, an Italian judge ordered that all bottles of Coca-Cola be removed from retail shelves because the ingredients were not properly labeled. Labeling is also harder in countries like Belgium and Finland, which require packaging to be bilingual.

Package *aesthetics* may also require some attention. Even though simple visual elements of the brand, such as a symbol or logo, can be a standardizing element across products and countries; marketers must stay attuned to cultural traits in host countries. For example, colors may have different connotations. Red is associated with witchcraft in some countries; green may be a sign of danger; and white may be symbolic of death. Such cultural differences could necessitate a packaging change if colors are chosen for another country's interpretation. In the United States, green typically symbolizes an eco-friendly product, but that packaging could keep customers away in a country where green indicates danger. Aesthetics also influence package size. Soft drinks are not sold in six-packs in countries that lack refrigeration. In some countries, products such as detergent may be bought only in small quantities because of a lack of storage space. Other products, such as cigarettes, may be bought in small quantities, or even single units because of the low purchasing power of buyers.

Extreme climates and long-distance shipping necessitate sturdier and more durable packages for goods sold overseas. Spillage, spoilage, and breakage are all more important concerns when products are shipped long distances or frequently handled during shipping and storage.

cigdem/Shutterstock.com

Packages may also need to ensure a longer product life if the time between production and consumption lengthens significantly.

10-6 Product Warranties

10-6 Describe why product warranties are important marketing tools

Just as a package is designed to protect the product, a warranty protects the buyer and gives essential information about the product. A **warranty** confirms the quality or performance of a good or service. An **express warranty** is a written guarantee. Express warranties range from simple statements—such as "100 percent cotton" (a guarantee of quality) and "complete satisfaction guaranteed" (a statement of performance)—to extensive documents written in technical language. In contrast, an **implied warranty** is an unwritten guarantee that the good or service is fit for the purpose for which it was sold. All sales have an implied warranty under the Uniform Commercial Code.

Congress passed the Magnuson–Moss Warranty–Federal Trade Commission Improvement Act in 1975 to help consumers understand warranties and get action from manufacturers and dealers. A manufacturer that promises a full warranty must meet certain minimum standards, including repair "within a reasonable time and without charge" of any defects and replacement of the merchandise or a full refund if the product does not work "after a reasonable number of attempts" at repair. Any warranty that does not live up to this tough prescription must be "conspicuously" promoted as a limited warranty.

---

warranty a confirmation of the quality or performance of a good or service

express warranty a written guarantee

implied warranty an unwritten guarantee that the good or service is fit for the purpose for which it was sold

wichayada suwanachun/Shutterstock.com

Chapter 11

Developing and Managing Products

Learning Outcomes

After studying this chapter, you will be able to . . .

11-1 Describe the six categories of new products

11-2 Explain the steps in the new-product development process

11-3 Summarize why some products succeed and others fail

11-4 Discuss global issues in new-product development

11-5 Explain the diffusion process through which new products are adopted

11-6 Explain the concept of product life cycles

11-1 The Importance of New Products

New products are important to sustain growth, increase revenues and profits, and replace obsolete items. Each year *Fast Company* rates and ranks its most innovative companies, based on the ability to buck tradition in the interest of reaching more people, building a better business, and spurring mass-market appeal for unusual or highly technical products or services. In 2022, the top five companies were Stripe, Solugen, Twelve, BlocPower, and Climate Trace.[1] All of these firms have reputations for relying heavily on technology and are deeply committed to sustainability initiatives.

11-1a Introduction of New Products

Some companies spend a considerable amount of money each year developing new products. At Pfizer, the world's largest research-based pharmaceutical company, nearly $14 billion is spent annually on research and development.[2] Other companies with high research and development (R&D) spending include Amazon ($42.74 billion per year), Apple ($18.75 billion per year), and Samsung ($18.75 billion per year).[3]

Sometimes, it is difficult to decide when to replace a successful product. Gillette Company has a history of introducing new shaving systems (razors and accompanying blades) before the previous generation of products begins experiencing a sales decline. In fact, Gillette *expects* to cannibalize the sales of older models with its newer introductions. In 2022, Apple released the newest edition of its MacBook Air laptops, one of the company's most popular laptop lines. Apple executives agreed that the MacBook Air needed to be replaced to keep customers satisfied, but the design of the new laptop required complex decisions, trade-offs, and risks. The new version features a thinner design, a larger screen and memory, and a longer battery life.[4] Clearly, the introduction of a new product is a monumental undertaking with a lot of open-ended questions—even for an established, multibillion-dollar company like Apple.

11-1b Categories of New Products

The term **new product** is somewhat confusing because its meaning varies widely. In fact, the term has several "correct" definitions. A product can be new to the world, the market, the producer, the seller, or some combination of these. There are six categories of new products as follows:

1. **New-to-the-world products** (also called discontinuous innovations)**:** These products create an entirely new market. For example, Withings, a health-tech company, recently introduced a smart scale that not only measures weight, but can also monitor nerve activity, heart rate, and vascular age. The scale syncs with an app so users can keep track of their health stats and easily share them with their medical care providers.[5] New-to-the-world products represent the smallest category of new products.

   On average, consumer packaged goods companies introduce a total of about 30,000 new products every year.

2. **New-product lines:** These products, which the firm has not previously offered, allow it to enter an established market. For example, Brooklinen is a brand best known for luxurious pillows, sheets, and blankets. More recently, the company has expanded its product offerings to include bath robes and a line of eco-friendly laundry detergent.[6]

3. **Additions to existing product lines:** This category includes new products that supplement a firm's established line. Fast-food restaurant chain McDonald's recently added the "McPlant"—a plant-based hamburger—to its menu. To promote the new vegan burger, McDonald's teamed up with Snapchat to create a virtual reality game on the social media platform in which users could create their own McPlant burger, choosing ingredients and placing them in a specific order. According to Snapchat, the campaign was a success, resulting in a significant increase in awareness and intentions to purchase the product.[7]

4. **Improvements or revisions of existing products:** The "new and improved" product may be significantly

Introducing McDonald's "McPlant," a plant-based version of the company's iconic hamburger.

---

new product a product new to the world, the market, the producer, the seller, or some combination of these

or only slightly changed. For example, motivated by new government regulations and consumer demand for healthier products, Capri Sun recently revised the recipe for its popular Orange, Blackcurrant, and Tropical flavored beverages. The new recipe decreased the amount of sugar in these products by about 40 percent by replacing traditional sugar with a monk fruit sweetener.[8]

5. **Repositioned products:** These are existing products targeted at new markets or market segments or products that are repositioned to change the current market's perception of the product or company, which may be done to boost declining sales. For many years, Gucci primarily targeted older consumers, who typically have more money to spend on luxury goods, but after several years of declining sales, the brand launched a repositioning campaign to market to millennial consumers more effectively. To reach these consumers, Gucci focused on growing their social media presence and significantly increased their spending on influencer marketing. These strategies were successful in repositioning the brand, and in recent years, over half of Gucci's sales have come from consumers under the age of 35.[9]

6. **Cost reductions:** This category refers to products that provide performance similar to competing brands at a reduced price. The HP Color LaserJet Pro MFP is a scanner, copier, printer, and fax machine combined. This new product is priced lower than many conventional color copiers and much lower than the combined price of the four items purchased separately.

11-2 The New-Product Development Process

11-2 Explain the steps in the new-product development process

The management consulting firm Booz Allen Hamilton has studied the new-product development process since the early 1980s. Analyzing five major studies undertaken during this period, the firm has concluded that the companies most likely to succeed in developing and introducing new products are those that take the following actions:

- Make the long-term commitment needed to support innovation and new-product development.

- Use a company-specific approach, driven by corporate objectives and strategies, with a well-defined new-product strategy at its core.

- Capitalize on experience to achieve and maintain competitive advantage.

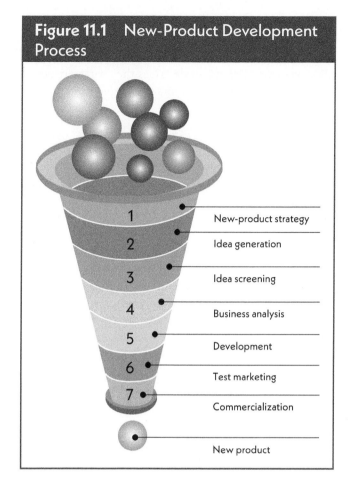

Figure 11.1 New-Product Development Process

1. New-product strategy
2. Idea generation
3. Idea screening
4. Business analysis
5. Development
6. Test marketing
7. Commercialization

New product

- Establish an environment—a management style, organizational structure, and degree of top management support—conducive to achieving company-specific new-product and corporate objectives.

Most companies follow a formal new-product development process, usually starting with a new-product strategy. Figure 11.1 illustrates the seven-step process, which is discussed in detail in this section. The figure is funnel-shaped to highlight the fact that each stage acts as a screen to filter out unworkable ideas.

11-2a New-Product Strategy

A **new-product strategy** links the new-product development process with the objectives of the marketing department, the business unit, and the corporation. A new-product strategy must be compatible with these objectives, and in turn all three of the objectives must be consistent with one another.

A new-product strategy is part of the organization's overall marketing strategy. It sharpens the focus and

new-product strategy a plan that links the new-product development process with the objectives of the marketing department, the business unit, and the corporation provides general guidelines for generating, screening, and evaluating new-product ideas. The new-product strategy specifies the roles that new products must play in the organization's overall plan and describes the characteristics of products the organization wants to offer and the markets it wants to serve.

11-2b Idea Generation

New-product ideas come from many sources, including customers, employees, distributors, competitors, R&D, consultants, and other experts.

Customers

The marketing concept suggests that customers' wants and needs should be the springboard for developing new products. Companies can derive insight from monitoring social media and customer reviews which often indicate early trends or areas consumers are interested in observing develop or change. Another approach for generating new-product ideas is using what some companies are calling "customer innovation centers." The idea is to provide a forum for meeting with customers and directly involving them in the innovation process.

Employees

Sometimes, employees know a company's products and processes better than anyone else. Many firms have formal and informal processes in place for employees to propose new-product ideas. To encourage participation, some companies run contests, hold votes, and set up idea kiosks.

Some companies even allow their employees time at work to try to produce new ideas. 3M encourages its employees to spend 15 percent of their time working on innovative independent projects. This policy has led to several successful new products, including the Post-It note.[10]

Some firms reward employees for producing creative new ideas. To encourage risk-taking through new ideas, companies like Google have begun implementing rewards for employees who fail after taking a big risk. Some of the most innovative Google ideas (such as driverless cars and Google Brain) were developed through the X program, formerly Google X. To promote innovative thinking and eliminate the fear of producing bad ideas among X employees, the company rewards failure. According to X CEO Astro Teller, "Google brain, the cars, Verily, everything else—those are symptoms. Side effects of trying weird things, things that are unlikely to work."[11] Programs like the X program make it safe for employees to fail, and, in doing so, encourage high levels of innovativeness.

Distributors

A well-trained sales force routinely asks distributors about needs that are not being met. Because they are closer to end users, distributors are often more aware of customer needs than manufacturers. The inspiration for Rubbermaid's Sidekick, a litter-free lunch box, came from a distributor who suggested that the company place some of its plastic containers inside a lunch box and sell the box as an alternative to plastic wrap and paper bags.

Competitors

No firms rely solely on internally generated ideas for new products. As discussed in Chapter 9, a big part of any organization's marketing intelligence system should be monitoring the performance of competitors' products. One purpose of competitive monitoring is to determine which, if any, of the competitors' products should be copied. There is plenty of information about competitors on the internet. Fuld & Company is a preeminent research and consulting firm in the field of competitive intelligence. Its clients include many companies on the Global Fortune 1000 list.[12]

Research and Development

R&D is carried out in four distinct ways. You learned about basic research and applied research in Chapter 4. The other two ways are product development and product modification. **Product development** goes beyond applied research by converting applications into marketable products. Product modification makes cosmetic or functional changes to existing products. Many new-product breakthroughs come from R&D activities.

Ride Snowboards R&D Lab is located near Seattle, close to Snoqualmie mountain, so that developers can create ideas in the lab and then easily test out new products at the nearby mountain. According to Ride, the R&D lab allows them "to take any ideas they have from imagination to reality and then put it through a barrage of wear and tests to make sure it passes muster."[13]

The United States and China are global leaders in research and development, and both countries spend heavily on R&D. The United States spends more than $600 billion annually on R&D, while China spends approximately $525 billion.[14]

Consultants

Outside consultants are always available to examine a business and recommend product ideas. Examples include the Weston Group, Booz Allen Hamilton, and Management Decisions Inc. Traditionally, consultants determine

---

product development a marketing strategy that entails the creation of marketable new products; the process of converting applications for new technologies into marketable products

whether a company has a balanced portfolio of products and, if not, what new product ideas are needed to offset the imbalance. For example, Continuum is an award-winning consultancy firm that designs new goods and services, works on brand makeovers, and conducts consumer research. Clients include Whole Foods, Nestlé, Procter & Gamble, Campbell Soup, IBM, and Freshly.[15]

Other Experts

A technique that is frequently to generate new-product ideas is called "crowdsourcing." General information regarding ideas being sought is provided to a wide range of potential sources such as industry experts, independent researchers, and academics. These experts then develop ideas for the company. In addition to field experts, firms such as Quirky and General Electric Company have used crowdsourcing to generate ideas from the general public and freelance inventors. Since the late 1990s, LEGO has used crowdsourcing to develop new product ideas through a program called LEGO Ideas. This program allows community members to submit ideas for new LEGO sets, after which other members can provide feedback on and ask questions about the potential new ideas. Once a new product idea has at least 10,000 votes of support, it is considered by LEGO for production.[16] For a more thorough discussion of crowdsourcing, refer to Chapter 18.

Creativity is the wellspring of new-product ideas, regardless of who produces them. A variety of approaches and techniques have been developed to stimulate creative thinking. The two considered most useful for generating new-product ideas are brainstorming and focus group exercises. The goal of **brainstorming** is to get a group to think of unlimited ways to vary a product or solve a problem. Group members avoid criticism of an idea, no matter how ridiculous it may seem. Objective evaluation is postponed. The sheer quantity of ideas is what matters. As noted in Chapter 9, an objective of focus group interviews is to stimulate insightful comments through group interaction. In the industrial market, machine tools, keyboard designs, aircraft interiors, and backhoe accessories have evolved from focus groups.

11-2c Idea Screening

After new ideas have been generated, they pass through the first filter in the product development process. This stage, called **screening**, eliminates ideas that are inconsistent with the organization's new-product strategy or are obviously inappropriate for some other reason. The new-product committee, the new-product department, or some other formally appointed group performs the screening review.

Concept tests are often used at the screening stage to rate concept (or product) alternatives. A **concept test** evaluates

Brainstorming is a time for thinking outside the box and exploring every avenue. When brainstorming, group members should avoid criticizing ideas no matter how ridiculous they may seem.

a new-product idea, usually before any prototype has been created. Typically, researchers get consumer reactions to descriptions and visual representations of a proposed product. Concept tests are considered fairly good predictors of success for line extensions. They have also been relatively precise predictors of success for new products that are not copycat items, are not easily classified into existing product categories, and do not require major changes in consumer behavior—such as Betty Crocker Tuna Helper. However, concept tests are usually inaccurate in predicting the success of new products that create new consumption patterns and require major changes in consumer behavior—such as microwave ovens, digital music players, and computers.

11-2d Business Analysis

New-product ideas that survive the initial screening process move to the **business analysis** stage, where preliminary figures for demand, cost, sales, and profitability are calculated. For the first time, costs and revenues are estimated and compared. Depending on the nature of the product and the company, this process may be simple or complex.

The newness of the product, the size of the market, and the nature of the competition all affect the accuracy

---

brainstorming the process of getting a group to think of unlimited ways to vary a product or solve a problem

screening the first filter in the product development process, which eliminates ideas that are inconsistent with the organization's new-product strategy or are obviously inappropriate for some other reason

concept test a test to evaluate a new-product idea, usually before any prototype has been created

business analysis the second stage of the screening process, where preliminary figures for demand, cost, sales, and profitability are calculated

of revenue projections. In an established market like soft drinks, industry estimates of total market size are available. Forecasting market share for a new entry in a new, fragmented, or relatively small niche is a bigger challenge.

Analyzing overall economic trends and their impact on estimated sales is especially important in product categories that are sensitive to fluctuations in the business cycle. If consumers view the economy as uncertain and risky, they will put off buying durable goods such as major home appliances, automobiles, and homes. Likewise, business buyers postpone major equipment purchases if they expect a recession. Understanding the market potential is important because costs increase dramatically once a product idea enters the development stage.

11-2e Development

In the early stage of **development**, the R&D or engineering department may develop a prototype of the product. A process called 3D printing, or additive manufacturing, is sometimes used to create three-dimensional prototypes quickly and at a relatively low cost. During this stage, the firm should start sketching a marketing strategy. The marketing department should decide on the product's packaging, branding, labeling, and so forth. In addition, it should map out preliminary promotion, price, and distribution strategies. The feasibility of manufacturing the product at an acceptable cost should be thoroughly examined. The development stage can last a long time and thus be very expensive. It took 10 years to develop Crest toothpaste, 15 years to develop the Polaroid Colorpack camera and the Xerox copy machine, 18 years to develop Minute Rice, and 51 years to develop the television. Video games typically take years to develop. Games that are rushed to market are often buggy, and some are even unplayable. Although Pokémon fans were initially excited for the release of the entertainment company's newest video games, *Pokémon Scarlet* and *Pokémon Violet*, many players were disappointed when they discovered technical issues and problems with the story upon playing the games. The company rushed the video games to market to meet launch deadlines, which resulted in an almost unplayable game and disappointed customers.[17]

The development process works best when all the involved areas (R&D, marketing, engineering, production, and even suppliers) work together rather than sequentially, a process called **simultaneous product development**. This approach allows firms to shorten the

development process and reduce costs. With simultaneous product development, all relevant functional areas and outside suppliers participate in all stages of the development process. Rather than proceeding through highly structured stages, the cross-functional team operates in unison. Involving key suppliers early in the process capitalizes on their knowledge and enables them to develop critical component parts.

The internet is a useful tool for implementing simultaneous product development. On the web, multiple partners from a variety of locations can meet regularly to assess new-product ideas, analyze markets and demographics, and review cost information. Ideas judged to be feasible can quickly be converted into new products. The best-managed global firms leverage their global networks by sharing best practices, knowledge, and technology.[18] Without the internet, it would be impossible to conduct simultaneous product development from different parts of the world. Some firms use online brain trusts to solve technical problems. Wazoku is a network of over 115,000 self-selected science problem solvers in 143 countries. Its clients include NASA, *Mastercard*, and *Bayer Crop Science*. When one of Wazoku's partners selects an idea for development, it no longer tries to develop the idea from the ground up with its own resources and time. Instead, it issues a brief to its network of thinkers, researchers, technology entrepreneurs, and inventors around the world, hoping to generate dialogue, suggestions, and solutions.

---

development the stage in the product development process in which a prototype is developed and a marketing strategy is outlined

simultaneous product development a team-oriented approach to new-product development

Customers use Zwift Forums to provide feedback about current products and to submit ideas for new products.

Innovative firms are also gathering a variety of R&D input from customers online. For example, Zwift, an indoor cycling and running company, created an online community called Zwift Forums. Customers can use this forum to provide feedback and ask questions about current products and to submit ideas for new products.[19]

Laboratory tests are often conducted on prototype models during the development stage. User safety is an important aspect of laboratory testing, which actually subjects products to much more severe treatment than that expected by end users. The Consumer Product Safety Act of 1972 requires manufacturers to conduct a "reasonable testing program" to ensure that their products conform to established safety standards.

Many products that test well in the laboratory are also tried out in homes or businesses. Examples of product categories well suited for such use tests include human and pet food products, household cleaning products, and industrial chemicals and supplies. These products are all relatively inexpensive, and their performance characteristics are apparent to users. For example, P&G tests a variety of personal and home care products in the community around its Cincinnati, Ohio, headquarters.

11-2f Test Marketing

After products and marketing programs have been developed, they are usually tested in the marketplace. **Test marketing** is the limited introduction of a product and a marketing program to determine the reactions of potential customers in a market situation. Test marketing allows management to evaluate alternative strategies and to assess how well the various aspects of the marketing mix fit together. Even established products are test marketed to assess new marketing strategies.

The cities chosen as test sites should reflect market conditions in the new product's projected market area. However, no "magic city" exists that can universally represent market conditions, and a product's success in one city does not guarantee that it will be a nationwide hit. When selecting test market cities, researchers should therefore find locations where the demographics and purchasing habits mirror the overall market. The company should also have good distribution in test cities. For example, Panera Bread uses Columbus, Ohio, as one of its test markets. Because the city has a nearly perfect cross section of America's demographic breakdown, it is the perfect testing ground for new products. Recently, Panera tested a new coffee and tea subscription in which consumers could pay a flat monthly fee and receive unlimited coffee or tea products. During the test marketing phase, Panera saw great success with this program. Nearly 25 percent of consumers that joined the program during the test phase were new to the MyPanera rewards program, indicating that the coffee and tea subscription program could be very effective at attracting new business. Additionally, consumers who joined the subscription program were visiting Panera locations nearly twice as often as they were previously. These successes led Panera to eventually launch the program in all of its locations.[20] This program is now referred to as the "Unlimited Sip Club" and has expanded to include all beverages that Panera offers, including fountain drinks and lemonades. Moreover, test locations should be isolated from the media. If the television stations in a particular market reach a very large area outside that market, the advertising used for the test product may pull in many consumers from outside the market. The product may then appear more successful than it really is.

The High Costs of Test Marketing

Test marketing frequently takes one year or longer, and costs can exceed $1 million. Some products remain in test markets even longer than a year. To expand its product offerings, Starbucks launched three new drinks made with extra virgin olive oil, including an olive oil latte, olive oil shaken espresso, and an olive oil cold brew. The drinks were initially launched in Italian Starbucks locations, and, after Starbucks saw initial success it that market, the drinks were expanded to Southern California stores to test the concept in the U.S. market.[21]

Despite the cost, many firms believe it is better to fail in a test market than in a national introduction. Because test marketing is so expensive, some companies do not test line extensions of well-known brands.

The high cost of test marketing is not just financial. One unavoidable problem is that test marketing exposes the new product and its marketing mix to competitors before its introduction. Thus, the element of surprise is lost.

---

test marketing the limited introduction of a product and a marketing program to determine the reactions of potential customers in a market situation

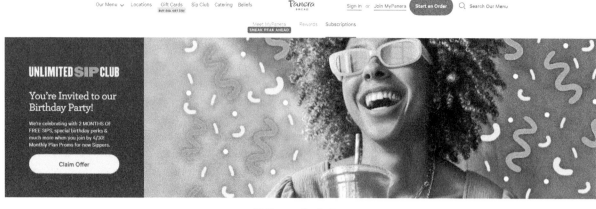

Panera test markets new products and promotional strategies, such as the Unlimited Sip Club, in Columbus, Ohio.

Competitors can also sabotage or "jam" a testing program by introducing their own sales promotion, pricing, or advertising campaign. The purpose is to hide or distort the normal conditions that the testing firm might expect in the market.

Alternatives to Test Marketing

Many firms are looking for cheaper, faster, safer alternatives to traditional test marketing. In the early 1980s, Information Resources Inc. (IRI) pioneered one alternative: scanner-based research (discussed in Chapter 9). Another alternative to traditional test marketing is **simulated (laboratory) market testing**. Advertising and other promotional materials for several products, including the test product, are shown to members of the product's target market. These people are then taken to shop at a mock or real store, where their purchases are recorded. Shopper behavior, including repeat purchasing, is monitored to assess the product's likely performance under true market conditions.

The internet offers a fast, cost-effective way to conduct test marketing. P&G uses the internet to assess customer demand for potential new products. Many products that are not available in grocery stores or drugstores can be sampled from P&G's website devoted to samples and coupons.[22]

Despite these alternatives, most firms still consider test marketing essential for most new products. The high price of failure simply prohibits the more-expensive widespread introduction of most new products without testing.

11-2g Commercialization

The final stage in the new-product development process is **commercialization**, the decision to market a product. The decision to commercialize the product sets several tasks in motion: ordering production materials and equipment, starting production, building inventories, shipping the product to field distribution points, training the sales force, announcing the new product to the trade, and advertising to potential customers.

The time from the initial commercialization decision to the product's actual introduction varies. The time for simple products that use existing equipment may be only a few weeks. Technical products that require custom manufacturing equipment could take several years until introduction, and the total cost of development and initial introduction can be staggering.

11-3 Why Some Products Succeed and Others Fail

11-3 Summarize why some products succeed and others fail

Despite the amount of time and money spent on developing and testing new products, a large proportion of new-product introductions fail. Products fail for many reasons.

---

simulated (laboratory) market testing the presentation of advertising and other promotional materials for several products, including a test product, to members of the product's target market

commercialization the decision to market a product

One common reason is that they simply do not offer any discernible benefit as compared with existing products. Another commonly cited factor in new-product failures is a poor match between product features and customer desires. For example, some smartphones on the market have more than 700 different functions, although the average user is happy with just 10 functions. Other reasons for failure include overestimation of market size, incorrect targeting or positioning, a price too high or too low, inadequate distribution, poor promotion, or simply an inferior product.

Estimates of the percentages of new products that fail vary. Many estimates range as high as 75 to 95 percent.[23] Failure can be a matter of degree, however. Absolute failure occurs when a company cannot recoup its development, marketing, and production costs—the product actually loses money for the company. A relative product failure results when the product returns a profit but fails to achieve sales, profit, or market share goals. Some notable product failures include McDonald's Mozzarella Sticks, Lululemon Astro Pants, Amazon Fire Phone, Keurig KKold, Google Glass, and Burger King's Satisfries, a healthier alternative to regular fries.[24]

High costs and other risks of developing and testing new products do not stop many companies, such as Newell Brands, Colgate-Palmolive, Campbell's, and 3M, from aggressively developing and introducing new products. These companies depend on new products to increase revenues and profits. The most important factor in successful new-product introduction is a good match between the product and market needs—as the marketing concept would predict. Successful new products deliver a meaningful and perceivable benefit to a sizable number of people or organizations and are different in some meaningful way from their intended substitutes. For example, Tylenol recently introduced a pain reliever in a dissolvable powder form. Many consumers do not like swallowing pills, so there was a need in the market for pain relief in a format other than a pill. Tylenol Dissolve Packs met this need and were voted by consumers as one of the best new products of 2022.[25]

11-4 Global Issues in New-Product Development

11-4 Discuss global issues in new-product development

Increasing globalization of markets and competition provides a reason for multinational firms to consider new-product development from a worldwide perspective. A firm that starts with a global strategy is better able to develop products that are marketable worldwide. In many multinational corporations, every product is developed for potential worldwide distribution, and unique market requirements are satisfied during development whenever possible.

Some global marketers design their products to meet regulations in their major markets and then, if necessary, meet smaller markets' requirements country by country. Nissan develops car models for these lead countries that, with minor changes, can be sold in most markets. With this approach, Nissan has been able to reduce the number of its basic models from 48 to 19. Some products, however, have little potential for global market penetration without modification. Succeeding in some countries (such as China) often requires companies to develop products that meet the unique needs of these populations. In other cases, companies cannot sell their products at affordable prices and still make a profit in many countries.

11-5 The Spread of New Products

11-5 Explain the diffusion process through which new products are adopted

Managers have a better chance of successfully marketing products if they understand how consumers learn about and adopt products.

11-5a Diffusion of Innovation

An **innovation** is a product perceived as new by a potential adopter. It really does not matter whether the product is "new to the world" or some other category of new. If it is

Initially launched as a limited edition, Kraft Macaroni & Cheese Ice Cream was surprisingly popular among consumers and ended up launching at Walmart's across the United States.

innovation a product perceived as new by a potential adopter

new to a potential adopter, it is an innovation in this context. **Diffusion** is the process by which the adoption of an innovation spreads. Five categories of adopters participate in the diffusion process.

Innovators

Innovators are the first 2.5 percent of all those who adopt the product. Innovators are eager to try new ideas and products; it is almost an obsession. In addition to having higher incomes, they are more worldly and more active outside their community than non-innovators. They rely less on group norms and are more self-confident. Because they are well educated and are more likely to get their information from scientific sources and experts. Innovators are characterized as being venturesome.

Early Adopters

Early adopters are the next 13.5 percent to adopt the product. Although early adopters are not the very first, they do adopt early in the product's life cycle. As compared with innovators, they rely much more on group norms and values. They are also more oriented to the local community, in contrast to the innovators' worldly outlook. Early adopters are more likely than innovators to be opinion leaders because of their closer affiliation with groups. Early adopters are a new product's best friends. Because viral, buzz, and word-of-mouth (WOM) advertising is on the rise, marketers focus a lot of attention identifying the group that begins the viral marketing chain—the influencers. Part of the challenge is that this group of customers is distinguished not by demographics, but by behavior. Influencers come from all age, gender, and income groups, and they do not use media any differently than the users who are considered followers. The characteristic influencers share is their desire to talk to others about their experiences with goods and services. A desire to earn the respect of others is a dominant characteristic among early adopters.

Early Majority

The next 34 percent to adopt are called the "early majority." Members of this group weigh the pros and cons before adopting a new product. They are likely to collect more information and evaluate more brands than early adopters, thereby extending the adoption process. They rely on the group for information but are unlikely to be opinion leaders themselves. Instead, they tend to be opinion leaders' friends and neighbors. Consumers trust positive WOM reviews from friends, family, and peers. According

---

diffusion the process by which the adoption of an innovation spreads

Seven Characteristics of Successful Product Introductions

Firms that routinely experience success in new- product introductions tend to share the following seven characteristics:

1. A history of listening carefully to customers
2. An obsession with producing the best product possible
3. A vision of what the market will be like in the future
4. Strong leadership
5. A commitment to new-product development
6. A project-based team approach to new-product development
7. Getting every aspect of the product development process right

to Nielsen research, 88 percent of consumers believe that recommendations from friends and family are the most trustworthy source of product information.[26] Product discussions often drive millennial conversations, so WOM marketing is particularly powerful among this demographic. In an effort to appeal to millennials and encourage them to discuss the brand on social media, L'Oréal Paris launched a campaign that encouraged social media users to post about things that truly mattered to them using the hashtag #WorthSaying. Many of the posts were focused on women's empowerment issues, and the campaign was heavily supported by several influential celebrities, including Jennifer Lopez.[27]

All WOM is not positive. A recent survey of U.S. and U.K. consumers found that 50 percent of consumers will tell friends and family about negative brand experiences.[28] The early majority is an important link in the process of diffusing new ideas because its members are positioned between earlier and later adopters. A dominant characteristic of the early majority is deliberateness.

Late Majority

The late majority is the next 34 percent to adopt. The late majority adopts a new product because most of their friends have already adopted it. Because they also rely on group norms, their adoption stems from pressure to conform. This group tends to be older and below average socioeconomic status. They depend mainly on WOM communication rather than on the mass media. The dominant characteristic of the late majority is skepticism.

Laggards

The final 16 percent to adopt are called laggards. Like innovators, laggards do not rely on group norms. Their independence is rooted in their ties to tradition. Thus, the past heavily influences their decisions. By the time laggards adopt an innovation, it is probably outmoded and has been replaced by something else. For example, they may have bought their first color television set after flat screen televisions were already widely diffused. Laggards have the longest adoption time and the lowest socioeconomic status. They tend to be suspicious of new products and alienated from a rapidly advancing society. The dominant value of laggards is tradition. Marketers typically ignore laggards, who do not seem to be motivated by advertising or personal selling and are virtually impossible to reach online.

Note that some product categories may never be adopted by 100 percent of the population. The adopter categories refer to all of those who will eventually adopt a product, not the entire population.

11-5b Product Characteristics and the Rate of Adoption

The following five product characteristics can be used to predict and explain the rate of acceptance and diffusion of a new product:

1. **Complexity:** the degree of difficulty involved in understanding and using a new product. The more complex the product, the slower is its diffusion.

2. **Compatibility:** the degree to which the new product is consistent with existing values and product knowledge, past experiences, and current needs. Incompatible products diffuse more slowly than compatible products.

3. **Relative advantage:** the degree to which a product is perceived as superior to existing substitutes. Because of significant improvements to the camera, including a larger size and better resolution, and the ability to send highlight videos directly to a user's phone, GoPro's HERO11 Black line of cameras had a clear relative advantage over previous versions of the camera.[29]

4. **Observability:** the degree to which the benefits or other results of using the product can be observed by others and communicated to target customers. For instance, fashion items and automobiles are highly visible and more observable than personal-care items.

5. **Trialability:** the degree to which a product can be tried on a limited basis. It is much easier to try a new toothpaste or breakfast cereal, for example, than a new personal computer.

11-5c Marketing Implications of the Adoption Process

Two types of communication aid the diffusion process: *WOM communication* among consumers and communication from marketers to consumers. WOM communication within and across groups, including social media and viral communication, speeds diffusion. Opinion leaders discuss new products with their followers and with other opinion leaders. Marketers must therefore ensure that the types of information they want to convey is available to opinion leaders in the media that they use. Suppliers of some products, such as professional and healthcare services, rely almost solely on WOM communication for new business.

Many large-scale companies like Procter & Gamble, Peloton, and Southwest Airlines seek out opinion leaders among their employees. Some companies conduct surveys to identify opinion leaders while others use technology to map connections between individuals and postings. Once identified, managers can provide training to these influential employees, discuss strategies for sharing information, and provide them with potential content. It is, however, important for these employee influencers, just as with any influencer marketing campaign, to share their authentic feelings and opinions to best connect with their audience. Influencers are frequently rewarded for their skills with promotions and other forms of recognition.[30]

The second type of communication aiding the diffusion process is communication directly from the marketer to potential adopters. Messages directed toward early adopters should normally use different appeals from messages directed toward the early majority, the late majority, or the laggards. Early adopters are more important than innovators because they make up a larger group, are more socially active, and are usually opinion leaders.

As the focus of a promotional campaign shifts from the early adopters to the early majority and the late majority, marketers should study the dominant characteristics, buying behavior, and media characteristics of these target markets. Then they should revise messages and the media strategy to fit. The diffusion model helps guide marketers in developing and implementing promotional strategies.

11-6 Product Life Cycles

11-6 Explain the concept of product life cycles

The **product life cycle (PLC)** is one of the most familiar concepts in marketing. Few other general concepts have been so widely discussed. Although some researchers and consultants have challenged the theoretical basis and managerial value of the PLC, many believe it is a useful

---

product life cycle (PLC) a concept that provides a way to trace the stages of a product's acceptance, from its introduction (birth) to its decline (death)

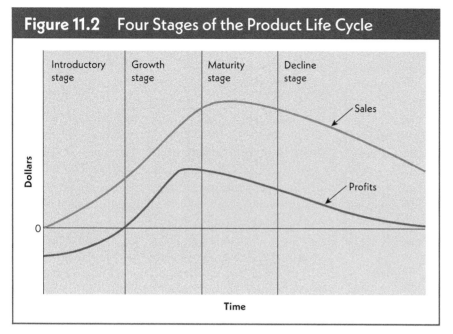

Figure 11.2 Four Stages of the Product Life Cycle

Introductory stage | Growth stage | Maturity stage | Decline stage

Dollars

Sales

Profits

0

Time

marketing management diagnostic tool and a general guide for marketing planning in various life-cycle stages.

The PLC is a biological metaphor that traces the stages of a product's acceptance, from its introduction (birth) to its decline (death). As Figure 11.2 shows, a product progresses through four major stages: introduction, growth, maturity, and decline.

The PLC concept can be used to analyze a brand, a product form, or a product category. The PLC for a product form is usually longer than the PLC for any one brand. The exception would be a brand that was the first and last competitor in a market for the product form. In that situation,

---

product category all brands that satisfy a particular type of need

introductory stage the full-scale launch of a new product into the marketplace

the brand and product-form life cycles would be equal in length. Product categories have the longest life cycles. A **product category** includes all brands that satisfy a particular type of need, such as shaving products, passenger automobiles, or soft drinks.

The time a product spends in any one stage of the life cycle may vary dramatically. Some products, such as fad items, move through the entire cycle in weeks. Fads are typically characterized by a sudden and unpredictable spike in sales followed by a rather abrupt decline. Examples of fad items are Fidget Spinners, Pokémon Go, and Crocs. Other products, such as electric clothes washers and dryers, stay in the maturity stage for decades. Figure 11.2 illustrates the typical life cycle for a consumer durable good, such as a washer or dryer. In contrast, Figure 11.3 illustrates typical life cycles for styles (such as formal, business, or casual clothing), fashions (such as miniskirts or baggy jeans), and fads (such as leopard-print clothing). Changes in a product, its uses, its image, or its positioning can extend that product's life cycle.

The PLC concept does not tell managers the length of a product's life cycle or its duration in any stage. It does not dictate marketing strategy. It is simply a tool to help marketers forecast future events and suggest appropriate strategies.

11-6a Introductory Stage

The **introductory stage** of the PLC represents the full-scale launch of a new product into the marketplace. Ring Car Cam, JBL's Tour Pro 2 earbuds with smart case, and GE's Smart Mixer are all products that have recently entered the PLC.[31] A high failure rate, little competition, frequent

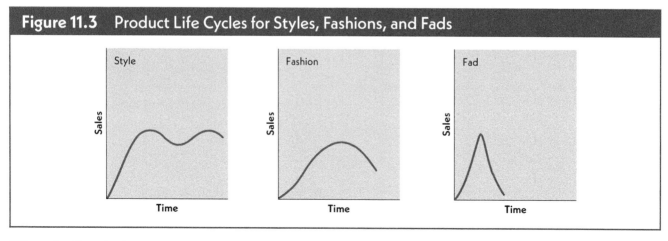

Figure 11.3 Product Life Cycles for Styles, Fashions, and Fads

Style — Sales / Time

Fashion — Sales / Time

Fad — Sales / Time

product modification, and limited distribution typify the introductory stage of the PLC.

Marketing costs in the introductory stage are normally high for several reasons. High dealer margins are often needed to obtain adequate distribution, and incentives are needed to get consumers to try the new product. Advertising expenses are high because of the need to educate consumers about the new product's benefits. Production costs are also often high in this stage, as product and manufacturing flaws are identified and corrected, and efforts are undertaken to develop mass production economies.

Sales normally increase slowly during the introductory stage. Moreover, profits are usually negative because of R&D costs, factory tooling, and high introduction costs. The length of the introductory phase is largely determined by product characteristics, such as the product's advantages over substitute products, the educational effort required to make the product known, and management's commitment of resources to the new item. A short introductory period is usually preferred to help reduce the impact of negative earnings and cash flows. As soon as the product gets off the ground, the financial burden should begin to diminish. Also, a short introductory period helps dispel some of the uncertainty about whether the new product will be successful.

Promotional strategy in the introductory stage focuses on developing product awareness and informing consumers about the product category's potential benefits. At this stage, the communication challenge is to stimulate primary demand—demand for the product in general rather than for a specific brand. Intensive personal selling is often required to gain acceptance for the product among wholesalers and retailers. Promotion of convenience products often requires heavy consumer sampling and couponing. Shopping and specialty products demand educational advertising and personal selling to the final consumer.

11-6b Growth Stage

If a product category survives the introductory stage, it then advances to the **growth stage** of the life cycle. In this stage, sales typically grow at an increasing rate, many competitors enter the market, and large companies may start to acquire small pioneering firms. Profits rise rapidly in the growth stage, reach their peak, and begin declining as competition intensifies. Emphasis switches from primary demand promotion (e.g., promoting ereaders) to aggressive brand advertising and communication of the differences between brands (e.g., promoting Kindle vs. promoting Nook).

Distribution becomes a major key to success during the growth stage as well as in later stages. Manufacturers scramble to sign up dealers and distributors and to build long-term relationships. Others are able to market directly to consumers using social media. Without adequate

Starbucks targets its gourmet line at new, young drinkers—the only segment that is growing.

distribution, it is impossible to establish a strong market position.

11-6c Maturity Stage

A period during which sales increase at a decreasing rate signals the beginning of the **maturity stage** of the life cycle. New users cannot be added indefinitely, and sooner or later, the market approaches saturation. Normally, this stage is the longest stage of the PLC. Many major household appliances are in the maturity stage of their life cycles.

For shopping products such as durable goods and electronics, and many specialty products, annual models begin to appear during the maturity stage. Product lines are lengthened to appeal to additional market segments. Service and repair assume more important roles as manufacturers strive to distinguish their products from others. Product design changes tend to become stylistic (How can the product be made different?) rather than functional (How can the product be made better?).

As prices and profits continue to fall, marginal competitors start dropping out of the market. Dealer margins also shrink, resulting in less shelf space for mature items, lower dealer inventories, and a general reluctance to promote the product. Thus, promotion to dealers often intensifies during this stage to retain loyalty.

Heavy consumer promotion by the manufacturer is also required to maintain market share. Cutthroat competition during this stage can lead to price wars. Another characteristic of the maturity stage is the emergence of "niche marketers" that target narrow, well-defined, underserved segments of a market. Starbucks Coffee

---

growth stage the second stage of the product life cycle, when sales typically grow at an increasing rate; many competitors enter the market; large companies may start to acquire small pioneering firms; and profits are healthy

maturity stage a period during which sales increase at a slower rate

targets its gourmet line at new, young, affluent coffee drinkers, the only segment of the coffee market that is growing.

11-6d Decline Stage

A long-run drop in sales signals the beginning of the **decline stage**. The rate of decline is governed by how rapidly consumer tastes change or substitute products are adopted. Many convenience products and fad items lose their market overnight, leaving large inventories of unsold items, such as designer jeans. Others die more slowly. Compact discs (CDs) are an example of a product in the decline stage of the product life cycle. For many years, CDs were the most popular way for people to listen to music. Many consumers owned portable CD players and many cars featured CD players. However, as the smartphone market grew, people could listen to music directly through their phones. Bluetooth technology advanced drivers being able to listen to music from their phones through their car's speakers. As a result, sales for both CDs and CD players dropped dramatically.

Some firms have developed successful strategies for marketing products in the decline stage of the PLC. They eliminate all nonessential marketing expenses and let sales decline as more and more customers discontinue purchasing the products. Eventually, the product is withdrawn from the market.

---

decline stage a long-run drop in sales

11-6e Implications for Marketing Management

The new-product development process, the diffusion process, and the PLC concept all have implications for marketing managers. The funnel shape of Figure 11.1 indicates that many new-product ideas are necessary to produce one successful new product. The new-product development process is sometimes illustrated as a decay curve, with roughly half of the ideas approved at one stage and rejected at the next. While the actual numbers vary widely among firms and industries, the relationship between the stages can be generalized. This reinforces the notion that an organized effort to generate many ideas from various sources is important for any firm that wishes to produce a continuing flow of new products.

The major implication of the diffusion process for marketing managers is that the message may need to change over time. The targeted adopter and media may need to shift based on how various categories of adopters gather product information. A message developed for and targeted toward early adopters will not be perceived similarly by late majority adopters.

Figure 11.4 shows the relationship between the adopter categories and stages of the PLC. The various categories of adopters buy products in different stages of the life cycle. Almost all sales in the maturity and decline stages represent repeat purchases.

Figure 11.4   Relationships Between the Diffusion Process and the Product Life Cycle

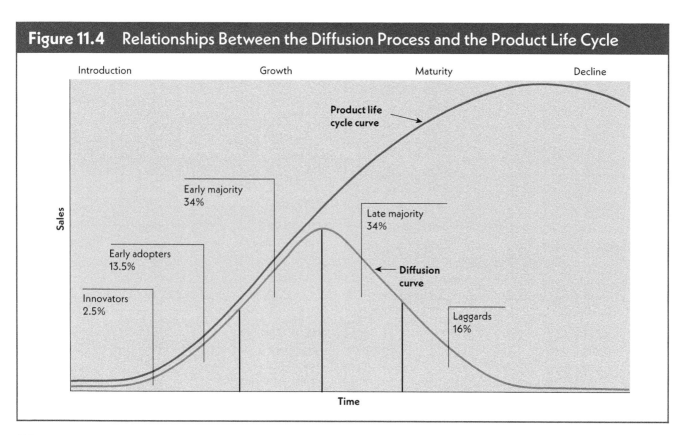

Jacob Lund/Shutterstock.com

Chapter 12

Services and Nonprofit Organization Marketing

Learning Outcomes

After studying this chapter, you will be able to . . .

12-1 Discuss the differences between services and goods

12-2 Describe the components of service quality

12-3 Develop marketing mixes for services

12-4 Discuss relationship marketing in services

12-5 Explain internal marketing in services

12-6 Describe nonprofit organization marketing

12-1 The Difference Between Services and Goods

12-1 Discuss the differences between services and goods

A **service** is the result of applying human or mechanical efforts to people or objects. Services involve a deed, a performance, or an effort that cannot be physically possessed. The service sector substantially influences the U.S. economy, accounting for nearly 80 percent of the country's economic output. The service-oriented industries contributing to much of this output include scientific and technological services, health care, financial services, and administrative services.[1]

The marketing process, described in Chapter, 1 is the same for all types of products, whether they are goods or services. In addition, although a comparison of goods and services marketing can be beneficial, in reality it is hard to distinguish clearly between manufacturing and service firms. Indeed, many manufacturing firms can point to service as a major factor in their success. For example, maintenance and repair services offered by the manufacturer are important to car buyers. Nevertheless, services have some unique characteristics that distinguish them from goods, and marketing strategies need to be adjusted for these characteristics. Services have four unique characteristics that distinguish them from goods. Services are intangible, inseparable, heterogeneous, and perishable.

12-1a Intangibility

The basic difference between services and goods is that services are intangible performances. Because of their **intangibility**, they cannot be touched, seen, tasted, heard, or felt in the same manner that goods can be sensed.

---

service the result of applying human or mechanical efforts to people or objects

intangibility the inability of services to be touched, seen, tasted, heard, or felt in the same manner that goods can be sensed

search quality a characteristic that can be easily assessed before purchase

experience quality a characteristic that can be assessed only after use

credence quality a characteristic that consumers may have difficulty assessing even after purchase because they do not have the necessary knowledge or experience

inseparability the inability of the production and consumption of a service to be separated; consumers must be present during the production

Evaluating the quality of services before or even after making a purchase is harder than evaluating the quality of goods because, compared to goods, services tend to exhibit fewer search qualities. A **search quality** is a characteristic that can be easily assessed before purchase—for instance, the color of an appliance or automobile. At the same time, services tend to exhibit more experience and credence qualities. An **experience quality** is a characteristic that can be assessed only after use, such as the quality of a meal in a restaurant. A **credence quality** is a characteristic that consumers may have difficulty assessing even after purchase because they do not have the necessary knowledge or experience. Medical and consulting services are examples of services that exhibit credence qualities.

These characteristics also make it harder for marketers to communicate the benefits of an intangible service than to communicate the benefits of tangible goods. Thus, marketers often rely on tangible cues to communicate a service's nature and quality. For example, Travelers, an American insurance company, uses an umbrella symbol as a tangible reminder of the protection that insurance provides.

The facilities that customers visit, or from which services are delivered, are a critical tangible part of the total service offering. Messages about the organization are communicated to customers through such elements as the décor, the clutter or neatness of service areas, and the staff's manners and dress. Hotels know that guests form opinions quickly and that great customer service, from the time that guests check-in until they check-out, is crucial. Some hotels go to great lengths to provide exceptional service to their guests. For example, Four Seasons Hotels and Resorts has begun utilizing chat technology to more efficiently communicate with guests who have checked in and respond to their needs.[2]

The company also gives all of its employees—from parking attendants to managers—the authority to act instantly when a guest makes a request. This allows Four Seasons to offer excellent personalized service to all guests throughout their stay.

12-1b Inseparability

Goods are produced, sold, and then consumed. In contrast, services are often sold, produced, and consumed at the same time. In other words, their production and consumption are inseparable activities. This **inseparability** means that, because consumers must be present during the production of services like haircuts or a medical exam, they are actually involved in the production of the services they buy. That type of consumer involvement is rare in goods manufacturing.

Simultaneous production and consumption also means that services normally cannot be produced in a centralized location and consumed in decentralized locations, as goods typically are. Services are also inseparable from the perspective of the service provider. Thus, the quality of service that firms are able to deliver depends on the quality of their employees.

12-1c Heterogeneity

One great strength of Jimmy John's is consistency. Whether customers order a Big John sub in Chicago or Seattle, they know exactly what they are going to get. This is not the case with many service providers. Because services have greater **heterogeneity**, or variability of inputs and outputs, they tend to be less standardized and uniform than goods. For example, physicians in a group practice or barbers in a barbershop differ within each group in their technical and interpersonal skills. Because services tend to be labor intensive and production and consumption are inseparable, consistency and quality control can be hard to achieve.

Standardization and training help increase consistency and reliability. In the information technology sector, a number of certification programs are available to ensure that technicians are capable of working on (and within) complex enterprise software systems. For example, professional certifications for big data engineers such as those at Microsoft, Oracle, SAS, and INFORMS ensure a consistency of knowledge and ability among those who can pass these programs' rigorous exams.[3]

12-1d Perishability

Perishability is the fourth characteristic of services. **Perishability** refers to the inability of services to be stored, warehoused, or inventoried. An empty hotel room or airplane seat produces no revenue that day. The revenue is lost. Yet service organizations are often forced to turn away full-price customers during peak periods.

One of the most important challenges in many service industries is finding ways to synchronize supply and demand. The philosophy that some revenue is better than none has prompted many hotels to offer deep discounts on weekends and during the offseason.

12-2 Service Quality

12-2 Describe the components of service quality

Because of the four unique characteristics of services, service quality is more difficult to define and measure than the quality of tangible goods. Business executives rank the improvement of service quality as one of the most critical challenges facing them today.

12-2a Evaluating Service Quality

Research has shown that customers evaluate service quality by the following five components:

1. **Reliability:** The ability to perform the service dependably, accurately, and consistently. Reliability is performing the service right the first time. This component has been found to be the one most important to consumers.

2. **Responsiveness:** The ability to provide prompt service. Examples of responsiveness include calling the customer back quickly, serving lunch fast to someone who is in a hurry, or mailing a transaction slip immediately. Many companies, including Netflix and Spotify, utilize their social media accounts to be more responsive to their customers—this allows these companies to not only quickly respond to customers, but also to connect with them in the process.[4] The ultimate in responsiveness is offering service 24 hours a day, seven days a week.

3. **Assurance:** The knowledge and courtesy of employees and their ability to convey trust. Skilled employees, who treat customers with respect and make customers feel that they can trust the firm, exemplify assurance.

4. **Empathy:** Caring, individualized attention to customers. Firms whose employees recognize customers and learn their specific requirements are providing empathy.

Many companies utilize their social media accounts to be more responsive with customers.

heterogeneity the variability of the inputs and outputs of services, which causes services to tend to be less standardized and uniform than goods

perishability the inability of services to be stored, warehoused, or inventoried

reliability the ability to perform a service dependably, accurately, and consistently

responsiveness the ability to provide prompt service

assurance the knowledge and courtesy of employees and their ability to convey trust

empathy caring, individualized attention to customers

The hotel-chain Hilton understands that offering personalized service is important in the hospitality industry. Hilton empowers its employees to anticipate and meet customers' wants and needs, which maximizes employee's opportunities to provide great service. According to a Hilton representative, "Customers are increasingly looking for truly personalized, one-of-a-kind experiences... This is why it is essential to create and foster a culture that is focused on people serving people—one where team members are inspired and empowered to go above and beyond for customers." This strategy has paid off and Hilton is often ranked as one of the top hotel chains in the world.[5]

5. **Tangibles:** The physical evidence of the service. The tangible parts of a service include the physical facilities, tools, and equipment used to provide the service, as well as the appearance of personnel.[6]

Overall service quality is measured by combining customers' evaluations for all five components.

12-2b The Gap Model of Service Quality

One model of service quality called the **gap model** identifies five gaps that can cause problems in service delivery and influence customer evaluations of service quality.[7] These gaps are illustrated in Figure 12.1:

1. **Gap 1:** The gap between what customers want and what management thinks customers want. This gap results from a lack of understanding or a misinterpretation of the customers' needs, wants, or desires. A firm that does little or no customer satisfaction research is likely to experience this gap. To close gap 1, firms must stay attuned to customer wishes by researching customer needs and satisfaction.

2. **Gap 2:** The gap between what management thinks customers want and the quality specifications that management develops to provide the service. Essentially, this gap is the result of management's inability to translate customers' needs into delivery systems within the firm. For example, KFC used to rate its managers according to "chicken efficiency," or how much chicken they threw away at closing; customers who came in late would either have to wait for chicken to be cooked or settle for chicken several hours old.

3. **Gap 3:** The gap between the service quality specifications and the service that is actually provided. If both gaps 1 and 2 have been closed, then gap 3 is due to the inability of management and employees to do what should be done. Management needs to ensure that employees have the skills and the proper tools to perform their jobs. Other techniques that help to close gap 3 are training employees so they know what management expects and encouraging teamwork.

4. **Gap 4:** The gap between what the company provides and what the customer is told it provides. This is clearly a communication gap. It may include misleading or deceptive advertising campaigns promising more than the firm can deliver or doing "whatever it takes" to get the business. To close this gap, companies need to create realistic customer expectations through honest, accurate communication about what the firms can provide.

5. **Gap 5:** The gap between the service that customers receive and the service they want. This gap can be positive or negative. For example, if a patient expects to wait 20 minutes in the physician's office before seeing the physician but actually waits only 10 minutes, the patient's evaluation of service quality will be high. However, a 40-minute wait would result in a lower evaluation. Nordstrom, a company whose service quality is legendary, consistently performs at a level above and beyond what customers expect, resulting in few to no signs of gap 5.[8]

When one or more of these gaps is large, service quality is perceived as low. As the gaps shrink, perceptions of service quality improve. Market research (discussed in Chapter 9) can help service firms close these gaps. Starbucks is consistently ranked as one of the top consumer-centric brands in the world, as well as one of the most valuable restaurant brands. Much of the brand's success comes from a heavy focus on market research to gain a better understanding of the wants and needs of its customers. For example, when Starbucks first released the popular Pumpkin Spice Latte (PSL), the fall beverage was not released until late September, but PSL fans loved the drink so much that they wanted it earlier in the year. Based on this feedback, Starbucks moved the launch of the PSL to August.[9]

Several other companies consistently get their service quality right. According to *Forbes*, some of the top service-based companies that offer exceptional customer service include Blue Cross Blue Shield, Airbnb, Illumnia Healthcare, Happy Money, and Mastercard.[10] These companies have three core beliefs in common: good service starts at the top; service is seen as a continual challenge; and companies work best when people want to work for them.

---

tangibles the physical evidence of a service, including the physical facilities, tools, and equipment used to provide the service

gap model a model identifying five gaps that can cause problems in service delivery and influence customer evaluations of service quality

Figure 12.1 Gap Model of Service Quality

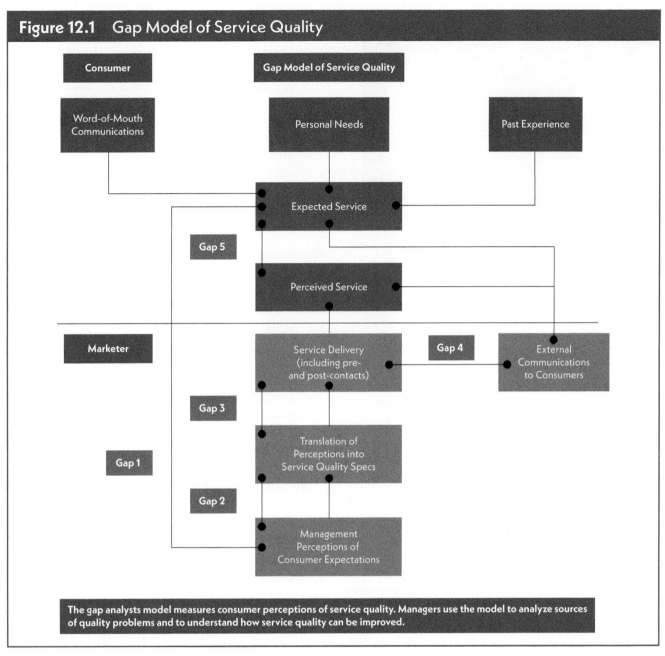

Source: Based on Valarie A. Zeithaml, Mary J. Bitner, and Dwayne Gremler, *Services Marketing*, 4/e, © 2006 (New York: McGraw Hill, 2006).

12-3 Marketing Mixes for Services

12-3 Develop marketing mixes for services

Services' unique characteristics—intangibility, inseparability of production and consumption, heterogeneity, and perishability—make marketing more challenging. Elements of the marketing mix (product, place, promotion, and pricing) need to be adjusted to meet the special needs created by these characteristics.

12-3a Product (Service) Strategy

A product, as defined in Chapter 10, is everything a person receives in an exchange. In the case of a service organization, the product offering is intangible and consists in large part of a process or a series of processes. Product strategies for service offerings include decisions on the type of process involved, core and supplementary services, standardization or customization of the service product, and the service mix.

Service as a Process

Two broad categories of things are processed in service organizations: people and objects. In some cases, the process is

Theater performances like are considered mental stimulus processing services.

physical, or tangible, while in others the process is intangible. Based on these characteristics, service processes can be placed into one of four categories:

1. People processing takes place when the service is directed at a customer. Examples are transportation services and health care.

2. Possession processing occurs when the service is directed at customers' physical possessions. Examples are lawn care, dry cleaning, and veterinary services.

3. Mental-stimulus processing refers to services directed at people's minds. Examples are theater performances and education.

4. Information processing describes services that use technology or brainpower directed at a customer's assets. Examples are insurance and consulting.[11]

Because customers' experiences and involvement differ for each of these types of services, marketing strategies may also differ. For example, people-processing services require customers to enter the *service factory*, which is a physical location, such as an aircraft, a physician's office, or a hair salon. In contrast, possession-processing services typically do not require the presence of the customer in the service factory. Marketing strategies for the former would therefore focus more on an attractive, comfortable physical environment and employee training on employee–customer interaction issues than would strategies for the latter.

Core and Supplementary Service Products

The service offering can be viewed as a bundle of activities that includes the **core service**, which is the most basic benefit the

---

core service the most basic benefit the consumer is buying

supplementary services a group of services that support or enhance the core service

mass customization a strategy that delivers customized services on a mass basis

customer is buying, and a group of **supplementary services** that support or enhance the core service. Figure 12.2 illustrates these concepts for a luxury hotel. The core service is providing rooms for a nightly fee, which involves people processing. The supplementary services, some of which involve information processing, include food services and reservations, parking, phone, and television services.

In many service industries, the core service becomes a commodity as competition increases. Thus, firms often emphasize supplementary services to create a competitive advantage. On the other hand, some firms position themselves in the marketplace by greatly reducing supplementary services, which can therefore lead to a decrease in prices.

Customization/Standardization

An important issue in developing the service offering is whether to customize or standardize it. Customized services are more flexible and respond to individual customers' needs. They also usually command a higher price. Standardized services are more efficient and cost less.

Instead of choosing to either standardize or customize a service, a firm may incorporate elements of both by adopting an emerging strategy called **mass customization**. Mass customization delivers customized services on a mass basis, which results in giving each customer whatever they ask for. To mass-customize pizzas, MOD pizza offers three different crusts, eight sauce options, and 30 different toppings, resulting in a diverse array of options for customers. Unlike many of its competitors, MOD does not charge customers

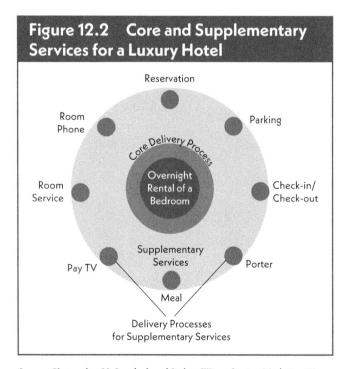

Figure 12.2   Core and Supplementary Services for a Luxury Hotel

Source: Christopher H. Lovelock and Jochen Wirtz, *Services Marketing*, 7/e, ©2011. Electronically reproduced by permission of Pearson Education, Inc., Upper Saddle River, New Jersey.

extra for additional toppings, so customers can get the exact pizza they want without having to worry about the price getting too high.[12]

The Service Mix

Most service organizations market more than one service. For example, TruGreen offers lawn care, shrub care, carpet cleaning, and industrial lawn services. Each organization's service mix represents a set of opportunities, risks, and challenges. Each part of the service mix should make a different contribution to achieving the firm's goals. To succeed, each service may also need a different level of financial support. Designing a service strategy, therefore, means deciding which new services to introduce to which target market, which existing services to maintain, and which services to eliminate.

12-3b Place (Distribution) Strategy

Distribution strategies for service organizations must focus on issues such as convenience, number of outlets, direct versus indirect distribution, location, and scheduling. A key factor influencing the selection of a service provider is *convenience*. An interesting example of this is an e-commerce solution to shopping that offers customers the convenience of an online marketplace and the reassurance of the in-person experience is the "try before you buy" option now offered by several companies. Customers select certain items to order (or personal stylist selects items for them), return what they don't like for free, and are then charged only for what they keep. For example, customers can visit Warby Parker's website and select five glasses frames to test out for five days, and the company will ship them for free. The customer can then try the different frames, select which frames they like the best, order those frames online with their prescription, and then return the test frames to Warby Parker with a pre-paid return shipping label. Stitch Fix customers fill out a style quiz and are then matched with a personal stylist who selects items that match the customer's style and price range. The customer then receives a box in the mail with the clothing items, picked specifically for them by their stylist. They can try on all of the items, purchase what they like and return what they do not like for free. There is a $20 styling fee, but this fee can be applied to items the customer ends up purchasing.[13]

An important distribution objective for many service firms is the number of outlets to use or the number of outlets to open during a certain time. Generally, the intensity of distribution should meet, but not exceed, the target market's needs and preferences. Having too few outlets may inconvenience customers; having too many outlets may boost costs unnecessarily. Intensity of distribution may also depend on the image desired. Having only a few outlets may make the service seem more exclusive or selective.

Stitch Fix lets customers shop using personal stylists that select clothes and mail them directly to the customer.

The next service distribution decision is whether to distribute services to end users *directly* or *indirectly* through other firms. Because of the intangible nature of services, many service firms have to use direct distribution or franchising. Examples include legal, medical, accounting, and personal-care services. The most-used form of direct distribution is the internet. All major airlines use online services to sell tickets directly to consumers, resulting in lower distribution costs for the airlines. Other firms with standardized service packages have developed indirect channels using independent intermediaries. Partnerships with technology firms also allow service firms more options for distribution. For example, Domino's Pizza has partnered with Nuro, a robotics firm, to test out a robot car that can deliver pizzas. When customers order their pizza and select the robot car as the delivery method, the customer receives a code via text message. When the robot car arrives, the customer is notified and must enter the code to open the car door and get their pizza. The robot car delivery service was initially launched in Houston, Texas, but, if it is successful, will be rolled out in other locations.[14]

The *location* of a service most clearly reveals the relationship between its target market strategy and distribution strategy. For time-dependent service providers such as airlines, physicians, and dentists, *scheduling* is often a more important factor.

How and where consumers interact with service organizations was impacted by the COVID-19 pandemic. The pandemic led to a huge increase in the use of services such as curbside pickup, also referred to as buy online pick up in store (BOPIS), local delivery and contactless payments. Although this shift in how consumers shop was initially triggered by the pandemic, the convenience that these services offer has led many consumers to continue utilizing them, even as the pandemic has subsided. Research has found that stores that do not offer BOPIS have noticed a decrease in online sales of nearly 5 percent in recent years.[15]

12-3c Promotion Strategy

Consumers and business users have more trouble evaluating services than goods because services are less tangible. In turn, marketers have more trouble promoting intangible services than tangible goods. Here are four promotion strategies they can try:

1. **Stressing tangible cues:** A tangible cue is a concrete symbol of the service offering. To make their intangible services more tangible, hotels turn down the bedcovers and put mints on the pillows.

2. **Using personal information sources:** A personal information source is someone consumers are familiar with (such as a celebrity) or someone they admire or can relate to personally. Service firms may seek to simulate positive word-of-mouth (WOM) communication among present and prospective customers by using real customers in their ads.

3. **Creating a strong organizational image:** One way to create an image is to manage the evidence, including the physical environment of the service facility, the appearance of the service employees, and the tangible items associated with a service (such as stationery, bills, and business cards). For example, McDonald's golden arches are instantly recognizable. Another way to create an image is through branding.

4. **Engaging in post-purchase communication:** Post-purchase communication refers to the follow-up activities that a service firm might engage in after a customer transaction. Postcard surveys, telephone calls, and other types of follow-up show customers that their feedback matters.

12-3d Price Strategy

Considerations in pricing a service are similar to the pricing considerations to be discussed in Chapter 19. However, the unique characteristics of services present two special pricing challenges.

First, to price a service, it is important to define the unit of service consumption. For example, should pricing be based on completing a specific service task (cutting a customer's hair), or should it be time based (how long it takes to cut a customer's hair)? Some services include the consumption of goods, such as food and beverages. Restaurants charge customers for food and drink rather than the use of a table and chairs.

Second, for services that are composed of multiple elements, the issue is whether pricing should be based on a "bundle" of elements or whether each element should be priced separately. A bundled price may be preferable when consumers dislike having to pay "extra" for every part of the service (e.g., paying extra for baggage or food

on an airplane), and it is simpler for the firm to administer. Alternatively, customers may not want to pay for service elements they do not use. Many furniture stores now have "unbundled" delivery charges from the price of the furniture. Customers who wish to can pick up the furniture at the store, saving on the delivery fee.

Marketers should set performance objectives when pricing each service. The following three categories of pricing objectives have been suggested:

1. Revenue-oriented pricing focuses on maximizing the surplus of income over costs. This is the same approach that many manufacturing companies use. A limitation of this approach is that determining costs can be difficult for many services.

2. Operations-oriented pricing seeks to match supply and demand by varying prices. For example, matching hotel demand to the number of available rooms can be achieved by raising prices at peak times and decreasing them during slow times.

3. Patronage-oriented pricing tries to maximize the number of customers using the service. Thus, prices vary with different market segments' ability to pay and methods of payment (such as credit) are offered that increase the likelihood of a purchase. Senior citizen and student discounts at movie theaters and restaurants are examples of patronage-oriented pricing.

A firm may need to use more than one type of pricing objective. In fact, all three objectives probably need to be included to some degree in a pricing strategy, although the importance of each type may vary depending on the type of service provided, the prices that competitors are charging, the differing ability of various customer segments to pay, or the opportunity to negotiate price. For customized services (such as construction services), customers may also have the ability to negotiate a price.

12-3e Global Service Marketing

The international marketing of services is a major part of global business, and the United States has become the world's largest exporter of services. Competition in international services is increasing rapidly, but many U.S. service industries have been able to enter the global marketplace because of their competitive advantages. U.S. banks, for example, have advantages in customer service and collections management.

For both for-profit and nonprofit service firms, the first step toward success in the global marketplace is determining the nature of the company's core products. Then the marketing-mix elements (additional services, place, promotion, pricing, and distribution) should be designed to take into account each country's cultural, technological, and political environment. McDonald's creates product offerings that reflect its varying global locations. For example, customers can get an iced milk tea or a McFloat in Hong Kong, tomato and mozzarella turnovers in Italy, and Poutine (fries with cheese curds and gravy) in Canada.[16]

12-4 Relationship Marketing in Services

12-4 Discuss relationship marketing in services

Many services involve ongoing interaction between the service organization and the customer. Thus, these services can benefit from relationship marketing, the strategy described in Chapter 1, as a means of attracting, developing, and retaining customer relationships. The idea is to develop strong loyalty by creating satisfied customers who will buy additional services from the firm and are unlikely to switch to a competitor. Satisfied customers are also likely to engage in positive WOM communication, thereby helping to bring in new customers.

Many businesses have found that it is more cost-effective to hang on to the customers they have than to focus only on attracting new ones. It has been estimated that marketing to new customers can be as much as 5 to 10 times more expensive than marketing to existing customers.[17]

Services that purchasers receive on a continuing basis (e.g., internet, banking, insurance) can be considered membership services. This type of service naturally lends itself to relationship marketing. When services involve discrete transactions (e.g., in a movie theater, at a restaurant, or on public transportation), it may be more difficult to build membership-type relationships with customers. Nevertheless, services involving discrete transactions may be transformed into membership relationships using marketing tools. For example, the service could be sold in bulk (e.g., a streaming service subscription or a commuter pass on public transportation). Or a service firm could offer special benefits to customers who choose to register with the firm (e.g., loyalty programs for hotels and airlines). The service firm that has a more formalized relationship with its customers has an advantage because it knows who its customers are and how and when they use the services offered.[18]

Relationship marketing can be practiced at four levels:

1. **Level 1: Financial.** The firm uses pricing incentives to encourage customers to continue doing business with it. Frequent-flyer programs are an example of level 1 relationship marketing. This level of relationship marketing is the least effective in the long term because its price-based advantage is easily imitated by other firms.

2. **Level 2: Social.** This level of relationship marketing also uses pricing incentives but further seeks to build social bonds with customers. The firm stays in touch with customers, learns about their needs, and designs services to meet those needs. One example of this is when a company sends its customers birthday cards. Level 2 relationship marketing is often more effective than level 1 relationship marketing.

3. **Level 3: Customization.** A customization approach encourages customer loyalty through intimate knowledge of individual customers (often referred to as *customer intimacy*) and the development of one-to-one solutions to fit customers' needs.

4. **Level 4: Structural.** At this level, the firm again uses financial and social bonds but also adds structural bonds to the formula. Structural bonds are developed by offering value-added services that are not readily available from other firms.[19] Travelers are both more health conscious and interested in special local experiences rather than experiences that are standardized across a hotel brand. Most hotels with spas have created signature treatments and products based on their locations. For example, the Ritz-Carlton in New Orleans, Louisiana, has a signature Voodoo Ritual spa treatment.[20]

12-5 Internal Marketing in Service Firms

12-5 Explain internal marketing in services

Services are performances, so the quality of a firm's employees is an important part of building long-term relationships with customers. Employees who like their jobs and are satisfied with the firm they work for are more likely to deliver superior service to customers. In other words, a firm that makes its employees happy has a better chance of retaining customers. Thus, it is critical that service firms practice **internal marketing**, which means treating employees as customers and developing systems and benefits that satisfy their needs. While this strategy may also apply to goods manufacturers, it is even more critical in service firms. This is because in service industries, employees deliver the brand promise—their performance as a brand representative—directly to customers. To satisfy employees, companies have designed and instituted a

---

internal marketing treating employees as customers and developing systems and benefits that satisfy their needs

Cisco Systems was the top ranked "Best Companies to Work For" by *Fortune Magazine* in 2023.

wide variety of programs such as flextime, on-site day care, and concierge services. Cisco Systems was the number-one ranked "Best Company to Work For" by *Fortune Magazine* in 2023, while Hilton and American Express were ranked second and third. The company encourages employees' philanthropy by giving them five paid days off per year to volunteer in their communities. The company offers many fully remote positions with no minimum days in office, so employees can create an optimal work/life balance. Many companies offer incentives to employees who refer new hires; Cisco Systems has a program, the Cisco Lotto Program, in which employees who make referrals are entered into a lottery for a chance to win prizes, such as a trip.[21]

12-6 Nonprofit Organization Marketing

12-6 Describe nonprofit organization marketing

A **nonprofit organization** is an organization that exists to achieve some goal other than the usual business goals of profit, market share, or return on investment. Both nonprofit organizations and private-sector service firms market intangible products, and both often require the customer to be present during the production process. Both for-profit and nonprofit services vary greatly from producer to producer and from day to day from the same producer.

In the United States alone, there are 1.5 million nonprofits accounting for revenues of more than $2.5 trillion.[22] The cost of government (i.e., taxes), the

---

nonprofit organization an organization that exists to achieve some goal other than the usual business goals of profit, market share, or return on investment

nonprofit organization marketing the effort by nonprofit organizations to bring about mutually satisfying exchanges with target markets

predominant form of nonprofit organization, has become the biggest single item in the American family budget—more than housing, food, or health care. Together, federal, state, and local governments collect tax revenues that amount to approximately one-fifth of the U.S. gross domestic product (GDP). In addition to government entities, nonprofit organizations include hundreds of thousands of private museums, theaters, schools, and churches.

12-6a What Is Nonprofit Organization Marketing?

Nonprofit organization marketing is the effort by nonprofit organizations to bring about mutually satisfying exchanges with target markets. Although these organizations vary substantially in size and purpose and operate in different environments, most perform the following marketing activities:

- Identify the customers they wish to serve or attract (although they usually use other terms, such as clients, patients, members, or sponsors)
- Explicitly or implicitly specify objectives
- Develop, manage, and eliminate programs and services
- Decide on prices to charge (although they use other terms, such as *fees, donations, tuition, fares, fines,* or *rates*)
- Schedule events or programs, and determine where they will be held or where services will be offered
- Communicate their availability through brochures, signs, public service announcements, or advertisements

Often, the nonprofit organizations that carry out these functions do not realize they are engaged in marketing.

12-6b Unique Aspects of Nonprofit Organization Marketing Strategies

Like their counterparts in business organizations, nonprofit managers develop marketing strategies to bring about mutually satisfying exchanges with target markets. However, marketing in nonprofit organizations is unique in many ways—including the setting of marketing objectives, the selection of target markets, and the development of appropriate marketing mixes.

Objectives

In the private sector, profit motives are both objectives for guiding decisions and criteria for evaluating results. Nonprofit organizations do not seek to make a profit for redistribution to owners or shareholders. Rather, their focus is often on generating enough funds to cover expenses.

PBS, the Public Broadcasting Service, receives its funding from donations.

Most nonprofit organizations are expected to provide equitable, effective, and efficient services that respond to the wants and preferences of multiple constituencies. These include users, payers, donors, politicians, appointed officials, the media, and the general public. Nonprofit organizations cannot measure their success or failure in strictly financial terms.

The lack of a financial "bottom line" and the existence of multiple, diverse, intangible, and sometimes vague or conflicting objectives make prioritizing objectives, making decisions, and evaluating performance hard for nonprofit managers. They must often use approaches different from the ones commonly used in the private sector.

Target Markets

Three issues relating to target markets are unique to nonprofit organizations:

1. **Apathetic or strongly opposed targets:** Private-sector organizations usually give priority to developing those market segments that are most likely to respond to particular offerings. In contrast, nonprofit organizations must often target those who are apathetic about or strongly opposed to receiving their services, such as vaccinations and psychological counseling.

2. **Pressure to adopt undifferentiated segmentation strategies:** Nonprofit organizations often adopt undifferentiated strategies (refer to Chapter 8) by default. Sometimes they fail to recognize the advantages of targeting, or an undifferentiated approach may appear to offer economies of scale and low per capita costs. In other instances, nonprofit organizations are pressured or required to serve the maximum number of people by targeting the average user.

3. **Complementary positioning:** The main role of many nonprofit organizations is to provide services, with available resources, to those who are not adequately served by private-sector organizations. As a result, the nonprofit organization must often complement, rather

than compete with, the efforts of others. The positioning task is to identify underserved market segments and to develop marketing programs that match their needs rather than target the niches that may be most profitable. For example, a university library may perceive itself as complementing the services of the public library rather than as competing with it.

Product Decisions

There are three product-related distinctions between business and nonprofit organizations:

1. **Benefit complexity:** Nonprofit organizations often market complex behaviors or ideas. Examples include the need to exercise and eat nutritional foods or the need to quit smoking. The benefits that a person receives are complex, long term, and intangible, and therefore, they are more difficult to communicate to consumers.

2. **Benefit strength:** The benefit strength of many nonprofit offerings is quite weak or indirect. What are the direct, personal benefits to you of driving 55 miles per hour or donating blood? In contrast, most private-sector service organizations can offer customers direct, personal benefits in an exchange relationship.

3. **Involvement:** Many nonprofit organizations market products that elicit very low involvement ("Prevent forest fires") or very high involvement ("Stop smoking"). The typical range for private-sector goods is much narrower. Traditional promotional tools may be inadequate to motivate adoption of either low- or high-involvement products.

Place (Distribution) Decisions

A nonprofit organization's capacity for distributing its service offerings to potential customer groups when and where they want them is typically a key variable in determining the success of those service offerings. For example, many large universities have one or more satellite campus locations to provide easier access for students in other areas. Some educational institutions also offer classes to students at off-campus locations through the use of interactive video technology or online classes.

The extent to which a service depends on fixed facilities has important implications for distribution decisions. Services like rail transit and lake fishing can be delivered only at specific points. Many nonprofit services, however, do not depend on special facilities.

Promotion Decisions

Many nonprofit organizations are explicitly or implicitly prohibited from advertising, thus limiting their promotion options. Most federal agencies fall into this category. Other nonprofit organizations simply do not have the resources to retain advertising agencies, promotion consultants, or marketing staff. Nonprofit organizations have a few special promotion resources to call on, however:

- **Professional volunteers:** Nonprofit organizations often seek out marketing, sales, and advertising professionals to help them develop and implement promotion strategies. In some instances, an advertising agency donates its services in exchange for potential long-term benefits. Donated services create goodwill; personal contacts; and general awareness of the donor's organization, reputation, and competency.

- **Sales promotion activities:** Sales promotion activities that use existing services or other resources are increasingly being used to draw attention to the offerings of nonprofit organizations. Sometimes nonprofit charities even team up with other companies for promotional activities. Recently, The Trevor Project, a nonprofit that supports the mental health of LGBTQIA+ youth, teamed up with SoulCycle to increase awareness of the organization's mission. SoulCycle is an indoor cycling studio with nearly 100 studios in the United States, Canada, and the United Kingdom. The partnership was promoted with the tagline "Ride as you are. Love as you are." In addition to increased awareness, The Trevor Project also received 10 percent of all proceeds from the sales of a class pack that was created by SoulCycle to help support the cause.[23] As another example, the Make-A-Wish Foundation has partnered with Disney for many years to give children who are battling serious illnesses the opportunity to have once in a lifetime Disney experiences. Since the partnership's launch in 1980, more than 145,000 children's wishes have been granted through the program.[24]

- **Public service advertising:** A **public service advertisement (PSA)** is an announcement that promotes a program of a federal, state, or local government or of a nonprofit organization. Unlike a commercial advertiser, the sponsor of the PSA does not pay for the time or space. Instead, it is donated by the medium. One of the most successful PSA campaigns of all time was a campaign run by the Ad Council entitled "Love Has No Labels." This campaign promoted the acceptance of all people regardless of race, religion, gender, sexual orientation, age, or ability. The campaign was so successful that it won an Emmy award in 2015. More recently, the Ad Council brought the campaign back through a partnership

SoulCycle partnered with The Trevor Project to help create awareness around the organizations mission of supporting the mental health of LGBTQIA+ youth.

with StoryCorp, a nonprofit that encourages people of different backgrounds to share their stories with each other in an effort to promote diversity, equality, and inclusion. The new campaign discusses how people can have meaningful conversations and make connections with people from backgrounds different from their own.[25]

Pricing Decisions

Five key characteristics distinguish the pricing decisions of nonprofit organizations from those of the for-profit sector:

1. **Pricing objectives:** The main pricing objective in the profit sector is revenue or, more specifically, profit maximization, sales maximization, or target return on sales or investment. Many nonprofit organizations must also be concerned about revenue. Often, however, nonprofit organizations seek to either partially or fully defray costs rather than to achieve a profit for distribution to stockholders. Nonprofit organizations also seek to redistribute income—for instance, through taxation and sliding-scale fees. Moreover, they strive to allocate resources fairly among individuals or households or across geographic or political boundaries.

2. **Nonfinancial prices:** In many nonprofit situations, consumers are not charged a monetary price but instead

public service advertisement (PSA) an announcement that promotes a program of a federal, state, or local government or of a nonprofit organization must absorb nonmonetary costs. The importance of those costs is illustrated by the large number of eligible citizens who do not take advantage of so-called free services in underprivileged communities. In many public assistance programs, about half the people who are eligible do not participate. Nonmonetary costs include time, embarrassment, and effort.

3. **Indirect payment:** Indirect payment through taxes is common to marketers of "free" services, such as libraries, fire protection, and police protection. Indirect payment is not a common practice in the profit sector.

4. **Separation between payers and users:** By design, the services of many charitable organizations are provided for those who are of lower socioeconomic status and are largely paid for by those who are of higher socioeconomic status. Although examples of separation between payers and users can be found in the profit sector (such as insurance claims), the practice is much less prevalent.

Keith J Finks/Shutterstock.com

Indirect payment through taxes is common to marketers of "free" services such as libraries, fire protection, and police protection.

5. **Below-cost pricing:** An example of below-cost pricing is university tuition. Virtually all private and public colleges and universities price their services below full cost.

Gorodenkoff/Shutterstock.com

Part 4

Chapter 13

Supply Chain Management and Marketing Channels

Learning Outcomes

After studying this chapter, you will be able to . . .

13-1 Discuss the importance of supply chain management

13-2 Discuss the concepts of internal and external supply chain integration

13-3 Identify the eight key processes of excellent supply chain management

13-4 Explain the importance of sustainable supply chain management to modern business operations

13-5 Discuss how new technology and emerging trends are impacting the practice of supply chain management

13-6 Describe channel intermediaries' functions

13-7 Describe the factors that influence channel strategy choice

13-8 Explain why omnichannel and multichannel marketing is important

13-1 Supply Chains and Supply Chain Management

13-1 Discuss the importance of supply chain management

In today's business environment, more and more companies are turning to effective supply chain management for a competitive advantage. A company's **supply chain** includes all the companies involved in the upstream and downstream flow of products, services, finances, and information, extending from initial suppliers (the point of origin) to the ultimate customer (the point of consumption). The goal of **supply chain management (SCM)** is to coordinate and integrate all the activities performed by supply chain members into a seamless and effective process, from the source of the raw materials to the point of consumption. Managing the supply chain ultimately gives the company "total visibility and control" of the materials, processes, money, and finished products inside and outside the company they work for. The underlying philosophy is that by visualizing and exerting control over the entire supply chain, companies can balance demand for their products and services as perfectly as possible with available supply. This approach maximizes customer outcomes while creating efficiency at each level of the chain. Understanding and integrating supply-and-demand–related information at every level enables supply chain managers to optimize their decisions, reduce waste, and respond quickly to sudden demand changes or other supply chain factors.

In today's marketplace, products are being driven by customer demand, and businesses need to balance demand with supply to ensure economic profits.

Following the modern realities of the marketplace, today's SCM reflects a completely customer-driven management philosophy. In the mass production era of the late 19th century, manufacturers produced standardized products that were "pushed" down through marketing channels to consumers, who were then convinced by salespeople to buy whatever was produced. In the modern marketplace, this logic is no longer valid, in fact the complete opposite is now true. Modern customers expect to receive product and service configurations matched to their unique needs, and this personalization is a catalyst that is increasingly driving demand. The focus of businesses has shifted to determining how products and services are being "pulled" into the marketplace by customers and on partnering with members of the supply chain to enhance customer value. For example, online retailer Spreadshirt offers customized shirts, hats, bags, phone cases, and other accessories which users can personalize with custom text, images, and designs. Customers are guided through a process where they can design products based on various materials, color palettes, and styles.[1] This differs dramatically from the mass-manufacturing approach apparel companies have historically taken, whereby a focus on efficiency led to a narrower range of selections and few opportunities for customization.

The reversal of demand flow from "push" to "pull" has resulted in a radical reformulation of traditional marketing, production, and distribution functions toward a philosophy of **supply chain agility**. Agile companies synchronize their activities through the sharing of supply-and-demand market information, spend more time than their competitors focusing on activities that create direct customer benefits, partner closely with suppliers and service providers to reduce customer wait times for products, and constantly seek to reduce supply chain complexity through the evaluation and reduction (or elimination) of stock-keeping units (SKUs) that customers aren't buying, among other strategies.

For example, the COVID-19 pandemic dramatically increased demand for many products and services. In situations like this, where customers behave unpredictably in response to a new crisis, businesses must react quickly by adjusting their purchasing and manufacturing processes to minimize the costs of making and holding incorrect inventory. The famous toy maker Lego is a company that manages agility in its supply chain, which is necessary when you sell more than 70 billion Lego bricks a year, which means that Lego must manufacture more than 200 million bricks a day. When Lego saw direct-to-consumer (D2C) demand for its iconic toys surge during the COVID-19 pandemic, it relied on communication within its agile supply chain to adjust for the change in consumer demand.[2] Shoppers want, and companies therefore promise, that items will be available faster, cheaper, and with greater convenience and choice than ever before. It is up to the supply chain managers of their favorite companies to deliver on those promises!

Because of the increasing complexity of supply chain operations, most companies do not manage their supply chains alone or in isolation. Effective SCM requires a team

---

supply chain the connected chain of all of the business entities, both internal and external to the company, that perform or support the logistics function

supply chain management (SCM) a management system that coordinates and integrates all of the activities performed by supply chain members into a seamless process, from the source to the point of consumption, resulting in enhanced customer and economic value

supply chain agility an operational strategy focused on creating inventory velocity and operational flexibility simultaneously in the supply chain effort between the firm and its partners. **Outsourcing**, or **contract logistics**, is a rapidly growing initiative in which a manufacturer or supplier turns over an entire logistical function (often buying and managing transportation, warehousing, and/or postponed manufacturing) to an independent **third-party logistics company (3PL)** that helps manage warehouse space, provides transportation solutions, assists with information sharing, or provides enhanced technological innovations. For example, ASOS, a U.K.-based fashion and cosmetic retailer, utilizes 3PL-operated fulfillment centers in Europe and the United States to speed up customer orders and returns. Not only did leveraging 3PL allow ASOS to keep up with increasing customer demand, but it also eliminated over 150 tons of CO_2 emissions in just one year.[3]

Outsourcing enables companies to cut inventories and locate stock at fewer plants and distribution centers while still providing the same level of service (or, sometimes, performing even better). While in the past, firms often looked around the globe for partners to help with customer service needs or manufacturing to secure lower costs, many companies are now seeking solutions within (**reshoring**) or close to (**nearshoring**) their primary base of operations, to reduce supply chain risk and maintain tighter control over operations. However, reshoring and nearshoring supply chain strategies are not the most efficient options for many companies. There are many reasons why a company might wish to globalize its supply chain. Foreign markets are attractive due to the increasing demand for imported products worldwide. Furthermore, cheap labor advantages and trade barriers/tariffs have encouraged firms to expand their global manufacturing operations. Unfortunately, globalization has brought about great uncertainty as well. Moving operations offshore exposes companies to risks associated with geopolitical conflict, foreign nationalization of assets, unintended knowledge leakage to foreign competitors, and highly variable quality standards. These risks were highlighted during the COVID-19 pandemic when international shipping and the ability to both import and export goods slowed to a crawl for many products and markets.

As the world continues to globalize, supply chain management will almost certainly continue to take on a multinational focus. Worldwide, the resources needed to manufacture and sell goods that are increasingly in demand are becoming scarcer, and market boundaries are melting together. Free trade markets continue to expand globally, and consumers living in nations with traditionally low demand now have access to previously unavailable goods and can place orders via the internet. The effort to achieve world-class global supply chain management means that the balancing of supply and demand—and the satisfaction of more and more customers worldwide—are becoming a reality for many companies. The United States and Great Britain have recently signaled that they may retreat to a less global and more protectionist stance with fewer imports being allowed. However, whether these changes will be sustainable in the long term is uncertain. In the meantime, nations such as China, India, Vietnam, and Singapore are extending the global reach of their supply chains into Africa and other less-developed parts of the planet.

13-1a Benefits of Effective Supply Chain Management

SCM is a crucial means of differentiation for a company and therefore represents a critical component in marketing and corporate strategy. Organizations with an intense focus on effective supply chain management commonly report lower inventory, transportation, warehousing, and packaging costs. These supply chain-centric companies also realize greater logistical flexibility, improved customer service, and higher revenues. Research has shown a clear relationship between supply chain performance and both profitability and company value. Additionally, because well-managed supply chains can provide better value to customers with only marginal incremental expenditure on company assets, best-in-class supply chain companies such as Amazon can use SCM as a means of demonstrating a competitive differential. The online retail giant uses strategic partnerships with suppliers, advanced inventory technologies, and state-of-the-art network design processes to stay competitive—all while providing consumers with thousands of essential needs at low prices. Amazon must keep its supply chain efficient to maintain its ability to procure and distribute products worldwide. Amazon also uses technologies such as **RFID** (radio-frequency identification) to track warehouse inventory locations. Amazon has also begun optimizing its delivery operations with machine learning and artificial intelligence technology.[4]

outsourcing (or contract logistics) a manufacturer's or supplier's use of an independent third party to manage an entire function of the logistics system, such as transportation, warehousing, or order processing

third-party logistics company (3PL) a firm that provides functional logistics services to others

reshoring the reinstitutionalization of a business process from an outsource location/country back to the original location to gain economic advantage

nearshoring the transfer of an outsourced activity from a distant to a nearby country

RFID radio-frequency identification; a device that uses radio waves as a means of locating a piece of inventory within a confined geographic space

Lean supply chains have become widespread in recent years, but a dark side to these lean systems emerged during the pandemic. A lean strategy requires balancing the inventory needs of a business while minimizing the possibility of overstocking goods and maximizing the company's cash flow. The COVID-19 pandemic exposed how delicate lean supply chains can be and supply chain managers had to learn the hard way to always be prepared for the unexpected. During the COVID-19 pandemic, some managers learned that their supply chains were just too lean and had to make the necessary adjustments. SCM managers are learning that adopting an agile strategy also carries risk, such as lost or incorrectly allocated inventories. A primary example was the toilet paper and hand sanitizer shortages in the early stages of the pandemic. Firms traditionally optimized manufacturing and distribution systems for two separate markets—commercial (office buildings, hotels, restaurants, etc.) and residential. However, during the COVID-19 pandemic, the market immediately switched to residential only, since almost everyone was working from home, shortages in the residential market were widespread. Later in the COVID-19 pandemic, similar commercial shortages emerged for aluminum can beverages, particularly aluminum packaging for soft drink and beer cans. In response to these supply chain problems, many businesses have begun rethinking what it means to be agile.

Redesigning a supply chain can do more than just improve the bottom line. For example, Patagonia strives to make the environmental impact of its supply chain a core aspect of its company, utilizing only natural and recycled materials. IKEA, a major home goods company has committed to becoming a circular business by 2030, meaning the company is trying to eliminate waste by creating products that can be reused, refurbished, remanufactured, and eventually recycled. IKEA has enforced multiple initiatives in its supply chain, including using sustainable materials and designing circular products.[5]

Due to ultra-lean supply chains, many customers experienced empty shelves on a multitude of products.

13-2 Supply Chain Integration

13-2 Discuss the concepts of internal and external supply chain integration

A key principle of supply chain management is that multiple entities (firms and/or their functional areas) should work together to perform tasks as a single, unified system, rather than as multiple individual units acting in isolation. Companies in a world-class supply chain combine their resources, capabilities, and innovations across multiple business boundaries so that they are used for the best interest of the entire supply chain. The goal of this cooperation is that the overall effectiveness and performance of the supply chain for all the participants will be greater than the sum of its parts.

As companies become increasingly focused on supply chain management, they develop a **supply chain orientation**. This means they implement management practices that are consistent with a "systems thinking" approach. Leading supply chain–oriented firms like Amazon, Siemens AG, IKEA, and Unilever possess five characteristics that, in combination, set them apart from their competitors:

1. **They are credible.** They can deliver on the promises they make.
2. **They are benevolent.** They are willing to accept short-term risks on behalf of others, are committed to others, and invest in others' success.
3. **They are cooperative.** They work *with* rather than *against* their partners when seeking to achieve goals.
4. **They have the support of top managers.** These managers possess the vision required to do things that benefit the entire supply chain in the short run so they can enjoy more meaningful company successes in the long run.
5. **They are effective at conducting and directing supply chain activity.** As a result, they are better off in the long run financially than those who are not as effective.

Management practices that reflect a highly coordinated effort between supply chain firms or across business functions within the same or different firms are "integrated." In other words, **supply chain integration** occurs when multiple firms or their functional areas in a supply chain coordinate business processes so they link seamlessly to one

---

supply chain orientation a system of management practices that are consistent with a "systems thinking" approach

supply chain integration when multiple firms or business functions in a supply chain coordinate, their activities and processes so that they are seamlessly linked to one another to satisfy the customer

another. In a world-class supply chain, the customer may not know where the business activities of one company or business unit end and where those of another begin—each actor keeps their interests in mind. Still, all appear to be reading from the same script, and from time to time, each makes sacrifices that benefit the system's performance.

In modern supply chain systems, integration can be either internal or external to a specific company or, ideally, both. From an internal perspective, the top supply chain integration companies develop a managerial orientation toward **demand–supply integration (DSI)**. Under the DSI philosophy, the functional areas in a company that creates customer demand (such as marketing, sales, or research and development) continually communicate and are fully synchronized with the areas of the business charged with fulfilling the created demand (purchasing, manufacturing, and logistics). Some companies, like Airbus, Ford Motor Company, and Nestlé colocate different divisions such as engineering, logistics, and research and development to build synergies between these divisions. Walmart has co-located many of its distribution centers with its retail stores to increase its last mile, or final delivery to the customer, efficiencies. With this strategy, Walmart distribution centers are within 10 miles of 90 percent of the U.S. population.[6] This type of alignment enhances customer satisfaction by ensuring that, for example, salespeople make promises to customers that can be delivered on by the company's logistics arm or that raw materials being purchased meet customer specifications before they are placed into production. At the same time, the company gains efficiencies from ordering and using only materials that lead directly to sales. In short, companies operating under a DSI philosophy are better at their business because all the divisions within the company work in sync with each other.[7]

In addition to being internally integrated, the group of connected organizations in a world-class supply chain behave as though they have a shared mission and leadership. To accomplish this task across companies that have different ownership and interests, five types of external integration are sought by firms interested in providing top-level service to customers:[8]

- Relationship integration is the ability of two or more companies to develop social connections that serve to guide their interactions when working together. More specifically, relationship integration is the capability to develop and maintain a shared mental framework across companies that describes how they will depend on one another when working together. This includes how they will collaborate on activities or projects so that the customer gains the maximum amount of total value possible from the supply chain.

- Measurement integration reflects the idea that performance assessments should be transparent and measurable across the borders of different firms; it should also assess the performance of the supply chain while holding each individual firm or business unit accountable for meeting its own goals.

- Technology and planning integration refers to the creation and maintenance of information technology systems that connect managers across the firms in the supply chain. It requires information hardware and software systems that can exchange information when needed between customers, suppliers, and internal operational areas of each of the supply chain partners.

- Material and service supplier integration requires firms to link seamlessly to those outsiders that provide goods and services to them so that they can streamline work processes and thereby provide smooth, high-quality customer experiences. Both sides need to have a common vision of the total value-creation process and be willing to share the responsibility for satisfying customer requirements to make supplier integration successful.

- Customer integration is a competency that enables firms to offer long-lasting, distinctive, value-added offerings to the customers who represent the greatest value to the firm or supply chain. Highly customer-integrated firms assess their own capabilities and then match them to customers whose desires they can meet and who offer large enough sales potential for the linkage to be profitable over the long term. Many companies, including Nike and BMW, utilize customer-integrated supply chains to offer their customers

demand–supply integration (DSI) a supply chain operational philosophy focused on integrating the supply-management and demand-generating functions of an organization

Source: Nike Inc.

Customers can customize their Nike shoes online with Nike By You.

high-quality, customized product offerings. For example, Nike allows customers to design their own pair of high-end athletic shoes on Nike By You. Many choices are made from the type of material to the color for each aspect of the shoe. Similarly, BMW's customers can choose what colors, body styles, and features they want in their car and order that car directly from the BMW website.

- Success in achieving both the internal and external types of integration is very important. Highly integrated supply chains (those that are successful in achieving many or all of these types of integration) are better at satisfying customers, managing costs, delivering high-quality products, enhancing productivity, and utilizing company or business unit assets, all of which translate into greater profitability for the firms and their partners working together in the supply chain.

Integration involves a balance between barriers and enablers. Companies that work closely with their suppliers encounter problems such as corporate culture, information hoarding, and trust issues. For example, Nestlé and Unilever strive for transparency and share information with partners in their supply chains to reduce waste and increase efficiency. Still, at the same time, there is a danger. Giving supply chain partners this information enables those partners to share it with competitors. On the other hand, these companies can improve integration through long-term agreements, cross-organizational integrated product teams, and improved communication between partners. These factors all aid in integrating supply chain operations.[9]

An unanticipated blind spot with agile supply chain systems materialized during the worldwide COVID-19 pandemic. In addition to hand sanitizer and toilet paper, consumers began to hoard products such as bottled water and Clorox wipes. In response, governments enacted restrictions on selected exports like medical supplies, ventilators, and personal protective equipment (PPE) for healthcare workers. These shortages affected some industries more than others, but almost all sectors in the marketplace were affected in some way. These supply side disruptions and the emphasis shift to customer and worker health and safety, as well as the need for continued distribution efficiency, dramatically slowed down supply chain responsiveness and increased costs. The harsh lesson for firms was to be better prepared for future disruptions to ensure supply chains continue to perform at a high level in the future. Moreover, the entire company's management team must be involved in developing solutions. Most companies had allocated insufficient resources to drive supply chain innovations, and yet innovations are among the most resilient forces to deal with a disaster or pandemic.

13-3 The Key Processes of Supply Chain Management

13-3 Identify the eight key processes of excellent supply chain management

When firms practice good supply chain management, their functional departments or areas, such as marketing, research and development, and/or production, are integrated both within and across the linked firms. Integration, then, is "how" excellent supply chain management works. The business processes on which the linked firms work together represent the "what" of supply chain management—they are what firms, departments, areas, and people focus on when working together to reduce supply chain costs or generate additional revenues. **Business processes** are composed of bundles of interconnected activities that stretch across firms in the supply chain. They represent key areas that some or all of the involved firms are constantly working on to reduce costs and/or generate revenues for everyone throughout supply chain management. The following are eight critical business processes on which supply chain managers must focus:

1. Customer relationship management
2. Customer service management
3. Demand management
4. Order fulfillment
5. Manufacturing flow management
6. Supplier relationship management
7. Product development and commercialization
8. Returns management[10]

13-3a Customer Relationship Management

The **customer relationship management (CRM) process** enables companies to prioritize their marketing focus on different customer groups according to each group's long-term value to the company or supply chain. Once higher-value customers are identified, firms should focus more on providing customized products and better service to this group than to others. The CRM process includes customer segmentation by value and subsequent generation of customer loyalty for the most attractive segments. This

---

business processes bundles of interconnected activities that stretch across firms in the supply chain

customer relationship management (CRM) process allows companies to prioritize their marketing focus on different customer groups according to each group's long-term value to the company or supply chain process provides a set of broad principles for initiating and maintaining customer relationships and is often carried out with the assistance of specialized CRM computer software. For example, international coffee retailer Starbucks leverages CRM to enhance its knowledge of customer preferences, creating unique value for its customers. The popular Starbucks app lets customers find drink choices that appeal to them based on their previous purchases. Customers can get rewards through coffee purchases but can also gain extra rewards through contests and games personalized for individual customers based on their preferences. In addition to being personalized and engaging, the Starbucks reward program draws in new customers and keeps existing customers engaged as they pursue Starbucks reward points.[11]

13-3b Customer Service Management

While the CRM process is designed to identify and build relationships with good customers, the customer service management process is designed to ensure that those customer relationships remain strong. The **customer service management process** presents a multi-company, unified response system to the customer whenever complaints, concerns, questions, or comments are voiced. When the process is well executed, it can have a strong positive impact on revenues, often because of a quick positive response to negative customer feedback and sometimes even in the form of additional sales gained through the additional customer contact. Customers expect service from when a product is purchased until it is ultimately disposed of. The customer service management process facilitates touchpoints between the buyer and seller throughout this life cycle. The use of customer care software enables companies to enhance their customer service

---

customer service management process presents a multi-company, unified response system to the customer whenever complaints, concerns, questions, or comments are voiced

demand management process seeks to align supply and demand throughout the supply chain by anticipating customer requirements at each level and creating demand-related plans of action before actual customer purchases

sales and operations planning (S&OP) a method companies use to align production with demand by merging tactical and strategic planning methods across functional areas of the business

order fulfillment process a highly integrated process, often requiring persons from multiple companies and multiple functions to come together and coordinate to create customer satisfaction at a given place and time

management process. Consider how the airline British Airways prides itself on providing consistent and continuous customer service. However, the travel industry is constantly evolving, and multiple travel options are available to customers. British Airways uses Teradata's CRM software platform to track customers and reengage through personalized deals and promotions with lapsed customers. British Airways can also monitor social media sites for conversations related to customer sentiment and directly reply to a customer who may be having an issue. Using CRM to automate these processes, keep current customers engaged, and reengage with lapsed customers, British Airways can reduce marketing costs while increasing customer communication.[12]

13-3c Demand Management

The **demand management process** seeks to align supply and demand throughout the supply chain by anticipating customer requirements at each level and creating customer-focused plans of action before actual purchases being made. At the same time, demand management seeks to minimize the costs of serving multiple customers with variable wants and needs. In other words, the demand management process allows companies in the supply chain to satisfy customers in the most efficient and effective ways possible. Collecting customer data, forecasting future demand, and developing activities that smooth out demand help align available inventory with customer desires.

Though it is challenging to predict exactly what items and quantities customers will buy before purchase, demand management can ease pressure on the production process and allow companies to satisfy most of their customers through greater flexibility in manufacturing, marketing, and sales programs. One fundamental way this occurs is by sharing customer demand forecasts and data during **sales and operations planning (S&OP)** meetings. During these meetings, the demand-generating functions of the business (marketing and sales) work together with the production side of the business (procurement, production, and logistics) in a collaborative arrangement designed to both satisfy customers and minimize waste. After implementing S&OP, U.S.-based auto manufacturer General Motors saved several millions of dollars in its operations, allowing the company to quickly pivot to emerging low-emission vehicle production.[13]

13-3d Order Fulfillment

One of the most fundamental processes in supply chain management is the order fulfillment process, which involves generating, filling, delivering, and providing on-the-spot service for customer orders. The **order fulfillment process** is highly integrated, often requiring persons from multiple companies and functions to come together and coordinate to create customer satisfaction at a given place and time. The best order fulfillment processes reduce **order cycle time**—the time between order and customer receipt—as much as possible, while ensuring that the customer receives exactly what they want. The shorter lead times are beneficial in allowing firms to carry reduced inventory levels and free up cash that can be used on other projects. Overall, the order fulfillment process involves understanding and integrating the company's internal capabilities with customer needs, and matching these together so that the supply chain maximizes profits while at the same time minimizing costs and waste. FedEx Fulfillment, a subsidiary of FedEx Corporation, was created to help small and medium-sized companies fulfill orders from multiple channels with streamlined efficiency while maximizing effectiveness. This service provider offers an integrated supply chain system with a user-friendly platform that provides users access to timely information about FedEx's transportation networks, warehouses, packaging, and even reverse logistics options for managing returns. With FedEx's infrastructure backing them, smaller companies can enhance their otherwise limited order fulfillment potential and can achieve better financial performance through faster and more accurate shipments.[14]

13-3e Manufacturing Flow Management

The **manufacturing flow management process** is concerned with ensuring that firms in the supply chain have the needed resources to manufacture with flexibility and to move products through a multistage production process. Firms with flexible manufacturing can create various goods and/or services with minimal costs associated with changing production techniques. The manufacturing flow process includes much more than the simple production of goods and services—it means creating flexible agreements with suppliers and shippers so that companies can accommodate unexpected demand bursts without disruptions to customer service or satisfaction.

The manufacturing flow management process centers on leveraging the capabilities held by multiple supply chain members to improve overall manufacturing output in terms of quality, delivery speed, and flexibility, all of which tie directly to profitability. Supply chain managers may choose between a lean or agile supply chain strategy depending on the product. In a lean supply chain, products are built before demand occurs, but managers attempt to reduce as much waste as possible. Lean supply chains first appeared within the Toyota Production System (TPS) as early as the 1950s. Agile strategies lie on the other end of the continuum—they prioritize customer responsiveness

more so than waste reduction. Instead of trying to forecast demand and reduce waste, agile supply chains wait for demand to occur and use communication and flexibility to fill that demand quickly.[15] One way U.S. auto manufacturer Tesla has created manufacturing agility is by building its **modular** battery systems, such that it can use the same battery system for multiple cars it manufactures. By using redundant parts and systems across different models, the company can quickly switch from producing one car model to another, reducing production machine downtime, and creating substantial cost savings. Additionally, this makes it more straightforward for customers to replace or repair the battery in their automobiles.[16]

13-3f Supplier Relationship Management

The **supplier relationship management process** is closely related to the manufacturing flow management process and contains several characteristics that parallel the customer relationship management process. The manufacturing flow management process is highly dependent on supplier relationships for flexibility. Furthermore, as in the customer relationship management process, supplier relationship management provides structural support for developing and maintaining supplier relationships. By integrating these two ideas, supplier relationship management supports manufacturing flow by identifying and maintaining relationships with highly valued suppliers.

Just as firms benefit from developing close-knit, integrated relationships with customers, close-knit, integrated relationships with suppliers provide a means to gain performance advantages. For example, careful management of supplier relationships is a critical step toward ensuring that firms' manufacturing resources are utilized to their maximum potential. It is clear, then, that the supplier relationship management process directly impacts each supply chain member's bottom-line financial performance.

---

order cycle time the time delay between the placement of a customer's order and the customer's receipt of that order

manufacturing flow management process process concerned with ensuring that firms in the supply chain have the needed resources to manufacture with flexibility and to move products through a multistage production process

modular a standardized form of component parts manufacturing designed so the parts are easily replaced or interchanged

supplier relationship management process supports manufacturing flow by identifying and maintaining relationships with highly valued suppliers

In certain instances, it can be advantageous for the supply chain to integrate via a formal merger. In 2020, French luxury goods conglomerate LVMH acquired American jeweler Tiffany & Co. for $16.2 billion. While the cost to acquire Tiffany & Co. was high, this merger allowed LVMH to vertically integrate its supply chain by adding Tiffany's jewelry production capabilities to its existing luxury brand portfolio. This ownership arrangement gives LVMH more control over its luxury goods supply chain.[17]

13-3g Product Development and Commercialization

The **product development and commercialization process** (discussed in detail in Chapter 11) includes the group of activities that facilitate the joint development and marketing of new offerings among a group of supply chain partner firms. In many cases, more than one supply chain entity is responsible for ensuring the success of a new product. Commonly, a multicompany collaboration is used to execute new-product development, testing, and launch, among other activities. The capability to develop and introduce new offerings quickly is critical for competitive success versus rival firms, so it is often advantageous to involve many supply chain partners in the effort. The process requires the close cooperation of suppliers and customers, who provide input and serve as advisers and co-producers for the new offering(s).

Designing a new product with the help of suppliers and customers can enable a company to introduce features and cost-cutting measures into final products. Customers provide information about what they want from the product, while suppliers can help design for quality and manufacturability. Research has shown that when each supply chain partner shares responsibility for designing and manufacturing a new product, more obstacles can be identified early and opportunities for cost reduction are made possible.

13-3h Returns Management

The final supply chain management process deals with situations in which customers choose to return a product to the retailer or supplier, thereby creating a reverse flow of goods

---

product development and commercialization process includes the group of activities that facilitates the joint development and marketing of new offerings among a group of supply chain partner firms

returns management process enables firms to manage volumes of returned product efficiently while minimizing returns-related costs and maximizing the value of the returned assets to the firms in the supply chain

The LVMH acquisition of Tiffany & Co. enables LVMH to bring the Tiffany & Co. brand and iconic Tiffany blue jewelry box to a more global market with a consistent message.

within the supply chain. The **returns management process** enables firms to manage volumes of returned products efficiently while minimizing returns-related costs and maximizing the value of the returned assets to the firms in the supply chain. Returns can potentially affect a firm's financial position in a significant and negative way if mishandled. In specific industries, such as apparel e-retailing, returns can amount to as much as 40 percent of sales volume.

In addition to the value of managing returns from a pure asset-recovery perspective, many firms are discovering that returns management can also create additional marketing and customer service touchpoints that firms can leverage to create additional customer value above and beyond regular sales and promotion-driven encounters. Handling returns quickly creates a positive image and gives the company an additional opportunity to please the customer. Customers who have positive experiences with the returns management process can become more confident buyers who are more willing to reorder since they know problems encountered with purchases will most likely be quickly corrected. In addition, the returns management process allows the firm to recognize potential weaknesses in product design and/or areas for potential improvement through direct customer feedback that initiates the return process.

Many retailers, such as Nordstrom, REI, and Trader Joe's, have implemented generous return policies to develop loyalty within their customer base and serve their needs. For example, Nordstrom, a large department store, has no time limit on when a customer must return a product. It assesses each return on a case-by-case basis to find a solution that benefits the customer and company. Additionally, REI has a 100 percent satisfaction guarantee and allows for returns to take place for up to a year with no questions asked.[18] Finally, grocery retailer Trader Joe's offers shoppers

Some major retailers, such as Amazon and Tesco, are limiting generous product return policies while others, such as Trader Joe's, continue with flexible return policies as a means of encouraging store loyalty.

a full refund on any private-label products and explicitly encourages the customer to return the product to the store if they are dissatisfied. Although Trader Joe's is unable to resell used grocery items after recovery, their liberal returns policy builds stronger relationships with their customers without creating too much inefficiency.[19]

The COVID-19 pandemic changed how companies viewed their supply chains, translating to how they handled customer returns. Major retailers have shifted how long customers have for returns in ways that both expand and limit customer returns. For example, Amazon and Walmart extended their window for most products but limited the return of certain items, such as hand sanitizer and other healthcare-related items.

13-4 Sustainable Supply Chain Management

13-4 Explain the importance of sustainable supply chain management to modern business operations

In response to the need for firms to reduce costs and act as leaders in protecting the natural environment, many are adopting sustainable supply chain management principles as a crucial part of their supply chain strategy. **Sustainable supply chain management** involves the integration and balancing of environmental, social, and economic thinking into all phases of the supply chain management process. In doing so, the organization better addresses current business needs and develops long-term initiatives that allow it to mitigate risks and avail itself of future opportunities to preserve resources for future generations and ensure long-term viability. Success at supply chain sustainability is measured using a concept known as the **triple bottom line**, which includes measures of economic success, environmental impact, and social well-being. The general logic is companies that fail to balance these performance objectives appropriately are susceptible to risks that, in the long term, can endanger the continuity of the business.

Sustainability activities within the supply chain include environmentally friendly materials sourcing; the design of products with consideration given to their social and environmental impact; and end-of-life product management that provides for easy recycling and/or clean disposal. By effectively enacting sustainable supply chain management principles, companies can simultaneously generate cost savings, protect the Earth's natural resources, and ensure that socially responsible business practices are enacted. Research has demonstrated a strong business case supporting many sustainability initiatives. For example, the recycling of used pallets is both an environmentally sustainable practice and cheaper than purchasing new ones.[20]

Companies such as UPS work continuously to develop a more sustainable supply chain. By integrating new transportation technologies into its fulfillment networks, UPS mechanics and employees can facilitate package delivery in ways that are more fuel- and emissions-efficient. For example, UPS has driven over 3 million miles on alternative fuels across its fleet. That's enough to drive to the planet Mars and back more than 12 times. UPS has begun deploying thousands of electric and plug-in hybrid electric vehicles in its operations in North America, Europe, and Asia. UPS plans to have 40 percent of its ground operations powered by alternative fuel sources by 2025.[21]

In addition to environmental sustainability, modern businesses are also balancing economic success with social sustainability practices like human rights, labor rights, employee-diversity initiatives, and quality-of-life concerns. The benefits of social sustainability efforts have been demonstrated by retailers such as Walgreens, where more than 1,000 workers with disabilities are currently working and the retention rate for these workers is 40 percent higher than those without disabilities. Companies like Walgreens have found that workers with disabilities are far less likely to miss work and are often as effective at performing job tasks as their able-bodied counterparts—while frequently exceeding them in terms of process execution and safety standards.[22]

sustainable supply chain management a supply chain management philosophy that embraces the need for optimizing social and environmental costs in addition to financial costs

triple bottom line the financial, social, and environmental effects of a firm's policies and actions that determine its viability as a sustainable organization

A misconception surrounding both the environmental and social aspects of sustainability is that their practice disproportionately increases costs and should be enacted only when business leaders are willing to act altruistically or for good public relations. In other words, some businesses believe investment in these green aspects necessarily trades off against corporate profitability. Companies that have been unable to successfully capture economic value from environmental or social initiatives sometimes practice **greenwashing**, whereby they use marketing techniques to portray that their operations are environmentally or socially friendly when they are not. For example, Volkswagen was accused of greenwashing after it was discovered that their "clean diesel" cars were producing far more pollutants than Volkswagen advertised.[23] However, emerging research has begun to conclusively demonstrate that positive long-term financial returns accrue as a result of environmentally and socially sustainable practices if firms are willing to commit sufficient resources to the sustainability effort.[24]

13-5 The Digitalization of the Supply Chain

13-5 Discuss how new technology and emerging trends are impacting the practice of supply chain management

Several technological advances and business trends are affecting the job of the supply chain manager today. The most impactful of these is the increasing digitalization of the supply chain. **Digitalization** refers to the use of digital technologies to change ways of doing business and to provide new revenue and value-producing opportunities. This is occurring throughout the sequence of events that make up modern SCM, including demand sensing and decision making (via the Internet of Things, big data, supply chain analytics, and AI/machine learning), digitalized process management (via advanced robotics and

greenwashing when a firm publicly feigns support for environmental or social sustainability but fails to live up to these standards in practice

digitalization the use of digital technologies to change a business model and provide new revenue or value

Internet of Things (IoT) a system of interrelated computing devices, mechanical and digital machines, objects, animals, or people that are connected and able to transfer data over a network without overt human effort

big data the rapidly collected and difficult-to-process large-scale data sets that have recently emerged and push the limits of current analytical capability

cloud computing), digitalized distribution (via automated vehicles/drones and three-dimensional printing/additive manufacturing), and digitalized product and supply chain integrity/verification (blockchain). These clusters of technologies are working together to improve the speed and accuracy with which supply chains can serve end users with desired products and services, but their best-case uses are only beginning to be fully understood.

13-5a Digitalized Demand Sensing and Decision Making

The first frontier on which the digital supply chain impacts business pertains to the heightened ability to acquire and process data to support decision making. First, a rapidly increasing prevalence of sensory equipment that connects physical objects to the internet allows for the collection of massive data sets that can be used to make better decisions about the best time, place, and form of products. This phenomenon is referred to as the **Internet of Things (IoT)**, which enables physical objects to relay chunks of information about themselves and their surroundings to people or computers over the internet in real time, without overt human interaction. There are currently more devices on Earth connected to the internet than people, and the number of devices is expected to grow exponentially faster than human connections in the future. The potential impact of the IoT is tantalizing. For example, connections between containers, cargo vessels or trucks, and transportation infrastructures are leading to the development of smart transportation modes that reroute vehicles in real-time based on local traffic patterns, weather events, and accidents. Alternatively, the traffic grid can react to a need for emergency supplies by enabling a sequence of green stoplights along a critical emergency route. The possibilities for the IoT to positively impact the supply chain are endless, and many companies have already launched projects related to developing IoT-enabled supply chain management strategies.

The increasing prevalence of sensors on products, their containers, and the transportation and storage modes that carry them has allowed for powerful data-capturing capabilities to develop in some companies, with the output taking the form of vast databases of customer, supplier, and company information. Over the past few years, the appearance of **big data** has presented both great opportunities and significant problems for supply chain managers. More information is available about supply chain operations than ever before, but the challenge of extracting usable data from this information is very expensive. When processed by humans, a pivotal aspect of dealing with big data is the ability to "make it small again," by developing a capability to extract only the elements critical for making a desired decision. This capability, as well as many others related to the linkage of data elements for SCM decision making, falls under the umbrella of **supply chain analytics**. Supply chain analytics programs that can interpret big data have great potential for improving supply chain operations. For example, the use of bigger (and better) data should allow supply chain forecasting to become more accurate; shipments to be rerouted in the event of traffic or bad weather; and warehouses to be stocked with exactly the products customers want (and none they don't want). Each of these ambitions, if realized, would offer lower prices for customers and lead to greater customer satisfaction.

However, not all the decisions required for the efficient and effective operation of a modern, global supply chain are made by humans anymore. In many cases, the data are so complex or unwieldy that it makes more sense for businesses to let computers not only calculate the answers to complicated problems but sometimes also to ask questions. **Artificial intelligence (AI)** refers to the field of computer science that creates machines capable of solving problems more quickly and accurately than humans can. Traditionally, AI applications work by analyzing a set of inputs and producing the correct output more reliably than humans can. In the supply chain context, AI enables decisions related to procurement, manufacturing, logistics, and planning by assessing many different data sets (often housed within different businesses) simultaneously and producing a solution that is as close to optimal as possible for all the parties involved. However, sometimes, supply chain managers are better off letting the application do more of the decision-making. **Machine learning** is a subset of artificial intelligence that reverses the traditional AI processing method. Rather than teaching the computer the required logic to solve a problem (by inputting data), machine learning gives the computer a set of known answers to the problem. Then the computer is responsible for generating, or learning, the logic it needs to solve similar problems. It then can begin to not only answer but also to ask questions about supply chain processes. For example, if the objective is to deliver a shipment to a retail store within a predefined time window, the application can look at patterns of inputs and outputs from similar usages in prior data and suggest several different route/mode combinations, and then ask the user which is most preferred. By engaging with AI and machine learning, supply chain managers take some of the heavy lifting out of the big data analysis process and can improve firm and supply chain performance as a result.

DHL and Engie, a French multinational electric utility company, are two companies that have used machine learning and AI to optimize their supply chains. DHL is now utilizing AI-powered robotic sorting machines, which they brand as "DHLBots," to perform package sorting work that could be tedious and dangerous for human workers. These changes have led to a 40 percent increase in sorting capacity. Engie transformed their procurement system to digitize spending and interactions with suppliers to make the savings more transparent. The prior lack of visibility and communication was inefficient and made tracing improvements difficult.[25]

13-5b Digitalized Supply Chain Processes

In addition to digitalized demand sensing and decision making, other applications and tools are useful for executing supply process tasks. To leverage useful information across organizational interfaces for better joint decision making, many companies are using **cloud computing** to collaborate on big data projects and analyze findings in a quick and cost-effective manner.

Advanced logistical technologies enabled by big data and analytics or AI is also improving supply chain operations at the tactical level. Increasingly, modern companies are automating many of their supply chain processes, substituting mechanized labor for human labor. Many tasks that are done repetitively and require significant precision can be accomplished more cheaply and accurately via **advanced robotics**. Zebra offers services in the warehousing, distribution, and manufacturing sector with their Fetch autonomous mobile robots, which provide their customers with automated solutions for order picking and just-in-time material delivery.[26] However, robotics is not the only form of automation that has emerged to assist with supply chain tasks. **Automated vehicles** and **drones** are in use to make complicated or costly deliveries

---

supply chain analytics data analyses that support the improved design and management of the supply chain

artificial intelligence (AI) the computer science area focused on making machines that can simulate human intelligence processes

machine learning (ML) an application of artificial intelligence that provides systems the ability to automatically learn and improve from experience without being explicitly programmed

cloud computing the practice of using remote network servers to store, manage, and process data

advanced robotics devices that act largely or partially autonomously, that interact physically with people or their environment, and that are capable of modifying their behavior based on sensor data

automated vehicles cars, trucks, or other ground transportation modes for which human drivers are not required to take control to safely operate the vehicle

drones unmanned aerial vehicles that can be controlled remotely or can fly autonomously when executing a task

of goods or information easier. Drones—unmanned aerial vehicles—are already being used in many nations to complete "final mile" deliveries to customers. India-based food delivery company Zomato acquired a drone startup company named TechEagle and have been using drones for food delivery since 2019. UPS has also partnered with a drone startup named Matternet to transport medical supplies in the state of North Carolina.[27] Some companies are also experimenting with unmanned surface transportation. Google's parent company Alphabet has created a division named Wing that is partnering with DoorDash in Australia to deliver food, grocery, and convenience items via the newly branded "DoorDash Air" to several parts of that country.[28]

13-5c Digital Distribution

Digital distribution is the most recent development in the logistics arena. Broadly defined, **digital distribution** includes any kind of product or service that can be distributed electronically, whether over traditional forms such as fiber-optic cable or through satellite transmission of electronic signals. Companies like Netflix, Apple (iTunes), and Spotify have built their business models around electronic distribution.

Soon, however, digital distribution will extend beyond products and services, mainly composed of electronic bits and bytes of information easily transferred via electronic connections. Experiments with **three-dimensional printing (3DP)** have succeeded in industries such as auto

New transportation technologies, such as drone delivery, are increasingly impacting digitalized distribution and ultimately fulfillment networks.

Flystock/Shutterstock.com

digital distribution includes any kind of product or service that can be distributed electronically, whether over traditional forms such as fiber-optic cable or through satellite transmission of electronic signals

three-dimensional printing (3DP) the creation of three-dimensional objects via an additive manufacturing (printing) technology that layers raw material into desired shapes

parts, biomedical, and even retail. Using 3DP technology, objects are built to precise specifications using raw materials at or near the location where they will be consumed. Even traditional retailers can find value in these new technologies. London-based retailer Harrods has partnered with a 3DP company named 3D Systems to bring its EKOCYCLE™ 3D printers into some Harrods retail locations. These printers allow customers to create personalized fashion, music accessories, and home décor. These 3D printers are also unique as they use old soda and water bottles in their printing, making them valuable not only to Harrods' shoppers but also to the environment.[29]

The potential uses for 3DP (also referred to as *additive manufacturing*) are virtually endless and are being utilized across many businesses. For example, while serving very different customers, both General Electric and Nike have begun using 3DP technology. General Electric heavily invested in 3DP technology and now uses its 3DP technology to produce industrial parts such as complex parts for Boeing 787 airplanes. This process can save Boeing up to $3 million per plane. Additionally, Nike can now use 3DP to create Flyprint shoes that are perfectly customized shoes tailored to an athlete's needs.[30]

Many industry experts project that 3DP will radically transform the ways global supply chains work by changing the basic platforms of business. With 3DP, smaller, localized supply chains will become the norm and small manufacturers will produce many more custom products than ever before with very short lead times. And because such platforms will remove much of the need for the transportation of finished goods to distribution centers and retailers, 3DP is expected to have a very positive impact on businesses' carbon footprints and the environment at large. The example of Harrods and its 3D

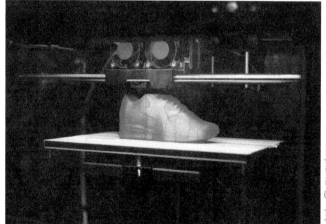

Using 3DP technology, objects as diverse as shoes and aircraft engines will be built to precise specifications at or near the location where they will be consumed, thereby disrupting supply chains.

asharkyu/Shutterstock.com

printing initiative reflects this benefit. Research shows that additive manufacturing will significantly decrease wasted materials, since parts can be printed on demand, reducing component-part waste, and providing large savings in energy and materials costs.

13-5d Digitalizing Supply Chain Integrity

In closing our discussion of supply chain digitalization, it is worth noting that as supply chains globalize, they get longer and more complex, often stretching around the world and including dozens of suppliers, intermediate customers, and service providers. And yet, end users of goods and services expect that the final output of the chain will be a perfect order, and there is little tolerance for error. But, because firms will inevitably make mistakes, **supply chain traceability**—the ability to map the paths of raw materials, component parts, subassemblies, and finished goods throughout the global network—has become a primary challenge for many businesses.

Until recently, achieving traceability has been a nearly impossible exercise that required extensive manual reporting and personal one-to-one communications. However, the digital era has brought with it a very important new reporting mechanism, **blockchain**, that has not only transformed traceability from a pipedream to a reality but has also ensured that any transactions between supply chain partners are impartially recorded and therefore beyond dispute. While blockchain is widely thought of exclusively for its part in the rise of cryptocurrency such as Bitcoin and Ethereum, its value and use has grown exponentially in recent years. A blockchain is a digital ledger of transactions that can be accessed by all parties in real time; it allows products or components to be traced from origin to destination including all stops in between. Because it is constantly visible and can be audited by any supply chain partner at any time, the blockchain eliminates fraud, lowers the cost of administration for shipments, increases accuracy, and reduces delays and disputes about the content of shipments. When combined with IoT, it can also be used to detect and record inventory locations and initiate automatic payments upon delivery. AB InBev, the Belgian drink and brewing company, has partnered with BanQu to utilize the blockchain to track the supply chain of African-grown crops, improving traceability and sustainability. Similarly, Swiss food and beverage giant Nestlé has partnered with OpenSC to use blockchain technology in its supply chain for palm oil and seafood products.[31] Though blockchain is relatively new to supply chain management applications, it is already proving to be a very effective tool for ensuring the integrity of global commercial trade.

Blockchain technology makes traceability of all global supply chain product movements and transactions.

VideoFlow/Shutterstock

13-6 Marketing Channels and Channel Intermediaries

13-6 Describe channel intermediaries' functions

A marketing channel can be viewed as a canal or pipeline through which products, their ownership, communication, financing and payment, and accompanying risk flow to the consumer. A **marketing channel** (also called a **channel of distribution**) is a business structure of interdependent organizations that reaches from the point of production to the consumer and facilitates the downstream physical movement of goods through the supply chain. Channels represent the "place" or "distribution" element of the marketing mix (product, price, promotion, and place), in that they provide a route for company products and services to flow to the customer. In essence, the marketing channel is the "downstream" portion of the supply chain that connects a producer with the customer. While "upstream" supply chain members are charged with moving component parts or raw materials to the producer,

---

supply chain traceability the degree to which a business can track a product's development through stages beginning with a raw material state and ending with delivery to the final consumer

blockchain a digital ledger in which transactions are made and recorded chronologically and publicly

marketing channel (channel of distribution) a set of interdependent organizations that eases the transfer of ownership as products move from producer to business user or consumer

members of the marketing channel propel finished goods toward the customer, and/or provide services that facilitate additional customer value.

Many different types of organizations participate in marketing channels. **Channel members** (also called *intermediaries*, *resellers*, and *middlemen*) negotiate with one another, buy and sell products, and facilitate the change of ownership between buyer and seller in the course of moving finished goods from the manufacturer into the hands of the final consumer. As products move toward the final consumer, channel members facilitate the distribution process by providing specialization and division of labor, overcoming discrepancies, and providing contact efficiency.

13-6a How Marketing Channels Work

According to the concepts of *specialization* and *division of labor*, breaking down a complex task into smaller, simpler ones and assigning these tasks to specialists create greater efficiency and lower average production costs via

channel members all parties in the marketing channel who negotiate with one another, buy and sell products, and facilitate the change of ownership between buyer and seller in the course of moving the product from the manufacturer into the hands of the final consumer

form utility the elements of the composition and appearance of a product that make it desirable

time utility the increase in customer satisfaction gained by making a good or service available at the appropriate time

place utility the usefulness of a good or service as a function of the location at which it is made available

exchange utility the increased value of a product that is created as its ownership is transferred

economies of scale. Marketing channels attain economies of scale through specialization and division of labor by aiding upstream producers (who often need more motivation, financing, or expertise) in marketing to end users or consumers. In most cases, such as for consumer goods like soft drinks, the cost of marketing directly to millions of consumers—taking and shipping individual orders—is prohibitive. For this reason, producers engage other channel members such as wholesalers and retailers to do what the producers are not well suited to do. Some channel members can accomplish certain tasks more efficiently than others because they have built strategic relationships with key suppliers or customers or have unique capabilities. Their specialized expertise enhances the overall performance of the channel.

Because customers, like businesses, are specialized, they also rely on other entities for the fulfillment of most of their needs. Imagine your life if you had to grow your food, make your clothes, produce your own television shows, and assemble your own automobile! Luckily, members of marketing channels are available to undertake these tasks for us. However, not all goods and services produced by channel members exist in the form we'd most prefer, at least at first. Marketing channels are valuable because they aid producers in creating time, place, and exchange utility for customers, such that products become aligned with their needs. Producers, who sit at the top of the supply chain, provide **form utility** when they transform oats grown on a distant farm into the Muesli or Cheerios that we like to eat for breakfast. **Time utility** and **place utility** are created by channel members, when, for example, a transport company hired by the producer physically moves boxes of cereal to a store near our homes in time for our next scheduled shopping trip. And the retailer, who is often the closest channel member to the customer, provides a desired product for some reasonable amount of money that we are willing to give, creates **exchange utility** in doing so.

13-6b Functions and Activities of Channel Intermediaries

Intermediaries in a channel negotiate with one another, facilitate the transfer of ownership for finished goods between buyers and sellers, and physically move products from the producer toward the final consumer. The most prominent difference separating intermediaries is whether they take title to the product. *Taking title* means they actually own the merchandise and control the terms of the sale—for example, price and delivery date. Retailers and merchant wholesalers are examples of intermediaries that take title to products in the marketing channel and resell them. **Merchant wholesalers** are organizations that facilitate the movement of products and services from the manufacturer to producers, resellers, governments, institutions, and retailers. All merchant wholesalers take title to the goods they sell. Most operate one or more warehouses where they receive finished goods, store them, and reship them to retailers, manufacturers, and institutional clients. Since wholesalers do not dramatically alter the form of a good or sell it directly to the consumer, their value hinges on their providing time and place utility and contact efficiency to retailers.

Other intermediaries do not take title to goods and services they market but do facilitate exchanges of ownership between sellers and buyers. **Agents and brokers** facilitate the sales of products downstream by representing the interests of retailers, wholesalers, and manufacturers to potential customers. Unlike merchant wholesalers, agents or brokers only facilitate sales and generally have little input into the terms of the sale. However, they get a fee or commission based on sales volume. For example, grocery chains often employ the services of food brokers, who provide expertise for a range of products within a category. The broker facilitates the sale of many different manufacturers' products to the grocery chain by marketing the producers' stocks, but the broker never actually takes ownership of any of the products.

Many different variations in channel structures are possible, with choices made based on the numbers and types of wholesaling intermediaries that are most desirable. Generally, product characteristics, buyer considerations, and market conditions determine the types and number of intermediaries the producer should use, as follows:

- Customized or highly complex products such as computers, specialty foods, or custom uniforms are usually sold through an agent or broker, who may represent one company or multiple companies. In contrast, standardized products such as soda or toothpaste are often sold through a merchant wholesaler and retailer channel.

- Buyer considerations such as purchase frequency or customer wait time influence channel choice. When there is no time pressure, customers may save money on books by ordering online and taking direct distribution from a wholesaler. However, if a book is needed immediately, it will have to be purchased at retail—for example, at the school bookstore—and will include a markup.

- Market characteristics such as how many buyers are in the market and whether they are concentrated in a general location also influence channel design. In a home sale, the buyer and seller are localized in one area, which facilitates the use of a simple agent–broker relationship, whereas mass-manufactured goods such as automobiles may require parts from all over the world and therefore many intermediaries.

Retailers are the firms in the channel whose primary function is to sell directly to consumers. A critical role fulfilled by retailers within the marketing channel is that they provide contact efficiency for consumers. Suppose you had to buy your milk at a dairy, your meat at a stockyard, and so forth. You would spend a great deal of time, money, and energy just shopping for just a few groceries. Retailers simplify distribution by reducing the number of transactions required by consumers and by making an assortment of goods available in one location. Consider the example illustrated in Figure 13.1. Four consumers each want to buy a game console. Without a retail intermediary like Best Buy, video game console manufacturers Sony, Microsoft, Nintendo, Sega, and Valve would each have to make four contacts to reach the four consumers in the target market for a total of 20 transactions. But when Best Buy acts as an intermediary between the producer and consumers, each producer needs to make only one contact, reducing the number to nine transactions. This benefit to customers accrues whether the retailer operates in a physical store location or online.

---

merchant wholesaler an institution that buys goods from manufacturers and resells them to businesses, government agencies, and other wholesalers or retailers and that receives and takes title to goods, stores them in its own warehouses, and later ships them

agents and brokers wholesaling intermediaries who do not take title to a product, but facilitate its sale from producer to the end user by representing retailers, wholesalers, or manufacturers

retailer a channel intermediary that sells mainly to consumers

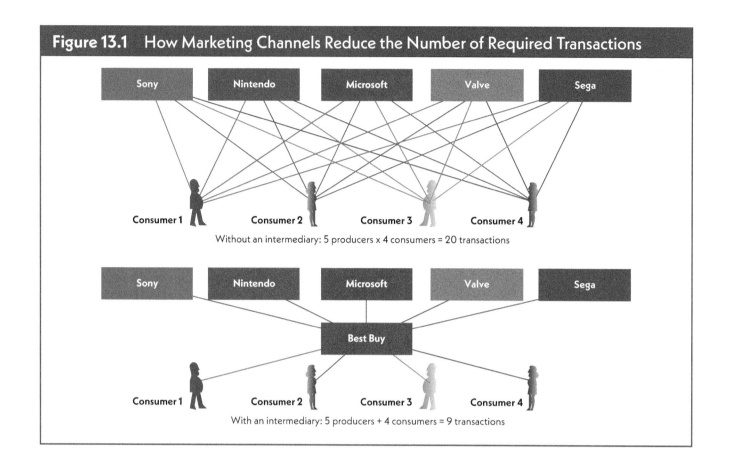

Figure 13.1 How Marketing Channels Reduce the Number of Required Transactions

Without an intermediary: 5 producers x 4 consumers = 20 transactions

With an intermediary: 5 producers + 4 consumers = 9 transactions

13-6c Channel Functions Performed by Intermediaries

Intermediaries in marketing channels perform three essential functions that enable goods to flow between producer and consumer. *Transactional* functions involve contacting and communicating with prospective buyers to make them aware of existing products and to explain their features, advantages, and benefits. Intermediaries in the channel also provide *logistical* functions. *Logistical* functions typically include the transportation and storage of assets, as well as their sorting, accumulation, consolidation, and/or allocation to conform to customer requirements. *Facilitating* includes research and financing. Research provides information about channel members and consumers by getting answers to the key questions: Who are the buyers? Where are they located? Why do they buy? Financing ensures channel members have the money to keep products moving through the channel to the ultimate consumer. Although individual members can be added to or deleted from a channel, someone in the channel must perform these essential functions. Producers, wholesalers,

retailers, or consumers can perform them, and sometimes nonmember channel participants such as service providers elect to perform them for a fee.

13-7 Channel Structures

13-7 Describe the factors that influence channel strategy choice

A product can take any of several possible routes to reach the final consumer. Marketers and consumers each search for the most efficient channel among many available alternatives. Constructing channels for a consumer convenience good such as candy differs from doing so for a specialty good like a Prada handbag. Figure 13.2 illustrates four ways manufacturers can route products to consumers. When possible, producers use a **direct channel** to sell directly to consumers to keep purchase prices low. Direct marketing activities—including telemarketing, mail order and catalog shopping, and forms of electronic retailing such as online shopping and shop-at-home television networks—are good examples of this type of channel structure. There are no intermediaries. Producer-owned stores and factory outlet stores—like Sherwin-Williams, Patagonia, Oneida, Zara, and WestPoint Home—are also examples of direct channels.

---

direct channel a distribution channel in which producers sell directly to consumers

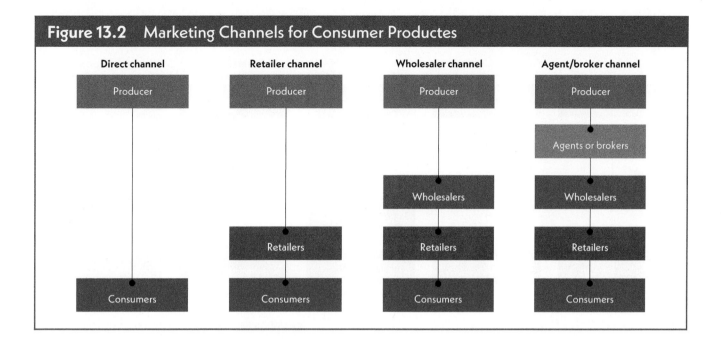

Figure 13.2 Marketing Channels for Consumer Productes

Direct channel	Retailer channel	Wholesaler channel	Agent/broker channel
Producer	Producer	Producer	Producer
			Agents or brokers
		Wholesalers	Wholesalers
	Retailers	Retailers	Retailers
Consumers	Consumers	Consumers	Consumers

By contrast, when one or more channel members are small companies that lack marketing power, an *agent–broker channel* may be the best solution. Agents or brokers bring manufacturers and wholesalers together for negotiations, but they do not take title to the merchandise. Ownership passes directly from the producer to one or more wholesalers and/or retailers, who sell to the ultimate consumer.

Most consumer products are sold through distribution channels similar to the other two alternatives: the retailer channel and the wholesaler channel. A *retailer channel* is most common when the retailer is large and can buy in large quantities directly from the manufacturer. Large and powerful retailers like Tesco, Walmart, and Amazon, as well as car dealerships are retailers that can often bypass a wholesaler. A *wholesaler channel* is commonly used for low-cost items that are frequently purchased, such as candy, cigarettes, and magazines.

Regardless of the number of channels used, managers must decide whether organizing channels around *customers* or *tasks*. Organizing channels around customers—for example, by creating a special distribution system for larger and more important customers—increases customer satisfaction at the expense of internal coordination and operating costs for the seller. On the other hand, organizing channels around tasks—for example, by using the company website to generate sales leads and the call center to handle after-sales service—enables the company to perform those tasks more efficiently across the customer base as a whole and to cut costs. Customer perceptions of the company's service quality may decrease, however, since there is not a single, one-stop point of contact.[32]

13-7a Channels for Business and Industrial Products

As Figure 13.3 illustrates, five-channel structures are common in business and industrial markets. First, *direct channels* are typical in business and industrial markets. For example, manufacturers buy large quantities of raw materials, major equipment, processed materials, and supplies directly from other producers. Manufacturers that require suppliers to meet detailed technical specifications often prefer direct channels. For instance, Apple uses a direct channel to purchase high-resolution retina displays for its innovative iPad tablet line. To ensure a sufficient supply for iPad manufacturing, Apple takes direct shipments of OLED screens from LG and Samsung.[33]

Alternatively, companies selling standardized items of moderate or low value often rely on *industrial distributors.* In many ways, an industrial distributor is like a supermarket for organizations. Industrial distributors are wholesalers and channel members that buy and take title to products. Moreover, they usually keep inventories of their products and sell and service them. Often small manufacturers cannot afford to employ their own sales forces. Instead, they rely on manufacturers' representatives or selling agents to sell to either industrial distributors or users. Additionally, the internet has enabled virtual distributors to emerge, forcing traditional industrial distributors to expand their business models. Many manufacturers and consumers bypass distributors and go directly to customers, often via the internet.

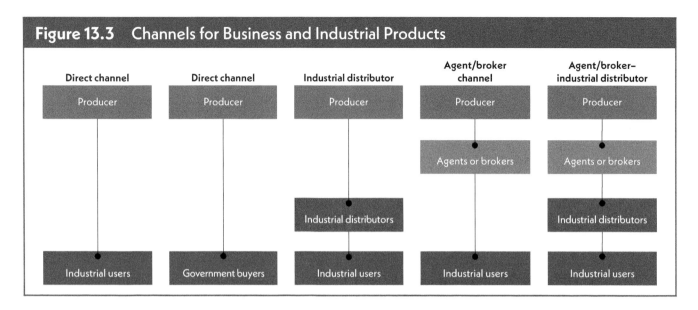

Figure 13.3 Channels for Business and Industrial Products

Direct channel	Direct channel	Industrial distributor	Agent/broker channel	Agent/broker–industrial distributor
Producer	Producer	Producer	Producer	Producer
			Agents or brokers	Agents or brokers
		Industrial distributors		Industrial distributors
Industrial users	Government buyers	Industrial users	Industrial users	Industrial users

13-7b Alternative Channel Arrangements

Rarely does a producer use just one type of channel to move its product. It usually employs several different strategies, which include the use of multiple distribution, nontraditional channels, and strategic channel alliances. When a producer selects two or more channels to distribute the same product to target markets, this arrangement is called **dual or multiple distribution**. Dual or multiple distribution systems differ from single-channel systems, and managers should recognize the differences. Multiple distribution channels must be organized and managed as a group, and managers must orchestrate their use in synchronization if the whole system is to work well. As consumers increasingly embrace online shopping, more retailers are employing a multiple distribution strategy. This arrangement allows retailers to reach a wider customer base but may also lead to competition between distribution channels through cannibalization (whereby one channel takes sales away from another). When multiple separate channels are used, they must all complement each other. Some customers use "showrooming" as a way of learning about products but may then also shop as a way of making price comparisons. Regardless of which channel customers choose when making the final purchase, they should receive the same messages and "image" of the products.

Peloton uses a showroom format for customers to experience what it would be like to own a Peloton.

The use of **nontraditional channels** may help differentiate a firm's product from the competition by providing additional information about products. Nontraditional channels include approaches such as mail-order television or video channels and infomercials. Although nontraditional channels may limit a brand's coverage, they can give a producer serving a niche market a way to gain market access and customer attention without having to establish physical channel intermediaries; they can also provide another sales avenue for larger firms.

Furthermore, companies often form **strategic channel alliances** that enable them to use another manufacturer's already-established channel. Alliances are used most often when the creation of marketing channel relationships may be too expensive and time consuming. For example, popular bedding and mattress e-tailer Casper partnered with multiple furniture companies such as Mattress Warehouse, Nordstrom, and Macy's, to increase consumer confidence in purchasing their products. By harnessing preestablished

---

dual or multiple distribution the use of two or more channels to distribute the same product to target markets

nontraditional channels nonphysical channels that facilitate the unique market access of products and services

strategic channel alliance a cooperative agreement between business firms to use the other's already established distribution channel

brick-and-mortar stores as a shared channel, Casper customers could try out mattresses before purchase, and stores like Mattress Warehouse and Nordstrom could more effectively advertise its chic bedroom furniture. The synergies created through the partnership benefitted both companies by creating more buying confidence in their shared consumer base.[34]

In addition to using primary traditional and nontraditional channels to flow products toward customer markets, many businesses also employ secondary channels, using either an active or passive approach. For example, though most automobile manufacturers sell their finished products to end users through networks of owned or franchised dealers, they also sell cars to rental agencies such as Enterprise or Hertz, that then rent them to potential customers. Similarly, fashion apparel companies might distribute their premium products, such as silk ties or branded watches, through primary channels such as department stores or specialty stores while using an off-brand or discount outlet for the distribution of low-end products. In each case, the goal of the company is the same: to engage a segment of customers who might otherwise never experience the product by offering it at a more easily affordable price or under trial conditions.

Marketers must also be aware, however, that some unintended secondary channels also exist. In some countries, **gray marketing channels** may be used to sell stolen or counterfeit products, which could detract from the profitability of the primary and secondary channels controlled by the business. Counterfeit products of popular brands like North Face outerwear, Rolex watches, Prada handbags, and even MAC cosmetics can be very difficult to distinguish from the real thing, and their presence provides unintended competition for the producer when such products are distributed through unauthorized intermediaries.

Along with marketing channels that move products downstream to end customers, retailers and manufacturers also manage channels that move products upstream, in the direction of the producer. These **reverse channels** enable consumers to return products to the retailer or manufacturer in the event of a product defect or at the end of the product's useful life to the consumer. The retailers or manufacturers can then recycle the product and use components to manufacture new products or refurbish and resell the same product in a secondary market. Several large companies, including Apple, Best Buy, IKEA, and Walmart, offer opportunities to recycle items ranging from plastic bags and batteries to televisions and Christmas trees. In certain countries, IKEA will buy back furniture from customers and recycle that furniture into new products or donate it to local charities.[35] Consumers and companies alike view reverse channels not just as a way to reduce

the firm's environmental impact but also as a means to gain some financial benefits. For example, electronics giant Apple offers a recycling program for its products, including iPhones, iPads, and Mac computers. Apple customers can trade their old devices for credit toward a new one. This endeavor allows Apple to offer new products to its existing customers and has helped the company's environmental initiatives. In fact, in 2021, almost 60 percent of all the aluminum shipped in Apple products came from recycled sources, with many products shipping with 100 percent recycled aluminum.[36] To incentivize customer cooperation in such initiatives, retailers are using **drop and shop** programs to get consumers to recycle products like batteries or cell phones during a regular trip to the store.

13-7c Digital Channels

With technology changing rapidly, many companies are turning to digital channels to facilitate product distribution. **Digital channels** are pathways for moving products and information toward customers so they can be sent and/or received with electronic devices, such as computers, smartphones, tablets, or video game consoles. Digital channels allow either push- or pull-based information and product flows—sometimes simultaneously. For example, a downloaded video game or music file purchased by a customer can also include a digital ad for more games or a new music player.

In response to the growth of digital channels, customers are turning in droves to **M-commerce**, whereby a mobile device is used to assess, compare, and/or buy products. For example, suppose you need a ride from one point in Prague to another. Instead of having to hail a cab or walk to the nearest elevated train station, you can use Bolt's smartphone app to contact a local driver who will take you directly to your destination. A key advantage of Bolt and similar apps is their frictionless payment interface. When you finish your ride, you leave the car and walk

---

gray marketing channels secondary channels that are unintended to be used by the producer, and which often flow illegally obtained or counterfeit product toward customers

reverse channels channels that enable customers to return products or components for reuse or remanufacturing

drop and shop a system used by several retailers that allows customers to bring used products for return or donation at the entrance of the store

digital channels electronic pathways that allow products and related information to flow from producer to consumer

M-commerce the ability to conduct commerce using a mobile device to buy or sell goods or services

away while the app charges your credit or debit card to pay the driver.[37]

M-commerce also enables consumers using wireless mobile devices to connect and shop online. Essentially, M-commerce goes beyond text message advertisements to allow consumers to purchase goods and services using wireless mobile devices. M-commerce users adopt the new technology because it saves time and offers more convenience in a greater number of locations. The use of M-commerce has become increasingly important as users grow in both number and purchasing power. Consumers have become more reliant on digital technologies, as shown in the world's first fully digital generation, the Millennials, and firms that fail to react to this trend risk losing a rapidly growing group of M-commerce customers.

Many major retail companies, ranging from Lowe's to Publix, already offer shopping on mobile phones, and the growth potential is huge. The retail M-commerce market is exploding, with mobile retail e-commerce sales projected at over $700 billion in 2025 and expected to grow at a compound annual rate of 27 percent.[38] Additionally, in 2023 the time spent on mobile shopping eclipsed over 100 billion hours globally. M-commerce is not just for online shopping, 49 percent of mobile shoppers said that they use a mobile device to compare retailer's prices to online alternatives. Mobile shopping experienced a boom during the COVID-19 pandemic, growing 18 percent from 2019 to 2020 when global lockdowns started taking place.[39]

Along with smartphone technology, companies are starting to look into other digital channels with which to connect with their customers. Social shopping allows multiple retailers to sell products to customers through social media sites. Most major social media companies such as Facebook, Instagram, Pinterest, Snapchat, and TikTok now have dedicated shopping sections of their sites that allow stores to sell directly to consumers without needing a traditional retail presence. TikTok Shop, for example, places a product cart next to the company's TikTok post and allows the viewer to purchase the product being shown. Services like TikTok Shop allow influencers to build product and brand loyalty without establishing a traditional retail channel.[40]

Firms are also using social media websites as digital channels—even in some cases without offering a purchasing opportunity. Companies create profiles on websites like Pinterest or Facebook and use them not only to give customers information about their products but also to collect customer information. According to one study, 38 percent of all online customers follow at least one retailer on a social networking site, and almost 40 percent of users are following their favorite brands on social media. Additionally, among internet users ages 18–34, 95 percent will follow at least one brand on social media. Many customers use these websites to find product information or get information on special deals, and those who follow a company's blog or profile on a social media site often end up clicking through to the firm's website.[41]

While some services group retailers together to bring products to customers, others allow consumers to combine and order larger amounts. Websites like Groupon, LivingSocial, Veepee, and Secret Escapes allow customers to fulfill their individual needs at group prices. Many of these sites are organized and managed by intermediaries between manufacturers and customers, but others may be customer initiated or even created by firms to better promote their own products and manage demand.[42]

13-7d Factors Affecting Channel Choice

Marketing managers must answer many questions before choosing a marketing channel. A book manufacturer must decide, for example, what roles physical and electronic distribution will play in the overall marketing strategy and how these two paths will fare against each other. In addition, managers must decide what level of distribution intensity is appropriate and must ensure that the channel strategy they choose is consistent with product, promotion, and pricing strategies. The choice of channels depends on a holistic analysis of market factors, product factors, and producer factors.

Market Factors

Among the most important market factors affecting distribution channel choices are market considerations. Specifically, managers should answer the following questions: Who are the potential customers? What do they buy? Where do they buy? When do they buy? How do they buy? Additionally, the choice of channel depends on whether the producer is selling to consumers directly or through other industrial buyers because of differences in the buying routines of these groups. The geographic location and size of the market are also important factors guiding channel

Options like TikTok Shop allow viewers to purchase products being featured in posts.

Chay_Tee/Shutterstock.com

selection. As a rule, if the target market is concentrated in one or more specific areas, then direct selling through a sales force is appropriate, whereas intermediaries would be less expensive in broader markets.

Product Factors

Complex, customized, and expensive products tend to benefit from shorter and more direct marketing channels. These types of products sell better through a direct sales force. Examples include pharmaceuticals, scientific instruments, airplanes, and mainframe computer systems. On the other hand, the more standardized a product is, the longer its distribution channel can be and the greater the number of intermediaries that can be involved without driving up costs. For example, except for flavor and shape, the formula for chewing gum is fairly standard from producer to producer. As a result, the distribution channel for gum tends to involve many wholesalers and retailers.

The product stage in the life cycle is also an important factor in choosing a marketing channel. In fact, the choice of channel may change over the life of the product. As products become more common and less intimidating to potential users, producers tend to look for alternative channels. Similarly, perishable products such as vegetables and milk have a relatively short life span, and fragile products like china and crystal require a minimum amount of handling. Therefore, both require fairly short marketing channels. Online retailers such as UncommonGoods and MoMA Design Store facilitate the sale of unusual or difficult-to-find products that benefit from a direct channel.

Producer Factors

Several factors about the producer itself are important to the selection of a marketing channel. In general, producers with large financial, managerial, and marketing resources are better able to perform their own marketing and thus will use more direct channels. These producers can hire and train their own sales forces, warehouse their own goods, and extend credit to their customers. Smaller or weaker firms, on the other hand, must rely on intermediaries to provide these services for them. Compared to producers with only one or two product lines, producers that sell several products in a related area can choose channels that are more direct. Therefore, sales expenses can be spread over more products.

A producer's desire to control pricing, positioning, brand image, and customer support also tends to influence channel selection. For instance, firms that sell products with exclusive brand images, such as designer perfumes and clothing, usually avoid channels in which discount retailers are present. Manufacturers of upscale products, such as Patek Philippe (watches), Perrier-Jouët (champagne), and Ladurée Macarons (baked goods), may sell

iStock.com/Denis_Zai

Perishable products spoil if they don't reach customers in time, so they tend to benefit from shorter, more direct marketing channels.

their wares only in expensive stores to maintain an image of exclusivity. Many producers have opted to risk their image, however, and test sales in discount channels. For example, Levi Strauss expanded its distribution network to include Kohl's, Target, and Walmart.

Timing Factors

A final consideration driving channel choice is the elapsed time between the introduction of a product into one channel and the secondary introduction of the same or a very similar product into another channel. Timing decisions such as when to release a product in different channels, how long to keep a product on the market, and when to launch new products are critical. For example, companies that offer products in multiple channels (such as online and in-store) must decide whether to launch in both channels simultaneously or to launch them sequentially—and if sequentially, in what order. They must also decide when to withdraw a product from a particular channel if that channel is no longer providing the expected value. Research shows companies that introduce movies into the primary channel (theater box office) often introduce the same movies into alternate channels (download, physical media, and streaming) as much as eight weeks too early, thereby suppressing aggregate revenues by up to 2.5 percent. This was especially true in the COVID-19 pandemic, where movies such as Disney's *Black Widow* and Warner Brother's *Dune* were released at the movie theater at the same time as they were on streaming platforms, a move many analysts say cost those studios money.[43] Similarly, aggregate revenues can decrease by as much as 2.5 percent if movies are released from theaters to a secondary channel too soon. One study found that 99 percent of the theater revenues are captured within the first four months, and 80 to 90 percent is captured in the first month, but the exact percentage depends on the success of the film.[44]

13-7e Levels of Distribution Intensity

Organizations have three options for the intensity of distribution: intensive, selective, and exclusive. **Intensive distribution** is a form of distribution aimed at maximum market coverage. Here, the manufacturer tries to have the product available in every outlet where potential customers might want to buy it. If buyers are unwilling to search for a product, it must be made very accessible to them. The next level of distribution, **selective distribution**, is achieved by screening dealers and retailers to eliminate all but a few in any single area. Because only a few are chosen, the consumer must seek out the product. John Deere products, for example, are only sold at selected authorized reseller locations. The same applies to certain high-end luxury brands such as Chanel and Louis Vuitton as well as clothing products such as Lululemon and Rolex watches. The most restrictive form of market coverage is **exclusive distribution**, which entails only one or a few dealers within a given area. Because buyers may have to search or travel extensively to buy the product, exclusive distribution is usually confined to consumer specialty goods, a few shopping goods, and major industrial equipment. Products such as Rolls-Royce automobiles, Chris-Craft powerboats, and Pettibone tower cranes are distributed under exclusive arrangements. Additionally, some consumer products also use exclusive distribution.

Emerging Distribution Structures

In recent years, rapid changes in technology and communication have led to the emergence of new, experimental distribution methods and channel structures. For example, fashion flash sale sites like Gilt, Groupon, and Doggyloothave recently boomed in popularity. On these fashion flash sites, new designer clothing items, services, or pet products are made available every day—often at a discount from 15 to 80 percent, and always for an extremely limited time. Veepee is a French

Luxury brands like Hermès use exclusive distribution which has very limited availability within a given area.

company that was one of the first retailers to experiment with this type of distribution method, and now it has similar sites for other product categories such as travel and home goods.

Another emerging channel structure involves renting items that are usually sold only to end consumers. For example, some websites allow customers to rent and return high fashion products (e.g., Rent the Runway), handbags and accessories (e.g., Bag Borrow or Steal), furniture (e.g., Fashion Furniture), and even children's clothes (e.g., The Dopple). Rental versus retail channels open up an entirely new customer base for certain products that were once reserved for a much smaller group.

For many years, subscription services such as book-of-the-month clubs have provided customers with products periodically over time. In recent times, subscription services have expanded their reach. Alongside the traditional subscription of magazines and books, customers can now find subscription services for things such as clothes (fabfitfun.com, statelymen.com), toys (lovevery.com), wine (wine.com), premade meals (simplyfresh.com) and much, much more. Streaming services are a primary way that many consume entertainment, and services like Spotify, OnLive, ZDF, and Netflix all charge a premium for a subscription to watch their content.

Digital marketplaces like Steam and the Google Play Store constitute another recent trend in marketing channels. Digital licensing adds an interesting facet to customer sales; instead of selling a tangible product, digital marketplaces sell the rights to songs, movies, and television shows through their websites and applications. Instead of leaving home to purchase a physical album, game, or movie, consumers can select specific media and download them directly to their computers or mobile devices.

---

intensive distribution a form of distribution aimed at having a product available in every outlet where target customers might want to buy it

selective distribution a form of distribution achieved by screening dealers to eliminate all but a few in any single area

exclusive distribution distribution to only one or a few dealers within a given area

13-8 Omnichannel Versus Multichannel Marketing

13-8 Explain why omnichannel and multichannel marketing is important

Marketing channels are valuable because they provide a route for products and services to reach the customer. Customers have different preferences, however, as to which channels to use when browsing, seeking information, comparing products to one another, and making a purchase. A single customer may use different channels for each of these activities, including both traditional and digital channels! For example, a customer might first learn about a new smartwatch when browsing a catalog, then research it on the company's website. They might later go to a physical retail location to try out the product before finally purchasing the device using a mobile app. Because of these varying preferences through different stages of the shopping cycle, many companies have begun to employ a multichannel marketing strategy, whereby customers are offered information, goods, services, and/or support through one or more synchronized channels. Some studies have demonstrated that customers who use multiple channels when shopping become more engaged during the purchase process and tend to spend more than customers who shop one channel only. The exception is when customers are buying simple, utilitarian products that are well-known and intended for frequent use. Since customers are already familiar with these product types, single-channel designs are just as effective.[45]

Because consumers use multiple channels during the shopping experience, it has become important for channel members to create a seamless shopping experience across all physical and digital channels. Facilitating such customer activities as checking a store's inventory online, purchasing an item through an app for in-store pickup, allowing online purchases to be returned in-store, and enabling mobile payment while shopping in a store are only a few strategies that producers and retailers are using to create customer perceptions that multiple channels are behaving as one.

However, it is important to understand that the multichannel design does create redundancy and complexity in the firm's distribution system. Selling through multiple channels is typically accompanied by the construction of multiple, parallel supply chains, each with its own inventory, processes, and performance metrics. Multichannel systems typically have meant that each channel would operate different transportation and distribution systems, hold and account for its own inventory, and otherwise act as independent sales and profit centers, with little knowledge of the operations of the other. This proved problematic for one retailer who was selling its products both in physical stores and on its website. The company had a distribution center in Kentucky for its internet retailing business and another near Chicago for its physical stores located there. When a customer in Chicago visited the local store looking for a certain product, the shelves were empty, and they were directed to order products from the company's website if they wanted one in time for the holidays. They did, and the product was shipped to the customer's home—at significant expense—from the Kentucky distribution center while unused product sat only miles from their home in the Chicago distribution center, waiting to be stocked on local store shelves.

Because of situations like these, many companies are transitioning to an omnichannel distribution operation that supports their multichannel retail operations and unifies their retail interfaces so that all customers receive equal and efficient service. For example, large retailers like Bloomingdales, The Home Depot, REI, and Zalando have systems that allow customers to browse in-store products online, make a purchase, and pick up that product at the retail store. These companies integrate that real-time inventory of the specific retail location to the customer as they are browsing. If the product is unavailable at a given store, the customer can find if any other stores in the area have it in stock. Since the COVID-19 pandemic, there has been a trend of curbside pickup, where customers can purchase online and have a retail employee bring the product to their car without even needing to enter the store. While allowing multiple ways to shop, these omnichannel retailers give more choices to customers, allowing them to control how they shop. This freedom to shop how you choose can increase customer satisfaction and loyalty. We discuss further implications of this strategy in Chapter 15.

Chapter 14

Retailing

Learning Outcomes

After studying this chapter, you will be able to . . .

14-1 Explain the importance of the retailer within the channel and the U.S. economy

14-2 List the different types of retailers

14-3 Explain the advantages of the different forms of nonstore retailing

14-4 Discuss why retailers vary in operation model strategies

14-5 Explain how retail marketing strategies are executed

14-6 Discuss how services retailing differs from goods retailing

14-7 Describe how retailers can address a product/service failure to turn it into an opportunity

14-8 Summarize current trends related to retail technology

14-1 The Importance of Retailing

14-1 Explain the importance of the retailer within the channel and the U.S. economy

Retailing represents all the activities directly related to selling goods and services to the ultimate consumer for personal, nonbusiness use. Retailing has enhanced the quality of our daily lives in countless ways. When we shop for groceries, hair care, clothes, books, or other products and services, we are doing business with **retailers**. The millions of goods and services provided by retailers mirror the diverse needs, wants, and trends of modern society. The U.S. economy depends heavily on the retail sector. On its own, the U.S. retail industry is responsible for generating 6 percent of gross domestic product (GDP), which equates to $3.9 trillion.[1]

Retailing affects everyone, both directly and indirectly. The retail industry consists of more than 1.8 million different U.S. retail entities and supports 52 million jobs, equal to about one in every four American jobs.[2] According to the U.S. Small Business Administration (SBA), 99.9 percent of all businesses in the United States employ fewer than 500 people, signifying that small businesses should comprise most of the retailing industry. However, the retail industry is dominated by only a few large companies. Walmart, for example, employs 2.1 million people around the world, 1.6 million of them in the United States alone; the company's global employment exceeds the total population of Iceland by nearly 6.5 times.[3] If its employees were an army, it would be the second largest army in the world—just behind China's.[4] As the retail environment changes, so do retailers. Trends and innovations relating to customer data, social media, and alternative forms of shopping are constantly developing, and retailers have no choice but to react. The *best* retailers actually lead the way by anticipating change and developing new and exciting ways to interact with customers. We discuss each of these issues and more in this chapter.

14-2 Types of Retailers and Retail Operations

14-2 List the different types of retailers

Retail establishments can be classified in several ways, such as type of ownership, level of service, product assortment, and price. These variables can be combined in several ways to create numerous unique retail operating models. Table 14.1 lists the major types of retailers and classifies them by their key differentiating characteristics.

14-2a Ownership Arrangement

Depending on its ownership arrangement, a retailer can gain advantages from having a broad brand identity or from having the freedom to take risks and innovate. Retail ownership takes one of three forms—independently owned, part of a chain, or a franchise outlet.

1. An **independent retailer** is owned by a person or group and is not operated as part of a larger network. Around the world, most retailers are independent, with each owner operating a single store in a local community.

2. A **chain store** is a group of retailers (of one or more brand names) owned and operated by a single organization. Under this form of ownership, a home office for the entire chain handles retail buying; creates unified operating, marketing, and other administrative policies; and works to ensure consistency across different locations. Target and Starbucks are retail chains.

3. A **franchise** is a retail business for which the operator is granted a license to operate and sell a product under the brand name of a larger supporting organizational structure, such as Subway or Supercuts. Under this arrangement, a **franchisor** originates the trade name, product, methods of operation, and so on. A **franchisee**, in return, pays the franchisor for the right

---

retailing all the activities directly related to the sale of goods and services to the ultimate consumer for personal, nonbusiness use

retailer a channel intermediary that sells mainly to consumers

independent retailer a retailer owned by a single person or partnership and not operated as part of a larger retail institution

chain store a store that is part of a group of the same stores owned and operated by a single organization

franchise a relationship in which the business rights to operate and sell a product are granted by the franchisor to the franchisee

franchisor the originator of a trade name, product, methods of operation, and the like that grants operating rights to another party to sell its product

franchisee an individual or business that is granted the right to sell another party's product

Table 14.1 Types of Stores and their Characteristics

Type of Retailer	Level of Service	Product Assortment	Price	Gross Margin
Department store	Moderately high to high	Broad	Moderate to high	Moderately high
Specialty store	High	Narrow	Moderate to high	High
Supermarket	Low	Broad	Moderate	Low
Drugstore	Low to moderate	Medium	Moderate	Low
Convenience store	Low	Medium to narrow	Moderately high	Moderately high
Full-line discount store	Moderate to low	Medium to broad	Moderately low	Moderately low
Specialty discount store	Moderate to low	Medium to broad	Moderately low to low	Moderately low
Warehouse club	Low	Broad	Low to very low	Low
Off-price retailer	Low	Medium to narrow	Low	Low
Restaurant	Low to high	Narrow	Low to high	Low to high

to use its name, product, and business methods and takes advantage of the franchisor's brand equity and operational expertise. Franchises can provide both goods and services, but increasingly, the most successful franchises are services retailers. Four of the top five franchises recognized by *Entrepreneur magazine* are fast-food restaurants.[5]

14-2b Level of Service

The service levels that retailers provide range from full service to self-service. Some retailers, such as exclusive clothing stores, offer very high or even customized service levels. They provide alterations, credit, delivery, consulting, liberal return policies, layaway, gift wrapping, and personal shopping. By contrast, retailers such as factory outlets and warehouse clubs offer virtually no service. After stock is set out for sale, the customer is responsible for any information gathering, acquisition, handling, use, and product assembly. At the extreme low end of the service continuum, a retailer may operate through a product kiosk or vending machine.

14-2c Product Assortment

Retailers can also be categorized by the width and depth of their product lines. *Width* refers to the assortment of products offered; *depth* refers to the number of different brands offered within each assortment. Specialty stores such as Kay Jewelers, Ashley Furniture, and Foot Locker

have the thinnest product assortments, usually carrying single or narrow product lines that are considerably deep. For example, a specialty home improvement store like Home Depot is limited to home-related products but may carry as many as 50 brands of refrigerators in a variety of colors and finishes with unique capacities and features. At the width end of the spectrum, full-line discounters typically carry very wide assortments of merchandise that are fairly shallow.

Stores often modify their product assortments to accommodate factors in the external environment. For example, a recent shift in customer preference toward high protein, plant-based, and health and wellness has led to the inclusion of on-the-go, conveniently packaged healthy meals on store shelves. Some of these options include bars, chips, and shakes featuring chickpeas, goji berries, and other nutritious ingredients. Large packaged food companies that haven't stayed on-trend with healthy options have suffered declining sales in recent years, demonstrating the importance of recognizing shifting customer lifestyles and offering new products to accommodate them.[6] Similarly, products ranging from baby formula to eye drops to mushrooms have been excluded from retail product lines via recalls to better ensure customer safety. However, the type of product can influence customers' expectations about product assortments. Researchers have found that customers expect less variety among items that are of higher quality.[7]

A shift in customer preferences toward plant-based and high-protein food options has led grocery stores, gas stations, and quick markets to offer healthier food and drink options.

14-2d Price

Price is the fourth way to position retail stores. Traditional department stores and specialty stores typically charge the full "suggested retail price." In contrast, discounters, factory outlets, and off-price retailers use low prices and discounts to lure shoppers. The last column in Table 14.1 shows the typical **gross margin**—how much the retailer makes as a percentage of sales after the cost of the goods sold is subtracted. (Margins are covered in more detail in Chapter 19.) Today, prices in any store format might vary not just from day to day, but from minute to minute! For example, bars and restaurants offer happy hours with discounted food items during times when business is typically slower than usual. Online retailers and traditional brick-and-mortar stores that have invested in electronic tagging systems are increasingly adopting dynamic pricing strategies that enable them to optimize price as an item's surging popularity or slow movement in real time.[8] The rise in the number of smartphones and other mobile devices has added a new layer of complexity to pricing decisions. Customers have more information than ever before with tools that can compare prices from dozens of retailers at once. Consequently, many are not willing to pay full price anymore. Recognizing this trend, some retailers have begun using pricing techniques to make customers believe that they are getting a bargain—even if they aren't. Some online retailers use customer information such as income, location, and browsing history to adjust their prices. That is, depending on the information that Amazon has about you, the price you find for a book on Amazon might be different from the price your instructor finds and the prices that your fellow classmates find. This practice can lead to negative reactions from consumers if they realize that they are not receiving equal prices or if they feel that their privacy has been invaded.[9]

14-2e Types of In-Store Retailers

Traditionally, retailers fall into one of several distinct types of retail stores, each of which features a product assortment, types of services, and price levels that align with the intended customers' shopping preferences. In recent years, however, retailers began experimenting with alternative formats that blend the features and benefits of the traditional types. For instance, supermarkets are expanding their nonfood items such as common cooking tools or cleaning products and offering services like health clinics; discounters are adding groceries; drugstores are becoming more like convenience stores; and department stores are experimenting with smaller stores. Nevertheless, many stores still fall into the traditional archetypes:

- **Department stores** such as Macy's and Spanish-based El Corte Inglés carry a wide range of products and specialty goods, including apparel, cosmetics, housewares, electronics, and sometimes furniture. Each department acts as a separate profit center, but central management sets policies about pricing and the types of merchandise carried.

- **Specialty stores** typically carry a deeper but narrower assortment of merchandise within a single category of interest. The specialized knowledge of their salesclerks allows for more attentive customer service. Office Depot, Ulta Beauty, and O'Reilly Auto Parts are well-known specialty retailers.

- **Supermarkets** are large, departmentalized, self-service retailers that specialize in food and some nonfood items. Some conventional supermarkets are being replaced by much larger *superstores*. Superstores offer one-stop shopping for food and nonfood needs, as well as services such as pharmacists, florists, salad bars, automotive services, and banking centers. Some examples include Food Lion, Kroger, and Publix.

---

gross margin the amount of money the retailer makes as a percentage of sales after the cost of goods sold is subtracted

department store a store housing several departments under one roof

specialty store a retail store specializing in a given type of merchandise

supermarket a large, departmentalized, self-service retailer that specializes in food and some nonfood items

- **Drugstores** primarily provide pharmacy-related products and services, but many also carry an extensive selection of cosmetics, health and beauty aids, seasonal merchandise, greeting cards, toys, and some refrigerated, nonrefrigerated, and frozen convenience foods. As other retailer types have begun to add pharmacies and direct-mail prescription services have become more popular, drugstores have competed by adding more services such as 24-hour drive-through windows and low-cost health clinics staffed by nurse practitioners. CVS Pharmacy, Rite Aid, and Walgreens are examples of drugstores.

- A **convenience store** resembles a miniature supermarket but carries a much more limited line of high-turnover convenience goods. These self-service stores are typically located near residential areas and offer exactly what their name implies: convenient locations, long hours, and fast service in exchange for premium prices. In exchange for higher prices, however, customers are beginning to demand more from convenience store management, such as higher-quality food and lower prices on staple items such as gasoline and milk. Quickie Mart, 7-Eleven, and Circle K are some convenience stores.

- **Discount stores** compete on the basis of low prices, high turnover, and high volume. Discounters can be classified into major categories, listed below:
  - **Full-line discount stores** such as Walmart offer consumers very limited service and carry a vast assortment of well-known, nationally branded goods such as housewares, toys, automotive parts, hardware, sporting goods, garden items, and clothing.
  - **Supercenters** extend the full-line concept to include groceries and a variety of services, such as pharmacies, dry cleaning, portrait studios, photo finishing, hair salons, optical shops, and restaurants. For supercenter operators such as Target, customers are drawn in by food but end up purchasing other items from the full-line discount stock.
  - Single-line **specialty discount stores** such as Staples offer a nearly complete selection of merchandise within a single category and use self-service, discount prices, high volume, and high turnover to their advantage. A **category killer** such as Home Depot is a specialty discount store that heavily dominates its narrow merchandise segment.

- A **warehouse club** sells a limited selection of brand-name appliances, household items, and groceries. These are sold in bulk from warehouse outlets on a cash-and-carry basis to members only. Currently, the leading stores in this category are Sam's Club, Costco, and BJ's Wholesale Club.

- **Off-price retailers** such as T.J. Maxx, Bed Bath & Beyond, and Saks Off Fifth sell at prices 25 percent or more below traditional department store prices because they buy inventory with cash, and they don't require return privileges. These stores often sell manufacturers' overruns, irregular merchandise, and/or overstocks that they purchase at or below cost. A **factory outlet** is an off-price retailer that is owned and operated by a single manufacturer and carries one line of merchandise—its own. Manufacturers can realize higher profit margins using factory outlets than they would by disposing of the goods through independent wholesalers and retailers. Nike Factory Store, L.L. Bean Outlet, and Bose Outlet are examples of factory outlets. **Used goods retailers** turn customers

---

drugstore a retail store that stocks pharmacy-related products and services as its main draw

convenience store a miniature supermarket, carrying only a limited line of high-turnover convenience goods

discount store a retailer that competes on the basis of low prices, high turnover, and high volume

full-line discount store a discount store that carries a vast depth and breadth of product within a single product category

supercenter a large retailer that stocks and sells a wide variety of merchandise including groceries, clothing, household goods, and other general merchandise

specialty discount store a retail store that offers a nearly complete selection of single-line merchandise and uses self-service, discount prices, high volume, and high turnover

category killer a large discount store that specializes in a single line of merchandise and becomes the dominant retailer in its category

warehouse club a large, no-frills retailer that sells bulk quantities of merchandise to customers at volume discount prices in exchange for a periodic membership fee

off-price retailer a retailer that sells at prices 25 percent or more below traditional department store prices because it pays cash for its stock and usually doesn't ask for return privileges

factory outlet an off-price retailer that is owned and operated by a manufacturer

used goods retailer a retailer whereby items purchased from one of the other types of retailers are resold to different customers

into suppliers: preowned items bought back from customers are resold to different customers. Used goods retailers can be either brick-and-mortar locations (such as Uptown Cheapskate) or electronic marketplaces (such as Thredup).

- **Restaurants** provide both tangible products—food and drink—and valuable services—food preparation and presentation, table service, and sometimes delivery. Most restaurants are also specialty retailers in that they concentrate their menu offerings on a distinctive type of cuisine—for example, Red Lobster restaurants and Caribou Coffee.

14-3 The Rise of Nonstore Retailing

14-3 Explain the advantages of the different forms of nonstore retailing

The retailing formats discussed so far entail physical stores where merchandise is displayed and to which customers must travel to shop. In contrast, **nonstore retailing** enables customers to shop without visiting a physical store location. Nonstore retailing adds a level of convenience for customers who wish to shop from their current locations. Broad changes in culture and society have led nonstore retailing currently growing faster than in-store retailing. In response to the successes found by nonstore retailers, many grocery stores have started offering curbside pick-up services. These services, such as Instacart Pickup and Kroger Grocery Pickup, offer consumers the ease of online shopping without the inconvenience of waiting days for a delivery.

Kroger shoppers use the app to clip coupons that can be redeemed at checkout in stores.

Besides pickup services, many retailers have created apps for smartphones to appeal to digital shoppers. This addition allows consumers to shop at their own convenience, including when the physical store is closed. Some changes to the physical store have resulted from these additions, including adding shelving or lockers by store entrances to make order pickup easier. In 2019, prior to the pandemic, Walmart, Target, and Home Depot were leading the way in their efforts for frictionless shopping experiences across channels (physical and online).[10] In the post-pandemic environment, top trends go beyond curbside pickup, but include stock visibility, in-store locator, same-day delivery, and easy returns. Given the supply shortages that resulted from the pandemic, many customers are taking advantage of these services as 51 percent of online shoppers reported checking for product availability at nearby stores.[11] The major forms of nonstore retailing are automatic vending, direct retailing, direct marketing, and internet retailing (or *e-tailing*).

- **Automatic vending** entails the use of machines to offer goods for sale—for example, the soft drink, candy, and snack vending machines commonly found in public places and office buildings. Retailers are continually seeking new opportunities to sell via vending. As a result, vending machines today sell merchandise such as ice cream, cosmetics, chargers, and even ice cream. A key aspect of their continuing success is the proliferation of cashless payment systems in response to consumers' diminishing preference for carrying cash. Automatic vending has allowed marketers to tap into a new, unlikely audience: customers seeking luxury items on the go. Some upscale hotels, including the Ritz-Carlton, Pendry Hotels, and the Mandarin Oriental, have champagne vending machines at some of their locations. Guests wishing to commemorate an event or simply partake in the perfectly chilled bottle of bubbly can find it in the hotel lobby.[12]
- **Self-service technologies (SST)** comprise a form of automatic vending where services are the primary focus.

restaurant a retailer that provides both tangible products—food and drink—and valuable services—food preparation and presentation

nonstore retailing shopping without visiting a store

automatic vending the use of machines to offer goods for sale

self-service technologies (SST) technological interfaces that allow customers to provide themselves with products and/or services without the intervention of a service employee

Automatic teller machines, pay-at-the-pump gas stations, and movie ticket kiosks allow customers to make purchases that once required assistance from a company employee. However, as with any sort of self-service technology, automatic vending comes with failure risks due to human or technological error. Unless customers expect that they can easily recover from such errors, they may end up shopping elsewhere. Naturally, some customers are frustrated with the growing trend toward self-service technology. Many can recall an incident of a self-service technology failure that left them begging to speak to a live human being. Some banks are attempting to avoid service failures at ATMs by reintroducing live interactions between customers and service employees. With virtual teller machines (VTMs), customers can video chat with a live teller to eliminate some technology errors.

- **Direct retailing** representatives sell products door to door, in offices, or at in-home sales parties. Companies like The Pampered Chef, Cutco, and Mary Kay have used this approach for years. Social media selling has flourished among direct sellers seeking to increase the number of products and services sold. Many direct sellers now host digital parties on social media, where people can shop from the comfort of their own homes for items ranging from do-it-yourself manicures to weight loss body wraps. Healthy Hands Cooking offers hands-on cooking classes to kids with an aim to fight obesity. Individuals become trained instructors through module courses to ensure proper food safety, licensing, and permits are in place. These instructors then teach kids to cook and keep 90 percent of the class revenue.[13]

- **Direct marketing (DM)** includes techniques used to elicit purchases from consumers while in their homes, offices, and other convenient locations. Common DM techniques include telemarketing, direct mail, and mail-order catalogs. Shoppers who

An increasing interest in personal health and wellness has led to essential oil products from Young Living being promoted for direct sale on Instagram.

use these methods are less bound by traditional shopping situations. Time-strapped consumers and those who live in rural or suburban areas are most likely to be DM shoppers because they value the convenience and flexibility it provides. DM occurs in several forms, as described below:

- **Telemarketing** is a form of DM that employs outbound and inbound telephone contacts to sell directly to consumers. Even in the age of digital marketing, telemarketing remains a highly effective marketing technique. For example, when individuals abandon high priced items in an online cart, telemarketing is an effective means of closing the sale. One survey indicates that in a business-to-business (B2B) setting, 14 percent of sales and marketing leads come from telemarketing activity alone, surpassing the impact of print advertising, organic social media, and account-based marketing.[14]

- Alternatively, **direct mail** can be a highly efficient or highly inefficient retailing method, depending on the quality of the mailing list and the effectiveness of the mailing piece. With direct mail, marketers can precisely target their customers according to demographic, geographic, and/or psychographic characteristics. Direct mailers are becoming more sophisticated in targeting the right customers. Direct mail has the highest return on investment at 112 percent across all mediums.[15]

---

direct retailing the selling of products by representatives who work door to door, office to office, or at home sales parties

direct marketing (DM) techniques used to get consumers to make a purchase from their home, office, or other nonretail setting

telemarketing the use of the telephone to sell directly to consumers

direct mail the delivery of advertising or marketing material to recipients of postal or electronic mail

Microtargeting based on data analytics of census data, lifestyle patterns, financial information, and past purchase and credit history allows direct mailers to pick out those most likely to buy their products.[16] According to one report, U.S. companies spend more than $43 billion each year on direct mail, and thanks to microtargeting initiatives, the customer response rates to direct mail is nine times greater than other digital channels.[17] Microtargeting is also an effective tool for online retailing. Many companies have purchased access to online search engine data, making it easier than ever to pinpoint customer preferences. A customer's online search history enables retailers to match their specific customer wants through targeted digital advertisements.

○ **Shop-at-home television networks** such as HSN and QVC produce television shows that display merchandise to home viewers. Viewers can phone in their orders directly on toll-free lines and shop with their credit cards. The shop-at-home industry has quickly grown into a multibillion-dollar business with a loyal customer following and high customer penetration. The Asia-Pacific region highly dominates the home shopping market. This includes China, the most prominent, South Korea, Singapore, Japan, and India. The growth is primarily due to expanding internet coverage to include 1,051.5 million users in China in 2022.[18]

• **E-tailing**, or **online retailing**, enables customers to shop over the internet and have items delivered directly to their door. Global online shopping accounts for about $5.7 trillion annually and is projected to hit $7 trillion by 2024. More than 70 percent of all retail website visits worldwide are via smartphones. Additionally, 2.14 billion people worldwide purchase goods online in a single year. Online retailer Amazon makes $4,722 each second and over $17 million per hour. Fifty-five percent of online shopping starts on Amazon.[19] Online, interactive shopping tools and live chats substitute for the in-store interactions with salespeople and product trials that customers traditionally used to make purchase decisions. Shoppers can use a variety of devices to look at a much wider variety of products online because physical space restrictions do not exist. While shopping, customers can take their time deciding what to buy. Research has demonstrated that as shoppers begin to engage multiple devices in a single shopping task, the likelihood of an eventual purchase increases—especially when the consumer progresses from more mobile devices, such as a phone or tablet, to more fixed devices such as a desktop computer.[20]

Travelers are increasingly using share economy services like Airbnb or VRBO for lodging rather than staying at a hotel.

Further, consumers who use computers to search are more likely to make a purchase using a computer.[21]

As consumers have become more connected, the **sharing economy** has emerged as a more efficient exchange of resources. Sharing economy refers to the way connected consumers exchange goods and services with one another through a digital marketplace. This phenomenon has given rise to online exchange communities such as ride-share and grocery delivery services. Other companies match people looking for specific services, such as vacation rentals (Airbnb and VRBO), crowd funding (GoFundMe), peer-to-peer loans (LendingClub), and freelance work (Task Rabbit). These companies provide a platform—not just to match buyers and sellers but also to track ratings and reviews for service providers and clients alike.

Besides retailer websites, consumers are increasingly using social media applications as shopping platforms. Social networking sites such as Facebook, Instagram, and Twitter, now known as X, enable users to immediately purchase items recommended by their social connections, a phenomenon known as *social shopping*. Companies are eager to establish direct linkages between social networking platforms and their own websites owing to the belief that a product or service

---

microtargeting the use of direct marketing techniques that employ highly detailed data analytics to identify potential customers with great precision

shop-at-home television network a specialized form of direct response marketing whereby television shows display merchandise, with the retail price, to home viewers

e-tailing (online retailing) a type of shopping available to consumers via access to the internet

sharing economy the way connected consumers exchange goods and services with each other through a digital marketplace

recommended by a friend will receive higher consideration from the potential customer. This is one reason influencer marketing has gained popularity. A message from someone we consider to be a friend feels less like promotional materials coming from organizations. Influencer marketing will be discussed more in Chapter 18.

14-4 Retail Operations Models

14-4 Discuss why retailers vary in operation model strategies

The retail formats covered so far are co-aligned with unique operating models that guide the decisions made by their managers. Each operating model can be summarized as a set of guiding principles. For example, off-price retailers deemphasize customer service and product selection in favor of lower prices, which are achieved through a greater focus on lean inventory management.

Alternatively, specialty shops generally adopt a high-service approach that is supported by an agile approach to inventory. By keeping a greater amount of **floor stock** (inventory displayed for sale to customers) and **back stock** (inventory held in reserve for potential future sale in a retailer's storeroom or stockroom) on hand, a broader range of customer demands can be accommodated. This operating model also implies higher prices for customers, however, retail managers must make sure that they deliver on the promises their firms make to customers to secure their loyalty. At the same time, these retail managers must control demand via promotions and other sales events to sell off slow-moving and perishable items, thereby making more room for items that are more popular.

Regardless of the type of stocking strategy a retailer chooses, there is always a chance that a wanted item will be out of stock leaving the consumer with having to make a choice—they can either seek the original product at another store or select a substitute item. While this could be bad for the retailer, research suggests that there may be a bright side to stockouts. One study found that customers view stockouts as an indication of how desirable a product is, and in turn will buy an item that is similar to the out-of-stock item, regardless of whether they even wanted the original item.[22]

These sorts of trade-offs have been partially responsible for the recent emergence of hybrid, or cross channel, retail operating models. As an example of a hybrid strategy,

Dikla is shopping for jeans at American Eagle. After trying on jeans in the dressing room, they realize that they need a different size, but that size is out of stock. The dressing room attendant gets the size Dikla is seeking, but it is not in the style desired. After Dikla confirms the size is correct, American Eagle places an order for Dikla for the appropriate size and style jeans that will be shipped directly to their home with no shipping fees. Dikla had the convenience of shopping in stores, but when an item was out of stock, the employee was still able to close the sale by crossing over to their online channel.

Likewise, with the growing trend of experiential shopping, some retailers carry no inventory at all. For instance, Nordstrom unveiled a new concept store in West Hollywood called Nordstrom Local in which shoppers can try on sample clothes, get manicures, and enjoy beer, wine or coffee while working with personal stylists on site to craft their desired look. Once the customer chooses an item to buy, the personal stylist will retrieve the good from one of six Nordstrom department store locations in Los Angeles or through its website.[23]

The trade-offs inherent in retail operating models have both spurred the recent success of online-only retailers and led to a surge in online storefront development among retailers who have traditionally operated in physical formats only. A key advantage of online retail is that no physical retail store space is needed for displaying and selling merchandise. Lower-cost remote distribution centers can be used, since all of the showcasing occurs on the company's website. By moving online, a specialty store can gain the operational benefits of a mass merchandiser. It can showcase exclusive or trendy items in an almost-free space to potential customers located around the world and can then fulfill demand from one of several localized distribution centers in a very short time. Fulfillment times are specified by the customer (according to their willingness to pay for greater

To cut delivery times to 30 minutes or less, Amazon is experimenting with drone delivery methods on some products.

---

floor stock inventory displayed for sale to customers

back stock inventory held in reserve for potential future sale in a retailer's storeroom or stockroom

shipping and delivery speed), and even this trade-off is becoming less of a sticking point every year. Amazon's Prime subscription program, for example, includes free same-day, one-, or two-day shipping depending on the item. The company has even introduced the use of drones to experiment delivering items in 30 minutes or less. Considering that there are more than 200 million Prime members worldwide, shipping speed is at the heart of what the Amazon customer values.

The Chicago-based software-as-a-service (SaaS) company Bringg is currently the leading delivery logistics solution for some of the world's best-known brands in more than 50 countries. Bringg helps its customers, including retail giant Walmart, to compete with Amazon and manage their challenging last-mile and delivery operations through its powerful retail delivery technology platform designed to enhance control, speed, visibility, and cost containment.[24] It is estimated that the last mile costs 41 percent of the total delivery costs. However, Bringg uses a wide variety of delivery vehicles, and routes with a goal of cost and time saving, translating to 20 to 25 percent delivery cost savings to retailers. Also, the platform communicates between the driver and customer to which the delivery is headed, in addition to the company and driver, thus keeping everyone informed.[25]

Today, most retail stores remain operationally and tactically similar to those that have been in business for hundreds of years, with one or more physical locations that the customer must visit to purchase a stocked product and strategies in place to attract customers to visit. The sorts of differences we have described among retail operating models imply that managing one type of store instead of another can involve very different experiences. But most of the decisions that retail managers make can be distilled down to six categories of activity, known as the retailing mix. These categories, described in the next section, are relatively universal to all forms of retailing but are applied in different ways based on the retail format.

14-5 Executing a Retail Marketing Strategy

14-5 Explain how retail marketing strategies are executed

Retail managers develop marketing strategies based on the goals established by stakeholders and the overall strategic plans developed by company leadership. Strategic retailing goals typically focus on increasing total sales, reducing costs of goods sold, and improving financial ratios such as return on assets or equity.

At the store level, more tactical retailing goals include increased store traffic, higher sales of a specific item, developing a more upscale image, and creating heightened public awareness of the retail operation and its products or services. The tactical strategies that retailers use to obtain their goals include having a sale, updating décor, and launching a new advertising campaign. The key strategic tasks that precede these tactical decisions are defining and selecting a target market and developing the retailing mix to successfully meet the needs of the chosen target market.

14-5a Defining a Target Market

The first and foremost task in developing a retail strategy is to define the target market. This process begins with market segmentation, the topic of Chapter 8. Successful retailing has always been based on knowing the customer. Sometimes retailing chains flounder when management loses sight of the customers the stores should be serving. Customers' desires and preferences change over their personal and professional life spans, and it is important for retailers to be sensitive to these changes by migrating their customers to new and different products as their buying patterns evolve.

Target markets in retailing are often defined by demographics, geographic boundaries, and psychographics because of the different needs that can be identified by these forms of segmentation. For example, European grocery apps for Pyaterochka and Tesco Groceries were among the top grocery apps downloaded during 2020, which made shoppers feel safer and shopping more convenient for its customers. App users can even request that their groceries be delivered directly to their homes to reduce shopping time. Long-term app use is targeted at millennials, who often have busy schedules and are technology savvy. In contrast, in the United States, Amazon's acquisition of Whole Foods was largely a strategic move to gain access to this highly coveted consumer demographic, as well as achieve a foothold in the brick-and-mortar world to create a true omnichannel experience for customers. Though Amazon has traditionally prided itself on offering affordable options for a diverse group of consumers, by purchasing Whole Foods, Amazon increased its access to a new class of consumers who are often affluent and educated and who value cultural knowledge above many other luxury items. By purchasing the preferred grocery store of millennials, Amazon can now easily become an integral part of their daily lives and shopping habits. Further, Amazon plan to implement more artificial intelligence at Whole Foods, which could include details on the history of the food being purchased and dynamic pricing that changes the price of goods as they approach the expiration date.[26]

14-5b Choosing the Retailing Mix

As previously noted, defining a retail operation entails combining the elements of the retailing mix to produce a single retailing method to attract the target market. The **retailing mix** consists of six Ps: the four Ps of the marketing mix (*product*, *promotion*, *place*, and *price*) plus *presentation* and *personnel* (refer to Figure 14.1). The combination of the six Ps projects a store's (or website's) image and influences customers' perceptions. Using these impressions, shoppers can position one store or website against another. Managers must make sure that the positioning is aligned with target customers' expectations.

Product

The first element in the retailing mix is the product offering, also called the "product assortment" or "merchandise mix." Developing a product offering is essentially a question of the width and depth of the product assortment. Price, store/website design, displays, and service are important to customers in determining where to shop, but the most critical factor is merchandise selection. This reasoning also holds true for online retailers. Alibaba, China's biggest online marketplace, for instance, offers enormous width in its product assortment with millions of different items, including books, music, toys, videos, tools and hardware, health and beauty aids, electronics, and software.

Conversely, online specialty retailers such as Giantnerd, a Chinese bike shop that operates exclusively online. They focus on a single category of merchandise, bicycles, but offer a wide variety of options including mountain bikes, road bikes, and electric bikes in the hopes of attracting loyal customers with a larger depth of products. Many online retailers purposely focus on single product-line niches that could never attract enough foot traffic to support a traditional brick-and-mortar store. For instance, websites such as dadant.com and glorybee.com sell beekeeping suits, hives, and supplies in the United States. After determining what products will satisfy target customers' desires, retailers must find sources of supply and evaluate the products. When the right products are found, the retail buyer negotiates a purchase contract.

Promotion

Retail promotion strategies include advertising, public relations and publicity, creator and influencer marketing, and sales promotions. The goal is to help position the store or website in customers' minds. Retailers design intriguing ads, stage special events, and develop promotions aimed at their target markets. Today's grand openings are a carefully orchestrated blend of advertising, merchandising, goodwill, and glitter. All the elements of an opening—press coverage, special events, media advertising, and store displays—are carefully planned. Other promotions that are often used successfully include sales events, coupons, and discounts for certain products or customer groups. Influencer marketing was previously reserved for celebrities, but today, individuals with dedicated social followers are finding their way into partnering with specific retailers to promote their products or services. In 2023, influencer marketing spending was estimated to be more than $21 billion. Also, of those using influencer marketing in 2023, 67 percent intend to increase their budgets in the future.[27]

One risk associated with store promotions, however, is **brand cannibalization**, a situation whereby the promotion intended to draw in new customers simply

---

retailing mix a combination of the six Ps—product, promotion, place, price, presentation, and personnel—to sell goods and services to the ultimate consumer

brand cannibalization the reduction of sales for one brand as the result of the introduction of a new product or promotion of a current product by another brand

---

Figure 14.1   The Retailing Mix

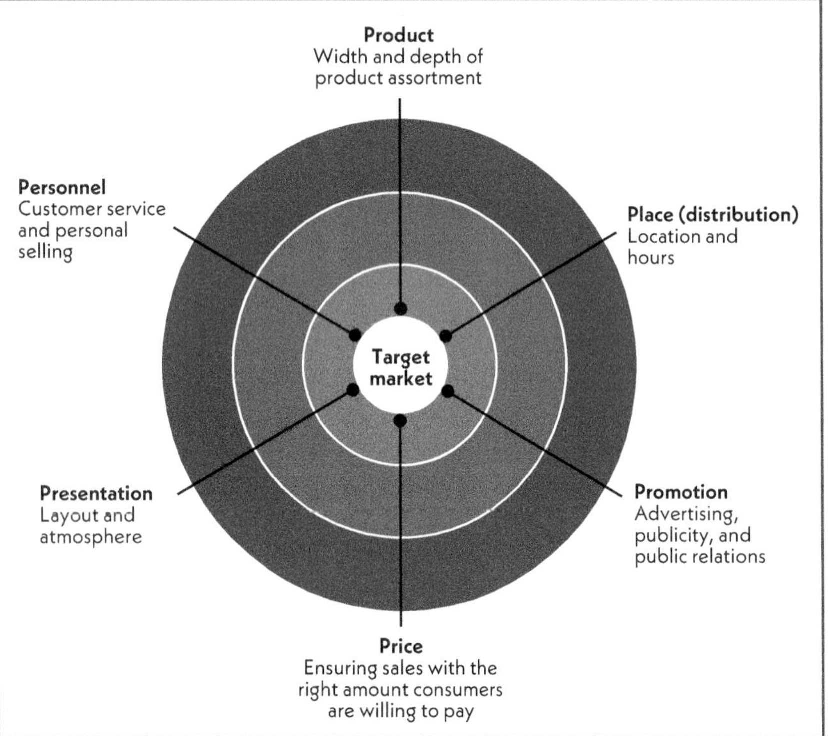

Product
Width and depth of product assortment

Personnel
Customer service and personal selling

Place (distribution)
Location and hours

Presentation
Layout and atmosphere

Promotion
Advertising, publicity, and public relations

Target market

Price
Ensuring sales with the right amount consumers are willing to pay

shifts current customers from buying one brand to another brand. Brand cannibalization is dangerous to the retailer for two reasons. First, the retailer incurs significant expense in executing the promotion itself. Second, the promotion creates inaccurate sales forecasts for both the promoted and cannibalized products, leading to stockouts of the promoted brand and financial losses from discounting the surplus inventory of the cannibalized brand. The latter types of losses can sometimes be significantly greater than the cost of the promotion itself. For example, promotions related to the release of a highly desired Nike shoe like the Air Max 270 can divert sales away from the Nike Air Force 1. Without having enough inventory of the Air Max 270 to fulfill demand, sales are lost. Further, the inventory of the Air Force 1 increases. Therefore, retail managers should design their promotional activities carefully, with gaining new customers being the primary objective.

Much retail advertising is focused on the local level. Local advertising by retailers usually provides specific information about their stores, such as location, merchandise, hours, prices, and special sales. In contrast, national retail advertising generally focuses on image. For example, Target uses advertisements similar to designer fashion advertisements to depict high-quality goods. Paired with the ubiquitous red target and tag line "Expect More. Pay Less," Target is demonstrating that it sells products that consumers normally aspire to own at prices they can afford.

Target's advertising campaigns also take advantage of cooperative advertising, another popular retail advertising practice. Traditionally, marketers would pay retailers to feature their products in store mailers, or a marketer would develop a television campaign for the product and simply tack on several retailers' names at the end. But Target's advertising uses a more collaborative trend by integrating products such as Tide laundry detergent or Coca-Cola into the actual campaign. Another common form of cooperative advertising involves promotion of exclusive products. Target often collaborates with fashion designers to provide designer fashion at affordable prices. Target's campaign catchphrase "Luxury for Every Woman Everywhere," depicted the essence of the collection that featured luxury fabrics like suede and cashmere. Other Target designer collaborations include Sergio Hudson, Kika Vargas, and La Ligne.[28]

Place

The retailing axiom "location, location, location" has long emphasized the importance of place to the retail mix. This is also known as marketing distribution. The physical *location* decision is important first because the retailer is making a large, semipermanent commitment of resources that can reduce its future flexibility. Second, the physical location will almost inevitably affect the store's future growth and profitability. Many retailers work with consultants and/or

city planners to determine the best sites for current sales as well as potential future growth. Wendy's uses geospatial data analytics to find new locations. The algorithms consider traffic patterns and average income of nearby businesses to select the area with the greatest earning potential.[29]

Physical site location begins by choosing a community. Important factors to consider are the area's economic growth potential, the amount of competition, and geography. For instance, retailers like T.J. Maxx and Walmart often build stores in new communities that are still under development. Convenience stores, such as RaceTrac or Speedway, often locate on the path of their customers' daily commutes, which regularly means choosing a space situated in or near a transit hub or along heavily trafficked routes. Specialty stores, like Sephora or Foot Locker, can benefit from locating themselves close to other shopping locations since their products, and the product offerings of other stores in the area, can complement one another. Furniture, automobile, or upscale clothing retailers often gain an advantage by locating their stores as far away from their rivals as possible so their customers will not be able to assess competing prices or easily comparison shop.[30] Even after careful research, however, the perfect location can be elusive in the face of changing markets. Mobile food trucks circumvent this problem by being able to relocate at will. By moving from spot to spot over the course of a day and parking outside events and heavily trafficked areas, mobile food trucks can maximize their exposure and adapt to changing markets.

After identifying a geographic region or community, retailers must choose a specific site. Besides growth potential, the important factors to consider are neighborhood socioeconomic characteristics, traffic flows, land costs, zoning regulations, and public transportation. A particular site's visibility, parking, entrance and exit locations, accessibility, and safety and security issues are also important considerations.

Dollar General locates its stores in rural or suburban areas where real estate costs are low to target consumers that often live miles away from a grocery store.

A retailer should consider how its store fits into the surrounding environment. Retail decision makers probably would not locate a Tractor Supply Company store next door to a Tiffany & Co. store. Furthermore, brick-and-mortar retailers have to decide whether to have a freestanding unit or to become a tenant in a shopping center or mall. Large retailers like Target and sellers of shopping goods like furniture and cars often use an isolated, freestanding location. A freestanding store location may have the advantages of low site cost or rent and no nearby competitors. On the other hand, it may be hard to attract customers to a freestanding location, and no other retailers are around to share costs. To be successful, stores in isolated locations must become "destination stores." A **destination store** is one that consumers seek out and purposely plan to visit. Websites can also be destinations for shoppers. Amazon is a destination website for a wide variety of products, and Google is a destination website for search information.

Freestanding units are increasing in popularity as brick-and-mortar retailers strive to make their stores more convenient to access, more enticing to shop, and more profitable. Freestanding sites now account for more than half of all retail store construction starts in the United States as more and more retailers are deciding not to locate in pedestrian malls. Perhaps the greatest reason for developing a freestanding site is greater visibility. Retailers often feel they get lost in huge shopping centers and malls, but freestanding units can help stores develop an identity with shoppers. Also, an aggressive expansion plan may not allow time to wait for shopping centers to be built. Drugstore chains like Walgreens have been purposefully relocating their existing shopping center stores to freestanding sites, especially street corner sites that offer drive-through accessibility.

Shopping centers first appeared in the 1950s when the U.S. population started migrating to the suburbs. The first shopping centers were *strip centers*, typically located along busy streets. They usually included a supermarket, a variety store, and perhaps a few specialty stores. Then *community shopping centers* emerged, with one or two small department stores, more specialty stores, a couple of restaurants, and several apparel stores. These community shopping centers provided off-street parking and a broader variety of merchandise. *Regional malls* offering a much wider variety of merchandise started appearing in the mid-1970s. Regional malls are either entirely enclosed or roofed to allow shopping in any weather. Most are landscaped with trees, fountains, sculptures, and the like

to enhance the shopping environment. They have acres of free parking. The *anchor stores* or *generator stores* (often major department stores) are usually located at opposite ends of the mall to create heavy foot traffic.

According to shopping center developers, *lifestyle centers* are emerging as the newest generation of shopping centers. Lifestyle centers typically combine outdoor shopping areas composed of upscale retailers and restaurants, with plazas, fountains, theaters, spas, coworking spaces, sports and entertainment facilities, hotels, residential units, and pedestrian streets. They appeal to retail developers looking for an alternative to the traditional shopping mall, a concept rapidly losing favor among shoppers. Though shopping malls bring multiple retail locations together, location is often not the most important motivator for a customer to choose a specific store. Instead, most shoppers look for stores that guarantee product availability, more service employees, and time-saving opportunities. Research indicates, for example, that to succeed, malls need to focus on transforming into *Consumer Engagement Spaces* based on the rising demand for things to do, rather than things to buy and own. Consumer Engagement Spaces focus heavily on experiential retail store formats complete with gyms, medical practices, nontraditional retailers, or ai augmented experiences for the consumer to enjoy a personalized brand experience. Also, pop-up shops are an important component since they give the shopper an unexpected treasure-hunting experience while simultaneously providing an experimental space for new retail concepts. Finally, these spaces need to include plenty of creative ways for visitors to spend their time, since time is the consumers' ultimate luxury, including options like restaurants, theaters, museums, and other engaging attractions.

Yet, despite the popularity of shopping malls in recent decades, the COVID-19 pandemic helped to accelerate the wide spread adoption of online shopping. Many traditional brick-and-mortar malls are struggling to survive. Anchor stores such as JCPenney and Macy's have closed hundreds of stores in recent years because of increased competition. Moreover, mall traffic is concentrating at fewer locations in affluent areas and tourist locations and is eroding in most other places.[31] As a result, online stores are also faced with the challenge of engagement with customers. Some of the online strategies include building communities, hosting webinars, encouraging co-creation, offering exclusive members-only content, and responding to feedback across a variety of channels and platforms.[32] Now that customers can easily travel from one site to the next without much effort, it will be important for retailers to find the strategy and channels that work best for their target market.

---

destination store a store that consumers purposely plan to visit prior to shopping

Price

Another important element in the retailing mix is price. Retailing's ultimate goal is to sell products to consumers, and the right price is critical to ensure sales. Because retail prices are usually based on the cost of the merchandise, an essential part of pricing is efficient and timely buying. Another pricing strategy is "value-based pricing," which focuses on the value of the product to the customer more than the cost of the product to the supplier. Price is also a key element in a retail store's positioning strategy. Higher prices often indicate a level of quality and help reinforce the prestigious image of retailers, as they do for Neiman Marcus (the United States), Printemps (France), Shinsegae (South Korea), Isetan (Japan), Daslu (Brazil), El Palacio de Hierro (Mexico), and Harrods (the United Kingdom). On the other hand, discounters and off-price retailers, such as Ross Stores and T.J. Maxx, offer a good value for the money.

Presentation

The presentation of a retail store helps determine the store's image and positions the retail store in consumers' minds. For instance, a retailer that wants to position itself as an upscale store would use a lavish or sophisticated presentation. The main element of a store's presentation is its **atmosphere**, the overall impression conveyed by a store's physical layout, decor, and surroundings. The atmosphere might create a relaxed or busy feeling, a sense of luxury or efficiency, a friendly or cold attitude, a sense of organization or clutter, or a fun or serious mood. Apple stores use a minimalist approach with all white, and clean surfaces to give customers a sleek, modern, and high-end sense of the organization. Apple's product packaging also reflects a sleek, modern approach. The following are the most influential factors in creating a store's atmosphere:

- **Employee type and density:** Employee type refers to an employee's general characteristics—for instance, neat, friendly, knowledgeable, or service oriented. Density is the number of employees per thousand square feet of selling space. While low employee density creates a do-it-yourself, casual atmosphere, high employee density denotes a readiness to serve the customer's every whim. Retailers must take care, therefore, to ensure that high employee density does not feel like "stalking" behavior to the customer. Research suggests that if shoppers feel as though store staff is too closely watching them, they can become uncomfortable and leave without completing their purchase.[33]

- **Merchandise type and density:** A prestigious retailer like Nordstrom or Neiman Marcus carries the best brand names and displays them in a neat, uncluttered arrangement. Discounters and off-price retailers often carry seconds or out-of-season goods crowded into small spaces and hung on long racks by category—tops, pants, skirts, and so on—creating the impression that "We've got so much stuff, we're practically giving it away."

- **Fixture type and density:** Fixtures can be elegant (rich woods) or trendy (chrome and smoked glass); they can even consist of old, beat-up tables, as in an antique store. The fixtures should be consistent with the general atmosphere the store is trying to create.

- **Sound:** Sound can be pleasant or unpleasant for a customer. Music can entice some customers to stay in the store longer and buy more or to eat quickly and leave a table for others. It can also control the pace of the store traffic, create an image, and attract or direct the shopper's attention. Studies show the type of music played can even influence a customer's choice of product or the perception of the amount of time spent in a store.[34] For example, when French or German music is played in a wine shop, more wines from that country are purchased. Moreover, when music that the customer normally listens to is played, they think little time has passed shopping.[35] Also, the presence of fast-tempo music has recently been demonstrated to entice customers to remain longer in crowded stores, which can increase the size of their purchases.[36]

- **Odors:** Smell can either stimulate or detract from sales. Research suggests that people evaluate merchandise more positively, spend more time shopping, and are generally in a better mood when an agreeable odor is present. Other research shows that certain scents empower consumers and lead to more premium purchases.[37] Retailers use fragrances as an extension of their retail strategy. Studies also show odors can imprint a strong image in a customer's mind and contribute to brand recall. That is why Auntie Anne's locates away from food courts—so the smell of its product does not compete with other food providers.

- **Visual factors:** Colors can create a mood or focus attention and therefore are an important factor in atmosphere. Red, yellow, and orange are considered warm colors and are used when a feeling of warmth and closeness is desired. Cool colors like

---

atmosphere the overall impression conveyed by a store's physical layout, decor, and surroundings

blue, green, and violet are used to open up closed-in places and create an air of elegance and cleanliness. Many retailers have found that natural lighting, either from windows or skylights, can lead to increased sales. Outdoor lighting can also affect a customer's choice of retailer.

The **layout** of retail stores is also a key factor in their success. The goal is to use all of the store's space effectively, including aisles, fixtures, merchandise displays, and non-selling areas. In addition to making shopping easy and convenient for the customer, an effective layout has a powerful influence on traffic patterns and purchasing behavior. Layout also includes where products are placed in the store. Many technologically advanced retailers are using a technique called *market-basket analysis* to sift through the data collected by their point-of-purchase scanning equipment. The analysis looks for products that are commonly purchased together to help retailers find ideal locations for each product. For example, a retailer may find that customers who purchase beer often also purchase salty snacks such as nuts or chips. Due to these findings, the merchant would try to place the two items in close proximity to one another.

Retailers can better acquire and use assets when they customize store layouts and merchandise mixes to the tastes of local consumer bases. For example, in large cities like New York, consumers live in smaller spaces and, therefore, would purchase items more frequently and in smaller packages compared to rural areas. Retailers in urban areas would offer a different layout compared to rural areas based on the more frequent trips to acquire basic necessities.

Retailers have had to adapt physical operations to a new normal that includes health and safety for both workers and customers, and experts expect many of these changes will be permanent. Retailers have also had to make the in-store experience more intriguing to draw customers out of the safety of their homes and into the physical space. A primary example has been the emergence of luxury cinemas. This redesign for delivery of luxury offerings is also evident in retailer electronic platforms. As an example, Artificial Intelligence enabled personal robot stylists are being used to assist in clothing selections. Moreover, in response to customer requests for social distancing and less contact, self-checkout and touchless payment systems are becoming the new norm.

Personnel

People are a unique aspect of retailing. Most retail sales involve a customer–salesperson relationship, if only briefly. Sales personnel provide their customers with the amount of service prescribed by the retail strategy of the store. For example, Peloton relies heavily on its salespeople since it uses the physical store merely as a showroom. The salesperson helps customers to experience what it would be like to own their product. Then an order is placed for home delivery.

Retail salespeople serve another important selling function: They persuade shoppers to buy. They must therefore be able to persuade customers that what they are selling is what the customer needs. Salespeople are trained in two common selling techniques: trading up and suggestion selling. *Trading up* means persuading customers to buy an item at a higher price than the one they originally intended to purchase. To avoid selling customers something they do not need or want, however, salespeople should take care when practicing trading-up techniques. *Suggestion selling*, a common practice among most retailers, seeks to broaden customers' original purchases with related items. For example, if you buy a new suit at Macy's the sales representative will ask if you would also like a new shirt or pair of shoes to complete the outfit. Suggestion selling by sales or service associates should always help shoppers recognize true needs rather than sell them unwanted merchandise.

Providing great customer service is one of the most challenging elements in the retail mix because customer expectations for service vary greatly. What customers expect in a department store is very different from what they expect in a discount store. Customer expectations also change. Ten years ago, shoppers wanted personal, one-on-one attention. Today, many customers are happy to help themselves as long as they can easily find what they need.

14-5c Enacting Shopper Marketing

Shopper marketing is an emerging retailing strategy that employs market data to best serve customers as they prepare to make a purchase. Shopper marketing focuses first on understanding how a brand's target consumers behave as shoppers in different channels and formats and then using this information in business-based strategies and initiatives that are carefully designed to deliver balanced benefits to all stakeholders—brands, channel members, and customers. It may sound simple, but it is

---

layout the internal design and configuration of a store's fixtures and products

shopper marketing understanding how one's target consumers behave as shoppers, in different channels and formats, and leveraging this intelligence to generate sales or other positive outcomes

anything but. While brand manufacturers used to advertise widely and tried to ensure that their products were available wherever consumers shopped, now they are placing far more emphasis on partnering with specific retailers or websites. Brand manufacturers work with retailers on everything from in-store initiatives to customized retailer-specific products. Shopper marketing brings brand managers and account managers together to connect with consumers along the entire path to purchase, whether it be at home, on the go via mobile marketing, or in the store. Both manufacturers and retailers now think about consumers specifically while they are in shopping mode. They use **shopper analytics** to dig deeply into customers' shopping attitudes, perceptions, emotions, and behaviors—and are thereby able to learn how the shopping experience shapes differences in these traits. Many multinational brands such as Procter & Gamble, Coca-Cola, Nestlé, Unilever, and PepsiCo use shopper analytics to develop targeted marketing strategies to optimize their distribution channels and overall sales.

Shopper marketing is becoming increasingly popular as businesses realize the implications of this new method of customer research. One implication is the strategic alignment of customer segments. Brands' core target consumers are compared to retailers' most loyal shoppers in an effort to find intersecting areas where brands and retailers can pool their resources. The ideal outcome is a more focused marketing effort and a three-way win for brands, channel members, *and* customers.

14-6 Retailing Decisions for Services

14-6 Discuss how services retailing differs from goods retailing

The fastest-growing part of our economy is the service sector. Although distribution in the service sector is difficult to visualize, the same skills, techniques, and strategies used to manage inventory can also be used to manage service inventory, such as hotel rooms, restaurant tables, or theatre seats. The quality of the planning and execution of distribution can have a major impact on costs and customer satisfaction.

Because service industries are so customer oriented, service quality is a priority. To manage customer relationships, many service providers, such as insurance carriers, physicians, hair salons, and financial services, use technology to schedule appointments, manage accounts, and disburse information. Service distribution focuses on four main areas:

1. **Minimizing wait times:** Minimizing the amount of time customers wait in line is a key factor in maintaining the quality of service.

2. **Managing service capacity:** If service firms don't have the capacity to meet demand, they must either turn down some prospective customers, let service levels slip, or expand capacity.

3. **Improving service delivery:** Service firms are now experimenting with different distribution channels for their services. Choosing the right distribution channel can increase the times that services are available or add to customer convenience.

4. **Establishing channel-wide network coherence:** Because services are to some degree intangible, service firms also find it necessary to standardize their service quality across different geographic regions to maintain their brand image.

14-7 Addressing Retail Product and Service Failures

14-7 Describe how retailers can address a product/service failure to turn it into an opportunity

In spite of retailers' best intentions and efforts to satisfy each and every customer, all retailers inevitably disappoint a subset of their customers. In some cases, customer disappointment occurs by design. No retailer can be everything to every customer, and by making strategic decisions related to targeting, segmentation, and the retailing mix, retailers implicitly decide which customers will be delighted and which will probably leave the store unsatisfied. In other cases, service failures are unintentional. A product may be located where customers cannot easily find it (or it may remain in the stockroom, entirely out of customer view), or an employee may provide mistaken information about a product's features or benefits. Customers are generally indifferent to the reasons for retailer errors, and their reactions to mistakes such as product stockouts and unexpectedly poor-quality products can range widely. Some may simply leave the store, while others will respond with anger or even revenge behaviors intended to prevent other customers from visiting the store.[38]

---

shopper analytics searching for and discovering meaningful patterns in shopper data for the purpose of fine-tuning, developing, or changing market offerings

The best retailers have plans in place to not only recover from inevitable lapses in service but perhaps even to benefit from them. For these top-performing stores, service recovery is handled proactively as part of an overarching plan to maximize the customer experience. Actions that might be taken include:

- Notifying customers in advance of stockouts and explaining the reasons why certain products are not available

- Implementing liberal return policies designed to ensure that the customer can bring back any item for any reason (if the product fails to work as planned or even if the customer simply doesn't like it)

- Issuing product recalls in conjunction with promotional offers that provide future incentives to repurchase

In short, the best retailers treat customer disappointments as opportunities to interact with and improve relations with their customers. Evidence indicates that successful handling of such failures can sometimes yield even higher levels of customer loyalty than if the failure had never occurred at all. The Ritz-Carlton prides itself on providing outstanding customer service even in the face of a service failure. A key to its success is empowering employees at all levels of the organization to resolve the situation without having to involve a superior.[39]

14-8 Retailer and Retail Customer Trends and Advancements

14-8 Summarize current trends related to retail technology

Though retailing has been around for thousands of years, it continues to change every day. Retailers are constantly innovating. They are always looking for new products and services (or ways to offer them) that will attract new customers or inspire current ones to buy in greater quantities or more frequently. Many of the most interesting and effective retail innovations that have recently taken hold are related to the use of purchase and shopping data to better understand customer wants and needs. Finding new and better ways to entice customers into a store—and then to spend more money once there—is another hotbed of innovation.

big data analytics the process of discovering patterns in large data sets for the purposes of extracting knowledge and understanding human behavior

This chapter concludes with an examination of emerging trends and recent advancements in retailing.

It is important to recognize that, fundamentally, retailers decide what to sell on the basis of what their target market wants to buy. They base these decisions on market research, past sales, fashion trends, customer requests, and other sources. Recently, the need for more and better information has led many retailers to use **big data analytics**, a process whereby retailers use complex mathematical models to make better product mix decisions. Costco is using big data to notify customers that purchased recalled products (based on their purchase history) rather than just sending out a major recall notice.[40] Groupon processes over one terabyte of data every day to match e-commerce sites with subscribers looking for discounts on travel, activities, and other goods or services.[41] The data that these and other companies collect at the point of sale and throughout their stores enable retailers and suppliers alike to gain better customer insights. For example, instead of simply unloading products into the distribution channel and leaving marketing, sales. and relationship building with local dealers, auto manufacturers use websites to stay connected with customers and prospects. They inquire about lifestyles, hobbies, and vehicle needs in an effort to develop long-lasting relationships in the hopes that these consumers will reward them with brand loyalty in the future.

For many years retail customers had become used to liberal return policies, for both instore and online purchases. This liberal policy on returns was made possible by retail data analytics systems. Retailers had no choice but to pause product returns at brick-and-mortar locations during state-mandated COVID-19 pandemic shutdowns. But after those closed businesses were opened, many encountered obstacles in setting up safe and effective returns management systems. As a result, companies are increasingly focusing on becoming more data driven in terms of forecasting returns. Some retailers are adjusting their traditional retail timelines to accommodate shopping patterns, including returns management and allowing time for products that have been in warehouses or returned to continue selling. For online retailers, using preventative steps to minimize returns is also helpful. Major reasons for returns include the item arriving damaged or broken and misleading item description. Monitoring customer reviews can also identify other factors. Resolving these issues may include better packaging and product descriptions, videos of products rather than static pictures, or the use of augmented reality or "fit true to size" reviews. Encouraging in-store returns has also been shown to result in 71 percent of individuals making an immediate purchase.[42]

Smart mirror technology can help businesses by allowing patrons to virtually try on clothes or ensure that a new hairstyle is something they will love before proceeding with the change.

Retailers are increasingly using **beacons**—devices that send out connecting signals to customers' smartphones and tablets. These devices recognize when a customer is in or near the store and indicate to an automated system that the customer is ripe to receive a marketing message via email or text. Beacons can also notify sales associates to offer (or not offer) a coupon at the point of sale. Some retailers are using an app called Swarm to map customer foot traffic data, which they use to make better decisions about product placement within the floor grid. Carefully designed beacons can even have an aesthetic appeal. At some retailers, cameras and beacons are built into mannequins located inside the store and in window displays. These beacons act not as only data-collection devices but also as primary displays for the clothing and jewelry that appeal to customers' eyes.[43]

RFID (radio-frequency identification) is not a new technology, but its use has diversified greatly over the past few years. Traditionally used for inventory management purposes before items reach the sales floor, retailers have begun using RFID to track items that customers pick up while shopping. This enables a retailer to instantly create a promotion for the specific item in a customer's hand. For example, if a customer picks up a set of sheets, the retailer can use RFID and digital advertising to suggest related items, such as pillowcases, blankets, and even paint colors that match the sheets. The advertisement can provide guidance as to where to find the promoted items in the store. Also, RFID has the potential to make the checkout process much faster by enabling an entire cart of products to be scanned in seconds.[44]

Retailers have begun using another emerging technology: facial recognition. Suppose a retailer scans a customer to determine the customer's age group. The retailer can then cross-reference these data with the customer's location in the store, providing promotions and information with pinpoint accuracy. Facial recognition even allows retailers to identify customers, call them by their names, and target them with personalized advertising based on their data as they walk through the retail space. Similarly, biometric sensors can be used to measure how long a customer views an ad or product in the store. These data can be used as a measure of interest and/or ad effectiveness.[45] Similarly, technology at self-checkout system can notify staff when to individuals appear to be underage when buying restricted items like alcohol, tobacco, or vapes.[46]

In 2022, 35 percent of all U.S. consumers owned a voice-assistant smart speaker device, like Alexa, Siri, or Google Home, with 52 percent of owners using the device on a daily basis.[47] Conversational artificial intelligence (AI) powers these voice technology systems and is quickly revolutionizing retail. Retailers use this emerging technology to develop highly personalized relationships with customers and to become their first and only choice, especially when reordering simple items. As conversational artificial intelligence continues to improve, retailers aspire to use its capabilities to provide a world-class customer service experience for shoppers, complete with AI-driven personalized recommendations and on-demand customer support. Also, by engaging in voice-assisted commerce, the consumer enjoys a dialogue throughout their product search process, which capitalizes on the recent trend toward experiential retailing. Retailers will find the most success from this emerging technology, however, if they are able to quickly and seamlessly integrate the voice-assisted commerce activity into their existing physical and digital channels to create an effective omnichannel experience for the user.[48] In fact, the emergence of voice-assisted commerce is motivating retailers to seek guidance on the most effective voice strategy to serve their customers.

Companies like REYDAR offer customers the opportunity to visualize new flooring in their own home by using augmented reality.

beacon a device that sends out connecting signals to customers' smartphones and tablets to bring them into a retail store or improve their shopping experience

14-8a Future Developments in Retail Management

A retailing trend with great growth potential is the leveraging of technology to increase touchpoints and engagement with customers and thereby generate greater profitability. The use of mobile devices and social media while browsing, comparison shopping, and actually making a purchase is becoming extremely pervasive, leading retailers to rethink how they should appeal to shoppers in the decision-making mode. Recall that customers who "showroom" visit a physical retail store to examine product features or quality firsthand, but then eventually make the purchase online. This practice has motivated a showrooming response from retailers themselves, who reduce the amount of stock kept on hand, rent or lease smaller spaces, and ramp up their fulfillment capabilities at distribution centers. Showrooming and data analytics have even led to the development of virtual reality apps and smart mirrors that enable customers to look at themselves wearing articles of desired clothing without physically putting them on! These approaches have led some retailers to pursue a strategy of **retail channel omnification** (recall the discussion of omnichannel distribution operations in Chapter 13). Retailers like Disney are making it easy for consumers to transition from online to in person experiences. Once customers book their vacation, they can begin planning using the My Disney Experience tool. Once in the park, the mobile app can be used to locate the experiences marked in the My Disney Experience tool. The app provides estimated wait times for attractions and works in combination with the Magic Band program. These bands allow customers to lighten the load when entering the park since the band serves as admission ticket, hotel key, FastPass, PhotoPass, and touchless charge to the credit card on file. The Magic Band can also make a great keepsake since some light-up and are customizable.[49] Customers of Disney can seamlessly transition between each of these channels when planning, shopping, enjoying the park, or scheduling reservations for dinner at Cinderella's castle!

However, not all retailers are embracing omnification as the way of the future. An alternative strategy, **click-and-collect**, also enables customers to make their purchases online. Rather than waiting for orders to arrive at their homes, customers drive to physical stores to pick their orders up.[50] Starbucks app users, for example, can eliminate waiting in line by placing an order and paying in advance. When retailers use this strategy, customers benefit from greater speed of delivery (in fact, they become the delivery vehicle), while retailers themselves benefit from the fact that customers must enter their stores to claim their purchases. Once inside, customers can be marketed to, increasing the likelihood that they will purchase add-on items or otherwise engage in impulse buying. It's not yet clear whether one or both of these strategies will stand the test of time, but it is certain that retailers are preparing for the inevitability of the internet as an important shopping and purchasing medium for the foreseeable future.

Another fascinating trend is the use of artificial intelligence as a touch point for customers. Robots are replacing or augmenting retail employees at restaurants, supermarkets, and airports across the globe. For example, Sam's Club deployed automated inventory analytics robots to scan inventory to ensure items are available for purchase. These robots relieve associates from this time-consuming task to devote their efforts to the member shopping experience.[51] Further, amid the labor shortage following the start of the COVID-19 pandemic, some restaurants began to utilize robots to fill in the gap. Not only can the robot work longer shifts than humans, but it doesn't need breaks and won't call in sick.[52] As technology progresses, customers will begin to notice virtual reality used in many retail contexts. Virtual reality enables customers to try items before they buy—even if those items don't actually exist yet The integration of these new technologies will bring customers a shopping experience like they have never had before—both highly interactive and customized.

Shopper marketing faced many challenges when the COVID-19 pandemic increased the demand for online shopping, one of which was the need to add omnichannel options. As a result, omnichannel was no longer a "nice to have" approach for retailers—it increasingly was a strategy retailers had to invest in to survive. At the same time, integration of inventory for brick and click operations motivated companies to rethink inventory strategies, and some found out cost savings were possible. The increase in online shopping produced higher demand for warehouse space, resulting in some price increases unless a better balance could be achieved between demand and manufacturing. Retailers have already begun thinking about whether better inventory balancing is possible and also evaluating whether to focus on improved forecasting accuracy or increasing warehousing space. In short, more storage space will

---

retail channel omnification the reduction of multiple retail channel systems into a single, unified system for the purpose of creating efficiencies or saving costs

click-and-collect the practice of buying something online and then traveling to a physical store location to take delivery of the merchandise

likely be needed unless retailers can more effectively integrate their inventory for brick and click operations as a single, coordinated system.

As retailers became accustomed to constrained supply during the pandemic, they recognized that narrower customer choice had become an unexpected benefit, thereby increasing profitability through cost savings that offset sales price reductions. At the same time, the long-held belief that more choice results in more revenue was adjusted by the realization that incremental variety can lead to incremental costs that outstrip the revenue gained from merchandise variety. Finally, as omnichannel distribution accelerated retail analytics has been increasingly applied to create real time automated/flexible pricing changes. This technology tool has enabled many retailers to better track, monitor and compare their product and pricing offers, and facilitated real-time reactions that have increased online competitiveness.

Stock-Asso/Shutterstock.com

Part 5

Chapter 15

Marketing Communications

Learning Outcomes

After studying this chapter, you will be able to...

15-1 Discuss the role of promotion in the marketing mix

15-2 Describe the communication process

15-3 Explain the goals of promotion

15-4 Discuss the elements of the promotional mix

15-5 Discuss how the AIDA concept relates to the promotional mix

15-6 Explain the concept of integrated marketing communications

15-7 Describe the factors that affect the promotional mix

15-1 The Role of Promotion in the Marketing Mix

15-1 Discuss the role of promotion in the marketing mix

Few goods or services, no matter how well developed, priced, or distributed, can survive in the marketplace without effective **promotion**—communication by marketers that informs, persuades, and reminds potential buyers of a product to influence an opinion or elicit a response.

Promotional strategy is a plan for the optimal use of the elements of promotion: advertising, public relations, personal selling, sales promotion, and digital and social media. Promotion is a vital part of the marketing mix, informing consumers of a product's benefits and thereby positioning the product in the marketplace. As Figure 15.1 shows, the marketing manager determines the goals of the company's promotional strategy in light of the firm's overall goals for the marketing mix—product, place (distribution), promotion, and price. Using these overall goals, marketers combine the elements of the promotional strategy (the promotional mix) into a coordinated plan. The promotion plan then becomes an integral part of the marketing strategy for reaching the target market.

The main function of a marketer's promotional strategy is to convince target customers that the goods and services offered provide a competitive advantage over the competition. A **competitive advantage** is the set of unique features of a company and its products that are perceived by the target market as significant and superior to those of the competition. Such features can include high product quality, rapid delivery, low prices, excellent service, or some feature not offered by the competition. Promotional strategies have changed a great deal over the years as many targeted customer segments have become more difficult to reach. Informative television advertisements are no longer enough, forcing marketers to think more creatively. Most campaigns utilize a variety of tactics—such as digital paid media, social media, and influencer marketing—in addition to more traditional media like television and print. Domino's is an example of a company that uses data analytics to develop campaigns and also to connect campaigns to pop culture. For example, partnered with the fourth season of *Stranger Things*, Domino's set out to target a younger demographic. Leveraging a combination of eye tracking, facial recognition and gesture control, Domino's launched a "mind-ordering" app. The app allowed users to levitate objects like *Stranger Things* character Eleven. The gamification eventually allowed players to order a pizza. Using Netflix data analysis related to *Stranger Things*, three themes were identified: supernatural, friendship, and nostalgia. Beyond the app, Domino's also deployed retro-themed pizza boxes to draw on the nostalgia theme. The 30-second ad titled "Stranger Order," landed Domino's in the top 20 percent for creative ads for their target market, but in the top 10 percent among *Stranger Things* fans, making the campaign a success.[1]

15-2 Marketing Communication

15-2 Describe the communication process

Promotional strategy is closely related to the process of communication. As humans, we assign meaning to feelings, ideas, facts, attitudes, and emotions. **Communication** is the process by which meanings are exchanged or shared through a common set of symbols. When a company develops a new product, changes an

---

Figure 15.1   Role of Promotion in the Marketing Mix

---

promotion communication by marketers that informs, persuades, and reminds potential buyers of a product to influence an opinion or elicit a response

promotional strategy a plan for the optimal use of the elements of promotion: advertising, public relations, personal selling, sales promotion, and social media

competitive advantage one or more unique aspects of an organization that cause target consumers to patronize that firm rather than competitors

communication the process by which we exchange or share meaning through a common set of symbols

old one, or simply tries to increase sales of an existing good or service, it must communicate its selling message to potential customers. Marketers communicate information about the firm and its products to the target market and various publics through their promotional programs.

15-2a Interpersonal Communication

Communication can be divided into two major categories: interpersonal communication and mass communication. **Interpersonal communication** is direct, face-to-face communication between two or more people. When communicating face-to-face, people notice the other person's reaction and can respond almost immediately. Since communication is comprised of 55 percent nonverbal, 38 percent vocal and 7 percent words only, being able to recognize the nonverbal cues and hear the tone of voice is the only means of gathering the full message.[2] For companies, being able to see and hear customers, as well as react and respond is one of the best ways to obtain the full intent of the message. Research has shown that emotionally intelligent salespeople, or those more aware of others' emotions, have improved relationships with their customers. Further, the customers of salespeople with high levels of emotional intelligence are more satisfied which increases sales performance compared to salespeople lacking in emotional intelligence.[3]

15-2b Mass Communication

Mass communication involves communicating a concept or message to large audiences. A great number of marketing communications are directed to consumers as a group, usually through a mass medium such as television or magazines. When a company advertises, it generally does not personally know the people with whom it is trying to communicate. Moreover, the company often cannot respond immediately to consumers' reactions to its messages unless they are using social media or digital-based tools. Clutter from competitors' messages or other distractions in the environment can reduce the effectiveness of mass-communications efforts. Microsoft, for example, uses many different mass media vehicles (including magazines and digital media) to reach its target audience.

Mass communication involves communicating a concept or message to large audiences. Electronic billboards are a means of targeting consumers through mass communication.

15-2c The Communication Process

Marketers are both senders and receivers of messages. As *senders*, marketers attempt to inform, persuade, and remind the target market to take actions compatible with the need to promote the purchase of goods and services. As *receivers*, marketers listen to the target market to develop the appropriate messages, adapt existing messages, and spot new communication opportunities. In this way, most marketing communication is a two-way, rather than one-way, process. The two-way nature of the communication process is shown in Figure 15.2.

The Sender and Encoding

The **sender** is the originator of the message in the communication process. In an interpersonal conversation, the sender may be a parent, a friend, or a salesperson. For an advertisement, press release, or social media campaign, the sender is the company or organization itself. Social media influencers are people who promote products and services on social media platforms like Instagram and TikTok; they are also considered senders on behalf of marketers. In fact, it sometimes is difficult to tell who the sender of a promotional message is, especially in the case of bold, unusual advertisements. For example, the Dove Real Beauty campaign set out to build self-confidence in women and teens by focusing on the positive elements of beauty and making women feel comfortable in their skin. The campaign focused on purpose rather than product. This strategy led to an increase in word-of-mouth (WOM) marketing and free marketing coverage from talk shows and radio discussions. Furthermore, it led to increased brand awareness as well as an increase in sales. Ad Age rated it in the top five campaigns of the 21st century which helped to bring awareness to the tradition of ads distorting reality.

---

interpersonal communication direct, face-to-face communication between two or more people

mass communication the communication of a concept or message to large audiences

sender the originator of the message in the communication process

Figure 15.2 Communication Process

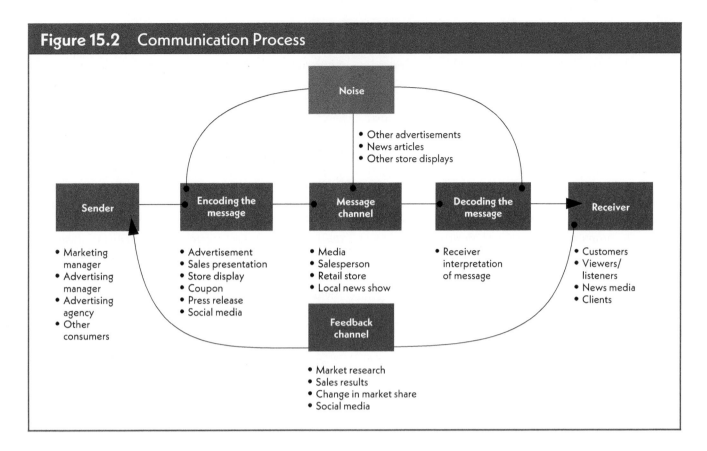

Most importantly, the campaign improved self-esteem and led the way for other companies to follow their success with unedited, body-positive messages.[4]

Encoding is the conversion of the sender's ideas and thoughts into a message, usually in the form of words, signs, images, or videos. A basic principle of encoding is that what the source says is not what matters, it is what the receiver hears. In the case of the Dove Real Beauty campaign, raw and emotional videos challenged stereotypes, including self-beliefs, to provoke thought and increase self-confidence.[5] One way of conveying a message the receiver will hear properly is to use concrete words and pictures.

Message Transmission

Transmission of a message requires a **channel**—a voice, radio, newspaper, computer, smartphone, social media platform, or other communication medium. A facial expression or gesture can also serve as a channel. For Dove, a centerpiece of the campaign was a video titled Dove Real Beauty Sketches, in which women described themselves to a forensic sketch artist who could not see them. Next, another individual described the same woman to the forensic artist. The result shows that women describe themselves more unfavorably than others describe them, with the powerful message, "you're more beautiful than you think."[6] The response to this specific ad created a lot of free publicity.

Reception occurs when the message is detected by the receiver and enters their frame of reference. In a two-way conversation such as a sales pitch given by a sales representative to a potential client, reception is normally high. Similarly, when the message is a recommendation from a friend, the reception is high. Even in social media, if the social media influencer responds to likes and comments, the reception is high. By contrast, the desired receivers may or may not detect the message when it is mass communicated because most media are cluttered by **noise**—anything that interferes with, distorts, or slows down the transmission of information. In some media overcrowded with advertisers, such as billboards and television, the noise level is high, and the reception level is low.

The Receiver and Decoding

Marketers communicate their message through a channel to customers, or **receivers**, who will decode the message. It is important to note that there can be multiple receivers, as consumers share their experiences and their

---

encoding the conversion of a sender's ideas and thoughts into a message, usually in the form of words or signs

channel a medium of communication—such as a voice, radio, or newspaper—for transmitting a message

noise anything that interferes with, distorts, or slows down the transmission of information

receiver the person who decodes a message

recommendations online through social networks and other types of social media. Online conversations are an influential way to promote products and services. Indeed, this empowerment of the receiver has transformed marketing and advertising. Receivers can easily share new information with their friends and followers on social media, and those new receivers can then also share that information. In fact, reviews and online comments have become important information for other receivers. This leads to a more diverse interrelationship between senders and receivers of social media messages. **Decoding** is the interpretation of the language and symbols sent by the source through a channel. A common understanding between two communicators, or a common frame of reference, is required for effective communication. Therefore, marketing managers must ensure a proper match between the message to be conveyed and the target market's attitudes and ideas.

Even though a message has been received, it may not necessarily be properly decoded because of selective exposure, distortion, and retention. When people receive a message, they tend to manipulate it to reflect their own biases, needs, experiences, and knowledge. Therefore, differences in age, social class, education, culture, and ethnicity can lead to miscommunication. Further, because people do not always listen or read carefully, they can easily misinterpret what is said or written. In fact, researchers have found that consumers misunderstand a large proportion of both printed and broadcast communications. Bright colors and bold graphics increase consumers' comprehension of marketing communications. But these techniques are not foolproof. The Dove Real Beauty campaign was easily decoded by its target audience, and it resonated with them. For example, research following the campaign showed improvements in women's self-esteem.[7]

Marketers targeting consumers in foreign countries must also worry about the translation and possible miscommunication of their promotional messages by other cultures. Global marketers must decide whether to standardize or customize the message for each global market in which they sell.

Feedback

In interpersonal communication, the receiver's response to a message is direct **feedback** to the source. Feedback may be verbal, as in saying "I agree" or "I do not like this new product." But it can also be nonverbal, as in nodding, smiling, frowning, or gesturing. Feedback can also occur digitally, as in a like or comment on social media platforms, a comment on a blog post, or a message sent through a website contact form. In the case of the Dove Real Beauty campaign, feedback is not only sales in support of the campaign, but also liking, commenting, or sharing the social media campaign is feedback. The feedback can be positive or negative. In fact, social media influencers do all they can to encourage engagement on social media platforms through comments, responses, or by getting people to share the message on their stories. Mass communicators are often cut off from some direct feedback, so they must rely on market research, social media, or analysis of viewer responses for indirect feedback. They may use such measurements as the percentage of television viewers who recognized, recalled, or stated that they were exposed to the company's messages. Indirect feedback enables mass communicators to decide whether to continue, modify, or drop a message.

With online advertising, marketers can get more feedback than before digital platforms became such a driving social force. Using web analytics, marketers can understand how long customers stay on a website and which pages they view. Moreover, social media enable companies such as Disney, Domino's, Adidas, and Nintendo to provide instant feedback by responding to consumers' posts on Facebook and to complaints on social network platforms such as Twitter, now known as X.

Digital platforms and social media have had an impact on the communication model in two major ways. First, consumers are now able to become senders (as opposed to only brands being senders). For example, a professional blogger or Instagram influencer who recommends a product, and thus influences a consumer's decision to buy it, is a sender. Similarly, everyday consumers who make casual recommendations on Facebook and Yelp are essentially senders as well. Clearly, the communication model is much more complicated today than it was just a few years ago. Second, the communication model displays the feedback channel as primarily impersonal and numbers driven. In the traditional communication process, marketers can view the results of customer behavior (e.g., a drop or rise in sales) but can explain those changes only by using their judgment. Today, customers use social media platforms like Facebook, X, and Instagram to comment publicly on marketing efforts. These platforms enable marketers to personalize the feedback channel by opening the door for direct conversations with customers. But because social media conversations occur in real time and are public, any negative posts or complaints are highly visible. Thus, many companies have crisis communication strategies to deal with negative information and to promote good brand reputations.

---

decoding interpretation of the language and symbols sent by the source through a channel

feedback the receiver's response to a message

Negative online customer reviews provide marketers with feedback and an opportunity for direct communication to resolve the issue.

15-3 The Goals of Promotion

15-3 Explain the goals of promotion

People communicate with one another for many reasons. They seek amusement, ask for help, give assistance or instructions, provide information, and express ideas and thoughts. Promotion, on the other hand, seeks to modify behavior and thoughts in some way. For example, promoters may try to persuade consumers to buy a Ford Bronco rather than a Jeep Wrangler. Promotion also strives to reinforce existing behavior—for instance, getting consumers to continue buying Jeep once they have switched. The source (the seller) hopes to project a favorable image or to motivate the purchase of the company's goods and services.

Promotion can perform one or more of four tasks: *inform* the target audience, *persuade* the target audience, *remind* the target audience, or *connect* with the audience. The ability to *connect* to consumers is one task that can be facilitated through social media. Often a marketer will try to accomplish two or more of these tasks at the same time.

15-3a Informing

Informative promotion seeks to convert an existing need into a want or to stimulate interest in a new product. It is generally more prevalent during the early stages of the product life cycle. People typically will not buy a product or service or support a nonprofit organization until they know its purpose and its benefits. Informative messages are important for promoting complex and technical products such as automobiles, computers, and investment services. For example, after the release of Uber Eats, the commercials released by Uber explained the Uber One membership that combines all of the benefits such as discounts on rides and orders, credits for late deliveries, and no delivery fees.[8] Informative promotion is also important for a "new"

brand being introduced into an "old" product class. Dyson, the maker of vacuum cleaners, Airblade Hand Dryers, and bladeless fans, utilized its knowledge of airflow to enter the hair dryer market. The high-performing hair dryer received rave reviews online across social media platforms which supported the company's efforts to inform consumers.[9] The customer reviews provided information outside of that which was being provided by the company which increased the credibility of the information as well. New products cannot establish themselves against more mature products unless potential buyers are aware of them, value their benefits, and understand their positioning in the marketplace.

15-3b Persuading

Persuasive promotion is designed to stimulate a purchase or an action. Persuasion typically becomes the main promotion goal when the product enters the growth stage of its life cycle. By the growth stage, the target market should have general product awareness and some knowledge of how the product can fulfill its wants. Therefore, the promotional task switches from informing consumers about the product category to persuading them to buy the company's brand rather than that of the competitor. The promotional message therefore emphasizes the product's real and perceived competitive advantages, often appealing to emotional needs such as love, belonging, self-esteem, and ego satisfaction. For example, Pringles used comedy to highlight the common mishap of consumers getting their hands wedged in the can trying to get the last of the chips. The commercial sought to persuade consumers by declaring the discomfort experienced is "worth it."[10]

As the market for electric vehicles grows, more manufacturers are entering the race. This increase in competition puts pressure on companies to differentiate while keeping prices in check. Consumers have choices beyond the initial sedan option, including the Jeep Wrangler 4xe, Hummer EV, Ford F-150 Lightning, and Volvo Recharge. Super Bowl commercials have been a major platform for highlighting unique qualities, such as the differences in electrical vehicles, compared to competitors as a persuasive technique.[11] Persuasion can therefore be an important goal for very competitive mature product categories, such as personal care items and soft drinks In a marketplace characterized by many competitors, the promotional message often encourages brand switching and aims to convert some buyers into loyal users. But some critics believe promotional messages and techniques can be too persuasive, causing consumers to buy products and services they don't really need.

15-3c Reminding

Reminder promotion is used to keep the product and brand name in the public's mind. This type of promotion prevails during the maturity stage of the life cycle. It assumes that the target market has already been persuaded of the merits of the good or service. Its purpose is to trigger a memory that leads to a purchase. Oreo cookies and other consumer products often use reminder promotions. Reminder advertising is often used for consumer services as well. Companies that produce products like tires and appliances advertise throughout the year to remind people about the brands when they are looking to purchase. In an April Fools' Day prank, Stouffer's posted to Instagram a reminder promotion targeted to younger generations. The post showed the image of a box of lasagna with a modified label with the company name, product name, and ingredients. Instead of Stouffer's, it read "Stouff's." The product was "Sagna with Mauce." The caption on the post read, "Saving time is the Stouff's way so we've shortened the product names of your favs! Other abbrevs you'd love to see? Drop 'em below!" The post not only reminds consumers of the product, but also targets a highly coveted demographic, and invites engagement.[12]

15-3d Connecting

The focus of social media is to form relationships with customers and potential customers through technological ties such as Instagram, TikTok, Facebook, or other social media platforms. In forming these relationships, the goal is for them to lead to customer engagement with the products or services, and ultimately to purchases. Indeed, some companies, such as Starbucks, have their own social networks that enable customers to share ideas, information, and feedback. By facilitating this exchange of information through a transparent process, brands are increasingly connecting with their customers in hopes that they become brand advocates who promote the brand through their own social networks. Tools for connection include social networks, social games, and social publishing tools as well as social commerce. For example, Breast Cancer Now, the research and care charity, uses personalized videos on social media to recognize donations to the campaign. In addition to regular tweets of appreciation on X, the organization sends special videos to the individuals. It also offers a themed photo frame for supporters to add to its Facebook profile picture and have a hashtag (#wearitpink) in which

Source: Stouffer's

supporters can join in the action by posting their efforts to dress up for Wear It Pink Day![13]

15-4 The Promotional Mix

15-4 Discuss the elements of the promotional mix

Most promotional strategies use several ingredients—which may include advertising, public relations, sales promotion, personal selling, and social media—to reach a target market. That combination is called the **promotional mix**. The proper promotional mix is the one that management believes will meet the needs of the target market and fulfill the organization's overall goals. Data and data analytics play a very important role in how marketers distribute funding among their promotional mix tactics. Spotify, for example, uses data analytics to compile a listener's year in a review called Wrapped. This visual, which is one of the world's most highly shared campaigns, shows listeners their musical statistics over the year. It also showcases the user's musical mood evolution from morning to night. Spotify then identifies each user into one of 16 "listening personalities" or personas from a marketing perspective, such as "The Adventurer" or "The Connoisseur." Then using the information from this data, Spotify has allowed artists to make special offers to their biggest fans, for products or early event tickets, which has resulted in record-breaking sales.[14]

15-4a Advertising

Almost all companies selling a good or a service use advertising, whether in the form of a multimillion-dollar campaign or a simple classified ad in a newspaper. **Advertising** is any form of impersonal paid communication in which the sponsor or company is identified. Media—such as television, radio, newspapers, magazines, pay-per-click search advertising, digital display advertising, social media advertising, direct mail, billboards, and transit advertising (such as on buses and taxis and at bus stops), product

---

promotional mix the combination of promotional tools—including advertising, public relations, personal selling, sales promotion, and social media—used to reach the target market and fulfill the organization's overall goals

advertising impersonal, one-way mass communication about a product or organization that is paid for by a marketer

placement (television, movie, or video game), websites, email marketing, blog, video, and interactive games—are often used to transmit advertisements to consumers. However, marketing budgets are shifting away from traditional communication media and toward digital options (such as social media). In fact, spending on digital advertising now exceeds spending on advertising through traditional media. And as digital marketing becomes a vital component of many companies' promotion and marketing mixes, consumers and lawmakers are increasingly concerned about possible violations of consumers' privacy or security. Several governments have restricted access to TikTok and other ByteDance-owned apps from government devices for fear of security threats.[15]

One of the primary benefits of advertising is its ability to communicate to a large number of people at one time. Cost per contact, therefore, is typically very low. Advertising has the advantage of being able to reach the masses (e.g., through national television networks), but it can also be microtargeted to small groups of potential customers, such as through television ads on a targeted cable network or shows on digital streaming services, such as Hulu or ESPN. Although the *cost per contact* in advertising is very low, the *total cost* to advertise, particularly for traditional media, is typically very high. This hurdle tends to restrict advertising on a national basis for many brands. Chapter 16 examines advertising in greater detail.

15-4b Public Relations

Concerned about how they are perceived by their target markets, organizations often spend large sums to build a positive public image. **Public relations** is the marketing function that evaluates public attitudes, identifies areas within the organization the public may be interested in, and executes a program of action to earn public understanding and acceptance. Public relations helps an organization communicate with its stakeholders, including customers, suppliers, stockholders, government officials, employees, and the community in which it operates. The Internet has expanded the role of public relations, as crisis communication and online stakeholder management become more important. Marketers use public relations not only to maintain a positive image, but also to educate the public about the company's goals and objectives, introduce new products, support the sales effort, and respond to customer-generated communications.

A public relations program can generate favorable **publicity**—public information about a company, product, service, or issue appearing in the mass media as a news item. Social media sites like X can provide large amounts of publicity quickly. Organizations generally do not pay for publicity and are not identified as the source of the

Source: ProductPlacementBlog.com

Advertising can show up in many ways, shapes, and forms. Product placement is prevalent in shows like *Riverdale*. Core Hydration's water product is prominently displayed in many episodes of the show.

information, but they can benefit tremendously from it. However, while organizations do not directly pay for publicity, it should not be viewed as free. Preparing news releases, staging special events, and persuading media personnel to broadcast or print publicity messages costs money. Public relations and publicity are examined further in Chapter 16.

15-4c Sales Promotion

Sales promotion consists of all marketing activities—other than personal selling, advertising, and public relations—that stimulate consumer purchasing and dealer effectiveness. Sales promotion is generally a short-run tool used to stimulate immediate increases in demand. Sales promotion can be aimed at end consumers, trade customers, or a company's employees. Sales promotions include free samples, contests, premiums, rebates, trade shows, vacation giveaways, and coupons. They also include experiential marketing whereby marketers create or participate in events that enable customers to connect with brands. For example, at a conference, Marvel had a photo booth in which participants walked away with not just a photo, but a printed personalized one-page comic strip where

---

public relations the marketing function that evaluates public attitudes, identifies areas within the organization the public may be interested in, and executes a program of action to earn public understanding and acceptance

publicity public information about a company, product, service, or issue appearing in the mass media as a news item

sales promotion marketing activities—other than personal selling, advertising, and public relations—that stimulate consumer buying and dealer effectiveness

they were a main character in the comic.[16] Companies like Groupon have combined social networks and sales promotions, and social media sites like Facebook are expanding their promotion platforms through built-in contests and sweepstakes tools.

Marketers often use sales promotion to improve the effectiveness of other ingredients in the promotional mix, especially advertising and personal selling. Research shows that sales promotion complements advertising by yielding faster sales responses. For example, MVMT Watches offers a first-time buyer discount code to help incentivize individuals and build the company's customer base. The promotion is conveyed in a popup message on its website.[17] In many instances, more marketing money is spent on sales promotion than on advertising.

15-4d Personal Selling

Personal selling is a purchase situation involving personal, paid-for communication between two people in an attempt to influence each other. In this dyad, both the buyer and the seller have specific objectives they wish to accomplish. The objective for the buyer, for example, may be to minimize cost or facilitate the selection of a quality product, while the seller often wants to maximize sales and profits.

Traditional methods of personal selling include a planned presentation to one or more prospective buyers to make a sale. Whether it takes place face to face or over the phone, personal selling attempts to persuade the buyer to accept a point of view. For example, an electronics salesperson may try to persuade a potential buyer of the benefits of a particularly high-end television. Once the buyer is somewhat convinced, the salesperson may attempt to elicit some action from the buyer, such as learning to program favorite channels or a purchase. Frequently, in this traditional view of personal selling, the objectives of the salesperson are at the expense of the buyer, creating a win–lose outcome.

More current notions of personal selling emphasize the relationship that develops between a salesperson and a buyer. Initially, this concept was more typical in business-to-business selling situations, involving the sale of products like automotive parts or electronics. More recently, both business-to-business (B-to-B) and business-to-consumer (B-to-C) selling focus on building long-term relationships rather than on making a onetime sale.

Relationship selling emphasizes a win–win outcome and the accomplishment of mutual objectives that benefit both buyer and salesperson in the long term. Rather than focusing on a quick sale, relationship selling attempts to create a long-term, committed relationship based on trust, increased customer loyalty, and a continuation of the relationship between the salesperson and the customer. In the case of the television sale previously mentioned, the salesperson seeks to satisfy the buyer so that if their needs change, they can not only help the buyer find other electronics but also can replace their televisions in the future. Personal selling, like other promotional mix elements, is increasingly dependent on digital communications. Most companies use their websites to attract potential buyers seeking information on products and services and to drive customers to their physical locations, where personal selling can close the sale. Personal selling is discussed further in Chapter 17.

15-4e Content Marketing and Social Media

As promotional strategies change, and since brands now can become publishers, content marketing is an increasingly crucial part of promotion. Recall from Chapter 7 that content marketing entails developing valuable content for interested audience members, and then using digital marketing, search engine optimization, paid search, and display advertising to pull customers to the company's website or social media channel so that the audiences can learn about the brand or make a purchase. Content created by brands is typically distributed through social media and other digital channels.

Recall that social media are promotion tools used to facilitate conversations and create engagement and other interactions among people online. When used by marketers, these tools facilitate consumer empowerment. Consumers can speak directly to other consumers, the company, and web communities. Social media includes blogs, microblogs (such as X), video platforms (such as YouTube), podcasting (online audio and video broadcasts), and social networks (such as LinkedIn, Pinterest, Instagram, and Snapchat).

Initially, individuals used social media tools primarily for self-expression. For example, a teacher might develop a video platform to showcase their songwriting because that is their hobby. Or a college freshman might develop a profile on Facebook to stay in touch with high school friends. But soon, businesses realized that these tools could be used to engage with consumers. Today, social media is everywhere. The rise of streaming video, and the internet infrastructure to support video streaming, for example, has created a completely new way for

---

personal selling a purchase situation involving a personal, paid-for communication between two people in an attempt to influence each other

With so many social media platforms, companies must determine the platforms that best integrate into their promotional mix to reach the desired target market.

marketers to manage their image, connect with consumers, and generate interest in, engagement with, and desire for their companies' products. Blogging has also led to a new type of influencer marketing, whereby social media influencers create their own digital channels (on YouTube, Instagram, and other social media platforms) to promote brands and products and earn income. Marketers are now using social media as integral components of their campaigns and as a way to extend the benefits of their use of traditional media. Social media is discussed in more detail in Chapter 18.

15-4f The Communication Process and the Promotional Mix

The Internet and digital communications have changed how businesses promote their brands. Traditionally, marketing managers have been in charge of defining the essence of the brand. This included complete brand control and mostly one-way communication between the brand and customers. All of the content and messages were focused on defining and communicating brand value. The focus for many campaigns was pure entertainment, and the brand created all of the content for promotional campaigns—from the website to television spots to print ads.

That approach has now changed. The consumer has much more control (which makes some brands quite nervous!) as the consumer increasingly controls the communication space and the brand message. Perception is reality, as consumers have more control to adapt the brand message to fit their ideas. Instead of repetition, social media relies on the idea of customization

and adaption of the message. Information is positioned as more valuable rather than being strictly entertaining. Probably the most important aspect is the idea of consumer-generated content, whereby consumers can both take existing content and modify it or create completely new content for a brand. For example, the Los Angeles-based Getty Museum, which is home to several historic artists such as Monet, Rembrandt, and Rubens, used X to challenge followers during the COVID-19 pandemic to recreate famous artwork with ordinary objects in their homes. Because so many people were bored at home with time to be creative, the challenge was highly successful.[18]

Because of the impact of social media as well as the proliferation of new platforms, tools, and ideas, promotional tactics can also be categorized according to media type—paid, earned, or owned, as shown in Figure 15.3. **Paid media** is based on the traditional advertising model, whereby a brand pays for media space. Traditionally, paid media has included television, magazine, outdoor, radio, or newspaper advertising. Paid media also includes display advertising on websites, pay-per-click advertising on search engines, paid ads on Facebook and Instagram, and even ads on Instagram Stories. Paid media is quite important, especially as it migrates to the web. Paid media is used with other media types to develop an integrated message strategy.

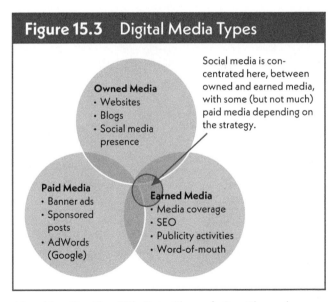

Figure 15.3   Digital Media Types

Social media is concentrated here, between owned and earned media, with some (but not much) paid media depending on the strategy.

Owned Media
• Websites
• Blogs
• Social media presence

Paid Media
• Banner ads
• Sponsored posts
• AdWords (Google)

Earned Media
• Media coverage
• SEO
• Publicity activities
• Word-of-mouth

Adapted from Dave Fleet, "Why Paying Bloggers for Posts Changes the Game," December 12, 2010, https://davefleet.com/2010/12/bloggers-money-posts-game (accessed May 2023).

paid media a category of promotional tactics based on the traditional advertising model, whereby a brand pays for media space

Earned media is based on a public relations or publicity model. The idea is to start people talking about the brand—whether through media coverage (as in traditional public relations) or through WOM. WOM traditionally occurred face-to-face. But the electronic word-of-mouth (eWOM)—for example, sharing a movie review on a social media site—has grown rapidly in recent years. Earned media is often created when people talk and share content on social media. Additionally, search engine optimization (SEO), whereby companies embed keywords into content to increase their positioning on search engine results pages (SERPs), can also be considered earned media. **Owned media** is a new promotional tactic in which brands are becoming publishers of their own content to maximize the brand's value to customers as well as increase their search rank in Google. Owned media includes the company's websites as well as its official presence on Facebook, X, YouTube channels,

blogs, and other digital platforms. These media are controlled by the brand but continuously keep customers' needs in mind as videos, blog posts, contests, photos, and other types of content are created. Owned media, also called "content marketing," is important for both B-to-B and B-to-C companies. The most effective campaigns typically employ all three types of media: owned media is created to increase WOM, while earned media and paid media are used to get the message out to target audiences.

The elements of the promotional mix differ in their ability to affect the target audience. For instance, promotional mix elements may communicate with the consumer directly or indirectly. The message flow may be one-way or two-way. Feedback may be fast or slow, a little or a lot. Likewise, the communicator may have varying degrees of control over message delivery, content, and flexibility. Exhibit 15.4 outlines characteristics among the promotional mix elements concerning the mode of communication, marketer's control over the communication process, amount and speed of feedback, direction of message flow, marketer's control over the message, identification of the sender, speed in reaching large audiences, and message flexibility.

From Table 15.1, you can tell that many elements of the promotional mix are indirect and impersonal when used to communicate with a target market, providing only one direction of message flow. For example, advertising, public

earned media a category of promotional tactics based on a public relations or publicity model that gets customers talking about products or services

owned media a new category of promotional tactics based on brands becoming publishers of their own content to maximize the brands' value to customers

Table 15.1 Characteristics of the Elements in the Promotional Mix

	Advertising	Public Relations	Sales Promotion	Personal Selling	Social Media
Mode of Communication	Indirect and impersonal	Usually indirect and impersonal	Usually indirect and impersonal	Direct and face-to-face	Indirect but instant
Communicator Control over Situation	Low	Moderate to low	Moderate to low	High	Moderate
Amount of Feedback	Little	Little	Little to moderate	Much	Much
Speed of Feedback	Delayed	Delayed	Varies	Immediate	Intermediate
Direction of Message	One-way	One-way	Mostly one-way	Two-way	Two-way, multiple ways
Control over Message Content	Yes	No	Yes	Yes	Varies, generally no
Identification of Sponsor	Yes	No	Yes	Yes	Yes
Speed in Reaching Large Audience	Fast	Usually fast	Fast	Slow	Fast
Message Flexibility	Same message to all audiences	Usually no direct control over message to audiences	Same message to varied targets	Tailored to prospective buyer	Some of the most targeted opportunities

relations, and sales promotion are generally impersonal, one-way means of mass communication. Because they provide little opportunity for direct feedback, it is more difficult to adapt these promotional elements to changing consumer preferences, individual differences, and personal goals.

Personal selling, on the other hand, facilitates direct two-way communication. The salesperson receives immediate feedback from the consumer and can adjust the message in response. Unlike other promotional tools, personal selling is very slow in dispersing the marketer's message to large audiences. Because a salesperson can communicate with only one person or a small group at one time, it is a poor choice if the marketer wants to send a message to many potential buyers. Social media are also considered two-way communications, though not quite as immediate as personal selling. Social media can disperse messages to a wide audience and allow for engagement and feedback from customers through Instagram Facebook, and blog posts.

15-5 Promotional Goals and the AIDA Concept

15-5 Discuss how the AIDA concept relates to the promotional mix

The ultimate goal of any promotion is to get someone to buy a good or service or, in the case of nonprofit organizations, to take some action (e.g., donate to a cause organization like the American Cancer Society). A classic model for reaching promotional goals is called the **AIDA concept**.[19] The acronym AIDA stands for *attention, interest, desire,* and *action*—the stages of consumer involvement with a promotional message. It mimics many "funnel-like" models that require audiences to move through a set of steps or stages.

15-5a The AIDA Model

This model proposes that consumers respond to marketing messages in a cognitive (thinking), affective (feeling), and conative (doing) sequence. First, a promotion manager may focus on attracting a consumer's *attention* by training a salesperson to use a friendly greeting and approach or by using loud volume, bold headlines, movement, bright colors, and the like in an advertisement. This could also include search ads that pop up on SERPs when a search occurs or a message from a social media influencer. The goal is to gain attention, which in a crowded marketplace is often quite difficult. Next, a good sales presentation, demonstration, or advertisement creates *interest* in the product and then, by illustrating how the product's features will satisfy the consumer's needs, arouses *desire*.

Finally, a special offer or a strong closing sales pitch may be used to motivate purchase *action.*

The AIDA concept assumes that promotion propels consumers along the following four steps in the purchase–decision process:

1. **Attention:** The advertiser must first gain the attention of the target market. A firm cannot sell something if the market does not know the good or service exists. When Adidas launches a new product and wants to show customers why they should buy its brand its, it often collaborates with famous people or well-known athletes. This generates awareness for the new product and directs the customer to the website for more information.

2. **Interest:** Simple awareness of a brand seldom leads to a sale. The next step is to create interest in the product. A print ad cannot tell potential customers all the features of the Adidas shoe. Therefore, Adidas has to use words on the website that generate curiosity and interest such as "new," "save up to," or "preorder" and target messages to innovators and early adopters to create interest in the new shoe.

3. **Desire:** Potential customers for the new Adidas shoe may like the concept, but they may not necessarily think that it is better than other brands or their current shoes. Therefore, Adidas has to create brand preference with famous people by releasing behind-the-scenes photos during the campaign shoot or creating an exclusivity of the brand that customers desire.

4. **Action:** Some potential target market customers may be persuaded to buy the new Adidas but had not yet made the actual purchase. To motivate them to take action, Adidas continues advertising using stores about well-known athletes with messages like "Impossible isn't a fact, it's an opinion…Impossible is nothing."[20]

Most buyers involved in high-involvement purchase situations pass through the four stages of the AIDA model on the way to making a purchase. The promoter's task is to determine where on the purchasing ladder most of the target consumers are located and design a promotion plan to meet their needs. For example, if Adidas learned from its market research and data analytics that many potential customers were in the desire stage but had not yet bought the new shoes for some reason, it could place advertising on Instagram and Google, and perhaps in video games, to

---

AIDA concept a model that outlines the process for achieving promotional goals in terms of stages of consumer involvement with the message; the acronym stands for attention, interest, desire, and action

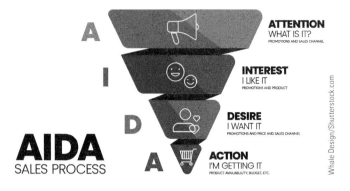

target younger individuals and professionals with messages motivating them to buy.

The AIDA concept does not explain how all promotions influence purchase decisions. The model suggests that promotional effectiveness can be measured in terms of consumers progressing from one stage to the next. However, the order of stages in the model, as well as whether consumers go through all steps, has been much debated. A purchase can occur without interest or desire, perhaps when a low-involvement product is bought on impulse. Regardless of the order of the stages or consumers' progression through these stages, the AIDA concept helps marketers by suggesting which promotional strategy will be most effective.[21]

15-5b AIDA and the Promotional Mix

Table 15.2 depicts the relationship between the promotional mix and the AIDA model. It shows that although advertising does have an impact in the later stages, it is most useful in gaining attention for goods or services. By contrast, personal selling reaches fewer people at first. Salespeople are more effective at developing customer interest in products and services and at creating desire. For example, advertising may help a potential camera purchaser gain knowledge about competing brands, but the salesperson may be the one who actually encourages the buyer to decide that a particular brand is the best choice. The salesperson also has the advantage of having the camera physically there to demonstrate its capabilities to the buyer.

Table 15.2	The Promotional Mix and AIDA			
	Attention	Interest	Desire	Action
Advertising	●	●	○	⬤
Public Relations	●	●	○	⬤
Sales Promotion	○	○	●	●
Personal Selling	○	●	●	●
Social Media	●	●	○	○
● Very effective ○ Somewhat effective ⬤ Not effective				

The greatest impact of public relations is as a method of gaining attention for a company, good, or service. Many companies can attract attention and build goodwill by sponsoring community events that benefit worthy causes such as mental health or disaster relief. Such sponsorships project a positive image of the firm and its products in the minds of consumers and potential consumers. Winemakers, for instance, push to get their products submitted to competitions to earn medals and awards as prestige. The vineyards may conduct tours and tastings to engage customers and promote the ingredients and processes used to make the product. They also frequently engage with fans on social media like Facebook and Instagram.

Sales promotion's greatest strength is in creating strong desire and purchase intent. Coupons and other price-off promotions are techniques used to persuade customers to buy new products. Frequent-buyer sales promotion programs, popular among retailers, enable consumers to accumulate points or dollars that can be redeemed for goods or to obtain discounts. ThredUP, the online consignment shop, rewards customers with points that can be redeemed for free shipping, money off an order, or waiving restock fees. Frequent-buyer programs tend to increase purchase intent and loyalty and encourage repeat purchases.

Social media are a strong way to gain attention and interest in a brand. It is particularly effective if the content goes viral and reaches large audiences. Social media are also effective at engaging with customers and enabling companies to maintain interest in the brand if properly managed.

15-6 Integrated Marketing Communications

15-6 Explain the concept of integrated marketing communications

Ideally, marketing communications from each promotional mix element (personal selling, advertising, sales promotion, social media, and public relations) should be integrated. That is, the message reaching the consumer should be the same regardless of whether it is from an advertisement, a salesperson in the field, a magazine article, a Facebook fan page, or a coupon sent via email. McDonald's "I'm lovin' it" campaign is a great example of an integrated marketing campaign. The campaign jingle is played on television, video, and radio. Social media posts also use campaign communication.

From the consumer's standpoint, a company's communications are already integrated. Consumers do not think in terms of the five elements of promotion: personal selling, advertising, sales promotion, public relations, and social media. Instead, everything is an "ad." The only people who recognize the distinctions among these communications elements are the marketers themselves. Unfortunately, too many marketers overlook this when planning promotional messages, and they fail to integrate their communication efforts across all elements of the promotional mix. The most common lack of integration is between personal selling and the other elements of the promotional mix.

The need for a common approach for all elements of the promotion mix has led many companies to adopt the concept of **integrated marketing communications (IMC)**. IMC is the careful coordination of all promotional messages—traditional advertising, direct marketing, social media, public relations, sales promotion, personal selling, event marketing, and other communications—for a product or service to ensure the consistency of messages at every point at which a company has contact with the consumer. Following the concept of IMC, marketing managers carefully work out the roles that various promotional elements will play in the marketing mix. The timing of promotional activities is coordinated, and the results of each campaign are carefully monitored to improve future use of the promotional mix tools. A marketing communications director is often appointed; this person has overall responsibility for integrating the company's marketing communications.

The IMC concept has been growing in popularity for several reasons. First, the proliferation of thousands of media choices beyond traditional television has made promotion a more complicated task. Instead of promoting a product just through mass-media options, like television and magazines, promotional messages today can appear in many varied sources.

Further, the mass market has also fragmented into more selectively segmented markets. The result has been an increase in niche marketing that has replaced the traditional broad market groups marketers promoted to in the past. Marketers have also slashed their advertising spending to focus on promotional techniques that generate immediate sales responses and are more easily measured, such as direct marketing. Online advertising has been allocated a bigger share of the budget as well because of its measurability. Thus, the interest in IMC is largely a reaction to the scrutiny that marketing communications have come under and, particularly, to suggestions that uncoordinated promotional activity leads to a strategy that is wasteful, inefficient, and ineffective.

15-7 Factors Affecting the Promotional Mix

15-7 Describe the factors that affect the promotional mix

Promotional mixes vary a great deal from one product and one industry to the next. Advertising and personal selling are typically used to promote goods and services. These primary tools are often supported and supplemented by sales promotion. Public relations help develop a positive image for the organization and the product line. Social media have been used more for consumer goods, but B-toB marketers are increasingly using social media. A firm may not use all five promotional elements in its promotional mix, or it may choose to use them in varying degrees. The particular promotional mix chosen by a firm for a product or service depends on several factors: the nature of the product, the stage in the product life cycle, target market characteristics, the type of buying decision, funds available for promotion, and whether a push or a pull strategy will be used.

15-7a Nature of the Product

The characteristics of the product itself can influence the promotional mix. For instance, a product can be classified as either a business product or a consumer product. (Refer to Chapters 7 and 10.) Business products are often custom-tailored to the buyer's exact specifications, so they generally are not well suited to mass promotion. As a result, most business goods rely more heavily on personal selling than on advertising, but advertising still serves a purpose in the promotional mix. Advertising in trade media can also help the sales force locate potential customers. For example, print media advertising often includes coupons soliciting the potential customer to visit a website and provide information to receive a discount code.

In contrast, since consumer products are seldom custom-made, they do not require the selling efforts of a company representative who can tailor them to the user's needs. Thus, consumer goods are promoted mainly through advertising or social media to create brand familiarity. Television and radio advertising, consumer-oriented magazines, and increasingly the Internet and other highly targeted media are used to promote consumer goods, especially nondurables. Sales promotion, the brand name, and the product's packaging are about twice as important for consumer goods as for business products. But persuasive

integrated marketing communications (IMC) the careful coordination of all promotional messages for a product or a service to ensure the consistency of messages at every point at which a company has contact with the consumer

Vehicles can send a nonverbal message about a person's social class and thus carry a degree of social risk.

personal selling is important at the retail level for goods such as electronics and sporting goods.

The costs and risks associated with a product also influence the promotional mix. As a general rule, as the costs or risks of buying and using a product or service increase, personal selling becomes more important. Inexpensive items cannot support the cost of a salesperson's time and effort unless the potential volume is high. On the other hand, expensive and complex machinery, technology, and financial services represent a considerable investment. For example, a high-end luxury car like a Ferrari comes with a financial investment. Ferraris also bring the owner an elevated social standing. Therefore, Ferrari consumers obtain

not only the benefits of transportation, but also high performance and status with their purchase. A salesperson must assure buyers that they are spending their money wisely and not taking undue financial risk.

Social risk is an issue as well. Many consumer goods do not have great social importance because they do not reflect social position. For example, people do not experience much social risk in buying a loaf of bread or a candy bar. However, buying many specialty products such as jewelry, clothing, vehicles, or buying a home in a particular neighborhood involves a social risk. When social risk is involved, many consumers depend on sales personnel for guidance in making the "proper" choice.

15-7b Stages in the Product Life Cycle

The product's stage in its life cycle is a big factor in designing a promotional mix (refer to Figure 15.4). During the *introduction stage*, the basic goal of promotion is to inform the target audience that the product is available. Initially, the emphasis is on the general product class—for example, global positioning system (GPS) trackers. This emphasis gradually changes to gaining attention for a particular brand, such as Apple, Garmin, Spytec, or Samsung. Typically, both extensive advertising and public relations inform the target audience about the product class or brand and heighten awareness levels. Sales promotion encourages early trial of the product, and personal selling gets retailers to carry the product.

Figure 15.4   Product Life Cycle and the Promotional Mix

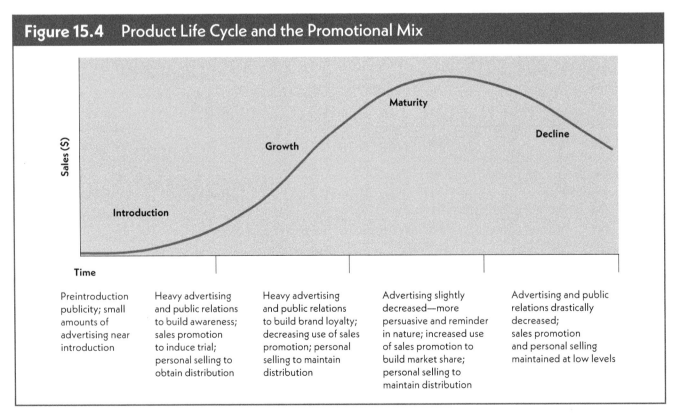

When the product reaches the *growth stage* of the life cycle, the promotion blend will often shift. Change is necessary because different types of potential buyers are targeted. Although advertising and public relations continue to be major elements of the promotional mix, sales promotion can be reduced because consumers need fewer incentives to purchase. The promotional strategy is to emphasize the product's differential advantage over the competition. Thus, persuasive promotion is used to build and maintain brand loyalty during the growth stage. By this stage, personal selling has usually succeeded in getting adequate distribution for the product.

As the product reaches the *maturity stage* of its life cycle, competition becomes fiercer, and persuasive and reminder advertising are therefore emphasized more strongly. Sales promotion also comes back into focus as sellers try to increase their market share.

All promotion, especially advertising, is reduced as the product enters the *decline stage*. Nevertheless, personal selling and sales promotion efforts may be maintained, particularly at the retail level.

15-7c Target Market Characteristics

A target market characterized by widely scattered potential customers, highly informed buyers, and brand-loyal repeat purchasers generally requires a promotional mix with more advertising and sales promotion and less personal selling. Sometimes, however, personal selling is required even when buyers are well informed and geographically dispersed. Although industrial installations may be sold to well-educated people with extensive work experience, salespeople must be present to explain the product and work out the details of the purchase agreement.

Often firms sell goods and services in markets where potential customers are hard to locate. Print advertising can be used to find them. The reader is invited to go online, call, or mail in a reply card for more information. As online queries, calls, or cards are received, salespeople are sent to visit potential customers.

15-7d Type of Buying Decision

The promotional mix also depends on the type of buying decision—for example, a routine decision or a complex decision. For routine consumer decisions like buying deodorant, the most effective promotion calls attention to the brand or reminds the consumer about the brand. Advertising, and especially sales promotion, are the most productive promotion tools to use for routine decisions.

If the decision is neither routine nor complex, advertising and public relations help establish awareness for the good or service. In honor of National Administrative Professionals Day, a colleague is looking to give their administrative professional a token of appreciation. The colleague is aware that the administrative professional enjoys chocolate even though they themselves do not. If the colleague had noticed a website ad in the *Washington Post* for Ghirardelli chocolates they would be more likely to buy it since they were aware of the brand. Online reviews are often important in this type of buying decision as well because reviews by other consumers are easily accessible to consumers.

By contrast, consumers making complex buying decisions are more extensively involved. They rely on large amounts of information to help them reach a purchase decision. Personal selling is most effective in helping these consumers decide. For example, if a hobbyist songwriter were thinking about purchasing recording equipment, they would typically research the various equipment online using corporate and third-party websites like Song Production Pros. An alternative method is to visit a studio and recording equipment sales location to try out the equipment firsthand. They depend on a salesperson to provide the information they need to reach a decision. In addition to online resources, print advertising may also be used for high-involvement purchase decisions because it often provides a large amount of information to the consumer.

15-7e Available Funds

Money, or the lack of it, may easily be the most important factor in determining the promotional mix. A small, undercapitalized manufacturer may rely heavily on free publicity if its product is unique. If the situation warrants a sales force, a financially strained firm may turn to manufacturers' agents, who work on a commission basis with no advances or expense accounts. Even well-capitalized organizations may not be able to afford the advertising rates of publications like *People Magazine*, *USA Today*, and *The Washington Post*, or the cost of running television commercials during the Super Bowl. The price of a high-profile advertisement in these media could support several salespeople for an entire year.

When funds are available to permit a mix of promotional elements, a firm will generally try to optimize its return on promotion dollars while minimizing the *cost per contact*, or the cost of reaching one member of the target market. In general, the cost per contact is very high for personal selling, public relations, and sales promotions like sampling and demonstrations. On the other hand, given the large number of people reached by national advertising and social media, they have a very low cost per contact. Usually, there is a trade-off among the funds available, the number of people in the target market, the quality of communication needed, and the relative costs of the promotional elements. In most instances, there are plenty of low-cost options available to companies that do not have a huge budget. Many of these include online strategies

Good Thins prominently displays "gluten-free" to help customers make routine buying decisions.

push strategy a marketing strategy that uses aggressive personal selling and trade advertising to convince a wholesaler or a retailer to carry and sell particular merchandise

pull strategy a marketing strategy that stimulates consumer demand to obtain product distribution

and public relations efforts in which the company relies on free publicity.

15-7f Push and Pull Strategies

The last factor that affects the promotional mix is whether a push or a pull promotional strategy will be used. Manufacturers may use aggressive personal selling and trade advertising to convince a wholesaler or a retailer to carry and sell their merchandise. This approach is known as a **push strategy** (refer to Figure 15.5). The wholesaler, in turn, must often push the merchandise forward by persuading the retailer to handle the goods. The retailer then uses advertising, displays, and other forms of promotion to convince the consumer to buy the "pushed" products. Some push examples include point-of-sale displays, direct marketing, direct mailers, display ads, and billboards. Good Thins prominently displays "gluten free" below the brand name on product packaging to help consumers during the decision-making process. This labeling is a push method to help move the gluten-free Good Thins products off the shelf. This vivid verbiage on the Good Thins packaging is helpful for those with dietary restrictions or wanting to reduce their gluten intake. These push strategies also work well with services.

At the other extreme is a **pull strategy**, which stimulates consumer demand for products to obtain better distribution. Rather than trying to sell to the wholesaler, the manufacturer using a pull strategy focuses its promotional efforts on end consumers or opinion leaders. Social media and content marketing are the most recent (and best)

Figure 15.5   Push Strategy Versus Pull Strategy

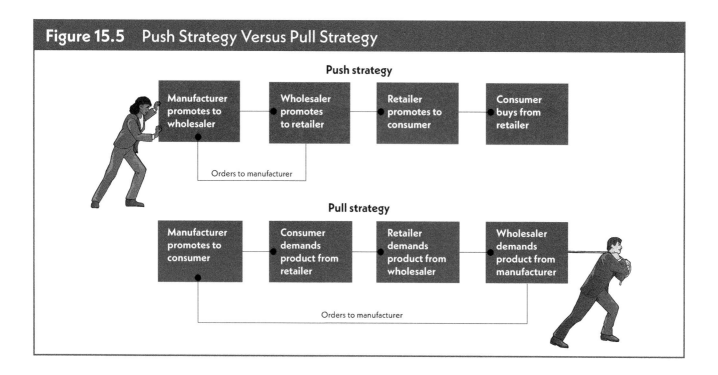

examples of a pull strategy. The idea is that social media content does not interrupt a consumer's experience with media (like a commercial interrupts your favorite television program). Instead, the content invites customers to experience it on social media or a website. Consumer demand pulls the product through the channel of distribution (refer to Figure 15.5). Heavy sampling, introductory consumer advertising, cents-off campaigns, and couponing are part of a pull strategy. Online retailer, Wayfair, has Way Day in which it promotes its 24-hour sale and free shipping on social media. The promotion for this event is to pull customers to the website. Wayfair notices an increased number of sales during this period which is a win for the company. Customers can save money on a vast number of goods in addition to receiving free shipping, which is a win for the customer.[22]

Rarely does a company use a pull or a push strategy exclusively. Instead, the promotional mix will emphasize a combination of these strategies. For example, pharmaceutical companies generally use a push strategy (personal selling and trade advertising) to promote their drugs and therapies to physicians. Sales presentations and advertisements in medical journals give physicians the detailed information they need to prescribe medication to their patients. Most pharmaceutical companies supplement this push promotional strategy with a pull strategy targeted directly to potential patients through advertisements in consumer magazines and on television.

iStock.com/Efenzi

Chapter 16

Advertising, Public Relations, and Sales Promotion

Learning Outcomes

After studying this chapter, you will be able to . . .

16-1 Discuss the effects of advertising on market share and consumers

16-2 List the major types of advertising

16-3 Discuss the creative decisions in developing an advertising campaign

16-4 Describe media selection techniques

16-5 Discuss the role of public relations in the promotional mix

16-6 Describe the tools used to achieve the objectives of sales promotion

16-1 The Effects of Advertising

16-1 Discuss the effects of advertising on market share and consumers

Advertising was defined in Chapter 15 as impersonal, mass communication about a product or organization that is paid for by a marketer. It is a popular form of promotion, especially for consumer packaged goods and services. Increasingly, as more and more marketers consolidate their operations, advertising is seen as an international endeavor. Promotion makes up a large part of most brands' budgets. Typically, promotional spending is divided into *measured* and *unmeasured media.* Measured media ad spending includes network and cable TV, newspapers, magazines, radio, outdoor, and internet (though paid search and social media are not included since these are typically counted as lead captures which is a part of the pipeline toward generating revenue).[1]

Unmeasured media spending includes direct marketing, promotions, co-op, coupons, catalogs, product placement, and event marketing. Forecasts for 2024 predict a 5 percent increase in total media spending in the United States and 7.5 percent worldwide. The Middle East and North Africa are expected to have the greatest increase of 13.5 percent.[2] The top 25 largest U.S. advertisers spent more than $80.56 billion in 2021. Amazon is the largest U.S. advertiser by spending $10.4 billion. Comcast spent $6 billion in the United States alone. Consumer goods companies like Procter & Gamble (P&G) ($5 billion), credit card provider American Express ($3.9 billion), and entertainment/media companies like Walt Disney ($3.7 billion) are also top spenders. Amazon is the largest global advertiser at $16.9 billion in 2021.[3]

Advertising and marketing services, agencies, and other firms that provide marketing and communications services employ millions of people across America. Just as the producers of goods and services need marketers to build awareness for their products, media outlets such as magazines and websites need marketing teams to coordinate with producers and transmit those messages to customers. The longer one thinks about the business of marketing, the more apparent become the unique positions within the industry.

One particular area that has continued to experience rapid growth is the data side of marketing. Companies are collecting huge amounts of information and need skilled, creative, web-savvy people to interpret the data coming in from web, mobile, and other digital ad campaigns. For example, Il Makiage, a beauty products and makeup brand, promotes its skincare products on Facebook and Instagram. As potential customers go to the website, they are given the opportunity to take a quiz to find the products that are most appropriate for them based on the results of the quiz. There are multiple quizzes for things like foundation, skincare products, or sunless tanning products. One study indicates that 97 percent of businesses are investing in data analytics and artificial intelligence programs believing that such programs are of strategic importance to their organizations. However, keeping up with data is a challenge since the average person produces 1.7 MB of data per second.[4]

16-1a Advertising and Market Share

The five most valuable U.S. brands for 2023 are Amazon ($299.28 billion in brand value), Apple ($297.51 billion), Google ($281.38 billion), Microsoft ($191.57 billion), and, Walmart ($113.78 billion).[5] Four of these brands were the top five brands in 2019, but some shifted in rank. Many of these are technology brands and many of these brands were built over the years by heavy advertising and by marketing investments made long ago. Walmart is the only brand that was not in the top five in 2019. Advertising budgets for most successful consumer brands in the United States are spent on maintaining brand awareness and market share.

New brands with a small market share tend to spend proportionally more of their promotion budget for advertising and sales promotion than those with a large market share, generally for two reasons. First, beyond a certain level of spending for advertising and sales promotion, diminishing returns set in. That is, sales and market share improvements slow down and eventually decrease no matter how much is spent on advertising and sales promotion. This phenomenon is called the **advertising response function**. Understanding the advertising response function helps marketers use promotion budgets wisely. A market leader like Procter & Gamble's Downy Fabric Softener typically spends proportionally less on advertising than a newer line, such as EnviroKlenz's Laundry Enhancer brand. Downy has already captured the attention of most of its target market. It only needs to remind customers that its product is available and where.

The second reason new brands tend to require higher spending for advertising and sales promotion is that a certain minimum level of exposure is needed to measurably affect purchase habits. If EnviroKlenz advertised its Laundry Enhancer in only one or two publications and bought only one or two television spots, it would not achieve the exposure needed to penetrate consumers' perceptual defenses, create awareness, and affect purchase intentions.

---

advertising response function a phenomenon in which spending for advertising and sales promotion increases sales or market share up to a certain level but then produces diminishing returns

16-1b The Effects of Advertising on Consumers

Advertising affects peoples' daily lives, informing them about products and services and influencing their attitudes, beliefs, and ultimately their purchases. Advertising affects the movies people watch, the content of the online articles they read, the politicians they elect, the personal care products they use, and the foods they eat. Consequently, the influence of advertising on the U.S. socioeconomic system has been the subject of extensive debate in nearly all corners of society.

Interestingly, despite a proliferation of new digital options, consumers still spend a lot of time-consuming traditional media (where much of advertising exists). The average person, for example, spends about 180 minutes a day watching live television programming and 397 minutes a day using digital media devices like smartphones, desktops, laptops, and tablets.[6] Americans report an average of 5.3 leisure hours a day, and most of it is spent watching TV. As a result, American consumers are exposed to thousands of advertising messages each year.[7]

Though advertising cannot change consumers' deeply rooted values and attitudes, advertising may succeed in transforming a person's negative attitude toward a product into a positive one. For instance, serious or dramatic advertisements are more effective at changing consumers' negative attitudes. Humorous ads, on the other hand, are more effective at shaping attitudes when consumers already have a positive image of an advertised brand.

Advertising also reinforces positive attitudes toward brands. A brand with a distinct personality is more likely to have a larger base of loyal customers and market share. The more consistent a brand's personality, the more likely a customer will build a relationship with that brand over their lifetime. Consider Apple, for example. Since 2018, more than 90 percent of iPhone users replace their smartphone with another iPhone.[8] This is why market leaders spend billions of dollars annually to reinforce and remind their loyal customers about the benefits of their products.

Advertising can also affect the way consumers rank a brand's attributes. In years past, credit cards emphasized such brand attributes as global acceptance and interest rates. Today, however, credit cards have added loyalty benefits and technology like chips and contactless payments.

16-2 Major Types of Advertising

16-2 List the major types of advertising

A firm's promotional objectives determine the type of advertising it uses. If the goal of the promotion plan is to improve the image of the company or the industry, **institutional advertising** may be used. In contrast, if the advertiser wants to enhance the sales of a specific good or service, **product advertising** should be used.

16-2a Institutional Advertising

Historically, advertising in the United States has been product and service oriented. Today, however, companies market multiple products and need a different type of advertising. Institutional, or corporate, advertising is designed to establish, change, or promote the corporation's identity as a whole. Institutional advertising is also important for hiring and recruitment. It usually does not ask the audience to do anything but maintain a favorable attitude toward the advertiser and its goods or services. A beer company running a series of television spots advocating the use of a designated driver is an example of institutional advertising.

A form of institutional advertising called **advocacy advertising** is typically used to safeguard against negative consumer attitudes and to enhance the company's credibility among consumers who already favor its position. Corporations often use advocacy advertising to express their views on controversial issues. Bud Light, owned by parent company Anheuser-Busch, in an effort to demonstrate its support of inclusivity, partnered with transgender woman and influencer, Dylan Mulvaney. Bud Light created a commemorative can with Mulvaney's image on the can. Mulvaney posted a video promoting Bud Light showcasing the can stating, "This month I celebrate my day 365 of womanhood." Mulvaney also comments, "Bud Light sent me possibly the best gift ever, a can with my face on it." While diversity, equity, and inclusion have been topics popular with many organizations, not all members of society are as supportive of the LBGTQIA+ population. As a result, Mulvaney's post was met with some anger, and a call was made to boycott Bud Light. From the brand's perspective, it is hoping to gain the support of younger legal drinkers by evolving the image of Bud Light by focusing on inclusivity.[9]

Alternatively, an advocacy campaign might also refute criticism or blame, or ward off increases in regulation, damaging legislation, or the unfavorable outcome of a lawsuit.

---

institutional advertising a form of advertising designed to enhance a company's image rather than promote a particular product

product advertising a form of advertising that touts the benefits of a specific good or service

advocacy advertising a form of advertising in which an organization expresses its views on controversial issues or responds to media attacks

A Samsung commercial shows Galaxy S4 users sharing a photo, then an iPhone user wants to do the same but lacks the capability.

16-2b Product Advertising

Unlike institutional advertising, product advertising promotes the benefits of a specific good or service. The product's stage in its life cycle often determines which type of product advertising is used: pioneering advertising, competitive advertising, or comparative advertising.

Pioneering Advertising

Pioneering advertising is intended to stimulate primary demand for a new product or product category. Heavily used during the introductory stage of the product life cycle, pioneering advertising offers consumers in-depth information about the benefits of the product class. Pioneering advertising also seeks to create interest and can be quite innovative in its own right. For example, Ring, the maker of video doorbells and security cameras, introduced the car cam. The product utilizes two high-definition cameras that record both inside and outside the car when in motion. It also includes night vision detectors when the car is in park and sends real-time alerts when there is activity in or around the vehicle. Ring released an "Install the Ring Car Cam" video on Instagram to demonstrate the ease of setting up.[10]

Competitive Advertising

Firms use competitive or brand advertising when a product enters the growth phase of the product life cycle and as other companies begin to enter the marketplace with similar products. Instead of building demand for the product category, the goal of **competitive advertising** is to influence demand for a specific brand. In the growth phase, promotion often focuses less on being informative and appeals more to emotions. Generally, this phase is where an emphasis on branding begins. Advertisements focus on showing subtle differences between competitive brands, building recall of a brand name, and creating a favorable attitude toward the brand. Hinge, the dating app, uses competitive advertising by discussing how Hinge focuses on finding the real thing and won't need the company any longer. The commercials comically display the Hinge app icon being destroyed as the owner of the app finds "the one." Hinge campaigns use humor to promote the brand above others in the industry but without actively comparing itself with other dating apps.

Comparative Advertising

Comparative advertising directly or indirectly compares two or more competing brands on one or more specific attributes. Some advertisers even use comparative advertising with their own brands. Products experiencing slow growth or those entering the marketplace against strong competitors are more likely to employ comparative claims in their advertising. A Samsung commercial uses comparative advertising by displaying the attributes of the Galaxy S4, how calls can be answered without touching the phone, photos can be shared from one Samsung to another by

pioneering advertising a form of advertising designed to stimulate primary demand for a new product or product category

competitive advertising a form of advertising designed to influence demand for a specific brand

comparative advertising a form of advertising that compares two or more specifically named or shown competing brands on one or more specific attributes

touching the phones together, and the ability to control the TV. The commercial uses humor to promote the brand above Apple since Apple iPhone users are shown trying to do the same with their phones and failing. One character asks, "So, some smartphones are smarter than other smartphones?" to which another responds, "Exactly!"[11]

Before the 1970s, comparative advertising was allowed only if the competing brand was veiled and unidentified. In 1971, however, the Federal Trade Commission (FTC) fostered the growth of comparative advertising by saying that the advertising provided information to the customer and that advertisers were more skillful than the government in communicating this information. Federal rulings prohibit advertisers from falsely describing competitors' products and allow competitors to sue if ads show their products or mention their brand names in an incorrect, misleading, or false manner. FTC rules also apply to advertisers making false claims about their own products.

16-3 Creative Decisions in Advertising

16-3 Discuss the creative decisions in developing an advertising campaign

Advertising strategies are typically organized around an advertising campaign. An **advertising campaign** is a series of related advertisements focusing on a common theme, slogan, and set of advertising appeals. It is a specific advertising effort for a particular product that extends for a defined period. For example, British Airways ran an ad campaign encouraging people to "Take Your Holiday Seriously." The campaign utilized the email out-of-office reply in the campaign with comical commentary. This campaign addresses the eight in ten individuals that desire to completely check out when on holiday, but the 61 percent that still check in.[12]

Before creative work can begin on an advertising campaign, it is important to determine what goals or objectives the advertising should achieve. An **advertising objective** identifies the specific communication task a campaign should accomplish for a specified target audience during a specified period. The objectives of a specific advertising campaign often depend on the overall corporate objectives and the product being advertised.

---

advertising campaign a series of related advertisements focusing on a common theme, slogan, and set of advertising appeals

advertising objective a specific communication task that a campaign should accomplish for a specified target audience during a specified period

In an ad campaign titled "Take Your Holiday Seriously," British Airways uses witty out-of-office replies to encourage customers to get away.

Source: Alison Hadley

The DAGMAR approach (defining advertising goals for measured advertising results) is one method of setting objectives. According to this method, all advertising objectives should precisely define the target audience, the desired percentage change in some specified measure of effectiveness, and the time frame in which that change is to occur.

Once objectives are defined, creative work can begin on the advertising campaign. Advertising campaigns often follow the AIDA model, which was discussed in Chapter 15. Depending on where consumers are in the AIDA process, the creative development of an advertising campaign might focus on creating attention, arousing interest, stimulating desire, and ultimately leading to the action of buying the product. Specifically, creative decisions include identifying product benefits, developing and evaluating advertising appeals, executing the message, and evaluating the effectiveness of the campaign.

16-3a Identifying Product Benefits

A well-known rule of thumb in the advertising industry is "Sell the sizzle, not the steak"—that is, in advertising, the goal is to sell the benefits of the product, not its attributes. Customers buy benefits, not attributes. An attribute is simply a feature of the product such as its easy-open package, special formulation, or new lower price. A benefit is what consumers will receive or achieve by using the product, such as convenience or ease of use. A benefit should answer the consumer's question, "What's in it for me?" Benefits might be such things as convenience, pleasure, improved health, savings, or relief. A quick test to determine whether you are offering attributes or benefits in your advertising is to ask "So?" Consider this example:

- **Attribute:** "OLIPOP is a new kind of soda that comes in nine flavors containing a blend of seven unique botanicals, plant fibers, and prebiotics with between 2–5 grams of sugar. ." "So . . . ?"
- **Benefit:** "So ....OLIPOP supports your gut health and provides great flavors to fulfill your craving for soda without adding extra calories from high sugar content."[13]

16-3b Developing and Evaluating Advertising Appeals

An **advertising appeal** identifies a reason for a person to buy a product. The challenging task of developing advertising appeals is typically the responsibility of the creative team (e.g., art directors and copywriters) in the advertising agency. Advertising appeals are based on findings from data analytics and typically play off consumers' emotions or address some need or want consumers have.

Advertising campaigns focus on one or more advertising appeals. Often the appeals are quite general, thus enabling the firm to develop several subthemes or mini-campaigns using advertising, sales promotion, and social media. Several possible advertising appeals are listed in Table 16.1. For example, profit appeals let customers know whether the product will save them money, make them money, or keep them from losing money. Health appeals to those who are body conscious or who want to be healthy, while fear can center around social embarrassment, safety, or losing one's health. Because of the power of fear, it requires advertisers to exercise care in the execution. Environmental centers around protecting the environment and being considerate of others which can be used to emphasize a product's ingredients or packaging.

Choosing the best appeal usually requires market research and data analytics. Criteria for evaluation include desirability, exclusiveness, and believability. The appeal first must make a positive impression on and be desirable

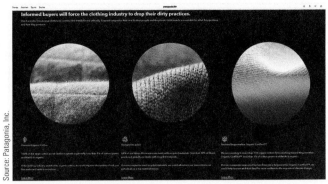

Patagonia's unique selling proposition is its dedication to preserving and restoring the planet.

to the target market. It must also be exclusive or unique. Consumers must be able to distinguish the advertiser's message from competitors' messages. Most importantly, the appeal should be believable. An appeal that makes extravagant claims not only wastes promotional dollars but also creates ill will for the advertiser.

The advertising appeal selected for the campaign becomes what advertisers call its **unique selling proposition**. The unique selling proposition often becomes all or part of the campaign's slogan. Patagonia proclaims, "We're in business to save our home planet." To accentuate this attribute, in the ad campaign titled "Buy Less, Demand More," Patagonia emphasizes the durability of its gear made from recycled materials. Further, the company asks consumers when shopping to ask themselves if the product is really needed or if can it be used in multiple ways. The company is encouraging people to buy fewer products and make existing products last longer for the good of the planet. This move helped the brand stand out in a crowded clothing market.[14]

16-3c Executing the Message

Message execution is the way an advertisement portrays its information. In general, the AIDA plan (refer to Chapter 15) is a good blueprint for executing an advertising message. Any ad should immediately draw the attention of the reader, viewer, or listener. The advertiser must then use the message to hold interest, create desire for the good or service, and ultimately motivate a purchase.

The style in which the message is executed is one of the most creative elements of an advertisement. Table 16.2 lists some examples of executional styles used by advertisers.

Table 16.1	Common Advertising Appeals
Appeal	**Examples**
Profit	Appliances that promote energy efficiency.
Health	Products that appeal to an individual's wellbeing.
Fear	Vehicles that discuss safety features for the prevention of an accident.
Admiration	Ads that utilize celebrity spokespeople.
Convenience	Ready-to-eat meals and delivery services that promote speed and ease.
Fun and Pleasure	Experiences and vacations that foster good times.
Vanity and Egotism	Cars or clothing that are expensive or allow an individual to stand out from the crowd.
Environmental Consciousness	Products made from recycled materials or reduce the usage of natural resources.

advertising appeal a reason for a person to buy a product

unique selling proposition a desirable, exclusive, and believable advertising appeal selected as the theme for a campaign

Table 16.2 Ten Common Executional Styles for Advertising

Executional Style	Description
Slice-of-Life	Depicts people in normal settings, such as at the dinner table or in their car. Oreo's often uses slice-of-life styles showing an adult and a child sharing an Oreo cookie by twisting the cookie apart, licking the filling, and then dunking the cookie in milk.
Lifestyle	Shows how well the product will fit in with the consumer's lifestyle. Nike commercials often depict individuals that go the extra mile and give it their all, then end the commercial with the tagline, "Just Do It."
Spokesperson/ Testimonial	Can feature a celebrity, company official, or typical consumer making a testimonial or endorsing a product. Lil Nas X represents Coach, while H.E.R. is an ambassador for L'Oréal Paris. Testimonials also include the growing area of social media influencers like Charli D'Amelio who promotes brands like Prada, Amazon, and Spotify.
Fantasy	Creates a fantasy for the viewer built around the use of the product. Carmakers often use this style to let viewers fantasize about how they would feel speeding around tight corners or down long country roads in their cars.
Humor	Often used by advertisers in their ads, such as Frito Lay's "Free Doritos" commercial, in which a snow globe used as a crystal ball was thrown into a Doritos vending machine, breaking the glass to access the product.
Real/Animated Product Symbols	Creates a character that represents the product in advertisements, such as Tony the Tiger for Frosted Flakes, or the M&M spokescharacters. GEICO's suave gecko has become a cult classic for the insurance company.
Mood or Image	Builds a mood or image around the product, such as peace, love, or beauty. Coca-Cola ads often depict an emotion of happiness or shared happy memories.
Demonstration	Shows consumers the expected benefit. Many consumer products use this technique. Dyson vacuum commercials demonstrate the high suction power of the machines which allows users to get cleaner floors.
Musical	Conveys the message of the advertisement through song. For example, T-Mobile enlisted the help of John Travolta to sing about the benefits of home internet with T-Mobile in a revised version of Grease's "Summer Nights."
Scientific	Uses research or scientific evidence to give a brand superiority over competitors. Allergy relief medicines like Allegra, Claritin, and Zyrtec use scientific evidence in their ads.

Execution styles often dictate what type of media is to be employed to convey the message. For example, scientific executional styles lend themselves well to print advertising, where more information can be conveyed. Testimonials by athletes are one of the more popular executional styles. This is particularly true for social media influencers whose following and influence are built on their testimonials for products and services.

Injecting humor into an advertisement is a popular and effective execution style. Humorous execution styles are more often used in radio and television advertising than in print or digital advertising, where humor is less easily communicated. Recall that humorous ads are typically used for lower-risk, low-involvement, routine purchases such as candy, cigarettes, and casual jeans, than for higher-risk purchases or for products that are expensive, durable, or flamboyant.[15] Although 94 percent of Gen Z and millennials prefer brands to be funny, 85 percent of business leaders do not feel they have the tools or data insights to successfully carry out humor.[16]

16-3d Postcampaign Evaluation

Evaluating an advertising campaign can be the most demanding task facing advertisers. How can an advertiser determine whether the campaign led to an increase in sales or market share or elevated awareness of the product? For traditional media, this is sometimes difficult. However, digital advertising and social media generate more data that enable marketers to better understand how well campaigns work. For example, Target, a large American retailer, has a large following on Instagram. Instagram has enhanced its shopping features making it easier to drive consumers from Instagram posts to purchases on the website. Target tags specific items in the post and these tags lead directly to the landing page. This allows Target to test different options and use marketing analytics to measure how well its Instagram marketing is working. Marketers spend considerable time studying advertising effectiveness and its probable impact on sales, market share, or awareness.

Testing ad effectiveness can be done before and/or after the campaign. Before a campaign is released, marketing managers use pretests to determine the best advertising appeal, layout, and media vehicle. After advertisers implement a campaign, they use several monitoring techniques to determine whether the campaign has met its original goals. Even if a campaign has been highly successful, advertisers still typically do a postcampaign analysis to identify how the campaign might have been more efficient and what factors contributed to its success.

16-4 Media Decisions in Advertising

16-4 Describe media selection techniques

A major decision for advertisers is the choice of **medium**—the channel used to convey a message to a target market. **Media planning**, therefore, is the series of decisions advertisers make regarding the selection and use of media, enabling the marketer to communicate the message optimally and cost-effectively to the target audience. Specifically, advertisers use marketing analytics to determine which types of media will best communicate the benefits of their product or service to the target audience and when and for how long the advertisement will run.

Promotional objectives and the appeal and executional style of the advertising strongly affect the selection of media. Both creative and media decisions are made at the same time: creative work cannot be completed without knowing which medium will be used to convey the message to the target market. In many cases, the advertising objectives dictate the medium and the creative approach to be used. For example, if the objective is to demonstrate how fast a product operates, a television commercial that shows this action may be the best choice.

In 2026, U.S. advertisers are expected to spend $405 billion on paid media: newspapers, magazines, radio, television, internet, and outdoor/cinema.[17] This represents a 41 percent increase over paid media spending in 2021.[18] More than 68 percent of every media dollar is expected to go toward paid internet advertising, which is an increase of 81 percent compared to 2021. Other increasing categories include podcasts ($1.8B projected for 2026), streaming music ($3.2B), trade magazines ($3.7B), and outdoor ($11B). Television is expected to remain constant at $72 billion along with video games ($1.8B), and cinema ($0.6B). Reductions are anticipated for newspaper ($9.9B) and radio ($16.7B).[19] As illustrated, the future growth lies in the digital realm, both in paid media (display ads, video ads, and search ads) as well as earned media (social media).

Digital advertising is growing rapidly, including video ads, display ads, search ads, and banner ads.

iStock.com/Rawpixel

16-4a Media Types

Advertising media are channels that advertisers use in mass communication. The eight major advertising media are newspapers, magazines, radio, television, digital, social, mobile, and outdoor media. Table 16.3 summarizes the advantages and disadvantages of some of these major channels.[20] But in recent years alternative media channels have emerged that offer advertisers innovative ways to reach their target audience and reduce advertising clutter.

Newspapers

Newspapers are one of the oldest forms of media. The advantages of newspaper advertising include geographic flexibility and timeliness. Although there has been a decline in circulation as well as in the number of newspapers, nationally, there are still several major newspapers including *The Wall Street Journal, USA Today, The New York Times, The Los Angeles Times*, and *The Washington Post*. Most newspapers, however, are local. Because newspapers are generally a mass-market medium, they may not be the best vehicle for marketers trying to reach a narrow market. Newspaper advertising also encounters distractions from competing ads and news stories. Further, newspapers are not viewed very long after the print date or shared with others, which increases the cost per reader. Therefore, one company's newspaper ad may not be particularly visible.

The main sources of newspaper ad revenue are local retailers, classified ads, and cooperative advertising. In

---

medium the channel used to convey a message to a target market

media planning the series of decisions advertisers make regarding the selection and use of media, allowing the marketer to communicate the message optimally and cost-effectively to the target audience

Table 16.3 Advantages and Disadvantages of Major Advertising Media

Medium	Advantages	Disadvantages
Newspapers	Geographic selectivity and flexibility; short-term advertiser commitments; news value and immediacy; year-round readership; high individual market coverage; co-op and local tie-in availability; short lead time	Little demographic selectivity; decreasing readership; limited color capabilities; low pass-along rate; high cost per reader
Magazines	Good reproduction, especially for color; demographic selectivity; regional selectivity; local market selectivity; relatively long advertising life; high pass-along rate	Long-term advertiser commitments; slow audience buildup; limited demonstration capabilities; lack of urgency; long lead time; can be expensive for good placement
Radio	Low cost; immediacy of the message; can be scheduled on short notice; relatively no seasonal change in audience; highly portable; short-term advertiser commitments; entertainment carryover; hyper-local targeting	No visual treatment; short advertising life of message; high frequency required to generate comprehension and retention; distractions from background sound; commercial clutter; decreased listeners due to streaming services particularly among younger audiences
Television	Ability to reach a wide, diverse audience; low cost per thousand; creative opportunities for demonstration; immediacy of messages; entertainment carryover; demographic selectivity with cable stations	The short life of message; some consumer skepticism about claims; high campaign cost; little demographic selectivity with network stations; long-term advertiser commitments; long lead times required for production; commercial clutter
Digital	Low cost; highly targetable; able to use programmatic ad buying for audience expansion; measurable performance; brand campaign can be managed for omnichannel	Relying completely on marketing analytics may result in questionable ad placement; highly competitive; dependent on technology; security and privacy issues.
Social	Many users; increased brand awareness; cost-effective	Time-consuming; need for qualified staff; heavy competition; reputation risk; long-term investment
Mobile	Fastest-growing medium; real-time access; people are spending an increasing amount of time on their phones each day	Sense of disruption; users must opt-in; costs users to receive advertisements
Outdoor Media	Repetition; moderate cost; flexibility; geographic selectivity	Short message; lack of demographic selectivity; high "noise" level distracting audience

cooperative advertising, the manufacturer and the retailer split the costs of advertising the manufacturer's brand. For example, Calvin Klein may split the cost of an advertisement with Dillard's department store, provided that the ad focuses on Calvin Klein's products. One reason manufacturers use cooperative advertising is the impracticality of listing all their dealers in national advertising. Also, cooperative advertising encourages retailers to devote more effort to the manufacturer's lines.

Magazines

Magazines are another traditional medium that continues to be successful. Some of the top magazines according to circulation include *People, Good Housekeeping, Allrecipes, AARP Magazine, Sports Illustrated, and Country Living*.[21] But the cost per contact in magazine advertising is usually high compared with the cost of advertising in other media,

particularly to obtain a favorable placement. The cost per potential customer may be much lower, however, because magazines are often targeted at specialized audiences and thus reach more potential customers.

Radio

Radio has several strengths as an advertising medium: hyper-local selectivity and audience segmentation, a large out-of-home audience, low unit and production costs, timeliness, and geographic flexibility. As with newspapers, radio also lends itself well to cooperative advertising. With the rise of streaming audio services, radio listening has experienced a decline over the years, particularly among younger listeners.[22]

Television

Television broadcasting media include network television, independent stations, cable television, and direct broadcast satellite television. Network television reaches a wide and diverse market, and cable television and direct broadcast satellite systems, such as DirecTV and DISH Network, broadcast a multitude of channels devoted to highly

---

cooperative advertising an arrangement in which the manufacturer and the retailer split the costs of advertising the manufacturer's brand

segmented markets. Because of its targeted channels, cable television is often characterized as "narrowcasting" by media buyers. DirecTV can show ads based on household data (as opposed to demographic and geographic data). To stay relevant amid new technologies, DirecTV and other television-focused companies recognize the need for better audience targeting. In addition, an increasing number of adults 18 or over (about 34 percent have become "cord cutters" and do not subscribe to traditional legacy cable or satellite TV; instead, they watch TV online.[23]

Advertising time on television can be very expensive, especially for network and popular cable channels. Special events and first-run prime-time shows for top-ranked television programs command the highest rates for a typical commercial. For example, running a 30-second spot during the CBS sitcom *Young Sheldon* costs $160,996, NBC's *The Voice* costs $220,476, and one spot during *NFL Thursday Night Football* runs $579,391 while *NFL Sunday Night Football* costs $828,501.[24] A 30-second spot during the Super Bowl costs approximately $7 million, which equates to $233,333 per second of advertising. Despite its high cost, many brands feel that a Super Bowl ad is a good investment. One survey indicated that 79 percent of Super Bowl viewers watched the commercials. Further, the Super Bowl, for many, is about the shared experience, not necessarily watching the game, but the commercials.[25] An alternative to a commercial spot is the **infomercial**, a 30-minute or longer advertisement, which is relatively inexpensive to produce and air. Advertisers say that infomercials are an ideal way to present complicated information to potential customers, which other advertising vehicles typically do not allow time to do. Approximately 35 percent of infomercials relate to fitness and health products.[26]

One of the most significant worrisome trends in terms of television advertising is the rise in popularity of on-demand viewing and streaming services. For every hour of television programming, an average of 20 minutes is dedicated to nonprogram material (ads, public service announcements, and network promotions), so the popularity of cloud recording or watching commercial-free streaming programs among ad-weary viewers is hardly surprising. Additionally, streaming services like Netflix and Hulu have allowed consumers to bypass cable TV altogether (along with much of the advertising should they desire by paying for the ad-free streaming service). With increased inflation, many budget-cautious households may find available streaming ad-supported options appealing and further shaping the way TV ads will be created and distributed in the future.[27]

Digital

Note that global digital advertising spending reached $567.59 billion in 2022, eclipsing television's $101 billion.[28] Digital advertising includes search engine marketing (e.g., pay-per-click ads like Google Ads), display advertising (e.g., banner ads, video ads), social media advertising (e.g., Instagram ads), email marketing, and mobile marketing (including mobile advertising and SMS). Some digital channels, like Google, previously offered the ability to buy a *similar audience* (whereby advertisers can purchase ad space targeted to a highly specific group), instead, marketers can optimize targeting or opt into audience expansion. These tools allow organizations to leverage their own data to reach the right audience and optimize their direct message.[29]

Programmatic advertising uses technology to match audiences and websites with marketers seeking to purchase advertising. It is a rapidly growing and evolving field that started with the auction model used by Google. Programmatic advertising has also been used to purchase display and social media advertising and is beginning to be used with more traditional media purchases. The rise of programmatic ad buying means advertisers can purchase ad space targeting specific groups in real-time, using audience insights and marketing analytics, thus maximizing reach and return on investment (ROI). Automation tools and AI platforms allow brands to measure their performance and easily manage their brand campaigns with an emphasis on omnichannel programmatic advertising. But some brands have elected to follow "brand safety" guidelines, whereby marketers determine a list of websites acceptable for media placement instead of relying completely on marketing analytics to determine programmatic advertising. This strategy is a result of ads showing up on websites with questionable content.

Popular internet sites and search engines generally sell advertising space to marketers to promote their goods and services. Internet surfers click on these ads to be linked to more information about the advertised product or service. Both leading advertisers and companies whose ad budgets are not as large have become big digital advertisers.

Americans check their phone an average of once per ten minutes, or 96 times per day.[30]

---

infomercial a 30-minute or longer advertisement that looks more like a television talk show than a sales pitch

Because of the relatively low cost and high targetability, search engines generate nearly half of all internet ad revenue. However, because of the low cost, this space is also highly competitive. It also is dependent on technology to operate and the possibility of a technological interruption.

Another popular digital advertising format is **advergaming**, whereby companies put ad messages in web-based, mobile, console, or handheld video games to advertise or promote a product, service, organization, or issue. *Gamification*, the process of using game mechanics and a gaming mindset to engage an audience, is increasingly important for marketers to know about and utilize. Challenges, rewards, incentives, and competition are all important aspects of social media games like *Criminal Case, Candy Crush Saga, and Pet Rescue Saga*.[31] Some games amount to virtual commercials. Other games encourage players to buy in-game items and power-ups to advance, while still others allow advertisers to sponsor games or buy ad space for product placements. Many of these are social games, played on Facebook, YouTube, Amazon Twitch or other mobile networks, where players can interact with one another, locally or globally. Social gaming has a global audience with gamers from the United States and the United Kingdom, and Germany playing mostly to pass the time, while South Koreans play to relieve stress.[32]

Privacy and security issues are a concern for all companies with a digital presence. Given the amount of personal information being collected by brands from consumers, protection from a data breach is an ongoing concern for companies with an online presence.

Social

With more than 3.5 billion social media users worldwide, it is no surprise that 73 percent of marketers are finding success by using social advertising. As one of the methods of digital advertising, social media are a cost-effective means of gaining brand awareness. When positioned properly, social media marketers can gain insights into their industry and their target market. This fast-paced environment can be very rewarding for those with the skills to utilize the data being collected but it can also be detrimental for companies if negative information is spread. Therefore, companies looking to tap this highly competitive market need to hire individuals that are qualified and familiar with how to advance their brands on the various platforms available. Opting for social advertising should be done with a long-term investment in mind and an understanding that this medium is very time-consuming. Increases to inbound web traffic is the most likely outcome of social advertising to convert the visit into a sale.[33]

Smartphones and other mobile devices are the most popular choice among gamers in the United States and the United Kingdom.

Mobile

The fastest-growing platform for digital advertising is mobile. In fact, mobile advertising is expected to make up 70 percent of all U.S. digital advertising by 2026.[34] About 97 percent of Americans have mobile phones, 85 percent of which are smartphones. Approximately 47 percent of all U.S. web traffic originates from a mobile device.[35] Mobile ads account for nearly all growth in digital advertising. The primary reason for this incredible growth is that people are spending more of their time (almost 5.5 hours per day) on mobile devices.[36] And this trend is not just in the United States. Globally, mobile advertising has substantial upside potential, given the more than 7.33 billion mobile phone users in the world, which equates to 91.4 percent of the global population, of which 86.29 percent have smartphones with internet access.[37] As advanced mobile devices continue to grow in popularity around the world, so too will mobile ad spending.

When using mobile advertising, companies have access to customers in real time. Therefore, if customers opt-in for mobile advertising, companies can send ads at the same time a customer enters a specific area or at a precise time to which the company may feel has the greatest impact based on a customer's shopping behavior. The downfall of course is that customers must opt-in to these advertisements. Furthermore, the customer may incur a charge for the receipt of the advertisement based on their mobile carrier plan. If ads are not what the customer expected, they can easily opt out as well.[38]

Outdoor Media

Outdoor media, also referred to as outdoor advertising, are a flexible, low-cost option that may take a variety of forms. Examples include billboards, skywriting, giant inflatables, mini billboards in malls and on bus stop shelters, signs in sports arenas, and lighted moving signs in bus terminals and airports, as well as ads painted on cars, trucks, buses, water towers, manhole covers, drinking glass coasters, and even people, called "living advertising." The plywood

---

advergaming placing advertising messages in web-based, mobile, console, or handheld video games to advertise or promote a product, service, organization, or issue

Alternative media like virtual reality, augmented reality, and holographic displays are other ways for companies to create awareness and stimulate interest in their target markets.

scaffolding surrounding downtown construction sites often holds ads, which in places like Manhattan's Times Square, can reach over a million viewers a day.

Outdoor advertising reaches a broad and diverse market and is therefore ideal for promoting convenience products and services as well as for directing consumers to local businesses. One of the main advantages of outdoor advertising over other media is that its exposure frequency is very high, yet the amount of clutter from competing ads is very low. Outdoor advertising also can be customized to local marketing needs, which is why local businesses are the leading outdoor advertisers in any given region. At the same time, outdoor advertising is noticing a lot of innovation by linking these ads to mobile phones and social media.

Alternative Media

To cut through the clutter of traditional advertising media, advertisers are developing new media vehicles, like shopping carts in grocery stores, computer screen savers, interactive kiosks in department stores, advertisements run before movies at the cinema, posters on bathroom stalls, and *advertainments*—mini-movies that promote a product and are shown online.

Marketers are looking for additional innovative ways to reach captive and often bored commuters. For instance, subway systems are now showing ads via lighted boxes installed along tunnel walls. Other advertisers seek consumers at home. Some marketers have begun replacing hold music on customer service lines with advertisements and movie trailers. This strategy generates revenue for the company being called and catches undistracted consumers for advertisers. The trick is to amuse and interest this captive audience without annoying them during their 10- to 15-minute wait.

16-4b Media Selection Considerations

An important element in any advertising campaign is the **media mix**, the combination of media to be used. Media mix decisions are typically based on several factors: cost per contact, cost per click, reach, frequency, target audience considerations, flexibility of the medium, noise level, and the life span of the medium.

Cost per contact, also referred to as **cost per thousand** or **cost per mille (CPM)**, is the cost of reaching one member of the target market. Naturally, as the size of the audience increases, so does the total cost. Cost per contact enables an advertiser to compare the relative costs of specific media vehicles (such as television versus radio or online advertising versus social media), or more specifically, within a media category (such as *Facebook* versus *Instagram*). Thus, an advertiser debating whether to spend local advertising dollars for television spots or radio spots could consider the cost per contact of each. Alternatively, if the question is which magazine to advertise in, the advertiser might choose the one with the greater reach. In either case, the advertiser can pick the vehicle with the lowest cost per contact to maximize advertising punch for the money spent. **Cost per click** is the cost associated with a consumer clicking on a display or banner ad. Although there are several variations, this option enables the marketer to pay only for "engaged" consumers—those who opted to click on an ad.

Reach is the number of target customers who are exposed to a commercial at least once during a specific period, usually four weeks. Media plans for product introductions and attempts at increasing brand awareness usually emphasize reach. For example, an advertiser might try to reach 70 percent of the target audience during the first three months of the campaign. Reach is related to a medium's ratings, generally referred to in the industry as *gross rating points*, or *GRP*. A television program with a higher GRP means that more people are tuning in to the show and the reach is higher. Accordingly, as GRP increases for a particular medium, so does cost per contact.

Because the typical ad is short-lived, and often only a small portion of an ad may be perceived at one time, advertisers repeat their ads so that potential customers will remember the

---

media mix the combination of media to be used for a promotional campaign

cost per contact (cost per thousand or cost per mille [CPM]) the cost of reaching one member of the target market

cost per click the cost associated with a consumer clicking on a display or banner ad

reach the number of target consumers exposed to a commercial at least once during a specific period, usually four weeks

message. **Frequency** is the number of times an individual is exposed to a given message during a specific period. Advertisers use average frequency to measure the intensity of a specific medium's coverage. Research suggests that the optimal number of exposure varies by medium, product category, and type of ad. Research from Facebook suggests that the ideal frequency is 1 to 2 impressions weekly over a 10-week campaign. Research on other media options suggests that a weekly frequency of 2 is good for radio ads, while 3 to 10 is needed for TV. Samsung, for example, would likely want an exposure frequency of 5 to 7 for its television ads, meaning that each of the television viewers saw the ad a minimum of 5 times and possibly as many as 7. However, this may lead to overexposure. The more people that notice the same ad, the less interested they become. Frequency caps can be put in place to prevent overexposure. Further, to increase touchpoints with customers, and heighten each ad's effectiveness, brands should use unique ads for separate channels while maintaining brand consistency.[39]

Media selection is also a matter of matching the advertising medium with the product's target market. If marketers are trying to reach teenage males, they might select *GamePro* or *Sports Illustrated* magazine. On social media, YouTube, TikTok, or Instagram would be the best medium to reach teen males. A medium's ability to reach a precisely defined market is its **audience selectivity**. Some media vehicles, like general newspapers and network television, appeal to a wide cross section of the population. Others—such as *Vegetarian Times*, *Ski Magazine*, *Yoga Journal*, *Teen Vogue*, Food Network, ESPN, and classical radio stations—appeal to very specific groups.

The *flexibility* of a medium can be extremely important to an advertiser. For example, because of layouts and design, the lead time for magazine advertising is considerably longer than for other media types, so it is a less flexible medium. By contrast, radio and internet advertising provides maximum flexibility. If necessary, an advertiser can change a radio ad on the day it is aired.

Noise level is the amount of distraction experienced by the target audience in a medium. Noise can be created by competing ads, such as when a street is lined with billboards or when a television program is cluttered with competing ads. While newspapers, outdoor media, and magazines have a high noise level, direct mail is a private medium with a low noise level. Typically, no other advertising media or news stories compete for the attention of direct mail's readers.

---

frequency the number of times an individual is exposed to a given message during a specific period

audience selectivity the ability of an advertising medium to reach a precisely defined market

media schedule designation of the media, the specific publications or programs, and the insertion dates of advertising

Media have either a short or a long *life span*, which means that messages can either quickly fade or persist as a tangible copy to be carefully studied. A radio commercial may last less than a minute, but advertisers can overcome this short life span by repeating radio ads often. In contrast, a magazine has a relatively long life span, which is further increased by a high pass-along rate.

Media planners have traditionally relied on the above factors in selecting an effective media mix, with reach, frequency, and cost often the overriding criteria. But the ability to measure impact is increasingly important. Well-established brands with familiar messages generally need fewer exposures to be effective, while newer or unfamiliar brands likely need more exposures to create awareness and be effective. In addition, today's media planners have more media options than ever before. For example, there are over 1,775 television stations across the United States, whereas up until the early 1990's there were only three major commercial networks.[40]

The proliferation of media channels is causing *media fragmentation* and forcing media planners to pay as much attention to where they place their advertising as to how often the advertisement is repeated. That is, marketers should evaluate reach *and* frequency in assessing the effectiveness of advertising. In certain situations, it may be important to reach potential consumers through as many media vehicles as possible. When this approach is considered, however, the budget must be large enough to achieve sufficient levels of frequency in all media vehicles to have an impact. In evaluating reach versus frequency, therefore, the media planner ultimately must select an approach that is most likely to result in the ad being understood and remembered when a purchase decision is being made.

Advertisers also evaluate the qualitative factors involved in media selection. These include such things as attention to the commercial and the program, involvement, program liking, lack of distractions, and other audience behaviors that affect the likelihood of a commercial message being seen and, hopefully, processed to long-term memory. While advertisers can advertise their product in as many media as possible and repeat the ad as many times as they like, the ad still may not be effective if the audience is not paying attention. In general, research confirms the benefits of cross-media advertising campaigns.[41]

16-4c Media Scheduling

After choosing the media for the advertising campaign, advertisers must schedule the ads. A **media schedule** designates the medium or media to be used (such as magazines, television, or digital), the specific vehicles (such as *Reader's Digest* magazine, the show *Chicago Fire* on television, or Instagram), and the dates of the advertising.

The following are four basic types of media schedules:

1. A **continuous media schedule** is designed so that the ad runs steadily throughout the advertising period. Examples include Nutella and Chobani Greek yogurt, which may have an ad on Instagram every Sunday and a television commercial on NBC every night during the week at 7:30 p.m. over three months. Products in the later stages of the product life cycle, which are advertised on a reminder basis, often use a continuous media schedule.

2. With a **flighted media schedule**, the advertiser may schedule the ads heavily every other month or every two weeks to achieve a greater impact with an increased frequency and reach at those times. Similarly, movie studios might schedule television advertising on Wednesday and Thursday nights, when moviegoers are deciding which films to watch that weekend.

3. A **pulsing media schedule** combines continuous scheduling with flighted scheduling; it is continuous advertising that is more frequent during the best sale periods. A retail department store, like Kohl's, may advertise on a year-round basis but place more advertising during certain sale periods, such as Thanksgiving, Christmas, and back to school. Or beer may be advertised more heavily during the summer months and football season, given the higher consumption levels at those times.

4. Certain times of the year call for a **seasonal media schedule**. Products like Theraflu cold and flu medicine and Yeti coolers, which are used more during certain times of the year, tend to follow a seasonal strategy.

Research comparing continuous media schedules and flighted ones suggests that continuous schedules are more effective than flighted ones at driving sales through television advertisements. Research also suggests that it is likely more important to reach a potential customer as close as possible to the time at which a purchase is being considered. Therefore, the advertiser should maintain a continuous schedule over as long a period as possible. Often called *recency planning*, this theory of scheduling is now commonly used for scheduling television advertising for frequently purchased products such as Quaker Chewy granola bars and Gain detergent. Recency planning's main premise is that advertising works by influencing the brand choice of people who are ready to buy. Mobile advertising is one of the most promising tactics for contacting consumers when they are thinking about a specific product. For example, a GPS-enabled mobile phone can get text messages for area restaurants around lunchtime to advertise specials to professionals working in a big city.

16-5 Public Relations

16-5 Discuss the role of public relations in the promotional mix

Public relations is the element in the promotional mix that evaluates public attitudes, identifies issues that may elicit public concern, and executes programs to gain public understanding and acceptance. Public relations is a vital link in a forward-thinking company's marketing communication mix. Marketing managers plan solid public relations campaigns that fit into overall marketing plans and focus on target audiences. These campaigns strive to maintain a positive image of the company in the eyes of the public. The campaigns should capitalize, therefore, on factors that enhance the firm's image and minimize the factors that could generate a negative image. The concept of earned media is based on public relations and publicity.

Publicity is the effort to capture media attention—for example, through articles or editorials in publications or through human-interest stories on radio or television programs. Companies usually initiate publicity through press releases that further their public relations plans. A company about to introduce a new product or open a new store may send press releases to the media in the hope that the story will be published or broadcast. Savvy publicity can often create overnight sensations or build up a reserve of goodwill with consumers. Corporate donations and sponsorships can also create favorable publicity.

---

continuous media schedule a media scheduling strategy in which advertising is run steadily throughout the advertising period; used for products in the later stages of the product life cycle

flighted media schedule a media scheduling strategy in which ads are run heavily every other month or every two weeks to achieve a greater impact with an increased frequency and reach at those times

pulsing media schedule a media scheduling strategy that uses continuous scheduling throughout the year coupled with a flighted schedule during the best sales periods

seasonal media schedule a media scheduling strategy that runs advertising only during times of the year when the product is most likely to be used

public relations the element in the promotional mix that evaluates public attitudes, identifies issues that may elicit public concern, and executes programs to gain public understanding and acceptance

publicity an effort to capture media attention, often initiated through press releases that further a corporation's public relations plans

16-5a Major Public Relations Tools

Public relations professionals commonly use several tools, many of which require an active role on the part of the public relations professional, such as writing press releases and engaging in proactive media relations. Sometimes, however, these techniques create their own publicity.

New-Product Publicity

Publicity is instrumental in introducing new products and services. Publicity can help advertisers explain what's different about their new product by prompting free news stories or positive word of mouth about it. During the introductory period, an especially innovative new product often needs more exposure than is provided by conventional, paid advertising. Public relations professionals write press releases or develop videos to generate news about their new products. They also jockey for exposure of their product or service at major events, on popular television and news shows, or in the hands of influential people. Social media and the use of celebrities are important for new product publicity. For example, Papa John's teamed up with Shaquille O'Neal and introduced an X-Large pepperoni pizza with extra pepperoni and extra mozzarella cheese that was called the Shaq-a-Roni pizza. This was a limited time released product that with the sale of each pizza, Papa John's donated one dollar to the Papa John's Foundation for Building Community fund. A contest on Twitter, now known as X, was also run in which the winner gets a "Shaq-sized" prize of free pizza for 22 years! Over $3 million were raised for the foundation with this limited-time product release.[42]

Product Placement

Marketers are increasingly using product placement to reinforce brand awareness and create favorable attitudes. **Product placement** is a strategy that involves getting one's product, service, or name to appear in a movie, television show, radio program, magazine, newspaper, video game, video, or audio clip, book, commercial for another product, on the internet, in conjunction with influencers, or at special events. Including an actual product, such as a bottle of Dasani

Positive publicity stimulates brand engagement and creates customer loyalty. Companies are increasingly choosing digital media alternatives, such as YouTube, to communicate with current and potential customers and enhance their brand equity.

Source: Target/YouTube, LLC

water, adds a sense of realism to a movie, television show, video game, book, or similar product that cannot be created by a bottle simply marked "water." Product placements are arranged through barter (trade of product for placement), through paid placements, or at no charge when the product is viewed as enhancing the vehicle in which it is placed. It is estimated that 70 percent of brands will dedicate 10 percent or more of their media budget to entertaining content product placement. This method is attractive since so many consumers opt out of ads or experience advertising fatigue.[43]

General Motors (GM) is partnering with Netflix to increase the use of electric vehicles in Netflix-produced shows and movies. The main goal of the partnership is to increase exposure to electric vehicles. Further, GM will educate the showrunners on the electric vehicles to integrate them into the storylines of the shows and movies so it feels natural.[44]

Global product placement expenditures total about $26.2 billion annually, with the United States accounting for 56 percent, of that spending. Nike has been featured over 3,000 times in movies or TV shows. MacBook has appeared over 2,145 times, and the iPhone has over 1,626 appearances in movies or TV shows.[45] More than two-thirds of product placements are in movies and television shows, but placements in alternative media are growing, particularly on the internet and in video games. Digital technology now enables companies to "virtually" place their products in any audio or video production. Virtual placement not only reduces the cost of product placement for new productions but also enables companies to place their products in previously produced programs, such as reruns of television shows. Overall, companies obtain valuable product exposure, brand reinforcement, and increased sales through product placement.

---

product placement a public relations strategy that involves getting a product, service, or company name to appear in a movie, television show, radio program, magazine, newspaper, video game, video or audio clip, book, or commercial for another product, on the internet, or at special events

As part of General Motors' "Everybody In" campaign, to accelerate the mass adoption of electric vehicles, it partnered with Netflix to increase the presence of electric vehicles in Netflix-produced shows and movies.

Consumer Education

Some major firms believe that educated consumers are more loyal customers. Financial planning firms often sponsor free educational seminars on money management, retirement planning, and investing in the hope that the seminar participants will choose the sponsoring organization for their future financial needs.

Sponsorship

Sponsorships are increasing both in number and as a proportion of companies' marketing budgets. U.S. sponsorship spending is likewise increasing and is currently about $47.8 billion annually.[46] Probably the biggest reason for the increasing use of sponsorships is the difficulty of reaching audiences and differentiating a product from competing brands through the mass media.

With **sponsorship**, a company spends money to support an issue, cause, or event that is consistent with corporate objectives, such as improving brand awareness or enhancing corporate image. The biggest category of sponsorships is sporting events.[47] Nonsports categories include entertainment tours and attractions, causes, arts, festivals, fairs and annual events, and association and membership organizations.

Although the most popular sponsorship events are still those involving sports, music, or the arts, companies have recently been turning to more specialized events such as tie-ins with schools, charities, and other community service organizations. Marketers sometimes even create their own events tied to their products. For example, Epic Games began hosting in-game concerts for the *Fortnite* community. These live virtual events have included performances by Travis Scott and DJ Marshmello. The Marshmello concert was attended by 10.7 million players.[48]

Corporations sponsor issues as well as events. Sponsorship issues are quite diverse, but the three most popular are education, health care, and social programs. Firms often donate a percentage of sales or profits to a worthy cause favored by their target market.

Experiential Marketing

While the internet enables consumers to connect with their favorite brands in a virtual environment, there is often nothing like experiencing the real thing live and in person. Experiential marketing involves engaging with consumers in a way that enables them to feel the brand—not just read about it. Experiential and event marketing have increased in recent years, with most of the growth coming from the world's largest brands. One example of experiential marketing is when M&Ms wanted to select its next flavor, the company created an immersive pop-up in New York, NY. This included "flavor rooms" including snack and drink lounges associated with each room theme. The fun element associated with the campaign appeared in many attendees' social pages and M&M's received feedback for the new flavors.[49]

Company Websites

Companies are increasingly using the internet in their public relations strategies. Company websites are used to introduce new products; provide information to the media, including social media news releases; promote existing products; obtain consumer feedback; communicate legislative and regulatory information; showcase upcoming events; provide links to related sites (including corporate and noncorporate blogs, Facebook, X, and Instagram); release financial information; interact with customers and potential customers; and perform many more marketing activities. In addition, social media are playing a larger role in how companies interact with customers online, particularly through sites like Facebook, Yelp, and X. Indeed, online reviews (good and bad) from opinion leaders and other consumers help marketers sway purchasing decisions in their favor.

---

sponsorship a public relations strategy in which a company spends money to support an issue, cause, or event that is consistent with corporate objectives, such as improving brand awareness or enhancing corporate image

16-5b Managing Unfavorable Publicity

Although marketers try to avoid unpleasant situations, crises do happen. In our free-press environment, publicity is not easily controlled, especially in a crisis. **Crisis management** is the coordinated effort to handle the effects of unfavorable publicity, ensuring fast and accurate communication in times of emergency.

When German grocery store chain, Aldi was accused of trademark infringement for offering its Cuthbert the Caterpillar cake, a similar product to British retailer Marks and Spencer's Colin the Caterpillar cake, the retailer took to X. Aldi launched a campaign using the hashtag #FreeCuthbert, which was highly supported and retweeted by Aldi fans with views from user-generated videos topping 30 million. The two supermarkets were able to resolve the issue in court. Although Cuthbert would undergo some changes, Aldi was pleased to announce, "Cuthbert is free and looking forward to seeing all his fans again very soon!"[50]

16-6 Sales Promotion

16-6 Describe the tools used to achieve the objectives of sales promotion

In addition to using advertising and public relations, marketing managers can use **sales promotion** to increase the effectiveness of their promotional efforts. Sales promotion consists of marketing communication activities other than advertising, personal selling, and public relations, in which a short-term incentive motivates consumers or members of the distribution channel to purchase a good or service immediately, either by lowering the price or by adding value.

---

crisis management a coordinated effort to handle all the effects of unfavorable publicity or another unexpected unfavorable event

sales promotion marketing communication activities other than advertising, personal selling, and public relations, in which a short-term incentive motivates consumers or members of the distribution channel to purchase a good or service immediately, either by lowering the price or by adding value

trade sales promotion promotion activities directed to members of the marketing channel, such as wholesalers and retailers

consumer sales promotion promotion activities targeted to the ultimate consumer market

trade allowance a price reduction offered by manufacturers to intermediaries such as wholesalers and retailers

Sales promotion is usually less expensive than advertising and easier to measure. A major national television advertising campaign can be expensive to run since production costs range from $100,000 to $8 million to produce. In addition, the placement for a single 30-second national ad slot runs about $350,000.[51] In contrast, promotional campaigns using the internet or direct marketing methods can cost less than half that amount. It is also very difficult to determine how many people buy a product or service as a result of radio or television ads. With sales promotion, marketers know the precise number of coupons or coupon codes redeemed or the number of contest entries received.

Sales promotion usually has more effect on behavior than on attitudes. Giving the consumer an incentive to make an immediate purchase is the goal of sales promotion, regardless of the form it takes. Sales promotion is usually targeted toward either of two distinctly different markets. **Trade sales promotion** is directed to members of the marketing channel, such as wholesalers and retailers. **Consumer sales promotion** is targeted to the ultimate consumer market. The objectives of a promotion depend on the general behavior of targeted customers (Table 16.4). For example, marketers who are targeting loyal users of their product need to reinforce existing behavior or increase product usage. An effective tool for strengthening brand loyalty is the *frequent-buyer program*, which rewards consumers for repeat purchases. Other types of promotions are more effective with customers who are prone to brand switching or with those who are loyal to a competitor's product. A cents-off coupon, free sample, or eye-catching display in a store will often entice shoppers to try a different brand.

Once marketers understand the dynamics occurring within their product category and determine the particular customers and behaviors they want to influence, they can then go about selecting promotional tools to achieve these goals.

16-6a Tools for Trade Sales Promotion

As we'll discuss in Section 16-6b, consumer promotions pull a product through the channel by creating demand. However, trade promotions *push* a product through the distribution channel (refer to Chapter 13). When selling to members of the distribution channel, manufacturers use many of the same sales promotion tools used in consumer promotions, such as sales contests, premiums, and point-of-purchase displays. Several tools, however, are unique to manufacturers and channel intermediaries:

- **Trade allowances:** A **trade allowance** is a price reduction offered by manufacturers to intermediaries such as wholesalers and retailers. The price reduction or rebate is given in exchange for doing something

Table 16.4 Types of Consumers and Sales Promotion Goals

Type of Buyer	Desired Results	Sales Promotion Examples
Loyal customers People who buy your product most or all of the time	Reinforce behavior, increase consumption, change purchase timing	• Loyalty marketing programs, such as frequent-buyer cards or frequent-shopper clubs • Bonus packs that give loyal consumers an incentive to stock up or premiums offered in return for proofs of purchase
Competitor's customers People who buy a competitor's product most or all of the time	Break loyalty, persuade to switch to your brand	• Sampling to introduce your product's superior qualities compared to their brand • Sweepstakes, contests, or premiums that create interest in the product
Brand switchers People who buy a variety of products in the category	Persuade to buy your brand more often	• Any promotion that lowers the price of the product, such as coupons, price-off packages, and bonus packs • Trade deals that help make the product more readily available than competing products
Price buyers People who consistently buy the least expensive brand	Appeal with low prices or supply added value that makes price less important	• Coupons, price-off packages, refunds, or trade deals that reduce the price of the brand to match that of the brand that would have been purchased

Source: From *Sales Promotion Essentials*, 2nd ed., by Don E. Schultz, William A. Robinson, and Lisa A. Petrison, published by McGraw Hill Education.

specific, such as allocating space for a new product or buying something during special periods. For example, a local Publix outlet could receive a special discount for running its own promotion on Pantene haircare products.

- **Push money:** Intermediaries receive **push money** as a bonus for pushing the manufacturer's brand through the distribution channel. Often the push money is directed toward a retailer's salespeople. When Dell introduced a new Latitude laptop model, it provided a bonus to the salespeople at Best Buy for every sale of the new model. This bonus is separate from any commissions the salesperson would normally receive from Best Buy.

- **Training:** Sometimes a manufacturer will train an intermediary's personnel if the product is rather complex—as frequently occurs in the computer and telecommunications industries. For example, an accounting software manufacturer may include training for employees with the purchase of a new software platform.

- **Free merchandise:** Often a manufacturer offers retailers free merchandise instead of quantity discounts. Occasionally, free merchandise is used as payment for trade allowances normally provided through other sales promotions. Instead of giving a retailer a price reduction for buying a certain quantity of merchandise, the manufacturer may throw in extra merchandise "free" (i.e., at a cost that would equal the price reduction).

- **Store demonstrations:** Manufacturers can also arrange with retailers to perform in-store demonstrations. Food manufacturers often send representatives to grocery stores and supermarkets to let customers sample a product while shopping.

- **Business meetings, conventions, and trade shows:** Trade association meetings, conferences, and conventions are an important aspect of sales promotion and a growing, multibillion-dollar market. At these shows, manufacturers, distributors, and other vendors have the chance to display their goods or describe their services to potential customers. Companies participate in trade shows to attract and identify new prospects, serve current customers, introduce new products, enhance corporate image, test the market response to new products, enhance corporate morale, and gather information on competing products.

push money money offered to channel intermediaries to encourage them to "push" products—that is, to encourage other members of the channel to sell the products

Trade promotions are popular among manufacturers for many reasons. Trade sales promotion tools help manufacturers gain new distributors for their products, obtain wholesaler and retailer support for consumer sales promotions, build or reduce dealer inventories, and improve trade relations. Car manufacturers annually sponsor dozens of auto shows for consumers. The shows attract millions of consumers, providing dealers with increased store traffic as well as good leads.

16-6b Tools for Consumer Sales Promotion

Marketing managers must decide which consumer sales promotion devices to use in a specific campaign. The methods chosen must suit the objectives to ensure success of the overall promotion plan. The popular tools for consumer sales promotion, discussed in the following pages, have also been easily transferred to online versions to entice internet users to visit sites, purchase products, or use services on the web.

Coupons and Rebates

A **coupon** is a certificate that entitles a consumer to an immediate price reduction when the product is purchased. Coupons are a particularly good way to encourage product trial and repurchase. They are also likely to increase the amount of a product bought. Coupons can be distributed in stores as instant coupons on packaging, on shelf displays with pull-off coupon dispensers, and at cash registers, printed based on what the customer purchased; through freestanding inserts (FSIs); and through various internet daily deal sites. Procter & Gamble (P&G), the makers of products like Tide laundry detergent and Pampers diapers, provide consumers an opportunity for savings on their brands. "P&G Good Everyday" is an online loyalty program that is free to join. Printable coupons and promo codes are available offering discounts on over 60 P&G brands.[52]

FSIs, the promotional coupon inserts found in newspapers, are the traditional way of circulating printed coupons. FSIs are used to distribute approximately 89 percent of coupons. Such traditional types of coupon distribution, which also include direct mail and magazines, have been declining for several years, as consumers use fewer coupons. About 168 billion coupons were circulated in 2021

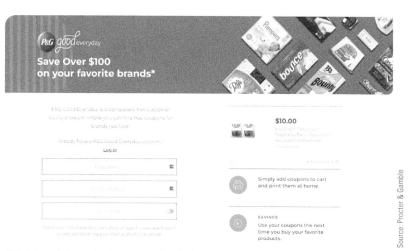

"P&G Good Everyday" is a completely free loyalty program for customers to find and print coupons at home for their favorite P&G brands.

which was down from 294 billion in 2015. However, the redemption rate for all printed and digital coupons in 2020 was a mere 0.5 percent. It is believed that the decline from 3.5 percent redemption in the 1980s is primarily due to dual-income households and time-strapped consumers not wanting to deal with the hassle. During recessionary times, coupon usage has experienced an increase.[53]

iDigital coupon sites such as Swagbucks and Rakuten, and social coupon sites such as Groupon and LivingSocial, there are also deal sites like DealSurf.com that aggregate offers from different sites for convenience. While daily deal sites have been quite popular with consumers, sites like Groupon and LivingSocial are coming under some fire as many small businesses claim they lose money or drown under the flood of coupon redemptions. Apple is using ApplePay to provide customers with incentives, and Capital One Shopping (formerly Wikibuy) helps consumers save money by providing shoppers with coupons or lower prices on another site. To help automate the process for shoppers, a browser extension for Edge, Chrome, Safari, and Firefox can be used.[54]

A **rebate** is similar to a coupon in that it offers the purchaser a price reduction. This is similar to a cashback program, but because the purchaser must mail in a rebate form and usually some proof of purchase, the reward is not immediate or automatic. Manufacturers prefer rebates for several reasons. Rebates allow manufacturers to offer price cuts directly to consumers. Manufacturers have more control over rebate promotions because they can be rolled out and shut off quickly. Further, because buyers must fill out forms with their names, addresses, and other data, manufacturers use rebate programs to build customer databases. Perhaps the best reason to offer rebates is that although rebates are particularly good at enticing purchases, most consumers never bother to redeem them. Redemption rates for rebates under $30 range from 10–30 percent.[55]

---

coupon a certificate that entitles a consumer to an immediate price reduction when the product is purchased

rebate a cash refund given for the purchase of a product during a specific period

Premiums

A **premium** is an extra item offered to the consumer, usually in exchange for some proof that the promoted product has been purchased. Premiums reinforce the consumer's purchase decision, increase consumption, and persuade nonusers to switch brands. A long-standing example of the use of premiums is the McDonald's Happy Meal, which rewards children with a small toy. Premiums can also include more products for the regular price, such as two-for-the-price-of-one bonus packs or packages that include more of the product. Some companies attach a premium to the product's package, such as a small sample of a complementary hair product, like a leave-in conditioner, attached to a shampoo bottle. Premium models like Breo Box and SingleSwag are subscription approaches in which customers pay a fee for delivery of a box of both full-size and sample products on a monthly or quarterly basis. These are great deals for marketers who want to get their beauty, tech, and home products into the hands of affluent customers.

Loyalty Marketing Programs

A **loyalty marketing program** builds long-term, mutually beneficial relationships between a company and its key customers. One of the most popular types of loyalty programs, the **frequent-buyer program**, rewards loyal consumers for making multiple purchases. The objective of loyalty marketing programs is to build long-term, mutually beneficial relationships between a company and its key customers.

More than 90 percent of companies have a form of loyalty or rewards program. These U.S. loyalty marketing programs are valued at over $5.5 billion and expected to be over $24 billion by the end of 2028.[56] Popularized by the airline industry through frequent-flyer programs, loyalty marketing enables companies to strategically invest sales promotion dollars in activities designed to capture greater profits from customers already loyal to the product or company. Co-branded credit cards are an increasingly popular loyalty marketing tool. Many stores like Kohls's, Best Buy, Macy's, and Amazon offer loyalty programs if a customer opens their branded credit card.

Through loyalty programs, shoppers receive discounts, alerts about new products, and other types of enticing offers. In exchange, retailers can build customer databases that help them better understand customer preferences. Since it is 5 to 25 times more expensive to obtain a new customer than keep existing ones, using loyalty programs that have a 60 to 70 percent chance of selling to an existing customer can be effective. Further, loyalty program members generate 12 to 18 percent additional revenue per year compared to non-members. For this reason, 80 percent of current loyalty program owners plan to increase their investment in these programs.[57]

Contests and Sweepstakes

Contests and sweepstakes are generally designed to create interest in a good or service, often to encourage brand switching. *Contests* are promotions in which participants use some skill or ability to compete for prizes. A consumer contest usually requires entrants to answer questions, complete sentences, or write a paragraph about the product and submit proof of purchase. Winning a *sweepstakes*, on the other hand, depends on chance, and participation is free. Sweepstakes usually draw about 10 times more entries than contests do.

While contests and sweepstakes may draw considerable interest and publicity, generally they are not effective tools for generating long-term sales. To increase their effectiveness, sales promotion managers must make certain the award will appeal to the target market. Offering several smaller prizes to many winners instead of one huge prize to just one person often will increase the effectiveness of the promotion, but there is no denying the attractiveness of a jackpot-type prize.

Sampling

Sampling allows the customer to try a product risk-free. This tactic is geared toward new customer acquisitions by building awareness but also reinforces the decision process among existing consumers. While in-store sampling at places like Costco and Sam's Club are common, sampling is not only an in-person opportunity. Chegg College Marketing sends millions of brand samples to students with textbook purchases. The program has been successful with many recipients organically promoting on social media and 67 percent reported making a first-time purchase after sampling a product. Sampling can also be added to loyalty programs or combined with company data to personalize the sampling program. Sephora customers can select two samples with their online order. Augmented reality can also be used as a form of sampling for products like cosmetics (Mac Cosmetics) or for viewing glasses on one's face (Zenni Optical).[58]

---

premium an extra item offered to the consumer, usually in exchange for some proof of purchase of the promoted product

loyalty marketing program a promotional program designed to build long-term, mutually beneficial relationships between a company and its key customers

frequent-buyer program a loyalty program in which loyal consumers are rewarded for making multiple purchases of a particular good or service

sampling a promotional program that allows the consumer the opportunity to try a product or service for free

Samples can be directly mailed to the customer, delivered door to door, packaged with another product, or demonstrated or distributed at a retail store or service outlet. Sampling at special events is a popular, effective, and high-profile distribution method that permits marketers to piggyback onto fun-based consumer activities—including sporting events, college fests, fairs and festivals, beach events, and chili cook-offs. Distributing samples to specific location types, such as grocery stores, health clubs, churches, or doctors' offices, is also one of the most efficient methods of sampling. Online sampling has grown with social media as well. Branded products not only run contests through Facebook, but also connect with fans, show commercials, and offer samples of new products in exchange for "liking" the brand or leaving a review.

Point-of-Purchase Promotion

A **point-of-purchase (POP) display** includes any promotional display set up at the retailer's location to build traffic, advertise the product, or induce impulse buying. POP displays include shelf "talkers" (signs attached to store shelves), shelf extenders (attachments that extend shelves so products stand out), ads on grocery carts and bags, end-aisle and floor-stand displays, television monitors at supermarket checkout counters, in-store audio messages, and audiovisual displays. One big advantage of the POP display is that it offers manufacturers a captive audience in retail stores. One study indicates that approximately 82 percent of all retail purchase decisions are made in-store. Sixty-two percent of shoppers buy more than they anticipated once in the store with 16 percent of those purchases influenced by in-store promotions, so POP displays can be very effective.[59] Other strategies to increase sales include adding cards to the tops of displays, changing messages on signs on the sides or bottoms of displays, adding

---

point of purchase (POP) display a promotional display set up at the retailer's location to build traffic, advertise the product, or induce impulse buying

inflatable or mobile displays, and using signs that advertise the brand's sports, movie, or charity tie-in.

16-6c Trends in Sales Promotion

The biggest trend in sales promotion on both the trade and consumer sides has been the increased use of the internet. Promotions based on social media, email, websites, and mobile apps have expanded dramatically in recent years. Marketers are now spending billions of dollars annually on such promotions. Sales promotions online have proved both effective and cost-efficient—generating response rates three to five times higher than offline promotions. The most effective types of online sales promotions are free merchandise, sweepstakes, free shipping with purchases, and coupons. One major goal of retailers is to add potential customers to their databases and expand marketing touch points.

Marketers have discovered that online coupon distribution provides another vehicle for promoting their products. Coupon redemption rates have seen a decline, while the users who *do* redeem coupons are increasingly inclined to make use of digital offers. These customers want coupons and discounts to be more available, making the shopping experience as simple as possible.[60] Online coupons can help marketers lure new customers, and with the speed of online feedback, marketers can measure channel effectiveness, track the success of a coupon in real time and make adjustments based on changing market conditions.[61]

Online versions of loyalty programs are also popping up, and although many types of companies have these programs, the most successful improve the experience for the customer and transcend the transaction.[62] A final major trend in sales promotion is the utilization of sales promotions on social media and at the point of purchase. Google's Zero Moment of Truth (ZMOT) insights illustrate how important consumer feedback is to consumer purchases, highlighting the importance of behavioral data and marketing analytics when executing a targeted sales promotion.[63]

Chapter 17

Personal Selling and Sales Management

Learning Outcomes

After studying this chapter, you will be able to . . .

17-1 Describe the sales environment and personal selling

17-2 Discuss social media's impact on personal selling

17-3 Discuss the key differences between relationship selling and transactional selling

17-4 List and explain the steps in the selling process

17-5 Explain the functions and roles of sales management

17-6 Describe the use of customer relationship management in the selling process

17-1 The Sales Environment and Personal Selling

17-1 Describe the sales environment and personal selling

Many people around the world work in some form of selling. Traditionally, salespeople engage in direct face-to-face contact with customers. This can take place either at the salesperson's place of business or at a secondary location (such as when a salesperson travels door to door or meets a customer at her office or home). Salespeople can be consumer-focused (as in the case of retail) or business-focused (selling to other firms).

17-1a The Sales Environment

In many cases, consumer-focused salespeople require customers to come directly to a retail store, shortening the sales process time. Even though many retailers use multiple customer relationship management processes (including information kiosks, websites, and self-checkouts), one-to-one interactions are often key to retail success. Most major retailers use trained salespeople—not just order takers—to enhance the customer experience. Electronics retailer Best Buy, for example, offers internships in its retail stores where interns can gain hands-on experience in sales and customer service.[1] By having knowledgeable salespeople, retailers can help their customers select the products or services that are best for them.

As previously indicated, some consumer-focused salespeople travel to their customers' locations. For example, many security alarm companies, such as ADT, Brink's, and Verisure, have salespeople meet potential customers at their homes to customize the options that make sense for customers looking to install a security alarm. Similarly, cosmetics, small appliances, and magazine subscriptions may be sold directly to customers at their homes. These salespeople are considered direct salespeople. Companies such as Herbalife Nutrition, Pampered Chef, and Mary Kay Cosmetics have been very successful in direct selling.

Business-focused salespeople call on other companies to sell their products. These business-to-business salespeople often spend a great deal of time traveling to customer locations to make sales calls, and the sales process generally takes a longer period than consumer-focused selling. Often, business-to-business (B2B) salespeople have more extensive sales training, are required to travel more, and in turn, receive a higher level of compensation.

The sales environment changes constantly as new competitors enter the market and old competitors leave. The ways customers interact with salespeople and learn about products and suppliers are changing because of the rapid increase in new sales technologies, including increased use of social media. Most salespeople are receptive to using social media, given that it has been shown to increase performance.[2] For companies to successfully sell products or services using a sales force, they must be very effective at personal selling, social media, technology, sales management, and customer relationship management—all of which play critical roles in building strong long-term relationships with customers.

17-1b Personal Selling

As mentioned in Chapter 15, personal selling is a purchase situation involving a personal, paid-for communication between two people in an attempt to influence each other. In a sense, all businesspeople are salespeople. An individual may become a project manager, a professor, a doctor, or a member of any profession, and yet still have to sell. For example, during a job search, applicants must "sell" themselves to prospective employers in an interview. Additionally, every time someone in a company asks a manager for a raise, or needs to communicate their needs for additional resources, they are engaging in communication to influence another. Personal selling offers several advantages over other forms of promotion:

- Personal selling provides a detailed explanation or demonstration of the product. This capability is especially needed for complex or new goods and services.

- The sales message can be personalized according to the motivations, needs, and interests of each prospective customer. Moreover, when the prospect has questions, concerns, or raises objections, the salesperson is there to provide explanations and guidance. By contrast, advertising and sales promotion can respond only to the questions and objections the copywriter *thinks* are important to customers. Importantly, any concern or objection addressed in an advertisement can never be changed in real-time. Personal selling, therefore, is considerably more effective than other forms of promotion in obtaining a sale and gaining a satisfied customer.

- Personal selling should be directed only toward qualified prospects. Other forms of promotion include some unavoidable waste because many people in the audience are not prospective customers. Think about how many advertisements you've noticed in the past 24-hour period. How many were for a product or service you would never purchase?

- Costs can be controlled by adjusting the size of the sales force (and resulting expenses) in one-person increments. On the other hand, advertising and sales promotion must often be purchased in fairly large amounts.

Table 17.1 Comparison of Personal Selling and Advertising/Sales Promotion

Personal selling is more important if . . .	Advertising and sales promotion are more important if . . .
The product has a high value.	The product has a low value.
It is a custom-made product.	It is a standardized product.
There are few customers.	There are many customers.
The product is technically complex.	The product is easy to understand.
Customers are concentrated.	Customers are geographically dispersed.
Examples: Insurance policies, custom windows, airplane engines	Examples: Soap, magazine subscriptions, cotton T-shirts

Personal selling also has limitations when compared to other forms of promotion:

- Cost per contact is much greater than for mass forms of communication, leading companies to be highly selective about where and when they use salespeople.
- If the sales force is not properly trained, or the salesperson's communication skills are lacking, the message provided can be unreliable and inaccurate. Hence, costly and continual sales force management and training are necessary.
- Salespeople may convince customers to buy unneeded products or services. This can lead to increased levels of cognitive dissonance among buyers if a salesperson is being pushed to meet certain quotas.

For certain products and services, personal selling often works better than other forms of promotion, given certain customer and product characteristics. Generally speaking, personal selling becomes more important when the number of potential customers decreases, as the complexity of the product increases, and as the value of the product grows (refer to Table 17.1). For highly complex goods, such as industrial equipment and large enterprise software solutions, a salesperson is needed to determine the prospective customer's needs and wants, explain the product's benefits and advantages, and propose the exact features and accessories that will best meet the client's needs. Many upscale clothing department stores, such as Bloomingdale's, Macy's, and Neiman Marcus, offer free personal shopping, whereby individual consultants select and suggest designer clothing and accessories they believe will fit the customer's style. Neiman Marcus, for example, offers free personal shopper services to its customers that can provide fashion advice and styling suggestions and can assist customers with clothing, accessories, beauty products, and more.[3]

17-2 Social Media's Impact on Selling

17-2 Discuss social media's impact on personal selling

Technology, including social media, plays an increasingly important role in personal selling. Instead of being handed traditional sales pamphlets and brochures, consumers are now able to easily learn about products and services by searching the internet before entering a store. Before the advent of widely available information, salespeople had an advantage over the customer in many situations simply because they knew more about the product than the customer. This advantage is no longer present. In fact, many consumers compare product features, prices, and quality online before even deciding which store to visit, and they are often influenced by social media.

Firms that succeed in having a consumer enter their retail store often find that today's consumer evaluates the products or services firsthand and then the internet to compare products for a potential purchase across several competing channels and companies—a process called showrooming (refer to Chapter 6).[4] In addition to their own research, consumers are constantly bombarded with messages, coupons, and sale information from retail locations on email and social media. Suffice it to say, consumers are more educated about products and services today than they have ever been before. If salespeople do not stay well informed about the products they are selling, consumers may enter the store knowing more than the salespeople do. This reduces the ability of the salesperson to build trust and confidence.

Like consumers, salespeople are increasingly using social media. When properly and strategically used, social media use by salespeople can lead to increased levels of customer engagement and increased sales.[5] LinkedIn, Facebook, Instagram, and YouTube are not only a place to make sales; they can also help establish a salesperson's expertise within a field. With more than 900 million members in more than 200 countries, LinkedIn positions itself as the world's largest professional network.[6] In addition to its networking function, LinkedIn offers sales solutions to help salespeople find and target prospects, more effectively qualify leads, and make quicker product recommendations to decision makers.[7] LinkedIn also provides advice on how to effectively sell using social media. For example, LinkedIn provides featured articles discussing topics such as the fundamentals of social selling, the differences between social selling and traditional selling, and strategies to measure social selling success.[8]

In most instances, firms cannot control the content on social media sites. They can only attempt to influence it. It is important for salespeople to be aware and to understand what is being distributed on social media regarding the firm, products, competitors, and the sales force itself. At the same time, customers' ability to share positive and negative service experiences with so many people dramatically increases the impact of both positive and negative word of mouth. For example, prospective customers evaluating several different home security alarm companies can review what recent alarm purchasers have posted about different companies through sites such as Angi and Trustpilot, which are platforms that provides customer reviews for home service professionals.[9] Social media also allows firms to monitor what customers, potential customers, or noncustomers say and share about the company. Social media, when used effectively, can provide a sophisticated method of measuring how marketers meet and interact with consumers. Finally, social media enables firms to have more direct and meaningful conversations, and even deeper relationships, with customers.

17-3 Relationship Selling

17-3 Discuss the key differences between relationship selling and transactional selling

Historically, marketing theory and practice concerning personal selling have focused almost entirely on planned presentations to prospective customers for the sole purpose of

relationship selling (consultative selling) a sales practice that involves building, maintaining, and enhancing interactions with customers to develop long-term satisfaction through mutually beneficial partnerships

sales process (sales cycle) the set of steps a salesperson goes through in a particular organization to sell a particular product or service

making sales. In the past, marketers were mainly concerned with making onetime sales and then moving on to the next prospect. The seller fulfilling their own needs was the primary focus of marketing activity. Transactional selling methods attempt to persuade the buyer to either accept a point of view or take a particular action. Frequently, the objectives of the salesperson were at the expense of the buyer, creating a win–lose outcome in favor of the seller. Although this type of sales approach has not disappeared entirely, professional salespeople are using it less and less often, especially in more relationship-dependent business-to-business situations.

By contrast, modern views of personal selling emphasize the relationship that develops between a salesperson and a buyer. **Relationship selling**, or **consultative selling**, is a multistage process that emphasizes personalization, win–win outcomes, and empathy as key ingredients in identifying prospects and developing them as long term, satisfied customers. The focus of modern personal selling, therefore, is building mutual trust between the buyer and seller through the delivery of long term, value-added benefits that are anticipated by the buyer.

Relationship or consultative salespeople, therefore, become consultants, partners, problem solvers, and even problem finders for their customers. Consultative salespeople strive to build long-term relationships with key accounts by working with customers as partners and developing trust over time. The emphasis shifts from a onetime transaction to a long-term relationship in which the salesperson works with the customer to develop solutions for enhancing the customer's bottom line. The result of relationship selling tends to be more loyal customers who purchase from the company time after time, often with an increased share of purchases. In general, acquiring new customers is more costly than cultivating existing customers. As such, a relationship-selling strategy focused on retaining customers is often less expensive. Relationship selling also provides many advantages over traditional transactional selling in business-to-consumer situations. Still, relationship selling is more often used in business-to-business situations, such as purchasing heavy machinery and computer systems, and services, such as airlines and insurance, than in business-to-consumer situations. Table 17.2 lists the key differences between transactional selling and relationship, or consultative, selling.

17-4 Steps in the Selling Process

17-4 List and explain the steps in the selling process

The **sales process**, or **sales cycle**, is the set of steps a salesperson goes through to sell a particular product or service. As stated earlier, modern sales approaches are customized

Table 17.2   Key Differences Between Transactional Selling and Relationship Selling

	Transactional Selling	Relationship Selling
Sales Techniques	Often canned, nonflexible presentations that are repetitive from one presentation to the next.	Flexible presentations that are customized for each buyer and are focused on identifying customer's needs and wants to reach the best solution(s).
Length of the Sales Cycle	Short term—focused on closing the sale as quickly as possible and moving to the next potential customer/sale. It has limited to no focus on customer development.	Long term—focused on maintaining the relationship over an extended period with the generation of higher-quality new customers who can be further developed over the long term.
Importance of Relationships Between the Parties	Low expectation and importance of the relationship between the two parties beyond the immediate transaction.	It is important for the relationship to develop between buyers and sellers.
Levels of Trust	Low-to-limited levels of trust are required beyond the actual transaction.	High levels of trust are required to develop and maintain the relationship over an extended period.
Outcomes	Win–lose—each party is trying to get the most benefit without considering the other party.	Win–win—each party is trying to create additional value for both parties.
Performance Assessment	Mainly output/sales-based and focused on the amount sold and/or profit per sale.	While the amount sold and profit per sale are important, customer satisfaction and support activities are also important and assessed.
Pros	Lower levels of employee training are required. Easy assessment of performance.	Highly customer-centric. More value-creation focused. Less price-focused. Higher levels of customer satisfaction.
Cons	Promotes more price-based competition. Can create an environment in which selling the customer more products than needed is acceptable. Lower levels of customer satisfaction. Lower levels of repeat business.	Higher cost per contact/presentation. More complex to assess salesperson performance. Requires highly skilled and knowledgeable salespeople.

for the specific situation; as such, the sales process for one situation is often different than another. The actual sales process depends on the features of the product or service, characteristics of customer segments, and internal processes in place within the firm (such as how leads are gathered).

Some sales take only a few minutes to complete, but others may take much longer. Sales of technical products (like a fleet of Volvo Construction Equipment excavators or an Airbus airplane) and customized goods and services typically take many months, perhaps even years, to complete. On the other end of the spectrum, sales of less technical products (like stationery) are generally more routine and often take less than a day to complete. Whether a salesperson spends a few minutes or a few

years on a sale, there are seven basic steps in the personal selling process as follows:

1. Generating leads
2. Qualifying leads
3. Approaching the customer and probing needs
4. Developing and proposing solutions
5. Handling objections
6. Closing the sale
7. Following up

Like other promotion forms, the selling steps follow the AIDA concept discussed in Chapter 15. Once a salesperson has located and qualified a prospect with the authority to buy, they attempt to get the prospect's attention. A thorough needs assessment turned into an effective sales proposal and the presentation should generate interest. After developing the customer's initial desire (preferably during the presentation of the sales proposal), the salesperson seeks action in the close by trying to get an agreement to buy. Follow-up after the sale, the final step in the selling process, not only lowers cognitive dissonance (refer to Chapter 6) but also may open up opportunities for repeat business, sales of related products and services, and new-customer referrals.

Transactional selling and relationship selling follow the same basic steps. They differ, however, in the relative importance they place on certain key steps in the process. Transactional selling is more focused on generating as many leads as possible, making as many presentations as possible, and closing as many sales as possible. Minimal effort is placed on asking questions to identify customer needs and wants, much less matching these needs and wants to the specific benefits of the good or service. Often, transactional selling allows little time for following up and ensuring that customers are satisfied. Perhaps not surprisingly, these types of sales usually result in lower customer satisfaction, less repeat business, more price-based competition, and more win–lose transactions for salespeople.

By contrast, a salesperson practicing relationship selling focuses on a long-term investment in the time and effort needed to uncover each customer's needs and wants and aligns those needs and wants with benefits offered by the product or service being sold. By doing their homework up front, relationship-focused salespeople often create the conditions necessary for a relatively straightforward close. Due to this customer-centric approach, customers are generally more satisfied, engage in more repeat business, and provide higher shares of purchase over more extended periods with relationship salespeople. In the following sections, we examine each step of the personal selling process.

---

lead generation (prospecting) identification of the firms and people most likely to buy the seller's offerings

cold calling a form of lead generation in which the salesperson approaches potential buyers without any prior knowledge of the prospects' needs or financial status

referral a recommendation to a salesperson from a customer or business associate

networking a process of finding out about potential clients from friends, business contacts, coworkers, acquaintances, and fellow members in professional and civic organizations

17-4a Step 1: Generating Leads

Initial groundwork must precede communication between the potential buyer and the salesperson. **Lead generation**, or **prospecting**, is the identification of firms and people most likely to buy the seller's offerings. These firms or people become "sales leads" or, more commonly, "prospects."

Sales leads can be obtained in many ways, most notably through advertising, networking events, trade shows and conventions, social media, webinars, or direct mail and telemarketing programs. Favorable publicity also helps to create leads. Company records of past purchases by clients are another excellent source of leads. Many sales professionals are also securing valuable leads from their firm's website, including questions posted by leads about a product or service.

An unsophisticated method of lead generation is done through **cold calling**—a form of lead generation in which the salesperson approaches potential buyers without any prior knowledge of the prospects' needs or financial status. In other words, the potential customer has no idea that this salesperson is going to contact them. Although cold calling is still used in generating leads, many sales managers have realized the inefficiencies of having their highly skilled top salespeople use their valuable time reaching out to entirely unaware leads. Passing the job of cold calling to a lower-cost employee, typically an internal sales support person, allows salespeople to spend more time and use their relationship-building skills on prospects who have already been identified.

Another way to gather a lead is through a **referral**—a recommendation from a customer or business associate. These referred leads are often welcomed by salespeople as they tend to consist of more highly qualified leads with higher closing rates, larger initial transactions, and shorter sales cycles. Referrals are often as much as 10 times more productive in generating sales than are cold calls. Unfortunately, beginning salespeople often miss these referrals since, although many clients are willing to give referrals, most salespeople do not ask for them. Effective sales training can help to overcome this reluctance to ask for referrals. To increase the number of referrals, some companies even pay or send small gifts to customers or suppliers that provide referrals. Generating referrals is one area that social media and technology can usually make much more efficient.

Salespeople should build strong networks to help generate leads. **Networking** is using friends, business contacts, coworkers, acquaintances, and fellow members in professional and civic organizations to identify potential clients. Indeed, several national networking clubs have been started for the sole purpose of generating leads and providing valuable business advice. Increasingly, sales professionals are also using online networking sites, like Indeed and LinkedIn, to connect with targeted leads and clients around the world—24 hours a day, 7 days a week.

17-4b Step 2: Qualifying Leads

When a prospect shows interest in learning more about a product, the salesperson has the opportunity to follow up, or qualify, the lead. Typically, an unqualified prospect will give vague or incomplete answers to a salesperson's specific questions, will try to evade questions on budgets, and will request changes in standard procedures like prices and terms of sale. In contrast, qualified leads are true potential customers that will answer questions, value the salesperson's time, and will be realistic about money and when they are prepared to buy.

Lead qualification involves determining whether the prospect has three things:

1. **A recognized need:** The most basic criterion for determining whether someone is a prospect for a product is a need that is not being satisfied. In other words, can they genuinely derive value from the salesperson's offering. The salesperson should first consider prospects who are aware of a need, but should not disregard prospects who have not yet recognized that they have one. Sometimes a customer may need to be made aware of a potential problem or inefficiency, and with a little more information about the product, they may decide they need it. Preliminary questioning can often provide the salesperson with enough information to determine whether there is a need.

2. **Buying power:** Buying power involves both authority to make the purchase decision and access to funds to pay for it. To avoid wasting time and money, the salesperson needs to identify the buyer's purchasing authority and ability to pay before making a presentation. Many times, salespeople must go through multiple rounds of qualifying before finding the person with buying authority. Organizational charts and information about a firm's credit standing can provide valuable clues.

3. **Receptivity and accessibility:** The prospect must be willing to meet up and be accessible to the salesperson. Some prospects simply refuse to consult salespeople. Others, because of their stature in their organization, will meet with only a salesperson or sales manager of similar stature.

In many organizations, the task of lead qualification is handled by a telemarketing team or a sales support person who prequalifies the lead for the salesperson. These kinds of prequalification systems free sales representatives from the time-consuming task of following up on leads to determine need, buying power, and receptiveness. Prequalification systems may even set up initial appointments with the prospect for the salesperson. The result is more time for the sales force to spend in front of interested potential customers.

Companies are increasingly integrating their websites and customer relationship management software to qualify leads. When qualifying leads online, companies want visitors to register, indicate the products and services they are interested in, and provide information on their time frames and resources. Leads from the internet can then be prioritized (potential customers indicating short time frames, for instance, can be given a higher priority) and then transferred to salespeople. Enticing visitors to register also enables companies to customize future electronic interactions.

Personally visiting unqualified leads wastes valuable salesperson time and company resources. Many leads often go unanswered because salespeople are given no indication as to how qualified the leads are in terms of interest and ability to purchase. Inside salespeople and sales support staff assess leads to maximize successful meetings, while CRM systems provide resources to increase lead follow-up rates. Still, salespeople follow up on only 10 to 15 percent of leads.

17-4c Step 3: Approaching the Customer and Probing Needs

Before approaching customers, the salesperson should learn as much as possible about the prospect's organization and the customers the organization serves. This process, called the **preapproach**, describes the "homework" that must be done by the salesperson before contacting the prospect. This may include visiting the company's website; consulting standard reference sources, such as Moody's, S&P, or Dun & Bradstreet; or contacting acquaintances or fellow salespeople who may have information about the prospect. Social media has become an invaluable tool for salespeople in the preapproach phase, with 76 percent of top salespeople stating that they use the potential customer's social media profiles to gather more information about them before the sales call.[10] Another preapproach task is to determine whether the actual approach should be

---

lead qualification determination of a sales prospect's (1) recognized need, (2) buying power, and (3) receptivity and accessibility

preapproach a process that describes the "homework" that must be done by a salesperson before they contact a prospect

a personal visit, a phone call, a letter, or some other form of communication. Note that the preapproach applies to most business-to-business sales and outside consumer sales, but it is usually not possible when consumers approach salespeople in the retail store environment.

During the actual sales approach, the salesperson either talks to the prospect or secures an appointment to question the prospect further about their needs. Experts on relationship selling suggest that salespeople should begin developing mutual trust with their prospect during the approach. Salespeople must sell themselves before they can sell their firm's products. Small talk that projects sincerity and some suggestion of friendship is encouraged to build rapport with the prospect, but remarks that could be construed as insincere should be avoided.

The salesperson's ultimate goal during the approach is to conduct a **needs assessment** to find out as much as possible about the prospect's situation. The salesperson should determine how to maximize the fit between what they can offer and what the prospective customer wants and communicate that to the customer as effectively as possible. As part of the needs assessment, the consultative salesperson must know everything there is to know about the following:

- **The product or service:** Product knowledge is the cornerstone for conducting a successful needs analysis. The consultative salesperson must be an expert on their product or service, including technical specifications, features and benefits, pricing and billing procedures, warranty and service support, performance comparisons with the competition, other customers' experiences with the product, and current advertising and promotional campaign messages. For example, a salesperson who is attempting to sell a Siemens Healthineers medical imaging machine to a doctor's office or hospital should be very knowledgeable about Siemens Healthineers' selection of imaging machines, their attributes, capabilities, technological specifications, and postpurchase servicing and maintenance costs.

- **Customers and their needs:** The salesperson should have a deep knowledge of the prospect, the needs and wants of the prospect's organization, and the needs of the organization's customers. This knowledge is crucial to relationship and consultative selling, where the salesperson acts not only as a supplier of products and services but also as a trusted consultant and adviser.

FizkesShutterstock.com

Financial planning, real estate, and other specialized service industries require a deep understanding of customer needs.

The professional salesperson brings business-building ideas and solutions to problems to each client. For example, suppose the Siemens Healthineers salesperson asks the "right" questions. In that case, they should be able to identify imaging-related areas where the doctor's office is wasting money or not meeting the needs of their patients. Rather than just selling an imaging machine, the Siemens salesperson can act as a consultant on how the doctor's office can save money and time and better meet patient needs.

- **The competition:** The salesperson must also know as much about the competitor's company and products as they know about their own company. Virtually no industries or companies exist in an environment free from competitors. Competitive intelligence includes many factors: who the competitors are and what is known about them, whether or not their products are comparable (and to what extent), advantages and disadvantages, and strengths and weaknesses. For example, if the competitor's Philips Healthcare imaging machine is less expensive than Siemens Healthineers', the doctor's office may lean toward purchasing Philips. The Siemens salesperson can point out that the cost of long-term maintenance is lower for the Siemens machine, offsetting its higher initial cost. In that case, the salesperson may persuade the doctor's office to purchase the Siemens machine.

- **The industry:** Knowing the industry requires active research by the salesperson. This means attending industry and trade association meetings, reading articles published in industry and trade journals, keeping track of legislation and regulations that affect the industry, being aware of product alternatives and innovations from domestic and foreign competition, understanding what is being said online and through social media sites, and having a feel for economic and

---

needs assessment a determination of the customer's specific needs and wants and the range of options they have for satisfying them

financial conditions that may affect the industry. It is also important to be aware of economic downturns, as businesses may be looking for less expensive financing options.

Creating a *customer profile* during the approach helps salespeople optimize their time and resources. This profile is then used to help develop an intelligent analysis of the prospect's needs in preparation for the next step, developing and proposing solutions. Customer profile information is typically stored and managed using sales force automation software packages designed for use on laptop computers, smartphones, or tablets. Sales force automation software provides sales reps with a computerized and efficient method of collecting customer information for use during the entire sales process. Further, customer and sales data stored in a computer database can be easily shared among sales team members. The information can also be appended with industry statistics, sales or meeting notes, billing data, and other information that may be pertinent to the prospect or the prospect's company. The more salespeople know about their prospects, the better they can meet their needs.

A salesperson should wrap up the sales approach and need-probing mission by summarizing the prospect's need, problem, and interest. The salesperson should also get a commitment from the customer to some kind of action, whether it is reading promotional material or agreeing to a demonstration. This commitment helps to qualify the prospect further and justify the additional time invested by the salesperson. When doing so, however, the salesperson should take care not to be too pushy or overbearing—a good salesperson will read a customer's social cues. The salesperson should reiterate the action they promise to take, such as sending information or calling back to provide answers to questions. The date and time of the next call should be set after the sales approach as well as an agenda for the next call in terms of what the salesperson hopes to accomplish, such as providing a demonstration or presenting a solution.

17-4d Step 4: Developing and Proposing Solutions

Once the salesperson has gathered the appropriate information about the client's needs and wants, the next step is to determine whether her company's products or services match the needs of the prospective customer. The salesperson then develops a solution, or possibly several solutions, in which the salesperson's product or service solves the client's problems or meets a specific need.

These solutions are typically presented to the client in the form of a sales proposal presented at a sales

Salespeople often present their sales proposals to potential customers. Presentations are particularly important in explaining sales solutions and overcoming objections.

presentation. A **sales proposal** is a written document or professional presentation that outlines how the company's product or service will meet or exceed the client's needs. The **sales presentation** is the formal meeting in which the salesperson has the opportunity to present the sales proposal. Incorporating visual elements that impart meaningful information, knowing how to operate the audio/visual or computer equipment used for the presentation, and ensuring the equipment works will make the presentation flow more smoothly.

Because the salesperson often has only one opportunity to present solutions, the quality of both the sales proposal and the presentation can often make or break the sale. Salespeople must be able to present the proposal and handle any customer objections confidently and professionally. For a powerful presentation, salespeople must be well prepared, make direct eye contact, ask open-ended questions, be poised, use hand gestures and voice inflection, and focus on the customer's needs. Presenting a boring or ill-prepared presentation can be detrimental to the salesperson's success, and equipment mishaps can consume valuable time for both the salesperson and the customer. Often, customers are more likely to remember how salespeople present themselves than what they actually say.

17-4e Step 5: Handling Objections

A prospect rarely purchases the product instantly without hesitation, questions, or concerns. Instead, the prospect often raises objections or questions about the proposal and the product. The potential buyer may insist that the salesperson lower the price or that the good or service will not satisfy the present need.

---

sales proposal a formal written document or professional presentation that outlines how the salesperson's product or service will meet or exceed the prospect's needs

sales presentation a meeting in which the salesperson presents a sales proposal to a prospective buyer

One of the first lessons every salesperson learns is that objections to the product should not be taken personally as confrontations or insults. The ability to deal with customer objections in a non-personal way is something that even advanced salespeople sometimes find difficult. Salespeople need to understand that objections are a legitimate part of every purchase decision. To handle objections effectively, the salesperson should anticipate specific objections (such as concerns about price); fully explore the objection with the customer; be aware of what the competition is offering; and, above all, stay calm and professional.

Often salespeople can use objections to close the sale. The customer may try to pit suppliers against each other to drive down the price, so the salesperson should be prepared to point out weaknesses in the competitor's offer and stand by the quality and value of their own proposal.

17-4f Step 6: Closing the Sale

At the end of the presentation, when all questions have been answered, and objections have been handled, the salesperson should then attempt to close the sale and ask for the purchase. Customers often give signals during or after the presentation that they are ready to buy or are not interested. Examples include changes in facial expressions, gestures, and questions asked. The salesperson should look for these signals and respond and adjust appropriately.

Effective closing requires courage and skill. Before making the close, the salesperson needs to understand that while a positive or negative outcome is possible, a negative result is not necessarily an indicator that the salesperson is ineffective.[11] Often, a salesperson will be told "no" flat out. In such a case, the salesperson must be resilient and must be able to handle this type of rejection gracefully and effectively. Salespeople need to remember that a prospect saying no to a product or service offering is not a personal rejection of the salesperson themselves. Salespeople can often make hundreds—potentially even thousands—of sales calls every year. Many of these are repeat calls to the same group of clients to make a single sale. Building and developing a good relationship with the customer is very important. Often, if the salesperson has developed a strong relationship with the customer, only minimal efforts are needed to close a sale (increasing the salesperson's closure rate).

Negotiating and closing the sale requires courage and skills. A team effort is often required for companies to complete a deal.

Negotiation often plays a key role in the closing of the sale. **Negotiation** is the process during which both the salesperson and the prospect offer special concessions in an attempt to arrive at a sales agreement. For example, the salesperson may offer a trial at a lower price, free installation, or expedited delivery. Effective negotiators, however, avoid using price as a negotiation tool and can show the greater value in their products or services. Because companies spend millions on advertising and product development to create value, when salespeople give in to price negotiations too quickly, it decreases the value of the product. Salespeople should also be prepared to ask for trade-offs and try to avoid giving unilateral concessions. Moreover, if the customer asks for a price discount, the salesperson should then ask for something in return, such as higher volume or more flexibility in delivery schedules.

More and more U.S. companies are expanding their marketing and selling efforts into global markets. Salespeople selling in foreign markets need to tailor their presentations and closing styles to each market. Different cultures require different adjustments for salespeople. A salesperson doing business in Latin America for the first time might need considerable time to build relationships as customers prefer to spend a long time building personal relationships with their suppliers. Similarly, personal space and physical contact are treated differently in various cultures. In many European and South American cultures, kissing a business associate on both cheeks is customary instead of shaking hands. In contrast, a softer handshake is standard in many Middle Eastern countries, while a firm handshake is more appropriate in Brazil.[12]

17-4g Step 7: Following Up

A salesperson's responsibilities do not end with making the sale and placing the order. One of the most critical aspects of the salesperson's job is **follow-up**—the final step

---

negotiation the process during which both the salesperson and the prospect offer special concessions in an attempt to arrive at a sales agreement

follow-up the final step of the selling process, in which the salesperson ensures delivery schedules are met, goods or services perform as promised, and the buyers' employees are properly trained to use the products

in the selling process, in which the salesperson must ensure delivery schedules are met, goods or services perform as promised, and buyers' employees are properly trained to use the products.

In the traditional sales approach, follow-up with the customer is generally limited to successful product delivery and performance. A basic goal of relationship selling is to motivate customers to come back again and again by developing and nurturing long-term relationships. During the follow-up, salespeople can begin this process by ensuring the customer is satisfied and gets the promised product and service.

Most businesses depend on repeat sales and repeat sales depend on thorough and continued follow-up by the salesperson. When customers feel abandoned, cognitive dissonance arises and repeat sales decline. This issue is more pertinent today because customers are far less loyal to brands and vendors. Buyers are more inclined to look for the best deal, especially when they experience poor postsale follow-up. Automated email follow-up marketing—a combination of sales automation and internet technology—is one tool that some marketers use to enhance customer satisfaction and bring in more business. After the initial contact with a prospect, a software program automatically sends a series of personalized email messages over a period of time. Another approach is to use contact software like Zoom, which facilitates live face-to-face exchanges via videoconferencing and direct access to cloud-based data centers.

17-4h Social Media and the Sales Process

Social media has impacted the sales process through what is referred to as "social selling." Social selling focuses on using social network sites (SNS), such as LinkedIn, Twitter, now known as X, and Facebook, to help with the sales process. Salespeople engage in social selling activities such as research, prospecting, networking, and relationship building.[13]

In 2022, 31 percent of salespeople closed deals over $500,000 through social selling channels without face-to-face contact with the buyer. Salespeople share and/or develop relevant content to answer questions posed by current and potential users. Relationships are built between salespeople providing the content and potential future customers. While the process may not generate immediate sales, foundations for relationships are already established when a prospect decides to move forward with the buying process. When that happens, the salesperson holds at least an initial advantage over the competition.

The modern sales presentation, using social media, can address likely concerns before they are raised. Success stories can be shared via Facebook, Instagram, and TikTok. Live streaming over platforms such as Facebook Live can be used to demonstrate how a product works in real-time.[14] Using home security alarms as an example, different options and installation procedures can be demonstrated for several different alarm systems available from the salesperson's company. For example, different types of security cameras, both inside and outside the house, can be demonstrated and highlighted through YouTube video presentations. With social media tools, updates and changes can be easily adjusted from one presentation to the next, unlike the use of a printed sales packet that requires more effort, time, and money to change.

As with the initial selling process and presentation stage, social selling is critical in the feedback stage. Many firms are asking customers not only to provide them feedback in person, but they are also requesting that customers complete reviews using social media platforms. Often, companies offer a free service call or discounts for future business if a customer completes an online review. Sales organizations are taking advantage of multiple tools that can not only monitor customer feedback but also remind buyers to submit reviews and encourage them to do so.[15]

While using social media tools might be more effective in certain stages of the sales process, research suggests that salespeople's use of social media tools often occurs early in the sales process, when sellers are attempting to build their personal brand and manage their impressions with the buyer, and during the latter stages, when listening to customer feedback is crucial.[16] This leaves handling objections and closing the sale better served by face-to-face interactions between the salesperson and buyer. If customers feel objections can be handled in a non–face-to-face context, however, then companies potentially would be better off with an inside sales force or possibly use of artificial intelligence, instead of the costly outside sales force.

17-5 Sales Management

17-5 Explain the functions and roles of sales management

There is an old adage in business that nothing happens until a sale is made. This is a way of saying that the sales process is potentially the most critical process in the firm. Without sales, there is no need for accountants, production workers, or even a company president. Sales provide the fuel that keeps the company engines humming. Companies such as SAP, IBM, Saint-Gobain, 3M, and thousands of other companies would cease to exist without successful salespeople. Even companies such as Unilever, Nestlé, and Coca-Cola which mainly sell consumer goods and use extensive advertising campaigns, still rely on salespeople to move products through the channel of distribution. Thus, sales management must be one of every firm's most critical specialties. Effective sales management stems from a success-oriented sales force that accomplishes its mission economically and efficiently. Poor sales management can lead to unmet sales and profit objectives or even to the downfall of the corporation.

Just as selling generally consists of a personal relationship, so does sales management. Although the sales manager's primary job is to maximize sales at a reasonable cost while maximizing profits, they also have many other essential responsibilities and decisions:

1. Defining sales goals and the sales process
2. Determining the sales force structure
3. Recruiting and training the sales force
4. Compensating and motivating the sales force
5. Evaluating the sales force

17-5a Defining Sales Goals and the Sales Process

Effective sales management begins with a determination of sales goals. Without specific goals to achieve, salesperson performance could suffer, and the company would likely fail. Like any marketing objective, the sales manager should state sales goals in clear, precise, and measurable terms and should always specify a time frame for their completion. Overall sales force goals are usually stated in terms of desired dollar sales volume, market share, and/or profit level. For example, a software sales company may have a goal of selling $70 million in services annually, attaining a 15-percent market share, and achieving $7 million in profits. Individual salespeople are also assigned goals in the form of quotas. A **quota** is a statement of the salesperson's sales goals, usually based on sales volume alone, but sometimes including other focuses, such as key accounts (those with greatest potential), new account generation, volume of repeat sales, profit margin, and specific product mixes sold. Although many salespeople would prefer to avoid quotas, when the sales manager sets them effectively, they should push the salesperson to increase their closing rate and then, in turn, their commissions.

17-5b Determining the Sales Force Structure

Because personal selling is so costly, no sales department can afford to be disorganized. Proper design helps the sales manager organize and delegate sales duties and provide direction for salespeople. Sales departments are

Part of sales management is defining sales goals for the sales force.

most often organized by geographic regions, product lines, marketing functions performed (such as account development or account maintenance), markets, industries, individual clients, or accounts. For example, the sales force for 3M could be organized into sales territories covering California, the Midwest, the South, and the East Coast or into distinct groups selling different product lines. 3M salespeople might also be assigned to specific industries or markets (such as the automotive industry), or to key clients (such as Ford, GM, and BMW).

Market or industry-based structures and key account structures are gaining popularity in today's competitive selling environment, especially with the emphasis on relationship selling. Being familiar with one specific industry or market allows sales reps to become experts in their fields, and thereby, offer better solutions and services. Further, by organizing the sales force around specific customers, many companies hope to improve customer service, encourage collaboration with other arms of the company, and unite salespeople in customer-focused sales teams.

17-5c Recruiting and Training the Sales Force

Sales force recruitment should be based on an accurate, detailed description of the sales task as defined by the sales manager. For example, Lenovo uses its website to provide prospective salespeople with explanations of different career entry paths and video accounts of what it is like to have a career at Lenovo. Aside from the usual characteristics, such as level of experience or education, what traits should sales managers look for in applicants?

- **Ego strength:** Great salespeople should have a strong, healthy self-esteem and the ability to quickly bounce back from rejection.
- **Sense of urgency and competitiveness:** These traits push their sales to completion, as well as help salespeople to persuade customers.
- **Assertiveness:** Effective salespeople can be firm in one-to-one negotiations, lead the sales process, and

quota a statement of the salesperson's sales goals, usually based on sales volume

get their point across confidently, without being over-bearing or aggressive.

- **Sociable:** Wanting to interact with others is a necessary trait for great salespeople.
- **Risk takers:** Great salespeople are willing to put themselves in less-than-assured situations, and in doing so, often can close unlikely sales.
- **Capable of understanding complex concepts and ideas:** Quick thinking and comprehension allow salespeople to quickly grasp and sell new products or enter new sales areas.
- **Creativity:** Great salespeople develop client solutions in creative ways.
- **Empathetic:** Empathy—the ability to place oneself in someone else's shoes—enables salespeople to understand the client.

In addition to these traits, the overwhelming majority of successful salespeople say their sales style is relationship oriented rather than transaction oriented.[17]

Social media has emerged as an ideal tool for recruiters searching for qualified salespeople. LinkedIn has emerged as the go-to site for recruiters to find information about potential sales recruits. This includes searching by industry, company, job title, and even geographic area. For potential recruits, understanding how to develop a complete profile emphasizing and talents viewed as desirable by prospective employers is crucial. Further, in the event recruiters examine a person's social media profile, it is critical that negative information (e.g., photos of questionable behavior) from other sites, including less professionally focused social media sites like Facebook, Instagram, or TikTok does not appear.

After the sales recruit has been hired and given a brief orientation, initial training begins. A new salesperson generally receives instruction in company policies and practices, selling techniques, product knowledge, industry and customer characteristics, and non-selling duties, such as filling out sales and market information reports and using the company's preferred customer relationship management software. Many companies provide new salespeople with mentorship from individuals or sales teams. These mentors can provide individualized one-on-one feedback in an experiential-based learning environment. Continuous training then keeps salespeople up to date on changes in products and services, technology, the competitive landscape, and sales techniques, and other issues that might arise. Continuous training can occur during sales meetings, annual reviews from sales managers, or during daily sales calls. Individuals seeking sales positions also need training in the basics of social selling and company policies on the use of sales media

platforms. This is especially true for salespeople who did not grow up with social media technologies. Another consideration is the generational differences that exist in today's salesforce. The older Generation X and the younger Generation Z cohorts prefer face-to-face communication, while millennials larger prefer electronic communication.[18] Thus, many salespeople entering the workforce may need to be encouraged and trained on how to successfully complete face-to-face selling.

Training can take place in a classroom environment, in the field, or using online modules. Given the growth in learning technologies, sales training has transformed from relying solely on traditional in-person methods (such as live sales calls, inside sales, and role playing) to eLearning methods, including the use of webinars and online tutorials. While some salespeople prefer face-to-face training, eLearning allows for on-the-go training, and complex training concepts, which can take hours or days in a face-to-face session, can be split up into more manageable and more flexible sessions.[19] When conducting job training in the field using a live sales call, the trainer should be a more experienced salesperson or sales manager. This type of training provides real-world experience for the trainee, but it may reduce the effectiveness of the call because it often entails reduced selling time. Another form of training involves the trainee working in inside sales, primarily phone-based sales, for an extended period before being given an outside territory to cover. This enables the trainee to develop selling skills with less important and/or less established accounts before facing the challenges of outside sales. Table 17.3 provides key differences between inside and outside sales.

Table 17.3   Inside Sales vs. Outside Sales

Outside Salespeople	Inside Salespeople
High need for interpersonal skills	High need for persistence
Must be well organization	Strong communication skills beyond face-to-face
Able to adapt their communication	Ability to be intuitive about others' needs
Possess analytical skills	Possess strong technology skills
Able to work without direct supervision	Open to direct supervision and feedback

Source: Adapted from: Ron Coxsom, "Inside Sales vs. Outside Sales: What's the Difference?" Indeed, https://www.indeed.com/career-advice/finding-a-job/inside-sales-vs-outside-sales, accessed April 9, 2023.

17-5d Compensating and Motivating the Sales Force

Compensation planning is one of the sales manager's most challenging jobs. Only good planning will ensure that compensation attracts, motivates, and retains good salespeople. Generally, companies and industries with lower levels of compensation suffer higher turnover rates. These issues increase costs (including training and recruiting costs), decrease sales effectiveness, and harm relationship management. Therefore, compensation needs to be competitive enough to attract and motivate the best salespeople. Firms sometimes take profit into account when developing their compensation plans. Instead of paying salespeople for overall volume, they pay according to the profitability achieved from selling each product.

Still, other companies tie a part of the salesperson's compensation to customer satisfaction. As the emphasis on relationship selling increases, there is emerging thought from sales managers that a portion of a salesperson's compensation should be tied to a client's satisfaction. To determine compensation for the salesperson, sales managers can use surveys to question clients about a salesperson's ability to create realistic expectations and their responsiveness to customer needs.

Although a compensation-based plan aims to motivate a salesperson to sell, sometimes more is needed to produce the sales volume or profit margin required by sales management. Sales managers, therefore, often offer rewards or incentives, such as employee recognition, plaques and trophies, individual parking spaces, and/or monetary-based rewards, such as vacations, merchandise, pay raises, and cash bonuses. Cash awards are the most popular sales incentive and are used by virtually all companies. For example, IBM, Salesforce, Gartner, and Microsoft reward their sales employees with over a million dollars in sales with entrance into their "Million Dollar Club," which often comes with a paid vacation. LinkedIn offers new salespeople with growth potential a "Rising Star Award" and a monetary bonus.

Recognition and rewards may help increase overall sales volume, add new accounts, improve salesperson morale, move slow-selling items, and bolster slow sales. They can also be used to achieve short- and long-term objectives, such as reducing overstocked inventory and meeting a monthly or quarterly sales goal.

17-5e Evaluating the Sales Force

The final task of sales managers is evaluating the effectiveness and performance of the sales force. To evaluate the sales force, the sales manager needs feedback—that is, regular information from salespeople. Typical performance measures include sales volume, contribution to profit, calls per order, sales or profits per call, customer satisfaction, or percentage of calls that achieve specific goals, such as sales of products that the firm is heavily promoting.

Performance information helps the sales manager monitor a salesperson's progress through the sales cycle and pinpoint where breakdowns might be occurring. For example, by learning the number of prospects an individual salesperson has in each step of the sales cycle process and determining where prospects are falling out of the cycle, a manager can determine how effective a salesperson might be at lead generation, needs assessment, proposal generation, presenting, closing, and follow-up stages. This information can then tell a manager which sales skills might need to be reassessed or retrained. For example, suppose a sales manager notices that a sales rep seems to be letting too many prospects slip away after presenting proposals. In that case, it might mean they need help developing proposals, handling objections, or closing sales.

Social media sites can also help assess the performance of salespeople. Using customer reviews, sales managers can better determine what salespeople are doing well and what could be better. Further, negative reviews can tell sales managers where salespeople may need to catch up. In our home security alarm example, alarm owners might post reviews about a company indicating the salesperson never showed up to an appointment, failed to follow up with a price quote, or failed to explain the actual installation and monthly monitoring fees correctly. This information can help a sales manager determine areas for improvement for an individual salesperson.

17-6 Customer Relationship Management and the Sales Process

17-6 Describe the use of customer relationship management in the selling process

As we have discussed throughout the text, customer relationship management (CRM) is the ultimate goal of a new trend in marketing that focuses on understanding customers as individuals instead of as part of a group. To do this, marketers are making their communications more customer-specific using the CRM cycle, covered in Chapter 8, and by developing customer relationships through touch points and data mining. CRM was initially popularized as a one-to-one marketing tool. However, CRM has transformed into a much broader approach to understanding and serving customer needs than simply one-to-one marketing.

Throughout the text, our discussion of a CRM system has assumed two key points. First, customers take center stage in any organization. Second, the business must manage the customer relationship across all points of customer contact throughout the entire organization. By identifying customer relationships, understanding the customer base, and capturing customer data, marketers and salespeople can leverage the information not only to develop deeper relationships but also to close more sales with loyal customers more efficiently.

17-6a Identify Customer Relationships

Companies that have CRM systems follow a customer-centric focus or model. **Customer-centric** is an internal management philosophy similar to the marketing concept discussed in Chapter 1. Under this philosophy, the company customizes its product and service offering based on data generated through interactions between the customer and the company. This philosophy transcends all functional areas of the business, producing an internal system in which all of the company's decisions and actions directly result from customer information.

Each business unit typically has its own way of recording what it learns, and perhaps, even has its own customer information system. The departments' different interests make it difficult to pull all the customer information together in one place using a standard format. To overcome this problem, companies using CRM rely on knowledge management. **Knowledge management** is a process through which customer information is centralized and shared to enhance the relationship between customers and the organization. Information collected includes experiential observations, comments, customer actions, and facts about the customer.

As Chapter 1 explained, *empowerment* involves delegating authority to solve customers' problems. Usually, organizational representatives, for example, salespeople, can make changes during interactions with customers through phone, fax, email, social media, or face-to-face interactions.

An **interaction** occurs when a customer and a company representative exchange information and develop learning relationships. With CRM, the customer—not the organization—defines the terms of the interaction, often by stating their preferences. The organization responds by designing products and services around customers' desired experiences.

The success of CRM—building lasting and profitable relationships—can be directly measured by the effectiveness of the interaction between the customer and the organization. In fact, the organization's ability to establish and manage interactions with its current customer base further differentiates CRM from other strategic initiatives. The more latitude (empowerment) a company gives its representatives, the more likely the interaction will conclude in a way that satisfies the customer.

17-6b Understand Interactions of the Current Customer Base

The interaction between the customer and the organization is the foundation on which a CRM system is built. Only through effective interactions can organizations learn about the expectations of their customers, generate and manage knowledge about them, negotiate mutually satisfying commitments, and build long-term relationships.

Figure 17.1 illustrates the customer-centric approach for managing customer interactions. Following a customer-centric approach, an interaction can occur through different communication channels, such as a phone, the internet, or a salesperson. Any activity or touch point a customer has with an organization, directly or indirectly, constitutes an interaction.

Companies that effectively manage customer interactions recognize that customer data consists of a wide variety of **touch points**. In a CRM system, touch points are all areas of a business where customers have contact with the company and from which the company can gather data.

Touch points might include a customer as follows:

- Registering for a particular service.
- Communicating with customer service for product information.
- Completing and returning the warranty information card for a product.
- Talking with salespeople, delivery personnel, and product installers.

Once interpreted, data gathered at these touch points provide information that affects touch points inside the company. The company may direct interpreted information to marketing research to develop profiles of extended

---

customer-centric a philosophy under which the company customizes its product and service offerings based on data generated through interactions between the customer and the company

knowledge management the process by which customer information is centralized and shared to enhance the relationship between customers and the organization

interaction the point at which a customer and a company representative exchange information and develop learning relationships

touch points areas of a business where customers have contact from which the company can gather data

Figure 17.1 Customer-Centric Approach for Managing Customer Interactions

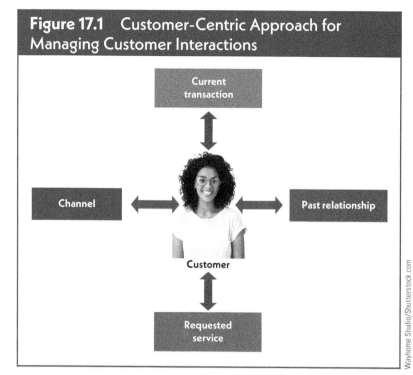

warranty purchasers, to production to analyze recurring problems and repair components, to accounting to establish cost-control models for repair service calls, and to sales for better customer profiling and segmentation.

Web-Based Interactions

Web-based interactions are an increasingly popular touch point for customers to communicate with companies on their own terms. Web users can evaluate and purchase products, make reservations, input preferential data, and provide customer feedback on services and products. Data from these web-based interactions are then captured, compiled, and used to segment customers, refine marketing efforts, develop new products, and deliver a degree of individual customization to improve customer relationships.

Social CRM

As social media have become more popular many companies have begun to use these media for "social CRM." Essentially, social CRM takes the most successful aspects of traditional CRM, such as behavioral targeting, and expands them to include ways to engage customers through social media platforms. This new paradigm includes a new customer recommendation value, called the *net promoter score*. The net promoter score measures how much a customer influences the behavior of other customers through recommendations on social media. Its ultimate purpose is to gather all consumer interactions into a single database so that they can be analyzed and used to improve communication. Social CRM also enables marketers to focus more on the relationship aspect of CRM. For example, Nike uses social CRM to listen to customer complaints about their products and reply in real-time. Coca-Cola utilizes social CRM through the "Create Real Magic" promotion that utilizes AI-powered experimentations which allows fans to utilize Coke's archived promotions and the Spencerian script logo to submit work that may be selected to be displayed on Coke's electronic billboards in London's Piccadilly Circus and New York's Time Square.[20] To use social CRM effectively, companies must understand which sites customers use, whether they post opinions, and who the major influencers in the category are. They can then marry this information with behavioral data like purchases and purchase frequency.

Domino's Pizza stimulates customer engagement with its Chatbot ordering system.

Point-of-Sale Interactions

Another touch point is through **point-of-sale interactions** in stores or at information kiosks. Many point-of-sale software programs enable customers to easily provide information about themselves without feeling violated. The information is then used for marketing and merchandising activities and to accurately identify the store's best customers and the types of products they buy. Data collected at point-of-sale interactions are also used to increase customer satisfaction through the development of in-store services and customer recognition promotions.

17-6c Capture Customer Data

Vast amounts of data can be obtained from the interactions between an organization and its customers. Therefore, in a CRM system, the issue is not how much data can be obtained, but rather what types of data should be acquired and how the data can be used effectively for relationship enhancement.

The traditional approach for acquiring data from customers is through channel interactions. Channel interactions include store visits, conversations with salespeople, interactions via the web, traditional phone conversations, and wireless communications. In a CRM system, channel interactions are viewed as prime information sources based on the channel selected to initiate the interaction, rather than on the data acquired. In some cases, companies use online chat to answer customer questions about products they are looking for. For example, Best Buy has an online chat window that guides the customer through writing a review on the Best Buy website. Customers can receive questions about products, services, or retail store information through this chat from a Best Buy representative. Domino's utilizes a chat bot, Dom, to allow customers to place their orders using this service as opposed to calling in their order. Customers can choose a new order, reorder something from their past orders, and track their order. The bots allow customers to select a restaurant and pick menu items. The bot then provides an estimated time for pickup.

Interactions between the company and the customer facilitate the collection of large amounts of data. Companies can obtain simple contact information (name, address, phone number) and data about the customer's current relationship with the organization—past purchase history, quantity and frequency of purchases, the average amount spent on purchases, sensitivity to promotional activities, and so forth.

In this manner, a large amount of information can be captured from one individual customer across several touch points. Multiply this by the thousands of customers

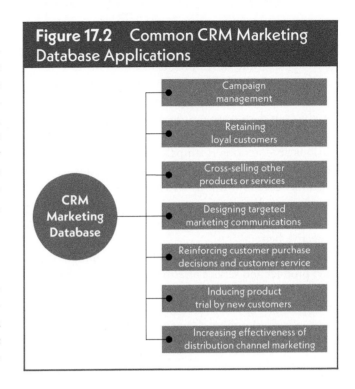

Figure 17.2   Common CRM Marketing Database Applications

CRM Marketing Database

- Campaign management
- Retaining loyal customers
- Cross-selling other products or services
- Designing targeted marketing communications
- Reinforcing customer purchase decisions and customer service
- Inducing product trial by new customers
- Increasing effectiveness of distribution channel marketing

across all of the touch points within an organization, and the volume of data can rapidly become unmanageable for company personnel. The large volume of data resulting from a CRM initiative can be managed effectively only through technology. Once customer data are collected, the question of who owns those data becomes extremely salient. In 2017, Equifax was hit with multiple scandals about misusing customer data. Equifax informed customers that hackers had stolen sensitive personal information such as names, Social Security numbers, birth dates, and addresses in a data breach. However, it later came out that this information was being sold to third parties without the customer's consent.

17-6d Leverage Customer Information

Companies can use data mining to identify the most profitable customers and prospects. Managers can then design tailored marketing strategies to best appeal to the identified segments. In CRM, this is commonly referred to as leveraging customer information to facilitate enhanced relationships with customers. Figure 17.2 shows some common CRM marketing database applications.

---

point-of-sale interactions   a touch point in stores or information kiosks that uses software to enable customers to easily provide information about themselves without feeling violated

Campaign Management

Through campaign management, all areas of the company participate in the development of programs targeted to customers. **Campaign management** involves monitoring and leveraging customer interactions to sell a company's products and increase customer service. Campaigns are based directly on data obtained from customers through various interactions. Campaign management includes monitoring the success of the communications based on customer reactions through sales, orders, callbacks to the company, and so on. If a campaign appears unsuccessful, it is evaluated and changed to achieve the company's desired objective better.

Campaign management involves developing customized product and service offerings for the appropriate customer segment, pricing these offerings attractively, and communicating these offers in a manner that enhances customer relationships. Customizing product and service offerings requires managing multiple interactions with customers and prioritizing the products and services that are viewed as most desirable for a specifically designated customer. Even within a highly defined market segment, individual customer differences will emerge. Therefore, customer interactions must focus on unique experiences, expectations, and desires.

Retaining Loyal Customers

If a company has identified its best customers, it should make every possible effort to maintain and increase their loyalty. When a company retains an additional 5 percent of its customers each year, profits will increase by as much as 125 percent. What's more, improving customer retention by a mere 2 percent can decrease costs by as much as 10 percent. Loyalty programs reward loyal customers for making multiple purchases. The objective is to build long-term, mutually beneficial relationships between a company and its key customers.

Cross-Selling Other Products and Services

CRM provides many opportunities to cross-sell related products. Marketers can use the database to match product profiles and consumer profiles so that they can cross-sell products to customers that match their demographic, lifestyle, or behavioral characteristics. The financial services industry uses cross-selling better than most other industries do. Retail firms often use cross-selling to sell more products to existing customers. For example, Starbucks's

rewards app or DoorDash food delivery services can remind you of products that you have ordered before that might pair well with the current order that you are placing. Cross-selling is a key part of Bank of America's digital banking strategy. Bank of America has more than 30 million users on its digital banking network and uses those digital platforms to sell more financial products to its existing customers. These digital sales accounted for almost 50 percent of Bank of America's sales in 2020.[21]

Internet companies use product and customer profiling to reveal cross-selling opportunities while customers surf their sites. Past purchases, tracking programs, and the site a surfer is referred from give online marketers clues about the surfer's interests and what items to cross-sell. Amazon, for example, uses profiling to better meet customer needs. The company systematically compares individuals' shopping habits and online activities to those of other Amazon customers to make better-tailored recommendations. Customers are also able to proactively rate products, review products, add products to wish lists, recommend products, and save products for a later purchase—all of which make for a more customized experience.[22]

Designing Targeted Marketing Communications

Using transaction and purchase data, a database allows marketers to track customers' relationships to the company's products and services and modify the marketing message accordingly.

Companies can also segment customers into infrequent users, moderate users, and heavy users. These firms can then develop a segmented communications strategy based on the customer's usage group. Communications to infrequent users might encourage repeat purchases through a direct incentive, such as a limited-time price discount for ordering again. Communications to moderate users may use fewer incentives and more reinforcement of past purchase decisions. Communications to heavy users would be designed around loyalty and reinforcement of the purchase, rather than around price promotions.

Reinforcing Customer Purchase Decisions and Customer Service As you learned in Chapter 6, cognitive dissonance is the feeling consumers experience when they recognize an inconsistency between their values and opinions and their purchase behavior. In other words, they doubt the soundness of their purchase decision and often feel anxious. CRM offers marketers an excellent opportunity to reach out to customers to reinforce their purchase decision. By thanking customers for their purchases and telling them they are important, marketers can help cement a long-term, profitable relationship. Updating customers periodically about the status of their order reinforces purchase decisions and offsets the feelings

---

campaign management developing product or service offerings customized for the appropriate customer segment and then pricing and communicating these offerings to enhance customer relationships

of cognitive dissonance. These CRM techniques are also increasingly being used to improve customer service and influence customer retention.

Inducing Product Trial by New Customers Although significant time and money are expended on encouraging repeat purchases by the best customers, a marketing database is also used to identify new customers. Because a firm using a marketing database already has a profile of its best customers, it can easily use the results of modeling to profile potential customers. REV, a regional telecommunications firm, uses modeling to identify prospective residential and commercial customers and successfully attracts their business. Marketing managers generally use demographic and behavioral data overlaid on existing customer data to develop a detailed customer profile that is a powerful tool for evaluating lists of prospects. For instance, if a firm's best customers are 35 to 50 years of age, live in suburban areas, own luxury cars, like to eat at Thai restaurants, and enjoy mountain climbing, then the company can find prospects already in its database or customers who currently are identified as using a competitor's product that match this profile.

Increasing Effectiveness of Distribution Channel Marketing In Chapter 13, you learned that a marketing channel is a business structure of interdependent organizations, such as wholesalers and retailers, which move a product from the producer to the ultimate consumer. Most marketers rely on indirect channels to move

their products to the end user. Thus, marketers often lose touch with the customer as an individual since the relationship is really between the retailer and the consumer. Marketers in this predicament often view their customers as aggregate statistics because specific customer information is difficult to gather. With CRM databases, manufacturers now have a tool to gain insight into who is buying their products.

With many brick-and-mortar stores setting up shop online, companies are now challenged to monitor purchases of customers who shop both in-store and online. This concept is referred to as multichannel marketing. One example of multichannel marketing is the partnership between Sephora and TikTok to connect TikTok creators with beauty products that are considered the best brands at Sephora. Sephora's Accelerate program provides educational training to help impact the content of the creator-driven perspective social media strategy.[23] Companies are also using radio-frequency identification (RFID) technology to improve distribution. The technology uses a microchip with an antenna that tracks anything from a soda can to a car from anywhere. The main implication of this technology is that companies will enjoy a reduction in theft and loss of merchandise shipments and will always know where merchandise is in the distribution channel. Moreover, as this technology is further developed, marketers can gather information on product usage and consumption.

Rawpixel.com/Shutterstock.com

Chapter 18

Social Media and Marketing

Learning Outcomes

After studying this chapter, you will be able to . . .

18-1 Describe how social media are used with integrated marketing communications

18-2 Explain how to create a social media campaign

18-3 Outline the various methods of measurement for social media

18-4 Explain consumer behavior on social media

18-5 Describe how social media tools are useful to marketers

18-6 Describe the impact of mobile technology on social media

18-7 Explain the aspects of developing a social media plan

18-1 What Are Social Media?

18-1 Describe how social media are used with integrated marketing communications

The most exciting thing to happen to marketing and promotion in recent years is the increasing use of digital platforms to promote brands, particularly using social media. Social media have changed the way marketers can communicate messages with their brands—from mass messages to intimate conversations. As marketing moves into social media, marketers must remember that for most people, social media are meant to be a social experience, not a marketing experience. In fact, the term *"social media"* means different things to different people, though most people think it refers to specific digital platforms like Facebook, Twitter, now known as X, or Instagram. **Social media** are any tool or service that uses the internet to facilitate conversations.[1] But social media can also be defined relative to traditional advertising like television and magazines: whereas traditional marketing media offer a mass media method of interacting with consumers, social media offer more one-to-one ways to meet consumers. However, social media should be an integral part of any promotional campaign, regardless of what other methods are used.

Several key usage numbers include:

- There are 4.9 billion social media users worldwide of the 8 billion people in the world, this is forecasted to be 5.85 billion by 2027.

- Eighty-five percent of the world's mobile phone users are on social media.

- China has the largest number of social media users, India is ranked second and the United States is ranked third.

- On average, social media users interact with 6.6 different social media platforms.

- Facebook is the largest social media platform, with nearly 3 billion active users.

- TikTok is the fastest growing network experiencing over 105 percent increase in two years.[2]

Social media imply several things for marketers and the ways they interact with their customers. First, marketers must realize that they often do not control the content on social media sites. Consumers are sharing their thoughts, wishes, and experiences about brands with the world through social media. Because of this level of visibility and discussion, marketers must understand that having a great campaign is not enough—the product or service must be great, too.

Second, the ability to share experiences quickly and with such large numbers of people amplifies the impact of word of mouth in ways that can affect a company's bottom line. Celebrities have taken advantage of their ability to

reach audiences through social media. Typically, celebrities will choose a platform like Instagram (Cristiano Ronaldo, Kylie Jenner, Selena Gomez) or X (Katy Perry, Justin Bieber, Rihanna) to reach their fans, and then use these platforms to influence their purchasing behaviors. Companies have also used social media to connect with customers. Seventy-two percent of Gen Z and millennials follow social media influencers. As a result, one in four marketers leverage influencer marketing.[3] For example, luxury brands like Dior and Versace use Instagram as a way to promote their products and luxury lifestyle. The total reach of these brands is difficult to quantify because of their celebrity influencers and advocates beyond their own direct efforts.[4]

Third, social media have enabled marketers to listen more effectively. Spectrum, Chipotle, and Netflix have taken social media monitoring to a whole new level, as they literally put social media at the center of their marketing efforts.[5] Through social media listening, Fitbit was able to identify and troubleshoot emerging customer issues. The company collects ideas from its communities and presents solutions to its engineering team. "Reminders to Move" is one outcome of this process. By not only monitoring but producing products based on customer engagement and feedback, brands are sending a message back to their customers letting them know they have been heard.[6]

Fourth, social media provide more sophisticated methods of measuring how marketers meet and interact with consumers than traditional advertising. Social media include tools and platforms like social networks, blogs, microblogs, and media-sharing sites that can be accessed through a growing number of devices, including smartphones, wearables, e-readers, digital assistants, televisions, tablets, smart watches, and video game consoles. This technology changes almost daily, offering consumers new ways to experience social media platforms. Therefore, social media must constantly innovate with new measurement

social media any tool or service that uses the internet to facilitate conversations

tools to keep up with consumer demands and the ability to measure their impact.

Finally, social media enable marketers to have much more direct and meaningful conversations with customers. Social media offer a form of relationship building that brings customers and brands closer. Indeed, the culture of *participation* that social media fosters may well prove to be a fifth "P" for marketing. For example, Target partnered with actress, author, and social media influencer, Tabitha Brown to create the Tabitha Brown Collection exclusively for Target. The collection contains products from a variety of categories including kitchenware, food, entertaining, swim, and apparel. Social media posts from both Target and Tabitha Brown spotlight and promote the products in the collection as well as one another.[7]

At the most basic level, consumers of social media want to exchange information, collaborate with others, and have conversations. Social media are designed for people to socialize with each other and have changed how and where conversations take place, even globalizing human interaction through rapidly evolving technology. Some technology enables companies to connect directly with consumers. Facebook Messenger Bots and Facebook Live, for example, enable customers to interact with companies in real time. BuzzFeed's election countdown ranks as the most-watched Facebook Live event. It racked up more than 50 million views leading up to the elections and was shared over 800,000 times.[8] This shows that conversations are happening online and events can progress over some time. It is up to marketers to decide whether engaging in those conversations will be profitable and to find the most effective method of entering the conversation.

Companies are beginning to understand the implications of their employees' activities on social media. In fact, there have been several examples of employees being fired for airing their personal feelings on social media platforms. To combat this, many companies have begun developing social media policies on what can be posted and what is inappropriate. Some companies have rules concerning corporate blogs, Facebook, X LinkedIn, and even online comments. Intel has a social media policy that is divided into three sections about disclosure, protecting trade secrets, and the use of common sense. The Air Force's social media policy is another example of a policy divided into three sections, but it extends beyond the employees. It separates the policy into sections as it relates to Leaders, Airmen, and Families to ensure safety and overall morale.[9] Having a social media policy can certainly help mitigate risk, but there is no guarantee that employees will not occasionally slip up.

Marketers are interested in online communication because it is wildly popular: brands, companies, individuals, and celebrities all promote their messages online. Some companies go as far as to require Facebook and

Security concerns about TikTok's connection to China have led many governments across the globe to ban the app on official devices.

Castleski/Shutterstock.com

X training for high-profile employees. Employees at Cisco can take advantage of training on how to use LinkedIn to attract candidates by acting as a talent influencer. The company occasionally allows employees to take over the company's social media for a day since the content feels less corporate-generated.[10]

18-1a How Consumers Use Social Media

Before beginning to understand how to leverage social media for brand building, it is important to understand which social media consumers are using and how they are using them. It is safe to assume that many customers are active on Instagram, X and Facebook. But targeting can also be accomplished by using less ubiquitous platforms. Sina Weibo, WeChat, and Douyin (China's version of TikTok), for example, are the largest social media platforms in China.[11] Hinge, Tinder, and Bumble are great platforms to reach young adult singles. Teens tend to use platforms like Snapchat, Instagram, YouTube, and TikTok. While Facebook is used widely by adults, its popularity among younger consumers is decreasing. Dedicated messaging apps have become more popular in terms of social media. These include WhatsApp, Viber, Telegram, Line, and Facebook Messenger.[12]

Videos are another of the most popular tools marketers can use to reach consumers, and YouTube is by far the largest online video repository—it has more content than any major television network. Vimeo is another popular video creation and sharing platform for events and live streaming.[13] TikTok is an app where users can create, watch, and share short videos shot on mobile devices or webcams. Similarly, Facebook Live, which enables live streaming of events, is becoming ever-more popular with consumers and brands alike. Visual content is 40 times more likely to be shared compared to text content. Therefore, it is no surprise that companies interested in high audience engagement are using online video content.[14]

Increased usage of alternative platforms like smartphones, tablets, and other mobile devices, has further contributed to the proliferation of social media usage.

In the United States:

- Ninety-seven percent of adults own a mobile phone, and 85 percent of these own a smartphone.

- Ownership of smartphones decreases as age increases, with 94 percent of 18- to 29-year-olds owning a smartphone while only 46 percent of individuals over 65 owning a smartphone.

Globally:

- China has the most smartphone users at 1.04 billion users, representing almost 74 percent of the population.

- Germany has the highest percentage of the population owning smartphones at 82.4 percent of all mobile devices.

- Returning to the United States, Further, 83 percent of urban dwellers have smartphones, while only 65 percent of rural citizens use smartphones.[15]

On the tablet side of electronics:

- Market growth is in the healthcare, education, and entertainment sectors.

- Users account for 16.2 percent (1.28 billion users) of the world's population, a decline from its 2017 peak.

- Almost 46 percent of table users are between the ages of 25 and 44.

- Users are almost equally divided between males and females.

- Over 50 percent of tablet interactions take place in the late evening (between 7 pm and 12 pm).[16]

Social Commerce

An area of growth in social media is social commerce, which combines social media with the basics of e-commerce. **Social commerce** is a subset of e-commerce that involves the interaction and user contribution aspects of social online media to assist online buying and selling of products and services.[17] Basically, social commerce relies on user-generated content on a website to assist consumers with purchases. Pinterest lets users collect ideas and products from all over the web and "pin" favorite items to individually curated pinboards. Other users browse boards by theme, keyword, or product; click on what they like; and either visit the originating sites or re-pin the items on their own pinboards. Companies like Michael Kors use

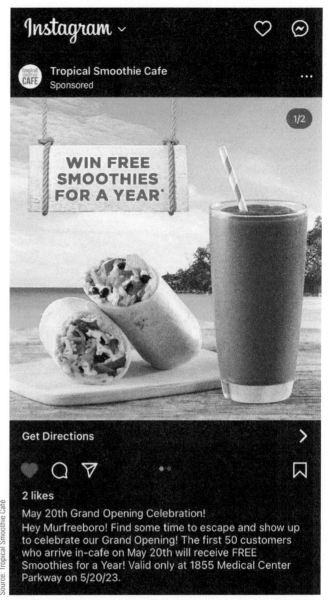

Source: Tropical Smoothie Café

To drive traffic and make locals aware of a new location, Tropical Smoothie Café uses sponsored Instagram ads and giveaways.

influencers who post photos of clothes and accessories on Instagram and encourage customers to purchase straight from Instagram. Social commerce sites often include ratings and recommendations (as Amazon does) and social shopping tools (as Groupon does). In general, social commerce sites are designed to help consumers make more informed decisions about which products and services to purchase. Tropical Smoothie used sponsored ads on Instagram to promote a new location. The goal of the ad is to increase awareness of the restaurant. Additionally, the giveaway mentioned in the sponsored ad incentivizes

---

social commerce a subset of e-commerce that involves the interaction and user contribution aspects of social online media to assist online buying and selling of products and services

consumers to visit early during the grand opening for the possibility of winning free smoothies for a year.

By 2026, global social commerce is expected to reach $2.9 trillion.[18] There are eight types of social commerce:

1. Peer-to-peer sales platforms (e.g., Mercari and Etsy)
2. Social networking websites driven by sales (e.g., Pinterest and Facebook)
3. Group buying platforms (e.g., Groupon and LivingSocial)
4. Peer recommendation sites (e.g., Yelp and Trustpilot)
5. User-curated shopping sites (e.g., Canopy and Lyst)
6. Participatory commerce platforms (e.g., Kickstarter and Threadless)
7. Social shopping sites (e.g., Buywith and Listia)
8. Shoppable videos (e.g., Wayfair and Kate Spade)[19]

As companies migrate to social commerce sites such as Instagram, consumer interactions across the sites may change. One way companies are leveraging Instagram's user base is by running promotions. For example, High Society Freeride, an outdoor and sporting goods store, wanted to engage users and promote its business. To do so, the company ran a hashtag contest called #OneLife-MakeItCount. Participants were entered to win a $100 gift certificate by posting a photo showing what they loved to do using the contest hashtag within the contest timeline.[20] This type of promotion can undermine the authenticity that many consumers rely on when using social commerce sites. But some companies hope to cultivate authentic relationships by staying away from promotions. Using Pinterest, Lush cosmetics pins behind-the-scenes information about the brand.[21] This transparent content is unique and helps customers build a relationship of trust.

18-1b Social Media and Integrated Marketing Communications

While marketers typically employ a social media strategy alongside traditional channels like print and broadcast, many budget pendulums are swinging toward social media. Globally, digital marketing spending is forecasted to grow from $523 billion in 2022 to almost $836 billion in 2026.[22] Paid search and online video advertising will account for over 50 percent of digital advertising by 2026.[23]

A unique consequence of social media is the widespread shift from one-to-many communication to many-to-many communication. Instead of simply putting a brand

advertisement on television with no means for feedback, marketers can use social media to have conversations with consumers, forge deeper relationships, and build brand loyalty. Social media also allow consumers to connect, share opinions, and collaborate on new ideas according to their interests.

With social media, the audience is often in control of the message, the medium, the response, or all three. This distribution of control is often difficult for companies to adjust to, but the focus of social marketing is unavoidably on the audience, and the brand must adapt to succeed. The interaction between producer and consumer becomes less about entertaining and more about listening, influencing, and engaging.

Using consumers to develop and market products is called **crowdsourcing**. Crowdsourcing describes how the input of many people can be leveraged to make decisions that used to be based on the input of only a few people.[24] Companies get feedback on marketing campaigns, new product ideas, and other marketing decisions by asking customers to share their thoughts. LEGO Ideas lets fans share creations and enter challenges for new LEGO Ideas sets. Submissions go through various stages including being voted on by fellow fans. Some products released as a result of LEGO Ideas include the *Home Alone* house, a motorized lighthouse, and Vincent van Gogh's *The Starry Night*, all LEGO brick sets that range in difficulty level and several pieces.[25] Crowdsourcing offers a way for companies to engage heavy users of a brand and receive input, which in turn increases those users' brand advocacy and lessens the likelihood that a change will be disliked enough to drive away loyal customers.

18-2 Creating and Leveraging a Social Media Campaign

18-2 Explain how to create a social media campaign

Social media offer exciting opportunities with the potential for enormous brand impact. Because the costs are often low and the learning curve is relatively quick, some organizations are tempted to dive headfirst into social media. As with any marketing campaign, however, it is always important to start with a strategy. For most organizations, this means starting with a marketing or communications plan. Important areas such as situation analysis, objectives, and evaluation are still essential. It is important to link communication objectives (e.g., improving customer service) to the most effective social media tools (e.g., TikTok) and to be able to measure the results to determine whether the objectives were met. It is also important to understand the various types of media involved.

The new communication paradigm created by a shift to social media marketing raises questions about categorization. In light of the convergence of traditional and

---

crowdsourcing using consumers to develop and market products

digital media, researchers have explored different ways that interactive marketers can categorize media types, namely owned, earned, and paid media (recall these concepts from Chapter 15). The purpose of owned media is to develop deeper relationships with customers. A brand's presence on Facebook, YouTube, X, Pinterest, and other social platforms constitutes owned media. Additional content such as videos, webinars, recommendations, ratings, and blog posts are also considered owned media since they are shareable on social media platforms. This can be referred to as "content marketing" to organize a brand's content across all platforms and expand the message using paid media and influencer marketing. Basically, brand marketers want to drive customers to a digital destination like a website to complete some type of conversation or to generate earned media.

In digital marketing, attention is *earned* through word of mouth or online buzz about something the brand is doing. Earned media include viral videos, reposts, comments on blogs, and other forms of customer feedback resulting from a social media presence. An example of earned media is consumers passing along brand information in the form of reposts, reposts comments, or ratings and recommendations. In other words, word of mouth is spread online rather than face-to-face. Paid media are similar to marketing efforts that utilize traditional media, like print publications, film, and television advertisements.

Most of the time marketers must put some money behind a campaign and cannot simply rely on earned media or a message going "viral." So, marketers turn to paid media. In digital marketing, paid media include social media advertising, display advertising, paid search words, and native advertising.[26] Ads purchased on Facebook, for example, are considered paid media, since the brand is paying for the text-based or visual ad that shows up on the right-hand side of Facebook profiles.

In some cases, social media can be thought of as an additional "layer" that many brands decide to develop. Some layers are quite deep—Doritos, Old Spice, and Nike can be said to have deeper layers of social media since these are brands people talk about a lot. Other brands, for example, many B-to-B brands, may have a more shallow social media layer and provide access to only one or two social media platforms. At the end of the day, it really depends on the type of product being sold and the customer's propensity to participate in social media. Regardless, marketers are including in their campaigns more social media that is owned, paid, and earned.

To leverage all three types of media, marketers must follow a few key guidelines. First, they must maximize owned media by reaching out beyond their existing websites to create portfolios of digital touchpoints. This is especially true for brands with tight budgets, since the organization may not be able to afford much-paid media. Second, marketers must recognize that public and media relations no longer translate into earned media. Instead, marketers must learn how to listen and respond to stakeholders. This will stimulate word of mouth. Finally, marketers must understand that paid media must catalyze to drive customer engagement and responses to increase earned media.[27] If balanced correctly, all three types of media can be powerful tools for interactive marketers.

18-2a The Listening System

The first action a marketing team should take when initiating a social media campaign is simple—it should just listen. Customers are on social media, and it is reasonable to assume the brand is there as well. Similarly, customers expect, and in some instances demand, a new level of engagement with brands. Developing an effective listening system is necessary for both understanding and engaging an online audience. Marketers must not only hear what is being said about the brand, the industry, the competition, and the customer, they must also pay attention to who is saying what and to act on that information. The specific ways that customers and noncustomers rate, rank, critique, praise, deride, recommend, snub, and generally discuss brands are all important. Thus, social media have created a new method of market research: customers telling marketers what they want and need (and do not want and do not need).

Once a company starts listening, it typically wants to develop a more formalized approach. **Social media monitoring** is the process of identifying and assessing what is being said about a company, individual, product, or brand. It can involve sentiment analysis and *text mining* specific keywords on social networking websites, blogs, discussion forums, and other social media. Negative comments and complaints are particularly important because they can illuminate unknown brand flaws, and also because negative comments and complaints are more likely to go viral. Listening is important because if consumers believe a brand is insincere based on whether negative comments go unanswered, consumers will take their business elsewhere.

Failure to respond to criticism typically leads to a larger crisis. Online tools such as Meltwater, Sprout Social, HootSuite, Cyfe, and Talkwalker are extremely helpful in monitoring social media. Larger companies typically use an enterprise system to monitor social media which

---

social media monitoring the process of identifying and assessing what is being said about a company, individual, product, or brand

may track images and logos as well.[28] Gatorade was one of the initial brands that created a mission control center to monitor social media interactions to understand how the brand is being perceived worldwide.[29]

18-2b Social Media Objectives

After establishing a listening platform, the organization should develop a list of objectives for its social media team to accomplish. These objectives must be developed with a clear understanding of how social media change the communication dynamic with and for customers. Remember, attempting to reach a mass audience with a static message will never be as successful as influencing people through conversation. For example, TikTok for Good seeks to inspire a new generation into having a positive impact on society and the planet. #EduTok is a popular challenge encouraging users to create educational content. The goal is to make educational content more accessible and engaging for younger audiences not typically drawn to traditional classroom settings.[30] Marketing managers must set objectives that reflect this reality. The following are some practical ideas marketing managers should consider when setting social media objectives:

- **Listen and learn:** Monitor what is being said about the brand and competitors, and glean insights about audiences. Use online tools and research to implement the best social media practices. Though an established a listening strategy, this objective should already have been accomplished.

- **Build relationships and awareness:** Open dialogues with stakeholders by giving them compelling content across a variety of media. Engage in conversations, and answer customers' questions candidly. This will both increase web traffic and boost your search engine ranking. This is where crowdsourcing can be useful for product development and communication campaign feedback.

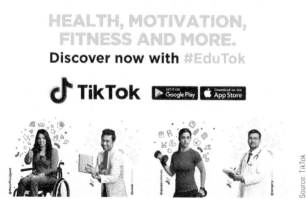

TikTok for Good strives to make educational content accessible and engaging.

- **Promote products and services:** The clearest path to increasing the bottom line using social media is to get customers talking about products and services, which ultimately translates into sales.

- **Manage your reputation:** Develop and improve the brand's reputation by responding to comments and criticisms that appear on blogs and forums. In addition, organizations can position themselves as helpful and benevolent by participating in other forums and discussions. Social media make it much easier to establish and communicate expertise.

- **Improve customer service:** Customer comments about products and services will not always be positive. Use social media to search out dissatisfied customers and engage them directly to solve their product or service issues.

18-3 Evaluation and Measurement of Social Media

18-3 Outline the various methods of measurement for social media

Social media have the potential to revolutionize the way organizations communicate with stakeholders. Given the relative ease and efficiency with which organizations can use social media, a positive return on investment (ROI) is likely for many—if not most—organizations. Social media ad spending in 2026 is expected to be 43 percent greater than 2023 spending. While it is recognized that social media spending is a worthwhile investment, most marketers have not been able to figure out how to measure the benefits of social media.[31]

As with traditional advertising, marketers lack hard evidence as to the relative effectiveness of these tools. Some marketers accept this unknown variable and focus on the fact that social media are less about ROI than about deepening relationships with customers. Others work tirelessly to better understand the measurement of social media's effectiveness. One survey found that 65 percent of marketers are either uncertain or they disagree that ROI on social media can be measured. Only 5 percent "strongly agree" and 30 percent "agree." Yet, in the same study, participants rank social media as the second-best way to generate sales, with email marketing being selected as the best.[32]

While the use of social media continues to increase (by both marketers and consumers), social media are difficult to measure, because there is no common denominator to measure ROI. Some ways to measure ROI include followers or fans, purchases from social media referrals, reposts, and shares. In truth, there are countless measures.

Regardless of the measure, there are four steps to help gauge the effectiveness of a social media effort:

1. **Calculate your total spending on social media.** No set number is appropriate. Items to consider include the cost of tools and platforms to manage social accounts, ad spending, content creation costs (in-house or externally created), social media manager/team salaries and training, and any other consultants that might be used.

2. **Define clear social media objectives that connect with the business goals.** Typical objectives include lead generation, awareness, conversions, sentiment, customer experience, satisfaction, confidence, sense of security or risk mitigation.

3. **Track metrics that align with social media objectives.** Some of the most common metrics include reach, audience engagement, site traffic, leads generated, sign-ups, conversions, or revenue generation. To determine the most appropriate metric, it is important to consider how the information will be used within the organization. The metrics should help the organization make decisions. It should also be a measure that the organization can measure effectively and regularly.

4. **Create an ROI report that illustrates the impact of social media.** The report should use a common language that can be understood by everyone. Therefore, avoid using acronyms or jargon. The reports should have a common layout. Using a template is helpful. Tie the result to the organization's objectives, using key performance indicators for tracking short-term progress. Finally, include any limitations about what may or may not be able to be measured and why.[33]

18-4 Social Behavior of Consumers

18-4 Explain consumer behavior on social media

Social media have changed the way that people interact in their everyday lives. Some say that social media have made people smarter by giving them (especially children) access to so much information and interactivity. Social media enable people to stay in touch in ways never before experienced. Social media have also reinvented civic engagement. Consider that #BlackLivesMatter and #MeToo all started on social media. Social media have drastically changed the advertising business from an industry based on mass-media models (such as television) to an industry based on relationships and conversations. For example, social media plays a huge part in politics helping to engage voters and make content more accessible. According to Pew Research, around 71 percent of people get some of their news from social media. Top sources include Facebook, YouTube, X, and Instagram.[34] Since social media are designed to be intentionally fragmented because the content is curated by the user, pockets of like-minded individuals can be formed.[35] These pockets can be beneficial in bringing awareness to a cause or participation in rallies and other events. Clearly, these developments have implications for how consumers use social media and the purposes for which they use those media.

Once objectives have been determined and measurement tools have been implemented, it is important to identify which consumers the marketer is trying to reach. Who is using social media, and how often? What types of social media do they use? How do they use it? Are they just reading content, or do they actually create it? Does Instagram attract younger users? How are people using Snapchat? Do X users repost viral videos? These types of questions must be considered because they determine not only which tools will be most effective but also, more importantly, whether launching a social media campaign even makes sense for a particular organization.

Understanding an audience necessitates understanding how that audience uses social media. Charlene Li and Josh Bernoff of Forrester Research identify the following types of social media users:

1. **Creators:** Those who produce and share online content like blogs, websites, articles, and videos. This is the fastest-growing sector of the audience.

2. **Conversationalist:** This group is also creating content, but only to facilitate communication. They want to express themselves through status updates.

3. **Critics:** Those who post comments, ratings, and reviews of products and services on blogs and forums. They respond to status updates and are crucial to other types of users.

4. **Collectors:** Those who use RSS feeds to collect information and vote for websites online.

5. **Joiners:** Those who maintain a social networking profile and visit other sites.

6. **Spectators:** Those who read blogs, listen to podcasts, watch videos, and generally consume media. This is the largest category.

7. **Inactives:** This is the smallest group and makes up those who do none of the above.[36]

This type of classification gives marketers a general idea of who is using social media and how to engage them. It is similar to any type of market segmentation—especially the 80/20 rule. Those who are creating content and are active on social media could be those consumers most likely to actively engage with a brand as well as actively post negative comments on social media. The critics and collectors make up most of this group. However, it is important not to miss the joiners and spectators, because they are eager to follow and act on the comments of their fellow customers.

Another aspect of how consumers use social media is through their attention to social media influencers and how some people even become influencers themselves. There are five types of social media influencers.[37] At the top of the hierarchy, **Mega-influencers** are often celebrities like actors, singers, artists, or athletes who have more than a million followers on social media platforms. Some of these influencers have used their platforms as a voice for causes they care about while others have used social media to promote products. Some celebrities (like Selena Gomez and Kylie Jenner) have launched businesses based on their influence with their followers. These celebrities often get paid $10,000+ per post on Instagram to promote a brand.

Macro-influencers have between 500,000 and 1,000,000 followers on social media platforms. Macro-influencers may be a celebrity-turned-influencer or influencer-turned-celebrity. Examples include Jessi Malay and Elliot Choy. What makes this type of influencer is their reputation or created content. On Instagram, this level of influencer would receive between $5,000 - $10,000 per post.

Mid-tier influencers have between 50,000 and 500,000 followers on social media platforms. These individuals are not likely to have achieved celebrity status, yet. They are a powerful group of creators and have a dedicated group of followers. Sam Ushiro and Adam Gonon would be examples of mid-tier influencers. The content for this group is often professional, but the individuals still feel relatable to their followers. According to a post on Instagram, mid-tier influencers make between $500–$5,000 per post.

Micro-influencers have a smaller number of followers on social media with 10,000–50,000 followers but are still influential in specific areas. This level of influencer has provided an opportunity for ordinary people who have a unique voice and the ability to gain followers to connect with brands, like Allen Swan and Mary Sarge. Micro-influencers are also useful for more-local campaigns, since many times, their influence is location-based. On Instagram, these influencers make between $100–$500 per post.

Finally, we have the **nano-influencer** with the smallest follower count of 1,000–10,000 followers on social media. This group has the highest engagement rates of any influencer group. Examples include Emmy Rice and Noelle Graham. Content is considered ultra-authentic and personalized. Brands may not gain a lot of reach with nano-influencers, but the trade-off is a highly engaged, dedicated followers.

18-5 Social Media Tools: Consumer- and Corporate-Generated Content

18-5 Describe how social media tools are useful to marketers

Given that marketers need to engage with customers on social media for many reasons, some several tools and platforms can be employed as part of an organization's social media strategy. Blogs, microblogs, social networks, media creation and sharing sites, social news sites, location-based social networking sites, review sites, virtual reality/artificial intelligence, and online gaming all have their place in a company's social marketing plan. However, some platforms cross over multiple categories. These are all tools in a marketing manager's toolbox, available when applicable to the marketing plan but not necessarily to be used all at once. Because of the breakneck pace at which technology changes, this list of resources will surely look markedly different five years from now. More tools emerge every day, and branding strategies must keep up with the ever-changing world of technology. For now, the resources highlighted in this section remain a marketer's strongest set of platforms for communicating and strengthening relationships with customers.

18-5a Blogs

Blogs are staples in many social media strategies. A **blog** is a publicly accessible web page that functions as an interactive journal, where readers can post comments on the author's entries. Some believe that every company should have a blog that speaks to current and potential customers, not as consumers, but as people.[38] Blogs enable marketers to create content in the form of posts, which ideally build customer trust and a sense of authenticity about the posts. Once posts are made, audience members can provide feedback through comments. Because it opens a dialogue and

---

mega-influencers often celebrities who have more than a million followers on social media platforms

macro-influencers people who have between 500,000 and 1,000,000 followers on social media platforms

mid-tier influencers people who have between 50,000 and 500,000 followers on social media platforms

micro-influencers people who have a smaller number of followers on social media with 10,000–50,000 followers, but are still influential in specific areas

nano-influencers people who have the smallest number of followers on social media with 1,000–10,000 followers

blog a publicly accessible web page that functions as an interactive journal, where readers can post comments on the author's entries

gives customers a voice, the comments section of a blog post is one of the most important avenues of conversation between brands and consumers. Blogs also allow companies to develop long-term relationships with their customers. Posting content yields dividends over time, serving as a lasting resource for a brand's current and future customer base. Blogs are particularly important to B-2-B companies, since they provide thought leadership and recommendations to customers, and brands are increasingly using other blog formats like Medium which has a built-in following.

Blogs can be divided into two broad categories: corporate and professional blogs, and noncorporate blogs such as personal blogs. **Corporate blogs** are sponsored by a company or one of its brands and are maintained by one or more of the company's employees. They disseminate marketing-controlled information and are effective platforms for developing thought leadership, fostering better relationships with stakeholders, maximizing search engine optimization, attracting new customers, creating favorable impressions of the organization using anecdotes and stories about brands, and providing an active forum for testing new ideas. Many companies have moved away from corporate blogs and are replacing the in-depth writing and comment monitoring that are part of blog maintenance with the quick, easy, and more social Facebook, X, or Tumblr. IKEA Ideas, Hubspot, Home Depot's DIY Projects Done Right, and IBM operate some of the best big company corporate blogs. All are known for their creative and engaging content and the authenticity of their tone.[39]

On the other hand, **noncorporate blogs** are independent and not associated with the marketing efforts of any particular company or brand. Because these blogs contain information not controlled by marketers, they are perceived to be more authentic than corporate blogs. Personal finance is a topic area of noncorporate blogging. The Penny Hoarder, founded by Kyle Taylor, started in 2010 as a means for Taylor to document the ways of cutting costs while trying to pay off $50,000 in student debt.[40]

Because of the popularity of these and other types of blogs, many bloggers receive products and/or money from companies in exchange for a review. Many bloggers disclose where they received the product or if they were paid, but an affiliation is not always clear. Because of this, bloggers must disclose any financial relationship with a company per Federal Trade Commission rules. Marketing managers need to understand the rules behind offering complimentary products to bloggers before using them as a way to capitalize on the high potential for social buzz. For example, four out of five noncorporate bloggers post brand or product reviews. Even if a company does not have a formal social media strategy, chances are the brand is still out in the blogosphere, whether or not a marketing manager approached a blogger.

18-5b Microblogs

Microblogs are blogs that have shorter posts than traditional blogs. X is the most popular microblogging platform. There are several other platforms, including Pinterest, Instagram, and Tumblr. These platforms allow users to post text, videos, images, and links. The content posted on microblogs ranges from five-paragraph news stories to photos of sandwiches with the ingredients as captions. X was originally designed as a short messaging system used for internal communication. Now it is used as a communication and research tool by individuals and brands around the world. X is effective for disseminating breaking news, promoting longer blog posts and campaigns, sharing links, announcing events, and promoting sales. By following, reposting, responding to potential customers' posts, and posting content that inspires customers to engage the brand, corporate X users can lay a foundation for meaningful two-way conversation quickly and effectively. Celebrities also flock to X to interact with fans, discuss tour dates, and efficiently promote themselves directly to fans. Research has found that when operated correctly, corporate X accounts are well respected and well received. X can be used to build communities, aid in customer service, gain prospects, increase awareness, and in the case of nonprofit organizations, raise funds. However, the new CEO at X is making some changes to the original strategy of the organization.

Tumblr, a popular microblog social media platform, has more than 547 million monthly users. More than half of Tumblr's users are under the age of 35. While ranked in the top 10 platforms of social media, Tumblr ownership has changed hands several times. Beyond the ability to post daily blogs, Tumblr offers a liveblog function to account for real-time happenings. Tumblr experiences over 2,000 post creations per second.[41]

18-5c Social Networks

Social networking sites enable individuals to connect—or network—with friends, peers, and business associates.

---

corporate blogs blogs that are sponsored by a company or one of its brands and maintained by one or more of the company's employees

noncorporate blogs independent blogs that are not associated with the marketing efforts of any particular company or brand

microblogs blogs that have shorter posts than traditional blogs

social networking sites websites that allow individuals to connect—or network—with friends, peers, and business associates

Connections may be made around shared interests, shared environments, and personal relationships. Depending on the site, connected individuals may be able to send each other messages, track each other's activity, find each other's personal information, share multimedia, comment on each other's blog and microblog posts, or do all of these things. Depending on a marketing team's goals, several social networks might be engaged as part of a social media strategy: Facebook and YouTube are the largest social networks; Instagram, TikTok, and Snapchat are popular among younger audiences; LinkedIn is geared toward professionals and businesses who use it to recruit employees; and niche networks like Behance (creative people), Letterboxd (film lovers), Goodreads (book lovers), and Christian Mingle (dating service) cater to specialized markets. There is a niche social network for just about every demographic and interest. Beyond those already established, an organization may decide to develop a brand-specific social network or community. Although each social networking site is different, some marketing goals can be accomplished on any such site. Given the right strategy, increasing awareness, targeting audiences, promoting products, forging relationships, highlighting expertise and leadership, attracting event participants, performing research, and generating new business are attainable marketing goals on any social network.

Facebook

With nearly 3 billion Facebook users per month, it is the largest social networking site. Growth in new profiles is roughly 26 million per month. Further, approximately 37 percent of the global population use Facebook. Sixty-eight percent of the monthly active users log in each day.[42] Given the vast size of Facebook, many organizations utilize this platform to reach customers. Table 18.1 illustrates differences between nonindividuals (typically corporations) and individuals among four platforms Facebook, LinkedIn, TikTok, and Instagram.

LinkedIn

LinkedIn is used primarily by professionals who wish to build their personal brands online and businesses that are recruiting employees and freelancers. LinkedIn features many of the same services as Facebook (profiles, status updates, private messages, company pages, and groups), but is oriented around business and professional connections—it is designed to be information-rich rather than multimedia-rich. Therefore, companies use this platform

differently than Facebook. LinkedIn's question-and-answer forum, endorsement system, and job classifieds platform set it apart from Facebook as a truly business-oriented space. Additional features such as Audio Events, Company Pages, InMail, Groups, and Ads set LinkedIn apart as the optimal professional social media platform.[43] LinkedIn is the most effective social media platform for B-to-B marketing, as many use it for lead generation. Some companies use LinkedIn for recruiting, and others use it for thought leadership.

TikTok

TikTok has over 1 billion users in over 150 countries. There are over 5 million businesses actively using TikTok in the US. TikTok draws a younger demographic, with 32.5 percent between the ages of 10 and 19, and 29.5 percent between 20 and 29 years of age. Users spend 95 minutes per day on the platform. Further, 83 percent of users are creators and have posted a video. Engagement is also very high on TikTok compared to other platforms. For example, the same video posted by Jennifer Lopez on X (45 million followers) and TikTok (5 million followers) got 2 million views on X (45 million followers) and 71 million views on TikTok (5 million followers).[44]

Instagram

Instagram has over 1 billion users. Over 3.95 million photos and videos are shared every day on the platform. Users spend an average of 30 minutes on Instagram daily. Eighty percent of users engage with businesses. Sixty-seven percent of marketers use influencers. Accounts that post seven or more times per week have the greatest follower growth rates. Multi-photo posts gain the highest engagement rates. Seventy-five percent of adults in the U.S. aged 18–24 use Instagram.[45]

18-5d Media Sharing Sites

Media sharing sites enable users to upload and distribute multimedia content like videos and photos. YouTube, TikTok, Instagram, BeReal, Twitch and Snapchat are particularly useful to brands' social marketing strategies because they add a vibrant interactive channel on which to disseminate content. Suffice it to say, the distribution of user-generated content has changed markedly over the past few years. Today, organizations can tell compelling brand stories through videos, photos, and audio.

Photo-sharing sites enable users to archive and share photos. Dropbox, PhotoCircle, Google Photos, 500px, and VSCO all offer free photo-hosting services that can be utilized by individuals and businesses alike.[46] Instagram is often used by brands to engage younger audience members. Instagram Stories is a wildly popular tool for visual storytelling for both individuals and brands. Snapchat is

---

media sharing sites websites that allow users to upload and distribute multimedia content like videos and photos

Table 18.1 Differences in Social Media Non-Individual vs. Individual

Facebook

Nonindividual (Usually a Business)	Individual
Page	Profile
Fan of a page, tells fan's friends that the user is a fan, creates mini-viral campaign	Friend a person, send private messages, write on the wall, see friend-only content
Public, searchable	Privacy options, not searchable unless user-enabled

LinkedIn

Nonindividual (Usually a Business)	Individual
Page	Profile
Connections	Followers
Can run ads	Can not run ads
Sections: Overview, About, Jobs, and People	Sections include: Activity, Experience, Skills & Endorsements, Recommendations, and Interests

TikTok

Nonindividual (Usually a Business)	Individual
Pro Account	Personal Account
Downloadable Analytics	In-App Analytics Only

Instagram

Nonindividual (Usually a Business)	Individual
All the features of an Individual account and able to insert links into stories, able to tag products, and more information in bio like email, phone number, website, address, and location.	For posting pictures, videos, live streaming, adding to stories, and direct messaging
Can only connect to one Facebook page	Allowed to link to multiple Facebook pages and profiles
Real-time analytics with details about posts and demographics of those interacting	Analytics include likes and comments
Options to boost and promote posts	Organic reach

also useful, but since photos and videos are only visible for a few seconds, complex marketing messages cannot easily be conveyed. To get around this, Snapchat developed Snapchat Discover, a storytelling feature that lets brands engage consumers more effectively.

Video creation and distribution have also gained popularity among marketers because of video's rich ability to tell stories. YouTube, the highest-trafficked video-based website and the second-highest-trafficked site overall, allows users to upload and stream their videos to an enthusiastic and active community.[47] YouTube is not only large (in terms of visitors), but also attracts a diverse base of users: age and gender demographics are remarkably balanced.

Many entertainment companies and movie marketers have used YouTube as a showcase for new products, specials, and movie trailers. User-generated content can also be a powerful tool for brands that can use it effectively. While YouTube is still the champ, Instagram is quickly becoming another popular platform for corporate promotion.

A podcast, another type of user-generated media, is a digital audio or video file that is distributed serially for other people to listen to or watch. Podcasts can be streamed online, played on a computer, streamed through a mobile device, or downloaded onto a smartphone or other mobile devices. Podcasts are like radio shows that are distributed through various means and not linked to a scheduled time slot. Podcasts have amassed a steadily growing number of loyal devotees. For example, #LIPSTORIES by Sephora Collection tells the story of the influential woman behind different lipstick lines. ZipRecruiter's "Rise and Grind" podcast focuses on learning from hardworking, successful people in a variety of fields. Finally, "Innovation" by Johnson & Johnson discusses important new concepts in personal and healthcare and how Johnson & Johnson are working to advance those areas.[48]

18-5e Social News Sites

Social news sites enable users to decide which content is promoted on a given website by voting that content up or down. Users post news stories and multimedia on crowdsourced sites such as Reddit for the community to vote on. The more interest from readers, the higher the story or video is ranked. Marketers have found that these sites are useful for promoting campaigns, creating conversations around related issues, and building website traffic.

If marketing content posted to a crowdsourced site is voted up, discussed, and shared enough to be listed among the most popular topics of the day, it can go viral across other sites, and eventually the entire web. Social bookmarking sites such as Pinterest are similar to social news sites, but the objective of their users is to collect, save, and share interesting and valuable links. On these sites, users categorize links with short, descriptive tags. Users can search the site's database of links by specific tags or can add their own tags to others' links. In this way, tags serve as the foundation for information gathering and sharing on social bookmarking sites.

18-5f Location-Based Social Networking Sites

Based on Global Positioning System (GPS), location-based social apps are paired with smartphones to help people find others based on where they are. City Hour is a business networking app that connects people with common interests within a 50-mile radius.[49] Essentially, **location-based social networking sites** combine the fun of social networking with the utility of location-based GPS

---

social news sites websites that allow users to decide which content is promoted on a given website by voting that content up or down

location-based social networking sites websites that combine the fun of social networking with the utility of location-based GPS technology

technology. MapMyFitness not only allows users to track their training but results and routines can be shared with others. Wearables can be synchronized to the app and live tracking can be shared in real-time to give loved ones peace of mind.[50]

Location service providers such as Foursquare, are the underlying location provider to many brands like Uber, Snapchat, and Coca-Cola. These services are particularly useful social marketing tools for local businesses, especially when combined with sales promotions like coupons, special offers, contests, and events. Location information can be harnessed to forge lasting relationships and deeply ingrained loyalty among customers. For example, a local restaurant can encourage customers to "check-in" on Foursquare using their smartphones and receive coupons for that day's purchases. Location-based technology makes it possible for people to share their location with their online friends. Beyond just providing the location information, Foursquare information is used to provide information about how busy a location generally is at a given time.[51]

18-5g Review Sites

Individuals tend to trust other people's opinions when it comes to purchasing. According to GlobeNewswire, 95 percent of online consumers read online reviews before buying but 67 percent will not trust a high rating unless there are many reviews. Further, 83 percent said relevance and recency are meaningful when considering trustworthiness.[52] Online reviews are important for marketers hoping to influence consumers in the early stages of the purchase cycle who don't yet have an established plan for what and how to purchase. The percentage of individuals trusting

frantic00/Shutterstock.com

One form of advertising used in the cosmetics and fashion industry is a #Brandtrip. Initially, these trips were offered to YouTubers but later extended to TikTok influencers. However, the desire for transparency and drama has brands questioning their use in the future.

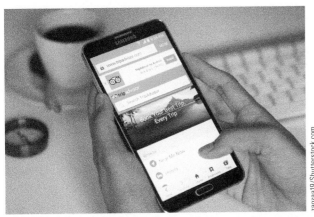

Social travel and review site Tripadvisor helps consumers make more informed decisions on things to do, places to stay, and where to eat.

other people's online opinions is much higher than that of consumers who trust traditional advertising. Based on the early work of Amazon.com and eBay to integrate user opinions into product and seller pages, countless websites allowing users to voice their opinions have sprung up across every segment of the internet market.

Review sites enable consumers to post, read, rate, and comment on opinions regarding all kinds of products and services. For example, Yelp, the most active local review directory on the web with more than 53 percent of consumers reported using Yelp, combines customer critiques of local businesses with business information and elements of social networking to create an engaging, informative experience.[53] On Yelp, users scrutinize local restaurants, fitness centers, tattoo parlors, and other businesses, each of which has a detailed profile page. Business owners and representatives can edit their organizations' pages and respond to Yelp reviews both privately and publicly. Yelp even rewards its most popular (and prolific) reviewers with Elite status. Businesses like Johnston's in San Diego, California, will throw Elite-only parties to enable these esteemed Yelpers to try out their restaurant, hoping to receive a favorable review. This event garnered Johnston's 40 reviews averaging five out of five stars.[54] By allowing marketers to respond to their customers directly and put their businesses in a positive light, review sites certainly serve as useful tools for local and national businesses.

18-5h Virtual Worlds and Online Gaming

Online gaming presents additional opportunities for marketers to engage with consumers. These include massive multiplayer online (MMO) games such as *Final Fantasy XIV, Destiny 2, Lost Ark,* and *World of Warcraft,* and most recently, the popular Fortnite game. Other possibilities include competitive online games such as *Valorant, Counter-Strike Global Offensive, League of Legends,* and online communities (or virtual worlds) such as *Decentraland, The Sandbox,* and *Hyperfy.* Although these virtual worlds are unfamiliar to and even intimidating for many traditional marketers, they are becoming an important, viable, and growing consideration. Over 215 million U.S. citizens play video games which accounts for about 65 percent of the population. China has the most video gamers in the world with over 742 million players.[55]

One particular area of growth is social gaming. The number of people playing games on Facebook like *Criminal Case, Candy Crush Saga,* and *Dragon City* peaked in 2022. However, Facebook Gaming still holds the third highest market share in game-streaming market following Twitch and YouTube Gaming.[56] Social gaming has gained popularity in the past few years, but consumers are changing the way they play. Many users are playing games on their smartphones, which has pulled them away from the extremely popular games offered on Facebook, and in turn away from Facebook's advertisers.[57]

The average U.S. player of online games is a 33-year-old male (users who play on mobile devices tend to be younger), but women make up nearly 48 percent of gamers. The average time spent playing video games per week is 7.71 hours in the United States, 12.39 hours in China, and 8.45 hours is the global average.[58]

Many mobile games use advertising to generate revenue for the game developers and publishers. As long as the ads are not overly intrusive, most users opt to play free versions of games with ads over paid versions that do not have ads. Another popular strategy is to give an ad-free game away for free and then charge small sums of money for in-game items and power-ups. The worldwide in-game advertising market is anticipated to generate nearly $13 billion in revenue by 2028 with North America accounting for approximately $4.7 billion of that total.[59]

Massively multiplayer online games (MMOs) are an environment that draws thousands of people playing simultaneously. Regardless of the type of experience, brands must be creative in how they integrate ads into games. Social and realistic titles are the most appropriate for marketing and advertising (as opposed to fantasy games). Promotions typically include special events, competitions, and sweepstakes, and for some games, having ads actually increases the authenticity. For example, EA

review sites websites that allow consumers to post, read, rate, and comment on opinions regarding all kinds of products and services

Chapter 18: Social Media and Marketing **319**

Games, Jeremy Scott, and luxury fashion brand Moschino partnered together to create in-game fashion packs in *The Sims* that can be unlocked. Furthermore, fashion-themed career paths are an option and avatar models appear in the game wearing signature Moschino outfits.[60]

18-6 Social Media and Mobile Technology

18-6 Describe the impact of mobile technology on social media

While much of the excitement in social media has been based on website and new technology uses, much of the growth lies in new platforms. These platforms include a multitude of smartphones and wearables as well as iPads and other tablets. The major implication of this development is that consumers can now access popular websites like Facebook, YouTube, Instagram, Reddit, and Netflix from all their various platforms.

18-6a Mobile Marketing

Worldwide, there are more than 7.33 billion mobile phones in use, about 86 percent of which are smartphones.[61] It is no surprise, then, that the mobile platform is such an effective marketing tool—especially when targeting a younger audience. Smartphones up the ante by allowing individuals to do nearly everything they can do with a computer—from anywhere. With a smartphone in hand, reading a blog, writing an email, scheduling a meeting, posting to Instagram, playing a multiplayer game, watching a video, taking a picture, using GPS, conducting

Mobile technology is on the rise which includes the increasing usage of artificial intelligence (AI). Beyond Siri, Cortana, Alexa, Google Assistant, or other voice recognition software, more apps are incorporating AI to improve the customer experience.

banking transactions, and surfing the internet might all occur during one 10-minute bus ride. Smartphone technology, often considered the crowning achievement in digital convergence and social media integration, has opened the door to modern mobile advertising as a viable marketing strategy.

Mobile advertising is driving digital advertising spending annually in the United States to more than $360 billion. This number is more than double the amount in 2018.[62] There are several reasons for the popularity of mobile marketing. First, an effort to standardize mobile platforms has resulted in a low barrier to entry. Second, especially given mobile marketing's younger audiences, there are more consumers than ever acclimating to once-worrisome privacy and pricing policies. Third, because most people carry their smartphones with them at all times, mobile marketing is uniquely effective at garnering customer attention in real time. Fourth, mobile marketing is measurable: metrics and usage statistics make it an effective tool for gaining insight into consumer behavior. Fifth, in-store notification technology using Bluetooth can send promotional messages and in-store product locations based on real-time interactions with customers. Finally, mobile marketing's response rate is higher than that of traditional media types like print and broadcast advertisements. Video and banner advertising are the two most popular types of mobile advertising. Native advertising is also becoming more popular as a result of its ability to customize. Some common mobile marketing tools include:

- **RCS (rich communication service):** promoted as a replacement protocol for SMS, lets subscribers of different carriers and countries communicate with one another through rich messaging of group chats, video, audio, and high-resolution images with real-time viewing.[63]

- **SMS (short message service):** 160-character text messages sent to and from cell phones. SMS is typically integrated with other tools.

- **MMS (multimedia messaging service):** Similar to SMS but allows the attachment of images, videos, ringtones, and other multimedia to text messages.

- **Mobile website:** Website designed specifically for viewing and navigation on mobile devices.

- **Mobile ads:** Visual advertisements integrated into text messages, applications, and mobile websites. Mobile ads are often sold on a cost-per-click basis.

- **Bluetooth marketing:** A signal is sent to Bluetooth-enabled devices, allowing marketers to send targeted messages to users based on their geographic locations.

- **Smartphone applications (apps):** Software designed specifically for mobile and tablet devices.

Smartwatches, which look like traditional watches, but connect to users' mobile phones or directly to the internet, are an easy way for advertisers to gain the attention of consumers, but advertising on smartwatches is starting slowly. As smartwatch advertising develops, it will likely focus more on branded notifications and alerts than on the traditional forms of advertising seen on mobile phones and PCs. The watch is the starting point, but connected wearables open up a whole new avenue for advertisers.[64]

18-6b Apps and Widgets

Given the widespread adoption of Apple's iPhone, Android-based phones, and other mobile devices, it is no surprise that millions of apps have been developed for the mobile market. Dozens of new and unique apps that harness mobile technology are added to mobile marketplaces every day. While many apps perform platform-specific tasks, others convert existing content into a mobile-ready format. Whether offering new or existing content, when an app is well branded and integrated into a company's overall marketing strategy, it can create buzz and generate customer engagement.

Web widgets, also known as gadgets and badges, are software applications that run entirely within existing online platforms. Essentially, a web widget allows a developer to embed a simple application such as a weather forecast, social media feed, or stock market ticker into a website, even if the developer did not write (or does not understand) the application's source code. From a marketing perspective, widgets enable customers to display company information (such as current promotions, coupons, or news) on their own websites or smartphone home screens. Widgets are often cheaper to develop than apps, can extend an organization's reach beyond existing platforms, will broaden the listening system, and can make an organization easier to find.[65]

18-7 The Social Media Plan

18-7 Explain the aspects of developing a social media plan

To effectively use the tools in the social media toolbox, it is important to have a clearly outlined social media plan. The social media plan is linked to larger plans such as a promotional plan or marketing plan and should fit appropriately into the objectives and steps in those plans (for more information, review Chapters 2 and 16). It is important to research throughout the development of the social media plan to keep abreast of the rapidly changing social media world. The following are six stages involved in creating an effective social media plan:

1. **Listen to customers:** This is covered in more detail in Section 18-2a.

2. **Set social media objectives:** Set objectives that can be specifically accomplished through social media, with special attention to how to measure the results. Numerous metrics are available, some of which are mentioned throughout the chapter.

3. **Define strategies:** This includes examining trends and best practices in the industry and mapping out the approach by designing the messaging that will appear across the campaign along with the timeline for delivery.

4. **Identify the target audience:** This should line up with the target market defined in the marketing plan, but in the social media plan, pay special attention to how that audience participates and behaves online.

5. **Select the tools and platforms:** Based on the result of Step 4, choose the social media tools and platforms that will be most relevant. These choices are based on the knowledge of where the target audience participates on social media.

6. **Implement and monitor the strategy:** Social media campaigns can be fluid, so it is important to keep a close eye on what is successful and what is not by utilizing metrics. Then, based on the observations and metrics, make changes as needed. It also becomes important, therefore, to go back to the listening stage to interpret how consumers are perceiving the social media campaign.

Listening to customers and market trends as well as continually revising the social media plan to meet the needs of the changing social media market are keys to successful social media marketing. Numerous industry leaders are sharing their best practices, and sources such as *Fast Company* and *The Wall Street Journal* report regularly on how large and small companies are successfully using social media to enhance engagement, gain market share and increase sales. A good example of using social media strategies is Red Bull, a company that creates engaging experiences for its target audience using digital channels like social media. Red Bull focuses on two aspects, extreme sports or adventures and high-quality content that is relatable to the audience.[66]

18-7a The Changing World of Social Media

Some of the trends noted in this chapter may already seem ancient to you. The rate of change in social media is astounding—usage statistics change daily for sites like Facebook, Instagram, TikTok, Snapchat, and X. Some things in the rumor mill as we write this may

Table 18.2 Social Media Trends

Trend	Change
Edutainment	The rise of entertaining informative content.
Video Production Budgets	Increased investments in quality video production equipment and staff to aid in brand storytelling.
Creator Economy	Influencer content is watched 13 times more than branded content and will continue to be leveraged.
Employee Advocacy	Employees speak on behalf of the organization, like an inside influencer.
Authentic Sustainability	To avoid issues related to greenwashing, corporate social responsibility announcements are accurate and transparent.
Customer Surprise and Delight	Going above and beyond when interacting with customers to create a personalized experience.
Social and Legal	Legal teams are involved to ensure brand content doesn't cross the line.
Metaverse Technology	Augmented reality (AR) and virtual reality (VR) are still on the rise.
Artificial Intelligence	Companies using artificial intelligence like ChatGPT to create tailored and engaging human-like text to increase human productivity

have exploded in popularity, while others may have fizzled out without even appearing on your radar. In Table 18.2, we have listed some of the items that seem to be on the brink of exploding onto the social media scene.[67] Periodically taking an inventory of the state of social media highlights not only the speed with which social media changes but also the importance of keeping tabs on rumors. Doing so may give you a competitive advantage by being able to understand and invest in the next big social media site.

Part 6

Chapter 19

Pricing Concepts

Learning Outcomes

After studying this chapter, you will be able to . . .

19-1 Discuss the importance of pricing decisions to the individual firm

19-2 Describe the different types of pricing objectives

19-3 Explain the role of demand in price determination

19-4 Describe the concepts of dynamic pricing

19-5 Describe cost-oriented pricing strategies

19-6 Discuss the different factors that can affect price

19-7 Describe the procedure for setting the right price

19-8 Explain how different pricing tactics can be used to fine-tune a base price

19-9 Identify the legal constraints on pricing decisions

19-1 The Importance of Price

19-1 Discuss the importance of pricing decisions to the individual firm

Price means one thing to the consumer and something else to the seller. To the consumer, it is the cost of something. To the seller, price is revenue—the primary source of profits. Marketing managers are frequently challenged by the task of price setting because they know that setting the right price can have a significant impact on the firm's bottom line. Organizations that successfully manage prices do so by creating a pricing infrastructure within the company. This means defining pricing goals, searching for ways to create greater customer value, and creating tools and systems to continually improve pricing decisions. The importance of creating the right pricing strategy cannot be overstated.

19-1a What Is Price?

Price is that which is given up in an exchange to acquire a good or service. Price also plays two roles in the evaluation of product alternatives: as a measure of sacrifice and as an information cue. To some degree, these two effects are opposing.

The Sacrifice Effect of Price

Price is, again, "that which is given up," which means what is sacrificed to get a good or service. In the United States, the sacrifice is usually money, but it can be other things as well. It may also be time lost while waiting to acquire the good or service. For a college student, paying tuition might mean skipping a vacation, buying a less luxurious car, or waiting longer to buy a first house.

The Information Effect of Price

Consumers do not always choose the lowest-priced product in a category, such as shoes, cars, or wine, even when the products are otherwise similar. One explanation of this behavior, based on research, is that we infer quality information from price—that is, higher quality equals higher price. The information effect of price may also extend to favorable price perceptions by others because higher prices can convey the prominence and status of the purchaser to other people. Thus, both a Swatch and a Rolex can tell time accurately, but they convey different meanings. The price–quality relationship will be discussed later in the chapter.

---

price that which is given up in an exchange to acquire a good or service

revenue the price charged to customers multiplied by the number of units sold

profit revenue minus expenses

Trying to set the right price is one of the most stressful and pressure-filled tasks of the marketing manager.

Value Is Based on Perceived Satisfaction

Consumers are interested in obtaining a "reasonable price." "Reasonable price" really means "perceived reasonable value" at the time of the transaction. Imagine a consumer that purchased a new juice machine for around $60 so they could quickly prepare fresh-squeezed orange juice in the morning. The machine worked just fine for a few months, but one morning, it made a strange noise and that was the last of the fresh orange juice. This consumer did not receive the expected perceived reasonable value from the juice machine.

19-1b The Importance of Price to Marketing Managers

As noted in the chapter introduction, prices are the key to revenues, which in turn are the key to profits for an organization. **Revenue** is the price charged to customers multiplied by the number of units sold. Revenue is what pays for every activity of the company: production, finance, sales, distribution, and so on. What is left over (if anything) is **profit**. Managers usually strive to charge a price that will earn a fair profit.

$$\text{Price} \times \text{Units} = \text{Revenue}$$

To earn a profit, managers must choose a price that is not too high or too low—a price that equals the perceived value to target consumers. If, in consumers' minds, a price is set too high, the perceived value will be less than the cost, and sale opportunities will be lost.

19-2 Pricing Objectives

19-2 Describe the different types of pricing objectives

To survive in today's highly competitive marketplace, companies need pricing objectives that are specific, attainable, and measurable. Realistic pricing goals, then, require continual monitoring to determine the effectiveness of the company's strategy. For convenience, pricing objectives can be divided into three categories: profit oriented, sales oriented, and status quo.

19-2a Profit-Oriented Pricing Objectives

Profit-oriented pricing objectives include profit maximization, satisfactory profits, and target return on investment.

Profit Maximization

Profit maximization means setting prices so that total revenue is as large as possible relative to total costs. Profit maximization does not always signify unreasonably high prices, however. Both price and profits depend on the type of competitive environment a firm faces, such as whether it is in a monopoly position (being the only seller) or in a much more competitive situation. Also, remember that a firm cannot charge a price higher than the product's perceived value. Sometimes managers say that their company is trying to maximize profits—in other words, trying to make as much money as possible. Although this goal may sound impressive to stockholders, it is not good enough for planning.

In attempting to maximize profits, managers can try to expand revenue by increasing customer satisfaction, or they can attempt to reduce costs by operating more efficiently. A third possibility is to attempt to do both. Some companies may focus too much on cost reduction at the expense of the customer. Lowe's lost market share when it cut costs by reducing the number of associates on the floor. Customer service declined—and so did revenue. When firms rely too heavily on customer service, however, costs tend to rise to unacceptable levels. Many airline companies in the United States used to serve full meals on two-hour flights and offered pillows and blankets to tired customers. This proved to be unsustainable. A company can maintain or slightly cut costs while increasing customer loyalty through customer service initiatives, loyalty programs, customer relationship management programs, and allocating resources to programs that are designed to improve efficiency and reduce costs.

Satisfactory Profits

Satisfactory profits are a reasonable level of profits. Rather than maximizing profits, many organizations strive for profits that are satisfactory to the stockholders and management—in other words, a level of profits consistent with the level of risk an organization faces. In a risky industry, a satisfactory profit may be 35 percent. In a low-risk industry, it might be 7 percent.

Target Return on Investment

The most common profit objective is a target **return on investment (ROI)**, sometimes called the firm's return on total assets. ROI measures management's overall effectiveness in generating profits with the available assets. The higher the firm's ROI, the better off the firm is. Many companies use a target ROI as their main pricing goal. In summary, ROI is a percentage that puts a firm's profits into perspective by showing profits relative to investment.

Return on investment is calculated as follows:

$$\text{Return on investment} = \frac{\text{Net profit after taxes}}{\text{Total assets}}$$

Assume that a company has assets of $4.5 million, net profits of $550,000, and a target ROI of 10 percent. This was the actual ROI:

$$\text{ROI} = \frac{\$550,000}{\$4,500,000} = .122\ (12.2\%)$$

As you can tell, the ROI for this company exceeded its target, indicating a successful year for the company.

Comparing the 12.2 percent ROI with the industry average provides a more meaningful picture, however. Any ROI needs to be evaluated in terms of the competitive environment, risks in the industry, and economic conditions. Generally speaking, firms seek ROIs in the 10 to 30 percent range. In some industries, such as the grocery industry, however, a return of under 5 percent is common and acceptable.

A company with a target ROI can predetermine its desired level of profitability. The marketing manager can use an industry standard, such as 10 percent ROI, to determine whether a particular price and marketing mix are feasible.

In addition, however, the manager must weigh the risk of a given strategy even if the return is in the acceptable range.

19-2b Sales-Oriented Pricing Objectives

Sales-oriented pricing objectives are based on market share as reported in dollar or unit sales. Firms strive either for market share or to maximize sales.

Market Share

Market share is a company's product sales as a percentage of total sales for that industry. Sales can be reported in dollars or units of product. It is very important to know whether market share is expressed in revenue or units because the results may be different. Consider four companies competing in an industry with 2,000 total unit sales and total industry revenue of $4,000 (refer to Table 19.1). Company A has the largest unit market share at 50 percent, but it has only 25 percent of the revenue market share. In contrast, Company D has only a 15 percent unit share but the largest revenue share: 30 percent. Usually, market share is expressed in terms of revenue and not units.

Many companies believe that maintaining or increasing market share is an indicator of the effectiveness of their marketing mix. Larger market shares have indeed often meant higher profits, thanks to greater economies of scale, market power, and the ability to compensate top-quality management. Conventional wisdom also says that market share and ROI are strongly related. For the most part, they are; however, many companies with low market share survive and even prosper. To succeed with a low market share, companies

---

return on investment (ROI) net profit after taxes divided by total assets

market share a company's product sales as a percentage of total sales for that industry

Table 19.1	Two Ways to Measure Market Share (Units and Revenue)					
Company	Units Sold	Unit Price	Total Revenue	Unit Market Share	Revenue Market Share
A	1,000	$1.00	$1,000	50	25
B	200	4.00	800	10	20
C	500	2.00	1,000	25	25
D	300	4.00	1,200	15	30
Total	2,000		$4,000		

often need to compete in industries with slow growth and few product changes—for instance, industrial supplies. Otherwise, they must vie in an industry that makes frequently bought items, such as consumer convenience goods.

The conventional wisdom about market share and profitability is not always reliable, however. Because of extreme competition in some industries, many market share leaders either do not reach their target ROI or actually lose money. Procter & Gamble (P&G) switched from market share to ROI objectives after realizing that profits do not automatically follow from a large market share.

Sales Maximization

Rather than strive for market share, sometimes companies try to maximize sales. A firm with the objective of maximizing sales ignores profits, competition, and the marketing environment as long as sales are rising.

If a company is strapped for funds or faces an uncertain future, it may try to generate a maximum amount of cash in the short run. Management's task when using this objective is to calculate which price–quantity relationship generates the greatest cash revenue. Sales maximization can also be effectively used temporarily to sell off excess inventory. It is not uncommon to find holiday cards, gift wrapping materials, and other seasonal items discounted at 50 to 70 percent off retail prices after the holiday season has ended.

Maximization of cash should never be a long-run objective because cash maximization may mean little or no profitability.

19-2c Status Quo Pricing Objectives

Status quo pricing seeks to maintain existing prices or to meet the competition's prices. This third category of pricing objectives has the major advantage of requiring little planning. It is essentially a passive policy.

Often, firms competing in an industry with an established price leader simply meet the competition's prices. These industries typically have fewer price wars than those

---

status quo pricing a pricing objective that maintains existing prices or meets the competition's prices

LP Design/Shutterstock.com

with direct price competition. In other cases, managers regularly shop at competitors' stores to ensure that their prices are comparable.

Status quo pricing often leads to suboptimal pricing. This occurs because the strategy ignores customers' perceived value of both the firm's goods or services and those offered by its competitors. Status quo pricing also ignores demand and costs. Although the policy is simple to implement, it can lead to a pricing disaster.

19-3 The Demand Determinant of Price

19-3 Explain the role of demand in price determination

After marketing managers establish pricing goals, they must set specific prices to reach those goals. The price they set for each product depends mostly on two factors: the demand for the good or service and the cost to the seller for that good or service. When pricing goals are mainly sales oriented, demand considerations usually dominate. Other factors, such as distribution and promotion strategies, perceived quality, needs of large customers, the internet, and the stage of the product life cycle, can also influence the price.

19-3a The Nature of Demand

Demand is the quantity of a product that will be sold in the market at various prices for a specified period. The quantity of a product that people will buy depends on its price. The higher the price, the fewer goods or services consumers will demand. Conversely, the lower the price, the more goods or services they will demand.

Supply is the quantity of a product that will be offered to the market by a supplier or suppliers at various prices for a specified period. At higher prices, manufacturers earn more capital and can produce more products.

19-3b Elasticity of Demand

To appreciate the concept of demand, you should understand elasticity. **Elasticity of demand** refers to consumers' responsiveness or sensitivity to changes in price. **Elastic demand** is a situation in which consumer demand is sensitive to price changes. Conversely, **inelastic demand** means that an increase or a price decrease will not significantly affect demand for the product.

Factors That Affect Elasticity

Several factors affect the elasticity of demand, including the following:

- **Availability of substitutes:** When many substitute products are available, the consumer can easily switch from one product to another, making demand more elastic. The same is true in reverse: A consumer who drives a gas-powered car will have to pay whatever is charged for a gallon of gas because there is no substitute.

- **Price relative to purchasing power:** If a price is so low that it is an inconsequential part of an individual's budget, demand will be inelastic. If the price of pepper doubles, for example, people won't stop putting pepper on their eggs or buying more when they run out.

- **Product durability:** Consumers often have the option of repairing durable products (like cars and washing machines) rather than replacing them, thus prolonging their useful life. In other words, people are sensitive to the price increase, and demand is more elastic.

- **A product's other uses:** The greater the number of different uses for a product, the more elastic demand tends to be. If a product has only one use, as may be true of a new medicine, the quantity purchased probably will not vary as price varies. A person will consume only the prescribed quantity, regardless of price. On the other hand, a product like steel has many possible

People who identify strongly with local traditions and local communities tend to be less price sensitive when shopping in local or regional stores.

applications. As its price falls, steel becomes more economically feasible in a wider variety of applications, thereby making demand relatively elastic.

- **The consumer mindset—local or global:** Researchers have found that consumers with a local identity are less sensitive to price increases (inelastic demand) than persons with a global identity. *Local identity* refers to a consumer's mindset that pertains to their respect for local traditions and cultures while also identifying with people in their local communities. These individuals patronize local stores and buy local (or regional) products. They tend to be less price sensitive to price increases, which leads to more inelastic demand.[1] Research has found that many consumers are willing to pay 20 percent more to purchase local products.[2] *Global mindset, on the other hand,* refers to an interest in global culture and identification with people around the world. These individuals are often less influenced by "buy local" promotions, resulting in demand being more elastic.

- **Customer satisfaction:** Researchers have found a strong relationship between overall customer satisfaction and

---

demand the quantity of a product that will be sold in the market at various prices for a specified period

supply the quantity of a product that will be offered to the market by a supplier at various prices for a specified period

elasticity of demand consumers' responsiveness or sensitivity to changes in price

elastic demand a situation in which consumer demand is sensitive to changes in price

inelastic demand a situation in which an increase or a decrease in price will not significantly affect demand for the product

willingness to tolerate a price increase (inelastic demand).[3] Specifically, they showed that a 1 percent increase in consumer satisfaction should be associated with a 0.06 percent decrease in price sensitivity.[4] Porsche owners tend to be very satisfied with their vehicles and willingly pay for new vehicles despite price increases. Singapore Airlines can slightly increase prices because it is the perennial winner of the "world's best airline" award.[5]

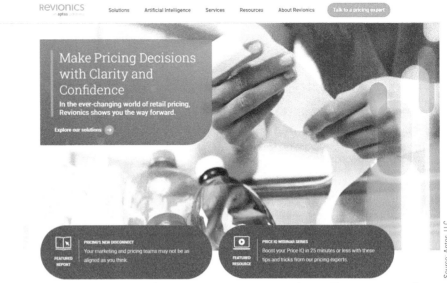

Revionics is a technology company focused on AI-driven pricing software. The company works with retailers in many different industries including home improvement, beauty, and grocery.

Source: Aptos, LLC

19-4 Dynamic Pricing Concepts

19-4 Describe the concepts of dynamic pricing

When competitive pressures are high, a company must know when it should raise or lower prices to maximize its revenues. More and more companies are turning to **dynamic pricing** to help adjust prices. Although dynamic pricing originated with airlines, which are limited by fixed capacity, the new thinking is that dynamic pricing can be used in any industry in which demand or supply fluctuates. Amazon, for example, analyzes and updates prices every 10 minutes.[6] Uber uses dynamic pricing by raising fares when more people need rides and vice versa. This is referred to as **surge pricing**. Dynamic pricing is the ability to adjust prices very quickly, often in real time using software programs. This technology has come to the aid of brick-and-mortar retailers, enabling them to compete more effectively with online alternatives.

19-4a The Growing Use of Artificial Intelligence (AI) in Dynamic Pricing

Many companies are using newer software that move beyond traditional dynamic pricing models, which often

---

dynamic pricing the ability to change prices very quickly, often in real time using software programs

surge pricing occurs in a fluid market, where demand changes rapidly, often hourly. When demand increases, so do prices, and vice versa.

---

used simple rules. Examples of old rules might include always increasing the price of economy tickets "X" percent when "Y" number of seats have been sold on the 10:30 A.M. flight from Chicago to San Francisco; Charge "X" percent more for full-size rental cars between 7:00 am and 10:30 am because this is when business customers typically pick up their cars. New systems incorporate huge amounts of historical and real-time data, both traditional structured data sources of information, for example, purchased items, price, financing, and newer nonstructured or semistructured data sources such as videos, emails, photos, and blogs, social media posts, and audio files.

New AI pricing software constantly updates the algorithms. The updates are based on what the AI software has learned. Updates are created to more efficiently reach a preestablished objective such as an overall average gross profit of 28 percent. Revionics, a technology company that created an AI-driven pricing software program, works with many different retailers including.[7] The Home Depot and Sally Beauty, to optimize pricing strategies. As another example, Walmart uses AI to more efficiently price certain grocery items. Supply chain issues caused by the COVID-19 pandemic led to shortages across many different product categories, such as meat. Walmart was able to utilize AI to quickly increase prices on products that were suddenly in short supply.[8] Some AI pricing software will even raise prices on an item when it learns, from a competitor's website, that the competitor has run out of stock on a similar item.

The more AI learns about you, including your interests, hobbies, lifestyle, and past behavior, the more effective it can be about targeting you with "the right price." For example, structured online data regarding your purchasing behavior will include:

- What types of goods and services you perused online.
- How long you were on each web page.
- The items you put in your shopping cart.
- The goods and services you actually bought.

Unstructured data might include:

- The brands you wear or use in your photos.
- What your lifestyle reveals about your pricing sensitivity.
- What people who have the same psychographic and behavioral profile as yours pay for items.
- What brands you discuss on social media and whether your comments are positive or negative.

These are but a few of the data sources that AI pricing software can use to learn about you.

19-5 The Cost Determinant of Price

19-5 Describe cost-oriented pricing strategies

Sometimes companies minimize or ignore the importance of demand and decide to price their products largely or solely based on the company's costs. Prices determined strictly based on costs may be too high for the target market, thereby reducing or eliminating sales. On the other hand, cost-based prices may be too low, causing the firm to earn a lower return than it should. An entrepreneur might say, "I know what it costs to make this item, so I'll just add 40 percent to the cost, sell it for $70, and feel good about it." But what if the product creates $1,000 worth of value for the buyer? In that case, the seller created a lot of value but failed to capture it. Nevertheless, costs should generally be part of any price determination, if only as a floor below which a good or service must not be priced in the long run.

The idea of cost may seem simple, but it is actually a multifaceted concept, especially for producers of goods and services. A **variable cost** is a cost that varies with changes in the level of output; an example of a variable cost is the cost of materials. In contrast, a **fixed cost** does not change as output is increased or decreased. Examples include rent and executives' salaries. Costs can be used to set prices in a variety of ways. While markup pricing is relatively simple, break-even pricing uses more complicated concepts of cost.

19-5a Markup Pricing

Markup pricing, a method used by some wholesalers and retailers to establish a selling price, does not directly analyze the costs of production. Instead, **markup pricing** uses the cost of buying the product from the producer, plus amounts for profit and expenses not otherwise accounted for. The total determines the selling price.

A retailer, for example, may add a certain percentage to the cost of the merchandise received to arrive at the retail price. An item that costs the retailer $1.80 and is sold for $2.20 carries a markup of 40 cents, which is a markup of 22 percent of the cost ($0.40 ÷ $1.80). Retailers tend to discuss markup in terms of its percentage of the retail price—in this example, 18 percent ($0.40 ÷ $2.20). The difference between the retailer's cost and the selling price (40 cents) is the gross margin.

The formula for calculating the retail price given a certain desired markup is as follows:

$$\text{Retail price} = \frac{\text{Cost}}{1 - \text{Desired returns on sales}}$$

$$\frac{\$1.80}{1.00 - 0.18} = \$2.20$$

If the retailer wants a 30 percent return, then:

$$\text{Retail price} = \frac{\$1.80}{1.00 - 0.30}$$

$$= \$2.57$$

The reason that retailers and others speak of markups on selling price is that many important figures in financial reports, such as gross sales and revenues, are sales figures, not cost figures.

To use markup based on cost or selling price effectively, the marketing manager must calculate an adequate gross margin—the amount added to cost to determine the price. The margin must ultimately provide adequate funds to cover selling expenses and profit. Once an appropriate margin has been determined, the markup technique has the major advantage of being easy to employ.

Markups are often based on experience. For example, many small retailers mark up merchandise 100 percent over cost. (In other words, they double the cost.) This tactic is called **keystoning**. Some other factors that influence markups are the merchandise's appeal to customers, past response to the markup (an implicit demand consideration), the item's promotional value, the seasonality of the good, the fashion appeal of the good, the product's traditional selling price, and competition. Most retailers

---

variable cost a cost that varies with changes in the level of output

fixed cost a cost that does not change as output is increased or decreased

markup pricing the cost of buying the product from the producer, plus amounts for profit and expenses not otherwise accounted for

keystoning the practice of marking up prices by 100 percent, or doubling the cost

avoid any set markup because of such considerations as promotional value and seasonality.

19-5b Break-Even Pricing

Now, let's take a closer look at the relationship between sales and cost. **Break-even analysis** determines what sales volume must be reached before the company breaks even (its total costs equal total revenue) and no profits are earned.

The typical break-even model assumes a given fixed cost and a constant average variable cost (total cost

---

break-even analysis a method of determining what sales volume must be reached before total revenue equals total costs

---

divided by the quantity of output). Suppose that Creative Cookies, a hypothetical firm, has fixed costs of $2,000 and that the cost of labor and materials for each unit produced is 50 cents. Assume that it can sell up to 6,000 units of its product at $1 without having to lower its price.

Figure 19.1a illustrates the break-even point for Creative Cookies. As Figure 19.1b indicates, Creative Cookies' total variable costs increase by 50 cents every time a new unit is produced, and total fixed costs remain constant at $2,000 regardless of the level of output. Therefore, for 4,000 units of output, Creative Cookies has $2,000 in fixed costs and $2,000 in total variable costs (4,000 units × $0.50), or $4,000 in total costs.

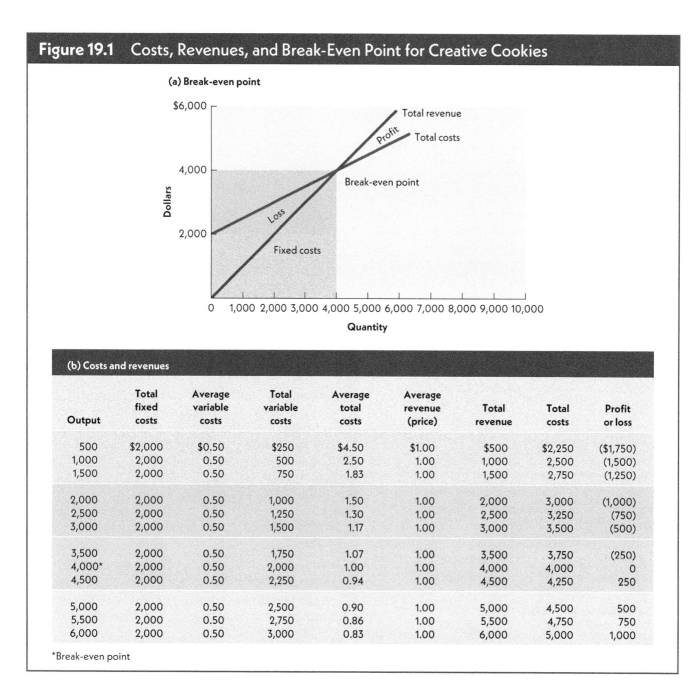

Figure 19.1 Costs, Revenues, and Break-Even Point for Creative Cookies

(a) Break-even point

(b) Costs and revenues

Output	Total fixed costs	Average variable costs	Total variable costs	Average total costs	Average revenue (price)	Total revenue	Total costs	Profit or loss
500	$2,000	$0.50	$250	$4.50	$1.00	$500	$2,250	($1,750)
1,000	2,000	0.50	500	2.50	1.00	1,000	2,500	(1,500)
1,500	2,000	0.50	750	1.83	1.00	1,500	2,750	(1,250)
2,000	2,000	0.50	1,000	1.50	1.00	2,000	3,000	(1,000)
2,500	2,000	0.50	1,250	1.30	1.00	2,500	3,250	(750)
3,000	2,000	0.50	1,500	1.17	1.00	3,000	3,500	(500)
3,500	2,000	0.50	1,750	1.07	1.00	3,500	3,750	(250)
4,000*	2,000	0.50	2,000	1.00	1.00	4,000	4,000	0
4,500	2,000	0.50	2,250	0.94	1.00	4,500	4,250	250
5,000	2,000	0.50	2,500	0.90	1.00	5,000	4,500	500
5,500	2,000	0.50	2,750	0.86	1.00	5,500	4,750	750
6,000	2,000	0.50	3,000	0.83	1.00	6,000	5,000	1,000

*Break-even point

The advantage of break-even analysis is that it provides a quick estimate of how much the firm must sell to break even and how much profit can be earned if a higher sales volume is obtained. If a firm is operating close to the break-even point, it may want to understand what can be done to reduce costs or increase sales.

Break-even analysis is not without several important limitations. Sometimes it is hard to know whether a cost is fixed or variable. If labor wins a tough guaranteed-employment contract, are the resulting expenses a fixed cost? More important than cost determination is the fact that simple break-even analysis ignores demand. How does Creative Cookies know it can sell 4,000 units at $1? Could it sell the same 4,000 units at $2 or even $5?

19-6 Other Determinants of Price

19-6 Discuss the different factors that can affect price

Other factors besides demand and costs can influence the price. For example, the stages in the product life cycle, the competition, the product distribution strategy, the internet and extranets, the promotion strategy, price transparency, customer loyalty, the appearance of being informed, the demands of large customers, and the perceived quality can all affect pricing.

19-6a Stages in the Product Life Cycle

As a product moves through its life cycle (refer to Chapter 11), the demand for the product and the competitive conditions tend to change:

- **Introductory stage:** When not using pricing software, management often sets prices high during the introductory stage. One reason is that it hopes to recover its development costs quickly. In addition, demand originates in the core of the market (the customers whose needs ideally match the product's attributes) and thus is often relatively inelastic. On the other hand, if the target market is highly price sensitive, management often finds it better to price the product at market level or lower. When companies introduce highly innovative products such as consumer electronics, medical devices, and pharmaceuticals, they must properly estimate the elasticity of demand for those products. This is particularly true today when some life cycles are measured in months, not years.

- **Growth stage:** As the product enters the growth stage, prices generally begin to stabilize for several reasons. First, competitors have entered the market, increasing the available supply. Second, the product has begun to appeal to a broader market. Finally, economies of scale are lowering costs, and the savings can be passed on to the consumer in the form of lower prices.

- **Maturity stage:** Maturity usually brings further price decreases as competition increases and inefficient, high-cost firms are eliminated. Logistics become a significant cost factor, however, because of the need to offer wide product lines for highly segmented markets, extensive service requirements, and the sheer number of dealers necessary to absorb high-volume production. The manufacturers that remain in the market toward the end of the maturity stage typically offer similar prices. At this stage, price increases are usually cost initiated, not demand initiated. Nor do price reductions in the late phase of maturity stimulate much demand. Because demand is limited and producers have similar cost structures, the remaining competitors will probably match price reductions.

- **Decline stage:** The final stage of the life cycle may result in further price decreases as the few remaining competitors try to salvage the last vestiges of demand. When only one firm is left in the market, prices begin to stabilize. In fact, prices may eventually rise dramatically if the product survives and moves into the specialty goods category, as horse-drawn carriages and vinyl records have.

19-6b Competition, Price Matching, and Customer Loyalty

Competition varies during the product life cycle, of course, and so at times, it may strongly affect pricing decisions. Although a firm may not have any competition at first, the high prices it charges may eventually induce another firm to enter the market.

Fast-food giants McDonald's, Burger King, and Wendy's have been going head-to-head for years in their efforts to attract cost-conscious customers. McDonald's has seen much success with its $1, $2, and $3 Dollar Menu. With this menu, consumers can get a Sausage McMuffin for around $2 or a 4-piece McNuggets for around $3. One way to counter a competitor's prices is price matching. For

Gorodenkoff/Shutterstock.com

example, Best Buy offers a price match guarantee in which the retailer will match prices offered by its biggest competitors including Amazon, Dell, and Hewlett-Packard (HP).[9] Best Buy has been able to reverse its sales decline, caused primarily by online retailers, by offering price matching.

On the face of it, it seems that fierce competition is driving down prices. And this is often the case. However, economists warn that price matching may actually result in higher prices. A car dealership worried about losing clients to a lower-priced rival may offer a price-matching guarantee. The hope is that the guarantee will persuade customers not to shop around; they will always pay the lowest price available by sticking with the usually higher-priced dealership. As a result, cutting prices no longer wins the competitor new business. Instead, it means lower profits on existing sales. Thus, the competitor will likely conclude that prices and profit margins are better left high.

Price matching and other pricing strategies can be used as tools for building customer loyalty. One approach is to offer discounts to regular patrons. This can lead to a loyalty-discount cycle, whereby loyal customers receive deeper discounts that in turn further increase their customer loyalty—resulting in downward pressure on the issuing firm's long-term pricing strategy.[10] Discounts can be an excellent tool to build customer loyalty, but care must be taken not to compromise profit goals. There are many other creative and industry-specific ways to reward loyalty. For example, airlines use unfilled seats to award free travel and upgrades to loyal customers. Some companies give branded gifts to drive customer loyalty. Hotel chains build databases on their most loyal customers so they can automatically service the room and amenity preferences of frequent customers.

19-6c Distribution Strategy

An effective distribution network can sometimes overcome other minor flaws in the marketing mix. For example, although consumers may perceive a price as being slightly higher than normal, they may buy the product anyway if it is being sold at a convenient retail outlet.

Adequate distribution for a new product can often be attained by offering a larger-than-usual profit margin to distributors. A variation on this strategy is to give dealers a large trade allowance to help offset the costs of promotion and further stimulate demand at the retail level.

19-6d The Impact of the Internet and Extranets

The internet, **extranets** (private electronic networks), and wireless setups are linking people, machines, and

---

extranet a private electronic network that links a company with its suppliers and customers

companies around the globe—and connecting sellers and buyers as never before. These links are enabling buyers to quickly and easily compare products and prices, putting them in a better bargaining position. At the same time, the technology allows sellers to collect detailed data about customers' buying habits, preferences, and even spending limits so that sellers can tailor their products and prices.

Using Shopping Bots

A shopping bot is a program that searches the web for the best price for a particular item that you wish to purchase. "Bot" is short for robot. Shopping bots theoretically give pricing power to the consumer. The more information that the shopper has, the more efficient their purchase decision will be.

There are two general types of shopping bots. The first is the broad-based type that searches (trawls) a wide range of product categories such as Google Shopping and PriceGrabber. These sites operate using a Yellow Pages type of model in that they list every retailer they can find. The second is the niche-oriented type that searches for prices for only one type of product such as consumer electronics (CNET), event tickets (SeatGeek), or travel-related services (Kayak).

Shopping bots have been around for quite some time, and security protocols have been developed by some internet retailers to limit bot trawls. Still, shopping bots remain a powerful and impactful marketing tool to this day.

Internet Auctions

The internet auction business is huge. Among the most popular consumer auction sites are:

- **eBay:** The most popular auction site, with more than 187 million buyers and sellers.

- **eBid:** The second largest internet auction site; fees are less than those for eBay.

- **Heritage Auctions:** The largest auction site focused specifically on collectibles, such as film and music memorabilia.

Even though consumers are spending billions on internet auctions, business-to-business auctions are likely to be the dominant form in the future. In a reverse auction, the buyer, rather than the seller, specifies the item or service that they are looking for. Sellers then compete to offer the lowest price to win the bid. A private company called Unison Marketplace (formerly called FedBid) has used reverse auctions to position itself between the federal government and private businesses. Unison Marketplace uses reverse auctions to put lucrative government contracts up for bid. In theory, since the lowest bid wins, the process can save taxpayers money by encouraging businesses to offer the best possible prices. Critics suggest that awarding government contracts based solely on price means that the government risks ending up with inferior products and services. For example, should the federal government award the next contract for a Navy aircraft carrier solely based on price? Supporters contend that many items that the government purchases (such as automobiles, tools, painting services, and groundskeeping services) are entirely suitable for a reverse auction.

19-6e Promotion Strategy

Price is often used as a promotional tool to increase consumer interest. In many cases, consumer perceptions of a store's prices are more impactful than the actual prices themselves. For example, Nordstrom is perceived as a pricier alternative to Macy's even though it has similar prices in many categories and lower prices in other categories. Clearly, price promotion alone does not always create a low-price image. Upscale ambiance, expensive specialty offerings, premier locations, a high level of service, and a lack of price matching contribute to a high-price image as well.

Often, the amount saved is the most important information when promoting a discount. For example, starting with a retail price of $80, a 40 percent discount creates a savings of $32, for a net sale price of $48. Of these four numbers—80, 40, 32, and 48—the most effective one to promote is the absolute savings of $32.[11]

19-6f Price Transparency

The worldwide proliferation of the internet has resulted in a huge increase in price transparency. Researchers analyzing the Italian highway system found that when prices of gasoline were posted for several service stations on a single sign, the average price of gas decreased by 1 euro per liter.[12] This doesn't sound like much, but it represented about 20 percent of the stations' profit margins. So, when drivers are better informed about gasoline prices, stations must compete by lowering prices. Now imagine how the internet has enabled consumers to compare prices in real time online. In the healthcare industry, a website that tracks drug and procedure prices across various providers and insurance agencies could result in lower consumer healthcare costs across the board. For example, going to a dentist for a root canal can cost you anywhere from $400 to $3,000 depending on where you live—lower prices tend to be in the Midwest and higher prices tend to be in larger cities. But if you saw on the internet that you could drive 10 miles outside your city to save thousands of dollars on a routine procedure—and did so—the industry would surely take notice.

19-6g The Appearance of Being Well-Informed or Not

Have you ever wondered if you paid too much for something because you had little knowledge of the product or service? Researchers have created an experiment using the auto repair shop business. Callers, using a script created by the researchers, requested a price quote for a radiator replacement on a Toyota Camry. The Auto MD database claimed that the price in that region should be around $365. A total of 2,778 independent repair shops were contacted. Three telephone scripts were used. The first script had callers disavow any knowledge about price (the uninformed consumer). The second script had callers claim that they had learned that the requested repair should cost about $365 (the informed consumer). In the third case, the caller stated that they understood the repair should cost around $510 (the misinformed consumer). Repair shop price quotes were not significantly different for the informed and uninformed callers. However, the shops quoted significantly higher prices to the misinformed callers.[13] The bottom line for consumers—go to the internet or other source and try to get pricing information when purchasing moderately priced or expensive items.

19-6h Demands of Large Customers

Manufacturers find that their large customers, such as department stores, often make specific pricing demands that the suppliers must agree to. Department stores are making greater-than-ever demands on their suppliers to cover the heavy discounts and markdowns on their own selling floors. They want suppliers to guarantee their stores' profit margins, and they insist on cash rebates if the guarantee is not met. They are also exacting fines for violations of ticketing, packing, and shipping rules. Cumulatively, the demands are nearly wiping out profits for all but the very biggest suppliers, according to fashion designers and garment makers.

Walmart is the largest retailer in the world, and the company uses that size to encourage companies to meet its needs. When Walmart decided that its grocery department needed to have everyday low prices instead of periodic rollbacks, it talked to its major suppliers, such as Conagra, Quaker Oats, and McCormick & Company, to discuss the

Walmart's pricing strategy is focused on providing grocery products at everyday low prices. The company's slogan "Save Money. Live Better" communicates this positioning to customers.

possibility of offering a consistently lower price to drive business. Some companies, like Conagra, struggled to lower costs while grain and other ingredients were steadily increasing in price. Other companies, like Kraft, had been steadily lowering costs and had an easier time meeting Walmart's demands. Walmart's demands are not all about keeping prices low, however. The company has instituted a policy requiring suppliers to evaluate and disclose the full environmental costs of their products. The risk of not working with Walmart? Either your product is important enough to drive traffic so that Walmart keeps the item, or you lose the world's biggest sales outlet.

19-6i The Relationship of Price to Quality

As mentioned at the beginning of the chapter, when a purchase decision involves uncertainty, consumers tend to rely on a high price as a predictor of good quality. Reliance on price as an indicator of quality seems to occur for all products, but it reveals itself more strongly for some items than for others. Among the products that benefit from this phenomenon are coffee, aspirin, shampoo, clothing, furniture, whiskey, education, and many services. In the absence of other information, people typically assume that prices are higher because the products contain better materials because they are made more carefully, or, in the case of professional services, because the provider has more expertise.

Researchers have found that price promotions of higher-priced, higher-quality brands tend to attract more business than do similar promotions of lower priced and lower-quality brands. Higher prices increase expectations and set a reference point against which people can evaluate their consumption experiences. Passengers on expensive full-service airlines like Delta, United, and American complain about service failures much more often than do customers of low-cost airlines like Spirit, Southwest, and EasyJet. A bad experience with a higher-priced product or service tends to increase the level of disappointment. Finally, products that generate strong emotions, such as perfumes and fine watches, tend to get more "bang for the buck" in price promotions.[14]

19-7 How to Set a Price on a Product

19-7 Describe the procedure for setting the right price

Setting the right price on a product is a four-step process, as illustrated in Figure 19.2 and discussed throughout this chapter:

1. Establish pricing goals.
2. Estimate demand, costs, and profits.

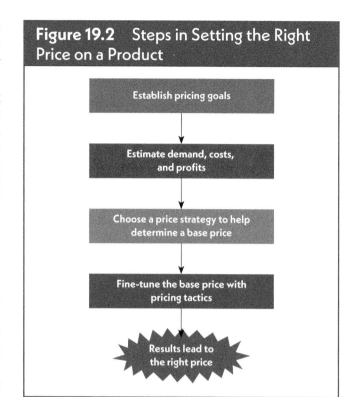

Figure 19.2 Steps in Setting the Right Price on a Product

Establish pricing goals

↓

Estimate demand, costs, and profits

↓

Choose a price strategy to help determine a base price

↓

Fine-tune the base price with pricing tactics

↓

Results lead to the right price

3. Choose a price strategy to help determine a base price.
4. Fine-tune the base price with pricing tactics.

19-7a Establish Pricing Goals

The first step in setting the right price is to establish pricing goals. Recall that pricing objectives fall into three categories: profit oriented, sales oriented, and status quo. These goals are derived from the firm's overall objectives. A good understanding of the marketplace and the consumer can sometimes tell a manager very quickly whether a goal is realistic.

All pricing objectives have trade-offs that managers must weigh. A profit-maximization objective may require a bigger initial investment than the firm can commit to or wants to commit to. Reaching the desired market share often means sacrificing short-term profit, because, without careful management, long-term profit goals may not be met. Meeting the competition is the easiest pricing goal to implement. But can managers really afford to ignore demand and costs, the life-cycle stage, and other considerations? When creating pricing objectives, managers must consider these trade-offs in light of the target customer, the environment, and the company's overall objectives. Pricing goals are a necessary input for pricing-AI software.

19-7b Estimate Demand, Costs, and Profits

Recall that total revenue is a function of price and quantity demanded and that quantity demanded depends on elasticity. Elasticity is a function of the perceived value to the buyer relative to the price. Often, pricing-AI software can answer this question. Some questions for pricing-AI software on demand and elasticity are as follows:

- What price is so low that consumers would question the product's quality?
- What is the highest price at which the product would still be perceived as a bargain?
- What is the price at which the product is starting to be perceived as expensive?
- What is the price at which the product becomes too expensive for the target market?

After establishing pricing goals, managers should estimate total revenue at a variety of prices. This may require marketing research. Next, they should determine the corresponding costs for each price. They are then ready to estimate how much profit, if any, and how much market share can be earned at each possible price. Managers can study the options in light of revenues, costs, and profits. In turn, this information can help determine which price base can best meet the firm's pricing goals.

19-7c Choose a Price Strategy

The basic, long-term pricing framework for a good or service should be a logical extension of the pricing objectives. The marketing manager's chosen **price strategy** defines the initial price and gives direction for price movements over the product's life cycle.

The price strategy, an integral part of pricing-AI software, sets a competitive price in a specific market segment based on a well-defined positioning strategy. Changing a price level from premium to super premium may require a change in the product itself, the target customers served, the promotional strategy, or the distribution channels.

A company's freedom in pricing a new product and devising a price strategy depends on the market conditions and the other elements of the marketing mix. If a firm launches a new item resembling several others already on the market, its pricing freedom will be restricted. To succeed, the company will probably have to charge a price close to the average market price. In contrast, a firm that introduces a totally new product with no close substitutes will have considerable pricing freedom.

The conventional wisdom is that store brands such as Target's Archer Farms should be priced lower than manufacturers' national brands. In fact, in the grocery industry, private-label products are priced an average of 40 percent less than their national-brand counterparts.[15] However, savvy retailers doing pricing strategy research have found that store brands do not necessarily have to be cheap. When store brands are positioned as gourmet or specialty items, consumers will even pay more for them than for gourmet national brands.

Companies that do serious planning when creating a price strategy and/or use pricing-AI software usually select from three basic approaches: price skimming, penetration pricing, and status quo pricing.

Price Skimming

Price skimming is sometimes called a "market-plus" approach to pricing because it denotes a high price relative to the prices of competing products. The term *price skimming* is derived from the phrase "skimming the cream off the top." Companies often use this strategy for new products when the product is perceived by the target market as having unique advantages. Often companies will use skimming and then lower prices over time. This is called "sliding down the demand curve." Manufacturers sometimes maintain skimming prices throughout a product's life cycle. Many luxury brands, including Chanel and Burberry, will destroy unsold inventory rather than selling it at a discount to protect the prestige of their brand name.[16]

Price skimming works best when there is strong demand for a good or service. Apple, for example, uses skimming when it brings out a new iPhone or Apple Watch. As new models are unveiled, prices on older versions are normally lowered. Firms can also effectively use price skimming when a product is well protected legally, when it represents a technological breakthrough, or when it has in some other way blocked the entry of competitors. Managers may follow a skimming strategy when production cannot be expanded rapidly because of technological difficulties, shortages, or constraints imposed by the skill and time required to produce a product (such as fine china, for example).

A successful skimming strategy enables management to recover its product development costs quickly. If the market perceives an introductory price as too high, managers can lower the price. Firms often believe that it is better to test the market at a high price and then lower the price if sales are too slow. Successful skimming strategies are not limited to products. Well-known athletes, lawyers, and celebrity hairstylists are experts at price skimming. Naturally, a skimming strategy will encourage competitors to enter the market.

---

price strategy a basic, long-term pricing framework that establishes the initial price for a product and the intended direction for price movements over the product's life cycle

price skimming a pricing policy whereby a firm charges a high introductory price, often coupled with heavy promotion

Penetration Pricing

Penetration pricing is at the opposite end of the spectrum from skimming. Penetration pricing means charging a relatively low price for a product when it is first rolled out as a way to reach the mass market. The low price is designed to capture a large share of a substantial market, resulting in lower production costs. If a marketing manager has made obtaining a large market share the firm's pricing objective, penetration pricing is a logical choice. For example, Kroger's Simple Truth Organic brand offers customers organic and free-from food options for prices that are significantly lower than many grocery competitors. This pricing strategy has paid off and in 10 years since the brand's launch, the company has seen over $3 billion in sales of this brand.[17]

Penetration pricing does mean lower profit per unit, however. Therefore, to reach the break-even point, it requires a higher volume of sales than would a skimming policy. The recovery of product development costs may be slow. As you might expect, penetration pricing tends to discourage competition.

A penetration strategy tends to be effective in a price-sensitive market. Price should decline more rapidly when demand is elastic because the market can be expanded through a lower price. The ultra-low-cost airline Spirit is now a very profitable U.S. airline. Its cut-rate fares include little more than a seat—nearly everything else is sold à la carte. The only complimentary item in the cabin is ice. If you want water with your ice, it costs $3.00 per bottle. Yet this airline maintains a high passenger load number and it continues to grow. Clearly, price matters.[18]

If a firm has a low fixed-cost structure and each sale provides a large contribution to those fixed costs, penetration pricing can boost sales and provide large increases in profits—but only if the market size grows or if competitors choose not to respond. Low prices can attract additional buyers to the market. The increased sales can justify production expansion or the adoption of new technologies, both of which can reduce costs. And, if firms have excess capacity, even low-priced business can provide incremental dollars toward fixed costs.

Penetration pricing can also be effective if an experience curve will cause costs per unit to drop significantly. The experience curve proposes that per-unit costs will go down as a firm's production experience increases. Manufacturers that fail to take advantage of these effects will find

Ulta Beauty utilizes both skimming and penetration pricing to effectively reach a broader range of consumers.

themselves at a competitive cost disadvantage relative to others that are further along the curve.

The big advantage of penetration pricing is that it typically discourages or blocks competition from entering a market. The disadvantage is that penetration means gearing up for mass production to sell a large volume at a low price. If the volume fails to materialize, the company will face huge losses from building or converting a factory to produce the failed product.

Ulta Beauty has been able to successfully utilize both price skimming and penetration pricing policies. The retailer sells its own store-branded beauty products at price levels significantly lower than many of its competitors, while also selling luxury beauty brands, such as Dior Beauty, at premium prices. To effectively integrate these two policies, Ulta has designed its store layout so that lower price-point brands are on one side of the store and higher price-point brands are on the other.[19]

Status Quo Pricing

The third basic price strategy a firm may choose is status quo pricing. Recall that this pricing strategy means charging a price identical to or very close to the competition's price. Although status quo pricing has the advantage of simplicity, its disadvantage is that the strategy may ignore demand or cost, or both. If the firm is comparatively small, however, meeting the competition's price may be the safest route to long-term survival.

19-8 Tactics for Fine-Tuning the Base Price

19-8 Explain how different pricing tactics can be used to fine-tune a base price

After managers understand both the legal and the marketing consequences of price strategies, they should set a **base price**—the general price level at which the company expects to sell the good or service. The general price level is

---

penetration pricing a pricing policy whereby a firm charges a relatively low price for a product when it is first rolled out as a way to reach the mass market

base price the general price level at which the company expects to sell the good or service

correlated with the pricing policy: above the market (price skimming), at the market (status quo pricing), or below the market (penetration pricing). The final step, then, is to fine-tune the base price often using pricing-AI software.

Fine-tuning techniques are approaches that do not change the general price level. They do, however, result in changes within a general price level. These pricing tactics allow the firm to adjust for competition in certain markets, meet ever-changing government regulations, take advantage of unique demand situations, and meet promotional and positioning goals. Fine-tuning pricing tactics include various sorts of discounts, geographic pricing, and other pricing strategies.

19-8a Discounts, Allowances, Rebates, and Value-Based Pricing

A base price can be lowered through the use of discounts and the related tactics of allowances, rebates, low or zero-percent financing, and value-based pricing. Managers use the various forms of discounts to encourage customers to do what they would not ordinarily do, such as paying cash rather than using credit, taking delivery out of season, or performing certain functions within a distribution channel. The following are the most common tactics:

- **Quantity discounts:** When buyers get a lower price for buying in multiple units or above a specified dollar amount, they receive a **quantity discount**. A **cumulative quantity discount** is a deduction from the list price that applies to the buyer's total purchases made during a specific period; it is intended to encourage customer loyalty. In contrast, a **noncumulative quantity discount** is a deduction from the list price that applies to a single order rather than to the total volume of orders placed during a certain period. It is intended to encourage orders in large quantities.

- **Cash discounts:** A **cash discount** is a price reduction offered to a consumer, an industrial user, or a marketing intermediary in return for prompt payment of a bill. Prompt payment saves the seller carrying charges and billing expenses and allows the seller to avoid bad debt.

- **Functional discounts:** When distribution channel intermediaries, such as wholesalers or retailers, perform a service or function for the manufacturer, they must be compensated. This compensation, typically a percentage discount from the base price, is called a **functional discount** (or **trade discount**). Functional discounts vary greatly from channel to channel, depending on the tasks performed by the intermediary.

- **Seasonal discounts:** A **seasonal discount** is a price reduction for buying merchandise out of season. It

shifts the storage function to the purchaser. Seasonal discounts also enable manufacturers to maintain a steady production schedule year-round.

- **New customer discounts:** Many firms offer an initial discount to new customers. The objective is to create a long-term relationship with the new client and therefore a long-term revenue stream. Researchers have found that this is often an effective strategy. It was noted that a discount of approximately 15 to 20 percent was recommended to maximize customer lifetime revenues. An initial discount of 40 to 60 percent was not recommended, as it was too costly and also creates expectations of receiving large discounts in the future.[20]

- **Reframing discount and markdown math:** During the holidays, it has become quite common for large retail chains and other retailers to layer discounts one on top of the other. In some cases, this layering has confused shoppers, resulting in consumers both overestimating and underestimating the final price. Some retailers, such as Kohl's and JCPenney, are making price reductions easier to understand. These retailers now show online shoppers the final price after all discounts on the product page and have been increasingly advertising sales with final dollar amounts, rather than percentage discounts. On its app, Kohl's offers a "Your Price" feature that shows the final cost after all discounts. For example, if a Disney Princess Palace, regularly priced at $79.99, were on sale on the Kohl's app for $54.99 and eligible for an extra 25 percent off, the "Your Price" would be displayed as $41.24. Researchers have approached the "clarifying of discount math for consumers" a bit differently. In an experiment, using "was X% higher," the researchers determined that this simple technique can often increase consumers

---

quantity discount a price reduction offered to buyers buying in multiple units or above a specified dollar amount

cumulative quantity discount a deduction from list price that applies to the buyer's total purchases made during a specific period

noncumulative quantity discount a deduction from list price that applies to a single order rather than to the total volume of orders placed during a certain period

cash discount a price reduction offered to a consumer, an industrial user, or a marketing intermediary in return for prompt payment of a bill

functional discount (or trade discount) a discount to wholesalers and retailers for performing channel functions

seasonal discount a price reduction for buying merchandise out of season

purchase intentions. This technique was found to be more successful if the retailers served either older or less-educated consumers.[21] The technique had a minimal impact on all consumers if the actual discount was small. Other researchers examined the concept of "double mental discounting." For example, a promotion might advertise: "Spend $200 now and receive a $50 gift card to spend in the future!" Double mental discounting occurs when a potential buyer mentally deducts the $50 from $200 thinking "this product only cost me $150." Later on, when they receive the $50 gift card, the consumer may purchase an item for $75 but thinks "this only cost me $25 because I have a $50 gift card." The double mental discount perception is that their cost for the two items was lower than they actually were. This perception may trigger higher expenditures. The researchers found that consumers double mental discounts promotion credits (e.g., $50 gift card) are perceived as a greater discount over other types (e.g., mail-in rebates, percent off, and cash-back offers).[22]

- **Promotional allowances:** A **promotional allowance** (also known as a **trade allowance**) is a payment to a dealer for promoting the manufacturer's products. It is both a pricing tool and a promotional device. As a pricing tool, a promotional allowance is like a functional discount. If, for example, a retailer runs an ad for a manufacturer's product, the manufacturer may pay half the cost.

- **Rebates:** A **rebate** is a cash refund given for the purchase of a product during a specific period. The advantage of a rebate over a simple price reduction for stimulating demand is that a rebate is a temporary inducement that can be taken away without altering the basic price structure. A manufacturer that uses a simple price reduction for a short time may meet resistance when trying to restore the price to its original, higher level.

- **Coupons:** A coupon is a discount offered via paper, a card, a printable web page, or an electronic code. U.S. marketers issue over 165 billion coupons each year. Many coupons are still printed and distributed through newspaper inserts and mail, but the use of

Zappos uses free shipping and returns to build customer loyalty and gain new customers.

digital coupons is increasing rapidly. The majority of coupons distributed by retailers are still printed, but approximately one-third of coupons that are ultimately redeemed by consumers are digital.[23]

- **Zero percent financing:** To get consumers into automobile showrooms, manufacturers sometimes offer zero percent financing, which enables purchasers to borrow money to pay for new cars with no interest charge. This tactic creates a huge increase in sales but is not without its costs. A five-year interest-free car loan typically represents a loss of more than $3,000 for the car's manufacturer.

- **Free shipping:** Free shipping is another method of lowering the price for purchasers. Zappos and Nordstrom offer free shipping with no minimum order amount. However, since shipping is an expense to the seller, it must be built into the cost of the product. It is estimated that there are over 268 million digital shoppers in the United States. Free shipping is a prime motivation for shopping online, and high shipping costs are one of the top reasons for online cart abandonment.[24] Only 20 percent of online retailers offer free shipping on all purchases, while about 60 percent offer it as an option if a minimum purchase amount is reached.[25] Additionally, nearly one in three consumers will purchase more to meet a free-shipping threshold.

Value-Based Pricing

Value-based pricing, also called *value pricing*, is a pricing strategy that has grown out of the quality movement. Value-based pricing starts with the customer, considers the competition and associated costs, and then determines the appropriate price. The basic assumption is that the firm is customer driven, seeking to understand the attributes customers want in the goods and services they buy and the value of that bundle of attributes to customers. Because very few firms operate in a pure monopoly, however, a

---

promotional allowance (trade allowance) a payment to a dealer for promoting the manufacturer's products

rebate a cash refund given for the purchase of a product during a specific period

value-based pricing setting the price at a level that seems to the customer to be a good price compared to the prices of other options

marketer using value-based pricing must also determine the value of competitive offerings to customers. Customers determine the value of a product (not just its price) relative to the value of alternatives. In value-based pricing, therefore, the price of the product is set at a level that seems to the customer to be a good price compared with the prices of other options.

19-8b Geographic Pricing

Because many sellers ship their wares to a nationwide or even a worldwide market, the cost of freight can greatly affect the total cost of a product. Sellers may use several different geographic pricing tactics to moderate the impact of freight costs on distant customers. The following methods of geographic pricing are the most common:

1. **FOB origin pricing: FOB origin pricing**, also called "FOB factory" or "FOB shipping point," is a price tactic that requires the buyer to absorb the freight costs from the shipping point ("free on board"). The farther buyers are from sellers, the more they pay, because transportation costs generally increase with the distance merchandise is shipped.

2. **Uniform delivered pricing:** If the marketing manager wants total costs, including freight, to be equal for all purchasers of identical products, the firm will adopt uniform delivered pricing, or "postage stamp" pricing. With **uniform delivered pricing**, the seller pays the actual freight charges and bills every purchaser an identical, flat freight charge. This is sometimes called *postage stamp pricing* because a person can send a letter across the street or across the country for the same price.

3. **Zone pricing:** A marketing manager who wants to equalize total costs among buyers within large geographic areas—but not necessarily all of the seller's market area—may modify the base price with a zone-pricing tactic. **Zone pricing** is a modification of uniform delivered pricing. Rather than using a uniform freight rate for the entire United States (or its total market), the firm divides it into segments or zones and charges a flat freight rate to all customers in a given zone.

4. **Freight absorption pricing:** In **freight absorption pricing**, the seller pays all or part of the actual freight charges and does not pass them on to the buyer. The manager may use this tactic in intensely competitive areas or as a way to break into new market areas or increase sales (refer to "Free shipping").

5. **Basing-point pricing:** With **basing-point pricing**, the seller designates a location as a basing point and charges all buyers the freight cost from that point, regardless of the city from which the goods are shipped. Thanks to several adverse court rulings, basing-point pricing has waned in

popularity. Freight fees charged when none were actually incurred, called *phantom freight*, have been declared illegal.

19-8c Other Pricing Tactics

Unlike geographic pricing, other pricing tactics are unique and defy neat categorization. Managers use these tactics for various reasons—for example, to stimulate demand for specific products, to increase store patronage, and to offer a wider variety of merchandise at a specific price point. Such pricing tactics include a single-price tactic, flexible pricing, professional services pricing, price lining, leader pricing, bait pricing, odd–even pricing, price bundling, and two-part pricing.

Single-Price Tactic

A merchant using a **single-price tactic** offers all goods and services at the same price (or perhaps two or three prices). Dollar Tree and Family Dollar chains sell everything for $1 or less. Such a strategy can be quite successful.

Flexible Pricing

Flexible pricing (or **variable pricing**) means that different customers pay different prices for essentially the same merchandise bought in equal quantities. This tactic is often found in the sale of shopping goods, specialty merchandise, and most industrial goods except supply items. Car dealers and many appliance retailers commonly follow the practice. It allows the seller to adjust for competition by meeting another seller's price. Thus, a marketing manager with a status quo pricing objective might readily adopt the tactic.

FOB origin pricing a price tactic that requires the buyer to absorb the freight costs from the shipping point ("free on board")

uniform delivered pricing a price tactic in which the seller pays the actual freight charges and bills every purchaser an identical, flat freight charge

zone pricing a modification of uniform delivered pricing that divides the United States (or the total market) into segments or zones and charges a flat freight rate to all customers in a given zone

freight absorption pricing a price tactic in which the seller pays all or part of the actual freight charges and does not pass them on to the buyer

basing-point pricing a price tactic that charges freight from a given (basing) point, regardless of the city from which the goods are shipped

single-price tactic a price tactic that offers all goods and services at the same price (or perhaps two or three prices)

flexible pricing (variable pricing) a price tactic in which different customers pay different prices for essentially the same merchandise bought in equal quantities

Flexible pricing also enables the seller to close a sale with a price-conscious consumer.

The obvious disadvantages of flexible pricing are the lack of consistent profit margins, the potential ill will of high-paying purchasers, the tendency for salespeople to automatically lower the price to make a sale, and the possibility of a price war among sellers.

Professional Services Pricing

Professional services pricing is used by people with lengthy experience, training, and often certification by a licensing board—for example, lawyers, physicians, and family counselors. Professionals sometimes charge customers at an hourly rate, but sometimes fees are based on the solution of a problem or performance of an act (such as an eye examination) rather than on the actual time involved.

Those who use professional pricing have an ethical responsibility not to overcharge a customer. Because demand is sometimes highly inelastic, such as when a person requires heart surgery to survive, there may be a temptation to charge "all the traffic will bear."

Price Lining

When a seller establishes a series of prices for a type of merchandise, it creates a price line. **Price lining** is the practice of offering a product line with several items at specific price points. For example, Honda cars are priced as follows: Civic, $23,750; Accord, $27,295; Pilot, $36,300; Odyssey, $37,490; and Passport, $41,100. Cars that are bigger or have more advanced features start at higher price points. Many cell phone companies also utilize price lining. The Apple iPhone pricing usually starts at $799, whereas the iPhone Plus, which features a larger screen, usually starts at $899.[26]

Price lining reduces confusion for both the salesperson and the consumer. The buyer may be offered a wider variety of merchandise at each established price. Price lines may also enable a seller to reach several market segments. For buyers, the question of price may be quite simple: all they have to do is find a suitable product at the predetermined price. Moreover, price lining is a valuable tactic for the marketing manager because the firm may be able to carry a smaller total inventory than it could without price lines. The results may include fewer markdowns, simplified purchasing, and lower inventory carrying charges.

Price lines are used in many different industries, including cars and technology.

Mikbiz/Shutterstock.com

Price lines also present drawbacks, especially if costs are continually rising. Sellers can offset rising costs in three ways. First, they can begin stocking lower-quality merchandise at each price point. Second, sellers can change the prices, although frequent price-line changes confuse buyers. Third, sellers can accept lower profit margins and hold quality and prices constant. This third alternative has short-run benefits, but its long-run handicaps may drive sellers out of business.

Leader Pricing

Leader pricing (or **loss-leader pricing**) is an attempt by the marketing manager to attract customers by selling a product near or even below cost in the hope that shoppers will buy other items once they are in the store. This type of pricing appears weekly in the newspaper advertising of supermarkets, drug stores, and other retailers. Leader pricing is normally used on well-known items that consumers can easily recognize as bargains. Leader pricing is not limited to products. Health clubs often offer a one-month free trial as a loss leader.

---

price lining the practice of offering a product line with several items at specific price points

leader pricing (loss-leader pricing) a price tactic in which a product is sold near or even below cost in the hope that shoppers will buy other items once they are in the store

A new condo in a prime location may be listed for $1,000,000 and not $999,999. The even price implies quality and prestige.

Alstock Productions/Shutterstock.com

Bait Pricing

In contrast to leader pricing, which is a genuine attempt to give the consumer a reduced price, bait pricing is deceptive. **Bait pricing** tries to get consumers into a store through false or misleading price advertising and then uses high-pressure selling to persuade them to buy more expensive merchandise. For example, imagine that you see an ad for a brand-new Ford Mustang for $20,000, nearly $8,000 dollars less than the typical starting price for this car. This is bait. You go to the dealer to test drive the car, but when you get there, the salesperson tells you that particular car is no longer in stock, but they have another similar Mustang with upgraded features in stock for $30,000. This is the switch that may cause a susceptible consumer to walk out with a more expensive car. The dealership never had any intention of selling a new Ford Mustang for $20,000, but used that deceptive claim to lure consumers in. The Federal Trade Commission considers bait pricing a deceptive act and has banned its use in interstate commerce. Most states also ban bait pricing, but sometimes enforcement is lax.

Odd–Even Pricing

Odd–even pricing (or **psychological pricing**) means pricing at odd-numbered prices to connote a bargain and pricing at even-numbered prices to imply quality. For years, many retailers have priced their products in odd numbers—for example, $99.95—to make consumers feel they are paying a lower price for the product. Even-numbered pricing is often used for "prestige" items, such as a fine perfume at $100 a bottle or a good watch at $1,000. The demand curve for such items would also be saw-toothed, except that the outside edges would represent even-numbered prices and, therefore, elastic demand.

Price Bundling

Price bundling is marketing two or more products in a single package for a special price. For example, travel websites, such as Travelocity, bundle flights, hotel, and a car rental into one price, so the consumer must only consider one cost for their entire vacation rather than three separate costs. Price bundling can stimulate demand for the bundled items if the target market perceives the price as a good value. Consumers expect to pay less for a bundle than they do for each item sold individually.[27]

Services like hotels and airlines sell a perishable commodity (hotel rooms and airline seats) with relatively fixed costs. Bundling can be an important income stream for these businesses because the variable costs tend to be low—for instance, the cost of cleaning a hotel room. To account for this variability, hotels sometimes charge a resort fee that covers things like the use of the gym, pool, and Wi-Fi.

Bundling is also widely used in the telecommunications industry. Companies offer internet service, wireless, and cable television in various bundled configurations. Telecom companies use bundling as a way to protect their market share and fight off competition by locking customers into a group of services. For consumers, comparison shopping may be difficult since they may not be able to determine how much they are really paying for each component of the bundle.

You inevitably encounter bundling when you go to a fast-food restaurant. Taco Bell Combo boxes are bundles. Customers can build their own combo box, which includes one specialty item, such as a Cheesy Gordita Crunch, one classic item, such as a soft taco, one side, such as cinnamon twists, and a drink for only $5.99. If purchased individually, all of these items would be nearly $9.

Two-Part Pricing

Two-part pricing means establishing two separate charges to consume a single good or service. Consumers sometimes prefer two-part pricing because they are uncertain about the number and the types of activities they might use at places like an amusement parks. Also, the people who use a service most often pay a higher total price. Two-part pricing can increase a seller's revenue by attracting consumers who would not pay a high fee even for unlimited use. For example, a health club might be able to sell only 100 memberships at $700 annually with unlimited use of facilities, for a total revenue of $70,000. However, it could sell 900 memberships at $200 with a guarantee of using the racquetball courts 10 times a month. Every use over 10 would require the member to pay a $5 fee. Thus, membership revenue would provide a base of $180,000, with some additional usage fees throughout the year.

Pay What You Want

To many people, paying what you want or what you think something is worth is a very risky tactic. Obviously, it would not work for expensive durables like automobiles. Imagine someone paying $1 for a new BMW! Yet this model has worked to varying degrees in digital media marketplaces, restaurants, and other service businesses. The Metropolitan

---

bait pricing a price tactic that tries to get consumers into a store through false or misleading price advertising and then uses high-pressure selling to persuade consumers to buy more expensive merchandise

odd–even pricing (psychological pricing) a price tactic that uses odd-numbered prices to connote bargains and even-numbered prices to imply quality

price bundling marketing two or more products in a single package for a special price

two-part pricing a price tactic that charges two separate amounts to consume a single good or service

Museum of Art in New York City allows visitors to pay what they want for admission. The museum does provide suggestions for admission prices, but visitors can choose whether they want to pay the suggested amount, less than the suggested amount, or potentially more if they want to provide greater support for the museum. Social pressures can come into play in a "pay what you want" environment because an individual does not want to appear poor or cheap to their peers.

19-8d Consumer Penalties

More and more businesses are adopting **consumer penalties**—extra fees paid by consumers for violating the terms of a purchase agreement. Airlines often charge a fee for changing a return date on a ticket. Businesses impose consumer penalties because they will allegedly suffer an irrevocable revenue loss and/or incur significant additional transaction costs should customers be unable or unwilling to complete their purchase obligations. For the company, these customer payments are part of doing business in a highly competitive marketplace. With profit margins in many companies increasingly coming under pressure, organizations are looking to stem losses resulting from customers not meeting their obligations. Some medical professionals charge a penalty fee if you don't show up for an appointment. However, the perceived unfairness of a penalty may affect some consumers' willingness to patronize a business in the future.

19-9 The Legality of Price Strategy

19-9 Identify the legal constraints on pricing decisions

As mentioned in Chapter 4, some pricing decisions are subject to government regulation. Among the issues that fall into this category are unfair trade practices, price fixing, price discrimination, and predatory pricing.

19-9a Unfair Trade Practices

In many states in the United States, **unfair trade practice acts** put a floor under wholesale and retail prices. Selling

---

consumer penalty an extra fee paid by the consumer for violating the terms of the purchase agreement

unfair trade practice acts laws that prohibit wholesalers and retailers from selling below cost

price fixing an agreement between two or more firms on the price they will charge for a product

below cost in these states is illegal. Wholesalers and retailers must usually take a certain minimum percentage markup on their combined merchandise cost and transportation cost. The most common markup figures are 6 percent at the retail level and 2 percent at the wholesale level. If a specific wholesaler or retailer can provide conclusive proof that operating costs are lower than the minimum required figure, lower prices may be allowed.

The intent of unfair trade practice acts is to protect small local firms from giants like Walmart and Amazon, which often operate very efficiently on razor-thin profit margins. State enforcement of unfair trade practice laws has generally been lax, however, partly because low prices benefit local consumers.

However, enforcement is not always so lax. Amazon was recently investigated for unfairly pricing diapers, supposedly with the intention of forcing Quidsi, a company that ran the website diapers.com, out of business. For several years, diapers.com was a leading diaper retailer. The website sold diapers at low prices, often with overnight shipping. To compete with diapers.com, Amazon decreased diaper prices by 30 and had to take a $200 million loss. The impact on diapers.com's sales, however, was devastating, and Quidsi was eventually forced to accept a merger agreement with Amazon. The Federal Trade Commission (FTC) and Attorney General's Offices in California and New York investigated the case and found emails proving that Amazon's actions were intentional.[28]

19-9b Price Fixing

Price fixing is an agreement between two or more firms on the price they will charge for a product. Suppose two or more executives from competing firms meet to decide how much to charge for a product or to decide which of them will submit the lowest bid on a certain contract. Such practices are illegal under the Sherman Antitrust Act and the FTC Act. Offenders have received fines and sometimes prison terms. Price fixing is one area where the law is quite clear, and the U.S. Justice Department's enforcement is vigorous.

19-9c Price Discrimination

The Robinson–Patman Act of 1936 prohibits any firm from selling to two or more different buyers, within a reasonably short time, commodities (not services) of like grade and quality at different prices where the result would be to substantially lessen competition. The act also makes it illegal for a seller to offer two buyers different supplementary services and for buyers to use their purchasing power to force sellers into granting discriminatory prices or services.

The Robinson–Patman Act provides three defenses for sellers charged with price discrimination (in each case the burden is on the sellers to defend themselves):

1. **Cost:** A firm can charge different prices to different customers if the prices represent manufacturing or quantity discount savings.

2. **Market conditions:** Price variations are justified if designed to meet fluid product or market conditions. Examples include the deterioration of perishable goods, the obsolescence of seasonal products, a distress sale under court order, and a legitimate going-out-of-business sale.

3. **Competition:** A price reduction may be necessary to stay even with the competition. Specifically, if a competitor undercuts the price quoted by a seller to a buyer, the law authorizes the seller to lower the price charged to the buyer for the product in question.

19-9d Predatory Pricing

Predatory pricing is the practice of charging a very low price for a product with the intent of driving competitors out of business or out of a market. Once competitors have been driven out, the firm raises its prices. This practice is illegal under the Sherman Antitrust Act and the FTC Act. To prove predatory pricing, the Justice Department must show that the predator—the destructive company—explicitly tried to ruin a competitor and that the predatory price was below the predator's average variable cost.

Prosecutions for predatory pricing suffered a major setback when a federal judge threw out a predatory pricing suit filed by the Department of Justice against American Airlines. The Department of Justice argued that the definition should be updated and that the test should be whether there was any business justification, other than driving away competitors, for American's aggressive pricing. Under that definition, the Department of Justice attorneys thought they had a great case. Whenever a fledgling airline tried to get a toehold in the Dallas market, American would meet its fares and add flights. As soon as the rival retreated, American would jack its fares back up.

Under the average variable cost, however, the case would have been almost impossible to win because, like a high-tech industry, the airline industry has high fixed costs and low marginal costs. Once a flight is scheduled, the marginal cost of providing a seat for an additional passenger is almost zero. Thus, it is very difficult to prove that an airline is pricing below its average variable cost. The judge was not impressed by the Department of Justice's argument, however, and kept to the average variable cost definition of predatory pricing.

---

predatory pricing the practice of charging a very low price for a product with the intent of driving competitors out of business or out of a market

Marketing Analytics Appendix

Learning Outcomes

After studying this chapter, you will be able to . . .

A-1 Explain the importance of marketing analytics

A-2 Identify different sources of data

A-3 Describe data management

A-4 Explain the steps used to engage in marketing analytics initiatives

A-1 The Growing Importance of Marketing Analytics

Has the cost of a product, an interaction with customer service, or the environment of a store ever influenced how satisfied you were as a customer? Have you ever responded to a digital marketing campaign by searching for more information about a product or making a purchase? Do you frequently purchase more than one product at the same time, such as purchasing milk, cereal, and bread during a single visit to the grocery store? Are your purchase habits influenced by the weather, time of day, or day of the week? Do your social media interactions affect your purchase decisions? These are behaviors that marketers, such as those for Walmart, Target, and Nordstrom explore among the millions of customers each week using their marketing analytics programs. In this appendix, we introduce you to the new and exciting world of marketing analytics and explain its tremendous popularity and endless possibilities.

Throughout the text, you have learned that marketing consists of processes that provide value and benefits to customers through products and services, communications, distribution, and pricing strategies. As described in Chapter 1, it is the marketers' responsibility to assess the wants and satisfactions of present and potential customers, design and manage product offerings, determine prices and pricing policies, develop distribution strategies, communicate with present and potential customers, and maintain long-term customer relationships. The survival of companies depends on these marketing capabilities since more customers typically translates into higher profitability. So

how do marketers make critical decisions that facilitate these capabilities? They use insights that can be accurately understood only through marketing research and analytics.

Marketing analytics applies quantitative techniques that enable companies to identify hidden customer shopping patterns and produce actionable insights. The value of marketing analytics, however, is dependent on the data that companies possess. Companies collect an abundance of data from different exchange relationships with channel partners and customers. But they also collect external data such as economic, competitor, and weather events. The large amount of data now available through traditional and digital sources—such as in-store sales, e-commerce sites, social media, digital connectivity, and other technologies—provides marketers with a unique resource to improve and expand their businesses. Considering the use of "always connected" smartphones, wearables such as the Apple Watch, and intelligent personal assistants such as the Amazon Echo, it is evident that technology has drastically changed the way customers search for information, interact with companies, and purchase products.

When was the last time you searched online for product information, or jumped on social media to explore your friend's latest updates? These technologies impact not only the customer's journey but also produce data to enhance a company's ability to understand and respond to customers. Can you imagine the amount of data generated from millions of customers each day? Although having so much data can be an asset, the large amount of data can also produce significant challenges. As a result, marketers rely on information systems to capture and manage these data collections.

Marketers often access much of the information they need from customer relationship management (CRM) systems or marketing information systems (MIS). Recall that CRM is a company-wide business strategy designed to optimize profitability, revenue, and customer satisfaction by focusing on highly defined and precise customer groups. A marketing information system is a **management information system (MIS)** designed to support marketing

---

marketing analytics the application of quantitative techniques to identify customer shopping patterns and produce actionable insights

management information system (MIS) a system that stores data about customers, supply chain partners, and other data internal and external to a company

decision making. These systems store data about customers, supply chain partners, and other data internal and external to the company, such as weather patterns, locations, and competitor decisions. For example, a CRM system might store multichannel customer data from mobile apps, online websites, in-store locations, social media sites, and call centers that indicate how and where customers are engaging with the company. Whether you call customer service, purchase a product in a store, browse a company website, or place an order through social media, the data you generate is stored in a CRM system. Information from each touchpoint is captured to enhance the potential that companies can meet the needs and wants of customers. You can easily recognize the value as marketers leverage information from these databases to optimize profitability, determine marketing strategy, differentiate themselves from competitors, personalize experiences, and identify their best customers. Regardless of the specific strategy, data are used in marketing analytics to identify patterns and get to know customers on a personal level. Marketing analytics converts data into actionable information. Consequently, the information can then be used to improve customer satisfaction, drive innovative ideas, assess performance, and develop more effective marketing strategies.

Kroger, like many other major retailers, has lots of data. The company has 11 million consumers that shop at the grocery retailer's more than 1,300 locations—all of these transactions result in huge data sets! Kroger has invested in creating its own data science organization, called 84.51° and, clearly, has high expectations for the potential of marketing analytics, with the goal of engaging with customers more effectively.[1] For example, using marketing analytics insights, Kroger can determine what coupons to send to each customer and when to send these coupons so that they are more likely to result in a purchase. Similarly, Stitch Fix, an online subscription shopping service, has grown rapidly in the personalized retail industry by using data and marketing analytics. When customers initially open an account, Stitch Fix gathers personal style information and preferences. The company then integrates preferences with prior customer selections and runs analytics assessments to determine what products will best satisfy the customer. As new data become available through purchase behavior and customer feedback, marketing analytics software updates the information to improve performance.[2] Other retailers such as Amazon and Target have successfully implemented similar recommender systems online that suggest products for customers based on search history and items placed in the basket.

As described in the previous examples, company data can be used to understand behavioral patterns and optimize customer engagement and experiences. Walmart, for example, built an advanced analytics lab driven by artificial intelligence (AI) inside one of its existing stores. **Artificial intelligence** is the development of computer systems that can perform tasks that are normally performed by a person, such as visual perception, decision making, and speech recognition. The big-box retailer is examining the use of video camera systems to detect inventory-control management issues and to identify customers that might need assistance to prevent them from leaving the store when they cannot find what they want.[3] The benefit of developing marketing strategies based on these metrics is that increasing customer retention rates by 5 percent can increase profits by as much as 125 percent. Thus, there is a clear financial benefit for proactively sensing and responding to customers who might decide to make purchases elsewhere. Depending on the business strategy, companies distinctly investigate data to achieve different goals. These examples demonstrate why more and more companies are embracing a culture focused on collecting and analyzing data to make better and more timely decisions.

Companies often have more data than they realize. But the data are valuable only if companies use it to improve decision making. Unfortunately, some companies do not realize the value of data early enough. JCPenney collected behavioral data on customer attitudes for many years. But until recently, the company relied on intuition rather than on marketing analytics and customer trends. The company was surprised to discover through its marketing analytics program that customers were more receptive to discounts and coupons than to everyday low pricing. While the strategic move toward analytics occurred several years ago, JCPenney still faces challenges in identifying core customers. On the other hand, companies such as Airbnb, Nike, Johnson & Johnson, and Samsung chose to use marketing analytics to examine patterns in their data and improve strategic decision making, expand sales, and increase customer satisfaction. Clearly, marketers can leverage data using analytics to create a competitive advantage and provide a more personalized experience to customers.

A-1a Data Types

What types of data do companies collect? They collect all types of data, including both structured and unstructured data.

Structured data is easily defined and organized and can include text, such as names, and numeric fields. For example, ZIP Codes, sales figures, and numerical or categorical survey results are all structured data. This type of data

---

artificial intelligence (AI) the development of computer systems that can perform tasks normally performed by a person

structured data data that is easily defined and organized

provides an efficient way to run statistical analyses to identify purchasing patterns, but it sometimes limits potential insights. Let's consider that a company wants to know the number of purchases occurring online from different geographic areas. The company can extract cities, states, or ZIP Codes from CRM systems to obtain this information. But what type of data can be used when a company is interested in understanding why customers are purchasing products or how customers feel about the products? In this situation, companies can use **unstructured data** (data that are not organized in a predefined manner) from social media posts, online communications, customer service call records, or emails with the company. This type of data consists of images, videos, audio files, and text—such as reviews or social media posts—and typically makes up about 80 to 90 percent of a company's data. Social media and digital marketing environments are contributing to the growing availability of unstructured data. Combining structured with unstructured data enables companies to capture a broader view of the customer.

A-2 Data Sources and Collection

Data sources involve both primary data and secondary data. Recall from Chapter 9 that primary data are collected for the first time to solve a specific problem or answer specific questions. Results from surveys, interviews, and experiments are examples of primary data—the research is conducted to achieve a specific purpose. For instance, companies that develop surveys and collect responses often do so to accomplish a specific objective. Perhaps the company initiates a survey to understand recent shopping experiences at a particular store, or they might inquire specifically about customer perceptions regarding a new product. Eye-tracking technology is also increasingly being used by companies to better understand consumption behaviors. Toyota has adopted this approach and conducts experiments inside a simulated vehicle showroom.[4] The company utilizes eye-tracking technology to better understand what features car shoppers focus on and to explore what types of marketing communications best capture consumers' attention. This information can then be used to design vehicle showrooms and create more effective communication materials and displays. These examples illustrate how companies design methods of data collection for which there is a specific purpose in mind. Primary data has a significant advantage in that this type of data can answer specific questions. But it can also be costly and require a lot of time to collect. In contrast, secondary data are data that have been previously collected for another reason. Secondary data might not be capable of answering a specific question but is usually available immediately and might provide an initial starting point to assist in the further development of a research study. It is also much less expensive to gather than primary data.

Examples of secondary data include those from various digital channels such as computers, smartphones, tablets, and video game consoles. People are often willing to share ideas with others via social media. The best conversations are often organically derived, with customers offering advice and feedback about product quality and use. The Clorox Company, the owner of Hidden Valley Ranch brands, recognized this as a source of secondary data. Through social media listening, researchers discovered a new trend—customers were mixing packets of Hidden Valley Ranch seasoning into jars of pickles to create "ranch pickles."[5] These insights played a pivotal role in inspiring the company to create a pickle-flavored Hidden Valley ranch dressing. Through interacting with others, searching for information, purchasing products, and playing video games, people generate a variety of data from these digital channels. Companies capture conversations on social media websites such as Instagram or TikTok, but they also collect data from customer purchases on websites, location data from smartphones, and other sources.

There are many sources of secondary data, such as the following:

- **Government:** Companies can access data such as Census or North American Industry Classification System (NAICS) details through government websites. Census data can be integrated with internal customer data to improve understanding of other drivers of purchasing behavior. For example, do specific demographics in an area have an impact on sales of particular products or brands? Business-to-business salespeople might also explore NAICS codes, a format that provides a classification of industries, to develop an understanding of a particular industry or type of customer.

- **Channel partners:** There are often many partners in a channel—suppliers, manufacturers, wholesalers, distributors, and retailers—that can provide important data. Each channel partner collects data of value to them. Manufacturers or retailers might share sales data or customer preferences with each other to benefit production or inventory control. As an example, Ford Motor Company utilizes the retail inventory management system from Syncron, a software company focused on providing solutions to inventory

---

unstructured data data that is not easily organized in a predefined manner

management and pricing issues, to integrate many sources of data to make inventory recommendations to the dealer network.[6] As a result of sharing this information, dealers acquire the inventory with models, styles, and features that customers in their market want to purchase.

- **Commercial entities:** Data brokers collect and sell data. Retailers might be interested in credit card purchasing history to investigate whether customers are also purchasing from a competitor. Similarly, to identify high-risk patients, hospitals have purchased data so that they can examine lifestyles to determine whether patients might be more likely to experience specific medical issues.[7] Hospitals use the data to target specific types of patients in their market area and in general to improve medical decision making.

- **Corporate:** Companies collect data that are stored internally in a variety of databases. Data can be integrated across the organization from accounting, finance, sales, customer service, and marketing to gain a better understanding of sales and customer satisfaction.

- **Mobile and social media:** Companies can obtain valuable feedback about products and brands from online sources such as Facebook, TikTok, and Instagram. For example, companies such as L'Oréal, Netflix, and Chipotle collect consumer opinions by exploring social media posts. Using marketing analytics, cosmetics brand NYX, which is owned by L'Oréal, recognized that a nostalgic, Y2K beauty aesthetic, including white eyeliner, was beginning to emerge among consumers. In response to this trend, NYX shifted its social media strategy to focus on the multiple ways that its white eyeliner product could be used, including as a traditional eyeliner but also as a brow or face contour tool. Within a few days of posting this content to its social media account, NYX white eyeliner was sold out in multiple stores and online.[8]

- **Online websites:** Existing websites are sources of secondary data. Some companies use weather data to predict consumer behavior.[9] Weather patterns can predict emotions or result in different habits in consumer behavior, such as the desire to attend a movie, plan a spa day, or remain inside. A rainy day might cause consumers to stream a movie rather than venture out to shop. Retailers can also use weather data in combination with demographic and sales data to personalize communications or sales in specific geographical areas.

A-3 Data Management

Walmart processes huge amounts of internal and external data every hour, 24/7. The company collects transactional data from its approximately 245 million customers per week, analyzes the nearly 300,000 social media mentions per week, and collects data from 200 other sources.[10] Walmart might collect weather data or data about local area events to promote certain products or they might use the data to determine strategic pricing for different geographic regions. They also rely on economic data and social media data to help design solutions to other problems. Walmart's massive amount of data is considered big data, which was introduced in Chapter 9. Big data requires special tools to manage, process, and analyze the massive amounts of data. In the case of Walmart, the company has created a data management system that helps them improve marketing decisions. The proper management of data creates an efficient method for employees throughout the company to access the data and efficiently solve business problems.

To create value from big data, an integration process that combines three stages is executed: extract data, transform data, and load data. The process, referred to as **ETL**, *extracts* data from the original source, *transforms* the data into a usable format, and *loads* the data into a system designated for storing data. Multichannel retailers rely on this process to integrate customer data from multiple channels, sort records, and provide a more complete profile of customers. ETL enables data that are complex and dynamic to be collected and integrated from various sources. Integrating data from these different sources improves the measurement of market potential, and marketing analytics software uses data to develop new insights, identify business trends, and discover opportunities.

A-3a Databases and Data Warehousing

With technology enhancements and collaboration between the marketing and information technology departments, the same guidance is now applied to understand databases and data warehousing. Although marketers may not be responsible for maintaining these systems, they should have an understanding of the terminology and processes.

ETL integration process that creates value from big data through extracting the data, transforming the data, and loading the data

Table A.1 Relational Database Example

Record Number	Customer ID	Purchase Amount	Products Purchased	Name
1	4	55	2	Liang
2	1	78	5	Marco
3	2	17	1	Katrina
4	3	104	6	Hugo

A **database** is a collection of data that is organized for efficient retrieval and analysis by people throughout a company. These systems store, manage, and track current business information. Recent CRM transactions, such as customer names and recent purchase information, are commonly stored in **relational databases** (Table A.1). These types of databases are organized into structured tables that contain neatly separated rows and columns.

A-3b Data Warehouse

Although companies often use databases to store current data such as customer transactions that occurred in a particular week and to monitor events in real time, data that represents previous points in time and multiple sources are often contained in a data warehouse. A **data warehouse** is a centralized storage area that includes historical data from multiple databases used by different departments throughout the company. The data warehouse stores a combination of data relating to areas such as customers, sales, human resources, and financial data. Data warehouses are structured for simplicity, yet offer powerful, high-speed querying performance for historical data analysis.

A-4 Bridging the Gap Between Data and Business Needs

Similar to the marketing research process introduced in Chapter 9, there is an established method that is commonly used when engaging in marketing analytics initiatives.

---

database collection of data that is organized for efficient retrieval and analysis

relational database collection of data relating to customer relationship management transactions

data warehouse centralized storage area that includes historical data from multiple databases

It is a sequence of six stages to guide data analysis:

1. Business understanding
2. Data understanding
3. Data preparation
4. Data modeling
5. Evaluation of results
6. Deployment of a plan

It is important for marketers to first understand the business situation when applying this method since data analysis is dependent on the type of questions that need to be answered. Researchers cannot use customer age, for example, to answer questions about weather patterns and purchase history.

A-4a Marketing Analytics Tools and Techniques: Application in Marketing

Once there is a complete understanding of the business and available data, the information can be used with the correct analytics technique to answer marketing questions. It might seem unlikely that you will need to understand marketing analytics techniques. But if you pursue a marketing career, you will likely be expected to know something about analytics techniques. Marketing analytics is increasingly being used by companies to make decisions and improve their operations.

Analytics techniques vary in complexity and are often classified as producing results that are descriptive, predictive, or prescriptive. *Descriptive analytics* are explanatory and provide results such as how many products are sold each day or how often customers visit a website. *Predictive analytics* assists companies in forecasting what is likely to occur in the future, such as how customers will respond to certain products or whether a customer might decide to purchase from a competitor. Companies also use *prescriptive analytics* to identify optimal business outcomes, such as knowing what pricing approaches to use to achieve increased sales or reduce costs.

A-4b Marketing Analytics

Marketing analytics includes a variety of statistical techniques that can be categorized into supervised or unsupervised learning. *Supervised learning* is when an output has been determined for analysis. Let's say you are interested in why customers remain loyal to a particular company. Why would a customer decide to continue purchasing from the company versus seeking a competitor's alternative? When you use marketing analytics, you specify an input for supervised learning, such as whether customers have remained loyal to your business or have started buying from a competitor. The objective is to determine whether the customer's decision to stay or leave is based on their perceptions of the quality of products, product pricing, loyalty toward the brand, or something else. On the other hand, *unsupervised learning* is when there is no designated outcome. A company might want to understand how customer markets are segmented. What similarities do customers share and how are they clustered together by needs and wants? When we discuss advanced analytics, we are referring to a broad concept used to describe quantitative analysis techniques that use high-speed technology and processing. We now describe a few examples of advanced analytics and how marketers can use insights to make better decisions.

Market Basket Analysis

Are certain products most frequently purchased together? For example, when a customer purchases cereal, do they also purchase milk? Market basket analysis determines, for example, the strength of association between the likelihood that cereal and milk will be purchased at the same time. Market basket techniques use association rules to detect products that are commonly purchased together.

Understanding that the purchase of one item might lead to the purchase of another item is helpful to marketers. Market basket analysis might also take into consideration seasonal baskets of behavior as a response to anticipated weather-related events, such as snow or hurricanes. Retailers can use this information to maintain levels of inventory that ensure that items are always on the shelf, determine product placement on store shelves or websites, and identify how a customer might respond to a coupon.

Social Media Network Analytics

Who are the influencers of the social media group? Do subgroups exist in social networks? Are messages being viewed or shared? What is the number of unique or return visitors? What is the length of follower comments? Social media are used to generate brand awareness, brand engagement, and word of mouth. Social networks or people participating in social media have the potential to provide an immediate return by rapidly increasing conversations about the brand. In general, social media network analytics help discover basic performance metrics such as how many likes a post possesses or how frequently a person responds to posts. However, measures such as centrality can identify more complex relationships such as trends and clusters of people that are connected.

Web Analytics

What factors are attracting visitors to the website? Are email campaigns highlighting seasonal sales and driving people to the site? How are visitors navigating through the website? How long are visitors spending on the website before converting to a sale or leaving? Companies dedicate substantial budgets to driving traffic to their websites, where a significant number of people visit each day. Web analytics offers companies an understanding of basic visitor behavior through click stream and customer browsing behavior.

Results from web analytics provide insights into whether companies should refocus efforts on driving visitors to their website or which webpage designs result in more online purchases. Attracting customers to a website is one way to expose them to more information about products and services. Whether customers visit websites to investigate products or to actually make purchases, understanding their behavior is valuable as the company plans future digital initiatives. Tools such as Google Analytics, Adobe Analytics, and Adobe Target have been developed to comprehensively analyze website performance.

A-4c Marketing Metrics

Acquiring and retaining customers is necessary to achieve financial success. Resources are used to attract new customers and retain loyal customers. Measuring *customer acquisition costs (CAC)* helps companies determine whether resources associated with gaining customers result in a return on investment. If you watch *Shark Tank,* you are familiar with the "sharks" frequently asking about what types of marketing the companies use and the customer acquisition costs. How much are they really spending to gain a single customer? Understanding customer acquisition costs can help companies determine whether they are spending too much to acquire customers or too little. Marketing spending that is not acquiring customers should be eliminated or allocated to other marketing opportunities.

When the company has acquired good customers, it should focus on managing those relationships to increase satisfaction and achieve loyalty. The greater the satisfaction and loyalty, the more likely a customer is to remain with the company. *Customer retention rate* and *churn ratios* provide an understanding of the company's ability to retain customers; they also identify customers at risk of leaving.

The *customer retention rate,* or the percent of customers that have been retained within a certain time frame, is calculated as:

[(The number of customers at the end of a specified period − the number of new customers acquired during the period) ÷ the number of customers at the start of the period] × 100.

For example, if a taco shop started the month with 1,000 customers, ended the month with 950 customers, and acquired 100 new customers during that month, the customer retention rate would be calculated as follows:

$$\text{Customer retention rate} = \frac{950 - 100}{1,000} \times 100 = 85\%$$

Customer churn is when a customer ceases to make purchases. Although companies might include other variables, a simple measure of customer churn within a given period (month) can be measured as:

(The number of customers lost last month ÷ the total customers at the beginning of that month) × 100.

If the taco shop mentioned previously started the month with 1,000 customers and lost 150 customers during that month, the customer churn would be calculated as follows:

$$\text{Customer churn rate} = \frac{150}{1,000} \times 100 = 15\%$$

Companies that increase acquisition and reduce churn improve the value over the lifetime that a customer remains a customer.

The measure of *customer lifetime value (CLV)* is focused on the long term, future relationship with a customer. Profits generated by a customer over their lifetime can be useful to companies in assessing the value of the relationship. Is the cost of acquiring and maintaining the relationship worth the investment? Although it might be surprising, companies sometimes stop pursuing relationships when discovering that they are no longer valuable. As the customer's lifetime value decreases, so does the company's financial performance. Thus, CLV also provides companies with information on forecasting future financial performance. The CLV relies on several values. First, companies should know the gross margin of a customer—the sales revenue minus the cost of the service to the company. Next, companies should have an idea of the acquisition cost of each customer and how many customers are being retained. Finally, companies understand the time value of money. That is, the value of money today is worth more than it will be next year. Therefore, companies determine a discount rate to reflect this difference in value.

As this appendix shows, big data and data analytics have important implications for marketers. The vast amounts of data that marketers collect allow them to better understand consumers, their motivations, and their purchase habits. Marketers can use this knowledge to create marketing mixes that better meet the wants and needs of their consumers, thereby increasing customer satisfaction and profits from the company.

Glossary

A

80/20 principle a principle holding that 20 percent of all customers generate 80 percent of the demand

absolute advantage when a country can produce a product or service at a lower cost than any other country or when it is the only country that can provide the product or service

accessory equipment goods, such as portable tools and office equipment, which are less expensive and shorter-lived than major equipment

advanced robotics devices that act largely or partially autonomously, that interact physically with people or their environment, and that are capable of modifying their behavior based on sensor data

advergaming placing advertising messages in web-based, mobile, console, or handheld video games to advertise or promote a product, service, organization, or issue

advertising appeal a reason for a person to buy a product

advertising campaign a series of related advertisements focusing on a common theme, slogan, and set of advertising appeals

advertising impersonal, one-way mass communication about a product or organization that is paid for by a marketer

advertising objective a specific communication task that a campaign should accomplish for a specified target audience during a specified period

advertising response function a phenomenon in which spending for advertising and sales promotion increases sales or market share up to a certain level but then produces diminishing returns

advocacy advertising a form of advertising in which an organization expresses its views on controversial issues or responds to media attacks

agents and brokers wholesaling intermediaries who do not take title to a product, but facilitate its sale from producer to end user by representing retailers, wholesalers, or manufacturers

AIDA concept a model that outlines the process for achieving promotional goals in terms of stages of consumer involvement with the message; the acronym stands for attention, interest, desire, and action

applied research research that attempts to develop new or improved products

artificial intelligence (AI) the computer science area focused on making machines that can simulate human intelligence processes

aspirational reference group a group that someone would like to join

assurance the knowledge and courtesy of employees and their ability to convey trust

atmosphere the overall impression conveyed by a store's physical layout, decor, and surroundings

audience selectivity the ability of an advertising medium to reach a precisely defined market

automated vehicles cars, trucks, or other ground transportation modes for which human drivers are not required to take control to safely operate the vehicle

automatic vending the use of machines to offer goods for sale

B

back stock inventory held in reserve for potential future sale in a retailer's storeroom or stockroom

bait pricing a price tactic that tries to get consumers into a store through false or misleading price advertising and then uses high-pressure selling to persuade consumers to buy more expensive merchandise

balance of payments the difference between a country's total payments to other countries and its total receipts from other countries

balance of trade the difference between the value of a country's exports and the value of its imports over a given period

base price the general price level at which the company expects to sell the good or service

basic research pure research that aims to confirm an existing theory or to learn more about a concept or phenomenon

basing-point pricing a price tactic that charges freight from a given (basing) point, regardless of the city from which the goods are shipped

beacon a device that sends out connecting signals to customers' smartphones and tablets to bring them into a retail store or improve their shopping experience

behavioral norms standards of proper or acceptable behavior. Several modes of social control are important to marketing

behavioral segmentation the process of grouping customers based on the behaviors they exhibit, including what they buy, where they buy, when they buy, and how they buy

behavioral targeting (BT) a form of observation marketing research that combines a consumer's online activity with psychographic and demographic profiles compiled in databases

benefit segmentation the process of grouping customers into market segments according to the benefits they seek from the product

big data analytics the process of discovering patterns in large data sets for the purposes of extracting knowledge and understanding human behavior

big data the discovery, interpretation, and communication of meaningful patterns in data

big data the exponential growth in the volume, variety, and velocity of information and the development of complex, new tools to analyze and create meaning from such data

big data the rapidly collected and difficult-to-process large-scale data sets that have recently emerged and push the limits of current analytical capability

blockchain a digital ledger in which transactions are made and recorded chronologically and publicly

blog a publicly accessible web page that functions as an interactive journal, whereby readers can post comments on the author's entries

brainstorming the process of getting a group to think of unlimited ways to vary a product or solve a problem

brand a name, term, symbol, design, or combination thereof that identifies a seller's products and differentiates them from competitors' products

brand cannibalization the reduction of sales for one brand as the result of the introduction of a new product or promotion of a current product by another brand

brand equity the value of a company or brand name

brand loyalty consistent preference for one brand over all others

brand mark the elements of a brand that cannot be spoken

brand name that part of a brand that can be spoken, including letters, words, and numbers

break-even analysis a method of determining what sales volume must be reached before total revenue equals total costs

business analysis the second stage of the screening process, where preliminary figures for demand, cost, sales, and profitability are calculated

business marketing (industrial, business-to-business, B-to-B, or B2B marketing) marketing goods and services to individuals and organizations for purposes other than personal consumption

business processes bundles of interconnected activities that stretch across firms in the supply chain

business product (industrial product) a product used to manufacture other goods or services, to facilitate an organization's operations, or to resell to other customers

business services expense items that do not become part of a final product

business-to-business online exchange an electronic trading floor that provides companies with integrated links to their customers and suppliers

buyer for export an intermediary in the global market that assumes all ownership risks and sells globally for its own account

buying center all the people in an organization who become involved in the purchase decision

C

campaign management developing product or service offerings customized for the appropriate customer segment and then pricing and communicating these offerings for the purpose of enhancing customer relationships

cannibalization a situation that occurs when sales of a new product cut into sales of a firm's existing products

capital intensive using more capital than labor in the production process

captive brand a brand manufactured by a third party for an exclusive retailer, without evidence of that retailer's affiliation

cash cow in the portfolio matrix, a business unit that generates more cash than it needs to maintain its market share

cash discount a price reduction offered to a consumer, an industrial user, or a marketing intermediary in return for prompt payment of a bill

casuist ethical theory ethical theory that compares a current ethical dilemma with examples of similar ethical dilemmas and their outcomes

category killer a large discount store that specializes in a single line of merchandise and becomes the dominant retailer in its category

cause-related marketing the cooperative marketing efforts between a for-profit firm and a nonprofit organization

central-location telephone (CLT) facility a specially designed phone room used to conduct telephone interviewing

chain store a store that is part of a group of the same stores owned and operated by a single organization

channel a medium of communication—such as a voice, radio, or newspaper—for transmitting a message

channel members all parties in the marketing channel who negotiate with one another, buy and sell products, and facilitate the change of ownership between buyer and seller in the course of moving the product from the manufacturer into the hands of the final consumer

click-and-collect the practice of buying something online and then traveling to a physical store location to take delivery of the merchandise

closed-ended question an interview question that asks the respondent to make a selection from a limited list of responses

cloud computing the practice of using remote network servers to store, manage, and process data

co-branding placing two or more brand names on a product or its package

code of ethics a guideline to help marketing managers and other employees make better decisions

cognitive dissonance inner tension that a consumer experiences after recognizing an inconsistency between behavior and values or opinions

cold calling a form of lead generation in which the salesperson approaches potential buyers without any prior knowledge of the prospects' needs or financial status

commercialization the decision to market a product

communication the process by which we exchange or share meaning through a common set of symbols

comparative advertising a form of advertising that compares two or more specifically named or shown competing brands on one or more specific attributes

competitive advantage a set of unique features of a company and its products that are perceived by the target market as significant and superior to those of the competition

competitive advantage one or more unique aspects of an organization that cause target consumers to patronize that firm rather than competitors

competitive advertising a form of advertising designed to influence demand for a specific brand

component parts either finished items ready for assembly or products that need very little processing before becoming part of some other product

Comprehensive and Progressive Agreement for Trans-Pacific Partnership (CPTPP) a trade agreement between Canada and 10 Asia-Pacific countries, which include: Australia, Brunei, Darussalam, Chile, Japan, Malaysia, Mexico, New Zealand, Peru, Singapore, and Vietnam

concentrated targeting strategy a strategy used to select one segment of a market for targeting marketing efforts

concept test a test to evaluate a new-product idea, usually before any prototype has been created

connected self-schema a perspective whereby a consumer perceives themself as an integral part of a group

consumer behavior processes a consumer uses to make purchase decisions, as well as to use and dispose of purchased goods or services; also includes factors that influence purchase decisions and product use

consumer behavior processes a consumer uses to make purchase decisions, as well as to use and dispose of purchased goods or services; also includes factors that influence purchase decisions and product use

consumer decision-making process a five-step process consumers use when buying goods or services

consumer penalty an extra fee paid by the consumer for violating the terms of the purchase agreement

consumer product a product bought to satisfy an individual's personal wants or needs

Consumer Product Safety Commission (CPSC) a federal agency established to protect the health and safety of consumers in and around their homes

consumer sales promotion promotion activities targeted to the ultimate consumer market

content marketing a strategic marketing approach that focuses on creating and distributing content that is valuable, relevant, and consistent

continuous media schedule a media scheduling strategy in which advertising is run steadily throughout the advertising period; used for products in the later stages of the product life cycle

contract manufacturing private- label manufacturing by a foreign company

control provides the mechanisms for evaluating marketing results in light of the plan's objectives and for correcting actions that do not help the organization reach those objectives within budget guidelines

convenience sample a form of nonprobability sample using respondents who are convenient or readily accessible to the researcher—for example, employees, friends, or relatives

convenience store a miniature supermarket, carrying only a limited line of high-turnover convenience goods

cooperative advertising an arrangement in which the manufacturer and the retailer split the costs of advertising the manufacturer's brand

core service the most basic benefit the consumer is buying

corporate blogs blogs that are sponsored by a company or one of its brands and maintained by one or more of the company's employees

corporate social responsibility (CSR) a business's concern for society's welfare

cost competitive advantage being the low-cost competitor in an industry while maintaining satisfactory profit margins

cost per click the cost associated with a consumer clicking on a display or banner ad

cost per contact (cost per thousand [CPM]) the cost of reaching one member of the target market

countertrade a form of trade in which all or part of the payment for goods or services is in the form of other goods or services

countervailing duty a tax on imported goods to offset a subsidy or other financial assistance given to a foreign exporter by its government that enables the foreign exporter to sell at an artificially low price in the global marketplace

coupon a certificate that entitles a consumers to an immediate price reduction when the product is purchased

credence quality a characteristic that consumers may have difficulty assessing even after purchase because they do not have the necessary knowledge or experience

crisis management a coordinated effort to handle all the effects of unfavorable publicity or another unexpected unfavorable event

cross-tabulation a method of analyzing data that lets the analyst look at the responses to one question in relation to the responses to one or more other questions

crowdsourcing using consumers to develop and market products

culture the set of values, norms, attitudes, and other meaningful symbols that shape human behavior and the artifacts, or products, of that behavior as they are transmitted from one generation to the next

cumulative quantity discount a deduction from list price that applies to the buyer's total purchases made during a specific period

customer relationship management (CRM) a company-wide business strategy designed to optimize profitability, revenue, and customer satisfaction by focusing on highly defined and precise customer groups

customer relationship management (CRM) process allows companies to prioritize their marketing focus on different customer groups according to each group's long-term value to the company or supply chain

customer satisfaction customers' evaluation of a good or service in terms of whether it has met their needs and expectations

customer service management process presents a multicompany, unified response system to the customer whenever complaints, concerns, questions, or comments are voiced

customer value the relationship between benefits and the sacrifice necessary to obtain those benefits

customer-centric a philosophy under which the company customizes its product and service offerings based on data generated through interactions between the customer and the company

D

decline stage a long-run drop in sales

decoding interpretation of the language and symbols sent by the source through a channel

demand management process seeks to align supply and demand throughout the supply chain by anticipating customer requirements at each level and creating demand-related plans of action prior to actual customer purchases

demand the quantity of a product that will be sold in the market at various prices for a specified period

demand-supply integration (DSI) a supply chain operational philosophy focused on integrating the supply-management and demand-generating functions of an organization

demographic segmentation segmenting markets by age, gender, income, ethnic background, and household life cycle

demography the study of people's vital statistics, such as age, race and ethnicity, and location

deontological theory ethical theory that states that people should adhere to their obligations and duties when analyzing an ethical dilemma

department store a store housing several departments under one roof

derived demand the demand for business products

destination store a store that consumers purposely plan to visit prior to shopping

development the stage in the product development process in which a prototype is developed and a marketing strategy is outlined

diffusion the process by which the adoption of an innovation spreads

digital channels electronic pathways that allow products and related information to flow from producer to consumer

digital distribution includes any kind of product or service that can be distributed electronically, whether over traditional forms such as fiber-optic cable or through satellite transmission of electronic signals

digitalization the use of digital technologies to change a business model and provide new revenue or value

direct channel a distribution channel in which producers sell directly to consumers

direct mail the delivery of advertising or marketing material to recipients of postal or electronic mail

direct marketing (DM) techniques used to get consumers to make a purchase from their home, office, or other nonretail setting

direct retailing the selling of products by representatives who work door-to-door, office-to-office, or at home sales parties

discount store a retailer that competes on the basis of low prices, high turnover, and high volume

diversification a strategy of increasing sales by introducing new products into new markets

diversity people's race, religion, gender, ethnicity, nationality, socioeconomic status, age, and abilities

dog in the portfolio matrix, a business unit that has low growth potential and a small market share

Dominican Republic-Central America Free Trade Agreement (CAFTA-DR) a trade agreement instituted in 2005 that includes Costa Rica, the Dominican Republic, El Salvador, Guatemala, Honduras, Nicaragua, and the United States

drones unmanned aerial vehicles that can be controlled remotely or can fly autonomously when executing a task

drop and shop a system used by several retailers that allows customers to bring used products for return or donation at the entrance of the store

drugstore a retail store that stocks pharmacy-related products and services as its main draw

dual or multiple distribution the use of two or more channels to distribute the same product to target markets

dumping the sale of an exported product at a price lower than that charged for the same or a like product in the "home" market of the exporter

dynamic pricing the ability to change prices very quickly, often in real time using software programs

E

earned media a category of promotional tactic based on a public relations or publicity model that gets customers talking about products or services

elastic demand a situation in which consumer demand is sensitive to changes in price

elasticity of demand consumers' responsiveness or sensitivity to changes in price

empathy caring, individualized attention to customers

empowerment delegation of authority to solve customers' problems quickly—usually by the first person the customer notifies regarding a problem

encoding the conversion of a sender's ideas and thoughts into a message, usually in the form of words or signs

environmental scanning collection and interpretation of information about forces, events, and relationships in the external environment that may affect the future of the organization or the implementation of the marketing plan

environmental scanning the continual collection and evaluation of environmental information to identify market opportunities and threats

environmentalism a concern about, and action aimed at protecting the environment

equity fairness in procedures, processes, and distribution of resources

ethics the moral principles or values that generally govern the conduct of an individual or a group

ethnicity shared cultural characteristics such as language, ancestry, practices, and beliefs

ethnographic research the study of human behavior in its natural context; involves observation of behavior and physical setting

European Union (EU) a free trade zone encompassing 27 European countries

evaluation gauging the extent to which the marketing objectives have been achieved during the specified time period

evoked set (consideration set) a group of brands resulting from an information search from which a buyer can choose

exchange people giving up something in order to receive something else they would rather have

exchange rate the price of one country's currency in terms of another country's currency

exchange utility the increased value of a product that is created as its ownership is transferred

exclusive distribution distribution to only one or a few dealers within a given area

executive interview a type of survey that usually involves interviewing business people at their offices concerning industrial products or services

experience curves curves that show costs declining at a predictable rate as experience with a product increases

experience quality a characteristic that can be assessed only after use

experiment a method of gathering primary data in which the researcher alters one or more variables while observing the effects of those alterations on another variable

export agent an intermediary who acts like a manufacturer's agent for the exporter; the export agent lives in the foreign market

export broker an intermediary who plays the traditional broker's role by bringing buyer and seller together

exporting selling domestically produced products to buyers in other countries

express warranty a written guarantee

extensive decision making the most complex type of consumer decision making, used when buying an unfamiliar, expensive product or an infrequently bought item; requires use of several criteria for evaluating options and much time for seeking information

external information search the process of seeking information in the outside environment

extranet a private electronic network that links a company with its suppliers and customers

F

factory outlet an off-price retailer that is owned and operated by a manufacturer

family branding marketing several different products under the same brand name

Federal Trade Commission (FTC) a federal agency empowered to prevent persons or corporations from using unfair methods of competition in commerce

feedback the receiver's response to a message

field service firm a firm that specializes in interviewing respondents on a subcontracted basis

fixed cost a cost that does not change as output is increased or decreased

flexible pricing (variable pricing) a price tactic in which different customers pay different prices for essentially the same merchandise bought in equal quantities

flighted media schedule a media scheduling strategy in which ads are run heavily every other month or every two weeks to achieve a greater impact with an increased frequency and reach at those times

floating exchange rates a system in which prices of different currencies move up and down based on the demand for and the supply of each currency

floor stock inventory displayed for sale to customers

FOB origin pricing a price tactic that requires the buyer to absorb the freight costs from the shipping point ("free on board")

focus group 7 to 10 people who participate in a group discussion led by a moderator

follow-up the final step of the selling process, in which the salesperson ensures delivery schedules are met, goods or services perform as promised, and the buyers' employees are properly trained to use the products

Food and Drug Administration (FDA) a federal agency charged with enforcing regulations against selling and distributing adulterated, misbranded, or hazardous food and drug products

Foreign Corrupt Practices Act (FCPA) a law that prohibits U.S. corporations from making illegal payments to public officials of foreign governments to obtain business rights or to enhance their business dealings in those countries

foreign direct investment a business investment in a foreign country, either by establishing business operations or by acquiring business assets in that country

form utility the elements of the composition and appearance of a product that make it desirable

frame error an error that occurs when a sample drawn from a population differs from the target population

franchise a relationship in which the business rights to operate and sell a product are granted by the franchisor to the franchisee

franchise a relationship in which the business rights to operate and sell a product are granted by the franchisor to the franchisee

franchisee an individual or business that is granted the right to sell another party's product

franchisor the originator of a trade name, product, methods of operation, and the like that grants operating rights to another party to sell its product

free trade policy of permitting individuals and businesses in a country to buy and sell in other countries without restrictions

freight absorption pricing a price tactic in which the seller pays all or part of the actual freight charges and does not pass them on to the buyer

frequency the number of times an individual is exposed to a given message during a specific period

frequent-buyer program a loyalty program in which loyal consumers are rewarded for making multiple purchases of a particular good or service

full-line discount store a discount store that carries a vast depth and breadth of product within a single product category

functional discount (trade discount) a discount to wholesalers and retailers for performing channel functions

G

gap model a model identifying five gaps that can cause problems in service delivery and influence customer evaluations of service quality

gender identity an individual's internal perception of their gender and how they label themselves

generic product name identifies a product by class or type and cannot be trademarked

geodemographic segmentation segmenting potential customers into neighborhood lifestyle categories

geographic segmentation segmenting markets by region of a country or the world, market size, market density, or climate

global brand a brand that obtains at least one-third of its earnings from outside its home country, is recognizable outside its home base of customers, and has publicly available marketing and financial data

global marketing marketing that targets markets on a worldwide scale

global marketing standardization production of uniform products that can be sold the same way all over the world

global vision recognizing and reacting to international marketing opportunities, using effective global marketing strategies, and being aware of threats from foreign competitors in all markets

gray marketing channels secondary channels that are unintended to be used by the producer, and which often flow illegally obtained or counterfeit product toward customers

green marketing the development and marketing of products designed to minimize negative effects on the physical environment or to improve the environment

greenwashing Adding a minimal number of green product attributes in order to promote it as green

greenwashing when a firm publicly feigns support for environmental or social sustainability but fails to live up to these standards in practice

gross domestic product (GDP) the total market value of all final goods and services produced in a country for a given time period

gross margin the amount of money the retailer makes as a percentage of sales after the cost of goods sold is subtracted

Group of Twenty (G-20) a forum for international economic development that promotes discussion between industrial and emerging-market countries on key issues related to global economic stability

growth stage the second stage of the product life cycle, when sales typically grow at an increasing rate; many competitors enter the market; large companies may start to acquire small pioneering firms; and profits are healthy

H

hedonic value a value that acts as an end in itself rather than as a means to an end

heterogeneity the variability of the inputs and outputs of services, which causes services to tend to be less standardized and uniform than goods

household life cycle (HLC) a series of stages determined by a combination of age, marital status, and the presence or absence of children

I

ideal self-image the way an individual would like to be perceived

implementation the process that turns a marketing plan into action assignments and ensures that these assignments are executed in a way that accomplishes the plan's objectives

implied warranty an unwritten guarantee that the good or service is fit for the purpose for which it was sold

inclusion the action of including people of diverse backgrounds

independent retailer a retailer owned by a single person or partnership and not operated as part of a larger retail institution

individual branding using different brand names for different products

inelastic demand a situation in which an increase or a decrease in price will not significantly affect demand for the product

inflation a measure of the decrease in the value of money, expressed as the percentage reduction in value since the previous year

infomercial a 30-minute or longer advertisement that looks more like a television talk show than a sales pitch

informational labeling a type of package labeling designed to help consumers make proper product selections and lower their cognitive dissonance after the purchase

innovation a product perceived as new by a potential adopter

inseparability the inability of the production and consumption of a service to be separated; consumers must be present during the production

inshoring returning production jobs to the United States

institutional advertising a form of advertising designed to enhance a company's image rather than promote a particular product

intangibility the inability of services to be touched, seen, tasted, heard, or felt in the same manner that goods can be sensed

integrated marketing communications (IMC) the careful coordination of all promotional messages for a product or a service to ensure the consistency of messages at every point at which a company has contact with the consumer

intensive distribution a form of distribution aimed at having a product available in every outlet where target customers might want to buy it

interaction the point at which a customer and a company representative exchange information and develop learning relationships

internal information search the process of recalling information stored in the memory

internal marketing treating employees as customers and developing systems and benefits that satisfy their needs

International Monetary Fund (IMF) an international organization that acts as a lender of last resort, providing loans to troubled nations, and also works to promote trade through financial cooperation

Internet of Things (IoT) a system of interrelated computing devices, mechanical and digital machines, objects, animals, or people that are connected and able to transfer data over a network without overt human effort

interpersonal communication direct, face-to-face communication between two or more people

introductory stage the full-scale launch of a new product into the marketplace

involvement the amount of time and effort a buyer invests in the search, evaluation, and decision processes of consumer behavior

J

jilting effect anticipation of receiving a highly desirable option only to have it become inaccessible

joint demand the demand for two or more items used together in a final product

joint venture when a domestic firm buys part of a foreign company or joins with a foreign company to create a new entity

K

keiretsu a network of interlocking corporate affiliates

keystoning the practice of marking up prices by 100 percent, or doubling the cost

knowledge management the process by which customer information is centralized and shared in order to enhance the relationship between customers and the organization

L

layout the internal design and configuration of a store's fixtures and products

lead generation (prospecting) identification of the firms and people most likely to buy the seller's offerings

lead qualification determination of a sales prospect's (1) recognized need, (2) buying power, and (3) receptivity and accessibility

leader pricing (loss-leader pricing) a price tactic in which a product is sold near or even below cost in the hope that shoppers will buy other items once they are in the store

learning a process that creates changes in behavior, immediate or expected, through experience and practice

licensing the legal process whereby a licensor allows another firm to use its manufacturing process, trademarks, patents, trade secrets, or other proprietary knowledge

limited decision making the type of decision making that requires a moderate amount of time for gathering information and deliberating about an unfamiliar brand in a familiar product category

location-based social networking sites websites that combine the fun of social networking with the utility of location-based GPS technology

loyalty marketing program a promotional program designed to build long-term, mutually beneficial relationships between a company and its key customers

M

machine learning (ML) an application of artificial intelligence that provides systems the ability to automatically learn and improve from experience without being explicitly programmed

macro-influencers people who have between 500,000 and 1,000,000 followers on social media platforms

major equipment (installations) capital goods such as large or expensive machines, mainframe computers, blast furnaces, generators, airplanes, and buildings

management decision problem a broad-based problem that uses marketing research for managers to take proper actions

manufacturer's brand the brand name of a manufacturer

manufacturing flow management process concerned with ensuring that firms in the supply chain have the needed resources to manufacture with flexibility and to move products through a multi-stage production process

market development a marketing strategy that entails attracting new customers to existing products

market opportunity analysis (MOA) the description and estimation of the size and sales potential of market segments that are of interest to the firm and the assessment of key competitors in these market segments

market orientation a philosophy that assumes that a sale does not depend on an aggressive sales force but rather on a customer's decision to purchase a product; it is synonymous with the marketing concept

market penetration a marketing strategy that tries to increase market share among existing customers

market share a company's product sales as a percentage of total sales for that industry

marketing audit a thorough, systematic, periodic evaluation of the objectives, strategies, structure, and performance of the marketing organization

marketing channel (channel of distribution) a set of interdependent organizations that eases the transfer of ownership as products move from producer to business user or consumer

marketing concept the idea that the social and economic justification for an organization's existence is the satisfaction of customer wants and needs while meeting organizational objectives

marketing mix (four Ps) a unique blend of product, place (distribution), promotion, and pricing strategies designed to produce mutually satisfying exchanges with a target market

marketing myopia defining a business in terms of goods and services rather than in terms of the benefits customers seek

marketing objective a statement of what is to be accomplished through marketing activities

marketing plan a written document that acts as a guidebook of marketing activities for the marketing manager

marketing planning designing activities relating to marketing objectives and the changing marketing environment

marketing research objective the specific information needed to solve a marketing research problem; the objective should be to provide insightful decision-making information

marketing research problem determining what information is needed and how that information can be obtained efficiently and effectively

marketing research the process of planning, collecting, and analyzing data relevant to a marketing decision

marketing strategy the activities of selecting and describing one or more target markets and developing and maintaining a marketing mix that will produce mutually satisfying exchanges with target markets

marketing the activity, set of institutions, and processes for creating, communicating, delivering, and exchanging offerings that have value for customers, clients, partners, and society at large

marketing-controlled information source a product information source that originates with marketers promoting the product

markup pricing the cost of buying the product from the producer, plus amounts for profit and for expenses not otherwise accounted for

Maslow's hierarchy of needs a method of classifying human needs and motivations into five categories in ascending order of importance: physiological, safety, social, esteem, and self-actualization

mass communication the communication of a concept or message to large audiences

mass customization a strategy that uses technology to deliver customized services on a mass basis

maturity stage a period during which sales increase at a slower rate

M-commerce the ability to conduct commerce using a mobile device for the purpose of buying or selling goods or services

measurement error an error that occurs when there is a difference between the information the researcher desires and the information the measurement process provides

media mix the combination of media to be used for a promotional campaign

media planning the series of decisions advertisers make regarding the selection and use of media, allowing the marketer to communicate the message optimally and cost-effectively to the target audience

media schedule designation of the media, the specific publications or programs, and the insertion dates of advertising

media sharing sites websites that allow users to upload and distribute multimedia content like videos and photos

medium the channel used to convey a message to a target market

mega-influencers often celebrities who have more than a million followers on social media platforms

merchant wholesaler an institution that buys goods from manufacturers and resells them to businesses, government agencies, and other wholesalers or retailers and that receives and takes title to goods, stores them in its own warehouses, and later ships them

MERCOSUR the largest Latin American trade agreement; full members include Argentina, Brazil, Paraguay, Uruguay. Associate members are Suriname, Guyana, Chile, Colombia, Ecuador, Peru, and Bolivia

microblogs blogs that have shorter posts than traditional blogs

micro-influencers people who have a smaller number of followers people who have a smaller number of followers on social media with 10,000–50,000 followers, but are still influential in specific areas

microtargeting the use of direct marketing techniques that employ highly detailed data analytics to isolate potential customers with great precision

mid-tier influencers people who have between 50,000 and 500,000 followers on social media platforms

mission statement a statement of the firm's business based on a careful analysis of benefits sought by present and potential customers and an analysis of existing and anticipated environmental conditions

modified rebuy a situation in which the purchaser wants some change in the original good or service

modular a standardized form of component parts manufacturing designed so the parts are easily replaced or interchanged

moral relativism a theory of time-and-place ethics; that is, the belief that ethical truths depend on the individuals and groups holding them

morals the rules people develop as a result of cultural values and norms

motive a driving force that causes a person to take action to satisfy specific needs

multidomestic strategy when multinational firms enable individual subsidiaries to compete independently in domestic markets

multinational corporation a company that is heavily engaged in international trade, beyond exporting and importing

multiplier effect (accelerator principle) phenomenon in which a small increase or decrease in consumer demand can produce a much larger change in demand for the facilities and equipment needed to make the consumer product

multisegment targeting strategy a strategy that chooses two or more well-defined market segments and develops a distinct marketing mix for each

mystery shoppers researchers posing as customers to gather observational data about a store

N

nano-influencers people who have the smallest number of followers on social media with 1,000–10,000 followers

nearshoring the transfer of an outsourced activity from a distant to a nearby country

need recognition result of an imbalance between actual and desired states

needs assessment a determination of the customer's specific needs and wants and the range of options they have for satisfying them

negotiation the process during which both the salesperson and the prospect offer special concessions in an attempt to arrive at a sales agreement

networking a process of finding out about potential clients from friends, business contacts, coworkers, acquaintances, and fellow members in professional and civic organizations

neuromarketing a field of marketing that studies the body's responses to marketing stimuli

new buy a situation requiring the purchase of a product for the first time

new-product strategy a plan that links the new-product development process with the objectives of the marketing department, the business unit, and the corporation

niche competitive advantage the advantage achieved when a firm seeks to target and effectively serve a small segment of the market

niche one segment of a market

noise anything that interferes with, distorts, or slows down the transmission of information

nonaspirational reference group a group with which an individual does not want to associate

noncorporate blogs independent blogs that are not associated with the marketing efforts of any particular company or brand

noncumulative quantity discount a deduction from list price that applies to a single order rather than to the total volume of orders placed during a certain period

non-marketing-controlled information source a product information source that is not associated with advertising or promotion

nonprobability sample any sample in which little or no attempt is made to get a representative cross section of the population

nonprofit organization an organization that exists to achieve some goal other than the usual business goals of profit, market share, or return on investment

nonprofit organization marketing the effort by nonprofit organizations to bring about mutually satisfying exchanges with target markets

nonstore retailing shopping without visiting a store

nontraditional channels nonphysical channels that facilitate the unique market access of products and services

norm a value or attitude deemed acceptable by a group

North American Industry Classification System (NAICS) a detailed numbering system developed by the United States, Canada, and Mexico to classify North American business establishments by their main production processes

nudge a small intervention that can change a person's behavior

O

observation research a research method that relies on four types of observation: people watching people, people watching an activity, machines watching people, and machines watching an activity

odd-even pricing (psychological pricing) a price tactic that uses odd-numbered prices to connote bargains and even-numbered prices to imply quality

off-price retailer a retailer that sells at prices 25 percent or more below traditional department store prices because it pays cash for its stock and usually doesn't ask for return privileges

on-demand marketing delivering relevant experiences, integrated across both physical and virtual environments, throughout the consumer's decision and buying process

e-tailing (online retailing) a type of shopping available to consumers via access to the internet

open-ended question an interview question that encourages an answer phrased in the respondent's own words

opinion leader an individual who influences the opinions of others

optimizers business customers who consider numerous suppliers (both familiar and unfamiliar), solicit bids, and study all proposals carefully before selecting one

order cycle time the time delay between the placement of a customer's order and the customer's receipt of that order

order fulfillment process a highly integrated process, often requiring persons from multiple companies and multiple functions to come together and coordinate to create customer satisfaction at a given place and time

original equipment manufacturers (OEMs) individuals and organizations that buy business goods and incorporate them into the products they produce for eventual sale to other producers or to consumers

outsourcing (contract logistics) a manufacturer's or supplier's use of an independent third party to manage an entire function of the logistics system, such as transportation, warehousing, or order processing

outsourcing sending U.S. jobs abroad

owned media a new category of promotional tactic based on brands becoming publishers of their own content to maximize the brands' value to customers

P

Pacific Alliance a single region for the free movement of goods, services, investment, capital, and people between Chile, Colombia, Mexico, and Peru

paid media a category of promotional tactic based on the traditional advertising model, whereby a brand pays for media space

penetration pricing a pricing policy whereby a firm charges a relatively low price for a product when it is first rolled out as a way to reach the mass market

perceived value the value a consumer *expects* to obtain from a purchase

perception the process by which people select, organize, and interpret stimuli into a meaningful and coherent picture

perceptual mapping a means of displaying or graphing, in two or more dimensions, the location of products, brands, or groups of products in customers' minds

perishability the inability of services to be stored, warehoused, or inventoried

personal selling a purchase situation involving a personal, paid-for communication between two people in an attempt to influence each other

personality a way of organizing and grouping the consistencies of an individual's reactions to situations

persuasive labeling a type of package labeling that focuses on a promotional theme or logo; and consumer information is secondary

pioneering advertising a form of advertising designed to stimulate primary demand for a new product or product category

place utility the usefulness of a good or service as a function of the location at which it is made available

planned obsolescence the practice of modifying products so those that have already been sold become obsolete before they actually need replacement

planning the process of anticipating future events and determining strategies to achieve organizational objectives in the future

point of purchase (POP) display a promotional display set up at the retailer's location to build traffic, advertise the product, or induce impulse buying

point-of-sale interactions a touch point in stores or information kiosks that uses software to enable customers to easily provide information about themselves without feeling violated

pop culture the products and forms of expression and identity that are frequently encountered or widely accepted, commonly liked, or approved, and characteristic of a particular society at a given time

portfolio matrix a tool for allocating resources among products or strategic business units on the basis of relative market share and market growth rate

position the place a product, brand, or group of products occupies in consumers' minds relative to competing offerings

positioning developing a specific marketing mix to influence potential customers' overall perception of a brand, product line, or organization in general

preapproach a process that describes the "homework" that must be done by a salesperson before they contact a prospect

predatory pricing the practice of charging a very low price for a product with the intent of driving competitors out of business or out of a market

premium an extra item offered to the consumer, usually in exchange for some proof of purchase of the promoted product

price bundling marketing two or more products in a single package for a special price

price fixing an agreement between two or more firms on the price they will charge for a product

price lining the practice of offering a product line with several items at specific price points

price skimming a pricing policy whereby a firm charges a high introductory price, often coupled with heavy promotion

price strategy a basic, long-term pricing framework that establishes the initial price for a product and the intended direction for price movements over the product life cycle

price that which is given up in an exchange to acquire a good or service

primary data information that is collected for the first time; used for solving the particular problem under investigation

primary membership group a reference group with which people interact regularly in an informal, face-to-face manner, such as family, friends, and coworkers

principle of comparative advantage each country should specialize in the products or services that it can produce most readily and cheaply and trade those products or services for goods and services that foreign countries can produce most readily and cheaply

private brand a brand name owned by a wholesaler or a retailer

probability sample a sample in which every element in the population has a known statistical likelihood of being selected

problem child (question mark) in the portfolio matrix, a business unit that shows rapid growth but poor profit margins

processed materials products used directly in manufacturing other products

product advertising a form of advertising that touts the benefits of a specific good or service

product category all brands that satisfy a particular type of need

product development a marketing strategy that entails the creation of marketable new products; the process of converting applications for new technologies into marketable products

product development a marketing strategy that entails the creation of new products for present markets

product development and commercialization process includes the group of activities that facilitates the joint development and marketing of new offerings among a group of supply chain partner firms

product differentiation a positioning strategy that some firms use to distinguish their products from those of competitors

product everything, both favorable and unfavorable, that a person receives in an exchange

product item a specific version of a product that can be designated as a distinct offering among an organization's products

product life cycle (PLC) a concept that provides a way to trace the stages of a product's acceptance, from its introduction (birth) to its decline (death)

product line a group of closely related product items

product line depth the number of product items in a product line

product line extension adding additional products to an existing product line in order to compete more broadly in the industry

product mix all products that an organization sells

product mix width the number of product lines an organization offers

product modification changing one or more of a product's characteristics

product placement a public relations strategy that involves getting a product, service, or company name to appear in a movie, television show, radio program, magazine, newspaper, video game, video or audio clip, book, or commercial for another product, on the Internet, or at special events

product/service differentiation competitive advantage the provision of something that is unique and valuable to buyers beyond simply offering a lower price than that of the competition

production orientation a philosophy that focuses on the internal capabilities of the firm rather than on the desires and needs of the marketplace

profit revenue minus expenses

promotion communication by marketers that informs, persuades, and reminds potential buyers of a product to influence an opinion or elicit a response

promotional allowance (trade allowance) a payment to a dealer for promoting the manufacturer's products

promotional mix the combination of promotional tools—including advertising, public relations, personal selling, sales promotion, and social media—used to reach the target market and fulfill the organization's overall goals

promotional strategy a plan for the optimal use of the elements of promotion: advertising, public relations, personal selling, sales promotion, and social media

protectionism where a nation protects its home industries from foreign competitors by establishing artificial barriers, such as tariffs and quotas

psychographic segmentation segmenting markets based on personality, motives, lifestyles, and geodemographics

public relations the element in the promotional mix that evaluates public attitudes, identifies issues that may elicit public concern, and executes programs to gain public understanding and acceptance

public relations the marketing function that evaluates public attitudes, identifies areas within the organization the public may be interested in, and executes a program of action to earn public understanding and acceptance

public service advertisement (PSA) an announcement that promotes a program of a federal, state, or local government or of a nonprofit organization

publicity an effort to capture media attention, often initiated through press releases that further a corporation's public relations plans

publicity public information about a company, product, service, or issue appearing in the mass media as a news item

pull strategy a marketing strategy that stimulates consumer demand to obtain product distribution

pulsing media schedule a media scheduling strategy that uses continuous scheduling throughout the year coupled with a flighted schedule during the best sales periods

purchasing power a comparison of income versus the relative cost of a standard set of goods and services in different geographic areas

push money money offered to channel intermediaries to encourage them to "push" products—that is, to encourage other members of the channel to sell the products

push strategy a marketing strategy that uses aggressive personal selling and trade advertising to convince a wholesaler or a retailer to carry and sell particular merchandise

pyramid of corporate social responsibility a model that suggests corporate social responsibility is composed of economic, legal, ethical, and philanthropic responsibilities and that a firm's economic performance supports the entire structure

Q

quantity discount a price reduction offered to buyers buying in multiple units or above a specified dollar amount

quota a statement of the salesperson's sales goals, usually based on sales volume

R

random error an error that occurs when the selected sample is an imperfect representation of the overall population

random sample a sample arranged in such a way that every element of the population has an equal chance of being selected as part of the sample

raw materials unprocessed extractive or agricultural products, such as mineral ore, lumber, wheat, corn, fruits, vegetables, and fish

reach the number of target consumers exposed to a commercial at least once during a specific period, usually four weeks

real self-image the way an individual actually perceives themself

rebate a cash refund given for the purchase of a product during a specific period

rebate a cash refund given for the purchase of a product during a specific period

receiver the person who decodes a message

recession a period of economic activity characterized by negative growth, which reduces demand for goods and services

reciprocity a practice whereby business purchasers choose to buy from their own customers

reference group all of the formal and informal groups in society that influence an individual's purchasing behavior

referral a recommendation to a salesperson from a customer or business associate

relationship commitment a firm's belief that an ongoing relationship with another firm is so important that the relationship warrants maximum efforts at maintaining it indefinitely

relationship marketing a strategy that focuses on keeping and improving relationships with current customers

relationship selling (consultative selling) a sales practice that involves building, maintaining, and enhancing interactions with customers in order to develop long-term satisfaction through mutually beneficial partnerships

reliability the ability to perform a service dependably, accurately, and consistently

repositioning changing consumers' perceptions of a brand in relation to competing brands

research design specifies which research questions must be answered, how and when the data will be gathered, and how the data will be analyzed

reshoring the reinstitutionalization of a business process from an outsource location/country back to the original location for the purpose of gaining economic advantage

responsiveness the ability to provide prompt service

restaurant a retailer that provides both tangible products—food and drink—and valuable services—food preparation and presentation

retail channel omnification the reduction of multiple retail channel systems into a single, unified system for the purpose of creating efficiencies or saving costs

retailing all the activities directly related to the sale of goods and services to the ultimate consumer for personal, nonbusiness use

retailing mix a combination of the six Ps—product, promotion, place, price, presentation, and personnel—to sell goods and services to the ultimate consumer

return on investment (ROI) net profit after taxes divided by total assets

returns management process enables firms to manage volumes of returned product efficiently while minimizing returns-related costs and maximizing the value of the returned assets to the firms in the supply chain

revenue the price charged to customers multiplied by the number of units sold

reverse channels channels that enable customers to return products or components for reuse or remanufacturing

review sites websites that allow consumers to post, read, rate, and comment on opinions regarding all kinds of products and services

RFID radio-frequency identification; a device that uses radio waves as a means of locating a piece of inventory within a confined geographic space

routine response behavior the type of decision making exhibited by consumers buying frequently purchased, low-cost goods and services; requires little search and decision time

S

sales and operations planning (S&OP) a method companies use to align production with demand by merging tactical and strategic planning methods across functional areas of the business

sales orientation the belief that people will buy more goods and services if aggressive sales techniques are used and that high sales result in high profits

sales presentation a meeting in which the salesperson presents a sales proposal to a prospective buyer

sales process (sales cycle) the set of steps a salesperson goes through in a particular organization to sell a particular product or service

sales promotion marketing activities—other than personal selling, advertising, and public relations—that stimulate consumer buying and dealer effectiveness

sales promotion marketing communication activities other than advertising, personal selling, and public relations, in which a short-term incentive motivates consumers or members of the distribution channel to purchase a good or service immediately, either by lowering the price or by adding value

sales proposal a formal written document or professional presentation that outlines how the salesperson's product or service will meet or exceed the prospect's needs

sample a subset from a larger population

sampling a promotional program that allows the consumer the opportunity to try a product or service for free

sampling error an error that occurs when a sample somehow does not represent the target population

satisficers business customers who place an order with the first familiar supplier to satisfy product and delivery requirements

scaled-response question a closed-ended question designed to measure the intensity of a respondent's answer

scanner-based research a system for gathering information from a single group of respondents by continuously monitoring the advertising, promotion, and pricing they are exposed to and the things they buy

screening the first filter in the product development process, which eliminates ideas that are inconsistent with the organization's new-product strategy or are obviously inappropriate for some other reason

search quality a characteristic that can be easily assessed before purchase

seasonal discount a price reduction for buying merchandise out of season

seasonal media schedule a media scheduling strategy that runs advertising only during times of the year when the product is most likely to be used

secondary data data previously collected for any purpose other than the one at hand

secondary membership group a reference group with which people associate less consistently and more formally than a primary membership group, such as a club, professional group, or religious group

segmentation bases (variables) characteristics of individuals, groups, or organizations

selective distortion a process whereby a consumer changes or distorts information that conflicts with their feelings or beliefs

selective distribution a form of distribution achieved by screening dealers to eliminate all but a few in any single area

selective exposure a process whereby a consumer notices certain stimuli and ignores others

selective retention a process whereby a consumer remembers only that information that supports their personal beliefs

self-concept how consumers perceive themselves in terms of attitudes, perceptions, beliefs, and self-evaluations

self-service technologies (SST) technological interfaces that allow customers to provide themselves with products and/or services without the intervention of a service employee

sender the originator of the message in the communication process

separated self-schema a perspective whereby a consumer perceives themself as distinct and separate from others

service the result of applying human or mechanical efforts to people or objects

service the result of applying human or mechanical efforts to people or objects

sharing economy the way connected consumers exchange goods and services with each other through a digital marketplace

shop-at-home television network a specialized form of direct response marketing whereby television shows display merchandise, with the retail price, to home viewers

shopper analytics searching for and discovering meaningful patterns in shopper data for the purpose of fine-tuning, developing, or changing market offerings

shopper marketing understanding how one's target consumers behave as shoppers, in different channels and formats, and leveraging this intelligence to generate sales or other positive outcomes

showrooming the practice of examining merchandise in a physical retail location without purchasing it, and then shopping online for a better deal on the same item

simulated (laboratory) market testing the presentation of advertising and other promotional materials for several products, including a test product, to members of the product's target market

simultaneous product development a team-oriented approach to new-product development

single-price tactic a price tactic that offers all goods and services at the same price (or perhaps two or three prices)

social class a group of people in a society who are considered nearly equal in status or community esteem, who regularly socialize among themselves both formally and informally, and who share behavioral norms

social commerce a subset of e- commerce that involves the interaction and user contribution aspects of social online media to assist online buying and selling of products and services

social control any means used to maintain behavioral norms and regulate conflict

social media any tool or service that uses the Internet to facilitate conversations

social media monitoring the process of identifying and assessing what is being said about a company, individual, product, or brand

social media monitoring the use of automated tools to monitor online buzz, chatter, and conversations

social networking sites websites that allow individuals to connect—or network—with friends, peers, and business associates

social news sites websites that allow users to decide which content is promoted on a given website by voting that content up or down

socialization process how cultural values and norms are passed down to children

societal marketing orientation the idea that an organization exists not only to satisfy customer wants and needs and to meet organizational objectives but also to preserve or enhance individuals' and society's long-term best interests

specialty discount store a retail store that offers a nearly complete selection of single-line merchandise and uses self-service, discount prices, high volume, and high turnover

specialty store a retail store specializing in a given type of merchandise

sponsorship a public relations strategy in which a company spends money to support an issue, cause, or event that is consistent with corporate objectives, such as improving brand awareness or enhancing corporate image

stakeholder theory ethical theory stating that social responsibility is paying attention to the interest of every affected stakeholder in every aspect of a firm's operation

star in the portfolio matrix, a business unit that is a fast-growing market leader

status quo pricing a pricing objective that maintains existing prices or meets the competition's prices

stimulus any unit of input affecting one or more of the five senses: sight, smell, taste, touch, hearing

stimulus discrimination a learned ability to differentiate among similar products

stimulus generalization a form of learning that occurs when one response is extended to a second stimulus similar to the first

straight rebuy a situation in which the purchaser reorders the same goods or services without looking for new information or investigating other suppliers

strategic alliance (strategic partnership) a cooperative agreement between business firms

strategic business unit (SBU) a subgroup of a single business or collection of related businesses within the larger organization

strategic channel alliance a cooperative agreement between business firms to use the other's already established distribution channel

strategic planning the managerial process of creating and maintaining a fit between the organization's objectives and resources and the evolving market opportunities

subculture a homogeneous group of people who share elements of the overall culture as well as unique elements of their own group

supercenter a large retailer that stocks and sells a wide variety of merchandise including groceries, clothing, household goods, and other general merchandise

supermarket a large, departmentalized, self-service retailer that specializes in food and some nonfood items

supplementary services a group of services that support or enhance the core service

supplier relationship management process supports manufacturing flow by identifying and maintaining relationships with highly valued suppliers

supplies consumable items that do not become part of the final product

supply chain agility an operational strategy focused on creating inventory velocity and operational flexibility simultaneously in the supply chain

supply chain analytics data analyses that support the improved design and management of the supply chain

supply chain integration when multiple firms or business functions in a supply chain coordinate, their activities and processes so that they are seamlessly linked to one another in an effort to satisfy the customer

supply chain management (SCM) a management system that coordinates and integrates all of the activities performed by supply chain members into a seamless process, from the source to the point of consumption, resulting in enhanced customer and economic value

supply chain orientation a system of management practices that are consistent with a "systems thinking" approach

supply chain the connected chain of all of the business entities, both internal and external to the company, that perform or support the logistics function

supply chain traceability the degree to which a business is able to track a product's development through stages beginning with a raw material state and ending with delivery to the final consumer

supply the quantity of a product that will be offered to the market by a supplier at various prices for a specified period

surge pricing occurs in a fluid market, where demand changes rapidly, often hourly. When demand increases, so do prices and vice versa

survey research the most popular technique for gathering primary data, in which a researcher interacts with people to obtain facts, opinions, and attitudes

sustainability the idea that socially responsible companies will outperform their peers by focusing on the world's social problems and viewing them as opportunities to build profits and help the world at the same time

sustainable competitive advantage an advantage that cannot be copied by the competition

sustainable supply chain management a supply chain management philosophy that embraces the need for optimizing social and environmental costs in addition to financial costs

SWOT analysis identifying internal strengths (S) and weaknesses (W) and also examining external opportunities (O) and threats (T)

T

tangibles the physical evidence of a service, including the physical facilities, tools, and equipment used to provide the service

target market a group of people or organizations for which an organization designs, implements, and maintains a marketing mix intended to meet the needs of that group, resulting in mutually satisfying exchanges

teamwork collaborative efforts of people to accomplish common objectives

telemarketing the use of the telephone to sell directly to consumers

test marketing the limited introduction of a product and a marketing program to determine the reactions of potential customers in a market situation

the Regional Comprehensive Economic Partnership (RCEP) a trade agreement that began in 2022 with 15 member countries including Australia, Brunei, Cambodia, China, Indonesia, Japan, South Korea, Laos, Malaysia, Myanmar, New Zealand, the Philippines, Singapore, Thailand, and Vietnam, with seven of the countries also included in CPTPP

third-party logistics company (3PL) a firm that provides functional logistics services to others

three-dimensional printing (3DP) the creation of three-dimensional objects via an additive manufacturing (printing) technology that layers raw material into desired shapes

time utility the increase in customer satisfaction gained by making a good or service available at the appropriate time

touch points areas of a business where customers have contact with the company and from which the company can gather data

trade allowance a price reduction offered by manufacturers to intermediaries such as wholesalers and retailers

trade sales promotion promotion activities directed to members of the marketing channel, such as wholesalers and retailers

trademark the exclusive right to use a brand or part of a brand

triple bottom line the financial, social, and environmental effects of a firm's policies and actions that determine its viability as a sustainable organization

trust the condition that exists when one party has confidence in an exchange partner's reliability and integrity

two-part pricing a price tactic that charges two separate amounts to consume a single good or service

U

undifferentiated targeting strategy a marketing approach that views the market as one big market with no individual segments and thus uses a single marketing mix

unfair trade practice acts laws that prohibit wholesalers and retailers from selling below cost

uniform delivered pricing a price tactic in which the seller pays the actual freight charges and bills every purchaser an identical, flat freight charge

unique selling proposition a desirable, exclusive, and believable advertising appeal selected as the theme for a campaign

United States–Mexico–Canada Agreement (USMCA) free trade agreement between the United States, Mexico, and Canada which replaces the North American Free Trade Agreement (NAFTA)

universal product codes (UPCs) a series of thick and thin vertical lines (bar codes) readable by computerized optical scanners that represent numbers used to track products

universe the population from which a sample will be drawn

Uruguay Round a trade agreement to dramatically lower trade barriers worldwide and created the World Trade Organization (WTO)

used goods retailer a retailer whereby items purchased from one of the other types of retailers are resold to different customers

utilitarian ethical theory ethical theory that is founded on the ability to predict the consequences of an action

utilitarian value a value derived from a product or service that helps the consumer solve problems and accomplish tasks

V

value a personal assessment of the net worth one obtains from making a purchase, or the enduring belief that a specific mode of conduct is personally or socially preferable to another mode of conduct

value-based pricing setting the price at a level that seems to the customer to be a good price compared to the prices of other options

variable cost a cost that varies with changes in the level of output

virtue a character trait valued as being good

W

want recognition of an unfulfilled need and a product that will satisfy it

warehouse club a large, no-frills retailer that sells bulk quantities of merchandise to customers at volume discount prices in exchange for a periodic membership fee

warranty a confirmation of the quality or performance of a good or service

World Bank an international bank that offers low-interest loans, advice, and information to developing nations

World Trade Organization (WTO) a trade organization with 164 nations that replaced the General Agreement on Tariffs and Trade (GATT)

Z

zone pricing a modification of uniform delivered pricing that divides the United States (or the total market) into segments or zones and charges a flat freight rate to all customers in a given zone

Endnotes

Chapter 1

1. "Definition of Marketing," American Marketing Association, www.ama.org.com/AboutAMA/Pages/DefinitionofMarketing.aspx (accessed January 18, 2023).

2. Raymond Fabius and Sharon Phares, "Companies That Promote a Culture of Health, Safety, and Wellbeing Outperform in the Marketplace," https://journals.lww.com/joem/fulltext/2021/06000/companies_that_promote_a_culture_of_health,.2.aspx, https://journals.lww.com/joem/fulltext/2021/06000/companies_that_promote_a_culture_of_health,.2.aspx, June 2021.

3. Roula Amire, "Here are the 100 Best Companies to Work For According to nearly 1 Million Employees," https://www.greatplacetowork.com/press-releases/here-are-the-fortune-100-best-companies-to-work-for®-in-2022%2C-according-to-nearly-1-million-employees, April 11, 2021.

4. Philip Kotler and Kevin Lane Keller, *A Framework for Marketing Management*, 6th ed.

5. Joan Verdon, "Green Is the Hottest Color in the Toy Box, As Manufacturers Embrace Sustainability," https://www.forbes.com/sites/joanverdon/2020/02/26/green-is-the-hottest-color-in-the-toy-box-as-manufacturers-embrace-sustainability/?sh=3c13b90d6f76, February 26, 2020.

6. "Auto Dealer Service Departments Trying to Navigate Parts and Staffing Challenges, J.D. Power Finds," https://www.jdpower.com/business/press-releases/2022-us-customer-service-index-csi-study, March 9, 2022.

7. "Auto Dealer Service Departments Trying to Navigate Parts and Staffing Challenges, J.D. Power Finds," https://www.jdpower.com/business/press-releases/2022-us-customer-service-index-csi-study, March 9, 2022.

8. Rebecca Elliott, "What if Tesla Is…Just a Car Company?" https://www.wsj.com/articles/tesla-stock-elon-musk-electric-vehicle-11673623093, January 20, 2023.

9. Susan B. Noyes and Ann Marie Scheidler, "U.S. Companies That Excel at Corporate Social Responsibility in 2022," https://better.net/philanthropy/corporate-social-responsibility/10-u-s-companies-that-excel-at-corporate-social-responsibility/, January 24, 2022.

10. A. G. Laffey and Ron Charon, cited in George S. Day and Christine Moorman, *Strategy from the Outside In: Profiting from Customer Value* (New York, NY: McGraw Hill, 2010), 235.

11. Princie Kim, "101 customer service quotes to keep your team motivated at work," https://www.zendesk.com/blog/get-motivated-customer-service-quotes/, January 11, 2023 .

12. George Day and Christine Moorman, *Strategy from the Outside In* (New York, NY: McGraw Hill, 2010).

13. Ibid.

14. Lucas Newman, "6 Reasons People Love Apple Products So Much," https://www.makeuseof.com/reasons-people-love-apple-products/, June 18, 2022.

15. Samuel Stebbins, Michael B. Sauter, and Evan Comen, "Customer Service Hall of Shame," https://247wallst.com/special-report/2017/08/24/customer-service-hall-of-shame-6/2/, August 24, 2017 (accessed October 25, 2018).

16. Shep Hayken, "Trader Joe's Loyalty Program Has Nothing To Do With Points or Perks," https://www.forbes.com/sites/shephyken/2022/12/04/trader-joes-loyalty-program-has-nothing-to-do-with-points-or-perks/?sh=374f77536662, December 4, 2022.

17. "How Top 15 Brands Use Customer Feedback Effectively," https://qualaroo.com/blog/the-best-ways-big-companies-use-customer-feedback/, February 8, 2023.

18. Gabrielle Pickard-Whitehead, "Motivational Sales Quotes to Inspire You," https://smallbiztrends.com/2020/02/motivational-sales-quotes.html, February 25, 2020.

19. David Vanamburg, "National Banks Improve Customer Experience," ACSI Matters, December 29, 2016, https://acsimatters.com/2016/12/29/national-banks-improve-the-customer-experience/ (accessed October 25, 2018).

20. "4 Examples of Businesses Leveraging CRM to Improve Productivity and Efficiency," Salesforce.com, February 8, 2017, https://www.salesforce.com/crm/examples/ (accessed October 25, 2018).

21. Adam Shell, "Invest in These Great Places to Work," Kiplinger's Personal Finance, pp. 26–29, February 2021.

22. "Creating a Culture of Innovation and Care," Fortune, March 2018, ad section.

23. David Kirkaldy, "12 Service Values Ritz Carlton Uses (And You Can Too)," David Kirkaldy, www.davidkirkaldy.com/12-service-values-ritz-Carlton (accessed January 21, 2023).

24. "Does Costco Really Pay $21 an Hour?" https://www.aisleofshame.com/does-costco-really-pay-21-an-hour/, May 17, 2022.

25. https://www.microsoft.com/en-us/about/values (accessed February 9, 2023).

26. "The IKEA Vision and Values, "https://www.ikea.com/us/en/this-is-ikea/about-us/the-ikea-vision-and-values-pub9aa779d0 (accessed February 8, 2023).

27. Adrianne Pasquarelli, "How a Millennial Mindset Is Helping This 116-Year-Old Retailer," *Advertising Age,* January 30, 2017, https://adage.com/article/cmo-strategy/a-millennial-mindset-helping-116-year-retailer/307734/ (accessed February 8, 2023).

28. Julie Jargon, "Restaurants See Value in Big Data," *The Wall Street Journal*, October 3, 2018, p. R5.29.

29. Aaron Brooks, 30 Killer Examples of Personalised Customer Experiences, https://www.ventureharbour.com/personalised-experiences-examples/

30. Christopher Wanamaker, "How Much Food Do Americans Eat?" https://caloriebee.com/nutrition/Food-Consumption-by-The-Numbers, May 25, 2022.

Chapter 2

1. Ben Cohen, "Hershey's Turnaround Story Isn't Sweet, It's Salty," https://www.wsj.com/articles/halloween-hershey-stock-chocolate-candy-11666831636, October 28, 2022.

2. Shirley Brady, "Ford Pivots from Passenger Cars in Massive Transformation of Business," https://www.brandchannel.com/2018/04/25/ford_exits_passenger_cars_transformation_042518/, April 25, 2018.

3. George Anderson, "Amazon Looks to Undercut Rivals with Monthly RX Prescription Plan," https://retailwire.com/discussion/amazon-looks-to-undercut-rivals-with-monthly-rx-prescription-plan/ January 24, 2023.

4. Shelly Banjo, "Amazon's Path to Profitability," *Bloomberg Gadfly,* January 28, 2016, https://www.bloomberg.com/gadfly/articles/2016-01-28/amazon-holiday-earnings-a-glimpse-at-retail-s-future (accessed January 28, 2023).

5. https://www.cvs.com/extracare/home, and https://www.cvshealth.com/news/pharmacy/cvs-pharmacy-pilots-new-carepass-program-in-boston.html (accessed March 3, 2023).

6. Daniel Anderson, "CVS's Business Model, Generic Strategy and Intensive Growth Strategies," https://www.rancord.org/cvs-business-model-generic-competitive-intensive-growth-strategies, March 29, 2019.

7. pharmaphorum Editor, "What CVS's Signify Health Acquisition Means for the Future of Healthcare," https://pharmaphorum.com/views-and-analysis/what-cvss-signify-health-acquisition-means-for-the-future-of-healthcare, October 19, 2022.

8. Betsy Guzior, "Food: You can now get Blue Apron meal kits on Amazon," https://www.bizjournals.com/bizwomen/news/latest-news/2022/10/you-can-now-get-blue-apron-meal-kits-on-amazon.html?page=all,, October 14, 2022.

9. Best 10 BCG Matrix Examples for Students, https://www.edrawmind.com/article/best-10-bcg-matrix-examples-for-students.html (accessed February 10, 2023).

10. "BCG Matrix of Samsung | BCG Matrix Analysis of Samsung," https://heartofcodes.com/bcg-matrix-of-samsung/; Gennaro Cuofano. "BCG Matrix: The Growth-Share Matrix in a Nutshell." FourWeekMBA, What Is The FourWeekMBA, 9 March 2023, https://fourweekmba.com/bcg-matrix/ (accessed February 11, 2023).

11. Shascha Brodsky, "Why Some People Still Love Apple's iPod," https://www.lifewire.com /why-some-people-still-love-apples-ipod-5322900, May 23, 2022.

12. "Mobile Vendor Market Share Worldwide—February 2023," https://gs.statcounter.com/vendor -market-share/mobile (accessed March 4, 2023).

13. Anshul, "BCG Matrix of Samsung/BCG Matrix Analysis of Samsung," https://heartofcodes .com/bcg -matrix-of-samsung/, July 25, 2018.

14. Fahad Usmani, "GE McKinsey Matrix: Definition, Examples, and Limitations," https:// parsadi.com/ge-mckinsey-matrix/, April 29, 2022.

15. Elise Dopson, "How to Build a Marketing Plan That Actually Works," https://www.shopify .com/blog/marketing-plan, July 19, 2022 (accessed February 11, 2023).

16. "Ben & Jerry's Ice Cream—Ben & Jerry's Mission Statement," www.benjerry.com/activism /mission-statement (accessed February 15, 2023).

17. Lia Sestric, "How Your Favorite Brands Reinvented Themselves and Made Big Money," *Go Banking Rates,* September 5, 2016, https:// www .gobankingrates.com/personal-finance /favorite -brands-reinvented-themselves-made -big-money/ (accessed February 11, 2023).

18. Lia Sestric, "How Your Favorite Brands Reinvented Themselves and Made Big Money," *Go Banking Rates,* September 5, 2016, https:// www .gobankingrates.com/personal-finance /favorite -brands-reinvented-themselves-made -big-money/ (accessed February 11, 2023).

19. https://www.ikea.com/us/en/this-is-ikea /about-us/the-ikea-vision-and-values (accessed January 28, 2023).

20. Gennaro Cuofano, https://fourweekmba.com /experience-curve, August 7, 2022).

21. https://corporate.aldi.us/fileadmin/fm-dam /Press_Releases/ALDI_Newsroom_Story_FINAL .pdf (accessed February 1, 2023).

22. Kimberley Amadeo, https://www .thebalancemoney.com/government-subsidies -definition-farm-oil-export-etc-3305788, March 31, 2022.

23. "Cipla Is Undergoing a Big Transformation and Is Doing Something It Once Eschewed." *The Economic Times,* https://m.economictimes.com /industry/healthcare/biotech/pharmaceuticals /cipla-is-undergoing-a-big-transformation-and -is-doing-something-it-once-eschewed/articleshow /69179068.cms.

24. Rebecca Fannin, https://www.cnbc.com/2022 /09/25/what-kroger-walmart-target-learned-from -china-about-grocerys-future.html, September 25, 2022.

25. Daniel Periera, https://businessmodelanalyst .com/southwest-airlines-business-model/, July 17, 2022.

26. https://www.prnewswire.com/news-releases /petsmart-partners-with-interior-designers-nate -berkus-and-jeremiah-brent-to-launch-a-new -collection-that-brings-style-beauty-and-function -to-pet-parents-301632994.html, September 26, 2022).

27. Sara Eisenberg, https://www.wrike.com/blog /niche-marketing-strategies/, June 15, 2022).

28. Geronimo Colt, https://toughnickel.com /industries/Sustained-Competitive-Advantage-of -Starbucks, September 29, 2022.

29. Shep Hayken, https://www.forbes.com /sites/shephyken/2021/01/03/nobody-has-a -sustainable-competitive-advantage/?sh =2c934c2f7374, January 3, 2021.

30. https://www.cbinsights.com/research/corporate -innovation-product-fails/, October 4, 2021.

31. Chad Brooks, "Digital Disrupt: What We can Learn From the Netflix Model," https://www .business.com/articles/digital-disrupt-what-we -can-all-learn-from-the-netflix-model/, February 21, 2023; Dawn Chmielewski and Lisa Richwine, 'Netflix Targets Global TV Ad Market as Next Business to Disrupt," https://www.reuters.com /technology/netflix-targets-global-tv-ad-market -next-business-disrupt-2022-10-19/, October 19, 2022; "How the Rise of Netflix Has Reshaped the Media Industry," https://www.adamsfunds.com /insights/how-the-rise-of-netflix-has-reshaped-the -media-industry/, March 15, 2019; Mallory, "The Netflix Effect is Real," https://mix106radio.com /the-netflix-effect-is-real/, December 5, 2020.; Julius Mansa, "How Netflix is Changing the TV Industry," https://www.investopedia.com/articles /investing/060815/how-netflix-changing-tv -industry.asp, September 20, 2022 (accessed February 15, 2023); Andy Robinson, "The Netflix Effect and How Pop Culture Impacts Ecommerce," https://venturestream.co.uk/blog /the-netflix-effect-how-pop-culture-impacts -ecommerce/, January 14, 2021.

Chapter 3

1. "Social Control: From Hunter-Gatherer Bands to the United Nations," *Anthropology Now,* April 17, 2014, https://anthropologynow.wordpress.com /tag/social-control (accessed January 16, 2015).

2. Grace Dean, "A California man is suing the maker of Texas Pete hot sauce for false advertising because it's made in North Carolina, not Texas," *Business Insider,* October 11, 2022.

3. Dom McAndrew, "You now need to ask for a straw at Starbucks," *KTLA5,* June 1, 2022.

4. April Rubin, "8 Million Laundress Products Recalled Over Bacteria Risk," *The New York Times,* https://www.nytimes.com/2022/12/03/business /the-laundress-recall-bacteria.html?searchResult Position=1, December 3, 2022.

5. "Yaqub M., "20+ Ethical Consumption Statistics: The State of Ethical Consumer in 2022," *BusinessDIT,* October 4, 2022.

6. Paul Skeldon, "More than half of UK consumers would avoid buying from brands accused of work- ing with unethical suppliers," *Internet Retailing,* September 29, 2021.

7. Catherine Rainbow, "Descriptions of Ethical Theories and Principles," Davidson College, https://www.bio.davidson.edu/people/kabernd /indep/carainbow/Theories.htm (accessed January 10, 2015).

8. Ashley Capoot "SEC fines Oracle $23 million, says the company bribed foreign officials for business," *CNBC,* September 27, 2022.

9. Amna Kirmani, Rebecca W. Hamilton, Debora V. Thompson, and Shannon Lantzy, "Doing Well versus Doing Good: The Differential Effect of Underdog Positioning on Moral and Competent Service Providers," *Journal of Marketing,* January 2017, 103–117.

10. Anusorn Singhapakdi, Scott Vitell, and Ken- neth Kraft, "Moral Intensity and Ethical Decision Making of Marketing Professionals," *Journal of Business Research,* 36, no. 3 (1996): 245–255; Ishmael Akaah and Edward Riordan, "Judgments of Marketing Professionals about Ethical Issues in Marketing Research: A Replication and Exten- sion," *Journal of Marketing Research,* 26, no. 1 (1989): 112–120; see also Shelby Hunt, Lawrence Chonko, and James Wilcox, "Ethical Problems of Marketing Researchers," *Journal of Marketing Research,* 21, no. 3 (1984): 309–324; Kenneth Andrews, "Ethics in Practice," *Harvard Business Review,* September 1989, 99–104; Thomas Dun- fee, Craig Smith, and William T. Ross Jr., "Social Contracts and Marketing Ethics," *Journal of Mar- keting,* 63, no. 3 (1999): 14–32; Jay Handelman and Stephen Arnold, "The Role of Marketing Actions with a Social Dimension: Appeals to the Institutional Environment," *Journal of Marketing,* 63, no. 3 (1999): 33–48; David Turnipseed, "Are Good Soldiers Good? Exploring the Link between Organizational Citizenship Behavior and Personal Ethics," *Journal of Business Research,* 55, no. 1 (2002): 1–15; and O. C. Ferrell, John Fraedrich, and Linda Ferrell, *Business Ethics: Ethical Decision Making and Cases,* 10th ed. (Stamford, CT: Cengage Learning, 2015), 128–137.

11. Lena Eisenstein, "5 steps to Creating an Ethical Organizational Culture," *Board Effect,* July 15, 2021.

12. *Research Report: The State of Ethics in Large Companies," Ethics Research Center,* https://www. ethics.org/wp-content/uploads/2015-ECI-WP -State-of-Ethics-Large-Companies.pdf *(accessed January 30, 2023).*

13. Mia Salas, "8 Fast-Food Chains That Use the highest Quality Ingredients," Eat This, Not That!, January 17.2023, https://www.eatthis.com/fast -food-chains-that-use-highest-quality-ingredients / (accessed January 30, 2023).

14. Marina Pitofsky, "Phthalates on the fast-food menu: Chemicals linked to health problems found at McDonalds, Taco Bell," *USA Today,* October 27, 2021.

15. "The State of Ethics & Compliance in the Workplace," The Ethics & Compliance Initiative, https://www.ethics.org/wp-content/uploads/2022 -ECI-GBES-Small-Medium-Large-Enterprise -Report-v2.pdf (accessed February 2, 2023).

16."Gender Bias in Search Algorithms Has Effect on Users, New Study Finds," *NYU,* https://www .nyu.edu/about/news-publications/news/2022/july /gender-bias-in-search-algorithms-has-effect-on -users--new-study-.html, July 12, 2022.

17. Ibid.

18. "China party says nearly 5 million member probed for graft," October 17, 2022, https:// apnews.com/article/health-china-business-covid -economy-6618e65ef6148e0c75fce4dc2a28011f (accessed January 30, 2023).

19. "Takata Airbag Recall: Everything You Need to Know," December 30, 2022, https://www.consumerreports.org/car-recalls-defects/takata-airbag-recall-everything-you-need-to-know-a1060713669/ (accessed January 30, 2023).

20. Freshworks IPO: Indian Tech Startup Creates 500 Millionaires in Trading Debut, *The Quint World*, September 24, 2021, https://www.thequint.com/news/breaking-news/indian-software-as-a-service-company-freshworks-went-public-and-made-its-trading-debut-in-nasdaq (accessed January 30, 2023).

21. Saurabh Mishra and Sachin B. Modi, "Corporate Social Responsibility and Shareholder Wealth: The Role of Marketing Capability," *Journal of Marketing*, January 2016, 26–46.

22. "Free Exchange-Believing Is Seeing," *The Economist*, August 27, 2016, 58.

23. Christian Homburg, Marcel Stierl, and Torsten Bornemann, "Corporate Social Responsibility in Business-to-Business Markets: How Organizational Customers Account for Supplier Corporate Social Responsibility Engagement," *Journal of Marketing*, November 2013, 53–72; Daniel Korschun, C. B. Bhattacharya, and Scott Swain, "Corporate Social Responsibility, Customer Orientation, and the Job Performance of Frontline Employees," *Journal of Marketing*, May 2014, 20–37; Farnoosh Khodakarami, J. Andrew Petersen, and Rajkumar Venkatesan, "Developing Donor Relationships: The Role of the Breadth of Giving," *Journal of Marketing*, July 2015, 77–93; Charles Kang, Frank Germann, Rajdeep Grewal, "Washing Away Your Sins? Corporate Responsibility, Corporate Social Irresponsibility, and Firm Performance," *Journal of Marketing*, March 2016, 59–79 and "Good Behavior, Heavenly Returns," *Fortune*, September 1, 2018, 45–48.

24. "16 Brands Doing Corporate Social Responsibility Successfully," *Digital Marketing Institute*, November 10, 2022.

25. "The Halo Effect," *The Economist*, June 27, 2015, 56.

26. Jason Stern, "The Business Benefits of Corporate Social Responsibility Impact Assessments," *Forbes*, January 24, 2022, https://www.forbes.com/sites/forbestechcouncil/2022/01/24/the-business-benefits-of-corporate-social-responsibility-impact-assessments/?sh=554b0a8d3209 (accessed February 1, 2023).

27. "The Walt Disney Company: 2021 Corporate Social Responsibility Report," *Walt Disney Company*, https://thewaltdisneycompany.com/disney-releases-2021-corporate-social-responsibility-report/ (accessed January 31, 2023).

28. "'Performance with Purpose': Indra Nooyi Imparts Wisdom to USC MBCs," Yahoo, https://www.yahoo.com/now/performance-purpose-indra-nooyi-imparts-172217566.html

29. Kailynn Bowling, "How Corporate Responsibility is Influencing Consumer Buying Decisions," *Forbes*, May 2, 2022, https://www.forbes.com/sites/theyec/2022/05/02/how-corporate-responsibility-is-influencing-consumer-buying-decisions/?sh=2e4807235c6d (accessed February 1, 2023).

30. United Nations Global Compat, https://www.unglobalcompact.org (accessed February 1, 2023).

31. https://bcorporation.net (accessed February 1, 2023).

32. https://bimpactassessment.net/case-studies/elissa-loughman (accessed February 1, 2023).

33. Katrijn Gielens, Inge Geyskens, Barbara Deleersnyder, and Max Nohe, "The New Regulator in Town: The Effect of Walmart's Sustainability Mandate on Supplier Shareholder Value," *Journal of Marketing*, March 2018, 124–141.

34. "It's Now illegal in NY to Sell Many Popular Laundry Detergents," *WPDH*, https://wpdh.com/its-now-illegal-in-ny-to-buy-many-popular-laundry-detergents/ January 5, 2023 (accessed February 1, 2023).

35. "GreenPrint Survey Finds Consumers Want to Buy Eco-Friendly Products, but Don't Know How to Identify Them," *Business Wire*, https://www.businesswire.com/news/home/20210322005061/en/GreenPrint-Survey-Finds-Consumers-Want-to-Buy-Eco-Friendly-Products-but-Don't-Know-How-to-Identify-Them, March 22, 2021. (accessed February 1, 2023). Jeonggyu-Lee, Siddharth Bhatt, and Rajneesh Suri, "When Consumers Penalize Not So Green Products," *Psychology & Marketing*, December 13, 2017, https://onlinelibrary.wiley.com/doi/full/10.1002/mar.21069 (accessed October 7, 2018).

36. Ibid.

37. "The Green Guides," Federal Trade Commission, https://www.ftc.gov/news-events/topics/truth-advertising/green-guides (accessed February 1, 2023).

38. Lesley Fair, "$5.5 million total FTC settlements with Kohl's and Walmart challenge "bamboo" and eco claims, shed light on Penalty Offense enforcement," Federal Trade Commission, April 8, 2022, https://www.ftc.gov/business-guidance/blog/2022/04/55-million-total-ftc-settlements-kohls-and-walmart-challenge-bamboo-and-eco-claims-shed-light (accessed February 2, 2023).

39. Emily Bobrow, "Ryan Gellert Wants Patagonia to Be Part of the Environmental Solution," *The Wall Street Journal*, February 3, 2023, https://www.wsj.com/articles/ryan-gellert-wants-patagonia-to-be-part-of-the-environmental-solution-11675444847 (accessed February 20, 2023).

40. Grace O'Donnell, "Sustainability 'contributes to the bottom line,' Unilever CEO says," *Yahoo! Finance*, November 5, 2022.

41. "The Fresh Scent of Success," *Businessweek*, September 4, 2017, 46–51.

42. Sarah Flis, "The Rise of Cause Marketing," *Business 2 Community*, https://www.business2community.com/social-business/the-rise-of-cause-marketing-02286159, December 9, 2022 (accessed February 2, 2023).

43. Ibid.

44. *Walgreens*, https://www.walgreens.com/topic/promotion/rednoseday.jsp (accessed February 1, 2023).

Chapter 4

1. Thomas Hum, "Ford Chief Futurist talks sustainability and the F-150 Lightning," *Yahoo! News*, December 31, 2021, https://news.yahoo.com/ford-chief-futurist-talks-sustainability-and-the-f-150-lightning-210718820.html

2. Getting ahead of the curve," https://www2.deloitte.com/us/en/insights/industry/financial-services/consumer-payment-survey.html, February 26, 2020.

3. Niamh Carroll, "Mars Petcare on approaching innovation as 'platforms not projects'," https://www.marketingweek.com/mars-petcare-innovation-platforms/, August 23, 2022.

4. "How to turn sugar cane into Lego bricks?" https://www.linkedin.com/pulse/how-turn-sugar-cane-lego-bricks-wenzhou-superchen-nonwoven-technol/?trk=organization-update-content_share-article, January 13, 2022.

5. Nic Newman, "Journalism, media, and technology trends and predictions 2023," https://reutersinstitute.politics.ox.ac.uk/journalism-media-and-technology-trends-and-predictions-2023, January 10, 2023.

6. Gilda Raczkowski, "How social values influence consumer purchase behavior and brand performance," https://www.surveymonkey.com/curiosity/how-social-values-influence-consumer-purchase-behavior-and-brand-performance/ (accessed February 22, 2023).

7. Dorothy Neufeld, "The world's most influential values, in one graphic," https://www.weforum.org/agenda/2020/11/values-graphic-care-behaviour-family-love-tradition-free-speech/, November 12, 2020.

8. Fiona Lomas, "Understanding the impact of culture on marketing content," https://www.smartinsights.com/digital-marketing-strategy/understanding-the-impact-of-culture-on-marketing-content/, February 3, 2020.

9. Matt Graywood, "How Brand Loyalty Differs Among the Generations," https://modernrestaurantmanagement.com/how-brand-loyalty-differs-among-the-generations/, February 2, 2018.

10. "Global Social Media Statistics," https://datareportal.com/social-media-users, January 2023.

11. Sarah McNaugton, "Tech Can Make Calving Season Easier," https://www.farmprogress.com/cattle-news/tech-can-make-calving-season-easier, January 6, 2023.

12. Adam Hayes, "What Video Marketers Should Know in 2023, According to Wyzowl Research," https://blog.hubspot.com/marketing/state-of-video-marketing-new-data, February 6, 2023.

13. Tim Delany, "Pop Culture: An Overview," www.ou.edu/pop-culture-an-overview (accessed March 11, 2023).

14. Ibid.

15. Jeremy deSouza, "Pop Culture in Marketing—Why and How You Need to Use It," https://www.engati.com/blog/pop-culture-marketing, February 3, 2023.

16. Ibid.

17. Maya Yang, "Americans Go 'Westerncore' As Yellowstone Fans Adopt Cowboy Look," https://www.theguardian.com/tv-and-radio/2023/jan/15/americans-go-westerncore-as-yellowstone-fans-adopt-cowboy-look, January 15, 2023.

18. "10 Top Retail Brands to Watch in 2023," https://go.placer.ai/wp/10-top-retail-brands-to-watch-in-2023 (accessed March 12, 2023).

19. Kwak Yeons, "Teens Feel Peer Pressure To Buy Luxury Goods Endorsed By K-Pop Stars," https://www.koreatimes.co.kr/www/culture/2023/03/135_344743.html, February 3, 2023.

20. Caryll Cabuhat, "A Deep Dive on Why K-Pop is at the Forefront of Fashion," https://mega.onemega.com/a-deep-dive-on-why-k-pop-is-at-the-forefront-of-fashion/, January 18, 2023.

21. Julianna Lopez, "What is DEI? Defining Diversity, Equity, and Inclusion," https://www.uschamber.com/co/start/strategy/what-is-dei, February 19, 2023.

22. Constantine von Hoffman, "By the Numbers: Diversity and Inclusion are Good Business," https://martech.org/by-the-numbers-diversity-and-inclusion-are-good-business, April 5, 2022.

23. Cecília Cury, "Customers Are Now More Than Ever, Choosing Brands They Feel Represented By," https://rockcontent.com/blog/customers-want-to-be-represented/, August 4, 2022.

24. "TIAA Ranks 9th on DiversityInc's Top 50 Companies List," https://www.businesswire.com/news/home/20200507005956/en/TIAA-Ranks-9th-on-DiversityInc's-2020-Top-50-Companies-List, May 7, 2020.

25. Cury *op cit*.

26. "The Rise of the Inclusive Consumer," https://www.mckinsey.com/industries/retail/our-insights/the-rise-of-the-inclusive-consumer, February 8, 2022.

27. Ibid.

28. Danni White, "What are Diversity, Equity and Inclusion, and Why Do Marketers Need Them?" https://martech.org/what-are-diversity-equity-and-inclusion-and-why-marketers-need-them/, July 18, 2022.

29. Daisy Rogozinsky, "9 Brands Winning With Inclusive Marketing (and How You Can Too)," https://promo.com/blog/9-brands-winning-with-inclusive-marketing-and-how-you-can-too, January 19, 2022.

30. "13 Inclusive Marketing Campaigns to Inspire Your 2023 Marketing Strategy," https://sharethis.com/data-topics/2023/01/2022-inclusive-marketing-campaigns/, February 21, 2023.

31. https://worldpopulationreview.com/state-rankings/average-family-income2023, (accessed March 7, 2023).

32. Jack Flynn, "25+ Essential Average American Income Statistics [2023]: Household + Personal Income in the Us," https://www.zippia.com/advice/average-american-income/, October 26, 2022.

33. "Median Income by Country 2023," https://wisevoter.com/country-rankings/median-income-by-country/, (accessed March 7, 2023).

34. "Low-Income Countries 2023," https://worldpopulationreview.com/country-rankings/low-income-countries, (accessed March 7, 2023).

35. "How Does a College Degree Improve Graduates' Employment and Earnings Potential?" https://www.aplu.org/our-work/4-policy-and-advocacy/publicvalues/employment-earnings/ (accessed March 8, 2023).

36. "Real Personal Consumption Expenditures by State and Real Personal Income by State and Metropolitan Area, 2021," *Bureau of Economic Analysis,* https://www.bea.gov/news/2022/real-personal-consumption-expenditures-state-and-real-personal-income-state-and, December 15, 2022; The Average Income in Every State—And What It's Really Worth," *Money,* May 2018, 67–69. https://usinflationcalculator.com/inflation/current-inflation-rates.

37. "Monthly 12-month Inflation Rate in the United States from January 2020 to January 2023," https://www.statista.com/statistics/273418/unadjusted-monthly-inflation-rate-in-the-us/ (accessed March 8, 2023).

38. Matt Egan, "First on CNN: 71% of Workers say Their Pay Isn't Keeping Up With Inflation," https://www.cnn.com/2022/09/27/economy/economy-inflation-savings/index.html, September 27, 2022.

39. Gwynn Guilford, "Baking Supplies Cost a Lot More This Year, So Did Flying, But That Flat-Screen TV Got Cheaper," https://www.wsj.com/articles/baking-supplies-cost-a-lot-more-this-year-so-did-flying-but-that-flat-screen-tv-got-cheaper-11671995514, December 26, 2022.

40. Jason Heinrich, Simon Henderson, Tom Holland and Megan Portanova, "6 Strategies to Help Your Company Weather Inflation," https://hbr.org/2021/09/6-strategies-to-help-your-company-weather-inflation, September 28, 2021.

41. Matthew Stern, "Will 2023 be All About Value?" https://retailwire.com/discussion/will-2023-be-all-about-value/, December 28, 2022.

42. Chris Bradley and Clayton O'Toole, "An Incumbent's Guide to Digital Disruption," https://www.mckinsey.com/business-functions/strategy-and-corporate-finance/our-insights/an-incumbents-guide-to-digital-disruption (accessed March 8, 2023).

43. "Best Buy is Back," *Business Week*, July 23, 2018, 44–49.

44. https://www.mckinsey.com/capabilities/quantumblack/our-insights/where-is-technology-taking-the-economy (accessed October 31, 2018).

45. John F. Sargent Jr. "U.S. Research and Development Funding and Performance: Fact Sheet," https://fas.org/sgp/crs/misc/R44307.pdf (accessed October 31, 2018).

46. "Federal Budget Authority for R&D and R&D Plant for National Defense and Civilian Functions Totaled $191 billion in FY 2023 Proposed Budget," https://ncses.nsf.gov/pubs/nsf23323 (accessed March 8, 2023).

47. "How Information Technology Helped Businesses Evolve During the Pandemic," https://www.iiba.org/professional-development/knowledge-centre/articles/how-information-technology-helped-businesses-evolve-during-the-pandemic/, November 30, 2021.

48. George Anderson, "Robo-Pharmacies Will Transform How Walgreens Operates its Business," https://retailwire.com/discussion/robo-pharmacies-will-transform-how-walgreens-operates-its-business/, October 4, 2022.

49. "Alo Yoga Debuts Virtual Reality Shopping Experience," https://www.retailcustomerexperience.com/news/alo-yoga-debuts-virtual-reality-shopping-experience/, February 8, 2023.

50. Survey of CMOs: Recession Fears Cause Companies to Double Down on Demand Activation," https://www.globenewswire.com/news-release/2023/02/23/2614386/0/en/Survey-of-CMOs-Recession-Fears-Cause-Companies-to-Double-Down-on-Demand-Activation.html, February 23, 2023.

51. https://www.washingtonpost.com/national/health-science/trump-administration-rewrites-aca-insurance-rules-to-give-more-power-to-states/2018/04/09/94b738fa-3c0f-11e8-a7d1-e4efec6389f0_story.html?noredirect=on&utm_term=.3ddd3426472d (accessed November 2, 2018).

52. Alison Bennett, "CFPB Targeting Largest U.S. Banks as it Cracks Down on Financial Industry," https://www.spglobal.com/marketintelligence/en/news-insights/latest-news-headlines/cfpb-targeting-largest-us-banks-as-it-cracks-down-on-financial-industry-72985438, November 16, 2022.

53. Jen Christensen, "FDA Fines E-cigarette Makers for Selling Products Illegally in 'Wakeup' Call to Tobacco Manufacturers," https://www.cnn.com/2023/02/22/business/fda-fines-ecigs/index.html, February 22, 2023.

54. Bureau of Consumer Protection, https://www.ftc.gov/about-ftc/bureaus-offices/bureau-consumer-protection (accessed March 8, 2023).

55. Mark Maremont, "Operator of LasikPlus Vision-Correction Clinics Lured Customers With Deceptive Advertising," https://www.wsj.com/articles/operator-of-lasikplus-vision-correction-clinics-lured-customers-with-deceptive-advertising-ftc-alleges-11674250221, January 20, 2023.

56. "Digital Ad Spend (2021–2026), https://www.oberlo.com/statistics/digital-ad-spend (accessed March 8, 2023).

57. https://www.acxiom.com/wp-content/uploads/2020/07/ac-2490-19-fs-acxiom-infobase.pdf, July 2020.

58. "Scraped Data from 500 Million LinkedIn Users Being Sold Online: 2 Million Records Leaked as Proof," https://cybernews.com/news/stolen-data-of-500-million-linkedin-users-being-sold-online-2-million-leaked-as-proof-2/, February 20, 2023.

59. "Europe Gets a Grip on Data," *Businessweek,* March 26, 2018, 42–43.

60. "Bed Bath & Beyond was a retail pioneer. Here's what went wrong," https://nbcpalmsprings.com/2023/02/08/bed-bath-beyond-was-a-retail-pioneer-heres-what-went-wrong/, February 8, 2023; Nathaniel Meyersohn, "Bed Bath & Beyond plans to liquidate all inventory and go out of business," https://www.cnn.com/2023/04/23/business/bed-bath-beyond-bankruptcy/index.html#:~:text=The%20company%27s%20360%20Bed%20Bath,Beyond%20will%20close%20some%20stores, April 24, 2023, Rob Wile, "Bed Bath & Beyond comes back as an online retailer," NBC News, August 1, 2023, https://www.nbcnews.com/business/business-news/bed-bath-beyond-comes-back-online-store-why-sale-overstock-rcna97286.

61. Michaela Ward, "32 Customer Loyalty Statistics You Need to Know in 2023," https://www.stampme.com/blog/customer-loyalty-stats, February 6, 2023.

62. Paul A. Laudicina and Erik R. Peterson, "Competition, Disruption, and Deception: Global Trends 2018–2023," https://www.kearney.com/web/global-business-policy-council/global-trends/2018-2023 (accessed March 9, 2023).

63. Arabella Ruiz, "51 Huge Environmentally Conscious Consumer Statistics 2023," https://theroundup.org/environmentally-conscious-consumer-statistics/ (accessed March 9, 2023).

64. Becky McKay, "Global Sustainability Trends – Insights from 42 Professional Experts," https://www.greenmatch.co.uk/blog/sustainability-trends, February 13, 2023.

65. Tanger Advances Towards Long-Term Environmental Goals," https://www.prnewswire.com/news-releases/tanger-advances-towards-long-term-environmental-goals-301732868.html, January 30, 2023.

66. Sheila Marikar, "A Shoe with No Footprint," *Fortune,* October 2020, 55–58.

67. Dennis Kamprad, "How Sustainable Is Patagonia? All You Need to Know," https://impactful.ninja/how-sustainable-is-patagonia/ (accessed March 10, 2023); https://www.patagonia.com (accessed March 10, 2023).

Chapter 5

1. Luca Ventura, "World's Largest Companies 2022," *Global Finance*, January 30, 2023, https://www.gfmag.com/global-data/economic-data/largest-companies (accessed January 23, 2023).

2. "About Us," Dunkin' Donuts, https://www.dunkindonuts.com/en/about/about-us (accessed January 23, 2023).

3. Hannah Fleishman, "13 Businesses With Brilliant Global Marketing Strategies," HubSpot.com, November 22, 2021, https://blog.hubspot.com/marketing/global-marketing-and-international-business (accessed January 23, 2023).

4. "U.S. Reaches Highest Recorded Mineral Import Reliance," National Mining Association, January 31, 2023, https://nma.org/2023/01/31/u-s-reaches-highest-recorded-mineral-import-reliance/#:~:text=Of%20the%2050%20mineral%20commodities,greater%20than%2050%25%20of%20apparent (accessed March 7, 2023).

5. "Global Dynamics," Global Trade Alert, https://www.globaltradealert.org/global_dynamics/day-to_0130/flow_all (accessed on January 30, 2023).

6. MacroTrends.net, https://www.macrotrends.net/countries/FRA/france/trade-gdp-ratio#:~:text=Trade%20is%20the%20sum%20of,a%204.2%25%20increase%20from%202020; https://www.macrotrends.net/countries/GBR/united-kingdom/trade-gdp-ratio; https://www.macrotrends.net/countries/DEU/germany/trade-gdp-ratio#:~:text=Germany%20trade%20to%20gdp%20ratio%20for%202021%20was%2089.39,a%208.28%25%20increase%20from%202020; https://www.macrotrends.net/countries/USA/united-states/trade-gdp-ratio#:~:text=Trade%20is%20the%20sum%20of,a%201.22%25%20decline%20from%202018; https://www.macrotrends.net/countries/CAN/canada/trade-gdp-ratio#:~:text=Canada%20trade%20to%20gdp%20ratio%20for%202021%20was%2061.37%25%2C%20a,a%201.04%25%20decline%20from%202018. (accessed January 30, 2023).

7. "Small and Medium-Sized Enterprises," Office of the United States Trade Representative, https://ustr.gov/trade-agreements/free-trade-agreements/trans-pacific-partnership/tpp-chapter-chapter-negotiating-8 (accessed January 30, 2023).

8. https://www.exim.gov/about (accessed March 7, 2023).

9. https://www.sba.gov/partners/lenders/7a-loan-program/types-7a-loans (accessed March 7, 2023).

10. https://sba.gov/about-sba (accessed March 7, 2023).

11. https://www.bea.gov/news/2022/activities-us-multinational-enterprises-2020; https://www.aei.org/carpe-diem/many-large-us-firms-sell-hire-and-invest-more-overseas-than-in-the-us-and-have-to-think-globally-to-survive/#:~:text=Other%20large%20American%20MNCs%20generate,global%20staffing%20outside%20the%20US; https://www.aei.org/carpe-diem/many-large-us-firms-sell-hire-and-invest-more-overseas-than-in-the-us-and-have-to-think-globally-to-survive/#:~:text=Other%20large%20American%20MNCs%20generate,global%20staffing%20outside%20the%20US (accessed January 30, 2023).

12. https://reshoringinstitute.org/more-companies-turn-to-reshoring-post-pandemic/ (accessed January 30, 2023).

13. https://go-gale-com.ezproxy.mtsu.edu/ps/i.do?p=AONE&u=tel_middleten&id=GALE%7CA715156769&v=2.1&it=r&sid=ebsco (accessed January 30, 2023).

14. https://tradetankmx.com/was-globalization-good-for-mexico/ (accessed January 30, 2023).

15. Robert E. Scott & Zane Mokhiber, "Growing China trade deficit cost 3.7 million American jobs between 2001 and 2018," Economic Policy Institute, https://www.epi.org/publication/growing-china-trade-deficits-costs-us-jobs/ (accessed March 7, 2023).

16. James Chen, "Multinational Corporation: Definition, How it Works, Four Types," Investopedia, https://www.investopedia.com/terms/m/multinationalcorporation.asp#:~:text=A%20multinational%20corporation%20is%20one,a%20business%20a%20multinational%20company (accessed February 1, 2023).

17. https://www.statista.com/statistics/382288/geographical-region-share-of-revenue-of-apple/ (accessed February 1, 2023).

18. https://www.insidermonkey.com/blog/5-biggest-multinational-companies-in-the-world-1087487/?singlepage=1; https://www.yahoo.com/video/15-biggest-multinational-companies-world-152339448.html?guccounter=1 (accessed February 1, 2023).

19. https://fortune.com/2023/01/11/how-covid-changed-supply-chains-forever-distinguished-professor-just-in-case-just-in-time-onshoring-technology/ (accessed February 1, 2023).

20. https://www.cnbc.com/2022/09/01/job-growth-investments-in-manufacturing-sector-tied-to-white-house-economic-plan-biden-says.html; https://www.whitehouse.gov/briefing-room/statements-releases/2022/08/09/fact-sheet-chips-and-science-act-will-lower-costs-create-jobs-strengthen-supply-chains-and-counter-china/ (accessed February 1, 2023).

21. https://www.apple.com/newsroom/2021/05/apple-awards-corning-45-million-from-its-advanced-manufacturing-fund/ (accessed February 1, 2023).

22. Theodore Levitt, "The Globalization of Markets," Harvard Business Review, May 1983, 92–100.

23. https://smallbusiness.chron.com/product-development-strategy-mcdonalds-12207.html (accessed February 1, 2023).

24. https://jtbbusinesstravel.com/business-culture-etiquette-around-world/ (accessed February 2, 2023).

25. https://www.data.worldbank.org/indicator/ny.gnp/pcap.cd (accessed February 2, 2023).

26. https://www.weforum.org/agenda/2022/12/world-most-expensive-cities/#:~:text=hardest%2Dhit%20places.-,New%20York%20and%20Singapore%20have%20topped%20the%20list%20of%20the,less%20affordable%20for%20ordinary%20people (accessed February 2, 2023).

27. https://www.bea.gov/news/2022/us-international-trade-goods-and-services-june-2022 (accessed February 3, 2023).

28. https://www.imf.org/en/Blogs/Articles/2022/10/14/how-countries-should-respond-to-the-strong-dollar (accessed February 3, 2023).

29. https://www.bea.gov/news/2022/us-international-trade-goods-and-services-june-2022 (accessed February 3, 2023).

30. https://www.chathamhouse.org/2022/10/brazils-new-president-inherits-huge-economic-challenges (accessed February 3, 2023).

31. https://carnegieendowment.org/politika/88664 (accessed Febrary 3, 2023).

32. https://som.yale.edu/story/2022/over-1000-companies-have-curtailed-operations-russia-some-remain (accessed February 3, 2023).

33. https://www.economicsobservatory.com/the-brics-countries-where-next-and-what-impact-on-the-global-economy#:~:text=This%20has%20been%20driven%20primarily,Russia%2C%20India%20and%20South%20Africa (accessed February 3, 2023).

34. https://www2.deloitte.com/us/en/insights/economy/asia-pacific/india-economic-outlook.html (accessed February 3, 2023).

35. https://www.morganstanley.com/ideas/investment-opportunities-in-india (accessed February 3, 2023).

36. https://digital.com/how-to-start-an-online-business/best-countries-to-start-a-business/ (accessed February 3, 2023).

37. https://www.investopedia.com/terms/e/exchangecontrol.asp (accessed February 4, 2023).

38. https://www.cfr.org/backgrounder/mercosur-south-americas-fractious-trade-bloc (accessed February 4, 2023).

39. https://www.gisreportsonline.com/r/mercosur-divided/ (accessed February 4, 2023).

40. *"New U.S.* Tariffs Hit China; Beijing Vows to Strike Back," *The Wall Street Journal,* September 18, 2018, A1, A10.

41. "Tariffs on China Take Their Toll on U.S. Factories," *The Wall Street Journal,* October 15, 2018, B1, N2.

42. "New Tariffs Pose Broad Economic Risks Amid Escalating Threat," *The Wall Street Journal,* June 4, 2018, A6.g.

43. "Peace Offering," *The Economist,* December 22, 2018–January 4, 2019, 91–93.

44. https://www.cfr.org/backgrounder/contentious -us-china-trade-relationship (accessed March 8, 2023).

45. https://www.reuters.com/legal/legalindustry /still-friends-review-us-mexico-canada-trade-two -years-under-new-nafta-2022-08-11/ (accessed February 5, 2023).

46. "USMCA, the New Trade Deal between the United States, Canada, and Mexico, Explained," https://www.vox.com/2018/10/2/17923638 /usmca-trump-nafta-trade-agreement (accessed October 5, 2018).

47. "NEWFTA," *The Economist,* October 6, 2018, 31–32.

48. "'Unprecedented Challenges' Confront Appellate Body, Chair Warns," https://www.wto .org/english/news_e/news18_e/ab_22jun18_e .htm (accessed February 5, 2023).

49. https://www.wto.org/english/tratop_e/dispu _e/dispu_e.htm#dsb (accessed February 5, 2023).

50. "Understanding the WTO," World Trade Organization, https://www.wto.org/english /thewto_e/whatis_e/tif_e/tif_e.htm (accessed February 5, 2023).

51. https://www.csis.org/programs/scholl-chair -international-business/world-trade-organization -appellate-body-crisis#:~:text=For%20roughly%20 two%20years%2C%20the,and%20concerns%20 over%20U.S.%20sovereignty (accessed February 6, 2023).

52. "TPP Points Way toward Other Deals," *The Wall Street Journal,* May 15, 2017, A2.

53. Louise Yaxley, "TPP Resurrected: Here's What's in the Latest Trans-Pacific Partnership Trade Deal and What It Means for You," https:// www.abc.net.au/news/2018-01-24/what-is-the -new-tpp-and-what-does-it-mean-for-australia /9357020 (accessed November 5, 2018).

54. https://crsreports.congress.gov/product/pdf /IF/IF11891#:~:text=The%20Regional%20 Comprehensive%20Economic%20Partnership, %2C%20Thailand%2C%20and%20Vietnam %2C%20and (accessed February 6, 2023).

55. https://www.fas.usda.gov/data/costa-rica -costa-rica-join-pacific-alliance#:~:text=Costa%20 Rica%3A%20Costa%20Rica%20to%20Join%20 Pacific%20Alliance,-December%2012%2C%20 2022&text=The%20members%20of%20the%20 Pacific,Peru%2C%20and%20Chile%20in%20 2023 (accessed February 6, 2023).

56. https://alianzapacifico.net/en/observant -countries/ (accessed March 7, 2023).

57. Kimberly Amadeo, "CAFTA Explained, with Its Pros and Cons," https://www.thebalance.com /what-is-cafta-3305580 (accessed November 4, 2018).

58. https://policy.trade.ec.europa.eu/eu-trade -relationships-country-and-region/countries-and -regions/united-states_en (accessed February 11, 2023).

59. https://www.itgovernance.eu/blog/en/how-much -does-gdpr-compliance-cost-in-2020#:~:text=But%20 when%20it%20comes%20to,spend%20more%20 than%20%2410%20million. (accessed February 11, 2023).

60. "Google, EU in Online Border War," *The Wall Street Journal,* September 10, 2018, B1–B4.

61. https://www.reuters.com/article/us-google -privacy-france/france-fines-google-57-million-for -european-privacy-rule-breach-idUSKCN1PF208 (accessed February 11, 2023).

62. https://www.cnn.com/2023/01/05/business /ukraine-economy/index.html#:~:text=%E2%80 %9CDuring%202022%2C%20Ukraine's%20 economy%20suffered,Russia's%20invasion%20in %20February%202022. (accessed February 12, 2023).

63. https://www.imf.org/en/About/FAQ /ukraine#:~:text=Ukraine%20was%20the%20 first%20IMF,window%20in%20early%20 October%202022. (accessed February 12, 2023).

64. "G20 Split over U.S. Trade Plan Deepens," *Wall Street Journal,* March 21, 2018, A9.

65. https://www.unfpa.org/world-population -trends (accessed February 12, 2023).

66. https://www.worldbank.org/en/topic/poverty /overview (accessed February 12, 2023).

67. https://www.brookings.edu/blog/future -development/2021/01/14/the-silver-economy-is -coming-of-age-a-look-at-the-growing-spending -power-of-seniors/ (accessed February 12, 2023).

68. https://www.mckinsey.com/cn/our-insights/our -insights/seven-segments-shaping-chinas-consumption -landscape (accessed February 12, 2023).

69. Andy Kiersz, "Here's What the Typical American Worker Earns at Every Age," https://www .businessinsider.com/typical-salary-americans-at -every-age-2018-6 (accessed November 16, 2018).

70. https://www.thinkimpact.com/average-college -graduate-salaries/#:~:text=Average%20Starting %20Salary%20for%20College,salaries%20of%20 the%20past%20year. (accessed February 12, 2023).

71. https://www.statista.com/statistics/282134 /china-labor-force/ (accessed February 12, 2023).

72. https://www.thaipbsworld.com/slumping -birth-rate-poses-urgent-policy-challenges -for-government/#:~:text=parents%20are%20 making-,The%20average%20Thai%20family%20 has%20only%201.3%20children%20while%20 it,children%2C%20according%20to%20health%20 experts. (accessed February 12, 2023).

73. https://www.reuters.com/business/energy /us-crude-output-rise-2023-while-demand-stay -flat-eia-2023-02-07/#:~:text=EIA's%20latest%20 forecast%20calls%20for,12.65%20million%20 bpd%20next%20year. Iaccessed February 12, 2023).

74. https://www.eia.gov/energyexplained/oil-and- petroleum-products/where-our-oil-comes-from. php (accessed February 12, 2023).

75. https://worldpopulationreview.com/country -rankings/natural-gas-by-country (accessed February 12, 2023).

76. www.unwater.org/water-facts/scarcity (accessed2/12/2023).

77. https://www.businessroundtable.org/new -study-trade-supported-over-40-million-american -jobs; https://www.trade.gov/feature-article /otea-publications; https://www.visualcapitalist .com/us-goods-exports-by-state/; https://www .bmwgroup-werke.com/spartanburg/en/news /2022/Eight-Years-in-a-Row-BMW-Manufacturing -is-Largest-Automotive-Exporter-in-the-United -States.html; https://www.trade.gov/us-commercial -service-office-map (accessed February 12, 2023).

78. https://www.franchise.com/blog/five-biggest -franchises-world/ (accessed February 13, 2023).

79. https://www.cnn.com/2010/LIVING/homestyle /04/08/fast.food/index.html (accessed February 13, 2023).

80. https://www.fastcompany.com/90724420 /most-innovative-companies-joint-ventures-2022 (accessed March 9, 2023).

81. https://telecoms.com/281201/ihs-to-take -over-mtn-nigerias-towers-through-joint-venture/ (accessed February 13, 2023).

82. https://www.bea.gov/data/intl-trade-investment /direct-investment-country-and-industry (accessed March 9, 2023).

83. https://www.bea.gov/news/2022/direct -investment-country-and-industry-2021 (accessed February 13, 2023).

84. https://ofii.org/report/foreign-direct -investment-in-the-united-states-2018 (accessed November 21, 2018).

85. https://www.bea.gov/data/intl-trade -investment/activities-us-affiliates-foreign-mnes (accessed February 13, 2023).

86. https://www.manufacturingdive.com/news /manufacturing-construction-projects-2023 -intel-enel-abbott-samsung-siemens/639995/ (accessed February 13, 2023).

87. https://www.aseanbriefing.com/news /the-philippines-amends-its-foreign-investment -act/#:~:text=The%20President%20has%20 the%20power,and%20well%2Dbeing%20of%20 Filipinos. (accessed February 13, 2023).

88. https://companiesmarketcap.com/supermarkets /largest-companies-by-market-cap/ (accessed March 9, 2023).

89. https://www.pginvestor.com/about-p-g /p-g-at-a-glance/default.aspx; https://www .macrotrends.net/stocks/charts/PG/procter -gamble/revenue#:~:text=Procter%20%26%20 Gamble%20revenue%20for%20the%20twelve%20 months%20ending%20December%2031,a%20 7.28%25%20increase%20from%202020 (accessed February 13, 2023).

90. https://theislamicinformation.com/fatwas/is -mcdonalds-halal/ (accessed March 9, 2023).

91. "Tesla Makes a U-Turn in China," *Fortune,* June 15, 2017, 129–136.

92. https://www.argusmedia.com/en/news /2185607-chinas-shanghai-continues-to-offer -free-ev-licences (accessed February 14, 2023).

93. https://www.npr.org/sections/money/2012/01 /27/145918343/rethinking-the-oreo-for-chinese -consumers (accessed February 14, 2023).

94. "How Japanese Kit Kats Got So Hot," *Fortune,* April 2, 2018.

95. https://janbox.com/blog/japanese-kit-kat -flavors/ (accessed February 14, 2023).

96. https://ux247.com/product-adaptation-in -foreign-markets-with-examples/ (accessed February 15, 2023).

97. "Trying to Speak India's Language(s)," *Businessweek,* November 13, 2017.

98. https://influencermarketinghub.com/influencer -marketing-statistics/#:~:text=Influencer%20 Marketing%20Industry%20Reached%20 %2416.4,billion%2C%20indicating%20a%20 steady%20growth.; https://www.statista.com /topics/2496/influence-marketing/#topicOverview (accessed February 15, 2023).

99. https://www.socialpilot.co/blog/micro -influencers (accessed February 15, 2023).

100. https://influencermarketinghub.com /influencer-marketing-benchmark-report/ (accessed February 15, 2023).

101. https://woosuite.com/stats/influencer -market-size/ (accessed February 15, 2023).

102. https://blog.unmetric.com/social-media -strategy-zara#:~:text=Zara's%20Facebook%20 page%20mostly%20showcases,of%20which%20 143%20were%20photos (accessed February 15, 2023).

103. https://www.businesswire.com/news /home/20230103005874/en/Perfect-Corp.-Partners -with-The-Good-Glamm-Group-to-Launch-AI -Powered-Skin-Analysis-and-AR-Makeup-Virtual -Try-On-Experiences-for-Beauty-Lovers-across -India; https://retail.economictimes.indiatimes.com /re-tales/trends-shaping-the-future-of-the-indian -beauty-and-personal-care-market/5278 (accessed February 15, 2023).

104. https://www.google.com/finance/quote /USD-JPY?sa=X&ved=2ahUKEwisucm3kZj9Ah XMk4kEHbTaDqcQmY0JegQIBhAd (accessed February 15, 2023).

105. https://www.fidelity.com/learning-center /trading-investing/strong-dollar#:~:text=The%20 dollar%20has%20been%20gaining,Reserve%20 keeps%20raising%20interest%20rates (accessed March 9, 2023).

106. https://www.npr.org/2022/09/27/1124284032 /strong-dollar-euro-pound-foreign-exchange-fx -inflation (accessed February 15, 2023).

107. https://catts.eu/updates/anti-dumping -duty/anti-dumping-duty-updates-january-2023/ (accessed February 15, 2023).

108. https://ustr.gov/countries-regions (accessed March 9, 2023).

109. https://bellroy.com/ (accessed March 18, 2023).

Chapter 6

1. Tonya Williams Bradford, "Beyond Fungible: Transforming Money into Moral and Social Resources," *Journal of Marketing,* March 2015, 79–97; "Budget Allocation Signals Consumers' Need States, Research Finds," *Marketing News,* April 2015, 7.

2. Tripp Mickle and Brian X. Chen, "Apple Extends Reach With $800 Watch, as New iPhone Inches Along," *The New York Times,* September 7, 2022, https://www.nytimes.com/2022/09/07 /technology/apple-new-iphone-watch.html.

3. Maryam Mohsin, "10 Google Search Statistics You Need to Know in 2023 [Infographic]," *Oberlo,* January 13, 2023, https://www.oberlo .com/blog/google-search-statistics.

4. "14 Stats That Prove Social Content Influences Consumer Buying Behavior," *Nosto,* https://www .nosto.com/blog/how-does-social-media-influence -customer-behavior/ (accessed March 13, 2023).

5. Bobby Marhamat, "Brick-And-Mortar Shoppers Have Spoken: Offer Great In-Store Experiences or Kiss Customers Goodbye," *Forbes,* May 16, 2022, https://www.forbes.com/sites /forbesbusinessdevelopmentcouncil/2022/05/16 /brick-and-mortar-shoppers-have-spoken-offer -great-in-store-experiences-or-kiss-customers -goodbye/?sh=1c8d917f1b70.

6. "Shoppers tapping phones for product research," *Retail Customer Experience,* October 10, 2022, https://www.retailcustomerexperience.com/news /shoppers-tapping-phones-for-product-research/.

7. Ashish Kumar, Ram Bezawada, Rishika Rishika, Ramkumar Janakiraman, and P.K. Kannan, "From Social to Sale: The Effects of Firm-Generated Content in Social Media on Customer Behavior," *Journal of Marketing,* January 2016, 7–25.

8. Giulio Piovaccari, "Ferrari, known for ultra-expensive sports cars, is getting into luxury fashion and opening a restaurant with a Michelin-starred chef," *Business Insider,* June 10, 2021, https:// www.businessinsider.com/ferrari-italian-luxury -sports-car-expands-to-luxury-fashion-restaurants -2021-6.

9. Uma Karmarkar, Baba Shiv, and Brian Kuntson, "Cost Conscious? The Neural and Behavioral Impact of Price Primacy on Decision Making," *Journal of Marketing Research,* August 2015, 467–481.

10. "Read the Story to Learn How Behavioral Economics Can Improve Marketing," *Marketing News,* January 2018, 32–41.

11. Ibid.

12. Destiny Torres, "Businesses Evolve with E-Commerce," *Los Angeles Business Journal,* October 10, 2022, https://labusinessjournal.com /featured/businesses-evolve-with-e-commerce/

13. Marie Jehanne, "Mobile vs Desktop Usage: What are the 2022 Consumer Trends," *ContentSquare,* April 6, 2022, https://contentsquare .com/blog/mobile-vs-desktop/.

14. Jessica Dickler, "Despite recession fears and fueled by 'revenge spending,' Americans spend $314 a month on impulse purchases, *CNBC,* August 20, 2022, *https://*www.cnbc.com/2022 /08/20/shoppers-spend-over-300-a-month-on -impulse-purchases-despite-recession-fears.html.

15. Shayna Walktower, "How to Encourage Buyers to Make Impulse Purchases With Your Business," *Business News Daily,* January 23, 2023, https://www.businessnewsdaily.com/2370 -impulse-purcahse-survey.html.

16. Iiro Jussila, Anssi Tarkiainen, Marko Sarstedt, and Joe Hair, "Individual Psychological Ownership: Concepts, Evidence and Implications for Research in Marketing," *Journal of Marketing Theory and Practice,* March 2015, 121–139; Bernadette Kamleitner and Silva Feuchtl, "'As If It Were Mine': Imaginary Works by Inducing Psychological Ownership," *Journal of Marketing Theory and Practice,* March 2015, 208–223.

17. Suzanne Shu and Joann Peck, "Psychological Ownership and Affective Reaction: Emotional Attachment Process Variables and the Endowment Effect," *Journal of Consumer Psychology,* March 2011, 439–452; Colleen Patricia Kirk, Bernard McSherry and Scott Swain, "Investing the Self: The Effect of Nonconscious Goals on Investor Psychological Ownership and Word-of-Mouth Intentions," *Journal of Behavioral and Experimental Economics,* January 2015, 186–194.

18. Colleen Patricia Kirk, Scott Swain, and James Gaskin, "I'm Proud of It: Consumer Technology Appropriation and Psychological Ownership," *Journal of Marketing Theory and Practice,* February 2015, 166–184.

19. Seren Morris, "20 Products that have Sold Out Because of TikTok Popularity," *Newsweek,* April 9, 2021, https://www.newsweek.com/20-products -sold-out-because-tiktok-popularity-1581946.

20. Aaron Garvey, "The 'Jilting' Effect: How Dashing Consumers' Hopes Isn't Always a Bad Thing," *Marketing News,* February 2018, 18–20.

21. Ronnie Gomez, "How 3 top brands provide social media customer service and support," *Sprout Social,* December 14, 2022, https://sproutsocial .com/insights/social-media-customer-service/.

22. "Bank of America's Erica Tops 1 Billion Client Interactions, Now Nearly 1.5 Million Per Day," *Bank of America Newsroom,* October 12, 2022, https://newsroom.bankofamerica.com/content /newsroom/press-releases/2022/10/bank-of -america-s-erica-tops-1-billion-client-interactions -now-.html.

23. "Forget 'Omni.' Just Help Me," *Quirk's Marketing Research Review,* October 2015, 44–49.

24. "Adventure Comes Standard: Ford Pro Reveals New 2023 Transit Trail," *Ford Media Center,* November 3, 2022, https://media.ford.com /content/fordmedia/fna/us/en/news/2022/11/03 /adventure-comes-standard--ford-pro-reveals-new -2023-transit-trai.html.

25. Raul Galera, "Word-of-Mouth: How Lush Cosmetics Hit Billion-dollar Revenues," *Referral Candy,* September 26, 2020, https://www.referralcandy .com/blog/lush-word-of-mouth-marketing.

26. "Why a Saturated Beauty Market Isn't a Bad Thing—And How You Can Stand Out," November 20, 2019, https://abcreativenyc.com /why-a-saturated-beauty-market-isnt-a-bad-thing -and-how-you-can-stand-out/.

27. "Alaska Airlines teams up with Lyft for new partnership to earn miles wherever you go," *Cision PR Newswire,* November 2, 2022, https://www .prnewswire.com/news-releases/alaska-airlines -teams-up-with-lyft-for-new-partnership-to-earn -miles-wherever-you-go-301665965.html.

28. David Edelman and Marc Singer, "Competing on Customer Journeys," *Harvard Business Review*, November 2015, https://hbr.org/2015/11/competing-on-customer-journeys (accessed September 26, 2018).

29. Shep Hyken, "58% of Customers Will Pay More For Better Customer Service," *Forbes*, April 24, 2022, https://www.forbes.com/sites/shephyken/2022/04/24/fifty-eight-percent-of-customers-will-pay-more-for-better-customer-service/?sh=5a032fb413f1.

30. David Aaker and Andrew Marcum, "The Satisfied vs Committed Brand Loyalist and What Drives Them," *Marketing News*, January 2017, pp. 24–25.

31. "Satisfaction Benchmarks by Company," *American Customer Satisfaction Index*, https://www.theacsi.org/industries/retail/online-retailers/ (accessed March 18, 2023).

32. *"2021's Top Brands Ranked by Customer Loyalty,"* *Marketing Charts*, https://www.marketingcharts.com/industries/retail-and-e-commerce-118573, *October 20, 2021.*

33. V. Kumar, Agata Leszkiewicz, and Angeliki Herbst, "Are You Back for Good or Still Shopping Around? Investigating Customers' Repeat Churn Behavior," *Journal of Marketing Research*, April 2018, 208–225.

34. Parker Morse, "3 Lessons Learned From McDonald's Latest Hispanic Ad Campaign," *MediaPost*, April 16, 2018, https://www.mediapost.com/publications/article/317681/3-lessons-learned-from-mcdonalds-latest-hispanic.html.

35. Claudia Aoraha, "World's most new expensive car is unveiled as one-of-a-kind Rolls Royce worth eye-watering £20MILLION," *The Sun*, May 21, 2022, https://www.the-sun.com/motors/5390589/world-most-expensive-car-rolls-royce-pearl/.

36. https://www.healthcare.gov/glossary/federal-poverty-level-fpl/ (accessed February 18, 2023).

37. "CDC's Tips From Former Smokers Returns With Powerful New Ads," *CDC*, February 28, 2022, https://www.cdc.gov/media/releases/2022/p0228-former-smoker-tips.html.

38. Tyler Lauletta, "Patrick Mahomes signed the richest deal in NFL history—here's how the Chiefs QB spends his money," *Business Insider* (https://www.insider.com/patrick-mahomes-net-worth-money-spends-career-earnings-2022-8).

39. "The State of Influencer Marketing 2023," Influencer Marketing Hub, https://influencermarketinghub.com/ebooks/Influencer_Marketing_Benchmark_Report_2023.pdf

40. "Creating sizzling demand for KFC's 'Best Chicken Sandwich Ever' with notable TikTok creators," TikTok for Business, https://www.tiktok.com/business/en-US/inspiration/kfc-435

41. Rick Suter, "The top 10 Super Bowl 57 commercials, according to USA TODAY Ad Meter, *USA Today*, https://admeter.usatoday.com/lists/top-10-best-super-bowl-57-commercials-usa-today-ad-meter/.

42. Ryan Holmes, "We Now See 5,000 Ads A Day…And It's Getting Worse," *LinkedIn*, https://www.linkedin.com/pulse/have-we-reached-peak-ad-social-media-ryan-holmes.

43. Girish Mallapragada, Sandeep R. Chandukala, and Qing Liu, "Exploring the Effects of 'What' (Product) and 'Where' (Website) Characteristics on Online Shopping Behavior," *Journal of Marketing*, March 2016, 21–38.

44. Nate Day, "Allstate to revive Dean Winters' Mayhem character," *Fox Business*, November 3, 2021, https://www.foxbusiness.com/lifestyle/allstate-revive-dean-winters-mayhem-character.

45. Manuela Lopex Restrepo, "Revenge travel' is surging. Here's what you need to know," *NPR*, June 16, 2022 (https://www.npr.org/2022/06/16/1105323610/flight-tickets-inflation-pandemic-revenge-travel-vacation-europe-recession).

46. https://www.mckinsey.com/capabilities/growth-marketing-and-sales/our-insights/emerging-consumer-trends-in-a-post-covid-19-world (Accessed February 18, 2023).

47. Annie Palmer, "Groceries and sporting goods were big gainers in the Covid e-commerce book of 2020," *CNBC*, February 19, 2021, https://www.cnbc.com/2021/02/19/e-commerce-surged-during-covid-groceries-sporting-goods-top-gainers-.html (accessed March 18, 2023).

Chapter 7

1. Michael D. Hutt and Thomas W. Speh, *Business Marketing Management: B2B*, 13th ed. (Boston, MA: Cengage, 2024).

2. "12th Annual B2B Content Marketing: Benchmarks, Budgets, and Trends," *Content Marketing Institute*, https://contentmarketinginstitute.com/wp-content/uploads/2021/10/B2B_2022_Research.pdf (accessed February 28, 2023).

3. Krista Fabregas and Kelly Main, "What is Shopify & How Does It Work (2023 Guide)," *Forbes*, https://www.forbes.com/advisor/business/software/what-is-shopify/.

4. Digital Ad Ratings," Nielsen, https://www.nielsen.com/solutions/audience-measurement/digital-ad-ratings/?gclid=CjwKCAiAr4GgBhBFEiwAgwORrc9vRQ0DqSd8vhRzfIJcTzyPfIMoz55cLeOD-LXnw-tpP_xJyKVs-RoCpHkQAvD_BwE&gclsrc=aw.ds (accessed March 1, 2023).

5. Ibid.

6. https://www2.deloitte.com/us/en/insights.html (accessed March 1, 2023).

7. AJ Agrawal, "3 Ways B2B Companies Must Market Themselves in 2016," *Forbes*, January 5, 2016, https://www.forbes.com/sites/ajagrawal/2016/01/05/3-ways-b2b-companies-must-market-themselves-in-2016/#25a22535b821 (accessed November 26, 2018).

8. John Koetsier, "Global Smartwatch Market: Apple 34%, Huawei 8%, Samsung 8%, Fitbit 4.2%," *Forbes*, May 27, 2021, https://www.forbes.com/sites/johnkoetsier/2021/05/27/global-smartwatch-market-apple-34-huawei-8-samsung-8-fitbit-42/?sh=55e6b67566c7 (accessed March 1, 2023).

9. "Starbucks and Nestlé to Bring Ready-to-Drink Coffee Beverages to Southeast Asia, Oceania, and Latina America," *Starbucks Stories & News*, July 26, 2021, https://stories.starbucks.com/press/2021/starbucks-and-nestle-to-bring-ready-to-drink-coffee-beverages-to-southeast-asia-oceania-and-latin-america/ (accessed March 1, 2023).

10. "John Deere and Volocopter Cooperate on Cargo Drone Technology," *Volocopter Newsroom*, November 7, 2019, https://www.volocopter.com/newsroom/john-deere-and-volocopter-cooperate-on-cargo-drone-technology/ (accessed March 4, 2023).

11. Robert M. Morgan and Shelby D. Hunt, "The Commitment-Trust Theory of Relationship Marketing," *Journal of Marketing*, 58, no. 3 (1994), 23.

12. Ibid.

13. Chase Shustack, "The Real Reason McDonald's Stopped Serving Heinz Ketchup," *Mashed*, February 8, 2022, https://www.mashed.com/756066/the-real-reason-mcdonalds-stopped-serving-heinz-ketchup/ (accessed March 4, 2023).

14. "Understanding Japanese Keiretsu," *Investopedia*, January 29. 2022, https://www.investopedia.com/articles/economics/09/japanese-keiretsu.asp (accessed March 13, 2023).

15. "Office 365 operated by 21Vianet," Microsoft 365, February 17, 2023, https://learn.microsoft.com/en-us/microsoft-365/admin/services-in-china/services-in-china?view=o365-21vianet (accessed March 4, 2023).

16. https://fiscaldata.treasury.gov/americas-finance-guide/ (accessed March 4, 2023

17. Ibid.

18. *"Selling Greener Products and Services to the Federal Government,"* *United States Environmental Protection Agency*, https://www.epa.gov/greenerproducts/selling-greener-products-and-services-federal-government.

19. Ibid.

20. Diana Olick, "Soaring lumber price adds nearly $19.000 to the cost of a new home," *CNBC*, February 15, 2022, https://www.cnbc.com/2022/02/15/soaring-lumber-price-adds-nearly-19000-to-the-cost-of-a-new-home.html (accessed March 4, 2023).

21. "Aluminum Association Launches Choose Aluminum Campaign Highlighting Infinitely Recyclable, Sustainable Material of Choice," *Aluminum Association*, December 2, 2021. https://www.globenewswire.com/en/news-release/2021/12/02/2345418/0/en/Aluminum-Association-Launches-Choose-Aluminum-Campaign-Highlighting-Infinitely-Recyclable-Sustainable-Material-of-Choice.html (accessed March 13, 2023).

22. Andrew Tangel and Jemal R. Brinson, "What's Holding Back Boeing's 787 Dreamliner," *The Wall Street journal*, June 26, 2022, https://www.wsj.com/articles/whats-holding-back-boeings-787-dreamliner-11656194652 (accessed March 4, 2023).

23. "Metro announces contract award to Hitachi Rail for 8000-series railcars," *Washington metropolitan Area Transit Authority*, March 17, 2021, https://www.wmata.com/about/news/Metro-announces-contract-award-to-Hitachi-Rail-for-8000-series-railcars.cfm (accessed March 4, 2023).

24. "10 Top U.S. States for Manufacturing," *Industry Select*, May 10, 2022, https://www.industryselect.com/blog/top-10-us-states-for-manufacturing (accesses March 4, 2023).

25. https://activities.alibaba.com/alibaba/following-about-alibaba.php?tracelog=footer_alibaba (accessed March 4, 2023).

26. Jack Ewing and Neal E. Boudette, "A Tine Part's Big Ripple: Global Chip Shortage Hobbles the Auto Industry," *The New York Times*, April 23, 2021, https://www.nytimes.com/2021/04/23/business/auto-semiconductors-general-motors-mercedes.html (accessed November March 4, 2023).

27. Michael D. Hutt and Thomas W. Speh, *Business Marketing Management: B2B*, 13th ed. (Boston, MA: Cengage, 2024).

28. Ibid.

29. Lee Frederiksen, "Marketing to C-Suite Executive Leadership," *Hinge Marketing*, June 12, 2022, https://hingemarketing.com/blog/story/marketing-to-c-suite-executives (accessed March 4, 2023).

30. Shukla, Khushboo, "How to Connect, Engage, and Approach C-Level Executives (CxO) and Decision Makers for B2B Companies, Grow Digitally, June 28, 2022, https://growdigitally.au/how-to-connect-engage-and-approach-c-level-executives-cxo-and-decision-makers-for-b2b-companies/ (accessed March 13, 2023).

31. Michael D. Hutt and Thomas W. Speh, *Business Marketing Management: B2B*, 13th ed. (Boston, MA: Cengage, 2024).

32. Ibid.

Chapter 8

1. Joris Zwegers and Dmitri Seredenko, "What's Wrong with Segmentation?" https://www.ama.org/partners/content/Pages/whats-wrong-with-segmentation.aspx (accessed December 2, 2018).

2. Hannah Fleishman, "13 Businesses with Brilliant Global Marketing Strategies," https://blog.hubspot.com/marketing/global-marketing-and-international-business, March 16, 2022.

3. Melissa Repko, "Dollar General's New Popshelf Stores Chase Inflation-Weary Shoppers in the Suburbs," https://www.cnbc.com/2022/12/13/inflation-dollar-general-chases-suburban-shoppers-popshelf.html, December 13, 2022.

4. "Geographic Segmentation Explained With 5 Examples," https://www.yieldify.com/blog/geographic-segmentation-real-world-examples/, August 27, 2020.

5. Dayna Winter, "Generation Alpha: Everything Brands Need to Know," https://www.shopify.com/blog/gen-alpha, November 11, 2022.

6. "Amazon Nurtures Young Readers with Prime Book Box Service," https://www.brandchannel.com/2018/05/01/amazon_prime_book_box/, May 1, 2018 (accessed February 16, 2023).

7. George Anderson, "Will Lowe's Become Birthday Party Central for Kids?" https://retailwire.com/discussion/will-lowes-become-birthday-party-central-for-kids/, January 20, 2023.

8. Tony Diapaolo, "Understanding Retail Through the Gen Z Filter," https://www.retailcustomerexperience.com/blogs/understanding-retail-through-the-gen-z-filter/, September 28, 2022.

9. Michelle Evans, 'How Gen Z Inspired Grocers to Reinvent Their Social Presence," https://www.forbes.com/sites/michelleevans1/2022/11/29/how-gen-z-inspired-grocers-to-reinvent-their-social-presence/?sh=6e8878c94692, November 29, 2022.

10. Erin Duffin, "Resident Population In The United States In 2021, By Generation," https://www.statista.com/statistics/797321/us-population-by-generation/, October 11, 2022.

11. Richard Fry, "Millennials Projected to Overtake Baby Boomers as America's Largest Generation," *Pew Research,* March 1, 2018, https://www.pewresearch.org/fact-tank/2016/04/25/millennials-overtake-baby-boomers/ (accessed December 3, 2018).

12. Ray A. Smith, "Retailers Stalk the Elusive Millennial Shopper," https://www.wsj.com/articles/retailers-stalk-the-elusive-millennial-shopper-1527692005, *Wall Street Journal,* May 30, 2018.

13. Erik D. Rosenstrauch, "Understanding Millennials' Purchasing Habits Regarding Private Label," https://progressivegrocer.com/understanding-millennials-purchase-habits-regarding-private-label, February 5, 2019.

14. William F. Schroer, "Generations X, Y, Z and the Others," *Social Librarian*, https://www.socialmarketing.org/newsletter/features/generation3.htm (accessed December 3, 2018).

15. Lira Stone, "What Makes Them Buy: Generation X," https://www.theshelf.com/the-blog/generation-x/, October 20, 2022.

16. Anna Grozdanov, "45+ Baby Boomer Spending Habits Statistics For 2022," https://www.lexingtonlaw.com/blog/credit-cards/baby-boomer-spending-habits.html, February 15, 2022

17. Lira Stone, "Marketing to Baby Boomers: What Makes Them Buy in 2023?" https://www.theshelf.com/the-blog/marketing-to-boomers/, January 9, 2023.

18. Eric Roth, "What Retailers Must Know About Consumers Over Age 50—Part 2." https://www.digitalcommerce360.com/2020/07/17/what-retailers-must-know-about-over-50-consumers-boomers-part-2/, July 17, 2020.

19. Alexis Abramson, "The Silent Generation Characteristics You Need to Know," https://www.alexisabramson.com/the-silent-generation-characteristics-and-facts-you-need-to-know/, July 3, 2018.

20. Axel Heyenga, "Silent Gen Shoppers: How Can Retail Brands Future-Proof Online and Offline Engagement?" https://business.adobe.com/uk/blog/perspectives/silent-gen-shoppers-how-can-retail-brands-future-proof-online-and-offline-engagement, November 24, 2020.

21. "Differences in shopping habits between men and women," *The Times of India*, October 26, 2021, https://timesofindia.indiatimes.com/life-style/fashion/buzz/differences-in-shopping-habits-between-men-and-women/articleshow/87263287.cms (accessed April 26, 2023).

22. Rebecca Batterton, "The Rising Purchasing Power Of Women: Facts And Statistics," https://www.bankrate.com/loans/personal-loans/purchasing-power-of-women-statistics/, January 4, 2023.

23. Amy Gesenhues, "Are brands behind the times when it comes to gender stereotypes in ads?" https://martech.org/are-brands-behind-the-times-when-it-comes-to-gender-stereotypes-in-ads/, January 28, 2019.

24. Anne Marie Chaker, "Supermarkets Lure in Male Shoppers," *The Wall Street Journal,* July 10, 2018, p. A9.

25. Robert Williams, "Moisturize This!" *Bloomberg Businessweek,* March 12, 2018, pp. 18, 19.

26. Sheila Savon, "Harrys Launches Flamingo Shaving Brand for Women," https://www.wsj.com/articles/espns-new-pitch-to-advertisers-we-reach-women-1515409200, October 17, 2018.

27. "Verizon LGBTQ pride campaign, "Love Calls Back," https://www.cbsnews.com/video/verizon-lgbtq-pride-campaign-love-calls-back/, May 21, 2020.

28. Mike Wilde, "Where did all the queer Super Bowl ads go in LVI?," *Queerty,* February 13, 2022, https://www.queerty.com/queer-super-bowl-ads-go-lvi-20220213 (accessed April 26, 2023).

29. Nikolett Lorinez, *Op Cit*

30. Elena Prokopets, "Gender-Neutral Marketing: It's More Than a Trend," https://latana.com/post/three-brands-gender-neutral/, May 3, 2022.

31. Hank Cardello, " Five Companies That are capitalizing on Helping The Poor Get Healthier," https://www.hudson.org/domestic-policy/five-companies-that-are-capitalizing-on-helping-the-poor-get-healthier, January 30, 2019.

32. https://www.census.gov/quickfacts/fact/table/US/IPE120221, July 1, 2022.

33. Racial and Ethnic Diversity in the United States: 2010 Census and 2020 Census, *United States Census Bureau,* August 12, 2021, https://www.census.gov/library/visualizations/interactive/racial-and-ethnic-diversity-in-the-united-states-2010-and-2020-census.html

34. Robert Williams, "McDonald's offers 'Golden Start' to Lunar New Year with 3 digital experiences," *Marketing Dive,* February 4, 2021, https://www.marketingdive.com/news/mcdonalds-offers-golden-start-to-lunar-new-year-with-3-digital-experienc/594493/

35. Morgan Strawn, "Excellence in Marketing to the Hispanic Community," https://www.ana.net/miccontent/show/id/ii-2023-01-marketing-to-hispanic-community, January 9, 2023.

36. Mia Gindia, "Black History Month 2023—How Apple, Nike, Spotify And Other Brands Are Celebrating," https://adage.com/article/marketing-news-strategy/black-history-month-2023-apple-nike-spotify-and-other-brand-plans/2474701, February 22, 2023; Portia Botchway, "Xbox Celebrates Black History Month," *Xbox Wire,* February 1, 2023, https://news.xbox.com/en-us/2023/02/01/xbox-celebrates-black-history-month/ (accessed April 26, 2023).

37. Morgan Strawn, "Excellence in Marketing to the Asian Community," https://www.ana.net/miccontent/show/id/ii-2023-01-marketing-to-asian-community, January 9, 2023.

38. "Comcast NBCUniversal Recognizes Native American Heritage Month," https://corporate.comcast.com/stories/comcast-nbcuniversal-native-american-heritage-month-2022, November 2, 2022.

39. Erin Duffin, "Percentage of U.S. households, by Type 1990–2022," https://www.statista.com/statistics/242244/percentage-of-us-households-by-type/, Dec 12, 2022; Census Bureau Releases New Estimates on America's Families and Living Arrangements, "*United States Census Bureau,* November 17, 2022, https://www.census.gov/newsroom/press-releases/2022/americas-families-and-living-arrangements.html (accessed April 26, 2023).

40. Vandita Grover, "Marketing to Kids Through Interactive & Experiential Marketing: World Children's Day Special," https://www.spiceworks.com/marketing/content-marketing/articles/marketing-to-kids-witsh-experiential-and-interactive-marketing/, December 16, 2021.

41. Monique Roberts, "Exploring New Career Paths for Empty Nesters," https://www.udacity.com/blog/2021/07/exploring-new-career-paths-for-empty-nesters.html, July 1, 2021.

42. Beth Hitchcock, "It's time to give PANKS (Professional Aunt, Ni Kids) a little respect," *Today's Parent,* March 29, 2018, https://www.todaysparent.com/family/family-life/give-aunts-a-little-respect/; Hillary Hoffower, "More and more women just want to be 'the cool' aunt instead of having their own kids," Insider, April 17, 2022, https://www.businessinsider.com/cool-aunt-aspirational-identity-childfree-women-instagram-tiktok-2022-4

43. "Why You Wear What You Wear," https://news.harvard.edu/gazette/story/2023/01/why-you-wear-what-you-wear/, January 31, 2023.

44. Gabrielle Policella, "How Lululemon Uses Lifestyle Marketing to create a strong brand community in 2023, " https://blog.smile.io/how-lululemon-uses-lifestyle-marketing-to-create-a-strong-brand-community/, (accessed March 17, 2023).

45. "Overview: Red Bull Ambassador Program," https://brandchamp.io/blog/red-bull-ambassador-program/, July 7, 2022.

46. "DuPont Nutrition & Health: Plant-Based Eating," https://www.preparedfoods.com/articles/121744-dupont-nutrition-health-plant-based-eating, November 16, 2018.

47. K.C. Karnes, "10 Behavioral Segmentation Examples and Strategies," https://clevertap.com/blog/behavioral-segmentation/#:~:text=Behavioral%20segmentation%20is%20the%20process,app%2C%20website%2C%20or%20business., January 27, 2022.

48. Rebecca Riserbato, "The 16 Best Abandoned Cart Emails to Win Back Customers," *Hubspot,* February 16, 2023, https://blog.hubspot.com/marketing/abandoned-cart-email

49. "What Is Behavioral Segmentation in Marketing? (And Examples)," https://www.indeed.com/career-advice/career-development/behavioral-segmentation, February 3, 2023.

50. Stephen Hourighan, "Twelve Effective Behavioural Segmentation Examples and Strategies," https://brandmasteracademy.com/behavioral-segmentation/ (accessed March 17, 2023).

51. Khalid Saleh, "The Importance of Customer Loyalty Programs—Statistics and Trends," https://www.invespcro.com/blog/customer-loyalty-programs/ (accessed April 28, 2023).

52. Toni Matthews, "Customers Baffled by Slow Checkout Line Then See Genius Sign Posted," https://www.inspiremore.com/tesco-relaxed-checkout/, January 2, 2018.

53. BigCommerce, https://www.bigcommerce.com (accessed May 1, 2023).

54. Stephanie Smittle, "Meet Black Paper Party, The Arkansas Company Shaking Up The Digital Gift Wrap Aisle," https://arktimes.com/entertainment/2020/12/04/meet-black-paper-party-the-arkansas-company-shaking-up-the-digital-gift-wrap-aisle, December 4, 2020.; "Black Paper Party Has Just What You Need To Make Your BAE Swoon This Valentine's Day!" https://www.bet.com/article/w3lxb0/black-paper-party-valentines-day-must-haves?xrs=BETPlus_PMAX_Google_campaignid=19319406201&gclid=EAIaIQobChMI2bf_irPr_QIVchh9Ch2s7AldEAMYASAAEgKjBfD_BwE (accessed March 20, 2023); Erin Hyatt and Moni Adeyi, "Black Paper Party: A Spotlight on Black-Owned Brands," https://www.rila.org/blog/2023/01/black-paper-party-a-spotlight-on-black-owned-brand, January 21, 2023; Mollie Belt, "Black Paper Party: Black-Owned, Woman-Owned Company Ensuring the Representation of The Black Family," https://dallasexaminer.com/black-paper-party-black-owned-woman-owned-company-ensuring-the-representation-of-the-black-family/, December 17, 2022; Samantha Doriska, "This Trio is Throwing a Black Paper Party This Holiday Season With Their Line of Inclusive Products," https://afrotech.com/black-women-holiday-products-black-families, November 24, 2021; Bloomberg Opinion, "50 States, 50 Startups: How Innovation Surged in 2022," https://www.bloomberg.com/features/2022-opinion-50-states-50-startups/, September 22, 2022.

55. "What is Undifferentiated Marketing; Basics," https://sendpulse.com/support/glossary/undifferentiated-marketing, February 16, 2022.

56. Mathew Turner, "15 Winning Niche Market Examples (Updated for 2023)," https://mirasee.com/blog/niche-market-examples/, February 8, 2023.

57. "31 Failed E-Commerce Startups & their Case Studies," https://www.failory.com/startups/e-commerce-failures, March 26, 2022.

58. Ibid.

59. "Market Segmenting, Targeting, and Positioning," https://learn.saylor.org/mod/book/view.php?id=53910&chapterid=38509 (accessed March 18, 2023).

60. Cascade Team, "How Toyota Went From Humble Beginnings to Automotive Giant," https://www.cascade.app/strategy-factory/studies/how-toyota-went-from-humble-beginnings-to-automotive-giant, February 22, 2023.

61. James Hetherington, "Apple and Samsung Smartphones May Struggle in 2018, and Its Their Own Fault," https://www.newsweek.com/apple-samsung-and-google-smartphones-may-struggle-2018-and-its-their-own-fault-845923, March 15, 2018.

62. Caroline Forsey, "The Ultimate Guide to Relationship Marketing," https://blog.hubspot.com/marketing/relationship-marketing, June 1, 2022.

63. Collage Group, "Iconic American Brands Connect with Black Consumers Using Culture, Partnerships," https://www.globenewswire.com/en/news-release/2023/02/08/2604151/0/en/Iconic-American-Brands-Connect-with-Black-Consumers-Using-Culture-Partnerships.html, February 8, 2023.

64. Lindsey Peacock, "7 Innovative Customer Loyalty Programs and How to Start," https://www.shopify.com/blog/loyalty-program, June 22, 2022.

65. "All Brands," Coca-Cola, https://www.thecocacolacompany.com/brands/brandlist.html (accessed March 19, 2023).

66. Guido Bartolacci, "14 Examples of Strong Brand Positioning and Why They Work," https://www.newbreedrevenue.com/blog/7-examples-of-strong-brand-positioning-and-why-they-work, October 20, 2022.

67. Ibid.

68. Jim Woodruff, "What is Premium Pricing Strategy?" https://smallbusiness.chron.com/premium-pricing-strategy-1107.html, February 6, 2019.

69. Amelia Lucas, "Vita Coco Wants Its Coconut Water to Be Your Cocktail Mixer—And Your Hangover Cure," https://www.cnbc.com/2023/02/10/vita-coco-coconut-water-cocktails-hangover.html, February 10, 2023.

70. "Our Brands," *Gap Inc.*, https://www.gapinc.com/content/gapinc/html/aboutus/ourbrands.html (accessed March 19, 2023).

71. "Positioning Product Class," https://www.zabanga.us/marketing-communications/info-nom.html, February 19, 2023.

72. Charlie Hobbs and Meredith Carey, "The Best Airbnb Experiences in the World, From Sailing in Rio to Shucking Oysters in Boston," https://www.cntraveler.com/story/best-virtual-airbnb-experiences-to-book-now, November 22, 2022.

73. Conor Bond, "9 Comparative Advertising Examples to Help You Get Ahead," https://www.wordstream.com/blog/ws/2020/01/13/comparative-advertising, February 11, 2023.

74. Khris Steven, "21 Interesting Emotional Marketing Statistics in 2023," https://khrisdigital.com/emotional-marketing-statistics/, December 17, 2022.

75. Jan Suski, "Brand Repositioning: How to Redefine Your Company's Image," https://brand24.com/blog/brand-repositioning/, November 4, 2022.

Chapter 9

1. "50 Camping Industry Statistics for North America (2022)," Amateur Adventure Journal, August 11, 2022, https://amateuradventurejournal.com/camping-industry-statistics-2022/ (accessed March 18. 2023).

2. Marcia Layton Turner "Retailers, 95% of Shoppers Want to be Left Along In-Store," Forbes, March 30, 2018.

3. Parks Associates: 38% of Households Own at Least One Smart Home Device, Up 2% From the Previous Year, PR Newswire, October 10, 2022, https://www.prnewswire.com/news-releases /parks-associates-38-of-households-own-at-least -one-smart-home-device-up-2-from-the-previous -year-301644694.html.

4. Alexander Kunst, "Does your household own wearables?," Statista, February 23, 2022, https://www.statista.com/forecasts/1101101 /wearable-devices-ownership-in-selected-countries

5. Lionel Sujay Vailshery, "IoT global annual revenue 2020-2030," Statista, November 23, 2022, https://www.statista.com/statistics/1194709 /iot-revenue-worldwide/

6. "Decoding the Product Page," Quirks Marketing Research Review, July 2018, 32–35.

7. https://datareportal.com/essential-facebook -stats (accessed March 18, 2023).

8. Avantika Monnappa, "How Facebook uses Big Data: The Good, the Bad, and the Ugly," Simple Learn, March 7, 2023, https://www.simplilearn. com/how-facebook-is-using-big-data-article.

9. Brandon A. Dorfman, "How Dollar Stores Sell Low-Income People a Sense of Belonging," talk poverty, https://talkpoverty.org/2020/02/19/dollar -stores-sell-low-income-people-sense-belonging/

10. "Mighty Neighborly," Quirks Marketing Research Review, January 2018, 12–14.

11. https://www.surveymonkey.com/welcome/sem -survey-respondents-3/?program=7013A000002Iel GQAS&utm_bu=AD&utm_campaign=7170000 0058890149&utm_adgroup=58700005410036437 &utm_content=43700075557173778&utm _medium=cpc&utm_source=adwords&utm_term =p75557173778&utm_kxconfid=s4bvpi0ju& gclid=CjwKCAjwiOCgBhAgEiwAjv5whNHSZ1r Gqf3WqzMIx42M_DprL1mlXUVO4TXxWXL _oq_U_7ckaxJ6ojhoC4LkQAvD_BwE&gclsrc=aw .ds (accessed March 20, 2023).

12. Carl McDaniel and Roger Gates, Marketing Research, 11th ed. (Hoboken: Wiley, 2018), 147.

13. "Taking Our Seat at the Table," Quirks Marketing Research Review, January 2018, 26–27.

14. https://www.statista.com/statistics/966543 /market-research-industry-mobile-surveys/ (accessed March 20, 2023).

15. Carl McDaniel ... Marketing Research, 148.

16. Danielle Wiener-Bronner, "How America turned into a nation of snackers," CNN, https:// www.cnn.com/2022/09/03/business/snacks -history/index.html

Chapter 10

1. Cara Salpini, "Adidas creates 'Virtual Gear' product category as it preps for metaverse future," Retail Dive, November 18, 2022, https://www. retaildive.com/news/adidas-creates-metaverse- virtual-gear-product-category-nft/636883/ (accessed March 29, 2023).

2. "Chobani unveils fall yogurt/creamer flavors," The Lewiston Tribune, https://www.lmtribune .com/business/chobani-unveils-fall-yogurt -creamer-flavors/article_b3d55801-9ec0-5f3a -8ed9-e14cdf4e36f1.html

3. Andy Boxall, "Apple's Ceramic Shield may change your mind about an iPhone 14 screen protector," digital trends, September 13, 2022, https://www.digitaltrends.com/mobile/iphone -ceramic-shield-glass-one-year-test/

4. Alex Leanse, "How 360-Degree Camera Systems Turn Your Into a Parking Pro," Motortrend, August 25, 2020, https://www.motortrend.com /features/360-degree-camera-systems/ (accessed March 29, 2023).

5. Maggie Ginsberg, "How Taco Bell Became 2020's Top Franchise," Entrepreneur, January 19, 2023, https://www.entrepreneur.com/franchise /how-taco-bell-became-2020s-top-franchise /363039 (accessed March 29, 2023).

6. Nathan Bomey, "Weight Watchers Rebrands as WW, Eliminates Artificial Ingredients in Focus on Wellness," https://www.usatoday.com/story /money/2018/09/24/weight-watchers-international -ww/1408238002/, September 24, 2018.

7. "Product of the Year USA Announces 2022 Award Winners," PR Newswire, https://www .prnewswire.com/news-releases/product-of-the -year-usa-announces-2022-award-winners -301479332.html (accessed April 10, 2023).

8. Michael Grothaus, "Coke is killing 200 brands: Here's the list of canceled products announced so far," Fast Company, October 23, 2020, https:// www.fastcompany.com/90567765/coke-is-killing -200-brands-heres-the-list-of-canceled-products -announced-so-far (accessed March, 28, 2023).

9. "Best Global Brands 2022," https://interbrand .com/best-brands/ (accessed March 29, 2023).

10. Errol Schweizer, "Why Private Label Brands are Having Their Moment," https://www.forbes .com/sites/errolschweizer/2022/06/30/why-store -brands-are-having-their-moment/?sh=388a27e 038bf, Forbes, June 30, 2022.

11. Katie Tarasov, "How Amazon's big private- label business is growing and leaving small brands to protect against knockoffs," CNBC, https:// www.cnbc.com/2022/10/12/amazons-growing -private-label-business-is-challenge-for-small -brands.html, October 12, 2022.

12. https://www.wholefoodsmarket.com /departments/365-products (accessed March 29, 2023).

13. Richard Mitchell, "Kroger's Simple Truth brand hits 10 year mark," Supermarket News, January 11, 2023, https://www.supermarketnews .com/organic-natural/kroger-s-simple-truth-brand -hits-10-year-mark (accessed March 29, 2023).

14. Mike Pomranz, "Oreo and Ritz Made a Cookie and Cracker Mashup Nobody Saw Coming," Food & Wine, May 24, 2022, https://www .foodandwine.com/news/oreo-ritz-cookies-crackers -sandwich (accessed March 29, 2023).

15. "13 Best Co-Branding Examples from Major Companies," Rockcontent, December 31, 2021, https://rockcontent.com/blog/co-branding -examples/ (accessed March 29, 2023).

16. Jordan Oloman, "Gaming is entering its fashion-forward phase," The Washington Post, July 12, 2021, https://www.washingtonpost.com /video-games/2021/07/12/video-game-fashion -esports-streetwear/ (accessed March 29, 2023).

17. "Trademark Applications—Intent-to-Use (ITU) Basis," https://www.uspto.gov/trademarks -application-process/filing-online/intent-use-itu -applications (accessed March 29, 2023).

18. Timothy Geigner, "Copyright Continues to be Abused to Censor Critics by Entities Both Big and Small," tech dirt, September 30, 2021, https:// www.techdirt.com/2021/09/30/copyright-continues -to-be-abused-to-censor-critics-entities-both-big -small/ (accessed March 29, 2023).

19. "Utah theme park sues Taylor Swift over 'Evermore' album," AP, February 3, 2021, https://apnews.com/article/lawsuits-utah-taylor- swift-trademark-infringement-trademarks- b57792e0e1408fc870a6705f0954aef1 (accessed March 29, 2023).

20. "Tiffany, Costco settle 8-year lawsuit over fake 'Tiffany' rings," CNBC, July 19, 2021, https:// www.cnbc.com/2021/07/19/tiffany-costco- settle-8-year-lawsuit-over-fake-tiffany-rings.html (accessed March 29, 2023).

21. The Fashion Law, "Louis Vuitton, Prada Targeted by Fake Stores in Chinese Cities," https://www.thefashionlaw.com/home/louis -vuitton-prada-targeted-by-fake-stores-in-chinese -cities, September 6, 2018.

22. U.S. Food and Drug Administration, "The New Nutrition Facts Label," https://www.fda .gov/food/nutrition-education-resources-materials /new-nutrition-facts-label (accessed March 29, 2023).

23. Government of Canada, "Consultation on proposed front-of-package labelling," https:// www.canada.ca/en/health-canada/programs /consultation-front-of-package-nutrition-labelling -cgi.html (accessed March 29, 2023).

24. "Color Packaging: The Color Wheel of Branding And Packaging," Johns Byrne, https:// www.johnsbyrne.com/blog/packaging-colors -say-brand/, February 16, 2017 (accessed April 1, 2023).

25. https://en.wikipedia.org/wiki/Wrap_rage (accessed March 29, 2023).

26. Lauren Manning, "Consumer demand for sustainable packaging holds despite pandemic," Food Dive, https://www.fooddive.com/news/consumer -demand-for-sustainable-packaging-holds-despite -pandemic/599013/, April 27, 2021.

27. Aleksandra Owczarek, "24 Eco Friendly Packaging Examples that Benefit your Brand," Packhelp, https://packhelp.com/eco-friendly -packaging-examples/ (accessed March 29, 2023).

28. Imperial College London "Food freshness sensors could replace 'use-by' dates to cut food waste," Science Daily, June 5, 2019, https://www.sciencedaily .com/releases/2019/06/190605100401.htm (accessed April 1, 2023).

29. https://greenseal.org/about/mission/ (accessed March 31, 2023).

30. Kristin Hohenadel, "One Designer's Lonely Crusade to Make Packing Disappear," Slate, April 2, 2014, https://slate.com/human-interest /2014/04/how-to-eliminate-packaging-waste-the -disappearing-package-by-aaron-mickelson.html (accessed August 30, 2023).

31. Mary Meisenzahl "This is how Dunkin' has changed since it dropped the 'Donuts'," *Business Insider*, April 15, 2021, https://www.businessinsider.com/dunkin-dropped-donuts-added-non-coffee-drinks-and-celebrity-partnerships-2021-8 (accessed April 1, 2023).

Chapter 11

1. "The World's Most Innovative Companies of 2022," *Fast Company*, https://www.fastcompany.com/most-innovative-companies/2022 (accessed April 11, 2023).

2. "Pharma's Top 20 R&D Spenders in 2021," *Drug Discovery & Development*, https://www.drugdiscoverytrends.com/pharmas-top-20-rd-spenders-in-2021/ (accessed April 11, 2023).

3. Prableen Bajpai, "Which Companies Spend the Most in Research and Development (R&D)?," *Nasdaq*, June 21, 2021, https://www.nasdaq.com/articles/which-companies-spend-the-most-in-research-and-development-rd-2021-06-21 (accessed April 11, 2023).

4. "Apple Unveils All-New MacBook Air, Supercharged by the New M2 Chip," *Apple Newsroom*, June 6, 2022, https://www.apple.com/newsroom/2022/06/apple-unveils-all-new-macbook-air-supercharged-by-the-new-m2-chip/ (accessed April 11, 2023).

5. Victoria Song, "Withings' New Scale has a Retractable Handle that Measures EKGs and Segmented Body Composition," *The Verge*, January 3, 2022, https://www.theverge.com/2022/1/3/22855714/withings-body-scan-ekg-body-fat-fda-ces-2022 (accessed April 11, 2023).

6. Victoria Giardina, "Brooklinen Just Launched Laundry Detergent—Get All the Details Here," *New York Post*, March 21, 2023, https://nypost.com/2023/03/21/shop-brooklinens-new-laundry-detergent-right-now// (accessed April 11, 2023).

7. "McDonald's Used Snapchat AR and Video Products to Drive a 4pt Increase in Purchase Intent for their McPlant Burger," *Snapchat*, https://forbusiness.snapchat.com/inspiration/mcdonalds-mcplant (accessed April 11, 2023.

8. Megan Poinski, "Capri Sun Cuts Sugar 40% by Reformulating with Monk Fruit," *Food Dive*, July 27, 2022, https://www.fooddive.com/news/capri-sun-cuts-sugar-monk-fruit-reformulation/628191/ (accessed April 15, 2023).

9. Irene Anna Kim and Jay Reed, "Why Millennials Love Gucci," *Insider*, March 5, 2021, https://www.businessinsider.com/gucci-millennials-teens-love-designer-comeback-2018-11 (accessed April 15, 2023).

10. Nate Klemp, "Google Encourages Employees to Take Time Off to Be Creative. Here's How You can Too, Without Sacrificing Outcomes," *Inc.*, November 14, 2019, https://www.inc.com/nate-klemp/google-encourages-employees-to-take-time-off-to-be-creative-heres-how-you-can-too-without-sacrificing-outcomes.html (accessed April 11, 2023).

11. Oliver Franklin-Wallis, "Inside X, Google's Top-Secret Moonshot Factory," *Wired*, February 17, 2020, https://www.wired.co.uk/article/ten-years-of-google-x (accessed April 11, 2023).

12. "About Fuld & Company," *Fuld & Company*, https://www.fuld.com/who-we-are/overview/ (accessed April 11, 2023).

13. "Winterstick Snowboards Opens R&D Site Near Sugarloaf," *Mainebiz*, March 9, 2017, https://www.mainebiz.biz/article/20170309/NEWS0101/170309942/winterstick-snowboards-opens-r&d-site-near-sugarloaf (accessed December 31, 2018).

14. "U.S. and Global Research and Development," *National Science Foundation*, https://ncses.nsf.gov/pubs/nsb20221/u-s-and-global-research-and-development (accessed April 15, 2023).

15. "Clients," *Continuum*, https://continuumcs.com/why-continuum/clients/ (accessed April 11, 2023).

16. Clive Reffell, "How LEGO Used Crowdsourcing to Achieve 21st Century Success," *Crowdsourcing Week*, November 19, 2021, https://crowdsourcingweek.com/blog/lego-success-through-crowdsourcing/ (accessed April 11, 2023).

17. Rachel Esposito, "10 Rushed Video Games That Were Unfinished on Launch," *CBR*, January 8, 2023, https://www.cbr.com/video-games-that-were-unfinished-on-launch/#pok-eacute-mon-scarlet-amp-violet-kept-its-glitches-in-for-a-holiday-release (accessed April 15, 2023).

18. Michael D. Hutt and Thomas W. Speh, *Mindtap Marketing for Business Marketing Management B2B*, 12th ed. (Boston: Cengage, 2017).

19. *Zwift Forums*, https://forums.zwift.com (accessed April 20, 2023).

20. Emma Liem Beckett, "Panera's Coffee Subscription Leverages Loyalty to Fight Breakfast Battle," *Restaurant Dive*, February 27, 2020, https://www.restaurantdive.com/news/paneras-new-coffee-subscription-leverages-loyalty-to-fight-breakfast-battl/573098/ (accessed April 15, 2023).

21. Danielle Wiener-Bronner, "One of the Biggest Launched We've Had': Starbucks New Drinks Have a Spoonful of Olive Oil," *ABC 7*, February 22, 2023, https://abc7.com/starbucks-olive-oil-drinks-coffee-oleato-latte-new-menu-item/12858675/ (accessed April 15, 2023).

22. "P&G Everyday," *Procter & Gamble*, https://www.pgeveryday.com/offers (accessed April 15, 2023).

23. Anish K, "75–95% of Product Launches Fail Every Year, Do You Know Why?," *LinkedIn*, December 16, 2020, https://www.linkedin.com/pulse/75-95-product-launches-fail-every-year-do-you-know-why-anish-k (accessed April 15, 2023).

24. "25 Biggest Product Flops of the Last 10 years," *Chicago Tribune*, January 12, 2023, https://www.chicagotribune.com/business/sns-25-biggest-product-flops-of-the-last-10-years-20230112-2u7636xcmjdzvo23trndcf7jtq-photogallery.html (accessed April 15, 2023).

25. 2022 Product of the Year Winners, https://productoftheyearusa.com/winners-2022/, (accessed April 20, 2023).

26. "Nielsen 2021 Trust in Advertising Study," *Nielsen*, https://www.nielsen.com/wp-content/uploads/sites/2/2021/11/2021-Nielsen-Trust-In-Advertising-Sell-Sheet.pdf (accessed April 15, 2023).

27. Pankaj Narang, "Social Media Hashtag Campaigns: 10 of the Very Best (+ A Few Fails)," *Mention*, February 21, 2023, https://mention.com/en/blog/social-media-hashtag-campaigns/ (accessed April 15, 2023).

28. Dan Berthiaume, "Consumers Share Brand Experiences—So Make Yours Positive," *Chain Store Age*, May 24, 2021, https://chainstoreage.com/consumers-share-brand-experiences-so-make-yours-positive (accessed April 15, 2023).

29. GoPro Launches Three New HERO11 Black Cameras That Send Highlight Videos to Your Phone," GoPro, https://gopro.com/en/us/news/hero11-black-mini-camera-launch, (accessed April 15, 2023).

30. Inna Semenyuk, "Employees As Influencers: A Blessing Or A Curse?" Forbes, February 14, 2020, https://www.forbes.com/sites/forbesagencycouncil/2020/02/14/employees-as-influencers-a-blessing-or-a-curse/?sh=723121de3d67 (accessed April 15, 2023).

31. Innovative Products Coming Out in 2023," *Tomorrow's World Today*, https://www.tomorrowsworldtoday.com/2023/01/16/9-innovative-products-coming-out-in-2023/

Chapter 12

1. "Service sector value added to the Gross Domestic Product (GDP) of the United States of America in 2021, by industry," https://www.statista.com/statistics/1233657/us-service-sector-value-added-gdp-industry/ (accessed April 18, 2023).

2. Justin Dawes, "Four Seasons Won't Let Tech Replace the Human Exchange Expected of Luxury," *Skift*, November 15, 2022, https://skift.com/2022/11/15/four-seasons-wont-let-tech-replace-the-human-exchange-expected-of-luxury/ (accessed April 24, 2023).

3. Ed Tittel and Kim Lindros, "Best Big Data Certifications," https://www.businessnewsdaily.com/10754-best-big-data-certifications.html, May 23, 2018.

4. Joei Chan "Social Customer Service: Lessons from 5 of Our Favorite Brands," *Mention,* https://mention.com/en/blog/social-customer-service/, February 21, 2023.

5. Candice Georgiadis "Hilton's Jonathan Witter: "The future of hospitality has to feel customized and personal," *Medium*, May 19, 2019, https://medium.com/authority-magazine/hiltons-jonathan-witter-the-future-of-hospitality-has-to-feel-customized-and-personal-c4d6a9c138bf.

6. Valarie Zeithaml, Mary Jo Bitner, and Dwayne Gremler, *Services Marketing: Integrating Customer Service Across the Firm,* 7th ed. (New York: McGraw Hill, 2018).

7. Ibid.

8. "Relationships, Not Retail: Nordstrom, Customer Service, and core Values," *Belief Agency,* February 1, 2023, https://www.beliefagency.com/blog/relationships-not-retail-nordstrom-customer-service-and-core-values (accessed April 19, 2023).

9. Caleb Wilson "Starbucks ranked most valuable restaurant brand," March 17, 2023, https://www.foodbusinessnews.net/articles/23433-starbucks-ranked-most-valuable-restaurant-brand (accessed April 20, 2023); Kathryn Lundstrom, "Yes, Pumpkin Spice IS Arriving Earlier Each Year – Driven by Gen Z and Millennial Demand," *Ad Week,* August 23, 2021, https://www.adweek.com/brand-marketing/pumpkin-spice-arriving-earlier-each-year-gen-z-millennials/ (accessed April 20, 2023).

10. Morgan, Blake. "The Top 100 Most Customer-Centric Companies of 2022." *Forbes,* 12 Oct. 2022, www.forbes.com/sites/blakemorgan/2022/05/01/the-top-100-most-customer-centric-companies-of-2022/?sh=1bf8f1f22b38.

11. Much of the material in this section is based on Jochen Wirtz and Christopher H. Lovelock, *Services Marketing: People, Technology and Strategy,* 8th ed. (Upper Saddle River, NJ: Prentice Hall, 2016).

12. Molly Allen, "The Untold Truth of MOD Pizza," *Mashed,* https://www.mashed.com/181208/the-untold-truth-of-mod-pizza/, February 1, 2023, (accessed April 24, 2023).

13. *Warby Parker,* https://www.warbyparker.com (accessed April 24, 2023); *StitchFix,* https://www.stitchfix.com/how-it-works (accessed April 24, 2023).

14. Alexis Benveniste, "Domino's is launching a pizza delivery robot car," *CNN Business,* April 13, 2021, https://www.cnn.com/2021/04/12/tech/dominos-pizza-delivery-robot/index.html (accessed April 24, 2023).

15. Colette Bennett, "Walmart, Target Made the Right Bet Based on What Customers Want," *The Street,* July 5, 2022, https://www.thestreet.com/investing/walmart-target-buy-online-pick-up-iin-store-harvard-report (accessed April 24, 2023).

16. Riley Cardoza, "35 Bizarre McDonald's Items from Around the World" *Eat This, Not That!,* April 10, 2021, https://www.eatthis.com/mcdonalds-food-around-the-world/ (accessed April 24, 2023).

17. "Returning Customers Spend 67% More Than New Customers—Keep Your Customers Coming Back with a Recurring Revenue Sales Model," *Business,* February 21, 2023, https://www.business.com/articles/returning-customers-spend-67-more-than-new-customers-keep-your-customers-coming-back-with-a-recurring-revenue-sales-model/ (accessed April 24, 2023).

18. Ibid.

19. Much of the material in this section is based on Valarie Zeithaml, Mary Jo Bitner, and Dwayne Gremler, *Services Marketing: Integrating Customer Service Across the Firm,* 7th ed. (New York: McGraw Hill, 2018).

20. "Why New Orleans' Ritz Carlton Hotel is a cut above the rest," *Luxury Gold,* September 11, 2022, https://blog.luxurygold.com/hotel-in-new-orleans/ (accessed April 24, 2023).

21. "Fortune 100 Best Companies to Work For 2023," *Fortune,* https://fortune.com/ranking/best-companies/ (accessed April 24, 2023); "Do rewards make a difference in employee referral?," *Medium,* March 9, 2018, https://medium.com/@referralrecruit/do-rewards-make-a-difference-in-employee-referral-a11a1faa396d (accessed April 24, 2023).

22. Sky Ariella, "26 Incredible Nonprofit Statistics [2023]: How Many Nonprofits Are in the U.S.?," *Zippia,* March 13, 2023, https://www.zippia.com/advice/nonprofit-statistics/#:~:text=5.7%25%20of%20the%20United%20States,annual%20revenue%20is%20%242.62%20trillion. (accessed April 24, 2023).

23. Korrin Bishop, "6 Creative Corporate Sponsorship Examples," *Classy Blog,* January 13, 2023, https://www.classy.org/blog/creative-examples-corporate-sponsorships/ (accessed April 24, 2023).

24. "Make-A-Wish, American Airlines, Disney and The Points Guy Take Off on The Best Flight Ever in support of 27 children battling critical illnesses," *PR Newswire,* April 05, 2023, https://www.prnewswire.com/news-releases/make-a-wish-american-airlines-disney-and-the-points-guy-take-off-on-the-best-flight-ever-in-support-of-27-children-battling-critical-illnesses-301790219.html (accessed April 24, 2023).

25. Ellen Ormesher, "Ad Council and StoryCorp take 'One Small Step' towards a meaningful conversation," *The Drum,* March 2, 2021, https://www.thedrum.com/news/2021/03/02/ad-council-and-storycorp-take-one-small-step-towards-meaningful-conversation (accessed April 24, 2023).

Chapter 13

1. "About Us," Spreadshirt, https://www.spreadshirt.com/about-us-C68 (assessed February 21, 2023).

2. "The Complexity of the Lego Supply Chain!," Supply Chain Game Changer, https://supplychaingamechanger.com/the-complexity-of-the-lego-supply-chain/; https://www.ascm.org/ascm-insights/scm-now-impact/lego-builds-a-resilient-supply-chain--brick-by-brick/; https://www.spglobal.com/marketintelligence/en/news-insights/latest-news-headlines/lego-s-supply-chain-agility-helps-build-sales-during-pandemic-60218745 (assessed February 21, 2023).

3. "ASOS PLC Annual Report and Accounts 2019," ASOS, https://www.annualreports.co.uk/HostedData/AnnualReportArchive/a/LSE_ASOS_2019.pdf (assessed February 21, 2023).

4. "Where machine learning models meet mobility and human behavior," Amazon, https://www.amazon.science/working-at-amazon/mahdieh-allahviranloo-last-mile-delivery-research (assessed February 25, 2023).

5. "Transforming into a circular business," IKEA, https://about.ikea.com/en/sustainability/a-world-without-waste (assessed March 27, 2023).

6. "Working as Fulfillment Centers, Walmart Stores are the Star of the Last Mile," Walmart, https://corporate.walmart.com/newsroom/2022/02/28/working-as-fulfillment-centers-walmart-stores-are-the-star-of-the-last-mile (assessed March 27, 2023).

7. Mark A. Moon, *Demand and Supply Integration: The Key to World-Class Demand Forecasting* (New York: Financial Times Press, 2013).

8. Much of this section is based on material adapted from Donald J. Bowersox, David J. Closs, and Theodore P. Stank, *21st Century Logistics: Making Supply Chain Integration a Reality* (Oak Brook, IL: Council of Logistics Management, 1999);

Barbara Flynn, Michiya Morita, and Jose Machuca, *Managing Global Supply Chain Relationships: Operations, Strategies and Practices* (Hershey, Pennsylvania: Business Science, 2010); and David Sims, "Integrated Supply Chains Maximize Efficiencies and Savings," *ThomasNet,* July 23, 2013, https://news.thomasnet.com/imt/2013/07/23/integrated-supply-chains-maximize-efficiencies-and-savings (accessed March 2019).

9. "Nestlé and Unilever CEOs: we will make our supply chains deforestation-free," *Financial Times,* https://www.ft.com/content/d0224863-6071-436d-a628-d7f3a71cb36f (assessed March 27, 2023).

10. Much of this and the following sections are based on material adapted from Douglas M. Lambert, ed., *Supply Chain Management: Processes, Partnerships and Performance* (Sarasota, FL: Supply Chain Management Institute, 2004); "The Supply Chain Management Processes," *Supply Chain Management Institute,* https://www.emeraldinsight.com/doi/pdfplus/10.1108/IJLM-12-2015-0242 (accessed March 18, 2019).

11. Haralalka, Amit, "Why Starbucks is the 'Apple' of CRM & Loyalty Programs!" https://www.linkedin.com/pulse/starbucks-apple-crm-loyalty-programs-heres-why-amit-haralalka/ (assessed February 25, 2023).

12. Neb, Vikrant "Customer Relationship Management," https://www.linkedin.com/pulse/customer-relationship-management-vikrant-neb/; "Companies with Successful CRM Strategies and how they did it." Hey Dan, https://heydan.ai/companies-with-successful-crm-strategies-and-how-they-did-it/ (assessed February 25, 2023).

13. Ruggles, Megan "GM secures 3 more supply agreements to boost EV production," Supply Chain Dive, https://www.supplychaindive.com/news/gm-secures-more-supply-agreements-for-electric-vehicles/628515/ (assessed February 25, 2023).

14. "20 Best Order Fulfillment Services & Companies of 2023," *Finances Online: Reviews for Business,* https://financesonline.com/top-20-order-fulfillment-services/ (accessed March 27, 2023).

15. https://electrek.co/2021/01/19/tesla-structural-battery-pack-first-picture/ (accessed February 26, 2023).

16. Lambert, Fred, "First look at Tesla's new structural battery pack that will power its future electric cars," *Electrek,* https://electrek.co/2021/01/19/tesla-structural-battery-pack-first-picture/ (assessed February 25, 2023).

17. Fedow, Lenore "What Tiffany's Acquisition Means for the Jewelry Industry," *National Jeweler,* https://nationaljeweler.com/articles/989-what-tiffany-s-acquisition-means-for-the-jewelry-industry (assessed February 26, 2023).

18. "Returns & Exchanges," REI, https://www.rei.com/help/returns (assessed February 26, 2023).

19. "23 Stores With the Best Return Policies," Retail Me Not, https://www.retailmenot.com/blog/stores-with-the-best-return-policies.html (assessed February 26, 2023).

20. Levy, Lauren, "Sustainable Pallets, Packages & More," *Food Logistics,* May 17, 2013, https://www.foodlogistics.com/article/10944473/sustainable-pallets-packages-more (accessed October 27, 2023).

21. "Trash to gas: UPS gets moving on Renewable Natural Gas," UPS https://about.ups.com/ae/en/social-impact/environment/sustainable-alternative-fuel---about-ups.html; "Electrifying our future," UPS, https://about.ups.com/us/en/social-impact/environment/sustainable-services/electric-vehicles---about-ups.html (assessed February 26, 2023).

22. "Walgreens Transitional Work Group sets the standard in disability hiring," Walgreens, https://news.walgreens.com/our-stories/walgreens-transitional-work-group-sets-standard-in-disability-hiring.htm (assessed March 26, 2023).

23. Hotten, Russell "Volkswagen: The scandal explained," BBC, https://www.bbc.com/news/business-34324772 (assessed February 26, 2023).

24. "Global CSR Risk and Performance Index 2018," Index.ecovadis.com (accessed March 26, 2023).

25. "We, Robot: How humans and AI are working together in logistics," DHL, https://www.dhl.com/global-en/delivered/digitalization/ai-in-logistics.html (assessed February 26, 2023); https://www.coupa.com/customers/using-coupa-sheds-light-engies-spend (accessed April 7, 2023).

26. https://fetchrobotics.com/ (assessed April 7, 2023).

27. Singh, Manish, "India's Zomato flies drone to deliver food in successful test," *TechCrunch,* https://techcrunch.com/2019/06/12/zomato-and-zee-dronezzz/ (assessed February 26, 2023).

28. Dickey, Megan Rose, "UPS partners with drone startup Matternet for medical sample deliveries," *TechCrunch,* https://techcrunch.com/2019/03/26/ups-partners-with-drone-startup-matternet-for-medical-sample-deliveries/; https://www.theverge.com/2022/11/8/23447502/alphabet-wing-drones-doordash-air-logan-australia (assessed February 26, 2023).

29. "3D Systems Brings EKOCYCLE ™ Cube® 3D Printer to Harrods," 3D Systems, https://www.3dsystems.com/press-releases/3d-systems-brings-ekocycle-tm-cuber-3d-printer-harrods (assessed March 26, 2023).

30. "Aviation and aerospace industry," GE, https://www.ge.com/additive/additive-manufacturing/industries/aviation-aerospace (assessed March 26, 2023), "How Nike is leveraging 3D Printing in the Footwear Industry," *Manufacturing 3D Mag,* https://manufactur3dmag.com/how-nike-isleveraging-3d-printing-in-the-footwear-industry/ (assessed March 26, 2023).

31. "BanQu Is Making a Brighter Future for Farmers," BanQU, https://www.banqu.co/news/banqu-is-making-a-brighter-future-for-farmers; https://www.nestle.com/media/pressreleases/allpressreleases/nestle-open-blockchain-pilot (assessed March 26, 2023).

32. Andreas Fürst, Martin Leimbach, and Jana-Kristin Prigge, "Organizational Multichannel Differentiation: An Analysis of Its Impact on Channel Relationships and Company Sales Success," *Journal of Marketing,* 81, no. 1 (2017): 59–82.

33. Lovejoy, Ben "LG matching Samsung's advanced OLED tech for 2022 iPad Air screens," 9to5Mac https://9to5mac.com/2021/08/18/2022-ipad-air-screens/ (assessed March 26, 2023).

34. Jansen, Caroline "Casper to open first branded shop-in-shop with Bed Bath and Beyond," Retail Dive, https://www.retaildive.com/news/casper-to-open-first-branded-shop-in-shop-with-bed-bath-beyond/603394/ (assessed March 26, 2023).

35. "IKEA Bordeaux contributes to ongoing product recycling push," INGKA, https://www.ingka.com/news/ikea-bordeaux-contributes-to-ongoing-product-recycling-push/ (assessed March 26, 2023).

36. "Apple expands the use of recycled materials across its products," Apple, https://www.apple.com/newsroom/2022/04/apple-expands-the-use-of-recycled-materials-across-its-products/ (assessed March 26, 2023).

37. "M-Commerce Market Share, Size, Trends, Industry Analysis Report, By Payment Modes (Near-field Communication (NFC), Premium SMS, Wireless Application Protocol (WAP), Direct Carrier Billing, Others); By Transactions; By End-Use; By Region; Segment Forecast, 2022 - 2030," *Polaris Market Research,* www.polarismarketresearch.com/industry-analysis/m-commerce-market (assessed March 26, 2023).

38. https://www.prnewswire.com/news-releases/mobile-commerce-sales-expected-to-double-to-700-billion-by-2025-301459912.html (accessed April 7, 2023).

39. Sapardic, Jelisaveta "Top 10+ Mobile Commerce Statistics for 2023 [Report]," Tidio, https://www.tidio.com/blog/mobile-commerce-statistics/ (assessed March 26, 2023).

40. "Grow your business with TikTok Shop," TikTok, https://shop.tiktok.com/merchant/en (assessed March 26, 2023).

41. LaMontagne, Liva, "MarketingSherpa Consumer Purchase Preference Survey: Demographics of customer reasons to follow brands' social accounts," MarketingSherpa, https://www.marketingsherpa.com/article/chart/demographics-why-customer-follow-brands-social-media (assessed March 26, 2023).

42. J.J. Wang, X. Zhao, and J.J. Li. "Group Buying: A Strategic Form of Consumer Collective," *Journal of Retailing,* 89, no. 3 (2013), 338–351.

43. Bentsen, Rick "Disney Reportedly Lost Over $600 Million on Black Widow to Piracy," Movie Web, https://movieweb.com/disney-black-widow-piracy/ (assessed March 26, 2023).

44. Granados, Dr. Nelson, Mooney, Dr. John. "Popcorn or Snack? Empirical Analysis of Movie Release Windows." *Pepperdine Business School,* November 2018, https://digitalcommons.pepperdine.edu/cgi/viewcontent.cgi?article=1005&context=graziadiowps

45. Taurn Kushwaha and Venkatesh Shankar, "Are Multichannel Customers Really More Valuable? The Moderating Role of Product Category Characteristics," *Journal of Marketing,* 77, no. 4, 67–85; Jennifer Lonoff Schiff, "Eight Ways to Create a Successful Multichannel Customer Experience," CIO, https://www.cio.com/article/2887285/e-commerce/8-ways-to-create-a-successful-multichannel-customer-experience.html (accessed December 2018).

Chapter 14

1. "Wholesale and Retail Trade Industries Labor Productivity," U.S. Bureau of Labor Statistics, https://www.bls.gov/productivity/highlights/wholesale-retail-trade-industries-labor-productivity.htm#:~:text=The%20retail%20trade%20sector%20employed,percent%20to%20value%2Dadded%20GDP (accessed February 17, 2023; Shearman, J. Craig, "NRF Says 2022 Holiday Sales Grew 5.3% to 936.3 Billion," National Retail Federation, January 18, 2023 https://nrf.com/media-center/press-releases/nrf-says-2022-holiday-sales-grew-53-9363-billion (accessed February 17, 2023).

2. "NAICS Code Description," NAICS Association, https://www.naics.com/naics-code-description/?code=44-45 (accessed February 17, 2023).

3. https://corporate.walmart.com/askwalmart/how-many-people-work-at-walmart (accessed March 18, 2023).

4. "2023 Employee Experience Trends Report," *Qualtrics,* https://www.qualtrics.com/ebooks-guides/2023-ex-trends-report/(accessed March 17, 2023); "How Americans View Their Jobs," *Pew Research Center,* October 6, 2016, https://www.pewsocialtrends.org/2016/10/06/3-how-americans-view-their-jobs/ (accessed March 17, 2023); "2022 Small Business Profile: United States," *U.S. Small Business Administration Office of Advocacy,* 2022, https://cdn.advocacy.sba.gov/wp-content/uploads/2022/08/30121338/Small-Business-Economic-Profile-US.pdf (accessed March 17, 2023); "Ask Walmart" *Walmart,* 2023, https://corporate.walmart.com/askwalmart/how-many-people-work-at-walmart (accessed March 17, 2023); "Countries in the World by Population (2023)," *Worldometers,* 2023, https://www.worldometers.info/world-population/population-by-country/ (accessed March 17, 2018).

5. "2023 Top 500 Franchise 500 Ranking," *Entrepreneur,* https://www.entrepreneur.com/franchises/500/2023 (accessed February 21, 2023).

6. Heather Carter, "5 food and beverage trends to watch in 2023," *Food & Beverage Insider,* January 13, 2023, https://www.foodbeverageinsider.com/market-trends-analysis/5-food-and-beverage-trends-watch-2023 (accessed February 21, 2023).

7. Kyuseop Kwak, Sri D. Duvvuri, and Gary J. Russell, "An Analysis of Assortment Choice in Grocery Retailing," *Journal of Retailing,* 91, no. 1 (2015): 19–33.

8. "How Dynamic Pricing is Disrupting Online Retail," *Intelligence Node* (accessed on February 25, 2023).

9. "Flexible Figures," *The Economist,* January 28, 2016, https://www.economist.com/news/business/21689541-growing-number-companies-are-using-dynamic-pricing-flexible-figures (accessed February 25, 2023).

10. April Berthene, "Walmart, Target and Home Depot win at omnichannel retailing," *Digital Commerce 360,* February 19, 2019, https://www.digitalcommerce360.com/2019/02/19/walmart-target-and-home-depot-win-at-omnichannel-retailing/ (accessed on February 26, 2023).

11. "2022 Omnichannel Report: Analyzing omnichannel trends in today's evolving retail world," *Digital Commerce 360,* https://www.digitalcommerce360.com/product/omnichannel-report/ (accessed on February 26, 2023).

12. "The Ritz Carlton in Naples Now Has a Vending Machine for Champagne," *Robb Report,* https://robbreport.com/travel/resorts/champagne-vending-machines-in-luxury-hotels-2841073/ (accessed on February 26, 2023).

13. "20 Unique Direct Sales Companies in 2022," *Finding Balance,* https://findingbalance.mom/unique-direct-sales-companies/ (accessed February 26, 2023).

14. "2023 B2B Marketing Mix Report," *Sagefrog Marketing Group,* 2023, https://sagefrog-website.s3.amazonaws.com/2022/11/Marketing-Mix-2023-Report.pdf (accessed February 26, 2023).

15. "47 Direct Mail Statistics Marketers Should Know in 2023," *Postalytics,* https://www.postalytics.com/blog/statistics-on-direct-mail/ January 12, 2023 (accessed February 26, 2023).

16. Tianyi Jiang and Alexander Tuzhilin, "Dynamic Microtargeting: Fitness-Based Approach to Predicting Individual Preferences," *Knowledge and Information Systems*, 19, no. 3 (2009): 337–360.

17. "47 Direct Mail Statistics Marketers Should Know in 2023," *Postalytics,* https://www.postalytics.com/blog/statistics-on-direct-mail/ January 12, 2023 (accessed February 26, 2023).

18. "Home Shopping Market – Growth, Trends, and Forecasts (2023-2028)," *Mordor Intelligence*, https://www.mordorintelligence.com/industry-reports/homeshopping-market (accessed, February 27, 2023).

19. "Online-Shopping and E-Commerce Worldwide: Statistics & Facts," *Statista*, 2022, https://www.statista.com/topics/871/online-shopping/#topicOverview (accessed February 27, 2023); Arishekar N, "Amazon Statistics (Seller, FBA, and Product) That'll Surprise You," *Sellerapp*, https://www.sellerapp.com/blog/amazon-seller-statistics/ (accessed February 27, 2023); Maryia Fokina, "Online Shopping Statistics: Ecommerce Trends for 2023," *TIDIO*, https://www.tidio.com/blog/online-shopping-statistics/ (accessed February 27, 2023).

20. Evert de Haan, Peter K. Kannan, Peter C. Verhoef, and Thorsten Wiesel. "Device Switching in Online Purchasing: Examining the Strategic Contingencies," *Journal of Marketing*, 82, no. 5, (2018) 1–19.

21. Sonika Singh, Sungha Jang, (2022), "Search, purchase, and satisfaction in a multiple-channel environment: How have mobile devices changed consumer behaviors?" *Journal of Retailing and Consumer Services*, 65, https://doi.org/10.1016/j.jretconser.2020.102200. (accessed February 28, 2023).

22. Yunhui Huang and Charles Zhang, "The Out-of-Stock (OOS) Effect on Choice Shares of Available Options," *Journal of Retailing*, 92, no. 1 (2015): 13–24.

23. Andrew Asch, "Nordstrom Local, the Americana at Brand Popping in Holiday Pop-up Shops," November 18, 2018, https://www.apparelnews.net/news/2018/nov/08/nordstrom-local-americana-brand-popping-holiday-po/

24. "Delivery Platform for Retail Logistics," *Bringg*, https://www.bringg.com/industries/retailers/ (accessed March 6, 2023); "Capitalizing on Its Tremendous Market Momentum, Bringg Appoints Guy Bloch as Its New Chief Executive Officer," *Cision*, September 26, 2018, https://www.prnewswire.com/news-releases/capitalizing-on-its-tremendous-market-momentum-bringg-appoints-guy-bloch-as-its-new-chief-executive-officer-860818369.html (accessed March 6, 2023).

25. https://www.forbes.com/sites/walterloeb/2022/04/29/how-bringg-solves-the-last-mile-in-supply-chain-delivery/?sh=5735bfef4b8a; https://www.forbes.com/sites/walterloeb/2022/04/29/how-bringg-solves-the-last-mile-in-supply-chain-delivery/?sh=5735bfef4b8a (accessed March 20, 2023).

26. Phil Dawsey, "Amazon's acquisition of Whole Foods will bring AI technology to grocery stores," *Venture Beat,* October 4, 2017, https://venturebeat.com/ai/amazons-acquisition-of-whole-foods-will-bring-ai-technology-to-grocery-stores/(accessed March 6, 2023).

27. "The State of Influencer Marketing 2023," *Influencer MarketingHub,* https://influencermarketinghub.com/ebooks/Influencer_Marketing_Benchmark_Report_2023.pdf (accessed March 6, 2023).

28. https://people.com/style/target-launches-new-designer-collaborations-with-sergio-hudson-la-ligne-and-kika-vargas/ (accessed March 20, 2023).

29. Shannon Flynn, "5 Powerful Examples of Retail Analytics," *Retail It,* August, 27, 2021, https://www.retailitinsights.com/doc/powerful-examples-of-retail-analytics-0001#:~:text=Both%20Wendy's%20and%20Starbucks%20use,areas%20hold%20the%20most%20potential (accessed March 6, 2023).

30. Shari Waters, "Choosing a Retail Store Location," *The Balance*, September 6, 2018, https://www.thebalancesmb.com/choosing-a-retail-store-location-2890245 (accessed December 6, 2018).

31. https://www.businessinsider.com/stores-closing-in-2023-list#jcpenney-2-stores-12 (accessed March 20, 2023).

32. https://articles.bplans.com/seven-creative-ways-to-engage-with-your-customers-online/ (accessed March 20, 2023).

33. Carl L. Esmark, Stephanie M. Noble, and Michael J. Breazeale, "I'll be Watching You: Shoppers' Reactions to Perceptions of Being Watched By Employees," *Journal of Retailing*, 93, no. 3, 336–349.

34. Adrian C. North, Lorraine P. Sheridan, and Charles S. Areni, "Music Congruity Effects on Product Memory, Perception, and Choice," *Journal of Retailing*, 92, no. 1 (2015): 82–95.

35. Yalch, Richard; Spangenberg, Eric, "Effects of Store Music on Shopping Behavior," *The Journal of Consumer Marketing*, Spring 1990; 7, 2; ABI/INFORM Global pg. 55 (accessed March 6, 2023).

36. Klemens M. Knoeferle, Vilhelm C. Paus, and Alexander Vossen, "An Upbeat Crowd: Fast In-store Music Alleviates Negative Effects of High Social Density on Consumers' Spending," *Journal of Retailing*, 93, no. 4, 541–549.

37. AdrienaV. Madzharov, Lauren G. Block, and Maureen Morrin, "The Cool Scent of Power: Effects of Ambient Scent on Consumer Preferences and Choice Behavior," *Journal of Marketing*, 79, no. 1 (2015): 83–96.

38. Haithem Zourrig, Jean-Charles Chebat, and Roy Toffoli, "Consumer Revenge Behavior: A Cross-Cultural Perspective," *Journal of Business Research*, 62, no. 10 (2009): 995–1001.

39. "The Power of Empowerment," *The Ritz-Carlton Leadership Center,* March 19, 2019, https://ritzcarltonleadershipcenter.com/2019/03/19/the-power-of-empowerment/ (accessed March 6, 2023).

40. "How 4 Major Retailers are Using Big Data," *Neil Patel,* https://neilpatel.com/blog/retailers-are-using-big-data/ (accessed March 7, 2023).

41. https://www.talend.com/resources/smart-retailing/ (accessed March 20, 2023).

42. Michael Simoncic & Alfredo Lozano, "Returns are the new growth strategy," *Retail Dive,* December 23, 2021, https://www.retaildive.com/news/returns-are-the-new-growth-strategy/611842/ (accessed March 7, 2023).

43. Christopher Ratcliff, "iBeacons: The Hunt for Stats," *Econsultancy.com*, August 26, 2014; Rachel Abrams, "Psst! It's Me, the Mannequin," *The New York Times*, 2015, A8.

44. Brian Laney, "5 Things Retailers Need to Know about RFID Technology," *Alert Tech,* June 16, 2015, https://alerttech.net/retail-rfid-technology/ (accessed December 15, 2018).

45. Richard Ventura, "Taking a Look at NRF16: Trends in Retail Industrial Technology," *Digital Signage Today,* February 18, 2016, https://www.digitalsignagetoday.com/articles/taking-a-look-at-nrf16-trends-in-retail-industry-technology/ (accessed November 30, 2018).

46. https://www.biometricupdate.com/202302/anonymized-demographic-data-targeted-advertising-added-to-itls-age-estimation (accessed March 20, 2023).

47. Ying Lin, "10 Voice search Statistics You Need to Know in 2023," *OBERLO,* January 28, 2023, https://www.oberlo.com/blog/voice-search-statistics#:~:text=An%20increasing%20number%20of%20people,week%20(UpCity%2C%202022) (accessed March 7, 2023).

48. Scott Clarke, "How Voice-Assisted Commerce Is Speaking Up in Retail," *ITProPortal*, March 6, 2018, https://www.itproportal.com/features/how-voice-assisted-commerce-is-speaking-up-in-retail/ (accessed March 7, 2023).

49. "5 Examples of Omnichannel Retail Experiences," *Emarsys,* October 5, 2016, https://emarsys.com/learn/blog/omnichannel-for-ecommerce-retailers/ (accessed March 7, 2023); "Access the Magic During Your Walt Disney World Vacation," *Disneyworld.disney.go.com.* https://disneyworld.disney.go.com/guest-services/access-the-magic/ (accessed March 7, 2023).

50. Stuart Miller, "Customers Have High Expectations for Click and Collect," Real Business, November 28, 2013, https://realbusiness.co.uk/article/24866-customers-have-high-expectations-for-click-and-collect (accessed December 6, 2018).

51. "Sam's Club Begins National Deployment of Automated Inventory Analytics Robots," *Sam's Club*, January 27, 2022, https://corporate.samsclub.com/newsroom/2022/01/27/sams-club-begins-national-deployment-of-automated-inventory-analytics-robots (accessed March 7, 2023).

52. Kathryn Rickmeyer, "Nashville-area restaurant rolls out robot server," *Tennbeat.com*, August 18, 2022, https://www.tennbeat.com/p/nashville-area-restaurant-rolls-out (accessed March 7, 2023).

Chapter 15

1. https://www.marketingdive.com/news/dominos-Netflix-stranger-things-app-Gen-Z-fans/634319/ (accessed on March 14, 2023).

2. https://online.utpb.edu/about-us/articles/communication/how-much-of-communication-is-nonverbal/#:~:text=It%20was%20Albert%20Mehrabian%2C%20a,%2C%20and%207%25%20words%20only (accessed April 8, 2023).

3. Yi, H. T., & Amenuvor, F. E. (2023). Emotional intelligence and boundary-spanning behavior among door-to-door salespeople. *Canadian Journal of Administrative Sciences/Revue Canadienne des Sciences de l'Administration*, https://onlinelibrary.wiley.com/doi/abs/10.1002/cjas.1711?casa_token=U-rE65VvCj4AAAAA:ChfnqgH3lcbiPeuBEPapRJu-fGxAws-xf6I3Ca8MZf4RV0h7XjAgVT0__zGQtXR-GkslatECueLnnLU (accessed April 8, 2023).

4. https://digitalmarketinginstitute.com/blog/dove-a-spotless-approach-to-digital-marketing#:~:text=As%20a%20result%20of%20the,Unilever's%20bestselling%20product%20company%2Dwide; https://www.studysmarter.us/explanations/marketing/marketing-campaign-examples/dove-real-beauty-campaign/ (accessed April 8, 2023).

5. https://www.liveoakcommunications.com/post/why-dove-s-real-beauty-campaign-was-so-successful (accessed April 10, 2023).

6. https://www.liveoakcommunications.com/post/why-dove-s-real-beauty-campaign-was-so-successful (accessed April 10, 2023).

7. https://www.studysmarter.us/explanations/marketing/marketing-campaign-examples/dove-real-beauty-campaign/ (accessed April 10, 2023).

8. https://www.youtube.com/@UberEats (accessed April 10, 2023).

9. https://www.forbes.com/sites/gabbyshacknai/2022/06/11/inside-the-success-of-dyson-hair-and-its-decision-to-redesign-the-bestselling-airwrap-tool/?sh=2311f83cc55e; https://www.cascade.app/strategy-factory/studies/dyson-strategy-study (accessed April 10, 2023).

10. https://www.marinsoftware.com/blog/5-persuasive-ads-to-inspire-you-in-2023 (accessed April 10, 2023)

11. https://www.insidehook.com/daily_brief/vehicles/gm-netflix-electric-car-war; https://www.caranddriver.com/features/g32463239/new-ev-models-us/ https://www.greencarreports.com/news/1138675_the-ev-price-war-is-here-and-its-no-pain-no-gain-for-automakers (accessed April 10, 2023).

12. https://thedieline.com/blog/2023/4/3/best-april-fools-day-pranks-of-2023? (accessed April 12, 2023).

13. https://breastcancernow.org/about-us/news-personal-stories/its-wear-it-pink-day; https://mention.com/en/blog/personalization-social-media-marketing/ (Accessed April 12, 2023).

14. https://www.fastcompany.com/90846952/most-innovative-companies-data-science-2023; https://sports.yahoo.com/16-personality-types-spotify-wrapped-195652285.html?guccounter=1&guce_referrer=aHR0cHM6Ly93d3cuZ29vZ2xlLmNvbS8&guce_referrer_sig=AQAAAKZlZvJqPSRt8FbIs0YOwGxkpQFB24z84TI2MI5xEvO7PJKv0EjPn0w_UwPxoprkZiP86u0a0olo6BRV901iC7B1gmmqyuhqOBlTxmAQCwqZvRjNok3x6irYxlR_pI2gwcrwPK8GK67zbQvMBBqjB_4-WSQDkWDH3yF42mtKWLOS (accessed April 21, 2023).

15. https://www.nytimes.com/article/tiktok-ban.html (accessed April 21, 2023).

16. https://www.forbes.com/sites/forbesagencycouncil/2023/02/06/15-industry-specific-examples-of-effective-experiential-marketing/?sh=434be2d97820 (accessed April 21, 2023)

17. https://wisepops.com/blog/sales-promotion-examples (accessed April 21, 2023)

18. https://www.searchenginejournal.com/social-media-marketing-examples/380202/#close (accessed April 22, 2023)

19. The AIDA concept is based on the classic research of E. K. Strong Jr. as theorized in *The Psychology of Selling and Advertising* (New York: McGraw Hill, 1925); "Theories of Selling," *Journal of Applied Psychology* 9, no. 1 (1925): 75–86.

20. https://www.sortlist.com/blog/adidas-ads/ (accessed May 5, 2023)

21. Thomas E. Barry and Daniel J. Howard, "A Review and Critique of the Hierarchy of Effects in Advertising," *International Journal of Advertising* 9, no. 2 (1990): 121–135.

22. https://www.wayfair.com/daily-sales/way-day (accessed April 24, 2023).

Chapter 16

1. https://www.obilityb2b.com/blog/how-to-measure-b2b-paid-search-and-paid-social-campaigns/ (accessed May 25, 2023).

2. https://www.statista.com/statistics/272314/advertising-spending-in-the-us/;https://www.statista.com/statistics/1174981/advertising-expenditure-worldwide/; https://www.statista.com/statistics/1175169/growth-of-advertising-spending-worldwide-by-region/.

3. https://adage.com/article/datacenter/bracing-recession-after-ad-spending-surge-worlds-largest-advertisers-2022/2432806; https://adage.com/datacenter/marketertrees2022; (accessed May 23, 2023).

4. https://www.zippia.com/advice/big-data-statistics/ (accessed May 11, 2023).

5. https://www.statista.com/statistics/264875/brand-value-of-the-25-most-valuable-brands/ (accessed May 4, 2023).

6. https://www.creditdonkey.com/television-statistics.html#:~:text=The%20average%20person%20watches%20about,home%20features%202.3%20TV%20sets.; https://www.oberlo.com/statistics/how-much-time-does-the-average-person-spend-on-the-internet#:~:text=On%20average%2C%20internet%20users%20worldwide,401%20minutes%E2%80%94414.5%20minutes%20less (accessed May 12, 2023).

7. https://www.bls.gov/opub/ted/2022/men-spent-5-6-hours-per-day-in-leisure-and-sports-activities-women-4-9-hours-in-2021.htm (accessed May 12, 2023).

8. https://9to5mac.com/2021/10/28/iphone-loyalty-rate-data-switchers/ (accessed May 12, 2023).

9. https://www.cnn.com/2023/04/12/business/bud-light-dylan-mulvaney/index.html (accessed May 12, 2023).

10. https://www.tomorrowsworldtoday.com/2023/01/16/9-innovative-products-coming-out-in-2023/; https://www.instagram.com/reel/Cpkb2UBjM68/ (accessed May 23, 2023).

11. https://www.youtube.com/watch?v=4Klv1Map2UY (accessed May 12, 2023).

12. https://www.alisonhadley.co.uk/british-airways-take-your-holiday-seriously-campaign/ (accessed May 24, 2023).

13. https://drinkolipop.com/pages/faq (accessed May 24, 2023).

14. https://www.patagonia.com/home/; https://www.youtube.com/watch?v=UAZ8Ts9CC6I; https://www.patagonia.com/mx/buy-less-demand-more/?s_kwcid=17928&utm_source=google&utm_medium=cpc&utm_campaign=Non+Brand++Dynamic+Search++Catch+All&utm_content=alwayson&gclid=CjwKCAjw04yjBhApEiwAJcvNoZIsinEbS_YQYNH6rTDiNOxRkTIUv0ih19d650aY8oW-tYGF-QqAAxoCfT4QAvD_BwE (accessed May 24, 2023) .

15. Lauren Cleave, "Using Humour to Cope, Is It Healthy?" https://talklaurentalk.wordpress.com/2018/08/16/using-humour-to-cope-is-it-healthy/ (accessed March 2019).

16. https://www.marketingdive.com/news/happiness-marketing-brand-consumer-oracle/625554/ (accessed on May 4, 2023).

17. https://www-statista-com.ezproxy.mtsu.edu/statistics/191926/us-ad-spending-by-medium-in-2009/ (accessed May 12, 2023).

18. Ibid.

19. Ibid.

20. Semenik, Richard J., et al. *Advertising and Integrated Brand Promotion*. Cengage, 2023.

21. https://www.agilitypr.com/resources/top-media-outlets/top-10-american-magazines/ (accessed May 25, 2023).

22. https://musicalpursuits.com/radio/ (accessed May 5, 2023)

23. https://www.zippia.com/advice/cord-cutting-statistics/ (accessed May 5, 2023)

24. https://adage.com/article/media/tv-commercial-prices-advertising-costs-2022-23-season/2437106 (accessed May 5, 2023)

25. https://stylecaster.com/super-bowl-commercial-cost/ (accessed May 5, 2023)

26. https://blog.gitnux.com/infomercial-industry -statistics/ (accessed May 5, 2023)

27. https://www.nexttv.com/news/2023-predictions -streaming-grows-with-advertising-measurement -follows (accessed May 5, 2023).

28. https://www.insiderintelligence.com/content /worldwide-digital-ad-spend-will-top-600-billion -this-year; https://www-statista-com.ezproxy.mtsu .edu/statistics/268666/tv-advertising-spending -worldwide-by-region/ (accessed May 5, 2023).

29. https://support.google.com/google-ads/answer /12463119?hl=en (accessed May 5, 2023).

30. https://www.zippia.com/advice/smartphone -usage-statistics/#:~:text=According%20to%20 our%20extensive%20research,or%20once%20 every%20ten%20minutes. (accessed May 7, 2023).

31. https://en.softonic.com/top/facebook-games (accessed May 7, 2023).

32. https://influencermarketinghub.com/facebook -gaming-stats/ (accessed May 7, 2023), https:// www.marketwatch.com/story/facebook-vs-non -facebook-social-network-gaming-ecosystem-and -market-analysis-2013-2018-2014-02-04 (accessed January 2019).

33. https://socialplanner.io/blog/social-media -marketing-advantages-and-disadvantages/; https://digitalcatalyst.in/blog/what-are-the -main-advantages-and-disadvantages-of-digital -marketing/ (accessed June 1, 2023).

34. https://www.odwyerpr.com/story/public/17584 /2022-03-02/mobile-account-for-70-digital-ads -by-2026.html#:~:text=Mobile%20platforms%20 accounted%20for%2060,and%2064%20percent %20in%202023 (accessed May 7, 2023).

35. https://www.zippia.com/advice/us-smartphone -industry-statistics/#:~:text=According%20to%20 Pew%20Research%20Center,t%20live%20without %20their%20smartphones (accessed May 7, 2023).

36. https://www.zippia.com/advice/smartphone -usage-statistics/#:~:text=According%20to%20 our%20extensive%20research,or%20once%20 every%20ten%20minutes (accessed May 7, 2023).

37. https://www.bankmycell.com/blog/how-many -phones-are-in-the-world (accessed May 7, 2023).

38. https://brandongaille.com/15-mobile -advertising-advantages-and-disadvantages/ (accessed June 1, 2023).

39. https://www.fox12marketing.com/blog/whats -the-optimal-frequency-for-running-your-ads (accessed May 10, 2023).

40. https://www.fcc.gov/edocs/search-results?t =advanced&titleText=broadcast%20station%20 totals; https://encyclopedia.pub/entry/37584 (accessed May 10, 2023).

41. https://www.marketingevolution.com /marketing-essentials/cross-channel-marketing (accessed May 10, 2023).

42. https://www.businesswire.com/news/home /20221017005130/en/Papa-Johns-Celebrates-the -Return-of-Shaq-a-Roni-Pizza-Highlighting-its -Footprint-in-a-Big-Way#:~:text=The%20Shaq%2 Da%2DRoni%20features,into%20eight%20Shaq %2Dsized%20slices; https://www.searchenginejournal .com/social-celebrity-endorsements/415568/#close (accessed May 10, 2023).

43. https://www.gartner.com/en/articles/what-will -marketing-focus-on-in-2023 (accessed May 10, 2023).

44. https://techcrunch.com/2023/02/02/netflix -evs-tv-shows-and-movies-part-new-partnership -with-gm/ (accessed May 10, 2023).

45. https://www.statista.com/topics/10118 /product-placement-worldwide/#topicOverview; https://www-statista-com.ezproxy.mtsu.edu /statistics/1376404/global-product-placement -spend-share/; https://advanced-television .com/2022/03/23/research-tv-shows-featuring -most-product-placement/ (accessed May 10, 2023).

46. "Zenith's 2021 US Media and Marketing- Services Spending Forecast: $487 billion," Advertising Age 2021 Edition Marketing Fact Pack, *Advertising Age,* https://adage.com/white -paper/ad-age-marketing-fact-pack-2021 (accessed May 10, 2023).

47. Ibid.

48. https://spotme.com/blog/13-event-marketing -examples/; https://en.as.com/meristation/2023 /02/03/news/1675455014_380837.html; https:// www.complex.com/pop-culture/best-fortnite-live -events-ranked (accessed May 10, 2023).

49. https://blog.hubspot.com/marketing/best -experiential-marketing-campaigns (accessed May 10, 2023).

50. https://sproutsocial.com/insights/crisis -communication-examples/; https://www .theguardian.com/business/2022/feb/01/marks -spencer-and-aldi-call-truce-in-colin-the-caterpillar -cake-war; https://www.standard.co.uk/reveller /caterpillar-cakes-rank-colin-cuthbert-aldi-m-s -b930107.html; https://www.bbc.com/news /business-60223220 (accessed May 10, 2023).

51. https://www.webfx.com/digital-advertising /pricing/cost-to-advertise-on-national-tv/ (accessed May 11, 2023).

52. https://www.pggoodeveryday.com/ (accessed May 11, 2023).

53. https://www.nytimes.com/2022/06/29/business /economy/grocery-coupons-inflation.html (accessed May 11, 2023).

54. https://millennialmoney.com/best-coupon-sites/ (accessed May 11, 2023).

55. https://www.tremendous.com/blog/why-rebates -are-a-great-consumer-promotion/ (accessed May 11, 2023).

56. https://queue-it.com/blog/loyalty-program -statistics/ (accessed May 11, 2023).

57. Ibid.

58. https://www.forbes.com/sites/forbesagencycouncil /2022/04/25/how-to-reinvent-your-sampling -efforts-in-2022-and-beyond/?sh=4f79afdc14c1; https://collegemarketing.chegg.com/insights /surprise-delight-samples/; https://www.zennioptical .com/help/after?a=What-is-Virtual-Try-On-and -how-do-I-use-it---id--MsGGANqaTqqc6IrSddy Axg (accessed May 11, 2023).

59. https://thedeltagroup.com/blog/how-in -store-signage-influences-consumer-purchasing -decisions/#:~:text=According%20to%20one%20 study%2C%2082,driven%20by%20in%2 Dstore%20promotions (accessed May 11, 2023).

60. https://www.bigcommerce.com/blog/coupon -marketing/ (accessed May 11, 2023).

61. https://www.bigcommerce.com/blog/coupon -marketing/ (accessed May 11, 2023).

62. https://queue-it.com/blog/loyalty-program -statistics/ (accessed May 11, 2023).

63. "Zero Moment of Truth (ZMOT)," Google, https://www.thinkwithgoogle.com/collections /zero-moment-truth.html (accessed May 11, 2023).

Chapter 17

1. "Retail" BestBuy, https://jobs.bestbuy.com /bby?id=career_area&content=retail&career _site=Retail&spa=1&s=req_id_num (accessed April 7, 2023).

2. Michael Rodriquez, Haya Ajjan, and Robert M. Peterson, "Social Media in Large Sales Forces: An Empirical Study of the Impact of Sales Process Capability and Relationship Performance," *Journal of Marketing Theory and Practice,* 24, no. 3 (2016), 365–379.

3. "Shopping made personal," Neiman Marcus, https://www.neimanmarcus.com/c/nm-services -of-nm-cat59720737 (accessed April 7, 2023).

4. Zimmerman, Ann. "Can retailers halt 'showroom- ing'?" *The Wall Street Journal* 259.1 (2012): B1–B8.

5. Chaker, Nawar N., Chaker, Nawar N., Edward L. Nowlin, Maxwell T. Pivonka, Omar S. Itani, and Raj Agnihotri. "Inside sales social media use and its strategic implications for salesperson- customer digital engagement and performance." *Industrial Marketing Management* 100 (2022): 127–144.

6. "About LinkedIn," LinkedIn, https://about .linkedin.com/ (accessed April 7, 2023).

7. "Sales Navigator Product Datasheet," LinkedIn, https://business.linkedin.com/sales-solutions/site -forms/sales-navigator-datasheet (accessed April 7, 2023).

8. "What Is Social Selling?" LinkedIn, https:// business.linkedin.com/sales-solutions/social-selling /what-is-social-selling (accessed April 7, 2023).

9. "How it works," Angie's List, https://www.angi .com/how-it-works.htm; "How reviews work," *Trust Pilot,* https://www.trustpilot.com/trust/how -reviews-work (accessed April 7, 2023).

10. "Global State of Sales 2022," LinkedIn, https://business.linkedin.com/sales-solutions/the -state-of-sales-2022-report; "6 Channels to find your new prospects online," PandaDoc, https:// www.pandadoc.com/blog/how-to-find-prospects -online/ (accessed April 13, 2023).

11. Friend, Scott B., Kumar Rakesh Ranjan, and Jeff S. Johnson. "Fail fast, sell well: The contingent impact of failing fast on salesperson performance." *Industrial Marketing Management* 82 (2019): 265–275.

12. "Different greetings across cultures," *Country Navigator,* https://www.countrynavigator.com /blog/greetings-across-cultures/ (accessed April 15, 2023).

13. "Global State of Sales 2022," LinkedIn, https:// business.linkedin.com/sales-solutions/the-state-of -sales-2022-report (accessed April 7, 2023).

14. Wongkitrungrueng, Apiradee, Nassim Dehouche, and Nuttapol Assarut. "Live streaming commerce from the sellers' perspective: implications for online relationship marketing." *Journal of Marketing Management* 36.5-6 (2020): 488–518.

15. "The Social Selling Sales Playbook," HubSpot, https://blog.hubspot.com/sales/sales-professionals-guide-to-social-selling (accessed April 14, 2023).

16. Terho, Harri, Marta Giovannetti, and Silvio Cardinali. "Measuring B2B social selling: Key activities, antecedents and performance outcomes." *Industrial Marketing Management* 101 (2022): 208–222.

17. Castleberry, Steven, and Jeff Tanner, *Selling*, 11th ed. New York: McGraw Hill, 2021.

18. Deeter-Schmelz, Dawn R. "Managing the latest generations of sales representatives: what Millennials and Generation Z want." *A Research Agenda for Sales.* Edward Elgar Publishing, 2021. 91–108.

19. "E-Learning and Its Role in Today's Sales Teams," SoCo Selling, https://www.socoselling.com/e-learning-for-sales-teams/ (accessed April 14, 2023).

20. https://www.passionateinmarketing.com/coca-cola-introduces-the-create-real-magic-ai-platform-as-part-of-its-new-promotion/ (accessed April 25, 2023).

21. "Bank of America set up a cross-sell opportunity by extending its digital engagement strategy across product lines," *Business Insider,* https://www.businessinsider.com/bank-of-america-mobile-refresh-advances-financial-ecosystem-2020-9 (accessed April 15, 2023).

22. "Recommendations," Amazon, https://www.amazon.com/gp/help/customer/display.html?nodeId=GE4KRSZ4KAZZB4BV (accessed April 15, 2023).

23. https://newsroom.sephora.com/sephora-and-tiktok-partner-to-pioneer-new-program-for-rising-beauty-brands-and-content-creators%EF%BF%BC/ (accessed April 26, 2023)

Chapter 18

1. Larry Bodine, "Building a Law Practice with Social Media," American Bar Association, November 8, 2018, https://abaforlawstudents.com/2018/11/08/building-a-law-practice-with-social-media/ (accessed May 12, 2023).

2. https://www.demandsage.com/social-media-users/#:~:text=So%20to%20answer%20your%20question,are%20on%20social%20media%20platforms (accessed May 12, 2023).

3. https://blog.hubspot.com/marketing/influencer-marketing-stats (accessed June 9, 2023).

4. https://www.rivaliq.com/live-benchmarks/designer-brands/

5. https://blog.hubspot.com/service/social-listening-examples (accessed May 15, 2023).

6. https://www.jeffbullas.com/social-listening-examples/ (accessed May 15, 2023).

7. https://www.prnewswire.com/news-releases/target-announces-ongoing-partnership-with-actress-author-and-social-media-phenomenon-tabitha-brown-301548364.html; https://www.instagram.com/iamtabithabrown/?hl=en; https://www.instagram.com/target/ (accessed May 15, 2023).

8. https://bloggingwizard.com/facebook-live-statistics/#:~:text=In%20fact%2C%20the%20most%20viewed,Live%20was%20'Chewbacca%20Mom'. (accessed May 16, 2023).

9. https://www.intel.com/content/www/us/en/legal/intel-social-media-guidelines.html; https://www.swaybase.com/social-media-policy-directory/us-air-force#:~:text=In%20general%2C%20the%20Air%20Force,must%20represent%20our%20core%20values. (accessed May 16, 2023).

10. https://www.forbes.com/sites/emmylucas/2023/04/07/bosses-are-training-employees-to-be-influencers-after-long-discouraging-social-media-posts-about-work/?sh=45df00f16d8e (accessed May 16, 2023).

11. https://www.meltwater.com/en/blog/top-chinese-social-media-apps-sites (accessed May 16, 2023).

12. https://www.similarweb.com/blog/research/market-research/worldwide-messaging-apps/ (accessed May 16, 2023).

13. https://riverside.fm/blog/video-platforms (accessed May 16, 2023).

14. https://imagen.io/blog/social-media-video/ (accessed May 16, 2023).

15. https://explodingtopics.com/blog/smartphone-stats; https://www.pewresearch.org/internet/fact-sheet/mobile/; https://www.statista.com/statistics/467160/forecast-of-smartphone-users-in-china/; https://www.worldometers.info/world-population/china-population/ (accessed May 16, 2023).

16. https://marketsplash.com/tablet-statistics/#:~:text=Google's%20Android%20is%20the%20leading,to%2060%25%20in%20recent%20quarters.&text=iOS%20has%20around%20a%20third,a%20little%20over%2010%25%20share. (accessed May 16, 2023).

17. Sid Gandotra, "Why Social Commerce Matters," *Social Media Today,* November 6, 2012, https://www.socialmediatoday.com/content/why-social-commerce-matters (accessed May 16, 2023).

18. https://www.prnewswire.com/news-releases/global-industry-analysts-predicts-the-world-social-commerce-market-to-reach-2-9-trillion-by-2026--301491332.html (accessed May 16, 2023).

19. https://rockcontent.com/blog/shoppable-video/ (accessed May 16, 2023).

20. https://blog.wishpond.com/post/113964795150/instagram-hashtag-contests-examples-and-best (accessed June 9, 2023).

21. https://www.creativemarketingltd.co.uk/blog/best-brands-on-pinterest/; https://www.pinterest.com/pin/774689573423110806/ (accessed May 16, 2023).

22. https://www.insiderintelligence.com/content/worldwide-digital-ad-spend-will-top-600-billion-this-year (accessed May 16, 2023).

23. https://www.statista.com/outlook/dmo/digital-advertising/worldwide#ad-spending (accessed May 16, 2023).

24. Eric Mosley, "Crowdsource your Performance Reviews," *Harvard Business Review*, June 15, 2013, https://blogs.hbr.org/cs/2012/06/crowdsource_your_performance_r.html (accessed May 16, 2023).

25. https://ideas.lego.com/; https://www.lego.com/en-us/themes/ideas (accessed May 16, 2023).

26. https://business.yelp.com/advertise/types-of-digital-advertising/#:~:text=The%20four%20main%20types%20of,convert%20prospects%20into%20real%20customers (accessed May 16, 2023).

27. https://www.mckinsey.com/capabilities/growth-marketing-and-sales/our-insights/beyond-paid-media-marketings-new-vocabulary (accessed May 16, 2023).

28. https://www.meltwater.com/en/blog/top-social-media-monitoring-tools (accessed May 16, 2023).

29. https://totempool.com/blog/social-media-command-center/#:~:text=One%20of%20the%20in%2Dhouse,customers)%20in%20real%2Dtime (accessed May 16, 2023).

30. https://m2comms.com/2023/04/04/5-content-creators-dominating-the-edutok-scene/#:~:text=Since%202019%2C%20content%20creators%20have,and%20engaging%20than%20ever%20before; https://www.tiktok.com/forgood?lang=en (accessed May 16, 2023).

31. https://www.theb2bhouse.com/social-media-marketing-statistics-trends-and-data/ (accessed May 17, 2023).

32. Ibid.

33. https://blog.hootsuite.com/measure-social-media-roi-business/ (accessed May 17, 2023).

34. https://www.socialmediatoday.com/news/new-research-shows-that-71-of-americans-now-get-news-content-via-social-pl/593255/ (accessed June 9, 2023).

35. https://blog.hootsuite.com/beginners-guide-to-content-curation/; https://blog.hootsuite.com/social-media-algorithm/ (accessed June 9, 2023).

36. Charlene Li and Josh Bernoff, *Groundswell: Winning in a World Transformed by Social Technologies,* revised ed. (Boston, MA: Harvard Business Press, 2011); What Are Types of Social Media Influencers?; https://epicmc2.com/insights/technographics-ladder-social-media-success/ (accessed May 2023).

37. https://www.simplilearn.com/types-of-influencers-article; https://www.shopify.com/blog/influencer-pricing#:~:text=Micro%20influencers%20(10%2C000%20%2D%2050%2C000%20followers,followers)%3A%20%2410%2C000%2B%20per%20post (accessed May 17, 2023).

38. https://www.techtarget.com/whatis/feature/Reasons-why-blogs-are-important-for-businesses (accessed May 18, 2023).

39. https://marketinginsidergroup.com/content-marketing/the-10-best-large-company-blogs-in-the-world/ (accessed May 18, 2023).

40. https://twinsmommy.com/personal-blogs/ (accessed, May 18, 2023).

41. https://blog.gitnux.com/tumblr-statistics/#:~:text=Tumblr%20is%20a%20popular%20microblogging,employees%20as%20of%20October%202021.; https://www.searchenginejournal.com/50-things-know-tumblr/84595/#close; https://mashable.com/article/how-tumblr-lost-its-way(accessed May 19, 2023).

42. https://datareportal.com/essential-facebook-stats#:~:text=Here's%20what%20the%20latest%20data,)%3A%202.989%20billion%20(April%202023)&text=Number%20of%20people%20who%20use,)%3A%202.037%20billion%20(April%202023)&text=Share%20of%20Facebook's%20monthly%20active,%3A%2068%25%20(April%202023) (accessed May 19, 2023).

43. https://www.socialmediacollege.com/blog/tiktok-for-business/#:~:text=TikTok%20users%20have%20the%20option,your%20business's%20performance%20on%20TikTok.; https://www.tiktok.com/creators/creator-portal/en-us/getting-started-on-tiktok/tiktok-business-vs-personal-account/; https://www.business.com/articles/instagram-business-account/; https://www.linkedin.com/pulse/linkedin-profile-page-which-better-use-why-manca-korelc/ (accessed June 15, 2023).

44. https://blog.hubspot.com/marketing/linkedin-vs-facebook; https://www.linkedin.com/business/marketing/blog/linkedin-pages/new-features; https://business.linkedin.com/marketing-solutions/why-advertise-on-linkedin?trk=lms-36c (accessed May 19, 2023).

45. https://wallaroomedia.com/blog/social-media/tiktok-statistics/ (accessed June 15, 2023). https://nealschaffer.com/instagram-statistics/ (accessed June 15, 2023).

46. https://www.tomsguide.com/best-picks/best-photography-sites (accessed June 12, 2023).

47. https://statisticsanddata.org/data/most-popular-social-media-in-history/ (accessed May 19, 2023).

48. https://backtracks-blog.com/10-successful-branded-podcasts/ (accessed June 12, 2023).

49. https://cityhour.weebly.com/ (accessed May 19, 2023).

50. https://www.myfitnesspal.com/apps/show/110 (accessed May 19, 2023).

51. https://www.cnbc.com/2022/06/16/remember-foursquare-the-location-tech-used-by-apple-uber-knows-you.html (accessed May 2023).

52. https://www.globenewswire.com/news-release/2022/01/13/2366090/0/en/Brand-Rated-Nine-out-of-ten-customers-read-reviews-before-buying-a-product.html (accessed May 20, 2023).

53. https://explodingtopics.com/blog/online-review-stats (accessed May 20, 2023).

54. https://www.yelp.com/biz/elite-event-johnstons-san-diego?start=10 (accessed May 20, 2023).

55. https://www.bankmycell.com/blog/how-many-people-play-video-games (accessed May 20, 2023).

56. https://influencermarketinghub.com/facebook-gaming-stats/ (accessed May 20, 2023).

57. https://techcrunch.com/2022/08/30/meta-shutting-down-facebook-gaming-app/?guccounter=1&guce_referrer=aHR0cHM6Ly93d3cuZ29vZ2xlLmNvbVS8&guce_referrer_sig=AQAAAEFK2HSX8czNdsOxTzM7GzqgpTdpsWZHaJ7AqqtAN0SRIxonKMafH1gFEzlkmijwFCTvQqD5TIcOSPFbr1ysGD0OdOpMDohsuqcvdk64srXOEIEdQ8HXq0ttRniJc9f9kNgj3vuPyG9mOKSkJLCAdnMZ9VaQdyxvIbt0BnX2Aap5#:~:text=Facebook%20is%20shutting%20down%20its%20standalone%20Gaming%20app%20in%20October,-Aisha%20Malik%40aiishamalik1&text=Just%20over%20two%20years%20after,and%20Android%20after%20that%20date (accessed May 20, 2023).

58. https://www.bankmycell.com/blog/how-many-people-play-video-games#section-5 (accessed May 20, 2023).

59. https://www.eskimi.com/blog/in-game-statistics (accessed May 20, 2023).

60. https://www.gamemarketinggenie.com/blog/brands-that-used-video-game-marketing (accessed May 20, 2023).

61. https://www.bankmycell.com/blog/how-many-phones-are-in-the-world (accessed May 20, 2023).

62. https://www.pocketgamer.biz/news/80585/ad-spend-predicted-to-hit-362bn-in-2023/#:~:text=Mobile%20ad%20spending%20will%20hit,the%20overall%20mobile%20gaming%20industry. (accessed May 20, 2023).

63. https://www.digitaltrends.com/mobile/what-is-rcs-messaging/ (accessed June 14, 2023).

64. https://www.moengage.com/blog/the-future-of-mobile-marketing-smartwatch/ (accessed May 20, 2023).

65. https://www.relevance.com/how-to-use-widget-marketing-to-improve-roi/ (accessed May 20, 2023).

66. https://digitalagencynetwork.com/red-bull-marketing-strategy-how-they-make-the-difference/#:~:text=An%20important%20aspect%20of%20Red,high%2Dquality%20content%20that%20resonates (accessed May 20, 2023).

67. https://sproutsocial.com/insights/social-media-trends/; https://www.hookle.net/post/how-to-use-chatgpt-for-social-media-posts-with-10-quick-examples#:~:text=ChatGPT%20can%20be%20useful%20for,up%20time%20for%20other%20tasks (accessed May 20, 2023).

Chapter 19

1. Huachao Gao, Yinlong Zhang, and Vikas Mittal, "How Does Local-Global Identify Affect Price Sensitivity," *Journal of Marketing*, May 2017, 62–70.

2. *Isabelle Gustafson, "Consumers Increasingly Value Local Food," CStore Decisions, January 30, 2020.*

3. Vikas Mittal, "Customer-Based Strategy for Raising Prices," *Marketing News*, November/December 2016, 20–22.

4. Ibid.

5. Chris Dong "This Airline Has Been Voted the No. 1 in the World for 27 Years in a Row," *Travel and Leisure*, March 28, 2023.

6. Kelly Main, "Amazon Accidently Inflation-Proofed Products. It's a Case Study in Pricing That You'll Want to Steal," *Inc.*, May 1, 2023.

7. https://revionics.com/about/customers.

8. Bryan Pearson, "Personalizing Price With AI: How Walmart, Kroger Do it," *Forbes,* September 7, 2021.

9. "Price Match Guarantee," *Best Buy*, https://www.bestbuy.com/site/help-topics/price-match-guarantee/pcmcat290300050002.c?id=pmcat290300050002.

10. "The Effect of Customer Loyalty on Retail Pricing," *Marketing News*, January 2016, 3.

11. Keith Coulter and Anne Roggeveen, "Price Number Relationships and Deal Processing Fluency: The Effects of Approximation Sequence and Number Multiples," *Journal of Marketing Research,* February 2014, 69–82.

12. Federico Rossi and Pradeep K. Chintagunta, "Price Transparency and Retail Price: Evidence from Fuel Price Signs in the Italian Highway System," *Journal of Marketing Research*, June 2016, 407–423.

13. Meghan Busse, Ayelet Israeli, and Florian Zettelmeyer, "Repairing the Damage: The Effect of Price Knowledge and Gender on Auto Repair Price Quotes," *Journal of Marketing Research*, February 2017, 75–95.

14. Aylin Aydinli, Marco Bertini, and Anja Lambrecht, "Price Promotion for Emotional Impact," *Journal of Marketing*, 78, no. 4 (July 2014): 80–96.

15. Jake Arky, "How Much Cheaper Are Store-Brand Groceries Than Name Brands?," *Yahoo!Finance*, May 15, 2023

16. Chiara Spagnolia Gabardi, "What Happens to Unsold Clothes May Surprise You," *Eluxe Magazine*, January 27, 2022.

17. Richard Mitchell, "Kroger's Simple Truth brand hits 10 year mark," *Supermarket News*, January 11, 2023.

18. "Spirit Airlines: The Power of a Clear Strategy," *Strongbrands*, February 23, 2015, https://timcalkins.com/branding-insights/spirit-airlines-power-clear-strategy/ (accessed February 28, 2015).

19. Dani James, "How Ulta is approaching its new store layout and the holidays," *Retail Dive*, December 19, 2022.

20. M.J. del Rio Olivares, Kristina Wittkowski, Jaakko Aspara Tomas Falk, and Pekka Mattila, "Relational Price Discounts: Consumers' Meta-cognitions and Nonlinear Effects of Initial Discounts on Customer Retention," *Journal of Marketing*, January 2018, 115–131.

21. Abhijit Guha, Abhijit Biswas, Dhruv Grewal, Swati Verma, Somak Banerjee, and Jens Nordfalt, "Reframing the Discount as a Comparison Against the Sales Price: Does It Make the Discount More Attractive?" *Journal of Marketing Research*, June 2018, 339–351.

22. Andong Cheng and Cynthia Cryder, "Double Mental Discounting: When a Single Price Promotion Feels Twice As Nice," *Journal of Marketing Research*, April 2018, 226–238.

23. Lydia DePillis, "As Prices Skyrocket, Coupons Are harder to Find Than Ever," *The New York Times*, June 30, 2022.

24. Elise Dopson, "30+ Shopping Cart Abandonment Statistics and Strategies for Recouping Lost Sales," *Shopify*, June 23, 2021.

25. Jimmy Duvall, "Shipping Is Critical To Keeping Online Shoppers Happy," *Forbes*, August 27, 2019, https://www.forbes.com/sites/forbestechcouncil/2019/08/27/shipping-is-critical-to-keeping-online-shoppers-happy/?sh=470e400e178c (accessed May 31, 2023).

26. *https://goldtoe.com/shop/mens/socks/dress* (accessed September 18, 2018).

27. Franklin Shaddy and Ayelet Fishbach, "Seller Beware: How Bundling Affects Valuation," *Journal of Marketing Research*, October 2017, 737–751.

28. Matt Day, "Amazon Emails Show Effort to Weaken Diapers.com Before Buying It," *Bloomberg*, July 29, 2020.

Appendix

1. Jessica Davis, "Grocery Giant Kroger's Data Side Hustle," Information Week, January 9, 2023.

2. Steven Li, "The Stitch Fix Story: How A Unique Prioritization of Data Science Helped the Company Create Billions in Market Value," February 17, 2020.

3. Matt Smith, "Walmart's New Intelligent Retail Lab Shows a Glimpse into the Future of Retail, IRL," *Walmart*, April 25, 2019.

4. "Examining buyer behavior in a car showroom for Toyota," *Tobii*, https://www.tobii.com/resource-center/customer-stories/examining-buyer-behavior-toyota-showroom

5. "Hidden Valley® Ranch Launches Dill-Icious New Flavor," *PR Newswire*, March 30, 2023, https://www.prnewswire.com/news-releases/hidden-valley-ranch-launches-dill-icious-new-flavor-301785420.html#:~:text=OAKLAND%2C%20Calif.%2C%20March%2030,Pickle%20Flavored%20Hidden%20Valley%20Ranch.

6. Synchrony to Help Optimize Service Parts Inventory and Enhance Customer Experience Across Sophisticated Dealer Network," *Businesswire*, January 11, 2022.

7. Bernardita Calzon, "21 Examples of Big Data Analytics In Healthcare That Can Save People," *Datapine*, June 2, 2022.

8. Kristina Monllos, "L'Oreal uses social listening, in-house teams to tap into beauty trends 'at the speed of culture'," *Digiday*, March 24, 2023.

9. Zach Brooke, "Marketers Are Using the Weather to Predict Buyer Behavior," https://www.ama.org/publications/MarketingNews/Pages/how-marketers-are-using-the-weather-to-predictbuyer-behavior.aspx (accessed January 2019); James Kobielus, "Weather Data Analytics: Helping Retailers Predict and Meet Customer Demand," https://www.ibmbigdatahub.com/blog/weatherdata-analytics-helping-retailers-predict-andmeet-customer-demand (accessed January 2019); Jeffrey F. Rayport. "Use Big Data to Predict Your Customers' Behaviors," https://hbr.org/2012/09/use-big-data-to-predict-your-c (accessed January 2019); Cindy Elliott, "Combining AI and Location Intelligence to Predict Market Demand," https://www.forbes.com/sites/esri/2018/05/30/combiningai-and-location-intelligence-to-predict-marketdemand/#1d93971838bf (accessed January 2019).

10. "How Big Data Analysis Helped Increase Walmart's Sales Turnover," *Project Pro*, April 24, 2023, https://www.projectpro.io/article/how-big-data-analysis-helped-increase-walmarts-sales-turnover/109#:~:text=World%27s%20Biggest%20Private%20Cloud%20at%20Walmart%2D%20Data%20Cafe,-Walmart%20is%20in&text=The%20data%20cafe%20pulls%20information,data%20for%2.

Index

Leads, gathering through social media, 111
Learning, 108–109
Leasing, use in B-to-B market, 119
Lefty's San Francisco, 22, 23
Legal factors, 52–56
    consumer privacy, 55–56
    federal legislation, 53
    regulatory agencies, 54–55
    state and local laws, 54
Legality, of price strategy, 342–343
Legal responsibilities, 38
LEGO, 4, 45, 181, 205, 310
    COVID-19 impact, 169
    crowdsourcing used by, 181
Lenovo, desirable qualities of salespeople, 298
Letterboxd, 316
Levi's, 169
Levi Strauss, 225
Levitt, Ted, 63
Lexus, product/service differentiation at, 23
LGBTQIA1+ community, 130
Licensing, global marketing and, 76
Li, Charlene, 313
Life events, influence of on consumer buying decisions, 105
Lifestyle, 44
    psychographic segmentation and, 132
Limited decision making, 93–94
LinkedIn, 290, 308, 316
    incentives for sales people, 300
    popularity of, 316
    usage
        for marketing, 316
        by salespeople, 289–290
        use for B-to-B content marketing, 113
Listening system, 311–312
Living advertising, 26
LivingSocial, 284
L.L. Bean, 5, 232
Local advertising, 239
Local identity, 327
Local laws, 54
Location-based social networking sites, 318
Location, of service, 197
Logistical functions, 220
L'Oréal, most ethical companies, 35
Loss-leader pricing, 340
Louis Vuitton, 104, 130, 171, 172
Love Calls Back campaign, 130
Lowe's Foods, 128, 129, 325
Low-involvement products, 97

Loyalty
    CRM and, 139
    customers, 331–332
Loyalty marketing programs, 285
Lucky, 171
Lululemon Astro Pants, 182
Lyft, 10, 46, 52
    price and quality positioning of, 141
Lynx, 175
Lysol, 167
Lyst, 310

M

Machine learning, 215
Macroenvironmental forces, 21
Macro-influencers, 314
Macy, 49, 56, 240, 285
    COVID-19 impact, 240
    diversity, equity, and inclusion, 49
    loyalty marketing program, 285
Magazines, cooperative advertising in, 274
Magnuson–Moss Warranty–Federal Trade Commission Improvement Act 1975, 176
Mahomes, Patrick, 102
Mail panels, 149
Mail surveys, 148–149
Maintenance, repair, or operating supplies (MRO) market, 121
Major equipment (installations), 119
Management
    corporate social responsibility to, 37
    as stakeholders, 37
    uses of marketing research by, 143–144
Management decision problem, 145
Management Decisions Inc., 180
Mandarin Oriental, 233
Manufacturer's brand vs. private brand, 169–170
Manufacturing flow management process, 211
March of Dimes, strategic planning of, 14
Market, 126
Market analytics, 146
Market attractiveness, 18
Market development, 15
Market factors, distribution channel choice and, 224–225
Market grouping, 67
Marketing
    B-to-B. See B-to-B marketing
    cause-related, 41–42
    changing behavior, 47
    content, 311
    definition of, 2–3
    demographic factors, 46–47
    in everyday life, 12

    gender and, 104
    global. See Global marketing
    implications of involvement, 95
    internal, 199–200
    management philosophies. See Philosophies, marketing management
    multisegment strategy, 136
    nonprofit organizations, 200–203
    pop culture, 47–48
    reasons for studying, 12
    sales vs. market orientations, 5–11
    services. See Service
    social media campaign, creating and leveraging, 310–312
    undifferentiated strategy, 136
    usefulness of want-got gap, 86
Marketing audit, 27, 28
Marketing channels
    for consumer products, 221
    definition of, 217
    factors affecting choice of, 224–225
    functions and activities of intermediaries, 219–220
    working of, 218
Marketing communication
    integrated, 260–261, 310
    promotional strategy and, 249–252
    targeted, 304
Marketing concept, 3–4
Marketing-controlled information source, 88
Marketing mix (four Ps), 26, 44
    definition of, 26
    global, 78–82
    place (distribution) strategy, 26, 197
    price strategy, 26, 198
    product (service) strategy, 195–197
    promotion strategy, 26, 198
    role of promotion in, 249
    for services, 195–199
Marketing myopia, 20
Marketing objectives, 25
Marketing planning, 19
Marketing plans, 19–20
    control of, 28
    definition of, 19
    elements, 19
    evaluation of, 28
    following up on, 26–38
    implementation of, 28
    need to write, 19
    postaudit tasks, 28
    setting objectives, 24–25
    writing, 19–20